HOUSING

HOUSING

SECOND EDITION

JOHN MACSAI F.A.I.A.

Architect
Professor, School of Architecture
University of Illinois/Chicago Circle

EUGENE P. HOLLAND

Structural Engineer

HARRY S. NACHMAN P.E.

Consulting Engineer

JAMES R. ANDERSON

Associate Professor, Housing Research and
Development Program and Department of Architecture
University of Illinois at Urbana-Champaign

JARED SHLAES C.R.E., M.A.I.

Real Estate Counselor

Illustrator

ALFRED J. HIDVEGI A.I.A.

Architect

A WILEY-INTERSCIENCE PUBLICATION

JOHN WILEY & SONS
New York · Chichester · Brisbane · Toronto · Singapore

Library of Congress Cataloging in Publication Data:
Main entry under title:

Housing.

"A Wiley-Interscience publication."
Bibliography: p.
Includes index.
1. Apartment houses. 2. Architecture, Domestic.
I. Macsai, John, 1926–. II. Hidvegi,
Alfred J.

TH4820.H68 1981   728.3′14   81-7584
ISBN 0-471-08126-4   AACR2

Printed in the United States of America

10 9 8 7 6 5 4 3 2 1

INTRODUCTION
TO THE SECOND EDITION

Five years have passed since the first edition of *Housing*. What was said in the introduction then, is still true.

In this introduction, I highlight the differences between the two editions. On the one hand, the corrections and additions reflect the changes that took place in the field of housing from 1975 to 1980; on the other hand, they attempt to respond to the comments I received about the first edition.

Many of the changes that have occurred in housing during the past five years have been demographic; housing for the elderly has become one of the largest unmet needs in the residential market. Today we are—if only reluctantly and prodded by codes— more aware of the plight of the handicapped. Also, the increasingly serious problem of energy has been brought to our minds. There have been useful advances in concrete technology for housing. We have become more sensitive to contextual issues in design, not only in preservation and rehabilitation, but also in new buildings. User research has reached the point where its results can—if only with some caveats—begin to guide the practitioner. There have been changes in the economy, in financing techniques, and in the market. Due to increased construction cost, there have been fewer highrises built, although an abundance of good midrises and ingenious lowrises has made up for the loss.

I attempt to respond to the above issues. There is a completely new chapter dealing with special users: the elderly and the handicapped. The issue of energy is referred to wherever it is meaningful and the HVAC chapter has a new section on energy conservation. The structural chapter has been expanded to include new concrete techniques, precast and prestressed. Context sensitivity is emphasized throughout the book and is dealt with specifically under sites. There is an entirely new chapter on user research, on the social and behavioral component of design. Changes in the economy are reflected in the revised chapter on financing. The abundance of midrises and lowrises is mirrored in the new projects added to or replacing those in the previous edition. As I look at these new projects now—they were selected for their architectural merit, not for user type or location—I find that there are more for upper- or middle-upper income users than for lower- or moderate-income residents; this also reflects what has happened to housing in the past five years.

The most critical comments about the first edition of this book referred to the overemphasis on highrise construction; in this edition, I enlarged the low- and midrise coverage, especially among the projects illustrated. I still use highrise, however, as a vehicle to introduce the reader to fundamental issues. Several reviewers suggested that I include specialized housing: dormitories, hotels, hostels, and housing for the elderly and the handicapped; the size of the book has limited me to including only the last of these. The same limitation prohibited me from satisfying those who wished the book contained a chapter on the history of housing. I was requested to incorporate a more practical section on site planning; with all the excellent books on the market about this topic, a detailed discussion would have been redundant. Nevertheless, I revised and enlarged the chapter about site planning and included my density studies. Suggestions were made that, for each project illustrated, I show all nontypical as well as typical floor plans; had I done so, the book would be much longer, and costlier. As it is, it costs too much on a student's budget. Lastly, I was told that the title is misleading because it does not include *all* housing; I thought of other less inclusive and more explicit titles, but they seemed too long and cumbersome; I decided to stick with brevity at the price of accuracy.

Since the first edition, several excellent books have been published that influenced my thoughts on housing: Davis's *Form of Housing*, Lawton's *Planning and Managing Housing for the Elderly*, and Arnheim's *Dynamics of Architecture*. If acknowledgments are due, they should go to these authors first. Gratitude expressed in the first edition to some who helped with particular chapters is still felt: to Frank Zimmerman of Westinghouse Corporation for the elevator data, to Rein Pirn of Bolt, Beranek & Newman, Inc., for acoustical information, and to Jerry Haag of National Loss Control Service Corporation for fire protection ideas. To these I add the name of Jack Catlin, graduate student in my design studio at the University of Illinois, Chicago Circle. He graciously let me use the results of his research on the handicapped. I am also grateful to Henry Hyatt of Technical Assistance Corporation for Housing and Ronald Weismehl of the Council for Jewish Elderly for their reading of the chapter on special users. I incorporated many of their suggestions and corrections. Whatever errors still remain are solely mine. Sincere appreciation is also expressed for assistance with the chapter on social and behavior components of design: to John Replinger, Department of Architecture, University of Illinois, Champaign-Urbana and to Sue Weideman, Department of Landscape Architecture and Housing Research and Development, University of Illinois, Champaign-Urbana.

Several illustrations in this chapter were developed for specific projects at the Housing Research and Development Program, University of Illinois, Champaign-Urbana. The many people who contributed to these projects, particularly Ronji Borooah, Guido Francescato, and Art Kaha, are gratefully acknowledged.

INTRODUCTION TO THE SECOND EDITION

Four people must be specially mentioned: William Dudley Hunt, FAIA, my architectural editor at Wiley, for constant help and encouragement; Al Hidvegi, my partner, for ideas, comments, and criticism; Marie Sporny, my secretary, for endless correspondence and typing; last, but foremost, my wife Jerry for editing, support, and love.

JOHN MACSAI

Chicago, Illinois
November 1981

INTRODUCTION
TO THE FIRST EDITION

Architectural design is a multileveled process. The designer—in this case the designer of housing—must consider simultaneously a multitude of tasks, a multitude of options.

To reproduce this complex thought process in words, a medium in which one is forced to put down one thought at a time sequentially, is impossible. The designer's concurrent awareness of program, regulations, budget, functional possibilities, structural and mechanical options, and architectural form is not reproducible. At best, the components can be identified and dealt with separately but not at once, as the architect must.

How much space should be allotted to each component? Each is of sufficient importance to have often been the topic of an entire study. It is neither necessary nor wise to try to be all encompassing for the purposes of this book; components of housing are treated only in their capacity as design generators.

This book is not a designer's Sweets Catalogue. It simply hopes to be: for the colleague already well versed in housing, a refresher course to clarify ideas or something to criticize and take issue with; for architects not so well acquainted with housing, a guide when a housing commission materializes; for architectural students, a reference when taking a course; and for others, such as developers and housing officials, an insight into the way architects think and therefore a tool to make their association more positive.

Because there are few absolutes in architecture, I am quite aware that there is no statement in this book with which a colleague could not disagree, based on his own experiences or architectural attitudes.

Writing about design inevitably reveals one's own prejudices and limited experiences in facets of housing and the avoidance or brief treatment of these areas. My own dislike of curtain walls in apartment buildings, disregard of industrialized housing, and extreme brevity in discussing steel framing all spring from the above. Aside from these prejudices and limitations, I must admit to other shortcomings: megastructures are not included; specialized housing types such as student accommodations and apartment hotels are not covered; regional differences such as earthquakes and climate are at best only touched on; site planning is covered in a much briefer manner than it deserves; examples are limited to the United States.

I must conclude with a warning: building types and apartment prototypes are not meant to be recipes. They are merely illustrations to cast light on a problem. No catalogue of solutions could be a substitute for architectural design: from the options inherent in the task, from the choices we make in responding to the task, based on our own theory of space born of the limitless combinations and permutations possible, a unique and individual architectural solution will be reached that no book can—or should—influence.

"True originality is to be found by those who, standing on the limits of the sphere of the known, reach out naturally to some apprehension and understanding of what is beyond; it is the next step in an orderly development."[1] This book attempts to cast light on the orderly development of housing design in the hope that it will help some of its readers who are about to take that next step.

CONTENTS

CONTENTS

CONTENTS

CONTENTS

HOUSING

DATA GATHERING   1

John Macsai

"The process of designing a building is really a path which you begin to travel as soon as you possibly can, in terms of the problems."—Kevin Roche, in *Conversations with Architects.* [2]

What hides behind the simple expression "in terms of the problems" is a mountain of data that the architect must have at hand in order to start the design process. Rare is the architect who can design well when information is missing, when programming is loose. The fact is that the more circumscribed the program and the more specific the data, the more challenged one feels and the more likely one is to respond to the challenge.

Most good design will rise out of the specificity of the program data, which are peculiar to this client, to this user, to this location. When we claim that the building grows out of the particularity of its conditions, we naturally do not mean that this outgrowth is "self-generated" or that it happens "in a sort of automatic pragmatism," [3] Far from it. The architect's response to the problem will be much influenced by the theory of form held. Obviously the same program data, the same site information, would be responded to differently by the offices of Mies van der Rohe and Davis Brody & Associates. Obviously, and inevitably, the solutions by the same architect to two entirely different building programs would still carry that architect's stamp of theory.

The chance to utilize theories of spatial organization is, however, somewhat limited in the field of housing. The program data—user needs, site conditions, local regulations, and marketing and financing constraints—allow the architect a more limited latitude of options than other areas of architecture. If these program data do not predetermine an architectural solution, they at least carry in themselves the kernel of a solution. Thorough understanding of the program data is a prerequisite to uncovering this kernel.

Naturally it is hard to avoid the temptation to "design" all through the process of data gathering. It is likely that the architect will concentrate on those data that seem most likely to affect design. More than that, architects may try to influence the program data—at least those about which their opinions are sought, such as the mix—to lead to more rational design solutions. They know that an even number of apartments on a typical floor is conducive to orderly exterior rhythm. They know that pairing apartments leads to various economies. They will have had enough experience with certain apartment designs to know whether they fit readily into a particular building type.

All this is unavoidable. Nevertheless, maximum objectivity can have its reward. One is never sure what specific data, what hitherto unknown piece of information, will suggest a new approach, a new solution, completely different from all the preceding notions.

Compiling the data in the form of a checklist to which to refer when the next housing job materializes is a helpful procedure. Each situation will have its own peculiarities and each architect will organize the data in an individual way. However, five major categories emerge: program, location, zoning, code, and budget.

PROGRAM

When designing multifamily housing—spaces in which human beings eat, sleep, relax, and make love—the architect naturally wants to know all about the people who will inhabit the buildings. Unfortunately the architect cannot meet, learn about, or interview the actual occupants. Rarely is there an opportunity to deal with a known group whose needs, desires, and idiosyncrasies can be sensed in first-hand contact. Usually this information will be handed to the architect, and although one can personally verify site data, zoning, or financial figures the chances of double checking the correctness of the information regarding the users are minimal. The normally heavy social responsibilities inherent in the design of housing are made even heavier by scanty or inaccurate information about the users and their needs.

On the one hand, programs prepared by various housing authorities are frozen in bureaucratic rule books that, if not already outdated when written, are obsolete by the time they are implemented. On the other hand, when the client is a private developer, when bureaucracy is not in control and there are no rule books, we expect more up-to-date program data. They, however, are not always provided. Few developers are large enough or sufficiently well organized to commission scientifically conducted market analyses. Even if they were, it often happens that when they first approach the architect they are gambling: they are not at all certain that the project will materialize. It all depends on whether they can obtain financing at the right terms. At the time they discuss the project with the architect they may not even own the land; at best they may hold an option on it. Until the mortgage is promised, they want to keep their financial exposure to a minimum. They will pay minimally for the architect's preliminary design, which is necessary to obtain financing. Even worse than the negligible compensation is the insufficiency of the data given the architect in a tentative project. It is likely that at this stage no proper survey will have been made of the lot. There will be no money to spend on soil investigation, certainly none for considering the kind of housing the architect is to design. Even if the developers want to spend money on user research, it is unlikely that there would be enough time for it.

Although user research, or environmental psychology, has progressed in the past 20 years, the dream of architects and social scientists working hand in hand has not materialized. "Few people are surprised to hear that occupants are affected by buildings or that people's images of the environment may be distorted in predictable ways."[4] While architects tend to accept such results of user research as territoriality, the need for surveillance, and the effects of clustering, these data, scattered in many books, are not readily available to the designer.

Brolin warns that generalized behavioral information is almost useless. Only specific information can lead to effective solutions.

In a study for apartment renovation in Puerto Rican Harlem, the firm of Brolin/Zeisel found that the kitchen was the center of family life—interesting information but not helpful in locating the kitchen in the apartment plan. Another observation was more helpful: the woman, who spends much of the day in the kitchen, must be able to monitor who comes and goes from the apartment. This specific information could be translated into a specific design inference: a person in the kitchen must be able to see the apartment entrance. This could be accomplished electronically, but the budget ruled this out. Therefore the kitchen had to be close to the entrance. With more information—should the sleeping areas be private; should people who come to the entrance be able to see into the living areas; should eating and entertaining areas be separated—the architect was able to locate the kitchen more precisely.

Although not all behavior patterns can or should be accommodated in design, the architect must know about the patterns so that his/her design does not obstruct them.[5]

Another warning by Brolin concerns the architect who generally resists the application of behavioral data. On the one hand, because these data are unlike engineers' calculations, they are imprecise and hard to apply. On the other hand, the fact that architects still believe they know how people want to live buttresses their resistance to social scientists.

Even when architects are thorough believers in behavioral research, very rarely, if ever, do their fees permit the hiring of people trained to apply behavioral science techniques to given projects. Nor, in most cases, is there adequate time to conduct meaningful investigation.

The dilemma is a serious one. One way to deal with it is to design into the project maximum user options. Sometimes, like at the Rokeby Condominium Apartments in Nashville, Tennessee, it is possible to predict the buyer's needs. There the architect devised 23 possible apartment plans from which buyers could select. As buyer commitment progressed, the architect fit the pieces together, within certain parameters. An exciting elevation was the serendipitous result of this process. Naturally, this procedure cannot be applied to rental housing, though some flexibility for tenant options is possible.

Because the quality of human life is strongly influenced by the kind of housing the architect designs, of all the data involved, the program—for whom and what—is the most important.

The following checklist attempts to cover the major program items architects should be informed about before starting to design a housing project. Naturally, some of the items are not applicable to all cases, and certain jobs may necessitate entirely new categories in the checklist. One should also be aware that the most complete list is only as good as the dialogue that is established between architect and client.

USER

1. AGE.   Different age groups—young, middle-aged, elderly—will require not only different structures but different amenities and services.
2. FAMILY SIZE.   Will the building serve singles, families with children, or both? If it serves both, in what mix?
3. OCCUPATION.   Occupations of the users, while often hard to predict with any certainty, are useful in reflecting living habits and recreational needs.

4. LIFE STYLE. Life style may be related to income levels, occupation, ethnic background, or education. It is frequently neglected and most buildings are designed for the common denominator.

5. PREVIOUS HOUSING. Whether families are moving from the suburbs to the city, from slums to better areas, from farm life to urban existence, their needs, habits, and degree of sophistication will vary.

MARKET

1. SPONSORSHIP. Whether with private developer or institutional sponsor, the architect deals with different rules, different requirements, different goals.

2. OWNERSHIP. Whether a building is a rental, cooperative, or condominium will affect the design of individual climate control, parking space, and extent of common facilities.

3. RENT OR SALES STRUCTURE. Knowledge of the proposed rental or sales price brackets will suggest limits in the design.

4. COMPETITION. Investigation of similar projects in the vicinity will indicate market preferences as well as pitfalls.

5. FINANCING. Financing is dealt with in a separate chapter. Here it is important to note that private lending institutions occasionally, and governmental financing sources inevitably, have their own requirements.

6. PHASING. Projects with large numbers of dwelling units should be built in marketable segments. The number of units that can be offered at one time without inundating the market should be determined.

7. FLEXIBILITY. If a project is phased, should the design allow for changes based on experience of the previous phase?

DWELLING UNIT

1. MIX. The percentages of various apartment types such as efficiencies (sometimes called studios), or units of one, two, three, or more bedrooms.

2. UNIT SIZE. Gross square footage of the dwelling unit is not adequate. How it is defined should be clarified. Does it include exterior walls? (In condominiums, these walls should be included because they are owned by the buyer.) Does it include corridor partitions or balconies?

3. ROOM SIZE. Room sizes should be given in approximate terms to keep design options flexible. It is also useful to state certain critical minimum dimensions. Height is currently assumed to be 8 ft from floor to ceiling unless otherwise specified.

4. LIVING SPACE. Options should be defined: formal living room with certain activities elsewhere; combined family–living room for all functions. Where can activities for which no specific space is designated take place (sewing, studying, and so on)?

5. DINING. Alternatives should be clearly stated: combined with living room; defined alcove in interior zone of the apartment; defined alcove along exterior wall; combined with kitchen; completely separate room.

6. KITCHEN. Amount of counter space, amount of cabinet space (base as well as wall) in linear feet and types of appliance should be specified. Is eating space to be provided in the kitchen? Is the room to accommodate other family activities?

7. BEDROOM. When more than one bedroom has been designated, should they be adjacent or split on each side of the living space? Should the use of bedrooms as living space be considered?

8.   BATHROOM.   How many? Complete bathrooms or powder rooms? Which should have shower stalls, which bathtubs? Compartmentalization? In case of multilevel apartments, on which level? Should the approach be directly from the bedrooms or from the common bedroom corridor?

9.   STORAGE.   Each type of storage space should be defined in terms of linear feet because depth is more or less standard.

10.   ENTRY.   Size and function of the entry should be stated. Will it serve any function other than reception?

11.   CIRCULATION.   Should circulation occur via defined channels such as corridors, or can some of the spaces, such as the living room, be used for traffic? To what extent should activities be isolated within the dwelling?

12.   EXTERIOR SPACE.   Depending on whether the unit is on ground level or elevated, will there be a terrace or balcony and in what size? What provisions are necessary to ensure security and privacy?

13.   SOUND SEPARATION.   What degree of sound separation should be provided between apartments, between apartments and other areas, within apartments.

BUILDING

1.   TYPE.   Preference such as low- or highrise, exterior- or interior-corridor, or multicore is often stated by the owner before the architect prepares any studies.

2.   PRIVACY VERSUS COMMUNITY.   This is stated primarily in terms of the maximum number of units that will share a common corridor or lobby.

3.   ORIENTATION.   Should sunlight penetrate every unit? Is there a preferred view and to what extent should it be visible from what percentage of the units? Is special protection to be considered?

SERVICES

1.   PARKING.   Minimum off-street parking is generally determined by zoning, but the client may have additional requirements. Controls? Self- or attendant parking? Provisions for guest parking? One-way or two-way traffic? Maximum walking distance from parking areas to units?

2.   LAUNDRY.   Will there be a washer/dryer in each unit or will a common laundry be provided? Where is it to be located? Is it to serve as a social magnet as well?

3.   REFUSE.   Methods of refuse handling and disposal should be determined.

4.   DELIVERY AND PICKUP.   Loading areas and controls should be defined. If the distribution is vertical, where should service elevators be located?

5.   MAIL.   Method of handling and distribution of letters, magazines, and parcels should be considered.

6.   WINDOW WASHING.   By resident or by management? If by management, access from inside the apartments or by scaffold? Decisions will strongly influence fenestration and type of operating sash.

STORAGE

1.   TENANT.   Tenant lockers should be specified in type, size, and location in the building.

2.   GENERAL.   Purpose should be stated: maintenance, repairs, vehicle storage.

3. BICYCLES.   How many and where to be stored; type of security?

4. BABY CARRIAGES.   Storage for how many? Relation to the entrance lobby?

SOCIAL AND RECREATIONAL

1. GOALS.   Is the purpose to ensure maximum privacy of units? To what degree should social intercourse between residents be promoted?

2. RECREATION.   Various desired activities should be defined in terms of the user: adult, child, or mixed? In terms of location: indoor, outdoor? Extent to which nontenants can use facilities should be considered.

3. CHILD CARE.   Local or state regulations should be followed governing these facilities if they are required in the program.

COMMERCIAL SPACE

To what extent does it depend on outside patronage? How will parking and deliveries be handled? One or more than one tenant?

SECURITY

1. NEEDS.   Locality and type of user will determine security provisions and surveillance required.

2. CONTROL.   Human: doorman, resident caretaker, other attendants. Mechanical: intercom systems, closed-circuit TV.

SPONSOR PECULIARITIES

1. BUILDER SKILLS.   When the developer is also a general contractor, there may be special preferences based on available skills related to structural systems, materials handling, or construction logistics.

2. EXPERIENCE.   Knowledge of sponsor's history of success—or failure—in similar projects will help to avoid mistakes.

3. MARKETING.   Should model apartments be set up in the building proper or in a separate temporary structure? Sales office requirements? Visitors' parking and routing?

MECHANICAL

1. HEATING, VENTILATING, AND AIR CONDITIONING
    a. Fuel for heating: gas, oil, coal, or electricity?
    b. Central or individual apartment heating plant(s)?
    c. Exposure control: quantity of fenestration, ordinary or insulating?
    d. Insulation in walls and roof; importance of initial versus operating cost.
    e. Is humidification wanted?
    f. Is cooling wanted? If so, by central or individual residence plant(s)? The owner should understand thoroughly the possibilities and implications of heating and cooling controls, which range from manual, through simple overall building, to sophisticated room-by-room. The latter may be an attractive point in rentals or sales but may also add substantially to maintenance costs and problems. In some types of all-electrical systems, however, room-by-room controls may be a normal

part of the equipment. Thus it behooves the owner to acquire a fair understanding of the many alternatives available. If cooling is desired, what should the inside temperature be? A straight 75° F for optimum comfort (or even lower?), or 10 to 12° F below the maximum outdoor temperature for minimum installation and operating costs?

g. Energy source for cooling. If natural fuel is used, the owner should be made aware of the possibilities of absorption refrigeration, using the same fuel. If electricity is used for heating, the potentialities of the heat pump should be made clear to the owner.

h. Will the owner, the individual occupant, or an organization of occupants pay fuel and energy costs for heating and/or cooling?

i. If individual heating and/or cooling systems are used, who will be responsible for their maintenance and replacement?

j. Ventilation for bathrooms and/or kitchens: central, individual, or a combination of individual control and central collection?

2. PLUMBING

a. Water centrally metered or individually metered?

b. Domestic water heating to be central or individual? Who will pay for the energy?

c. Water closets to be flush valve or tank operated?

d. Details of other sanitary fixtures; for example, lavatories to be free standing or cabinet type; kitchen sinks to be china or stainless steel; tub in every bathroom or shower only in some, quality of tub (cast iron or steel)?

e. Laundry facilities: central or individual? If central, will there be a concessionaire, or will the owner operate the facility?

f. Fire protection: should this be the minimum required by governing codes or does the owner want extra protection in the form of additional standpipes, fire extinguishers, and/or sprinklers? Will insurance charge reductions justify such additional costs?

3. ELECTRICAL

a. Is an owner-operated "total-energy" plant feasible, in which the owner provides all the electricity, heat, and cooling for the entire project?

b. If electricity from a utility company is purchased, the owner should understand the possibilities of various rates for different intensities of use and the overall costs, both installation and operating, for all alternatives. Any subsidies offered by the utility companies should be included in the consideration.

c. Will purchased electrical energy be individually or centrally metered and paid for? (The latter option is not available in Illinois, for example.)

d. Are the heating and cooling systems to be electrically powered? The same question applies to domestic water heating.

e. Quality of specialties such as switches and receptacles. The usual decision, low installation cost combined with higher maintenance and replacement costs for minimum quality specialties, or the converse?

f. Who will furnish and install lighting fixtures in the residential areas?

g. Electrical or gas ranges?

h. The spectrum of choices of auxiliary electrical systems is broad:

Front (and rear) door bell signals.

Voice communication with remote entrance doors.

Closed circuit television surveillance of entrances.

Central television antenna system.

Intercommunication systems of varying inclusiveness.

Burglar alarms and similar security systems.

Emergency alarms for persons in trouble in their apartments (particularly applicable in housing for the elderly).

Panic alarms for elevators.

Smoke and fire alarm systems.

Should any or all of these features be combined with the public telephone system?

i.   Emergency light and power. Should this be the minimum required by code or should such possibly noncovered uses as elevators, domestic water pressure pumps, heating boilers, and pumps be provided with standby power?

LOCATION

The decision to discuss the building program before location is arbitrary, and it can be fairly argued that location is probably the major contributor to the success or failure of any project.

The stigma attached to public housing in the United States is in no small measure due to location. Built in the most deteriorated parts of the city, in areas in which delinquency and crime are rampant, these projects are doomed to fail even if all other conditions—proper tenant selection and education, concerned management, and well-designed buildings—are properly met.

To realize the importance of location in the private sector of housing one only has to remember the often quoted statement by the developer who, when asked the secret of a successful apartment project, replied, "The secret lies in three factors. The first is location, the second is location, and the third is location."

A successful development starts out with the search for land. Whether the site is urban or exurban, the astute developer has to know a great deal about the property, not only its physical and environmental conditions but also the stability of the area.

For the architect the physical and environmental characteristics of the site become generators of design which, like the building program data, narrow the choices and lead to a solution. In the very best cases architectural design will be sensitive to its context.

SURFACE

1.   SIZE.   Accurate surveys must be available showing lot dimensions and lot line angles. Special attention must be paid to such possible limitations as deeded restrictions and permanent easements.

2.   BOUNDARIES.   Property line conditions often carry hidden hazards: party walls, adjacent foundations or basements to be protected, and proposed street widenings.

3.   TOPOGRAPHY.   Terrain elevations should be known at regular intervals not only on the property but also on adjacent properties, sidewalks, and curbs.

4.   ECOLOGY.   Surface drainage patterns, surface soil, flora, and natural features such as rocks and water should be investigated.

SUBSURFACE

1.   SOIL.   Composition, stability, and load bearing capacity must be analyzed by a qualified soil engineer.

2.   WATER.   Knowledge of the current water table alone is not enough; predictable rise of water level should also be considered.

3.   UTILITIES.   Proper survey should include all utilities, including water, sewer (storm and sanitary), and gas and electric lines.

4.   HINDRANCES.   As far as possible—by soil borings or historical investigation—underground hazards, such as rock formations, underground streams, peat areas, fills,

abandoned foundations, or filled-over structures like railroad beds and wharves should be uncovered.

CLIMATE

1.   TEMPERATURE.   Knowledge of the extremes and duration are needed to make decisions about environmental control systems.

2.   PRECIPITATION.   Maximum rain and snowfall will determine site issues such as drainage or snow removal. Humidity must also be known.

3.   SUN.   Direction and angles throughout the year; knowing where shadows are cast by adjacent structures is essential in locating and orienting buildings.

4.   WIND.   Awareness of direction, velocity, and unusual conditions created by adjacent structures will eliminate irreversible, faulty decisions.

HAZARDS

1.   POLLUTANTS.   Data on sources of smoke, fumes, and unpleasant odors and wind direction are necessary for proper building placement.

2.   NOISE.   Train lines, truck routes, and proximity to airports or other noise sources will influence the location of structures as well as the intensity of sound insulation.

3.   OTHER.   Presence of unusual hazards such as high-tension lines, adjacent subway, atomic plant, flooding and shore erosion, wave action, vibration, and earthquakes should be investigated.

VEHICULAR TRAFFIC

1.   VOLUME AND DIRECTION.   Maximum number of vehicles on adjacent roads at critical hours, one-way streets, traffic lights, speed limits; any proposed change in traffic direction; any proposed street widening or introduction of median strips.

2.   RESTRICTIONS.   Width of permitted curb cuts, their minimum distance from one another and from nearest intersection; special curb cut visibility requirements.

3.   PARKING.   Conditions of on-street parking; availability of public parking facilities in the vicinity.

ACTIVITY PATTERNS

1.   CIRCULATION.   Observation of human movement systems on or around the site will help the architect to locate the elements of the design in context.

2.   BEHAVIOR.   Individual and group behavior observable around or on the site will suggest responses to design criteria such as territoriality, socialization, and so on.

COMMUNITY FACILITIES

1.   REDUNDANCY.   Availability of recreational facilities such as parks, sport fields, or playgrounds will eliminate duplication in the project.

2.   LINKAGE.   Awareness of the location of educational and religious institutions, health and recreation facilities, commercial services, public transportation, and so on will influence pedestrian networks, especially on larger projects.

VISUAL CONDITIONS

1.   BUILDINGS.   Extent of physical stability and degree of deterioration of neighboring buildings; their architectural style, scale, predominant material, and fenestration.

2. STREETSCAPE. Buildings viewed as a total composition: continuity, height, and character of street facades. Is the existing pattern worth reinforcing?

3. PANORAMA. Is there anything worth looking at during the day or at night? Conversely: significant view channels of the neighborhood that will be influenced by the proposed project.

4. FEATURES. Significant structures, historical buildings, monuments, or natural features such as hills and forests worth relating to.

SERVICES

1. FIRE FIGHTING. Although building codes determine minimum safety requirements, it is essential to know the character and availability of local firefighting equipment, especially in exurban locations. The project should be discussed with the local fire chief in a small community with a limited fire department.

2. REFUSE COLLECTION. Private or public, frequency, type of vehicle.

3. STREET. Frequency and method of snow removal, street cleaning, maintenance, and lighting.

4. MAIL. Frequency of delivery and collection; any specific governmental requirements?

5. MISCELLANEOUS. Various services such as tree protection or anti-insect programs.

ZONING

> If there is any one rigid control that has the greatest influence on apartment house design, it is zoning. Although a community may realize the necessity of controlling land use to the best advantage of all, many of the zoning regulations are based on arbitrary standards and are fraught with political pressures. The objective is to provide controls so that residential living conditions will be at a high enough level to foster health, safety, and the public welfare, and to set a pattern for the orderly growth of the community in order to eliminate blight and congestion. But unless the zoning ordinance has a built-in process for adapting its provisions to meet changing conditions and advances in land planning, it can become archaic and defeat its very objectives.[6]

Unfortunately, after 50 years of zoning, blight is still with us. As David J. Mandel, eloquent and sincere advocate of no zoning at all, has said:

> Since zoning is only one of a host of forces shaping land use, it is difficult to measure its practical effects. There certainly is no evidence that the introduction of comprehensive zoning has improved the amenities of cities and substantial evidence that it has reduced them.[7]

A better understanding of the evolution of the zoning concept will clarify its purpose and spirit and encourage the architect to become concerned in shaping its future.

Zoning started in the United States in the 1920s and, simply stated, provided "all landowners with knowledge before the fact of what they could and could not do with their land."[8] It resulted in the simplistic subdivision of municipal areas into single-family, commercial, and industrial zones, with complete lack of preparation for future development. By the late 1950s most cities had rewritten their zoning ordinances using a more sophisticated division (several density areas in the residential zone) to control bulk, density, light and air, off-street parking, and loading by various formulas.

Unavoidably, the planners also formed an image that the ordinance was to achieve. Housing in the 1950s—based on Le Corbusier's early vision of towers in an urban park—led to serious zoning problems, the most obvious of which was the destruction of streets and city matrix, the lack of reference points, problems of safety and surveillance, and ultimately repetition and monotony. This type of zoning in each residential district in effect built in a preconceived prototype and led many to say that not the architect but the zoning ordinance designed the apartment buildings.

In this zoning "there is no sensitivity beyond generalized mapping for the various neighborhoods within the city. Both Greenwich Village and South Bronx are mapped R-6. No account is taken of the various geographic, social or economic conditions within these dramatically different areas."[9] High-density areas—with their high land values—are mapped to perpetuate existing real estate conditions and to protect and insulate the single-family areas. High-density housing along recent major rapid transit arteries, a development that would foster urban rejuvenation, becomes impossibly difficult under current mapping.

The social consequences of the zoning of the 1950s are equally serious. The poor are segregated from the rich (by minimum lot size per dwelling), the old from the young (by allowing no apartment buildings for the elderly in zones in which their children live). Based on the old theory that the glue factory has a deleterious effect on humans, zoning removes housing from other areas of human activity, such as shopping, restaurants, and crafts, and results in dormitory districts with dull, unsafe, unfriendly, and lifeless streets "because there is seldom any active reason for a good cross section of people to use them,"[10] thus robbing us of the richness of human interaction that has traditionally been a major attraction of the city. Looking at the cities of Europe, it becomes obvious that the strict separation of residential from other day-to-day activities is really not necessary and "zoning for diversity," as so admirably argued by Jane Jacobs, will result in richer, safer, and visually more stimulating neighborhoods.

As if all this were not enough as a condemnation, the zoning of the 1950s is obsolete and inflexible. It was based on knowledge and technology that tried to address itself to problems already decades old when the zoning plan was written. Not only was it therefore obsolete when it became law, but it was assumed to create an ideal world that would never need adjusting. Because the authors were looking through "clouded crystal balls,"[11] to use Babcock's term, zoning became a set of frozen rules.

To deal with this lack of flexibility several devices were introduced. One popular technique, still with us, was the special use permit, which allowed a review of each proposal that did not follow the existing ordinance.

A far more resilient instrument is the discretionary review, or the Planned Unit Development (PUD), which eliminates the ad hoc quality of the special use permit. Each project that usually requires a certain minimum land area to qualify, is judged on its own merit, in fact preempting existing zoning. "Pre-regulation gives way to negotiation."[12] This zoning technique is responsive to the pressure in the suburbs to increase density and to depart from the practice of having a single house on an individual lot to having clusters in which walls are shared and roads and utilities are economized on. The trouble with PUD is threefold: it requires an intelligent, flexible, architecturally sensitive, and politically independent staff to prevent zoning from becoming a political football; it is time consuming; the architect and the developer usually work with inadequate criteria, not knowing in advance what they will or will not be permitted to do.

Bonuses (rewards to the developer with larger building areas in exchange for various concessions such as larger apartments in Chicago or arcades and theaters in New York) did not make zoning more flexible.

DATA GATHERING

The most imaginative approach in recent years came from the Urban Design Corporation of New York in their proposal for zoning reform in New York City, a modified version of which has been added to the New York zoning laws. In contrast to current zoning practices, it does "not mandate all requirements nor offer voluntary bonuses for specific amenities. Instead, within given limits, the entire process would be elective, setting goals rather than minimum standards that effectively become maximum achievements."[13]

How does it work?

In order to put up a new residential building, a developer would have to earn a sufficient number of quality points in the four identified programs of quality; namely, neighborhood impact, recreation space, security and safety, and the apartment. The point system is delicately calibrated: different values are given for different elements and for varying degrees of compliance with each specific goal. For twenty-two of the elements, a minimum level of compliance is specified; extra points would be gained by going beyond that minimum. The degree of compliance of the other fifteen elements would be left to the discretion of the developer.

Although minimum compliance with the twenty-two basic elements would yield a project of acceptable quality, the scoring has been established in such a way that there is always an incentive to achieve higher levels of quality to the mutual benefit of developer and tenant alike. By its flexibility, the proposed zoning would offer a free choice system that for the first time accurately mirrors the selective process of actual planning and design. A developer and his architect could choose to amass points by enlarging room sizes while sacrificing some degree of visual privacy, or by providing larger windows but deleting balconies.

The proposed Housing Quality Program recognizes the diversity of neighborhoods and the different needs of an already-developed as opposed to a predominantly vacant area. The present limitations on ground coverage would be removed so as to produce the opportunity for lower buildings and economic efficiencies. Recreation activities would now be encouraged not only outdoors, but also on rooftops and even within the buildings. Increased security is envisioned, for example, by making elevator lobbies visible from the sidewalks.[14]

Notwithstanding all sincere attempts for reform, the frozen rules are still around and it is essential for the designer to understand them. Failure of thorough zoning investigation can result in serious and costly problems. Because the language of bureaucracy is not always clear, interpretation must be requested from the officials before making assumptions. When zoning is by Planned Unit Development, architects must be familiar with overall plans and the intentions of the planners who will negotiate with them and their clients and will give the final approval for solutions.

Zoning ordinances deal with land use, building bulk, density, light and air, parking, and loading.

LAND USE. Most cities are divided into residential, business, commercial, and manufacturing areas. The residential, "R" districts (in some cities denoted as "H" for housing), are further subdivided into R-1, R-2, R-3, and so on, as density increases from single-family detached houses (R-1) all the way to high-density highrises.

DENSITY.   The number of dwelling units—or families—permitted on any site, related to the size of the lot. There are generally two ways to determine density. The minimum lot area ratio establishes the area of land required per dwelling. If this ratio is 200 sf per dwelling and the property is 20,000 sf, the resultant number of dwellings is 100. Another way to define density is dwelling unit per acre (DUA).

BULK.   Most often the volume of the building is related to the lot size multiplied by a floor area ratio which can vary from 0.5 in single-family districts to 10 or more in highrise districts.

Some cities offer bonuses in density and/or bulk allowing an increase in density or in bulk above the normally permitted maximum if the developer meets certain conditions; for example, in Chicago both density and bulk can be increased when the lot faces an open public space of a certain size; floor area ratio, therefore bulk, can be increased if the developer decreases the density below the allowable maximum, thereby encouraging the construction of larger apartments.

Bulk is sometimes determined vertically by limiting the height of the buildings and horizontally by yard setbacks and/or percentage of permissible ground coverage—in fact, providing an envelope within which the structure must fit.

LIGHT AND AIR.   Light and air are provided by open space between other structures and the building on the site. Zoning ordinances have various formulas to determine setbacks for front, side, and rear yards or for distances between buildings. These formulas are related to the lot dimensions and the building height.

PARKING.   The minimum number of parking spaces to be provided, off the street, in relation to the number of dwellings.

LOADING.   The minimum number of loading stalls to be provided, off the street, based on the number of dwellings or the total floor area of the building.

BUILDING CODE

Next to zoning ordinances, building codes represent the severest restricting force in the design process. The purpose of the code is to protect life, to ensure safety, and to prevent the ignorant or the unscrupulous from endangering the well-being of the user or the public. If zoning determines "what and where," codes tell us "how."

Although we can quarrel about the necessity of zoning, there is little doubt about the need for a code; we only have to look at the shoddily built houses and apartment buildings that are possible under relatively stringent codes to make us shudder at what would happen in the absence of regulations. A visit to one of the rapidly growing, politically corrupt South American countries is enough to convince most of those who oppose codes.

This is not to say that codes are either perfect or fair. They can be products of selfish local interests, politically strong local unions, and manufacturers' associations.

Another shortcoming of building codes is their inflexibility. They, like zoning ordinances, are based on knowledge rooted in the past and are not updated often enough to allow the constantly appearing new materials and products.

The worst problem facing the architect regarding codes is the lack of uniformity from one city to the other. Some cities have adopted basic building codes. Others, usually large cities with adequate staffs, have written their own codes, which may then be adopted by some of the larger suburbs that lack help. Many small towns and suburbs have highly inadequate and scanty codes. The periodic enthusiasm for a nationwide uniform building code that would still recognize unique regional conditions such as climate or earthquakes dies fast in the face of vested local interests.

Because of these variations, when architects work in cities new to them, they are well advised to acquaint themselves thoroughly with the code.

In spite of the fact that codes vary to such a great extent, there is enough similarity among them to distill the common design generators. A large part of all codes is taken up with regulations that deal with materials, their properties, and installation methods. Although ultimately they do affect design, they are beyond the scope of this study.

USE

All codes recognize the differences between buildings according to their occupancy and use. Among the various categories—factories, commercial structures, institutional buildings, and assembly buildings—one is residential. Under this specific use codes define the rooms that are considered habitable and therefore in need of natural light and ventilation. They establish the minimum ceiling height, the maximum travel distance to exits, the minimal exit dimensions based on maximum possible occupancy. In mixed use the separation required between the residential part of the structure and hazardous use (garage) is stated.

CONSTRUCTION TYPES

Construction Type[a]	Fire Rating (hr)		Maximum Number of Floors[b]	Maximum Floor Area of Each Floor[c] (sf)
	Floors	Columns		
FIREPROOF All noncombustible with high rating of elements	2–3	3–4	7 and up	No limit
NONCOMBUSTIBLE All noncombustible with lower rating of elements	1–1½	2	5–6	8000–20,000
ORDINARY Combustible interior elements with protected exterior such as masonry	¾–1	¾–1	3–4	6000–8000
FRAME Interior and exterior combustible	½	½	1–2	5000–6000

[a] A separate table usually sets the rate of fire separation between different construction types such as a "fireproof" garage and the "ordinary" apartment building above it.

[b] Sometimes when a floor is below the level of adjacent street or grade it does not count as a "floor" according to the code, thereby increasing the allowable number of floors. However, it must be determined, probably elsewhere in the code, whether this below-grade floor can be used for habitation.

[c] Floor areas can be increased if adequate distance between the building and other structures provides accessibility for fire-fighting equipment. Some codes also permit an increase if the building is equipped with automatic sprinklers—a costly item in housing. However, sprinklers in the garage or portions of the garage falling under the residential section of the building are usually required by code even when the entire building has "fireproof" construction. Sprinklers are also required by HUD for certain areas of housing for the elderly.

CONSTRUCTION TYPES

For each use-category different floor-area and height limitations are set according to their degree of fireproofing under four basic construction types. Some cities limit some of these construction types to stated "fire districts" in the municipal area. The following table reflects in general terms the relation between the number of floors, their size, and the particular construction for residential occupancy. It is a distillation of many tables, and although it is not valid in any particular city, it is an indication of the limitations set by most building codes (see table on p. 14).

LIGHT AND AIR

Codes define for all habitable rooms the minimum amount of light (glass area) and natural ventilation (operating sash area) required. This is usually a set percentage of the floor area of each room, generally 10% for light and 5% for natural ventilation; if the room is exceedingly deep, these percentages are increased.

When windows required for light and natural ventilation are located in an exterior wall of a true court or a significant indentation of the building, most codes define these courts as inner, through, or outer, and regulate their size in relation to the height of the building.

EXITS

Exits are just one means of providing fire safety, an issue discussed in detail in a separate chapter. Here, we submit a brief summary of the exit elements, keeping in mind that codes vary in their requirements for maximum distance, dimensions, and even kind and number of exits.

CAPACITY.   The width of doors, corridor, and stairs is related to maximum occupancy load determined by the number of square feet of floor area per person or by the number of bedrooms per floor.

NUMBER OF EXITS.   In most cases a minimum of two exits is required, but in lowrise buildings of certain construction type, height, floor area, and number of dwellings, one exit may be permitted.

TRAVEL DISTANCE.   Maximum distance between apartment entrance and stair doors is defined as allowable travel distance. Codes also regulate the maximum length of dead-end corridors beyond the stairs. Inside the apartments the maximum distance between the entry and the remotest part of the apartment or the remotest door is sometimes stated. In large apartments this might necessitate two entries.

STAIRS.   Maximum riser height, minimum tread width, maximum number of risers between landings, landing width in relation to door swing, and fire rating of the stair shaft and its openings are defined. The code also determines whether any of the stairs can be open.

HORIZONTAL EXITS.   The code regulates whether stairs on the ground level must open directly to the outside, whether they can have a horizontal fireproof corridor leading to the outside, or whether they can lead into a lobby.

RAMPS.   In residential occupancies a ramp is a seldom-used means of egress. It is more important in the garage. The code limits the maximum degree of slope if the garage ramp is used as an exit.

SMOKEPROOF TOWER.   A smokeproof tower is achieved when the vestibule in front of the stair door opens to an exterior balcony or to a vertical shaft that will draw the smoke from the corridor before it can enter the stair shaft proper. The code defines size and details of shaft and vestibule and determines whether both of the required exit stairs or only one must be a smokeproof tower and at what building height.

ENERGY CONSERVATION

Some codes have recently adopted energy conservation regulations that deal with the maximum amount of heat loss through the building envelope. Glass areas must be minimized and dual-glazed, and solid walls and roofs must have high degrees of thermal insulation. These regulations place severe limitations on exterior design, the consequences of which are far reaching.

ACCESS BY THE HANDICAPPED

Many local codes have adopted special regulations to serve the handicapped, primarily the wheelchair-bound person. Various agencies, the state, HUD, or others may have their own requirements. Since these regulations entail more space than is needed in designs for normally functioning people, thorough understanding of them will prevent later compromises in the plan and embarrassment.

MISCELLANEOUS JURISDICTIONS

Some cities, or lending institutions, require that, in addition to the local code, the Life Safety Code (published by the National Fire Protection Association) be followed. Most cities—or the particular states in which they are located—have special regulations for the design of swimming pools and day care centers.

These rules by no means limit the agencies that may have jurisdiction over a project. They run the gamut from air pollution control to fire departments, street and highway departments, local park districts, and federal agencies covering a variety of matters such as aviation. When a building is constructed under federal mortgage insurance, minimum property standards must be followed. Regional HUD offices, state housing agencies, and local housing authorities have their own architectural staffs and consequently may have their own criteria for the architect to deal with.

Preliminary to understanding codes and regulations is the task of determining exactly what agencies have jurisdiction over a project and finding out whether they have set regulations. When they do not have set regulations, it is essential to have the preliminary site and building concept reviewed to avoid later changes.

BUDGET

"It is easy to design a great museum or office building, but so very difficult to design good housing"—I. M. Pei, in *Architecture Plus*, March 1973.

It is difficult enough because of the severe limitations of function and the limited options of architectural form, but it is even more difficult because of budget. This is not to say that other types of building are not budgeted.

The apartment must be built to a lower cost per square foot than any other type of building except single-family houses and certain industrial buildings. As an example, a medium highrise office building (without the office partitions) constructed by an owner-builder will cost at least 50 percent more than a medium highrise apartment project built also by an owner-builder, using the square foot or cubic foot basis as a standard for cost comparison. The apartment project will include all the partitioning as well as all kitchen and bathroom equipment. The reason why the builder can spend this difference on office buildings is that he can command two to three times the rent of an apartment project, again using the square foot as a comparable basis.[15]

Developers build apartment buildings in order to produce an income (or depreciation for tax calculations which for our purposes does not change the picture). The building itself is only one unknown, although the largest one, in a most complex economic equation, and slight variations of construction cost can have severe results in the last line of that equation called income.

In the public sector budget is equally important. Buildings for which federally insured mortgages are provided at favorable rates and long amortization periods have an even lower construction cost limit than those that are privately financed. Regardless of whether we are talking about the private or public sector, the building must make economic sense.

This does not mean that the lowest-cost solution is necessarily the most desirable one. Cost alone is meaningless. It gains meaning as part of a total equation where rent, market price, or profit are other components. It is meaningless to say that one building is costlier than another, that it is too expensive. It may not be if at the higher cost it still can be rented or marketed with a reasonable profit.

Because cost of construction is so important a factor, it must be looked at before the design process can start. Although public agencies and well-experienced builder-developer clients will set budgets without consulting the architect, it is essential that the architect be able to scrutinize these preestablished budgets. When budgets are set with the cooperation of the architect, there are no excuses.

At the top of the list is the proper definition of construction cost. Does it include the builder's profit, or in case of a builder-developer does it mean cost plus overhead only? By construction cost do they mean the bare building or are such items as appliances, corridor carpeting, landscaping, and furnishings in public areas included?

When a cost figure based on the square foot (the more common basis in housing) is established, it is usually related to the architect's or the developer's recent cost experience with similar building types, although we have to question how similar. It is certainly not enough that the building with which the cost figures were compared is also an apartment house. Before we can accept these cost figures, we have to consider all conditions to ensure that apples are not being compared with pears; for instance:

1.   If one structure has small one-bedroom apartments and efficiencies and therefore a high proportion of partitions, kitchens, and bathrooms per square foot, it cannot be compared in cost with a building that contains larger two-bedroom apartments.

2.   One project may need a large amount of site development, earth moving, and new roads; the other, on an urban site, will have few of these. In order to get a fair cost comparision, the cost of site development should be handled separately.

3.   Soil and foundation conditions on two projects must be taken into consideration when comparing unit costs.

4.   When we use the unit cost figures of a recent building of similar size, we still have to

make certain that the two buildings—the recently completed and the proposed—will have similar mechanical systems, quality of exteriors, and amenities.

5. When two buildings are compared, they should also contain a similar size and kind of parking structure. A most important caveat! Because garage floors cost less than apartment floors, an apartment building with an enclosed, multilevel parking garage will cost less per average square foot (including garage area) than a similar building with open, on-grade parking, but the cost per apartment naturally will be considerably higher.

6. Comparison must be made in terms of location and time. Construction costs vary from city to city, a point that should be carefully considered. When we say that a building—on which we have based our estimate—costs so much, it is important to realize that we do not mean the year in which it was completed but the year in which it was bid or bought, probably two years before. Had it been bid at the date of completion, it is likely that it would have cost more. Similarly, the time that elapses between the setting of the budget and the actual date of bidding, or buying, is crucial, especially so because neither the architect nor the owner has control over the time it will take to obtain financing. Attention must be paid to a proper inflation factor.

7. When the cost of the building volume is discussed (per square foot or cubic foot), we must make sure that everyone concerned—owner, architect, and contractor—uses the same basis to establish the volume. The following tabulation illustrates a generally accepted way to deal with such controversial oddities as balconies, arcades, and developed decks.

	Area	Floor Height	Volume
Penthouse	.... sf @	.... ft =	.... cf
Tower			
a. Enclosed: Typical floor area × number of floors	= .... sf @	.... ft =	.... cf
b. Balconies: Floor area of all balconies on typical floor × number of floors; total multiplied by 0.5	= .... sf @	.... ft =	.... cf
Intermediate Floor			
a. Enclosed floor area	= .... sf @	.... ft =	.... cf
b. Open area under tower multiplied by 0.66	= .... sf @	.... ft =	.... cf
Base			
a. Enclosed floor area	= .... sf @	.... ft =	.... cf
b. Arcade floor area multiplied by 0.66	= .... sf @	.... ft =	.... cf
Developed Roof Deck Area multiplied by 0.33 to 0.66, depending on extent of development	= .... sf @	.... ft =	.... cf
Basement Floor	= .... sf @	.... ft =	.... cf
Totals	.... sf		.... cf

Total square feet × $ per square foot = total cost
Total cost ÷ number of apartments = cost per apartment

18

It is important for the designer to be aware of how the average cost per square foot breaks down in trades or components of the building. Needless to say, this breakdown will vary from building to building. Although two buildings are seldom identical and it is dangerous to generalize, a highrise usually breaks down as follows:

Structural frame	22–30%
Plumbing, ventilation, heating, air conditioning, electrical	24–28%
Exterior skin	7–10%
Partitions	7– 9%
Elevators	3– 6%
Balance of trades	20–25%

The importance of design decisions regarding structural framing and mechanical systems cannot be overemphasized because the two together can constitute 50% or more of the building cost. Of the balance the three major cost items that involve early and basic architectural decisions are the exterior skin, the partitions, and the elevators.

COMPONENTS OF DESIGN— ARCHITECTURAL

2

John Macsai

Once the programming or data gathering has been completed the architect is ready to design. The design process will entail responding to the challenge of the program by utilizing knowledge of the component elements of housing.

The more an architect knows about these elements, the easier the work will be. This is not to say that acquaintance with the component elements and experience in housing will ensure good design! However, to have the components at one's fingertips will facilitate the design process considerably.

This knowledge is obtained in a variety of ways, from a variety of sources. Experience in housing, obviously the major source, is a storehouse of information. The less experienced designer will obtain knowledge by studying other buildings, from books and magazines, and from teammates and colleagues.

The purpose of the following chapters is to introduce these component elements. They are not a substitute for experience. They do not approximate the detailed data available in reference books. In the same manner, the structural and mechanical sections will not make the designer an engineer. They will, however, make communication with the engineering consultants more meaningful.

DWELLING UNIT

It is assumed that the client and the architect have jointly established a program for the building. At the heart of this program is the kind and size of dwelling, or apartment, that fits the particular group of users.

There is no "average" apartment. Demographic studies of the past decade have shown a large variety of emerging apartment types. The increasing average age of the population has led to the development of an apartment type for those who are leaving large homes after their families have moved out. A growing number of apartments are occupied by nonfamily households. Changes within the family structure itself have resulted in changing demands for apartment plans for families in which both parents work or in which there is only one parent.

Even if we have the results of reliable user research at hand and have determined the user type, we still do not know the actual persons who are going to live in the apartment—as we try to know the individuals for whom we may be designing a single-family home. Individual families live differently from each other, even if they belong to the same economic, age, occupation, and ethnic groups. Therefore in an apartment building the spaces themselves must be simple and universal enough to adapt to a variety of life styles.

Although much has been said about the universal nature of each space in an apartment, one should still be able to find criteria for the design of each space. These criteria result from the way people live or move through their apartments. A well-planned apartment provides maximum privacy for various activities and makes movement between rooms without crossing another possible.

ENTERING THE APARTMENT.   In inclement weather it should be possible to take off and put away outer clothing at the entrance, to store umbrellas and boots to prevent dirtying the floors of other rooms, and to put down packages.

ENTERING WITH GROCERIES OR LEAVING WITH GARBAGE.   Connection between entrance and kitchen should be as direct as possible, preferably through the entry hall and not the living space. A secondary entrance directly into the kitchen solves this problem.

CHILDREN COMING IN FROM PLAY OR ENTERING WHILE ADULT ACTIVITY IS TAKING PLACE.   Children should be able to reach the bathroom or their own rooms without crossing the living space.

DELIVERIES.   It should be possible to accept and pay for packages without having the deliverer enter the living space.

PASSING FROM BEDROOM TO BATHROOM.   It should not be necessary to cross the living space. Ideally, one should not be seen from the living space at all.

PASSING FROM KITCHEN TO BATHROOM.   This should be done, if possible, without crossing the living space.

SERVING FROM KITCHEN TO DINING ROOM.   Service should be as direct as possible without crossing any other space (except, if necessary, the entry hall).

Ideal circulation criteria are achieved by proper planning of the rooms around the core of the apartment, which consists of the entry hall and the bedroom corridor. In fact a well-planned apartment can be divided into two zones, living zone and sleeping zone, separated by the entry hall.

Neither this simple geometric division nor the ideal circulation pattern is always possible. Corner apartments, walk-ups, and row houses often require functional compromise to achieve economy.

As important as the relation of one room to another is the provision for daylight and fresh air. Ideally, every room in an apartment should have exterior exposure to ensure light and air. To plan for this, however, would increase the perimeter of the building to an extent that no one could afford to build it. Therefore bathrooms (almost invariably), kitchens (often), and dining rooms (sometimes) are handled as interior spaces. This is possible because building codes allow bathrooms and kitchens to be mechanically ventilated, because an inside dining alcove is really an extension of the living space, and because the kitchen can be situated to borrow light from the living or dining room. Thus the apartment plan is divided into outer and inner zones. Naturally, units with double exposure—row houses, duplex walk-ups, exterior gallery-type buildings, and corner apartments anywhere—can have kitchens and dining rooms in the outer zone without difficulty.

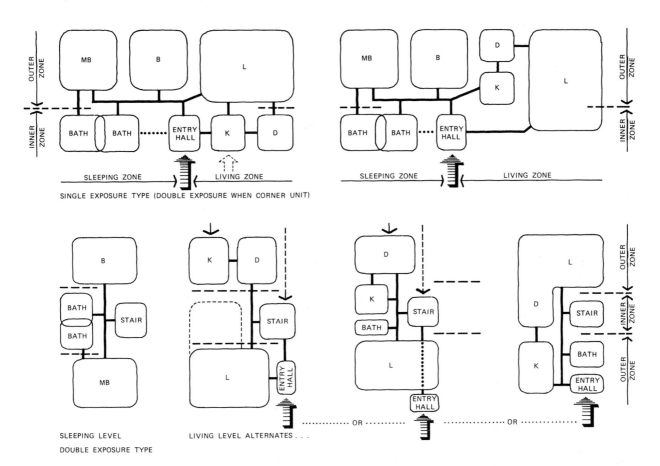

Roger Sherwood groups dwelling types into double-aspect 90 degree (corner units), double-aspect open-ended (single-family house, row house), single-aspect (high-rise).[16]

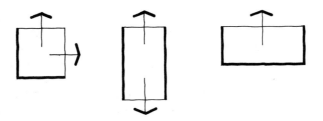

The approximate size and proportion of the rooms themselves must be included in the sponsor's program. Extreme care must be taken on public or federally assisted housing jobs because minimum dimensions given as guidelines cannot be accepted without scrutiny.

In the private building sector, market conditions and competition are the best gauge of room sizes. Awareness of the local housing market is essential, for market conditions

COMPONENTS OF DESIGN—ARCHITECTURAL

vary considerably not only from city to city but from neighborhood to neighborhood. As an example, the Chicago market above low income demands a separate alcove as a defined dining space; in New York the entry hall, often serves as a dining area. Considerably larger rooms are called for along Chicago's Lake Shore Drive than in Old Town, just a few blocks away.

MINIMUM ROOM SIZES

	Minimum Area (sf)					
Name of Space	LU with 0 BR	LU with 1 BR	LU with 2 BR	LU with 3 BR	LU with 4 BR	Least Dimension
MINIMUM ROOM SIZES FOR SEPARATE ROOMS						
LR	NA	160	160	170	180	11 ft 0 in.
DR	NA	100	100	110	120	8 ft 4 in.
BR (primary)	NA	120	120	120	120	9 ft 4 in.
BR (secondary)	NA	NA	80	80	80	8 ft 0 in.
Total area, BRs	NA	120	200	280	380	
MINIMUM ROOM SIZES FOR COMBINED SPACES						
LR-DA	NA	210	210	230	250	
LR-DA-SL	250	NA	NA	NA	NA	
LR-DA-K	NA	270	270	300	330	
LR-SL	210	NA	NA	NA	NA	
K-DA	100	120	120	140	160	

Abbreviations:

LU = living unit K = kitchen
LR = living room NA = not applicable
DR = dining room BR = bedroom
DA = dining area SL = sleeping area

The architect's most reliable guide is a thorough analysis of the function, furnishings, and circulation pattern of each space. In this respect HUD guidelines for minimum furniture requirements are quite reliable, assuming naturally that proper circulation space is provided. To ensure comfortable use and adequate dimensions we can safely refer to *Time Saver Standards*, latest edition (McGraw-Hill, New York).

LIVING ROOM (LIVING-DINING ROOM)

The living room should allow for group activities as well as individual relaxation: "entertaining, reading, writing, listening to music, watching television, and children's play."[17] It should be separated from the main circulation pattern of the apartment. It should be flexible enough to allow for various furniture arrangements and for the extension of the dining activity when occasion demands. Under certain conditions it should accommodate alternate activities such as study or music. HUD *Minimum Property Standards* calls for the following furniture as a minimum to be accommodated with the accompanying clearances:

One couch, 3 ft 0 in. by 6 ft 10 in.
Two easy chairs, 2 ft 6 in. by 3 ft 0 in.
    (one for efficiency apartment)
    (three for four or more bedroom units)
One desk, 1 ft 8 in. by 3 ft 6 in.
One desk chair, 1 ft 6 in. by 1 ft 6 in.

One television set, 1 ft 4 in. by 2 ft 8 in.
One table, 1 ft 6 in. by 2 ft 6 in.
60 in. between facing chairs or couch
24 in. where circulation occurs between furniture
30 in. in front of a desk
36 in. for main traffic
60 in. between television set and seating

The living room is the most impressive and largest of all rooms in the apartment, which is why many developers like it to be visible from the entry hall.

The living room in the average middle-income two-bedroom apartment is about 260 to 300 sf; combined living-dining room is about 400 sf. When the living room is also used for dining, its proportions, with minimum waste, become critical. Typical square (20 ft by 20 ft) living-dining rooms are far less efficient than the oblong (15 ft by 26 ft) of the same square footage.

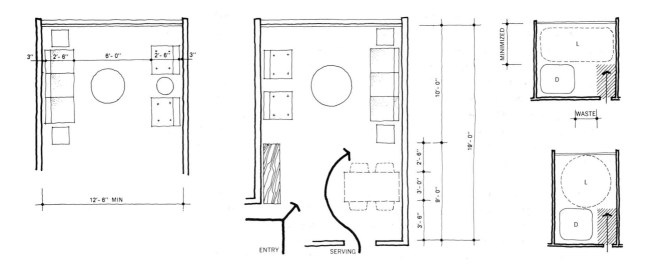

DINING

A truly separate dining room can be afforded only in row houses or luxury housing. The most common arrangement takes the form of an alcove off the living room. Although this alcove can occupy an inner zone, a windowed area is preferable even though it creates a larger building perimeter and consequently increases costs. When a large group of diners is to be accommodated, the table must be expanded into the living room and space should be provided for it without having to move heavy furniture.

HUD *Minimum Property Standards* calls for the table and chair requirements listed below. They should be considered not only with proper circulation space and pattern of food serving in mind but also in relation to space for storage.

Efficiency or one bedroom, two persons: 2 ft 6 in. by 2 ft 6 in.
Two bedrooms, four persons: 2 ft 6 in. by 3 ft 2 in.
Three bedrooms, six persons: 3 ft 4 in. by 4 ft 0 in. or 4 ft round
Four or more bedrooms, eight persons: 3 ft 4 in. by 6 ft 0 in. or 4 ft square
Dining chairs: 1 ft 6 in. square

In middle-income two-bedroom apartments an average dining alcove is about 100 sf, and a separate dining room is about 140 sf.

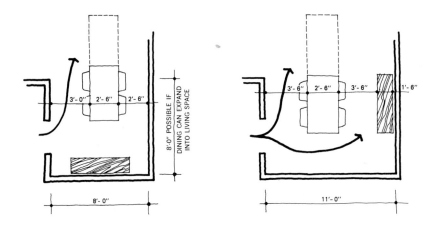

BALCONIES

There is much controversy about the need for balconies, which are costly, and it is questionable in profit-motivated housing whether they will result in increased rent or sales price. Besides the balcony's aesthetic factor (it allows strong articulation) and its symbolic significance (a visible indication of the presence of human beings), its functional role has pros and cons. Those who argue for it stress the delight of sitting outdoors when the weather is pleasant. They call attention to the visual extension of the living space, to extra storage space, and to the opportunity to grow plants or place condensing units. Those who oppose balconies claim that they cut off daylight, that they are dirt catchers and are hard to keep clean, and in many regions can be used only part of the year. Balconies are most popular in Europe:

> ...every dwelling should have some outdoor space—a terrace, loggia or balcony to enable the occupiers to sit or stay outside the enclosed living space. Even if the balcony can only be used for a few days or weeks of the year, it enables the town dweller, deprived of his association with the open countryside, to escape even in a block of flats from the artificial climate of his dwelling—albeit, as in inclement weather, for a moment only.[18]

Balconies must be wide enough for proper use (not less than 5 ft) and have adequate privacy.

KITCHEN

To provide for the most efficient food preparation, storage, and service, careful planning is required. *Architectural Graphic Standards* (latest edition), Ramsey and Sleeper (Wiley, New York), is an excellent guide and HUD *Minimum Property Standards* contains useful information on dimensional requirements for counter tops, fixtures, and storage cabinets. Storage space normally provided in cabinets or utility closets can be expanded by the addition of shallow pantries: floor-to-ceiling shelving behind hinged doors.

Unless space is extremely tight, kitchens should be equipped with a small eating space to augment the regular dining room or alcove. When the kitchen is part of a combined kitchen-dining or kitchen-family room, the food preparation–cooking space should be screened from the dining or family area to allow additional activities with some sense of privacy. In planning kitchens, the basic sequence of refrigerator-sink-stove, starting from the door and progressing toward the serving and eating areas, should be observed. The method of connecting with the dining room or alcove, pass-through or door, needs special attention. Well-planned kitchens in an inner zone should borrow daylight from the living or dining space to make working conditions in the kitchen pleasanter. Naturally kitchens with exterior light are preferred.

The proximity of the kitchen to the entry hall (deliveries, refuse) and to the dining room (serving) has already been covered. In certain housing types the kitchen gains an additional function of being a point for observation of children in the yard, or the entry to the unit, or both.

In a middle-income two-bedroom apartment an average kitchen with minimum eating space is about 100 sf.

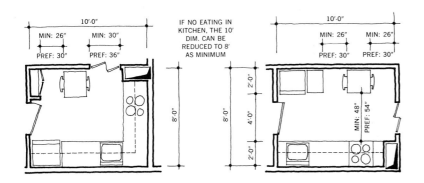
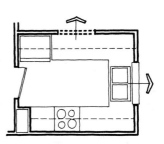

COUNTERTOPS AND FIXTURES

	Number of Bedrooms				
	0	1	2	3	4
Work Center	Minimum Frontages (lin in.)				
Sink	18	24	24	32[a]	32[a]
Countertop, each side	15	18	21	24	30
Range or cooktop space	21	21	24	30	30
Countertop, one side	15	18	21	24	30
Refrigerator space	30	30	36	36	36
Countertop, one side	15	15	15	15	18
Mixing countertop	21	30	36	36	42

[a] When a dishwasher is provided, a 24-in. sink is acceptable.

STORAGE AREA[a]

	Number of Bedrooms				
	0	1	2	3	4
Minimum shelf area (sf)	24	30	38	44	50
Minimum drawer area (sf)	4	6	8	10	12

[a] Wall cabinets over refrigerators and shelves above 74 in. shall not be counted as required storage area.

COMPONENTS OF DESIGN—ARCHITECTURAL

BEDROOM

Each bedroom should have enough space for double occupancy unless the client specifically agrees to its single use. In addition, one must make sure there is adequate space for chest of drawers, desk, chair, night table, and, in the master bedroom, crib and infant paraphernalia (or sewing machine). HUD *Minimum Property Standards* calls for the following basic furniture and clearances:

Two twin beds, 3 ft 3 in. by 6 ft 10 in.
One dresser, 1 ft 6 in. by 4 ft 4 in.
One chair, 1 ft 6 in. by 1 ft 6 in.
One crib, 2 ft 6 in. by 4 ft 6 in.
42 in. at one side or front of bed for dressing
6 in. between side of bed and side of chest
36 in. in front of chest of drawers
24 in. for major circulation path
22 in. on one side of bed for circulation
12 in. on least used side of double bed; the least used side of twin bed can be placed against the wall except in bedrooms for the elderly

In middle-income two-bedroom apartments average bedroom sizes (exclusive of closets) are 150 sf for secondary bedrooms and 180 sf for master bedrooms.

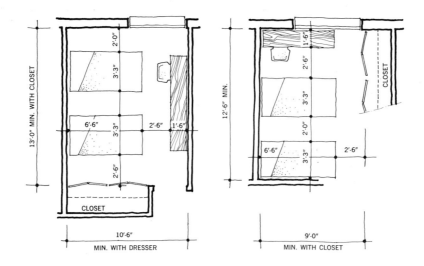

BATHROOMS

For the sake of economy a back-to-back arrangement of bathrooms is preferred either in the same apartment or with one that is adjacent. When there is only one bathroom, a tub and shower combination is standard equipment; when there are two, the second usually contains a stall shower. When an apartment has two or more bathrooms, one is customarily attached to the master bedroom; the others serve the remaining bedrooms. A powder room or lavatory is sometimes substituted for the second bathroom, although the savings are nominal compared with the convenience of having two baths. In luxury housing compartmentalization is an advantage that allows simultaneous multiple use. *Architectural Graphic Standards,* (latest edition) Ramsey and Sleeper (Wiley, New York) is a useful planning guide; for innovative ideas Alexander Kira's *The Bathroom* (Grosset & Dunlap, New York, 1967) is unsurpassed.

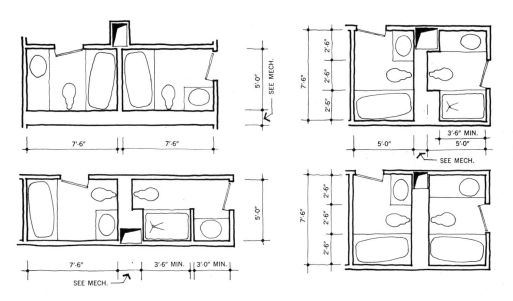

CLOSETS

Although overall apartment size is stated in a client's program, few clients pay attention in the early design stages to the amount and kind of closet space that is provided. It is generally accepted, however, that it is never enough for the tenant or buyer. The tabulation that follows is a guide to closet sizes at various rental levels.

CLOSET SIZES

		Length (lin ft)[a]			
	Depth	Low Rental	Middle	Luxury	HUD Minimum
Guest closet (in or near entry hall)	2 ft 3 in.	3	4	5	2
Utility closet (in or near kitchen)	2 ft 0 in.	2	2	2	2
Pantry (in kitchen)	8 to 10 in.	—	—	4	—
Linen closet (in bedroom hall)	1 ft 6 in.	2	2 to 3	3 to 4	1½
Master-bedroom closet (in bedroom)	2 ft 3 in.	8	10	12	5
Second-bedroom closet (in bedroom)	2 ft 3 in.	6	8	9	3
General storage closet (in entry or bedroom hall)	2 ft 0 in.	—	—	4	—

[a] Or equivalent linear feet in a walk-in closet.

Obviously additional storage space is provided for the user in row houses or attached single-family dwellings. In apartment buildings of other types, a so-called tenant locker has to be provided.

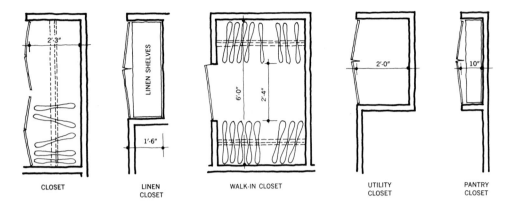

CLOSET LINEN CLOSET WALK-IN CLOSET UTILITY CLOSET PANTRY CLOSET

ENTRY HALL

The precise function of the entry hall should be stipulated. Is it merely for circulation or for other uses as well? For example, if it is to be used for telephoning, a small desk will be

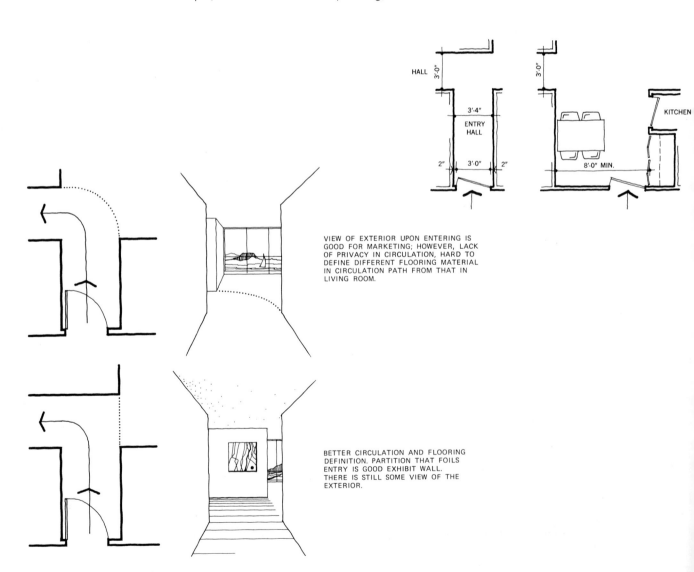

VIEW OF EXTERIOR UPON ENTERING IS GOOD FOR MARKETING; HOWEVER, LACK OF PRIVACY IN CIRCULATION, HARD TO DEFINE DIFFERENT FLOORING MATERIAL IN CIRCULATION PATH FROM THAT IN LIVING ROOM.

BETTER CIRCULATION AND FLOORING DEFINITION. PARTITION THAT FOILS ENTRY IS GOOD EXHIBIT WALL. THERE IS STILL SOME VIEW OF THE EXTERIOR.

required. It might also become an extension of the living room and made large enough for dining.

Entry halls present some special problems, aesthetic, functional, and marketing.

Certain building codes require that large apartments have two exits to the public corridor and that access be made easy to either one by obviating passing through the bedrooms. The ideal location for the second exit is in the kitchen (though it may make its planning more difficult). In this case the connection between the regular entry hall and the kitchen may be eliminated. The second exit, depending on the local code, may also open directly onto the stair landing (with "B" label door), though not when the stair is a smokeproof tower.

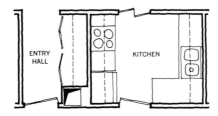

EFFICIENCY APARTMENTS

In efficiency apartments not only room functions but circulation patterns present different problems. Because one space serves for living, dining, and sleeping, precise demarcation is difficult. Still, an attempt must be made to define these areas. The kitchen is usually considerably smaller than those found in regular apartments, and because there is no bedroom, the bedroom closet should serve as a walk-in dressing room.

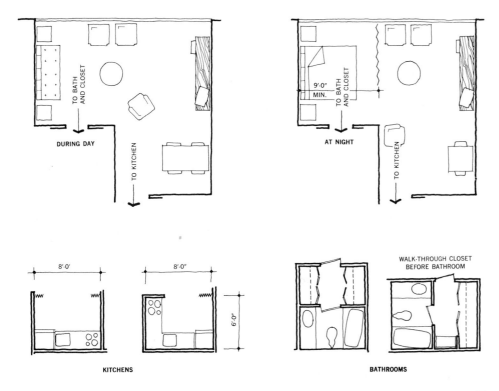

COMPONENTS OF DESIGN—ARCHITECTURAL

APARTMENT SIZES

Obviously there is a close relation between room sizes and the total dimensions of the apartment. As a rule of thumb all room areas (living, dining, bedrooms, kitchen, bathrooms, and closet spaces, but not entry hall) can be added to reach a total that should constitute 80 to 85% of the gross size, leaving 15 to 20% for circulation (entry hall, bedroom corridor), walls, columns, and shafts. Efficiency apartments naturally have less circulation space. In two-story apartments and row houses the space occupied on each floor by the stairs should also be taken into consideration as circulation space. It should be kept in mind that the most efficient apartment is not necessarily the largest but one that has the largest rooms within the smallest gross square-foot area and therefore the smallest possible circulation area. Although good, differentiated circulation is important, it should be handled with a minimum of wasted space.

What one developer considers a small apartment another may find medium; what would be considered medium in a plush suburb may be placed in the luxury class in Greenwich Village. Nevertheless, it is possible within the broadest parameters to propose some guidelines (the HUD minimums in the following table were arrived at by adding up HUD minimum room sizes and closets and adding 20% to them for circulation):

GROSS SIZES OF APARTMENTS

Unit	Low	Medium	Luxury	HUD Minimum
Efficiency (1 bath)	450	500 to 550	600+	380
1-bedroom (1 bath)	650	700 to 800	900+	580
2-bedroom (2 baths)	950	1100 to 1200	1250+	750
3-bedroom (2 baths)	1250	1350 to 1450	1600+	900

It is useful to know how apartment sizes are figured: from the exterior face of the exterior wall (in condominiums) and from the interior face of the exterior wall (in rentals) to the center line of the corridor partition, and from center line to center line of party walls (partitions between the apartments). Balconies are not included in these dimensions.

Apartments for the elderly fall into a special category and will be discussed in a separate chapter.

SEPARATORS–CONNECTORS

Apartments are separated vertically by floors and horizontally by party walls. Their rooms are defined by partitions, the purpose of which is not only physical and visual demarcation, but also protection from noise and, at least for a specified period of time, from fire.

The building code regulates the required fire rating of all floors and partitions. The publications of the Underwriters' Laboratories contain information that is based on various tests of floor and partition assemblies. Literature published by the manufacturers of gypsum-board partition systems, the most commonly used in housing today, provides additional data on fire ratings.

A far more complex problem is the reduction of noise transmission. The best planned, most generously sized apartment becomes unlivable if its privacy is inadequate. Because proper sound separation results in increased construction cost, some builders have tried to minimize the problem, but many lenders set their own requirements in order to protect their investments.

Sound is basically of two kinds: airborne and impact. Airborne sound has its source in the human voice, television and hi-fi, and is transmitted through the air. Impact sound originates when an object in motion comes in contact with the structure and causes it to vibrate. The sound-isolating qualities of walls and floors are expressed in STC (sound transmission class) for airborne sound and in IIC (impact insulation class) for impact noise. Obviously the higher the class rating, the better the results.

Some fundamental planning principles are used to avoid sound transfer problems. Wherever possible, noisy areas (elevators, mechanical rooms) should be carefully sound separated from residential areas. Likewise, bathrooms should be paired and not backed up against a bedroom or living room.

Partitions can block airborne sound. When heavy masonry walls were used to separate apartments, the problem was much simpler because mass or density is still the best control. In bearing-wall buildings the load-bearing partitions provide excellent sound insulation, as do the reinforced concrete shear walls in highrises. In today's stud partitions, with their small mass, the air spaces between the two layers play an important role. Naturally, adding to the density of the gypsum board layers will improve the rating, but with diminishing returns. The addition of sound-attenuating blankets in the air space helps considerably.

HUD *Minimum Property Standards* and manufacturers' literature provide STC ratings. With HUD these ratings vary if the background noise is low or high; that is, if it helps to reduce the airborne sound. Background noise is a tricky problem. To be effective it must be steady. Although the difference in noise levels between a downtown and a rural location is unquestionable, an acoustical engineer must be consulted if one is to rely on masking. This, of course, is a wise procedure in general except under the most routine conditions.

In arriving at recommended STC ratings, some manufacturers rate differently for low-, middle-, and high-income families. Such differentiation is unacceptable because it equates tenant sensitivity with income. Privacy should be equally available to all occupants.

The following STC ratings and illustrations reflect good, generally accepted practices (when a room is adjacent to noisy mechanical equipment STC should be increased by 5):

Between apartment and apartment (party wall)	55 STC
Between apartment and public corridor	50 STC
Within apartment between bedroom and another room	50 STC
Within apartment between bathroom and another room	40 STC
Within apartment between other rooms	40 STC

For sound rating of various wall assemblies, the reader is referred to the *Fire Resistance Design Manual* by the Gypsum Association (Evanston, Illinois). The following are well-tested partition types for highrises.

The effectiveness of the best partitions can be destroyed by poor detailing and workmanship. Most critical are the boundary details, where walls meet the floor and ceiling. Carefully placed caulking beads are essential. Another area of danger occurs where walls are pierced for pipes and electrical outlets. Outlets in party walls must be solidly caulked and should never occur back to back. The largest penetration of the wall takes place in bathrooms at the grilles of common exhaust ducts and at recessed medicine cabinets. These cabinets should be surface-mounted rather than recessed, and sound baffles should be installed in the ducts between bathroom grilles.

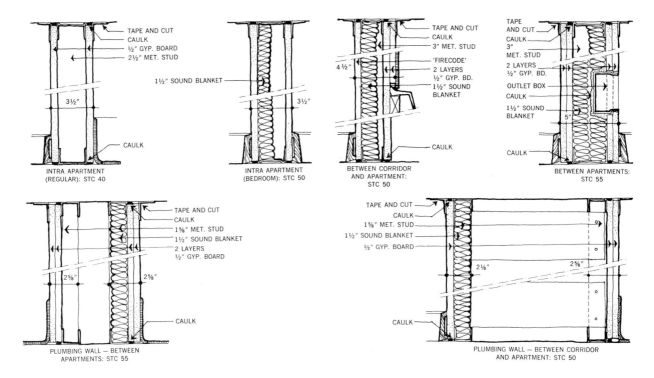

In concrete highrises in which the exterior columns are exposed there is movement of columns and slab edges as the outdoor temperature changes. This structural movement, called racking, causes partitions to crack and separate from the structural slab, especially when they occur between exterior and interior columns (tied on both ends). This racking action is worse on the upper floors of highrises. Another cause of cracking and separation is midspan deflection. Both problems can be ameliorated by using slip joints between partitions and slabs and control joints between partitions and columns, thus allowing the structure to move independently and preventing cracks and shielding separation—that is, maintaining the integrity of partitions as sound isolators.

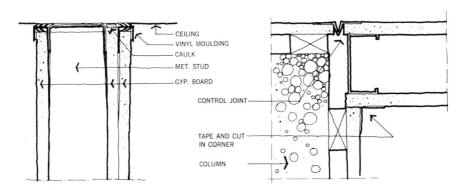

For floor construction the issue of mass versus air space in relation to airborne sounds is similar to the problems discussed in relation to partitions. Here, however, impact noise, caused by walking, dropping objects, or moving furniture, must also be taken into account. Mass or density is no great advantage in controlling impact noise. The best remedy is cushioning.

An STC rating of 55 is ideal but seldom reached. Ratings in the low 50s are acceptable, but in the high 40s complaints can occur. The low 40s are poor. The ideal

IIC rating of 70 is hardly ever reached. Satisfactory results can be obtained with 60 IIC in bedrooms, 55 IIC in living and dining rooms, and 50 IIC in kitchens.

The following chart lists STC and IIC ratings for the most common floor construc-tions. The ratings are rather pessimistic, assuming not the highest quality of workman-ship, especially in multilayered assemblies.

Construction Type		STC	With Blankets and Resilient Clips Added	IIC	With Blankets and Resilient Clips Added
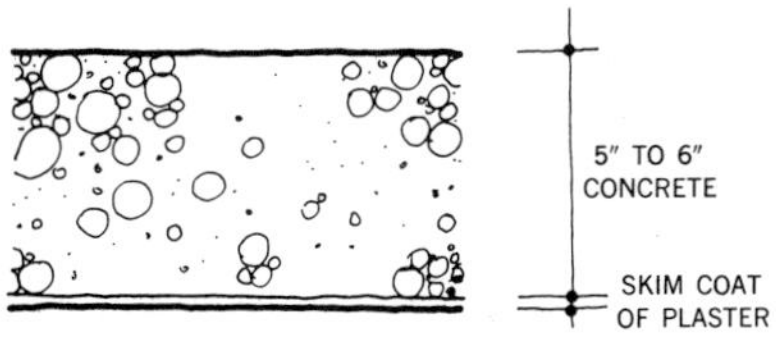 5" TO 6" CONCRETE / SKIM COAT OF PLASTER	w/carpet	48		65	
	w/⅛-in. resilient tile on underlayment	48		40	
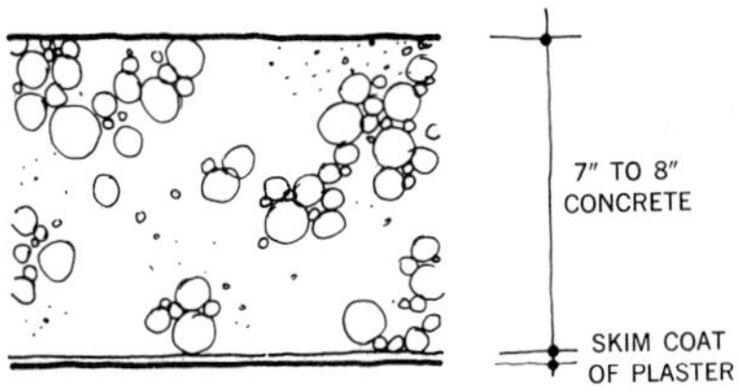 7" TO 8" CONCRETE / SKIM COAT OF PLASTER	w/carpet	51		66	
	w/⅛-in. resilient tile on underlayment	51		44	
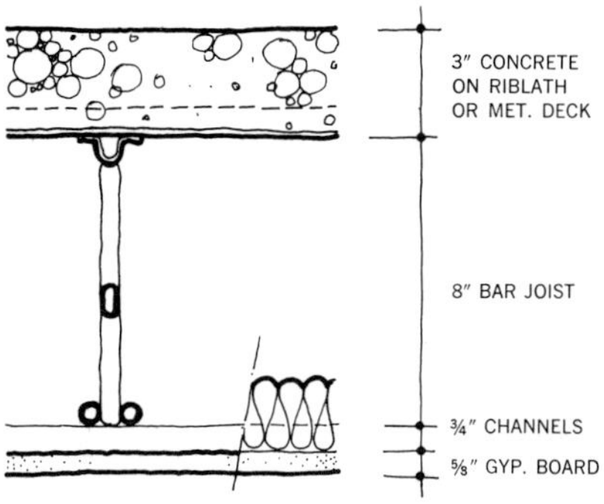 3" CONCRETE ON RIBLATH OR MET. DECK / 8" BAR JOIST / ¾" CHANNELS / ⅝" GYP. BOARD	w/carpet	48	56	63	68
	w/⅛-in. resilient tile on underlayment	48	56	38	52
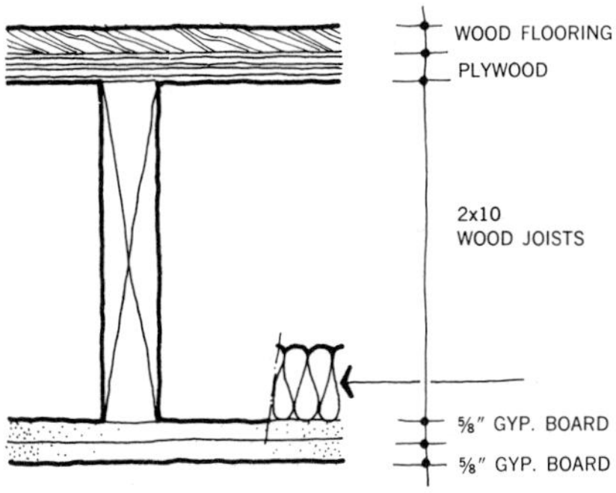 WOOD FLOORING / PLYWOOD / 2x10 WOOD JOISTS / ⅝" GYP. BOARD / ⅝" GYP. BOARD	w/carpet	40	52	55	63
	w/⅛-in. resilient tile on underlayment	40	52	35	48

The danger of poor performance (especially STC) is greatest in multilayered structures involving joints: sloppy workmanship results in inadvertent leaks, and where connec-tions are meant to be resilient but intact are tight and rigid instead, sound transmission increases. Best reliability is achieved with concrete slabs. Obviously the IIC ratings are greatest when the floors are carpeted. The figure given in the chart is a generalization, and it should not be forgotten that appreciable differences exist between carpet-pad combinations and tile underlayments. STC is not affected by the floor finish.

As partitions are the separators between apartment spaces, doors are the connectors. They should function and be sized according to the purposes they serve.

Apartment entrance doors are generally 3 ft wide. Most codes require them to have a 1-hour fire rating ("C" label) and have self-closers. Bathroom doors are 2 ft 4 in. wide and doors to bedrooms are 2 ft 6 in. or 2 ft 8 in. wide. In plans for the elderly and for the handicapped, bathroom and bedroom doors are 2 ft 8 in. All are hinged. The door between the kitchen and dining space presents a unique problem. Flexibility for swinging in each travel direction is desirable and a pair of double-acting doors is ideal in a 3-ft opening. Occasionally half doors (Dutch door, bar door) convey borrowed daylight from the dining space. Pocket-type sliding doors may save swing space but are hard to operate and should be avoided. The wall between kitchen and dining is sometimes entirely eliminated (based on market preference). This condition lends itself to the creation of a counter-type eating space and to an accordion-type door. Occasionally the connection between kitchen and dining is only a serve-through opening.

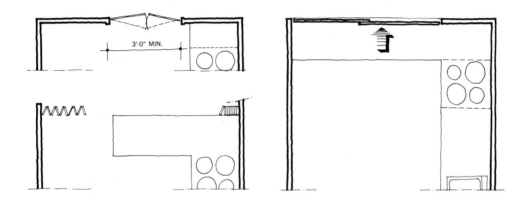

For closets the most commonly used door is the bifolding type (sliding doors limit the closet opening to half.) These doors, in contrast to standard hinged doors, do not require frames; a simple cased opening with ceiling track is adequate. Walk-in closets enjoy wide market preference; their standard hinged door width can be reduced to 2 ft 2 in. The walk-through dressing closets of efficiency apartments are generally equipped with bifolding doors in front of the hanging space.

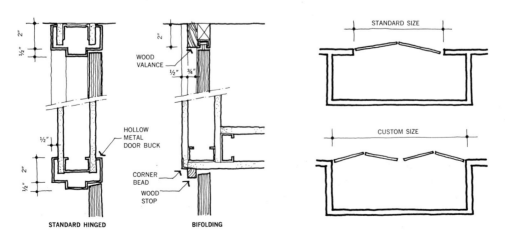

FIRE SAFETY

The floors of a multistory apartment building are connected vertically by stairs or stairs and elevators.

Although stairs in walk-ups and elevators in buildings of more than three stories serve both tenants and freight, they also play an important role when fire erupts: stairs provide an escape route for evacuation, and elevators carry the firemen quickly to the source of the fire.

Fire safety is an increasing concern when larger and larger numbers of people live in proximity and the threat to human life is heightened. Although statistically there has been far less loss of life by fire in highrises than in smaller buildings, the potential threat of a large number of people trapped in a highrise fire is ever-present. Notwithstanding the extensive fire safety regulations of present codes, most cities are in the process of writing special ordinances for highrises because of the panic caused by front-page publicity given the occasional highrise fire.

In order to understand the real need for stairs and elevators in a fire—and to help architects sitting on the committees that draft new ordinances—several excellent studies have been prepared by National Loss Control Service Corp., specialists in fire safety. Much of the following is excerpted from their report (prepared in 1971 for the Twin Oak Towers in Oak Park, Illinois) with grateful acknowledgment.

In case of fire special problems are related to the highrise structure. It is "beyond the reach of fire department aerial equipment," it "poses a potential for significant stack or chimney effect (vertical air movement due to temperature differential)," and it "requires unreasonable evacuation time."

FIRE PROPAGATION AND SPREAD

"The problems associated with fire propagation and spread in a building are not unique to highrise buildings but apply to all buildings." The solutions to these problems—fire-rated party walls and corridor walls, fire-rated floors, walls, and doors, limitation of interior finishes, and so on—are well covered by existing building codes.

SMOKE SPREAD

Unquestionably, smoke spread is the single most significant life hazard existing at the time of a fire in a high rise building. The movement of large quantities of smoke to areas remote from the fire is due to a number of factors including stack effect, ventilation system arrangements and inter-floor leakage. Vertical shafts for stairs, elevators, and utilities are primary avenues of smoke spread. Smoke can cause serious physical effects on building occupants, can block exitways and obscure exit signs, and can force evacuation from portions of the building far from the fire with resultant overloading of exits and rescue problems.

Smoke spread can be expected even in buildings which have a complete installation of automatic sprinklers because of the normal time lag associated with the heat activated sprinkler heads and because the contents and furnishings of high rise buildings are capable of producing relatively large volumes of smoke prior to the operation of the sprinklers. Complete or partial failure of a sprinkler system is also possible due to closed water supply valves, painted heads, inoperative fire pumps, fire shielded from the sprinkler head discharge, etc.

There are several ways to remedy this situation. Tamperproof automatic closers on all apartment entry doors will help to keep corridors smokefree. Making one or both stairways into smokeproof towers (traditionally required by codes) will keep the stairwells smokefree. Overpressurization of the stairs is another method of keeping smoke out.

Overpressurization of corridors might help contain the smoke inside the apartment where it was generated; however, once the smoke gets into the corridor (say, someone in a panic drops something, preventing the apartment door from closing) overpressurization can also force the smoke into the other apartments or the stairwell.

The best known method to prevent the spread of smoke (in addition to automatic door closers and smokeproof towers) is the compartmentation of the building. When smoke is detected, the doors in the corridor (otherwise held open) automatically close and, in fact, cut the floor into two compartments (each with its elevator, stair, and corridor air supply), one of them smokefree. The air supplied to the compartment that is smokefree equals the amount of air exhausted (through bathrooms and kitchens); in the other compartment, where the smoke is generated, all exhausts and air supply stop, thus preventing the smoke from spreading from one area to another.

Elevator shafts (especially in winter) tend to act as chimneys, sucking up the smoke from the lower floors and "exhaling" it on the upper ones. This so-called stack effect is practically unavoidable in tall structures.

OCCUPANT EVACUATION CONSIDERATIONS

At the time of a fire, a number of unique evacuation problems exist in a highrise building. In a residential building, the detection of a fire is frequently delayed as many of the occupants are either sleeping or at work a good portion of the day. Evacuation is further complicated by the fact that building codes do not require an effective means of notifying building occupants of a fire or, more importantly, what to do at the time of such an emergency.

Stairways, the traditional means for building evacuation, are normally designed to handle only a population load equal to the floor level having the highest number of persons based on the assumption that only a single floor needs to be evacuated. Thus, at the time of a fire, only a few floors can be simultaneously evacuated without seriously overcrowding the stairs. In addition, these stairs may become smoke filled due to the stack effect existing in the building.

It is also important to note that when a building height exceeds about twenty-five stories, total evacuation becomes impractical due to the excessive time needed to descend from such a height and the physical stress imposed on even a healthy individual.

Naturally, complete evacuation is seldom required. What is more important is an area of refuge. In fact, an apartment itself—surrounded by fire-rated floors and walls—can be safe enough until the arrival of the fire department. Even greater safety is provided by balconies.

FIRE CONTROL PROBLEMS

Fire control in a highrise building can be effected either automatically, as by installed fire extinguishing systems, or manually, by the fire department.

Usually fire department actions are also required to aid the automatic systems to effect extinguishment.

Automatic fire suppression has been utilized to only a limited extent to date in highrise buildings. While automatic sprinklers have been quite effective in controlling fires in many types of conventional buildings, their installation in highrise structures is relatively costly for several reasons and poses definite design problems, particularly for apartment buildings where a suspended ceiling is not normally provided.

The physical demands placed on a fire department in a highrise building fire are much more severe than that of a similar fire in a low building. Just getting to the fire floor high above the street level may be difficult or impossible if elevators are not available or are inoperative.

Ventilation of heat and smoke, an important fire control procedure, is often quite difficult in a highrise fire and greatly complicates firefighting operations.

Where effective means are not provided for communicating with building occupants, often the fire department must deploy already overtaxed manpower to individually notify occupants and direct evacuation. This can require more men than are needed for actual extinguishment of the fire itself. In addition, the internal communication system of the fire department may be ineffective because radio transmissions often will not reach outside the building due to the shielding effects of the structural frame.

Building codes call for water availability on the exterior of the building near the entrance (siamese connections) and standpipes with firehose in the stairways and corridors. Firemen, however, prefer to use their own hoses; those along the standpipes may be old and brittle and at best are good enough only for fighting small fires until the fire department arrives.

Most codes do not include, but should seriously consider, the following equipment:

Sensors in every apartment with direct connection to the fire department.

A voice communication system on all floors capable of being operated either selectively or on all floors together, from a central location in the first floor lobby.

A system of sound-powered telephone circuits paralleling the standpipe risers for the use of the fire department for fire scene command and control purposes.

Elevator controls arranged so that actuation of an emergency switch on the first floor will cause all elevators to disregard any floor calls and respond only to the first floor and remain there until returned to service. A light indicating that the elevators are out of service should show on each floor near the elevator call buttons. The freight elevator should be designated for fire department use, with all appropriate manual controls.

Highly dependable secondary source of emergency power supply for:

    a. Fire department elevator

    b. Fire pump

    c. Air handling units for corridor air supply

    d. Exit signs and exit lighting

    e. Internal communications system

COMPONENTS OF DESIGN—ARCHITECTURAL

An emergency Command and Communication Center for Fire Department use in the first floor lobby of each building and equipped as follows:

- a. Fire detector annunciator panel
- b. Emergency tenant communication system
- c. Floor plans of each floor
- d. Sound-powered phone handsets
- e. Keys for stair doors
- f. Elevator emergency controls
- g. Standpipe water pressure gauge

The one factor, other than carelessness, that causes maximum loss of life is panic. Most tenants do not know what to do when fire breaks out in their own apartments or when they smell smoke from a neighboring one. Most are unaware that elevators are not to be used or that escape is to be made via the stairs—assuming that they know where the nearest staircase is located. Proper tenant education, rarely attempted by management, should be a requirement for renewal of occupancy permits!

Many cities from New York to San Francisco have already revised their building codes to include special stringent requirements on highrise fire protection, as have some states in which a central code covers all construction. These measures have been taken in spite of statistics (in Chicago "93 percent of fire deaths in 1973 occurred in buildings under 80 ft"); in spite of the fact that "the typical concrete apartment structure is divided into small 1-hour-rated compartments already;" that "each apartment has its own air-handling system, so smoke spread is far less of a problem than in centralized office buildings;" and also that "windows are generally movable sash, so venting is possible."[19] Highrise in this context starts at 60 to 80 ft, depending on the reach of the fire department's equipment.

The new requirements include automatic closers on corridor-to-apartment doors, central control stations for the fire department in the lobby, automatic products-of-combustion detection systems, automatic recall of elevators, voice communication systems for the fire department, and emergency electrical systems. The requirement that automatic sprinkler systems be installed throughout is often questioned.

Because of the high cost of sprinkler systems, most codes permit alternate methods of fire prevention or what are commonly called trade-offs; the most usual of which is compartmentation. It is essential that designers understand clearly what it means and how it is interpreted by local building officials. It should be stated that under certain conditions where compartmentation is extremely difficult sprinklers are the logical alternative.

What we have presented here about stair, elevator, and corridor design is valid in locations in which no highrise fire ordinance has been passed, and even when one has been adopted it is valid for buildings under highrise height (as defined by the fire ordinance).

Compartmentation possibilities are covered in this chapter with the caveat that later chapters on stair, elevator, and corridor design should be read with such requirements in mind when the building is covered by a special highrise fire ordinance.

Although the idea of compartmentation varies from code to code, there are some constants. The most common method of compartmentation calls for continuous vertical 2-hour-rated partitions which divide each floor into two compartments in an area ratio not to exceed 3:1. Naturally each compartment must have a separate corridor air-supply system and each must contain one set of stairs, but because the code requires two means of egress, the 2-hour-rated partition, when it intersects the corridor, must have "B" label doors in each travel direction. These doors, if kept open, must have magnetic hold-open devices activated by electronic sensors responding to the products of combustion.

Because each compartment must have a separate enclosed staircase, the use of scissor-stairs in buildings covered by highrise fire ordinances is prohibited.

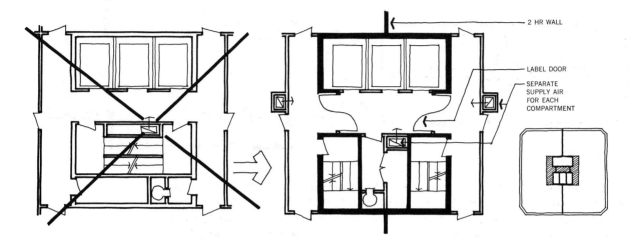

Codes also require an elevator in each compartment, of course easily achieved only in buildings with at least two banks of elevators.

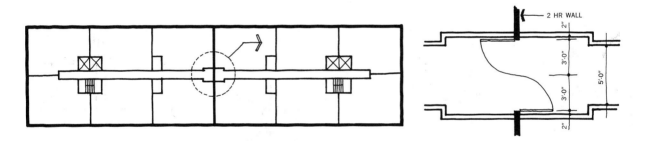

When there is only one bank of elevators, a compartment wall is required between the elevators unless the code permits handling the elevator bank as an independent compartment in lieu of one elevator being required in each compartment. Other fire

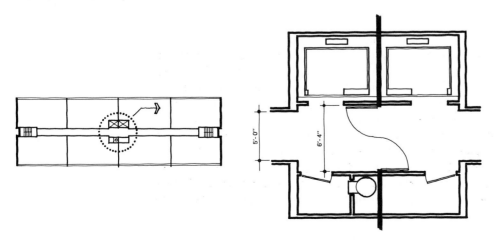

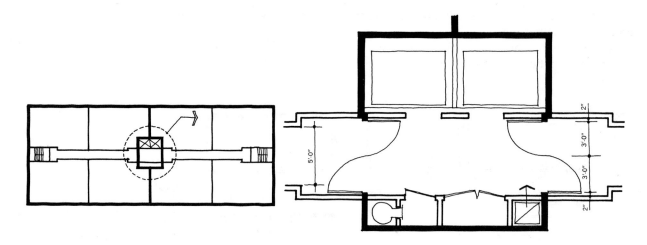

codes lean towards this third compartment by requiring that the elevator lobby at each level be separated from the remainder of the building by an effective smoke barrier.

Some highrise fire codes specify that all openings in exterior walls located vertically above one another shall be protected by approved flame barriers extending 30 in. beyond the exterior wall in the plane of the floor or by vertical panels not less than 3 ft or so in height; also, all exterior openings adjacent to the vertical 2-hour partition must be located not less than 3 ft, measured horizontally, from the vertical division wall. These stipulations pose severe limitations on the exterior options of the designer.

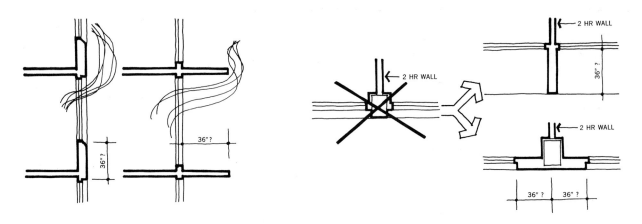

In dealing with lowrises the issue of fire safety is somewhat different. Codes permit a lower rate of fireproofing because complete evacuation is possible and because floors can be reached by the fire fighters with ladders and "cherry-pickers." The problem is to provide adequate access—fire lanes—to allow the fire equipment to reach the buildings. This is particularly difficult in lowrise projects in high-density areas. Whether driving isles, parking lots, or even the open space otherwise not required for vehicular traffic are to be used, the fire department should be consulted for the necessary turning radii and maneuvering space, distances between buildings (depending on building height and equipment reach), and location of fire hydrants. When it becomes impossible to plan roads or parking lots close enough to the buildings for the efficient deployment of fire equipment, areas that normally serve recreational purposes can be considered. The use of collapsible ballards will prevent normal vehicular traffic in fire lanes.

In suburban areas with less clearly defined regulations, one must consult with the local fire chief at an early stage of the design. The idiosyncrasies of the local fire department often exceed expectations and must be dealt with.

HUD has its own requirements for fire alarm and extinguishing systems (Revision No. 7, 1978 to MPS) requiring sprinklers in the public corridors, public spaces, and service areas of all buildings four stories or higher.

STAIRS

Stairs, required as escape routes in case of fire, are governed by codes. In apartment buildings with three-floors—occasionally four—in which stairs are the only means of access, their design is also determined by ease of climbing. In addition, stairs in walk-ups become important as visual architectural elements. In elevator buildings, on the other hand, their main function is as a means of escape, and more generous design than that required by code is unnecessary and economically unfeasible.

In most cases codes require two exits. Buildings of a certain height (three or four floors), limited floor area, particular construction type, and serving a limited number of families per floor often have only one staircase, but there are ways of "stretching" the number of floors in which only one stair is still permitted: the ground floor depressed below grade may not count as a "floor," depending on code definition, of course. When building codes limit the single exit to buildings of three stories, a second exit can be created from the top floor by providing access to the roof, to allow the occupants to reach the next staircase. Both devices need careful code analysis. In lowrises in high-crime areas single stairs add to security.

The location of stairs varies with codes. The maximum travel distance is usually 75 to 100 ft from the apartment entry door to the remotest fire stairs. (This dimension can be increased by 50% if the floor is sprinklered, not a usual practice in apartment buildings.) The distance from the entry door to the furthest point in the apartment is also defined by and varies with codes. When apartments are large, two entrances are necessary. There is much disagreement among codes regarding the question of permissible length of dead-end corridors. Some allow none, others define them as 50% of the maximum travel distance, and some as 20 or 25 ft; HUD allows 30 ft. It is obvious that unless a third staircase is introduced, travel distances determine the maximum length of the corridor, therefore of the building.

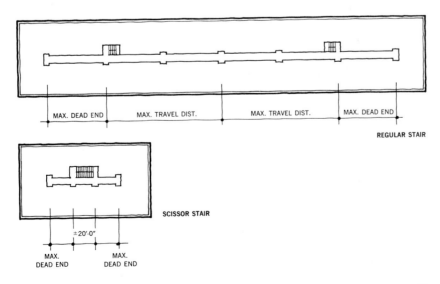

MAX. DEAD END   MAX. TRAVEL DIST.   MAX. TRAVEL DIST.   MAX. DEAD END

REGULAR STAIR

SCISSOR STAIR

±20'-0"

MAX.
DEAD END   MAX.
                  DEAD END

COMPONENTS OF DESIGN—ARCHITECTURAL

Exit width is also set by code and depends on the population of the floor, determined by multiplying bedrooms by 2 or dividing total square feet by 125 to 200. Doors are generally 3-ft wide, 2-hour fire-rated "B" label with automatic closers. The minimum width of stairs is 3 ft on floors housing about 45 persons. Maximum required width is usually 3 ft 8 in. The intermediate landing must be as wide as the stair itself. The width of floor landings is interpreted in a variety of ways, as illustrated. When it is more than the plan can take in that direction, it can be reduced by increasing the stair volume in the other direction and using the excess space for air supply ducts or something else.

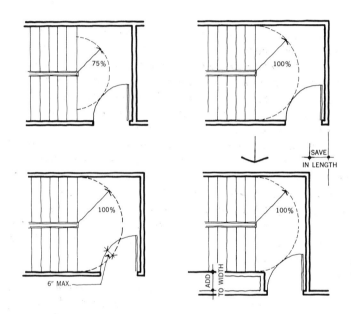

Winders in fire stairs are prohibited. The minimum number of risers between landings is three and the maximum vertical distance between landings is usually 12 ft. Maximum riser height is 7¾ or 8 in. Minimum tread width is 9 in., with 1 in. nosing. When the stair width is not more than 3 ft 8 in., railing is required on one side only, and the need for wall

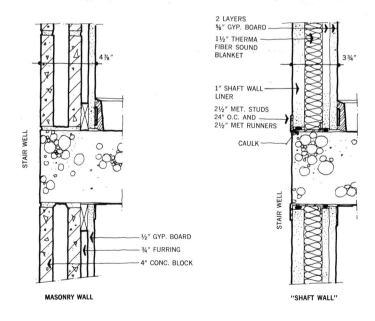

44

railings is eliminated. Railings may project 4 in. into the required stair width. Minimum headroom is usually 7 ft.

The construction of stairs, except in lowrises, is generally noncombustible. In highrises it is usually reinforced concrete. The stair shaft enclosure must provide 1-hour fire protection in lowrises, while highrises require 2-hour fire protection, which is achieved by 4-in. concrete blocks with furred gypsum board on the apartment or corridor side or by a gypsum board assembly called a "shaft wall," which is only 3¾ in. thick. This shaft wall is not only thinner and more economical than masonry but often eliminates beams that may be needed under masonry walls around openings. For various stair enclosure wall ratings the reader is referred to the *Fire Resistance Design Manual* by the Gypsum Association (Evanston, Illinois) (see illustration on p. 44).

Exterior open stairs are limited to a certain building height or to the number of floors they are to serve; as a rule, only 50% of the stairs required for exit can be open. Exterior stairs lend themselves to visual variety.

Codes also define how stairs should lead to the outside at ground level; either directly or via a 2-hour enclosed corridor called the horizontal exit. Sometimes the lobby will qualify in spite of its glass walls.

In order to provide two independent exits in a minimum floor area a special staircase, or scissor-stairs, is used in short corridors. Two completely separated stairs wind around each other in the same shaft like a double helix. Intermediate landings are eliminated. Each stair "runs" floor to floor without interruption. The length of a scissor-stair is greater than a regular stair but its floor area is less than that of the two regular stairs it replaces. The run dimensions obviously vary with floor height; the illustrations are based on an 8 ft 6 in. floor-to-floor dimension.

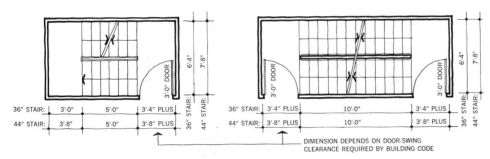

In tall buildings—the code defines the height limit—one or both of the required stairs must be a smokeproof tower to prevent smoke from entering the enclosure. This is done by providing a vestibule in front of the door to the stair so that when the vestibule door is opened—but before the stair door is reached—the smoke can be sucked out of the vestibule. The smoke is dispersed by opening this vestibule—like a balcony—directly to the outside or by a vertical shaft. The size of the shaft depends on whether it is mechanically exhausted or acts as a chimney to pull the smoke out naturally (see illustration on top p. 46).

Special attention must be paid to stairs on the first floor. This floor in most apartment buildings requires more height than the upper floors not only because of aesthetic reasons, but also because of the space needed for air ducts, pipes, and so on. The increased height results in longer stair runs on the first floor which sometimes (when the shaft is bordered by shear walls) cannot be accommodated. The problem is avoided by introducing two intermediate landings instead of the customary one. If the typical floor height is 8 ft 6 in., the first floor height should be three times one-half the typical, or 12 ft 9 in. The problem is similar on other floors of increased height (see illustration on p.46).

On occasion the function of the lower floors does not permit the stair enclosure to

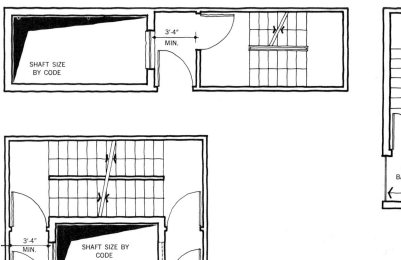

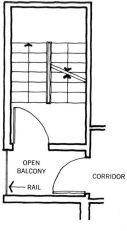

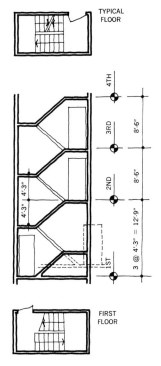

continue down in a straight line; the stairs will have to be transferred. Transfer can be a slight shift or a completely new location when the connection is made by a 2-hour-rated enclosed horizontal passage on the transfer floor (see illustration on p. 47).

It should also be noted that doors always swing in the direction of travel, on the upper floors from the corridor toward the stair, on the first floor from the stair out. One has to be careful that this stair door does not swing into a corridor or passage, thereby possibly injuring someone.

Code regulations are far more liberal for stairs that connect two levels of the same apartment. Some, as in row houses and other lowrises, might even have combustible construction; most, however, are allowed to have open risers and winders.

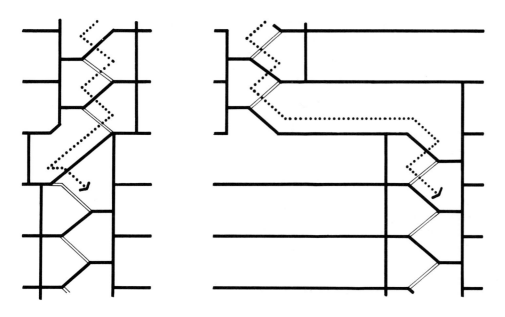

ELEVATORS

Elevator selection (the number, speed, and capacity of elevators) depends on a variety of interrelated factors such as population of the building, number of floors, number of stops, and speed of door operation. Because the calculations necessary for a reasonable decision are extremely involved and probability tables as well as empirical data must be used, the architect has to rely on the expert opinion of a consultant. Although years of experience will enable the designer to make some educated guesses, the responsibility is so heavy that a specialist should be called in for all but the simplest cases and certainly when the population of the building is more than 400.

Nevertheless the designer must have a schematic plan before calling on a consultant. To prepare such a plan involves some assumptions regarding the elevators. The following chart is no more than a number of "rules of thumb" to help in making these assumptions.

ELEVATORS FOR APARTMENT BUILDINGS

Number of Floors	Passenger Elevators (minimum 2000 lb; if used for service, 2500 lb)	Service Elevators (minimum 2500 lb)	Remarks
3–4	1 hydraulic (150 fpm)	1[a]	
5–6	2 hydraulic (150 fpm) or 2 electric (350 fpm)	1[a]	
7–12	2 electric (350 fpm)	1[a]	If population is more than 500, need more than 2
13–20 or 25	3 electric (350 fpm) or 2 electric (500 to 700 fpm)	1[a]	
20 or 25–40 or 45	3 electric (350 fpm) or 2 electric (500 to 700 fpm)	1 + 1[a]	
46–50	2 banks of 3 electric (500 to 700 fpm)	2	

[a] Indicates that a passenger elevator can be used as a service elevator as long as its capacity is 2500 lb.

COMPONENTS OF DESIGN—ARCHITECTURAL

It is obvious that one elevator is adequate for three- or four-story buildings. If the elevator breaks down or is being serviced, it is still possible to walk up to the top floor without serious discomfort. In five- or six-story buildings electric elevators are a luxury that can hardly be afforded. When a building reaches six floors, however, a borderline is also reached concerning hydraulic elevators because of their low speed. In 12 to 45-story buildings the choice is between three regular-speed and two high-speed passenger elevators, and much depends on availability of space in the floor plan.

Service elevator requirements are based on tenant turnover and travel distance (turnover in big cities runs 6 to 13% in the heaviest rental month; condominiums have minimal turnover but as a rule need more deliveries). As the chart indicates, buildings 20 to 25 stories get by with one service elevator which can also be used for passengers; buildings with more floors will need two service elevators, one of which can also double for passengers. The distinct advantage of having a service elevator in the same bank with the passenger elevators for multiple use is obvious. It is also desirable to load in the basement or on the first floor through a rear door to avoid passing through the main lobby. Side doors are possible but expensive. When the freight elevator is not located in the passenger bank, it should open into a small anteroom on each floor. It is important that service elevator cabs be 10 ft high—or have removable tops—for carrying large objects. When this provision is not made, objects of unusual length will have to be raised on top of the cab, a cumbersome and dangerous method.

An apartment building will have adequate passenger service when the following criteria are met (these should be documented by the consultant):

1.   It should be possible to move 6% of the population in less than 5 minutes.

2.   The traffic interval should not exceed 60 seconds. (If the traffic interval is more than 55 seconds, the car should be able to make a full run from the top of the building to the lobby in 45 to 50 seconds.)

To understand the consultant's recommendations, the architect must be familiar with some of the terminology commonly used in traffic studies:

POPULATION.   Population can vary from two persons per bedroom in low-rent housing to one-half person per bedroom in deluxe apartments. Recommended averages (not including public housing): 1 person per efficiency apartment of 350 sf or less and 1.5 above this size; 1.8 persons per one-bedroom apartment, 2.5 persons per two-bedroom apartment, 3.5 persons per three-bedroom apartment, and so on. Although the number of persons per elevator trip requires intricate calculations, the architect should know at least that a 2000-lb cab can hold 11 persons and a 2500-lb cab can hold 13 persons; maximum loading is seldom achieved, however.

TRAFFIC INTERVAL.   A traffic interval is an arbitrary time element calculated as follows: the number of stops (only the specialist can estimate it) multiplied by the sum of acceleration and deceleration time, plus door operation time, plus passenger loading and unloading time, plus other lost time. To this we add the round trip time of the elevator without stops. The total is then divided by the number of elevators to give the interval in seconds.

Example

Assume a building has 20 stories, with floor-to-floor heights of 8 ft 6 in. Then 20 stories times 8 ft 6 in. is 170 ft; travel is in two directions: 2 times 170 ft is 340 ft; an elevator that travels 350 fpm will make this round-trip run in approximately 1 minute.

ADD FOR EACH STOP

Acceleration and deceleration time of a 350 fpm elevator at each stop	2.35 sec
Time required to open and close the door at each stop	4.30 sec

(This time can be reduced by 1.4 sec if the door is center opening instead of single slide.)

Time required to load and unload passengers at each stop	2.00 sec
Other lost time: 0.1 × 2.35 (acceleration and deceleration) plus 0.1 × 4.30 (door opening and closing)	0.63 sec
	9.28 sec/stop
Assume 10 stops × 9.28 sec	92.80 sec

60 sec + 92.80 sec = 152.80 sec

152.80 ÷ 3 elevators = 50.93-sec interval; very good. If the interval is much shorter than 40, the building is probably overequipped.

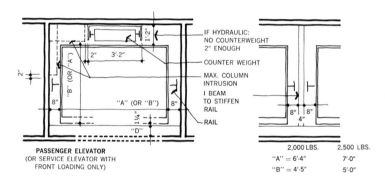

PASSENGER ELEVATOR
(OR SERVICE ELEVATOR WITH
FRONT LOADING ONLY)

IF HYDRAULIC:
NO COUNTERWEIGHT
2" ENOUGH

COUNTER WEIGHT

MAX. COLUMN INTRUSION

I BEAM TO STIFFEN RAIL

RAIL

	2,000 LBS.	2,500 LBS.
"A" =	6'-4"	7'-0"
"B" =	4'-5"	5'-0"

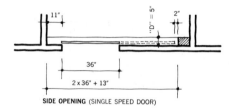

SIDE OPENING (SINGLE SPEED DOOR)

2 x 36" + 13"

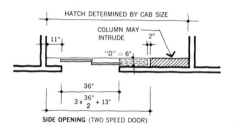

HATCH DETERMINED BY CAB SIZE

COLUMN MAY INTRUDE

"D" = 6"

3 x 36"/2 + 13"

SIDE OPENING (TWO SPEED DOOR)

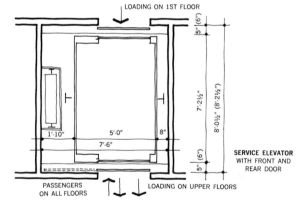

LOADING ON 1ST FLOOR

SERVICE ELEVATOR
WITH FRONT AND
REAR DOOR

PASSENGERS
ON ALL FLOORS

LOADING ON UPPER FLOORS

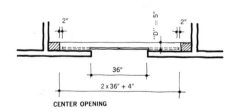

2 x 36" + 4"

CENTER OPENING

The hatch, cab, and door details illustrated here meet industry and building-code standards. Other cab dimensions may be used, but they can be costly and should be checked by the consultants.

The machinery (pump) for hydraulic elevators is housed in a small (approximately 8 by 10 ft) room near the lowest stop. A small (2 to 3 ft) protrusion on the roof accommodates overrun unless the top floor is higher than the average apartment floor, in which case the protrusion is eliminated.

Machinery for electric elevators (unless they are the underslung type hardly used in apartment buildings) is housed on the roof. The machine height *M* should be a minimum of 7 ft 6 in. for geared and 8 ft 6 in. for gearless elevators (those with speed in excess of 350 fpm). As the travel increases to 30 to 35 stories these figures should be checked by the elevator manufacturer or consultant.

Note that the dimensions given for the pit include space for the following: buffers to slow the car if it is approaching the bottom landing at full speed because of failure of controls, a space that must be allowed between the car striker plate and the buffer for cable stretch, and a safety device required under the car to allow for overspeed in the run. The car depth from platform to striker plate may be as much as 16 to 18 in. The code demands 2 ft under the compressed buffer to allow clearance for anyone caught in the pit under a falling car. In very tall buildings, which require higher speeds and more critical counterweight balance for landing, a form of cable compensation necessitates more pit depth. These facts will explain the need for the dimensions shown, which may otherwise appear excessive.

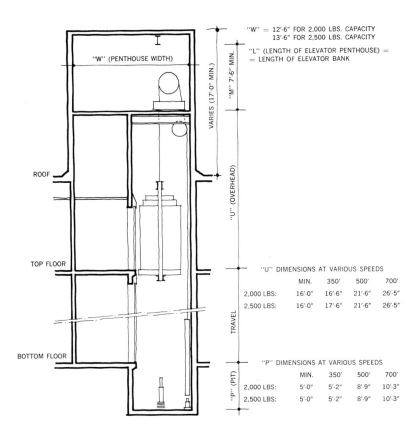

"W" = 12'-6" FOR 2,000 LBS. CAPACITY
13'-6" FOR 2,500 LBS. CAPACITY

"L" (LENGTH OF ELEVATOR PENTHOUSE) =
= LENGTH OF ELEVATOR BANK

"U" DIMENSIONS AT VARIOUS SPEEDS

	MIN.	350'	500'	700'
2,000 LBS:	16'-0"	16'-6"	21'-6"	26'-5"
2,500 LBS:	16'-0"	17'-6"	21'-6"	26'-5"

"P" DIMENSIONS AT VARIOUS SPEEDS

	MIN.	350'	500'	700'
2,000 LBS:	5'-0"	5'-2"	8'-9"	10'-3"
2,500 LBS:	5'-0"	5'-2"	8'-9"	10'-3"

How passenger elevators connect with the lobby and how service elevators connect with the receiving area of a building are discussed in a later chapter. It will be seen that direct connection between the service elevator and the receiving area is not always possible, or only at considerable cost, and sometimes loading will have to take place in the passenger lobby. This compromise is not recommended for senior citizen housing, in which the service elevator is frequently used for stretchers, a disturbing sight for other residents who like to congregate in the lobby. For this reason one of the elevators should be deeper and have a rear door connecting it directly with the receiving area. Cabs for the elderly and handicapped should have handrails at a height of 2 ft 9 in. and control buttons should not be higher than 4 ft 8 in.

The waiting space in front of the elevators and its relation to the public corridor as well as the elevator and main lobbies on the first floor are treated in Chapter 9.

VERTICAL CORE

Stairs are the primary vertical core elements in all multistory apartment buildings. When the building needs elevators, they are also part of what we call vertical core. The need for other vertical core elements (refuse chute, boiler stack, electric meter and transformer room, and corridor air supply duct) depends on various conditions.

Walk-ups seldom have boilers. Taller buildings might, but when the boiler room is located in a penthouse, there is no need for a stack. This obviously results in certain economies. However, the boiler on the roof is a source of noise and vibration, and careful separation should be considered to keep the top floor apartments comfortable. Electrically heated buildings have no boilers at all.

Other vertical core elements such as electric meter and transformer room or refuse chute are part of mid- or highrise buildings only.

A = STAIR
B = PASSENGER ELEVATOR
C = SERVICE ELEVATOR
D = OTHER CORE ELEMENTS

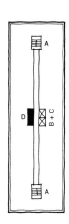
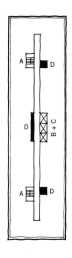

The location of all these elements is an essential part of the planning process and is discussed in detail in a later section of this book. Location criteria, however, can be established in advance.

Stairs, as determined by building codes, must be as far apart as possible to fulfill the criterion set for travel distance, but not farther apart than twice the maximum travel distance. Elevators on the other hand, in order to provide equal distribution on the typical floor, tend to be placed in the center of the building, though ground level conditions may require off-center location.

The refuse chute, even when individual garbage disposals are standard equipment, provides the tenants with a way of getting rid of a variety of waste. The ideal location is also in the center of the building, thus equalizing the walking distance from any of the apartments. Building code regulations stipulate that refuse chutes must be installed in 2-hour fire-rated enclosures (similar to stairs) with "B" label doors. It is advisable, to provide a small room in front of the refuse chute for the temporary storage of items such as boxes that will not fit into the chute. When garbage is stuffed through the door of the chute, some small waste occasionally drops and remains on the floor; the anteroom will prevent the public corridor from becoming littered. HUD requires that this anteroom measures at least 20 sf (see illustration on p. 52).

Unless the building is electrically heated or the boiler is located in the mechanical penthouse, the boiler room will be in the basement or on the first floor. The boiler stack, as part of the core, is ideally situated near the elevators because the stack must

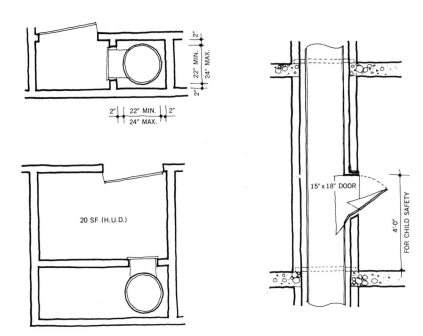

terminate above the elevator penthouse and it is easier to handle as part of that unit than as a separate element.

The size and configuration of electric meter and transformer rooms are discussed in the electrical section of this book. Ideally they are included in the building's central core in order to provide short distribution lines in both directions (the exception is in long buildings in which two risers and two electrical rooms may produce a more economical distribution, enough to outweigh the cost of the extra riser and room).

Because it is necessary to exhaust interior bathrooms and kitchens, apartment buildings would be under negative pressure, even though there is always some leakage through the windows, unless the lost air were somehow made up. For this reason make-up air is forced into the corridors, through corridor supply ducts, and into the apartments along the jambs of the apartment doors. The fan equipment which pushes the air into the corridors is generally on the roof unless in buildings of more than 40 stories the system is split in two: the upper section is then supplied from above, the lower from below. The space required for corridor supply ducts is discussed in the mechanical section of this book. Location in the center of the building permits the supply fans to be housed in the elevator penthouse. In long buildings and compartmented highrises the corridor supply is achieved by using two ducts (space for them can be borrowed from an apartment closet) and two fan housings on the roof. When the elevators form a third compartment in highrises this compartment must have its own air supply.

On occasion a restaurant may occupy a lower floor of an apartment building and its kitchen must be exhausted. If the site conditions do not permit exhausting the kitchen horizontally, the exhaust duct must penetrate the apartment tower. This duct is located wherever space can be found for it, assuming that the fan housing can be properly handled on the roof.

Although the various vertical core elements have their own location criteria based on function and economy, the roof housing required for this equipment will influence the design of the roof, an often neglected part of the building that is discussed in detail in Chapter 9, Design Methodology.

PARKING

Though many planners would prefer an automobile-free world, though malls and even entire city districts are being emptied of vehicular traffic, though those who live within walking distance of their jobs or along rapid transit lines can forego the automobile in getting to and from work, most people still rely on their cars for transportation. The automobile is an essential part of existence in the United States and it must be stored in conjunction with the dwelling.

As more and more families acquire two or more cars, it is becoming increasingly difficult to determine the amount of car storage required for a housing project. Although zoning establishes the minimum amount of off-street parking, the user's life style, economic status, proximity to public transportation, and other factors also play roles. Near-downtown housing may get by with 60% parking, condominium projects must have 100%, and on suburban sites the requirement can reach a 1 : 1.5 dwelling-to-car ratio. In housing for the elderly 20 to 30% parking is sufficient, and most authorities will permit it, even though the zoning ordinances require a higher ratio for regular housing.

The relation of parking to dwelling can be any of the following, depending on building type, site constraints, and budget:

1.   On grade, open parking (most common with lowrise housing and low-income mid- and highrise buildings around which there is adequate space).

2.   On grade, under the building (most common with midrises).

3.   In separate garage structures connected to one or several apartment towers (most common with highrises when land is plentiful).

4.   In a garage under the apartment tower (most common with highrises on limited land).

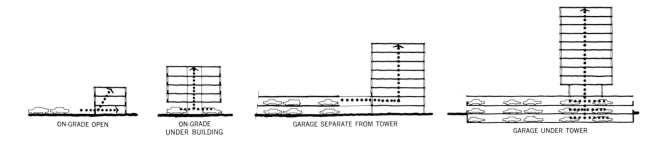

ON-GRADE OPEN   ON-GRADE   GARAGE SEPARATE FROM TOWER   GARAGE UNDER TOWER
                       UNDER BUILDING

Dimension data developed by HUD can be very useful (see p. 54).

Whether parking is along minor streets, in small off-street bays, or on large lots, after the basic technical issues of surfacing and drainage, bumpers, and safe lighting are taken care of, the visual aspects of these areas are of utmost importance. Large parking areas can become the familiar "sea of asphalt" and are quite unattractive, especially from upper floors. Smaller areas are more manageable. The partial sheltering of cars with lightweight umbrella structures is generally too costly. Trees, particularly those with dense branchwork for winter shielding, are ideal and can be located to provide minimal interference with the parking layout. Proper protection, drainage, and selection of species suggest consultation with a landscape architect.

Horizontal shielding of parking areas, especially in high-crime locations, should be carefully weighed against the fact that these become less visible, therefore potentially unsafe, areas. If shielding is decided on, it can be achieved in a variety of ways: with

COMPONENTS OF DESIGN—ARCHITECTURAL

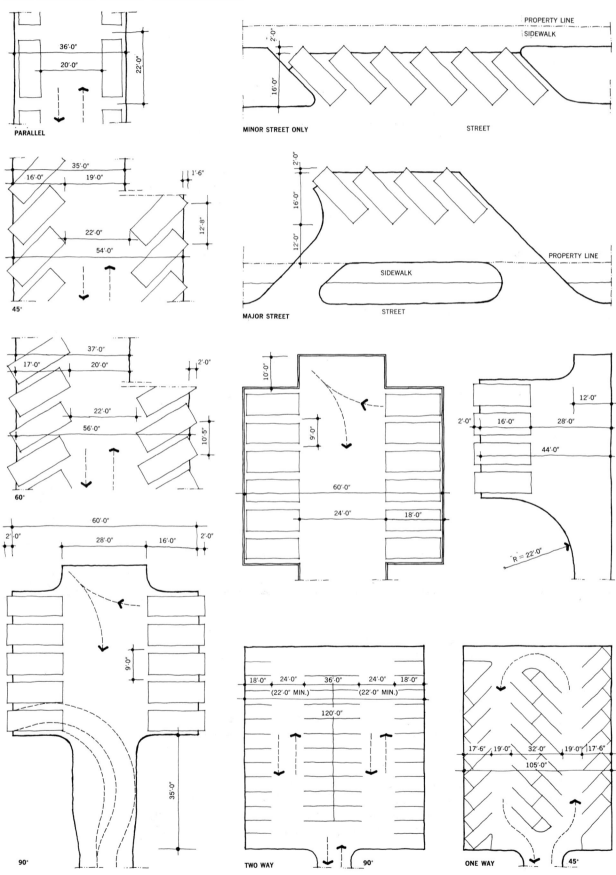

PARALLEL

MINOR STREET ONLY

STREET

PROPERTY LINE

SIDEWALK

45°

MAJOR STREET

STREET

SIDEWALK

PROPERTY LINE

60°

90°

TWO WAY   90°

ONE WAY   45°

54

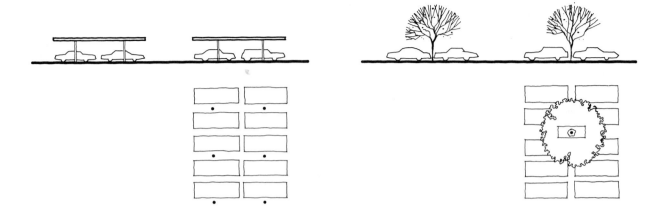

fences, garden walls, dense hedges, or earth mounding if space permits; a partly depressed parking lot can achieve a similar effect. Oscar Newman concludes[20] that a properly defined outdoor recreation area near the parking lot will add to the security.

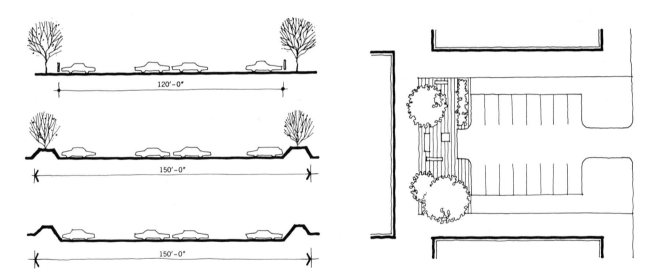

Because on-grade parking has the tendency to spread out, the distance between the automobile and the dwelling unit is critical. Preferred maximum dimensions are 100 ft for elderly residents, 150 ft for nonelderly, and 200 ft for visitors. HUD allows the following maximum distances: 150 ft for elderly residents, 250 ft for nonelderly, and 300 ft for guests.

Garage parking is six or seven times more expensive than open on-grade parking, and compact planning is essential. Special attention must be paid to insure that columns will interfere least with parking. HUD-recommended driving-aisle and parking-stall dimensions work well, especially when the parking structure is separated from the apartment tower (see illustration on top p. 56).

On small sites, particularly when parking is beneath the tower, dimensions must be tighter. By moving the columns away from the driving aisle, the width of parking stalls can be reduced (see illustration on p. 56).

Generally speaking, 90-degree parking, with automobiles on both sides of the driving aisle, will result in the best utilization of the available space; 45- or 60-degree parking requires one-way traffic, whereas the 22- to 24-ft driving aisle of 90-degree parking,

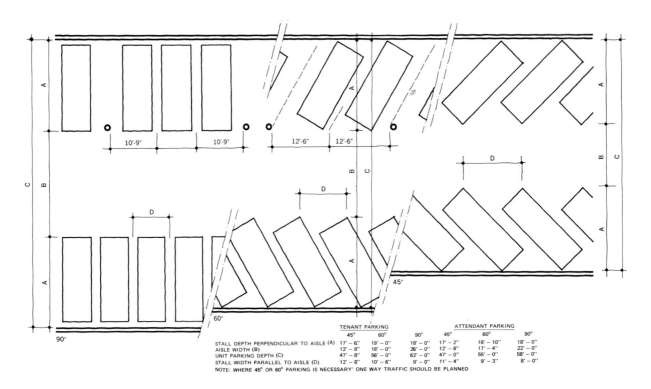

	TENANT PARKING			ATTENDANT PARKING		
	45°	60°	90°	45°	60°	90°
STALL DEPTH PERPENDICULAR TO AISLE (A)	17'-6"	19'-0"	18'-0"	17'-2"	18'-10"	18'-0"
AISLE WIDTH (B)	12'-8"	18'-0"	26'-0"	12'-8"	17'-4"	22'-0"
UNIT PARKING DEPTH (C)	47'-8"	56'-0"	62'-0"	47'-0"	55'-0"	58'-0"
STALL WIDTH PARALLEL TO AISLE (D)	12'-8"	10'-6"	9'-0"	11'-4"	9'-3"	8'-0"

NOTE: WHERE 45° OR 60° PARKING IS NECESSARY' ONE WAY TRAFFIC SHOULD BE PLANNED

which is wide enough for two-way traffic, produces more options. Even with the 90-degree, 22-ft aisle system, however, a one-directional traffic flow is preferred whenever possible.

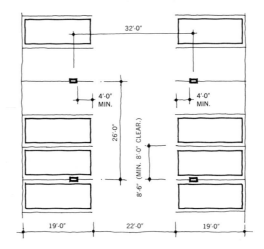

Before the preparation of actual layouts the parking capacity of a floor can be estimated. A typical bay in the 90-degree system is 26 by 60 ft or 1560 sf, which will accommodate six automobiles; 1560 divided by 6 is 260 sf per automobile. Taking into consideration cross aisles, space needed for ramps, stairs, and so on, no less than 350 sf should be allowed (300 sf is adequate for open on-grade parking). It should be kept in mind that attendant parking will improve this ratio. When attendant parking is provided, cars can be parked in double or even triple rows. It should be noted, however, that to satisfy zoning ordinances only those cars that are in the first row and directly accessible from the driving aisle can be counted among the required number of cars.

When parking is not under the apartment tower, 25- to 35-ft column spacing (with heavy 8- to 10-in. flat plate concrete slabs and shear heads on the columns) is adequate. Parking under the tower itself presents a different picture. Here column spacing is dictated by economical apartment planning and not by the best parking layout. Though columns can be transferred under the tower, this procedure is extremely costly and ought to be avoided wherever possible. Therefore the ratio of 350 sf per car is seldom achieved.

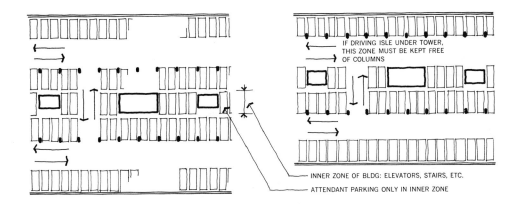

Apartment planning, especially with column rhythm along the exterior of the building, has serious consequences for the parking levels below. Everything else being equal, if there are choices of column location, parking is a factor that must be considered.

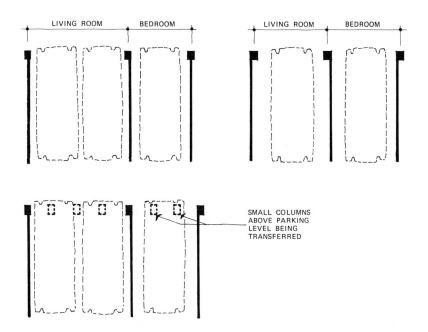

Ramps are the customary means of moving automobiles from level to level. When the lot is extremely tight, car elevators must be installed. Elevators are not only expensive but increase the operating costs, for 24-hour attendant service must be provided.

Ramp length, naturally, depends on floor-to-floor height. In determining this dimension, the need for sprinklers must be considered. Codes establish minimum headroom under sprinkler heads. Generally a 9-ft floor-to-floor dimension is adequate for structural slab and sprinklers. When the building code permits its use as a fire exit, the ramp must be less steep (maximum degree set by code) than when it is used only for driving. On circular ramps the minimum turning radius is 60 ft. Driving aisles used for turning on and off the ramp should be wider than normal aisles. It is possible to extend parking above the top and below the bottom level of a ramp as long as there is adequate headroom.

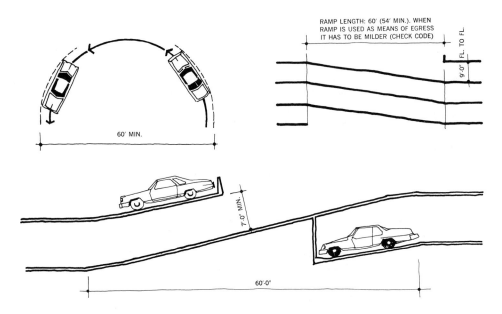

The difficult-to-handle ramp length can be reduced in two-level garages when they are depressed in relation to grade by half the floor-to-floor height.

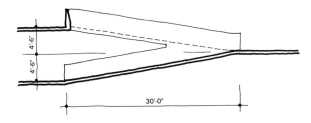

The following illustrations describe and give dimensions for a variety of ramp systems under apartment towers. It should be kept in mind that scissor ramps are costlier than normal ramps (see illustration on p. 59).

The principle of depressing the garage half a level below grade in order to shorten the ramp length can be applied to the entire garage. When all cars must be parked by the tenants, triple rows as shown in the diagrams are not acceptable. Therefore it becomes difficult to coordinate a 60-ft ramp with two stall lengths of 40 ft. However, the 40-ft length is more than adequate for a ramp spanning only half the regular floor-to-floor height. A further extension of this principle is the ramp garage in which driving aisle and parking stalls form a continuous mild ramp.

The integration of parking and apartment tower requires special attention in highrise projects. On tight lots much of the parking will be directly under the building (reducing the number of cars considerably) and so will the ramp (requiring careful column

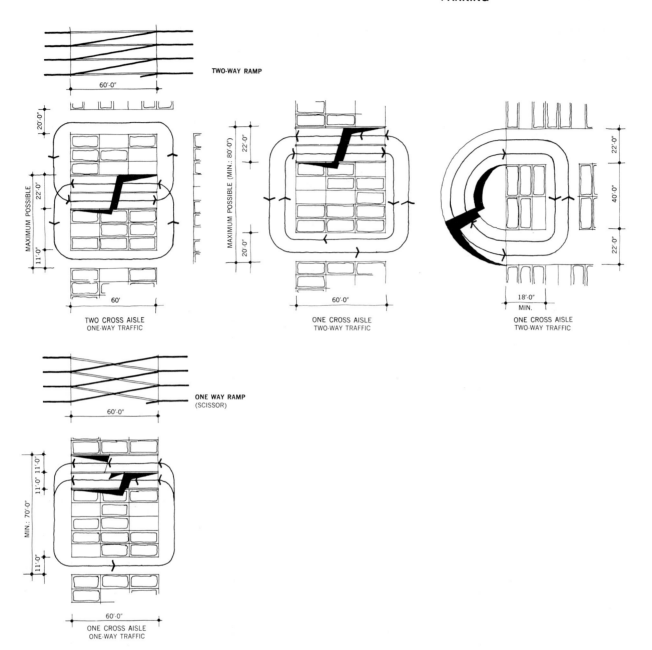

TWO-WAY RAMP

60'-0"

MAXIMUM POSSIBLE

20'-0"

22'-0"

11'-0"

60'

TWO CROSS AISLE
ONE-WAY TRAFFIC

MAXIMUM POSSIBLE (MIN.: 80'-0")

22'-0"

20'-0"

60'-0"

ONE CROSS AISLE
TWO-WAY TRAFFIC

22'-0"

40'-0"

22'-0"

18'-0"
MIN.

ONE CROSS AISLE
TWO-WAY TRAFFIC

ONE WAY RAMP
(SCISSOR)

60'-0"

MIN.: 70'-0"

11'-0" 11'-0"

11'-0"

60'-0"

ONE CROSS AISLE
ONE-WAY TRAFFIC

alignment). Even when the site is not so tight the outer bay under the tower is often used for parking. On these larger sites there is a broader choice of ramp locations. Large sites, where the tower sits on the parking volume in the middle, will need column alignment for drive-through aisles. The most efficient parking structure is completely independent of the tower, connected to it by a bridge (see p. 60).

No matter how the garage relates to the tower, vehicular entrance and exit must be easy. A thorough knowledge of local traffic conditions (direction, volume, pile-up conditions at traffic lights, maximum permitted width of curb cut, minimum distance of driveway from intersection, and so on) is essential. The basic criteria of good traffic flow can be summarized in three points:

1.   A cab can drive to the lobby entrance (without driving into the garage proper), drop off or pick up the passenger (under canopy or arcade), and leave.

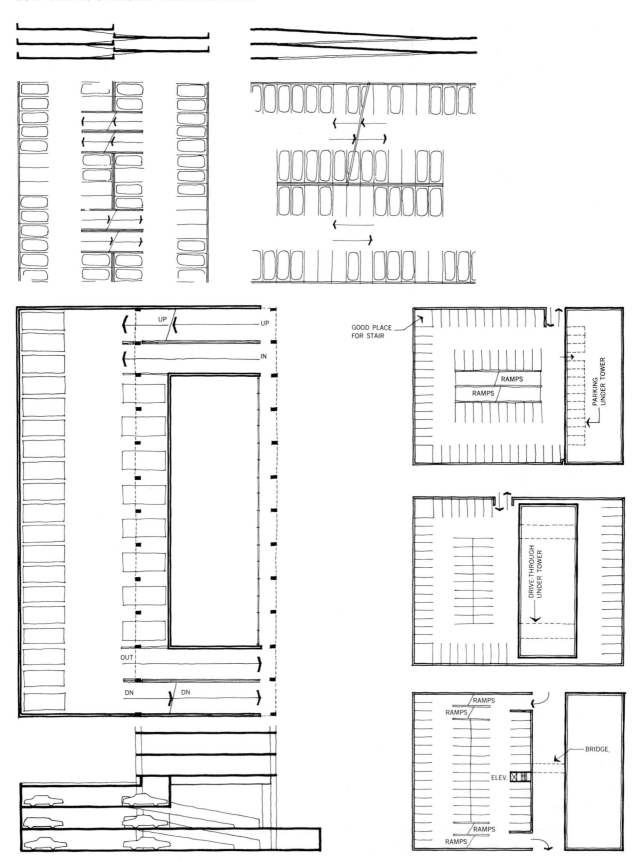

2.   A tenant can drive to the lobby entrance, drop off passengers, and drive on to the garage without having to drive back into the street.

3.   A tenant (or attendant) can pick up a car in the garage and bring it to the lobby entrance for loading without having to leave the property.

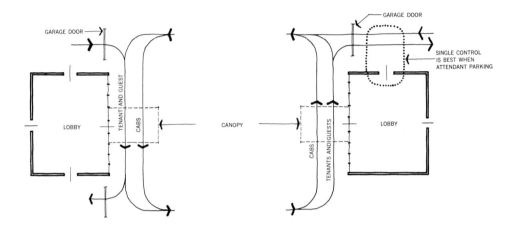

The required number of exits and maximum travel distance to the nearest exit are determined by the local code for garages. Under certain conditions the ramp can be used as one of the required means of egress and its maximum slope is regulated by code. Generally garages under apartment towers are required to be fully or partly (the part under the tower proper) sprinklered, and in this case the code usually stipulates more liberal distances between exits. When the garage is not extensive, the two stairs of the apartment tower proper may serve as exits for the garage as well. These stairs, like the elevators that connect the garage to the residential floors, must be separated from the garage by a fire vestibule of high rating, most commonly 4 hours with "A" label doors on both sides of the vestibule.

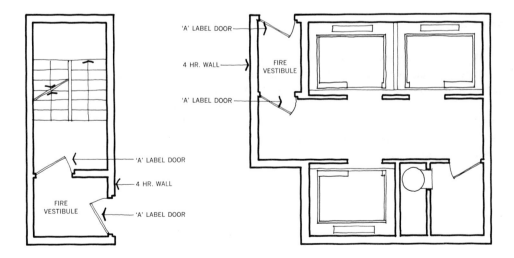

Garages are seldom heated. However, codes do require mechanical ventilation unless a required percentage, usually 50% or more, of the exterior walls is open. When possible and aesthetically acceptable, open-sided garages are obviously more economical. The pattern of garage lighting, needs special design attention in this case.

Enclosing the garage, while adding to the cost, will moderate freezing temperatures even without heating. Some codes require periodic access openings in the walls of enclosed garages when those walls face a public way to be made accessible for the fire department.

Garage roof decks serve as excellent outdoor recreation spaces. In highrise projects this is not only the cheapest but often the only space for these facilities.

Lowrise projects, consisting of several buildings, normally have adequate ground for both open parking and recreation. When the property is inadequate, however, the use of the roof deck of the garage as an elevated grade for circulation and play areas between buildings is a solution. It is not so economical when compared with open parking but it is an answer when land is scarce. Properly sized and spaced openings to the parking area below provide natural ventilation and daylight, and trees can be grown in the wells rather than in boxes on the deck. The cost problem is aggrevated by code requirements for fire separation (concrete deck) between parking and housing as well as waterproofing and wearing slab or other hard surfacing of the waterproof membrane. These costs should be weighted against the obvious planning advantages of the "deck" scheme.

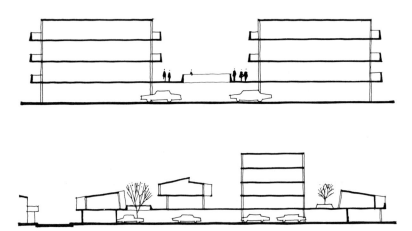

LOADING AND REFUSE REMOVAL

Apartment projects must allow for the delivery of goods and the disposal of refuse. The vertical movement of goods is handled by the service elevator and refuse is dropped into the refuse chute (except in walk-ups where both are handled manually).

The horizontal movement—goods in, refuse out—takes place on the ground level and both require vehicles: delivery and pickup vans and garbage trucks. Not only must the designer provide adequate space for parking these vehicles, but they must have access in some way to the service elevator or refuse room.

PICKUP AND DELIVERY

Zoning ordinances determine the number and size of off-street loading stalls on the basis of the number of dwellings served or the gross square footage of the buildings.

For the movement of pickup and delivery trucks on large-site projects with open parking the driving aisles of the parking lot will serve well, provided that loading areas are assigned at strategic locations to avoid interference with parking or pedestrian pathways. The loading areas, obviously, should be as close to each building as possible. In row house groups and other walk-ups with spread-out unit entrances ideal proximity is not possible.

Densely built sites with parking garages present an entirely different picture. Because of the minimum clearance of 14 ft required for trucks, to get the vehicles close to the freight elevator or to the refuse room without crossing automobile traffic is no small problem.

Many of these sites have limited access which sometimes is easiest through the garage, but its entire ground level would have to be raised to 15 ft, a terrible waste when 9 ft suffices for parking. To move the goods through the garage after unloading is a poor solution. Alternate possibilities are shown in the following illustrations.

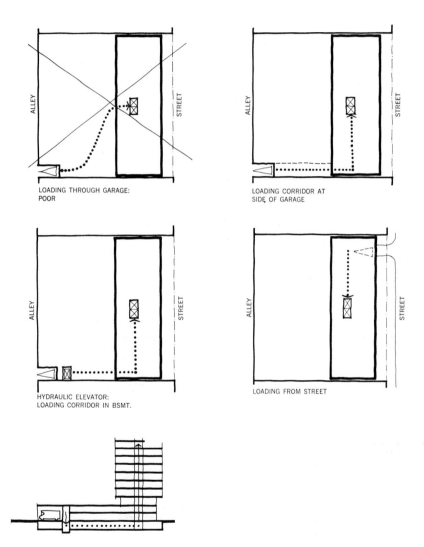

LOADING THROUGH GARAGE:
POOR

LOADING CORRIDOR AT
SIDE OF GARAGE

HYDRAULIC ELEVATOR:
LOADING CORRIDOR IN BSMT.

LOADING FROM STREET

The best spot for loading is the area in which the garage volume meets the apartment tower and in which there is no interference with the garage traffic or any need to introduce loading vehicles at the front of the building near the lobby. Such ideal loading conditions are possible only on corner lots or large sites on which buildings are freely positioned (see illustration on top p. 64).

The loading area proper is either a level one or a traditional raised dock. Although the dock is preferred, it cannot always be achieved. In either case loading is done best under cover; if not fully enclosed, at least it should be under a canopy. With an enclosed dock the garage doors help further to seal off the loading activity from the weather. There should also be a receiving room adjacent to the loading area where goods can be

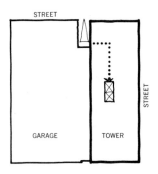

held until picked up by the tenant. Visual control of the loading dock should be possible from this receiving room. For the purpose of security the door leading from the dock to the elevator should be manned or controlled by intercom.

REFUSE REMOVAL

The line of movement of goods is also adequate for the removal of refuse. Therefore on large sites with open parking the driving aisles that serve delivery vans will also serve garbage trucks. Trucks can park in the area designated for loading. Because it is not possible to provide an assigned area for each row house or walk-up, the distance between the unit entrance and the loading area is more critical for refuse removal than for moving goods. Refuse removal is a daily occurrence, and the distance the tenant must walk to the garbage collection area in no case should exceed 100 to 150 ft. Visual shielding, or fencing of these areas demands attention. An alternate solution is provided by enclosed and properly ventilated trash rooms strategically located in the building complex.

In mid- and highrise apartments refuse dropped into a chute lands in a compactor which crushes it and from which it is then removed in carts. Incinerators are prohibited in most locations because of their contribution to air pollution.

In addition to the size of the compactor, the number of bins or carts will determine the size of the refuse room. With a compactor of approximately 1200 cf capacity and carts of 2-cubic-yard capacity, a 100-unit apartment building will need two carts and once-a-

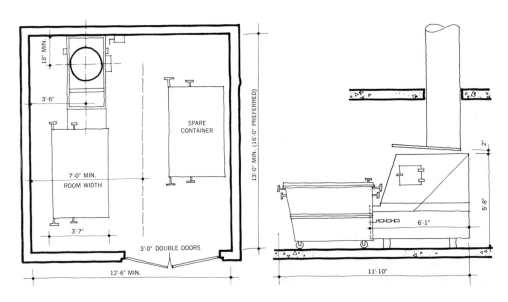

week pickup. A 200- to 250-unit apartment building with the same equipment will need two pickups a week or double the number of carts. Very large projects should have more than one chute.

The chute and compactor should be joined by an "accessible connection," which is not a permanent attachment, so that large items such as brooms and curtain rods can be removed.

A service corridor usually connects the refuse room with the loading dock (the same corridor that connects the loading area with the service elevator). In large buildings it is especially important that space be provided on the loading dock for refuse carts.

The location of the refuse room, whether in the basement or on the first floor, is determined by the position of the refuse chute. Clogged angles or offsets in the chute are dangerous because they can cause the garbage to back up. Refuse rooms as required by code are generally sprinklered.

LOBBY

The lobby of an apartment building (except those with direct access to the units) is the major connector between the exterior and the stairs of walk-ups or elevators of midrises and highrises. It is the first space entered in which an immediate impression is gained of the interior quality of the building. Therefore it can be, and often is, a showplace. Developers sometimes try to make up for the lack of amenities elsewhere by providing lavish lobby decoration.

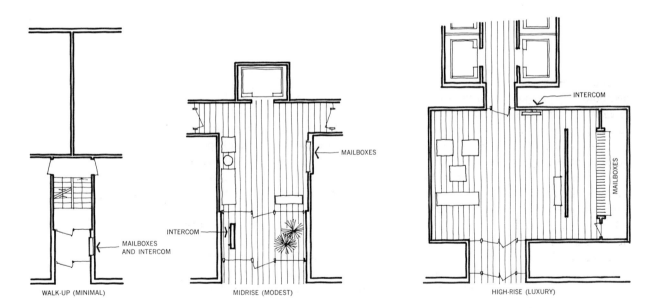

WALK-UP (MINIMAL)   MIDRISE (MODEST)   HIGH-RISE (LUXURY)

The lobby has several other functions: tenant directories hang on its walls and visitors can reach the occupants on an intercommunication device or wait for them to return. Here tenants can pick up their mail or whatever equipment they may have left in the storeroom.

There are no rules that indicate how large a lobby should be. Much depends on the sponsor's wishes. As a general rule, however, in walk-up buildings of limited magnitude the lobby is merely an oversized vestibule with intercom and mailboxes and usually without furniture. In midrises, which have more apartments, it is still a modest space but should be large enough to provide a small sitting area. In highrises that serve a large population the lobby can be quite elaborate, with large waiting areas, plants, and artwork.

At all times the lobby is a security checkpoint. The visitor can ring the occupant (on an independent intercom or telephone intercom system) before being admitted through—by remote control—the door leading to the elevator lobby or stairs in walk-ups. Sometimes for visual recognition and added security a closed-circuit television system is installed. When operating budget permits, the best security is provided by a doorman on the premises. He not only helps with packages and directions but his mere presence is a deterrent to prowlers. Unfortunately, in low-income housing located in troubled areas in which the doorman would be most useful there is seldom an adequate budget for such "luxury." In these buildings a certain amount of security can be achieved, according to the defensible space principles of Oscar Newman,[21] by facing the lobby toward the street and making it as well as the elevator doors visible from the outside. The possibility of being seen by the public acts as a deterrent to the potential criminal.

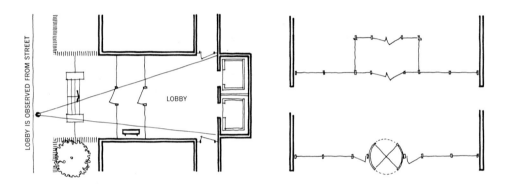

Because of frequent coming and going, the lobby needs a weatherbreak; that is, a vestibule or, in larger buildings, a revolving door. Because, however, the lobby may serve as a horizontal exit from the fire stairs to the outside, a hinged door is required in addition to the revolving door, which can substitute for only a portion of the width of the code-required exit. The hinged door is useful also for the delivery of packages that would not fit easily in a revolving door or for the handicapped for whom level passage between exterior and elevator must be provided. Most cities have ordinances for the handicapped that describe this on-grade passage (which can also be a slightly inclined ramp with rail) and the required door size.

The elderly as well have special needs. Because of the occupants' high incidence of sickness and accidents, in addition to the customary intercom, an alarm system that operates from both bedroom and the bathroom of the unit should be connected with the manager's office, superintendent's apartment, or lobby counter. The lobby itself is a social center. Often people enjoy sitting in the lobby and like to watch life in the street. Seating therefore should allow them to observe outdoor activities.

Although a building with a relatively small number of units can be served by front-loading mailboxes, larger apartment buildings should have rear-loading boxes with a small room behind them where, on a shelf, the letter carrier can sort out the mail and load the boxes undisturbed. In planning the space for mailboxes, it is necessary to keep in mind the number of rows that can be reached comfortably in order to arrive at the horizontal dimension needed for the total number of mailboxes. The architect should be aware of the federal standards for mailboxes and, in larger projects, of the delivery and collection processes followed by the local postal service (see illustration on top p. 67).

A constant problem is presented by packages or mail too large to fit into the

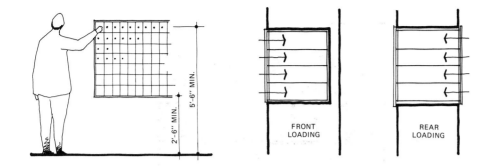

FRONT LOADING

REAR LOADING

mailboxes. When the addressee is not at home, the letter carrier can leave the package with the doorman or receiving clerk, if such person is on the premises, or take it back to the post office and leave a notice in the addressee's mailbox. When such personnel is provided, a secure area for packages must be located near the mailboxes or receiving room. In addition, a small closet or room near the doorman's stand is useful for various paraphernalia such as brooms, signs, and wheelchairs.

The preambulator (baby carriage) storage (pram room) should be close to the lobby. The need for this space, and its size, depends on the type of occupancy. It should open from the vestibule, especially if the lobby is carpeted, so that prams do not have to be dragged through the lobby.

If there is a connection (through a fire vestibule) between the lobby and the garage, no separate intercom security is required. If, however, the garage connection is beyond the elevator lobby, an intercom security system similar to the one at the loading dock entrance must be installed.

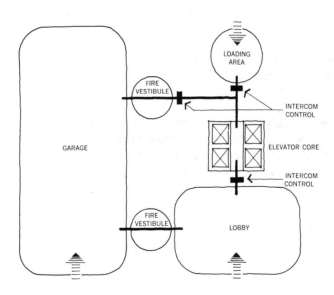

When parking is by attendant it is necessary to provide a continually operating manlift, office, and toilet for the manager and attendants, and waiting space for the tenants. This waiting space—approached through a fire vestibule—connects with the lobby. The entire complex should be designed to permit sufficient automobile pile-up space for both incoming and outgoing vehicles. It is usually a shabbily treated area between the utilitarian garage with its exposed concrete and the lavishly decorated lobby and deserves better design attention.

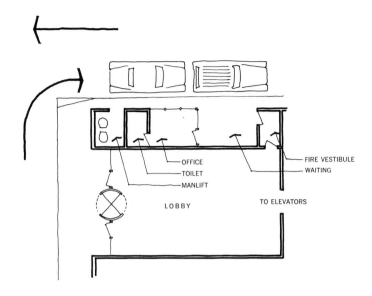

MAINTENANCE, MANAGEMENT, STORAGE

The general building storage is used for all kinds of maintenance materials and at least a small amount of work space for in-house painting and repairing. Maintenance areas should have workbench, tool storage, service sink, and toilet. Separate paint storage is required in larger projects. The size of the maintenance area depends largely on management needs and practices. If large outdoor areas are to be tended and their maintenance is not separately contracted, general storage includes lawn mowers and snow-moving equipment. Consequently it is placed on grade level in contrast to small-site, highrise projects which do not need heavy ground equipment and whose storage can be in the basement or on ground level, usually near the mechanical equipment room. Large-site projects with several buildings may have general storage and maintenance facilities in a separate centrally located structure or central recreation building.

Management space is generally smaller in condominiums and larger in rental projects, where it may even include a public waiting area with a rent-collection counter. The core of the management space is a private office, staff toilet, and supply storage. Rental projects with more than 100 units may need small interview rooms, record vault and janitor's closet. HUD requires the following spaces for management and maintenance:

Number of Dwelling Units	Management Space (sF)	Maintenance Space (sF)
50	325	400
100	500	800
200	775	1400
300	1000	1900
400	1200	2300
500	1375	2650

Storage for the use of occupants is provided in several sections of the building. Baby carriages are stored in the pram room near the main lobby, bicycles in a section of the garage, walled in or separated by wire partition, near the entrance.

Other tenant belongings that do not fit comfortably into the apartments—luggage, trunks, boxes, skis, tires, and so on—are stored in tenant lockers which are 3 by 5 or 4 by 4 ft spaces enclosed by partitions of metal frame and wire mesh, located in rows on each side of 3-ft aisles in a locker room. (Lockers may be planned one above the other, but each must have at least an 80-cf capacity.) For estimating the floor area needed for tenant lockers a minimum of 25 sf per apartment should be allowed (this includes locker as well as proportionate aisle space). The locker room, can be located anywhere in the building as long as it can be reached by the service elevator; it must also have two means of egress. The usual locations are on the top floor of the tower, an unused part of the garage, or the basement in highrises, the first floor or the basement in midrises, and the basement in walk-ups. Sometimes tenant lockers are located on the same floor as the apartments. This is a rather special case which occurs when the building configuration results in "wasted" space on the typical floor, space that cannot be otherwise utilized or when, because of site restrictions, no space can be found for lockers on the lower levels.

LAUNDRY

Some developers consider the laundry as an amenity, but like proper storage facilities, the laundry is a necessary adjunct of housing.

Although its purpose is tenant convenience, its provision, like so many other things in housing, is dictated by economy. The ideal arrangement which would provide every apartment dweller with a washer/dryer is the general practice in row houses, but in other multifamily housing it can be implemented—owing to cost and space limitations—only when the market can absorb the extra expense. When laundry facilities are part of each apartment, they are located in the kitchen or, more commonly, in a closet opening on the entry hall or bedroom corridor. The ultimate in luxury is a small utility room near the kitchen.

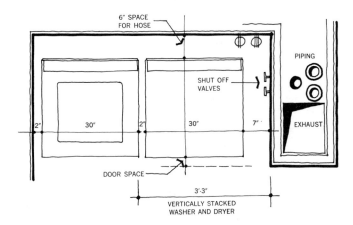

The next step, a small laundry room on each floor with one or two pairs of machines, is a distinct convenience. However, the use of such a small number of machines requires tight scheduling, a problem eliminated by a central facility equipped with many machines. Also, in addition to being uneconomical, a laundry on each floor is a source of odors and vibration. Only in housing for the elderly is this system occasionally used, but even here it is a luxury, for the elevator provides a perfectly acceptable means of access to the central laundry.

Obviously economy dictates the installation of a central laundry facility. This central laundry should be easily accessible from the freight elevator. Its location involves many factors and must depend on the type of occupancy. For families with many young children a room near the play area is ideal because it affords excellent supervision. When there are only a few youngsters in a building and recreation facilities are more formal, the laundry should not be part of the recreation complex. For the elderly the laundry provides an opportunity for socializing and its proximity to other recreational facilities is an advantage.

Physically the basement is the least desirable location. The ground floor is preferable because there it can have daylight. The recreation deck is even better because it interrelates with other community and recreational activities. The top floor is the ideal location not only because of its good view but also its accessibility to the roof terrace. It is important, however, that the service elevator stop at this floor.

Projects with several small buildings but a large enough site may have laundry facilities in a separate centrally located community building.

Regardless of its location, the central laundry should have toilets nearby, and two means of egress. In addition to washing machines and dryers (coin-operated in larger projects) the laundry room should be equipped with laundry sinks, space for folding tables, and a sitting area (with vending machines, coin changer, and soap dispenser). A 3-ft service space is required behind the dryers and 1 ft 6 in. for plumbing between the rows of washers.

The number of washers and dryers is proportionate to the number of apartments. In projects of 20 families, a washer and dryer for every seven apartments; 20 to 50 families, a washer and dryer for every 10 apartments; between 50 and 100 families, a washer and a dryer for every 15 apartments; for more than 100 families, a washer for every 20 apartments and a dryer for every 40 apartments. To determine the size of the laundry room, 25 sf of floor area should be allowed for each machine.

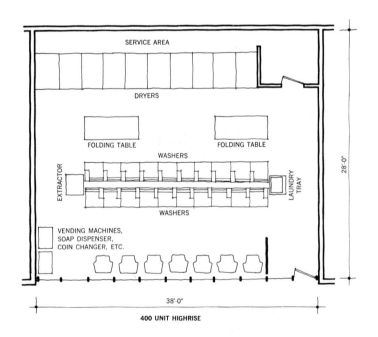

400 UNIT HIGHRISE

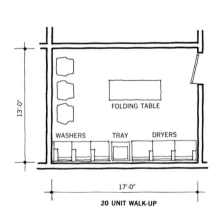

20 UNIT WALK-UP

RECREATION

The most ambiguous of all housing requirements is the space needed for recreation facilities. There are no useful standards to guide the architect in deciding the kind and quantity of recreation space to provide in a particular project. Zoning ordinances do not address themselves to this problem. At best they set "open space" requirements.

Because there are neither adequate guides nor meaningful regulations, developers tend to provide only as much recreation space as is needed to make the project marketable. This approach results in a relatively high level of recreational amenities for upper-income housing, where the renter or buyer can exercise financial options. While in public or federally assisted housing facilities are minimal, even the upper-income renter has only limited choices in a seller's market.

In all recent attempts to define recreational needs the one most sensitive to the problem is described by the Urban Design Corporation of the City of New York in "Housing Quality—A Program for Zoning Reform." It proposes that certain recreation facilities be made mandatory in all housing.

> Any proposed housing development will accommodate, within predictable limits, a fixed number of children and/or adults. Based upon these projections, specific types of recreation space must be provided for the exclusive benefit of the various age groups. The required recreation space is based upon a reasonable minimum need per person in the development, and may not be impinged upon for any other purpose, such as parking.

The New York proposal then defines what should be considered as recreation space. Its major innovations occur in its definitions. It considers public stoops, terraces, and laundry rooms as adult recreation areas and advocates that properly developed roofs be made available for the use of residents. The general requirements of the program are the following:

> The proposed development should provide child use space, mixed use space (children and adults) and adult use space in relation to projected tenancy characteristics. Computation is as follows:
>
> a. Compute the building occupancy according to the following schedule:

Apartment	Occupancy
Studio	1 Adult
1 BR	2 Adults
2 BR	2 Adults and 1 child
3 BR	2 Adults and 2 children
4 BR	2 Adults and 3 children

> b. Compute the amount of recreation space required according to the following schedule:
>
> For child use space multiply the number of children by 20 sf
>
> For mixed use space multiply the total number of residents (children plus adults) by 25 sf
>
> For adult space multiply the number of adults by 100 sf
>
> c. The facilities permitted to fulfill space requirements are the following:

Children	Adult	Mixed
Tot lot	Passive	Swimming pool
Intermediate playground	Rooftop terrace	Handball
	Health club	Tennis courts
Nursery daycare (public)	Terrace	Basketball
	Laundry room	Meeting rooms
Nursery daycare (private)		Volleyball
		Shops—craft
		Shops—automotive

COMPONENTS OF DESIGN—ARCHITECTURAL

Within these categories the developer can fulfill recreation requirements in relation to user characteristics and demands. Unfortunately this proposal, like all categorizations, has built-in restrictions; for instance, there are areas in which buildings containing two-bedroom apartments will be without children and consequently need no child-oriented recreation spaces. Also, some kinds of tenants such as the elderly, demand special recreation space.

The greatest difficulties appear to be in the square foot requirements, on the basis of which particular luxury condominium of 500 apartments in Chicago would need more than 140,000 sf in combined recreation space! This building, in which the residents are well satisfied with the area provided, actually has two open pools, two tennis courts, a putting green, shuffle boards, an enclosed handball court, saunas, day care facilities, game rooms, and large community rooms. Altogether approximately 40,000 sf are devoted to recreation, far less than the 140,000 required in the New York guide. Although the figures in the New York proposal seem valid for smaller projects, as the number of apartments increases the proposed space requirements become excessive. Taking into account simultaneous use, one should decrease them proportionately.

The grouping and definition of facilities in the New York proposal have wide validity with minor adjustments and amplification.

CHILDREN

In open-air tot-lots and intermediate-age playgrounds careful separation of young children from teenagers and provision of proper activities and identification for each is essential. It is important that these areas be observable. A level connection between the elevator stop and the tot-lot is necessary.

Day care or nursery facilities require space for supervisory personnel, storage, special toilets, and cooking facilities. For minimum requirements the regulations of local health boards or state agencies must be consulted. These agencies also regulate the necessary adjacent outdoor play area per child.

ADULT

Open air sitting and quiet areas must have some sort of shading, landscaping, lighting, and outdoor furniture.

Gardening plots are sometimes provided in housing for the elderly. The location of tool storage must be considered in this case.

A rooftop terrace must have an elevator stop at terrace level. It also needs proper surfacing, lighting, and screening from stacks, exhausts, and strong winds. Part of it should be covered to provide shelter from rain and sun, and public toilets must be nearby.

The laundry room, as a social magnet, can be counted among recreation spaces. The lounge area must be adequate for furniture grouping, and public toilets should be accessible. It is essential that it have daylight.

The health club contains sauna, dressing rooms, showers, and toilets, for men and women, and is usually located near the swimming pool. An exercise room—sometimes with massage tables, sleeping rooms, and even a steam bath—can be located between the men's and women's section of the sauna, making possible the use of a single facility by men and women in alternate schedules. As a rule of thumb, a health club consisting of sauna, showers, dressing space, and toilets (without exercise room or steam bath) for each sex requires the following square footage: for 100 apartments, 8 sf per apartment; 100 to 250 apartments, 5 to 6 sf per apartment; 250 to 500 apartments, 3.5 to 4 sf per apartment.

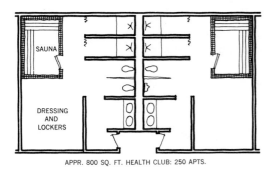

APPR. 800 SQ. FT. HEALTH CLUB: 250 APTS.

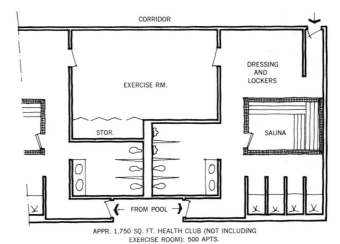

APPR. 1,750 SQ. FT. HEALTH CLUB (NOT INCLUDING
EXERCISE ROOM): 500 APTS.

MIXED

Sports such as tennis, handball, basketball, and volley ball are usually played in the open air unless a high budget permits enclosures. Dimensional standards, orientation, height, proper finishes, and lighting must be checked. Toilets, showers, and dressing rooms, needed for each sex, can double as pool facilities. Sometimes a small spectator space is provided.

An open-air putting green needs no adjacent facilities.

A swimming pool can be enclosed or in the open. When covered, the height of the space depends on the diving board, and an open-air sun bathing terrace must adjoin. The season for open-air swimming pools in northern climates can be extended by providing wind shielding around the deck. State health regulations will determine toilet and shower requirements as well as such details as gutters around the pool, foot bath, and filtering. Storage space must be built for deck furniture.

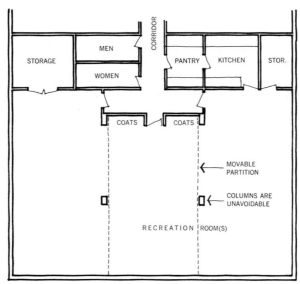

APPR. 3,200 SQ. FT. RECREATION FACILITY: 500 APTS.

Meeting rooms must have space for impromptu community gatherings or special events on a scheduled basis. Movable partitions permit multiple use of the space.

COMPONENTS OF DESIGN—ARCHITECTURAL

Separate toilets should be installed because the floor of the toilets that serve the sauna or the swimming pool is usually wet.

Meeting rooms also require coat space, storage for furniture, small kitchen, serving pantry for catered parties. In estimating meeting room space (including storage and kitchen) 15 sf per apartment is needed for buildings of 100 units. The square footage can be proportionately reduced to 8 sf per apartment for buildings of 500 units. HUD recommends that community facilities (meeting rooms and support spaces) should not exceed 8 sf per bedroom when the number of bedrooms served is under 100; when the number of bedrooms served is 100 or over, community facilities should not exceed 800 sf plus 4 sf for every bedroom over 100.

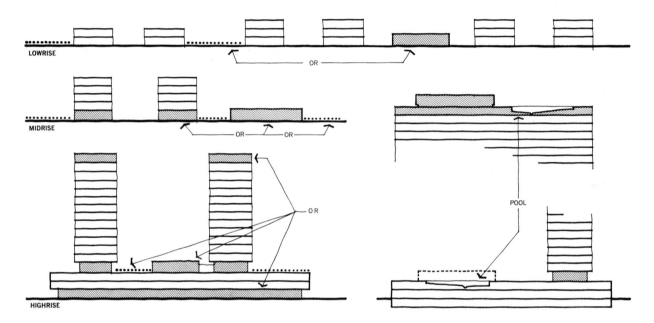

Game rooms for cards, pool, and ping pong are usually located near the meeting rooms.

Shops or craft rooms, also near the meeting rooms, require storage, special equipment, and plumbing.

The location of recreation space depends not only on functional requirements and interrelations but also on the physical character of the project it serves. The locations available for recreation depend on the type of project and the site.

COMPONENTS OF DESIGN— STRUCTURAL

3

Eugene P. Holland

FRAME SELECTION

The selection of the frame must result in the most economical structure within the bounds of the building function. The final product must be serviceable as well. What does "serviceable" mean? Deflection of floors and vibratory variations must be within reasonable limits; architectural elements interfacing with structural elements must suffer minimal distress; building drift must be limited to minimize partition cracking or crushing and adverse human response to building movement.

Unlike mechanical equipment, hardware, doors, or cabinetry, the structural system has no range of economic decision. The same well-designed structure could be used in minimal housing or in the most exclusive apartment construction. Having satisfied strength and serviceability, there is no way to make the structure "better." Additional quantity adds only to cost, not to quality.

Selection of the structure is bound by a multitude of interacting parameters. The program established by the building's sponsor tends to dictate the general type of structure. The number of type of desired units requires a specific expanse of building. Walk-up apartments are generally limited to three or four stories. Within this range, if allowed by code, the wood frame has most frequently proved to be economical from a first-cost standpoint. Aside from walk-ups, the number of apartments may be achieved by utilizing a large floor area and few floors or a smaller floor area and a greater number of floors. The choice is generally limited by the building code, zoning, and site conditions. If tolerance is allowed, the former will usually result in a more economical structure.

FLOOR AREA. A structure with a floor area of less than approximately 8000 sf cannot utilize a concrete crew efficiently; therefore a steel frame, concrete site or plant precast, or other "prefabricated" structure is generally competitively priced.

In two-story units stairs must be strategically placed to avoid undue structural complications. If allowed by code, spiral stairs offer the fewest structural disadvantages. In a concrete flat plate, stair openings are best arranged at the center of a bay, furthest away from columns. If this is not functionally possible, the flat plate system can accommodate any arrangement with appropriate structural variations (see section on slab openings). However, if the structural scheme consists of undirectional members (steel, wood, precast concrete) the run of stairs must be parallel to the secondary framing members and the stringers should bear on beam lines. For instance in a beam and joist floor system, the run of stairs should be planned to be parallel to the joists. To do the opposite requires heavy, expensive header beams and/or additional columns. Because the location of stairs is repeated in a typical two-story apartment complex, architectural planning of the units must be coordinated with the structure to be economical and serviceable.

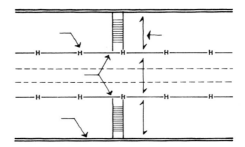

HEIGHT. A structure less than about seven stories high generally requires no significant lateral-load-resisting provisions. The gravity load elements of the building will be adequate to resist lateral loads with only slight modifications. Above this height consideration must be given to the integration and additional cost of bracing, shear walls, or moment connections. The use of a concrete flat plate requires about 8 ft 5 in. floor to floor, whereas a steel frame needs about 9 ft 6 in., a significant difference in multistory structures. Accordingly, more stories may be developed within the same overall building height with a flat plate. A good example is Chicago's requirement that a smokeproof tower be provided in buildings more than 264 ft high. Within this height four more stories could be provided by using a thin concrete flat plate instead of steel. Careful consideration of cost must also be given to the increased exterior wall surface, longer stair runs, increased pipes, and mechanical ducts in a structure with greater floor-to-floor heights.

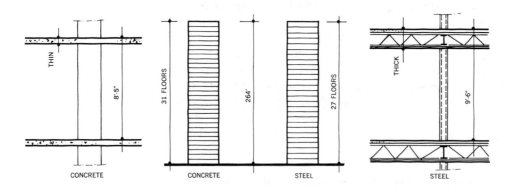

COLUMN TRANSFERS. Parking under the tower portion of the building requires careful coordination to avoid problems with the column layout. Column transfers are extremely costly and should be avoided. The most economical parking is outside the tower itself. The same problem exists for "air-tight" projects in which clear open spans at the lower levels are required. If major column transfers become unavoidable, the lightest frame possible should be used: either structural steel or lightweight concrete.

FOUNDATIONS. Similar consideration is required when foundation material is poor. If very deep foundations, such as piles, are recommended, the added cost must be taken into account when comparing structural frames.

MATERIALS. The availability and cost of materials may dictate the choice of structural frame. Especially in times of material shortages, the structural engineer must maintain current knowledge of material supply and costs. The time used in obtaining materials may also affect the decision. If the owners' financial commitment has generated inordinate interest costs, the choice of a more expensive structural frame that is available for earlier construction may be offset by the savings in interest and sometimes earlier occupancy.

CONSTRUCTION SEASONS. Seasonal variation in construction depends on the building's geographical location. In cold-weather country the brevity of good construction time in the winter season may dictate the use of a frame that can be erected without regard to climate. Many winter days do not permit on-site casting of concrete, whereas structural steel or precast concrete can readily be placed.

LABOR. Union and other labor practices may affect structural frame choice. For example, union rules vary concerning casting concrete. In the Midwest the same concrete crew may be required to stay with the castings process. If the concreting extends beyond the normal work day, the contractor is obligated to pay double and sometimes triple hourly rates. This minimizes the cost advantage of concrete. On the other hand, labor unions in other areas of the country permit entirely different crews to work the second and even third shifts of the work day, thereby allowing the contractor to complete the work in a shorter time without the "overtime" penalty. Another example concerns the tieing of reinforcing steel. Certain regions permit iron workers to carry tie wires with them; others require them to go back and forth from a designated tie wire storage area. Before selecting the framing system, the structural engineer therefore must review union regulations and also standard practices in the building's locale. The results may tip the scale in the selection of the frame.

STRUCTURAL FRAME

CAST-IN-PLACE CONCRETE

The cast-in-place reinforced concrete flat-plate structure is the most widely used system for highrise apartment structures in the United States. It is estimated that 90% of all apartment buildings of more than 10 stories are so constructed. Reasons for this high percentage are numerous.

1. Building height is reduced, which thereby reduces mechanical and electrical runs, facade, and wind loadings, which minimize lateral load-resisting elements and foundations.
2. Contractors have become adept at this type of construction.
3. Finishes are simplified, with paint or skim coat of plaster for final ceilings.

COMPONENTS OF DESIGN—STRUCTURAL

4. Fire rating is automatically provided with concrete. Normal slab design thicknesses satisfy most building code fire requirements.

5. Architectural planning is not hindered by consideration of rigid column layout because scattered columns may be used. Partition layout is not controlled by beams extending beneath the slab.

The use of "superplasticizers" (high-range water reducing admixtures) is relatively new in concrete technology. Although they have been used in Japan since the 1960s and in Europe since 1972, they have only recently been introduced into the United States. Many engineers feel that introduction of superplastizers has opened up a new era in concrete technology. The resulting concrete is used in a fully fluid state (while it maintains basic strength and other properties) allowing for a general increase in speed of concrete construction and thereby reducing labor costs. Because of the fluidity, concrete moves freely into forms and gives true, smooth surfaces in congested areas. Higher strength concretes are also more readily attained.

Major builders are predicting overall labor savings in the neighborhood of 30%, while the admixture adds about 5% to the cost of concrete.

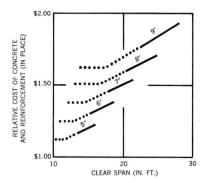
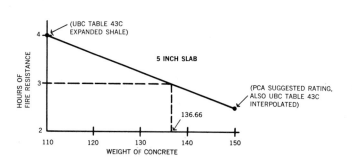

SLAB THICKNESS. Maximum economy is obtained when structures are devised requiring materials that work the least to resist applied loads. The object therefore is to minimize slab span by maintaining close column spacing. Additional columns do not substantially increase cost, but thinner slabs will decrease it. All but the most luxurious apartment structures can accommodate column spacings of about 15 ft. This span, measured from face to face of the columns requires a slab thickness of 5 in. Increased spans require increased reinforcing steel, which interferes with economy.

The rule of thumb for slab thickness is that the span length in feet, when divided by 3, will give the slab thickness in inches. In other words, the slab thickness must increase ½ in. for each 1.5 ft increase in span.

A slab thickness of 5 in., using normal weight concrete, will satisfy the majority of building code fire requirements; however, some codes require a 3-hour vertical separation, which necessitates using a lighter weight concrete or a thicker normal weight slab. The graph above shows that a 5-in. slab of 137-pcf (pounds per cubic foot) concrete will satisfy the 3-hour requirement. A 5½-in. slab of 150-pcf concrete would also be adequate.

MECHANICAL, ELECTRICAL, AND ARCHITECTURAL SLAB OPENING CONSIDERATIONS. Slab penetration for pipe chases, shafts, and duct work should be accomplished without adverse effect to the structure and with a minimum increase in structural element size. Larger shafts for elevators and stairs should be ideally located in the center half of the bay. To achieve this condition lightweight wall assemblies (shaft walls) are best. Lightweight walls avoid the need for edge beams. (Masonry walls could be used without edge beams, provided that the masonry passes the slab with adequate lateral ties or that it is allowed to span from column to column with only minimal load bearing on the slab span.) The most critical areas for openings are at or near columns. Openings at columns generally require an increase in column size to maintain equivalent slab capacity. The opening size and position greatly affect this condition. If large openings (stairs or elevators) are located at columns, it may be necessary to frame the opening with walls or at least additional columns.

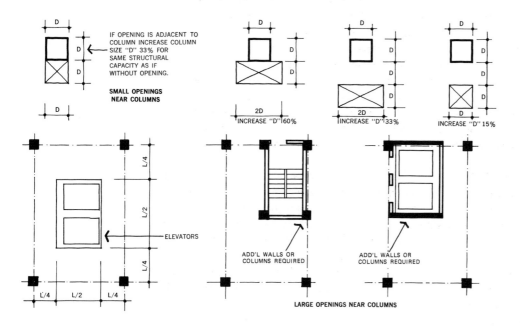

IN-SLAB CONDUITS.   The use of sleeves for pipes and vents, in lieu of totally open chases, offers considerable structural advantage. Electrical conduits in the plane of the slab (including crossovers) should never have dimensions greater than one-third of the slab thickness and should always be placed between the bottom and top layers of reinforcing material. If possible, the grouping of conduits, especially at columns, should be avoided. If this is not possible, the grouped conduits must be considered as creating an entire opening in the slab.

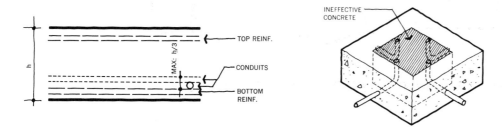

PLUMBING.   To fit within the floor slab standard plumbing traps require a minimum slab thickness of about 6 in. With a 5-in. slab the standard fittings project below the slab. The result is a suspended ceiling or some other architectural solution to disguise the trap. A fixture that discharges above the floor avoids the problem, as do the shallow traps that have been used on 5-in. slab projects in conjunction with prefabricated stacks.

SOUND CONSIDERATIONS.   Concrete flat plates provide excellent resistance to airborne transmission. As far as impact noise is concerned slab thickness does not discernibly influence the effectiveness of the floor. The major influence is the type of floor covering. With the same floor covering the difference between a 5- to 6-in. slab and a 7- to 8-in. slab is 3 (STC) and 1 (IIC).

COLUMN SPACING AND ARRANGEMENT.   Columns may be arranged in a rigid grid pattern or "scattered"—their placement determined by the best apartment plan. The rigid grid is ideal for a structural steel frame and is advantageous for a concrete frame in which "flying" forms are utilized. The "scattered" column layout, however, allows almost complete architectural freedom in apartment planning.

Except for a few cases, column spacing in apartment structures need not exceed 15 or 16 ft (maximum living room width). Thus, unlike practices in office buildings, a short-span framing system becomes possible. The small span will result in additional columns; however, unless foundation considerations are critical, the added cost is minimal when compared with the positive cost advantage of shorter spans.

COLUMN CONFIGURATIONS.   Columns are usually square or rectangular and, on occasion, circular (usually when free standing). The square column requires the least formwork and is therefore the most economical. Square and especially rectangular columns are generally more adaptable to apartment layouts than the round. Long narrow (6 to 8 in. wide) columns may be used to good advantage in limiting projections into rooms, fitting well into closets and corners and also minimizing slab spans. Unless the reduction of column sizes offers an extreme architectural advantage, columns should be reduced only every 10 to 15 stories. This reduction, however, need not be made symmetrical about the column centroid. Maintaining at least one flush face throughout the building height will eliminate dimensional problems and allow efficient form use.

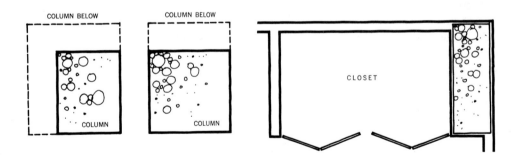

Architectural considerations can lead to a variety of column configurations and shapes on the exterior.

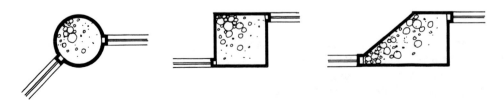

RIGID COLUMN PATTERN. The rigid column layout allows for the use of "flying forms" (see Flat Plate—Forms and Shores). Unfortunately the completely rigid layout generally requires longer spans and thicker slabs, which defeats or at least seriously reduces forming cost advantage.

SEMIRIGID COLUMN PATTERN. The semirigid grid with shorter spans (none longer than the 15 ft, dictated by living room width), which combines "flying forms" and ordinary forming may prove to be advantageous: column placement is not so inflexible that it hinders the floor plan and its regularity provides uniformity in construction procedures, details, and reinforcing.

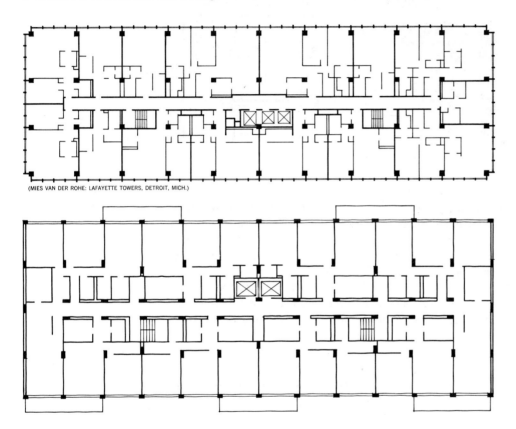

(MIES VAN DER ROHE: LAFAYETTE TOWERS, DETROIT, MICH.)

SCATTERED COLUMN PATTERN. The "scattered" column layout eliminates architectural restraints and allows placement of columns where they fit into the plan best. It is often advantageous to use long and narrow rectangular columns to minimize slab spans and even decrease the total number of columns.

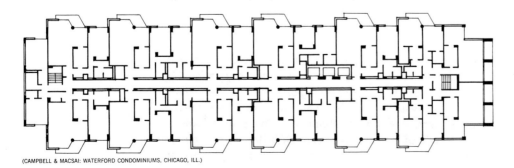

(CAMPBELL & MACSAI: WATERFORD CONDOMINIUMS, CHICAGO, ILL.)

COMPONENTS OF DESIGN—STRUCTURAL

EXTERIOR COLUMN SPACING.   Exterior column spacing is generally dictated by the exterior skin. To avoid problems of deflection and/or excessive cambers, close spacing is often needed to support the weight of a heavier exterior such as precast concrete or masonry. This closer spacing replaces spandrel beams, which should be avoided unless essential from an architectural standpoint. Exterior spans with a lightweight facade should be limited to 15 ft for thin slabs (5 in.+) and 21 ft for thicker slabs (8 in.+). Heavyweight facades limit the spans to about 12 ft and 18 ft for thin and thick slabs, respectively.

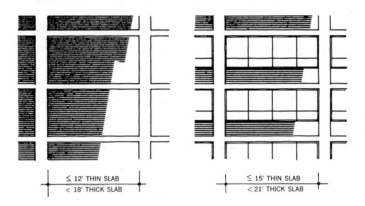

    ≤ 12′ THIN SLAB   ≤ 15′ THIN SLAB
    < 18′ THICK SLAB   < 21′ THICK SLAB

Exposed exterior columns require special design considerations for both column configuration and slab-to-column interface. The transfer of forces requires sufficient slab "bite" to the column. Thermal movements of exposed exterior columns need special structural analysis and construction details: exposed concrete may change vertical dimension by an inch or more in a 50-story structure.

Exterior column spacing may also be influenced by interior partition locations. A closely spaced column grid allows greater flexibility in partition layout. Close spacing of exterior columns, discussed later, offers a further structural advantage for resistance to lateral loads.

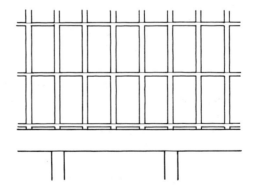

CANTILEVERS.   Apartment structures are often designed with cantilevered balconies or projecting bays. Maintaining a proper cantilever span-to-slab thickness relationship will prevent deflections. This is particularly true for projecting bays enclosed by walls at the free edges. The ratio of slab thickness to cantilever span shown may be extended with the understanding that serviceability may be impaired. The slab thickness, however, may be decreased at the end of the cantilever to provide drainage. (Caution should be exercised in arriving at the minimum thickness because of the anchoring requirement of railings.)

Type and placement of reinforcement should also be carefully considered. Normal practice is to extend interior bay reinforcement into the cantilever. However, in so doing concrete cover may be only ¾ in. This cover may not be adequate unless a coating is placed on the concrete to prevent the deleterious effects of de-icing salts and moisture penetrating the concrete and weakening it. Alternatively, the reinforcement should be placed with a concrete cover of at least 1½ in. Also, a concrete mix with a low water to cement ratio (0.45 to 0.5) and adequate air entrainment should be used.

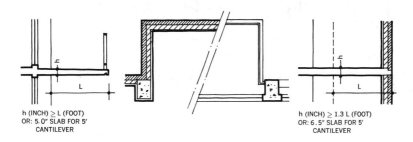

h (INCH) ≥ L (FOOT)
OR: 5.0″ SLAB FOR 5′
CANTILEVER

h (INCH) ≥ 1.3 L (FOOT)
OR: 6.5″ SLAB FOR 5′
CANTILEVER

A curb may be provided to prevent water intrusion, although some argue that it is dangerous or at least inconvenient. However, it has been used satisfactorily on luxury apartment buildings under sliding doors. Somewhat less efficient is the ¾-in. break in the slab proper. Efficient but costly is the balcony that utilizes a spandrel beam.

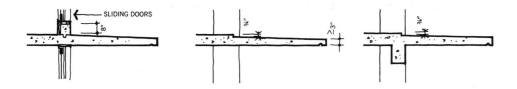

SLIDING DOORS

Continuous, exposed exterior balconies or corridors, popular in warmer climates, require considerations for thermal movement generally satisfied by the use of joints. Joints are normally placed in the range of 10 to 15 ft, depending on the architectural plan and balcony extent.

COLUMN TRANFERS. The interruption of column continuity is often desirable at the lower levels of apartment structures: the need is for larger spans at entrances,

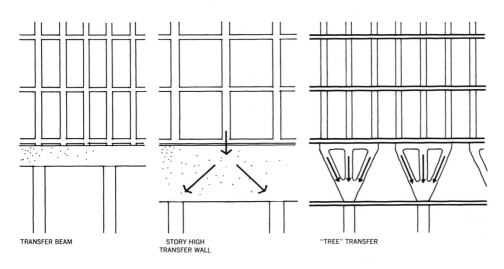

TRANSFER BEAM

STORY HIGH
TRANSFER WALL

"TREE" TRANSFER

community rooms, and lobby areas or parking and driving aisles under the tower. The best solution is to avoid the problem; when unavoidable, however, the methods generally employed utilize transfer beams, transfer walls, or transfer "trees." The last two are preferable because of their structural efficiency in force transfer.

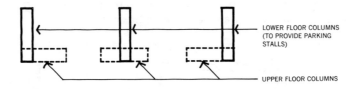

Occasionally the increased space on the lower level may be accomplished by changing the orientation of the columns.

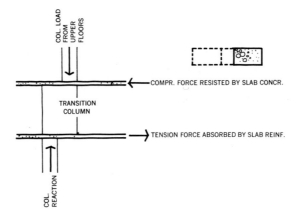

In addition, a complete offset in column location from upper to lower floors is made possible by using a "transition" column and utilizing the floor slabs to provide a resisting couple against the moment created by the eccentric load.

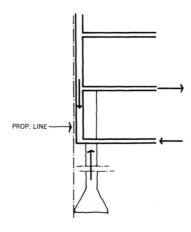

The same structural action may be readily adapted to other eccentric loads. The scarcity and cost of land in urban areas require the full use of the available property, and structures are often designed to extend from property line to property line. To prevent foundations from encroaching on adjacent property they must be set back from the lot line, thereby creating an eccentric load.

FLAT PLATE—FORMS AND SHORES. Although construction remains the contractor's responsibility, it is necessary to elaborate on the procedures required to form and shore a flat plate structure safely.

Careless shoring and early shore removal have resulted in numerous cases of nonlevel floors and, on occasion, catastrophic failures. The contractor must be made aware of the fact that "green" concrete has only a limited carrying capacity.

The problems can be minimized by removing only small portions of forming and reshoring as the forms are removed or utilizing "trapped" shores (shores that remain in place when the forms are stripped automatically become the "reshores").

The casting cycle is the primary factor in determining the number of shored and reshored floors required. Generally, the following sequence is necessary as a minimum shoring criterion: the first structural slab must be completely shored. The second structural slab must also be completely shored when the concrete is placed. When the second slab has gained at least 70% of its 28-day compressive strength and the first slab has gained at least 85% of its 28-day compressive strength, the first slab shores may be removed and reshores placed under the first slab. The second slab shores must remain in place. The third slab shores are then set and the third slab cast. When the third slab has gained at least 70% of its 28-day compressive strength and the second slab has gained at least 85% of its 28-day compressive strength, the second floor shores may be removed and reshores placed, and so on. The compressive strengths required are best determined by test cylinders cast and cured by the same procedure used in the actual slab construction.

For a 3- to 4-day casting cycle this "formula" results in the need for four sets of forms. Three floors are always fully shored and one set of forms is in transit. Three additional floors are reshored. A very large floor area (greater than about 16,000 sf) allows for staggered casting of half floors, thereby minimizing the number of forms needed and maximizing the efficiency of the casting cycle.

The contractor usually knows that certain deflections will occur and generally provides a small camber in the slab forms. Most contract specifications require the contractor to provide camber in accordance with ACI 347, "Concrete Formwork." This document outlines the responsibility of the contractor to provide camber for shortening of shores, mud sill settlement, and form deflection. It does not require camber for elastic deflections following shore removal or for long-term creep deflections. This is the structural engineer's responsibility, and, if deemed necessary, requirements must be contained in the contract documents.

The labor-intensive nature of traditional shoring and forming has led to considerable use of "flying forms." An entire bay of a building (that portion of a building defined by contiguous columns) is formed by a single section of form and shore. The unit is normally designed with story-high trusses and cross joists or beams with plywood. Most recently the flying forms has been adapted to function also as a form for spandrel beams and even architectural precast facade. Upon reaching adequate concrete strength the entire section is moved out of the building and lifted to the next story. The flying form system requires a rigid rectangular grid of columns, optimally with all columns oriented in the same direction, and the narrowest face parallel to the long building direction. Time requirements for removal and reshoring are the same as for the traditional system discussed above.

EXPANSION JOINTS. Changes in volume of concrete due to variations in temperature and moisture must be recognized as a detriment to the structure's serviceability.

COMPONENTS OF DESIGN—STRUCTURAL

Exposed vertical concrete elements such as columns or shear walls change dimensions when subjected to temperature variations. In highrise structures this dimension may be an inch or more. Slabs and partitions interfacing such elements will suffer distress if not detailed to allow for this movement.

Exposed horizontal concrete spandrels, balconies, walls, and roofs require expansion joints to provide for length changes due to temperature. The spacing of expansion joints in roofs is dependent to a great extent on thermal roof insulation. Requirements for expansion joint spacing vary between 150- and 250-ft intervals on roofs and a lesser distance in exposed concrete; particular attention must be paid to offsets. To be totally effective expansion joints should extend vertically through the building. They are not required, however, when structural elements supporting the subjected concrete are flexible enough to deform with the temperature movement; for instance, slender columns supporting a concrete roof may be flexible enough to drift with the expansion of the slab without deleterious effects. Expansion joints are also used on roofs of buildings with nonlinear plan geometry, Y-, T-, or L-shaped buildings with long or dissimilar wings should have expansion joints at the building core separating the wings. Joints that allow for differential settlement are required at the meeting of the tower columns and garage slabs.

GARAGE FRAMING.   Parking under the apartment tower offers many nonstructural advantages: reduced land coverage, shorter walking distance to the elevators, and increased security. With the most efficient 90-degree parking system, 20- to 22-ft aisles are used and therefore large spans and heavier slabs are required. Small spans, however, preferred from the point of view of structural economy, result in thinner slabs in the tower and transfer columns to facilitate parking, a rather costly solution. Methods of transfer have already been discussed. Cost advantages of close column spacing in the tower may be totally maintained if coordination of apartment layout and parking allow the apartment columns to continue down through the parking area without transfer. This, of course, requires other than 90-degree parking; for instance, with a 13 ft 6 in. one-directional travel aisle and 45-degree parking the close spacing of tower columns may not hinder a reasonable parking layout. Parking outside the tower area is more advantageous from a structural standpoint and produces the most efficient parking layout.

The framing system of the garage is dictated by column spacing. In concrete, a mild reinforced or post-tensioned flat slab with column capitals, ribbed slabs (pan joist or waffle), or precast, prestressed double-tee sections are used. The recent relaxation of fire-rating requirements for parking structures permits steel frames with concrete slabs to be considered more often.

Ninety-degree parking with 20-ft driving aisles requires 22 to 27 ft between columns. With an 8 ft 6 in. or 9 ft parking-stall width, columns in the transverse direction may then be spaced at a multiple of the stall width, for example, 18 or 27 ft. From these choices various column layouts may be selected. For a square (or nearly square) grid with minimum column spacing the flat slab with column capitals is generally the most economical and may be mild reinforced or post-tensioned. A two-way grid (waffle slab), also applicable, utilizes material to its best advantage; however, form costs (steel or fiberglass) are high. For a rectangular 18- by 27-ft bay, pan joist spanning in the long direction with a wide flat beam (in depth equal to the joist) in the 18-ft direction has proved to be economical. Narrow (8 to 12 in.) rectangular columns limit infringement on the parking spaces. Prestressed precast and structural steel frames are generally applicable to rectangular bays with much larger spans.

Caution should be exercised in specifying concrete mix and detailing reinforced concrete parking decks, particularly in northern climates where durability of the concrete is necessary to resist the deleterious effects of de-icing salts. Crack width control, increased concrete cover over reinforcing steel, a low water to cement ratio concrete mix, and a maintenance program defining washdowns, coatings, and/or sealers will extend the life of the structure under these adverse conditions.

OTHER CONCRETE SCHEMES

Although in highrise apartment construction mild reinforced, cast-in-place concrete predominates, other methods of concrete use are becoming prevalent, particularly in the midrise market.

POST-TENSIONED SLABS.   When the building's function or other restraints create the need for spans in excess of about 20 to 22 ft, prestressed concrete by post-tensioning, competitively priced, is gaining a considerable portion of the market.

Concrete cast-in-place slabs using slab forming and shoring procedures heretofore discussed contain high-strength prestressing cables or tendons. When the slab concrete has reached a specified strength the strands are tensioned by jacks at the slab edges. When desired tension is accomplished the strands are anchored. The concrete slab, being the resisting element to the tensioning, is put into compression. Transfer of force is accomplished by jack bearing on the slab edges. This structural action may be provided with or without grouting full the tendons. However, the use of ungrouted tendons is controversial.

The use of post-tensioned slabs provide the following advantages:

1.   Slab and beam thicknesses are reduced.
2.   Because of induced slab compression, cracks are minimized.
3.   Deflections are more controllable and reduce one of the most frequent problems with mild steel, cast-in-place concrete.

However, these advantages are not materialized without rigid controls on concrete strength, tendon placement, tensioning, and form and shore removal.

SITE PRECAST, ERECTED BY CRANE.   Cast-in-place concrete requires scores of laborers and craftspersons, alternating between work accomplished by fits and starts and waiting their turn. In addition to this inefficient utilization of labor, about 30% of the cost of the structure is spent on forming and shoring. Precasting, on the other hand, eliminates forming and can be organized in a rational, assembly-line fashion that yields a smooth flow of work.

If, however, we think in terms of the usual precast floor elements—voided planks 2, 4, or even 8 ft wide or double tees—various drawbacks become apparent. Neither the ceiling nor the floor is smooth or level. The architect may decide to live with this or spend money on camouflaging the ceiling and topping the floor. There is nothing anybody can do about the unidirectional structural behavior of these elements. They must be supported along lines, beams, or walls, as opposed to flat plates, which because of their two-way structural action require only point supports, that is, columns. To support planks or tees, beams amounting to an entire set of new structural elements must be introduced or bearing walls must be used.

A way to combine the advantages of precasting without the disadvantages of the unidirectional elements is to use large precast floor panels, each equal to several rooms in size. Thus the joints are hidden in the partitions, and the top and bottom surfaces of the panels are smooth and ready for floor finish and paint, respectively. These panels can be designed to provide two-way structural action; the panel does the job of the planks in one direction and the beams in the other. Moment continuity across the joint is not necessarily required, but it can be provided.

The panels are precast on the job site in layers. Casting beds are mud slabs, tennis courts, parking lots, or the first floor of the building. The slabs are lifted into place by crane. Readily available equipment can handle large and heavy panels economically.

The best way to ensure proper fit of the panels when on-site space is available is to fit-cast them on a single bed for an entire floor. Simple edgeforms and dividers between the panels, both raised for successive layers, are the only forming material needed. Special joint details, which provide for a grout key between panels in addition to bolted connections, produce an exact fit. They also transform the individual panels into a diaphragm needed for lateral stability of the building. This stability is otherwise achieved in a manner similar to the cast-in-place scheme.

Columns may be steel or precast concrete. Lateral loads are resisted by shear walls, shear panels, or steel bracing.

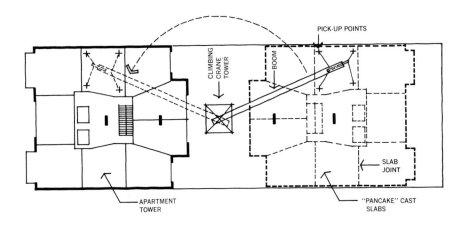

SITE PRECAST, LIFT SLAB.   The advantages of this precast scheme in relation to poured flat plates are also inherent in the "lift slab" approach. Rather than casting the slabs adjacent to the building, they are pancake-cast on a ground-floor slab in their final plan location. Sophisticated hydraulic lifting devices and procedures are necessary to raise the slabs at all lift points at an identical rate of climb. Also, cast-in-place concrete slab column joints may be readily designed for moment transfer, eliminating the need for other lateral load-resisting elements in midrise buildings, whereas lift-slab joint stiffness is difficult to achieve and thereby requires shear walls, bracing, and so on.

PLANT PRECAST.   Numerous plant-precast structural products are available, from individual elements such as hollow-core slabs, double tees, columns, and ledger girders to entire structures. Although most often applied on lowrise buildings in conjunction with steel-frame or bearing masonry walls, their use in highrise apartments is increasing. Structures of almost any height become feasible with precast wall panels and floor elements with proper connections. As on-site construction costs increase, assuming demands large enough to make precasting worthwhile, totally precast construction is becoming more and more competitively priced.

COMPOSITE CONCRETE.   Using precast prestressed concrete elements in concert with cast-in-place concrete offers a minimum of shoring, yields cost advantages of plant production, and allows for development of rigid joints. The type and shape of the precast prestressed elements vary. However, each serves as forming for the cast-in-place concrete. Particular schemes have captured a considerable portion of the low- to midrise and highrise markets. Normal span range is between 20 and 35 ft.

One scheme consists of thin precast prestressed soffit slabs (1½ in.) with protruding shear wires used for lifting and for developing composite action with the cast-in-place concrete. After it is cast and cured the prestressed slab provides the tension capacity for the composite section. The supporting beam elements are also formed with precast soffits and ultimately perform as a composite section. Mild reinforcement is added to the cast-in-place slab to minimize slab and beam moments. Because of the soffit slab thinness this scheme often requires some shoring, which is, however, minimal when compared to a totally cast-in-place slab.

Another composite floor system consists of precast prestressed concrete joists with a composite cast-in-place deck. A precast prestressed soffit forms the beams. Soffits are shored, and joists are supported on the soffits. Wood forms are used between the joist to complete the forming system. After reinforcement is placed, concrete is cast for slab and beam. Following concrete strength gain the wood forms are reused. Unless an architectural ceiling is used, the joists are exposed, which is apparently satisfactory for certain types of housing.

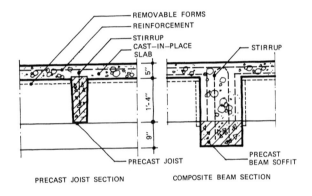

PRECAST JOIST SECTION   COMPOSITE BEAM SECTION

A similar scheme utilizes precast prestressed hollow-core slabs placed over precast prestressed beam soffits. In this case, negative reinforcement is placed only to provide a continuous composite beam, as cast-in-place concrete is only used structurally in the beam. The sole shoring required supports the beam soffit, the hollow-core slabs having adequate spanning strength to support either a structural or a nonstructural topping. As

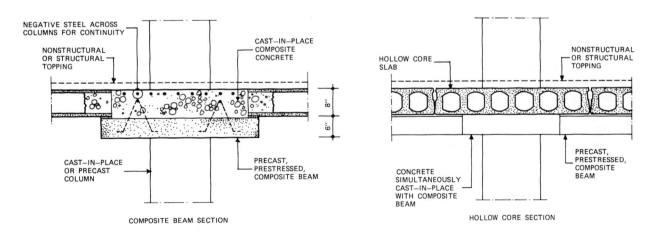

COMPOSITE BEAM SECTION   HOLLOW CORE SECTION

with the joist scheme, the overall soffit finish is not uniform in that the joints between hollow-core slabs and beams soffits are difficult to disguise.

As previously mentioned, because of the undirectional action of the precast prestressed members, floor system depths will be increased over cast-in-place flat plates. Any attempt to use such a scheme as a direct replacement for two-way action without appropriate changes is structurally impossible.

STRUCTURAL STEEL

Compared with concrete, relatively few apartment buildings of more than 10 or 12 stories have been constructed of structural steel. The advancement in structural design techniques, changes in code fireproofing requirements, the introduction of higher strength steels, and ease and speed of erection are factors that are increasing the attractiveness of using steel.

A rigid rectilinear column layout is normally required. Two or three column rows are used, depending on the width of the building and on the span and depth requirements of the secondary floor members and whether parking space is provided inside the building. A secondary-member span of 20 to 25 ft is reasonable. Spacing of columns at about 20 ft on center in the longitudinal direction produces an economical beam design.

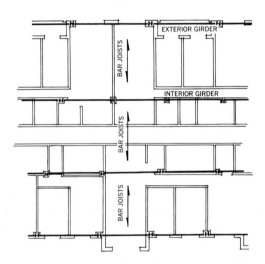

A floor plan of fewer than about 8000 sf is most economical when structural steel is used. As already discussed, pouring concrete for such a small area is inefficient, and prefabricated steel frames allow rapid erection and ease of materials handling. Columns are usually wide-flange sections, although steel tubes and pipes have been employed. The size of structural steel columns may be small when compared with concrete (even after fireproofing) because high-strength steels may be utilized in the design.

Most steel-frame structures use bolted connections, and high-strength A325 bolts predominate. Welded connections, which provide a simplified means of creating continuity of beams and columns that may be required for lateral loads, also minimize the weight and size of the flexural members. The testing of welded connection, however, is rather complicated and costly, and the acceptance criteria are vague, whereas simple procedures are available for testing bolted connections.

Open web steel joists 14 in. deep suffice for the spans discussed above, but simplification of the framing and ease of ceiling installation require that the joists be 2 in. deeper than the steel beams. With the 14-in. joist, therefore, a 12-in. beam should be used. For shorter spans a 12-in. joist and a 10-in. beam will satisfy this condition.

Joists are spaced at 20 to 30 in. on center. The greater spacing provides for more efficient use of the corrugated steel deck above. This deck, with 2½-in. cast-in-place concrete, is the most commonly used floor. A particularly critical design consideration relating to the use of bar joists is the minimization of vibrations. This flexible joist is likely to create a condition of adverse human response. Joist depth-to-span ratios that satisfy these conditions are discussed later.

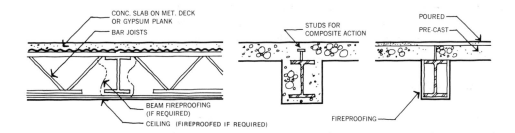

In addition to steel deck and cast-in-place concrete, gypsum planks spanning between joists spread to 48 in. on center may be used. A ¾-in. mastic is applied to the top of the gypsum plank. The resulting reduced weight tends to decrease the amount of structural steel considerably. The total savings, however, will depend on the number of floors.

Prestressed precast members spanning between steel girders may also be used. Hollow-core planks and double-tee sections offer the advantage of long spans. Concrete topping is required to level the floor and allow for placement of electrical conduits.

FIREPROOFING. Fireproofing requirements are constantly changing. The requirements for highrise structures in many codes have been or are in the process of being revised. "Trade-offs," such as compartmentation in lieu of sprinklers, will help the competitive status of structural steel because compartmented (or sprinklered) structures do not require the usual 3-hour fire separation between floors according to the most recent highrise fire codes. Modern methods of fireproofing in the form of spray-on materials have also lessened the cost of protecting structural steel. Cementous, vermiculite, and perlite are used with the spray-on technique. Fire ratings may also be obtained by boxing the structural members with gypsum board. Gypsum board or

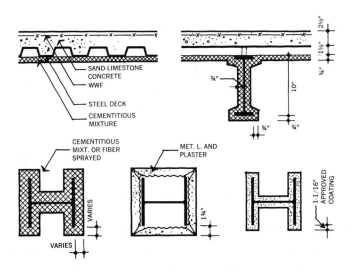

plaster ceilings can also be used to develop floor-system fire ratings, and the newer fireproofing paints or coatings, such as Albi-Clad, offer great promise. Underwriters Laboratory has rated this type of fireproofing for columns. A $\frac{3}{16}$-in. thickness will provide 1 hour; $\frac{1}{2}$-in., 2 hours; and $1\frac{1}{16}$ in., 3 hours.

STAGGERED TRUSS. A fairly recent development in structural steel for highrise apartment buildings is the "staggered truss" system. Story-high trusses supported on columns at the exterior span the width of the building. The trusses are arranged in a staggered pattern on adjacent column lines. Typical secondary members frame between the trusses. This scheme is particularly advantageous if there are air rights to consider or a substantial amount of parking under the tower.

MIDRISE STRUCTURAL VARIATIONS

Although the preceding framing systems are generally applicable to structures four stories or taller, apartment buildings in the 4- to 10-story range (and occasionally even walk-ups) may employ other combinations of steel, concrete, and bearing masonry walls more economically.

MASONRY BEARING. Floor-framing systems (joists, precast elements, and cast-in-place concrete) are often supported on masonry walls. Reinforced masonry bearing wall structures have been constructed to a height of about 18 stories, and 8-in. nonreinforced masonry has been used in 12-story buildings. The fact that the masonry bearing wall may function as architectural enclosure as well as structural support offers economic advantages. Structurally, the wall is designed to serve two functions: it acts jointly with the floors as a horizontal diaphragm. Both gravity and lateral loads are resisted.

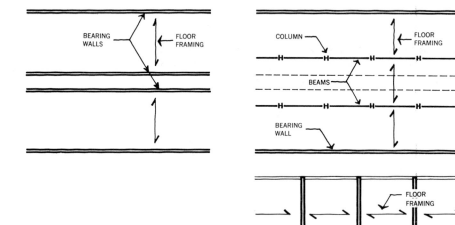

For years masonry design was dictated by rule of thumb and nebulous conservative code restrictions, primarily because of a lack of research. However, with the advent of design criteria established by the Brick Institute of America and the National Concrete

Masonry Association both major materials, clay brick and concrete block, may be engineered by a rational approach. Hence the use of engineering masonry for midrise buildings is now a more viable solution.

Precautions must be noted, however. Although design criteria have been established, construction expertise is lacking in engineered masonry buildings. Masons must be made aware that this type of structure requires greater control of the use of materials and construction techniques. Specifications necessary to ensure construction in accordance with design must be enforced. Mortar cubes and/or prisms (units + mortar) should be tested to ascertain that materials conform with those specified. In addition, cold-weather precautions, moisture-content limitations, and total filling of collar (slush) joints are required.

The most common application of masonry bearing walls is the double-loaded corridor, in which one or both corridor walls and the exterior walls are bearing, or a combination of exterior bearing wall and interior steel columns. If the apartment layout is repetitive, the party walls may be used for bearing.

FLAT PLATE/PIPE COLUMN.   The flat plate/pipe column system consists of cast-in-place or precast (on-site) thin slabs supported on pipe columns. Pipes 3 in. in diameter allow placement within standard stud partitions. This system has all the advantages of concrete construction. When more than a 2-hour fire rating is required for the columns, narrow (4 to 6 in.) cast-in-place or precast columns are used; otherwise the gypsum board will provide a 1-hour rating of the steel pipes. Lateral loads are resisted by braced bents, masonry walls, or shear panels.

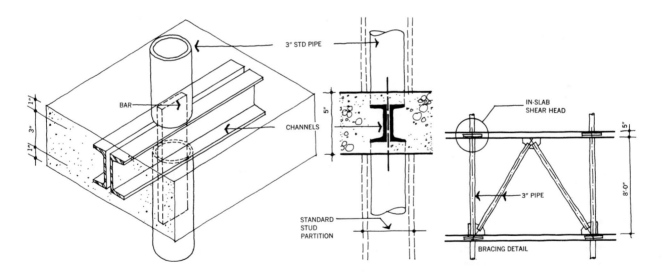

Because column spans are kept at a minimum so that these slabs can be used, they generally do not work well in parking areas if parking is under the tower. When this happens, a thick concrete slab above the parking floor will transfer the scattered pipe column loads to the regularly placed concrete columns. Concrete walls in the first apartment level have also served this transfer function.

WOOD FRAME

Wood frame apartment construction (often termed "ordinary construction") is usually restricted by code to walk-ups or elevator buildings of limited height (four stories). In this construction bearing walls and partitions and floor and roof framing are wholly or partly of wood. Exterior walls may be masonry veneer or bearing masonry. Partitions may be constructed of metal studs but most often wood 2 × 4's spaced at 16 or 24 in. are used. Light-gauge metal joists in lieu of the standard wood joist are gaining acceptance. The roof members are often lightweight prefabricated wood trusses.

Most wood frame structures are not "structurally designed," which sometimes leads to misbehavior and occasionally to structural failure. Nailing and other details of construction are usually left to the carpenter. Because of the lack of moisture control, some wood members, especially when subject to load, exhibit considerable creep and shrinkage, evidenced by partition and ceiling separation of disturbing magnitude and unsightly drywall cracking at locations such as lintels where varying load conditions are present. The result is expensive maintenance. Bearing of wood floor members on stud walls at one support and masonry at the other leads to floors that slope from the "rigid" masonry support to the shrinkage-prone stud support. These and numerous other serviceability problems could be minimized by using balloon framing in lieu of the standard stacking of stud on joist on stud, which results in cumulative shrinkage. Unfortunately the cost of balloon framing (first cost) is often prohibitive (probably because of a lack of the knowledge of carpentry in this method of construction). Another remedy is the use of a hybrid system that combines wood floor joists and steel columns and beams. Naturally the proper solution is engineering design even of the "simple" wood framing.

LATERAL LOADS AND RESISTING ELEMENTS

Requirements for lateral load resistance depend on two basic factors—the building plan and height. The shape of the building may inherently provide increased lateral load resistance. Long and narrow structures offer poor resistance to lateral loads on the broad face but are extremely stiff in the opposite direction.

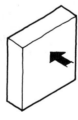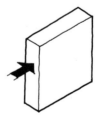

Combining rectangles to form more structurally efficient plans provides good but unequal resistance in both directions.

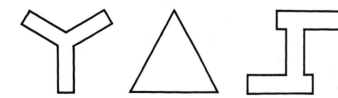

A square plan with equal resistance in both orthogonal directions is obviously the better solution. A circular plan has less applied wind load and is more economical in regard to wind resistance.

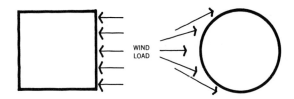

CONCRETE RIGID FRAME.   Building height dictates the means of the most economical resistance to lateral loads. From the point of view of lateral loading the concrete
frame (columns and slabs) is efficient to a height of about 10 stories, for within the
limitation of this height the addition of nominal reinforcing is sufficient to satisfy the
bending requirements caused by the lateral force.

To use only the frame to resist wind in higher structures requires increased
reinforcing and often increased slab thicknesses in the lower floors. This means of
resisting lateral loads (due to the flexible frame action) creates possible problems with
the interaction of structural and architectural elements. It necessitates special joinery
to prevent the partitions from crushing and cracking and special detailing for pipes and
ducts that may be in contact with the structure.

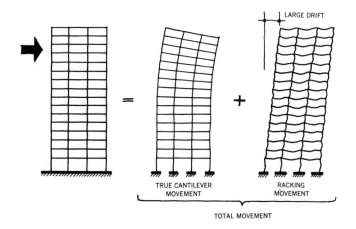

CONCRETE RIGID FRAME AND SHEAR WALLS.   Between 10 and about 40 stories
economy requires the addition of stiffer elements to supplement the frame resistance.
Shear walls generally satisfy this function. The lateral loads are distributed through the
slab, which behaves as a deep, thin beam in the horizontal plane (diaphragm) and

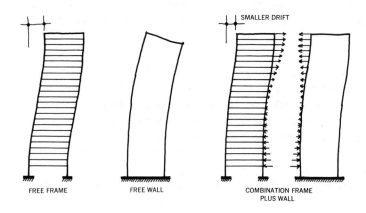

95

transfers the lateral loads to the shear walls and frame according to their relative stiffness. Vertically continuous shear walls are thought of as vertical cantilevered beams, restrained to the foundations, and resisting both axial (gravity) and lateral loads. The efficiency of the shear wall is dependent to a great extent on the amount of gravity load applied.

CONCRETE SHEAR PANELS.   The primary difference between the shear wall and shear panel is the purposeful vertical discontinuity of the shear wall, supported on columns, and placed strategically throughout the plan to mobilize the maximum amount of gravity load possible. In fact, the total horizontal force is distributed almost evenly among all the structural elements of the building. The increased gravity load counters the panel tension forces (uplift) created by lateral loads. Naturally the number of shear panels increases on the lower floors according to the increasing lateral load forces. Shear panels also minimize the diaphragm span.

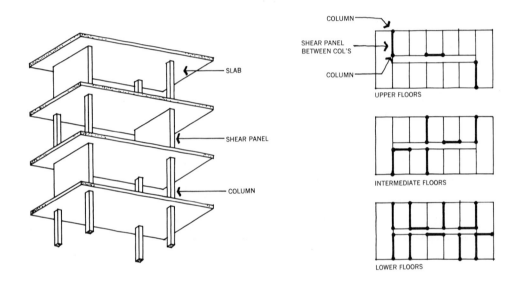

SHEAR ELEMENT LOCATIONS.   The location of shear walls or panels is dependent on the floor plan. Generally the more economical locations are corridor or apartment separation walls (due primarily to the relative ease of forming, when compared with exterior walls). Using shear elements as apartment separation offers an excellent barrier to sound transmission. When exterior (end walls) and core shear walls are used, cost should be seriously weighed. Increased forming considerations for this type of wall decreases its economic advantage. However, core walls with special forming systems (slip forms) have proved to be most efficient as shear-resisting elements with point-block type structures in the 60-story range.

CONCRETE TUBES.   Exterior concrete bearing walls which form a tube provide a uniquely efficient structural system. Variations in the tube have been used economically for apartment structures in the 40- to 60-story range. The extent of window openings dictates the structural behavior. Smaller openings allow a closer approximation to the pure tube behavior, with stiff columns and spandrels providing the tube effect. Increasing the size of openings diminishes the column and spandrel stiffness, and the structural response tends to approach frame action.

The tube effect becomes more efficient if a diagonal truss system is employed instead of vertical (column) and horizontal (beam) members. The diagonal members function

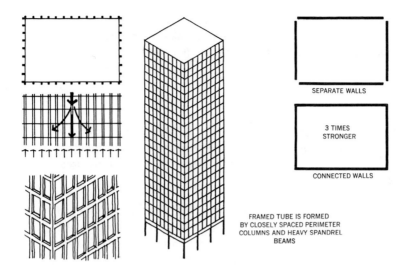

SEPARATE WALLS

3 TIMES
STRONGER

CONNECTED WALLS

FRAMED TUBE IS FORMED
BY CLOSELY SPACED PERIMETER
COLUMNS AND HEAVY SPANDREL
BEAMS

as columns to resist gravity loads and as a deep truss cantilevered from the foundations to resist lateral loads.

Economical lateral load resistance for apartment structures of more than 60 stories requires interaction of the exterior "bearing wall" and interior shear-resisting elements generally consisting of the core walls. To provide the necessary interaction stiff framing elements between the interior and exterior structure are required. These interconnecting elements need not occur at every floor but only as required to distribute the lateral forces.

The shear-resisting elements of a highrise can also be constructed of steel when the basic system is structural steel framing or a combination of concrete and structural steel. The rigid frame and tube structures are readily obtained in steel by providing moment connection between columns and girders. Equivalent shear walls or shear panels are provided by bracing between columns with angles, channels, wide flanges, plates, or pipes.

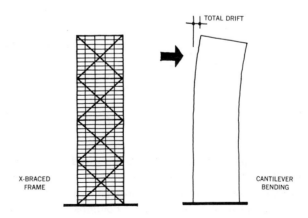

TOTAL DRIFT

X-BRACED
FRAME

CANTILEVER
BENDING

EARTHQUAKE CONSIDERATIONS.   The preceding discussion of schemes for lateral load resistance should be *generally* applicable to seismic conditions as well as wind loading. Code restrictions, however, on the use of a "box type" structure (shear walls or tubes) have limited their use in seismically active regions. However, recent proposed code limitations on building drift (to minimize architectural element distress during an earthquake) will require even stiffer structures. The existing code provisions, which demand a ductile moment-resisting space frame to resist 25% of the earthquake force (in addition to the shear walls resisting 100% of the earthquake force), necessitate thicker slabs, thereby negating the cost advantages of a thin flat plate.

FOUNDATIONS

Selection of the appropriate substructure for an apartment building depends on the available soil-bearing capacity and a multitude of other parameters including building height, column spacing, superstructure weight, water-table level, adjacent structures, and underground utilities.

SOIL REPORT.   A complete soil investigation should be made on any proposed building site. A report prepared by a soil engineer is required to determine the foundation type intelligently and economically. The architect and structural engineer generally prepare a project description for the soil engineer which includes information pertinent to conclusions such as building height, bay sizes, and column loads. The number and depth of borings should be left to the discretion of the soil engineers. The boring logs contain grade elevations, classification of each soil stratum, water-table elevations, blow count, unit weight, water content, and unconfined compressive strength of the various materials encountered. The soil report contains the logs and recommendations for foundation types, soil-bearing elevation, and anticipated settlements and construction abnormalities.

SPREAD FOOTINGS.   Spread footings are considered the most economical and have been used for structures of about 20 stories. They may be plain or reinforced concrete. Column loads from the superstructure are generally transferred by concrete piers extending to footings at an adequate bearing stratum. Continuous footings usually support the walls, whereas individual spread footings support isolated columns.

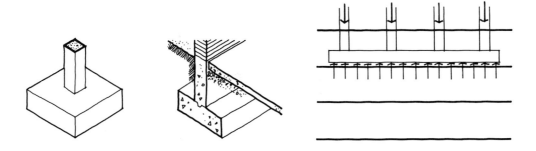

MATS.   Low bearing capacity and/or the possibility of differing settlement suggests the use of a mat foundation, which is simply a continuous slab of reinforced concrete that supports the columns as well as walls and is designed as an inverted flat plate, with the soil pressure loading the "flat plate" and the columns providing the reactions.

DEEP FOUNDATIONS.   When adequate bearing capacity is substantially below surface elevation, deep foundations are used. Drilled piers (sometimes called caissons) are employed when a bearing stratum of hardpan (stiff clays) or bedrock is available. The shaft is generally augured by mechanical means, and if it is bearing on hardpan, "bells" are formed at that level to increase the bearing area. Straight shafts are used when bedrock is reached for bearing strata. Temporary steel liners are used in the upper soft materials and anchored into stiffer clays to allow drilling without fear of cave-ins. The liner is generally withdrawn as concrete is cast. Permanent steel liners sometimes required by code or soil conditions prevent sloughing of the soil into the hole and may also be used as part of the load-carrying capacity of the caisson.

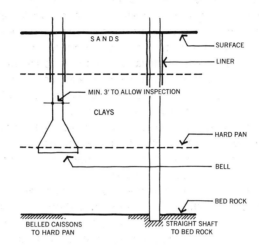

Piles are used when soil conditions and/or cost considerations do not warrant caissons. They develop their capacity to support the superstructure by skin friction and end bearing. The type of pile selected depends to a great degree on the soil being penetrated and the loads to be carried. Recommendations to this effect are given in the soil report. Depending on required capacities, piles may be used singly or in groups. Although column loads are directly applied to caissons, piles require a reinforced concrete cap, which greatly influences the economies of this type of foundation.

Piles may be driven, vibrated, or placed in prebored holes. Treated timber piles are used primarily for lightly loaded structures; their capacity is limited to about 25 tons. Precast prestressed concrete piles are manufactured in various shapes, with tapered or parallel sides. Capacities range up to 200 tons. Structural steel piles (H sections) can develop capacities equal to precast concrete. Composite piles are a combination of more than one material and often lead to economical solutions. Steel shell or pipe driven in and filled with concrete, precast concrete with steel sections embedded, timber with cast-in-place concrete, and various other combinations can be used.

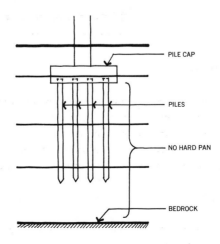

COMPONENTS OF DESIGN—STRUCTURAL

HYDROSTATIC PRESSURE.   Basements, parking garages, and pits to be constructed below the water table require special attention to counteract hydrostatis uplift. Construction procedures are complicated because of the need for pumps and well points to lower the water table temporarily to allow working "in the dry." Needless to say, this type of construction is costly and should be avoided if at all possible.

An accurate determination of the high water-table elevation is difficult because water fluctuates with the seasons and because means are lacking to separate the actual water-table measurement from trapped water (water trapped between earth seams). Therefore the high water table "design" elevation is usually conservative.

A highrise apartment structure with a mat foundation will readily resist a considerable uplift force due to its gravity load; for instance, a 30-story structure with 5-in. normal-weight concrete slabs developed a total dead load of about 1900 psf (pounds per square foot). To overcome this load would require about 30 ft of hydrostatic head; the weight of one 5-in. concrete slab is equal to 1 ft of hydrostatic water pressure. If the structure's column loads are supported by deep foundations, the lowest floor slab would be required to resist the uplift forces between columns. This may be accomplished by structurally designing the floor slab to resist the pressure, providing a massive concrete slab, or doing a combination of the two. A deep foundation adequately serves as a "hold-down" to prevent buoyancy. In parking garages and other lightly loaded structures deep foundations designed specifically to resist uplift forces are required.

Instead of using the structure to resist uplift, mechanical means of relieving hydrostatic pressures are sometimes used. Under-floor and perimeter drain tiles in conjunction with pumps to maintain a lower water level may prove to be more economical although not "fail safe."

Uplift is only a portion of the problem created by construction beneath the water table. Waterproofing is essential and costly to achieve. All walls and slabs below the water table must receive membrane waterproofing applications. All joints must have water stops. To protect the waterproof membrane "mud slabs" are often needed as a base for applying the waterproofing before casting the final structural elements.

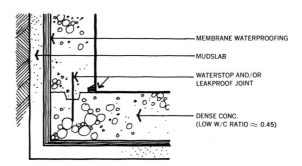

MEMBER SIZE SELECTION

The following simplified equations allow a rapid determination of *approximate* structural member sizes. The formulas are based on apartment loadings and are *not* to be used indiscriminately for all conditions. A slight variation in limiting parameters may substantially change the required value; therefore extrapolation should not be used. Span lengths are in feet, and resulting member depths are in inches.

CAST-IN-PLACE CONCRETE

1.   Solid slab supported on all sides by walls or stiff beams. Span range is 15 to 30 ft (recommended for heavier live loads):

$$\frac{L_1}{L_2} < 2 \quad (L_1 \text{ longer span})$$

Slab thickness:

$$h = \frac{L_1 + L_2}{7.5} \geqslant 4 \text{ in.}$$

Example

$$L_1 = 25 \text{ ft}, L_2 = 20 \text{ ft}$$

$$h = \frac{25 + 20}{7.5} = 6 \text{ in.}$$

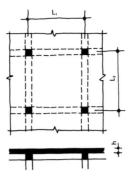

2. One-way solid slab supported by walls or stiff beams. Span range is 5 to 20 ft:

$$\frac{L_1}{L_2} \geqslant 2 \quad (L_1 \text{ longer span})$$

Slab thickness:

$$h = \frac{L_2}{2.8} \geqslant 4 \text{ in.} \quad \text{(continuous spans)}$$

$$h = \frac{L_2}{1.8} \geqslant 4 \text{ in.} \quad \text{(simple span)}$$

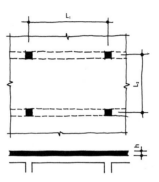

3. Pan joist supported by walls or stiff beams. Span range is 15 to 40 ft.

$$h = \frac{L}{2} \quad \text{(continuous spans)}$$

$$h = \frac{L}{1.5} \quad \text{(simple span)}$$

4. Flat plate supported only on columns. Span range is 14 to 22 ft:

$$\frac{L_1}{L_2} < 1.50 \quad (L_1 \text{ longer span})$$

Slab thickness:

$$h = \frac{L_1}{3} \geqslant 5 \text{ in.}$$

5. Flat slab supported only on columns. Span range is 18 to 30 ft; recommended for heavier live loads:

$$\frac{L_1}{L_2} < 1.50 \quad (L_1 \text{ longer span})$$

Slab thickness:

$$h = \frac{L_1}{3.3} \geqslant 5 \text{ in.}$$

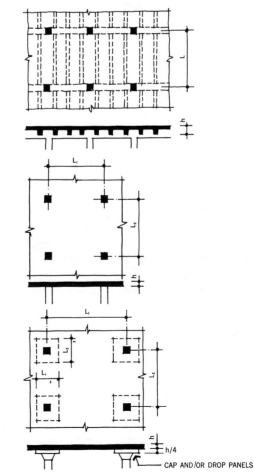

CAP AND/OR DROP PANELS

6. Beams.

   Beam thickness:

   $$h = \frac{L}{2} \quad \text{(continuous spans)}$$

   $$h = \frac{L}{1.5} \quad \text{(simple span)}$$

   $$h = \frac{L}{0.8} \quad \text{(cantilever span)}$$

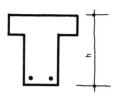

PRECAST PRESTRESSED CONCRETE

1. Beam.

   Beam thickness:

   $$h = \frac{L}{2.5} \quad \text{(continuous spans)}$$

   $$h = \frac{L}{2.0} \quad \text{(simple span)}$$

   $$h = \frac{L}{1.0} \quad \text{(cantilever span)}$$

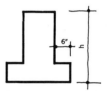

2. Secondary member (hollow-core slab and tee).

   Member thickness:

   $$h = \frac{L}{3} \quad \text{(floors)}$$

   $$h = \frac{L}{3.5} \quad \text{(roofs)}$$

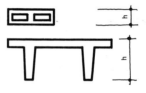

CONCRETE COLUMNS

Example

Assume an 18-story apartment building, completely braced. Normal-weight concrete: 24 by 24 ft bay size. Enter chart at 18 supported slabs, extend a line horizontally to intersect the solid (normal-weight concrete) diagonal line for 24 by 24 ft bay size. Drop a vertical line to intersect the "economical" and "uneconomical" lines. Move horizontally and read column area. The top value (870 sq in.) is an economical column size. The lower value (570 sq in.) is an uneconomical size. Both, however, satisfy structural conditions and either one or an area between the two may be used (see chart on p. 000).

STRUCTURAL STEEL

1. Girder.

   Girder depth:

   $$d = \frac{L}{1.5} \quad \text{(floors)}$$

   $$\frac{L}{2} \quad \text{(roofs with adequate slope for drainage)}$$

2. Beam.

   Beam depth:

   $$d = \frac{L}{2} \quad \text{(floors)}$$

   $$\frac{L}{2.5} \quad \text{(roofs with adequate slope for drainage)}$$

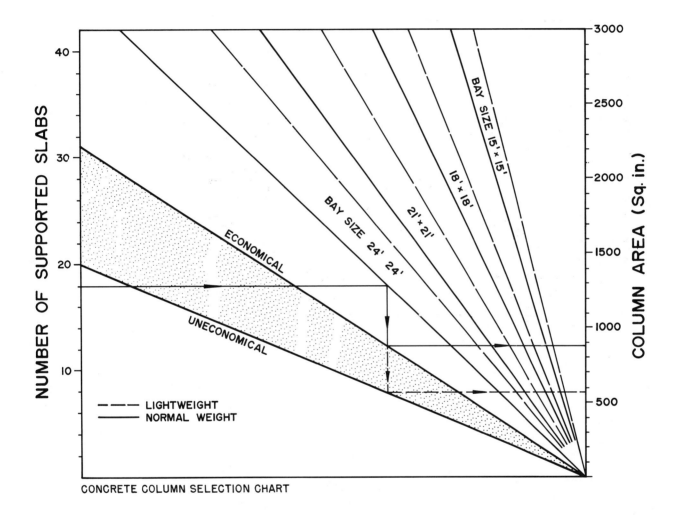

CONCRETE COLUMN SELECTION CHART

3. Bar joist (spacing—24- to 30-in. floors, 48- to 96-in. roofs).

   Joist depth:

   $$d = \frac{L}{1.4} \quad \text{(floors with no partitions, i.e., churches, offices)}$$

   $$\frac{L}{1.6} \quad \text{(floors with partitions, i.e., apartments)}$$

   $$\frac{L}{2.0} \quad \text{(roofs with adequate slope for drainage)}$$

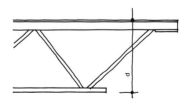

COMPONENTS OF DESIGN—STRUCTURAL

STEEL COLUMNS

Example

Assume a 24-story apartment building, complete braced. Floor dead load: 80 psf; tributary area to column, 500 sf; enter chart at 24 supported slabs, extend a line horizontally to intersect dead load = 80 diagonal line. Drop a vertical line to intersect tributary area = 500. Move horizontally and read column size required: W14 × 211.

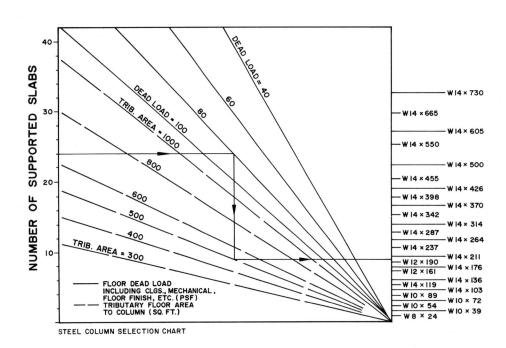

STEEL COLUMN SELECTION CHART

COMPONENTS OF DESIGN—HVAC   4

Harry S. Nachman

HEATING AND AIR CONDITIONING

The chapter heading, "Heating, Ventilating, and Air Conditioning," is really redundant. Air conditioning, correctly defined, is the science that deals with controlling temperature, humidity, cleanliness, and distribution of air in enclosed habitable spaces. Therefore the real name of our subject is "air conditioning." Somehow, however, this term has become equated with "cooling" in the public consciousness, and because of it we may as well employ the time-honored "HVAC" to avoid misunderstanding.

Stating the definition has not been an empty exercise in semantics. It reminds us that temperature is not the only factor of importance in our living environment. We may ignore humidity, cleanliness, and distribution for a number of perfectly acceptable reasons, but our selection of building air conditioning systems should be made only after considering all four factors. If we neglect one or more, that neglect should be deliberate, not inadvertent.

The necessity for *heating* in buildings is not universal. There are favored parts of the earth in which the temperature never falls below the comfort level and others in which outdoor temperatures under that level are so infrequent or so little below it, that no heating equipment is required. A critical need in all building plans is a history of climatic experience in the area. The important historical facts in regard to heating are those that set the lowest temperature likely to occur in any year. In most parts of the world records are kept over periods long enough for this minimum, called "design heating temperature," to be predicted. If that temperature is above 60° F, it is reasonably safe to say that no heating is necessary. If the design temperature is above 50° F, with the further proviso that this minimum occurs almost always at night, another factor which may be expressed as the expectations of the occupants or, more brutally, as "how much does it cost to live there," will influence the decision. Low-cost owners and low-rent tenants may be expected to put on sweaters against the evening chill. Their more affluent neighbors may demand heating to dispel the possibility of even mild discomfort. As a minimum in mild climates, fireplaces may heat the major rooms, if fuel is available.

In areas in which the heating design temperature is below 50° F, mechanical heating must be part of the building plan.

The temperature to which homes should be heated varies somewhat with custom, age, physical condition of the occupants, and personal preference. As world-wide diminution of fuel and energy supplies becomes more and more serious, pressure is being applied to reduce indoor design temperatures. In England many people have been accustomed to house temperatures of 65 to 68°F. In the United States accepted design has been 70–72°F, but it is no secret that thermostats are commonly set to 75°F and higher. Elderly persons usually demand temperatures some 5°F higher than "normal" design. Finally, air humidity, discussed later, has some effect on the comfort level.

When we turn to *cooling*, the emphasis is quite different. Although there are large parts of the earth in which heating is necessary for the survival of the human organism, there is almost no place on the globe in which temperatures are so high that people cannot live. Thus the "necessity" for cooling takes quite a different dimension, which is largely that of expectations and economics, discussed above. Even lacking accurate statistics, compare the number of residences cooled in an area of the United States with those in areas of similar size and climate in Africa or Asia.

Wherever cooling has become customary the same considerations of weather history and duration of hot spells apply. Cooling design temperatures are established by the records, which reflect the air temperature and the amount of moisture it carries. The latter factor is critically important to human comfort, as everyone knows. "It's not the heat, it's the humidity!" Consider what that cliche actually says. If the air is at 80°F and contains 2.2% water vapor (moisture), all of us will feel miserable, but if outside air at the same temperature contains only 1% moisture most of us will call it a pleasant summer day. Therefore our climate history must include a gauge of maximum atmospheric moisture to be anticipated as well as the highest temperature. Humidity is usually expressed as "relative" humidity, that is, the actual quantity of water vapor present compared with the maximum amount the air could carry. This proportion is conveniently measured and expressed as "wet bulb temperature." The regularly recorded air temperature is known as "dry bulb temperature."

If a family is building a new house, whether to cool is a matter of a few simple questions: How much will it cost to install cooling? How much to operate it? How often will we use it? In short, what is it worth to us? When a builder is planning multiple dwellings for sale or rent, the state of the market becomes crucial. Will the prospective tenants demand cooling? Will they pay the purchase or rental price made necessary by the installation cost? In rental housing who will pay the operating cost? If the owner is to shoulder this burden, will the rental market level cover his expense? If the tenants pay, will they accept this "hidden" rent, and will tenants in high exposure dwellings (such as the top floor of a multilevel building or an apartment with windows facing south and west) accept higher utility bills? The answers to some of these questions may be obvious, but they should still be checked off in the planning stage to make sure that the ground has been covered.

Ventilation is comparatively noncontroversial. Natural ventilation, in the form of windows or louvers, is mandated for residences by building codes and furthermore is an aesthetic consideration in the design of residential buildings. Mechanical ventilation is required for interior-occupied areas such as bathrooms and kitchens in which odors and quantities of water vapor may be generated. Interior spaces such as closets and dressing rooms usually do not require ventilation, but common sense consideration of special circumstances may sometimes dictate special treatment of these areas.

Mechanical ventilation of kitchens and bathrooms has long been understood to mean the removal of air from the subject space and expulsion of that air to the outdoors. A combination of building-code requirements and experience dictates that the removal rate should be such that a volume equal to the total cubic contents of the room be expelled at least every 5 minutes. For kitchens in high-cost or high-rental dwellings, in which occupant expectancies may correspond to the cost-rental level, the air change rate might be every 2 minutes.

It must be kept in mind that for every cubic foot of air exhausted from a building a cubic foot of air must enter. This replacement could be leakage around doors and windows, or it may be introduced in a controlled and purposeful way, but there is no escaping the necessity of having it come in. Of course, in winter that makeup air must be heated, and in summer, if the building is cooled, that air must be cooled.

Fuel and energy restrictions have lent and will continue to lend impetus to a means of reducing the expenditures for treating the replacement air. One dramatic method which removes odors from the exhausted air and then discharges the cleaned air back into the room instead of outdoors has been accepted by some building codes. Emphasis is laid on the word "remove." It has been found that chemically activated charcoal absorbs and stores particles in the air that cause odors; the exhausted air is then passed through activated charcoal before being returned to the room. After a period of time, usually three months to a year, the charcoal will have absorbed all it can store and must be replaced or regenerated. This process is in contrast to one that masks unpleasant odors by use of perfumes, small quantities of ozone, or the like, and which is unacceptable for residential ventilation purposes.

The use of odor control and recirculation of exhausted air, however, is not a complete solution for ventilating needs. Activated charcoal does nothing to remove accumulations of moisture due to cooking and bathing nor anything to replace the oxygen. Therefore ventilation of some kind is still needed either by leakage from the outdoors due to wind pressure or by mechanical means.

The subject of *humidity* has already been touched on. It is generally understood that air can hold more moisture at high temperatures than at low and that comfort is tied to *relative* humidity. Examine an illustration. Assume that outside air at 0°F and 100% relative humidity is holding as much moisture as it possibly can. As that air into is introduced into a building and heated to 70°F without the addition of any moisture, its relative humidity falls to approximately 7%!

One reaction to that revelation might be "So what? What is bad about very low or very high relative humidities?"

Extremely low humidities cause dryness of skin and other body surfaces such as the nasal passages. Many people, including many of those trained in medicine, believe that this nasal dryness adds to a person's susceptibility to respiratory disease. Skin dryness entails the rapid evaporation of body surface moisture, which has a cooling effect. This is not a critical effect, but it does mean that an individual in a room at 70°F and 7% relative humidity may be no more comfortable than at 67°F and 30% relative humidity. It is significant that by the judicious addition of moisture lower inside design temperatures may be tolerated and fuel saved.

Other objections to low humidities concern their effect on materials such as wood and fabric, which may become warped, embrittled, or damaged in similar ways.

Excessive humidities, on the other hand, can cause discomfort by inhibiting evaporation of moisture from the skin, leaving an oppressive or overwarm feeling. A familiar effect of high humidity is condensation on cold surfaces, particularly windows, although this occurs only in climates in which outside temperatures are low. In mild climates or in periods of prolonged high humidity anywhere wood and fabrics tend to rot.

In the design of residential air conditioning low humidity in winter is the primary concern. High humidities resulting from warm and moist outside conditions are reduced by the very fact of cooling the building. If there is no cooling, the occupants will have to live with the humidity as well as the temperature. Low winter humidities can often be improved at low cost in equipment and operation. Here, again, the factors of occupant expectations and return on investment should be weighed and should be decisive.

A note of caution is in order regarding winter humidification. Optimum relative humidity for comfort in the home is about 40% for most people. That level, however, will cause severe condensation on cold surfaces. In regions that have low outside temperatures double-pane glass, wood or tubular metal window frames, and well-insulated walls and roof will prevent this condition. If it is impractical to avoid some cold interior surfaces because of construction costs or other factors, a compromise can be reached by maintaining lower than optimum relative humidities, in the 20 to 30% range.

USE OF FUEL AND ENERGY

When western societies entered into the nineteenth century's industrial era, the passage was made possible by the exploitation of seemingly unlimited supplies of natural fuels. Burgeoning industrial development called for, and produced, new discoveries in fuel and energy sources. Despite a few voices citing obvious arithmetic facts, the earth's stores of fuel were gobbled up with little thought of the future. "They" would find a way when new energy sources were needed. "They" still may do so, but the present generation has suddenly confronted the unthinkable. Some day the well has to run dry.

That day is probably still quite distant, but the realization of it has added a new dimension to the selection of fuel and other energy sources for building heating, cooling, and other power needs. Best obtainable estimates of availability and cost trends during the expected life of the residential project must be weighed against immediate supplies and prices, and it is to be hoped the final decision will be made with some deference to the common good as well as to the advantage of the individual owner.

Let us list the sources of energy available to us, both practically and theoretically; they are placed in alphabetical order to avoid any hint of bias.

	Strengths	Drawbacks
1. COAL	Large reserves still exist Safe to use; nonexplosive Moderate cost at this writing Simple machinery needed to burn	Bulky; large storage requirements Dirty in handling and burning Difficult to ignite and extinguish Abrasive; short life of handling equipment Large equipment space needs, in addition to storage space
2. ELECTRICITY	No storage facilities required Easy to control Safe to use; nonexplosive Silent Clean Simple equipment; generally lowest capital investment; minimal space requirements	High cost per energy unit Lowest efficiency in use of natural fuels for generation of electricity, *except* if the natural flow of water can be used
3. GAS	Low cost at the time of this writing Simple equipment; generally modest capital investment Clean No storage facilities usually required	Potentially explosive Potentially toxic Reserves will probably be depleted before coal reserves

	Strengths	Drawbacks

4. NUCLEAR FISSION AND FUSION. At this time we cannot simply list the advantages and disadvantages of nuclear power. It is illegal for operators of residential building projects to own or use nuclear energy plants. Atomic fusion is not yet developed to the point at which its energy can be converted into useful heat or generation of electricity, although there are hopeful prospects. Atomic fission is being used for these purposes but only in large plants operated by major producers of energy federally licensed in the United States. The disposal of radioactive by-products has not been solved on a permanent basis and future pollution problems exist. The danger of explosion and other failure is small, but the results could be catastrophic. Fissionable material is limited. Equipment costs are enormous.

	Strengths	Drawbacks
5. OIL	High calorific value per unit weight Can be stored underground Low explosion potential	Uncertain reserves Pollution possibilities in handling High cost at this writing, due to monopolistic control Large storage requirements Not notably clean-burning Complex burners compared to coal and gas
6. SOLAR ENERGY	Supply inexhaustible Clean Quiet No cost at present	Dependent on weather conditions Conversion equipment very bulky and space consuming at this time Available supply is minimum at time of maximum need

EQUIPMENT LOCATION

From the designer's standpoint the space to be allocated for fuel storage and fuel utilization equipment is very important. It is particularly important that the selection of the source of energy be made early in the design process so that carefully drawn plans will not have to be scrapped or radically altered to accommodate unforeseen hundreds of square feet of mechanical equipment area. At the same time that the area is allotted, its location in the building should be fixed.

Heating, ventilating, and cooling equipment may be at the bottom, the top, or at some intermediate location in a building, preferably near the center. This revelation, though fundamental, may not be startling, but the fact of flexibility should always be borne in mind, whether the building is a lofty skyscraper or a three-story walk-up. A second fundamental is that, regardless of the location of the HVAC machinery, there must be space for mechanical and electrical equipment in the lowest level of the structure. Specifically, water service entrance and pumping equipment, electrical service entrance equipment, fuel storage if needed, gas service entrance piping and meter if gas is used in the project, and a means of garbage and rubbish disposal all require space "downstairs." It is sometimes sensible to combine these area allocations for mechanical and electrical equipment in one block, which must then be in the lowest level. An exception to "lowest level" can be the refuse collection room, which may be at ground level for ease of transportation, even in buildings with basements. Let us consider some of the pluses and minuses in the different locations.

1. *Lowest Level*

   ADVANTAGES: Weight of equipment can be carried directly on the earth.
   All equipment can be located in one area.

Equipment can be installed and placed in operation at earliest possible time.

Electrical feeders are usually short because the major equipment is close to the electrical service.

Depending on building design, there may be intervening floors between equipment rooms and the nearest living space, thus requiring less sound isolation of the equipment and consequently lower expense.

Major equipment can be installed early, checked out in operation, used for such purposes as temporary heat during construction, and even for heating and cooling to allow partial building occupancy.

Inflow of rental or sales cash may begin months before the building is finished.

DISADVANTAGES: If there is no basement, a potentially valuable first-floor area is surrendered to non-rent-paying equipment.

If there is a basement, substantial cost may be added to the building, particularly if soil and/or ground water conditions are unfavorable.

If natural fuel is burned, provision must be made through the entire height of the building for a chimney.

If there is a cooling tower which must be on the roof, long condensing water lines are needed at considerable cost. See the later discussion on cooling towers.

2. *Intermediate Level*

ADVANTAGES: In highrise buildings this location can sometimes serve as the logical level at which to change the typical floor plan (e.g., the upper floors may command higher rentals or prices and may consequently call for larger or more luxurious units). This change may also be used to create a visual break on building elevations.

Pipe sizes for HVAC systems may be reduced, with the result that pipe riser spaces may also be reduced. This may be a trifling gain, but, on the other hand, it may permit a pipe riser space width, for example, to fall in line with a column depth or partition thickness, thus saving useful space in the entire plan.

DISADVANTAGES: Rentable space is being lost at a usually desirable level in the building.

Special precautions must be made to avoid the transmission of sound, heat, or vibration both above and below.

Space must be allowed for a chimney, although only in that part of the building above the equipment room.

If natural fuel is used, it must be transported up to the level. For gas this becomes a minor factor, for oil a major nuisance, and for coal a negating fact. In other words, coal-burning equipment must be at the bottom of the building.

Although it need not be the case in a well-managed building, an "out of sight, out of mind" maintenance philosophy can creep in. The more remote the essential equipment, the more easily neglected.

Distress due to vibration and sound of moving machinery must be guarded against with special care, often at substantial expense.

3. *Roof Level*

ADVANTAGES: No boiler chimney is required, thus reducing construction cost and freeing space on each living floor.

Often a basement is not necessary, and, if no basement has been included in the plans, valuable ground floor space is released.

If the building has a central cooling plant, the water-saving device (cooling tower or air-cooled condenser, discussed later in this chapter) is usually best located on the roof. Thus, if the major HVAC equipment is also at the top of the building, the refrigeration machinery will be close to the water-saving equipment, shortening piping and electrical connections.

If the building is a highrise, an elevator machinery penthouse structure is required. Increasing this space to accommodate an equipment room is comparatively low in cost and can be an aesthetic improvement to the building.

DISADVANTAGES: Weight of heavy major equipment must be carried down through the building's structural system, partly offsetting the cost saving realized by elimination of the chimney.

Systems cannot be completed for operation until the building is structurally complete. This usually militates against early occupancy of lower floors and makes it impossible to use the permanent facilities for temporary heat (or cooling) during construction.

The cost of piping the major part of the fuel supply to the top of the building also cuts into the chimney saving. If the fuel is oil or gas, there is still the additional cost of electrical energy to lift it.

The same "out of sight, out of mind" maintenance danger cited above may exist.

Electrical supply and makeup water, both of which services enter at the bottom of the building, must be run all the way to the top.

Distress due to vibration and sound of moving machinery must be guarded against with special care, often at substantial expense.

FUEL-CONVERTING EQUIPMENT

Fuel, natural or electrical, is converted into heat in furnaces or boilers in most residential applications. The exceptions are those that use electric heat directly in the areas to be heated. The preponderance of installations are those that burn what we have called "natural" fuels (also frequently characterized as "fossil" fuels). These fuels require oxygen to support the combustion and a means of removing the waste gases, which are the products of that combustion, after they have yielded as much as possible of the heat they gained in the burning process. Electric central furnaces and boilers differ only in that they need no oxygen and produce no waste gases.

A furnace, in the nomenclature of residential heating, is a device in which air to be heated passes directly over a chamber in which the fuel is burned or the heat of electricity is released. The air is warmed by contact with the chamber walls and is then distributed to the spaces requiring warmth. The furnace is usually an assembly that includes air filters, a blower and a motor to move the desired quantity of air, a burner to mix air (containing the requisite oxygen) with the fuel if natural fuel is being burned, a smoke outlet to release the products, and a fireproof steel housing to contain all of it, including the combustion chamber itself. Depending on optimum convenience in the residence being heated, the furnace may be built with its greatest dimension vertical, the heated air discharging through the bottom or top, or with its longest dimension horizontal, with the heated air discharging through one end. Vertical furnaces are usually selected for installation in closets or basements, where a minimum of floor space is to be surrendered. Horizontal furnaces find application in attics or wherever headroom is sufficient to permit suspension of the furnace and leave occupiable space beneath it.

In any application that burns fuel it cannot be stressed too vehemently that there must *always* be an unobstructed supply of air, continually replaced, to support combustion, as well as a flue to carry the combustion products safely outdoors. Failure to allow combustion air to reach a furnace or boiler is literally a life-and-death matter.

"Boiler" is more often than not a misnomer. The name came from the boiling of water into steam, but in residential work in particular there are far more devices that just heat water for circulation than there are those that boil it. Nevertheless, all are called "boilers." They include a burner to mix fuel and air, if natural fuel is used, a combustion chamber, a container in which the water to be heated is held (and in the upper part of which steam collects, if it is a steam boiler), passages and an outlet for the gaseous products of combustion in fuel-burning boilers, and, again, a steel or cast-iron housing for the entire assembly. Depending on the space available, there is some latitude of selection in the type of boiler used. Some are long but relatively low. Others, when the floor area may be at a premium but there is plenty of height, are short and high. They may be long and narrow or nearly square. Some are built in sections and assembled on location, which is particularly convenient when a structure has been completed and no special doors have been provided for the movement of equipment.

In general, boilers not only contain the weight of the water but also must be strong enough to withstand some water pressure. Therefore they are much heavier than furnaces of like capacity and cannot be suspended. Their weight usually means that a location at any other than the lowest level of the building calls for structural strengthening beyond that required for normal loads.

Again, as in fuel-burning furnaces, there is an urgent reminder that fuel-burning boilers *must* have an adequate and unobstructed flow of air for combustion.

How many boilers or furnaces does a residential project require? Most often, a single residence heated by air will have one furnace, although larger houses not infrequently will boast of two, one for the general living quarters and one, perhaps, for the "bedroom wing," or one for the northern exposure and one for the southern. Almost invariably, if heating is by steam or water, a house will have only one boiler.

The question of the number of heating machines in multiple-residence-buildings is usually concerned with boilers only. An air-heating system, with a furnace, almost never serves more than one residence. In some localities it would be illegal and in all cases inadvisable to risk transmission of disease, cooking odors, or other perils and nuisances that could come from sharing an air distribution system.

With occasional exceptions the relation of the fewer boilers installed the lower the construction cost of a project, is somewhat balanced by a generally higher operating efficiency realized by more and smaller boilers. If cost alone is to be the criterion, the first advantage would usually dictate the selection of one boiler in the largest size commercially available for the project to be served. Obviously there is a major danger in using one boiler, for in the case of any malfunction, failure, or accident which would incapacitate the single machine the project would be without heat. Of course, a similar failure in a single small boiler serving one residence would leave its occupants just as cold and vulnerable as any of the tenants in a thousand-unit project. So it seems that the question is not whose ox is gored but how many.

The decision when to use multiple boilers may depend on many factors: climate, rental or sales value of the residences, type of occupancy expected, and legal requirements. Clearly, a cold climate, high cost of housing, and a large proportion of elderly residents, would support the use of multiple boilers. In regard to official requirements, some guidance may be found in the rules of the Federal Housing Administration of the United States, which has decreed that any project of 60 or more dwelling units must have more than one boiler, and that if two are used, the capacity of each must be at least two-thirds of the calculated heating load of all spaces served.

This appears to be a minimal requirement for multiple boilers. A project with 59 residences seems rather large to be served by only one boiler. Project planners here must use their best judgment in assaying the other factors involved, some of which are mentioned above.

In the following tables some rough rules of thumb are listed for sizes and space requirements for heating plants. There are, of course, too many variants to permit a complete tabulation. One of them is the use in large plants of many boilers of quite small size, which permits close regulation of the fuel burned to the actual heating load at any time. This kind of installation requires substantially more space than the conventional arrangement of a few large boilers, and its installation cost is usually not lower and frequently higher. It is not included in the space tabulation but often warrants serious special consideration in buildings in which there may be plenty of floor space allocable to a boiler room, often at the top of the building.

In the table a single boiler is designed to have a capacity equal to 100% of the actual heating load, two boilers are at 67% each, and three boilers at 33-1/3% each.

APPROXIMATE HEATING LOADS, BTU PER HOUR PER SQUARE FOOT OF FLOOR AREA FOR RESIDENTIAL OCCUPANCY (AVERAGE WINDOW AREAS ASSUMED)

Winter design temperature	30°F	20°F	10°F	0°F	−10°F	−20°F
Heating load, Btu/sf[a]	21	26	31	36	42	47

APPROXIMATE SPACE REQUIREMENTS FOR HEATING EQUIPMENT, INCLUDING ACCESS FOR SERVICING

Heating Load (Btu/hr)	Vertical Furnace			Horizontal Furnace		
	Length[b] (ft)	Width (ft)	Height (ft)	Length (ft)	Width (ft)	Height (ft)
FURNACES						
50,000	4.5	3	6.5	7.5	4.5	4
150,000	4.5	5	6.5	9	5	4

APPROXIMATE SPACE REQUIREMENTS FOR HEATING EQUIPMENT, INCLUDING ACCESS FOR SERVICING

		Minimum Boiler Room Dimensions								
		One Boiler			Two Boilers			Three Boilers		
Heating Load (Btu/hr)	Head-room Avail-able	Length (ft)	Width (ft)	Height (ft)	Length (ft)	Width (ft)	Height (ft)	Length (ft)	Width (ft)	Height (ft)
BOILERS										
1,000,000	Low	20	11	8.5	12	14	8.5	Not		
1,000,000	High	16.5	10	10.5	12	14	8.5	recommended		
5,000,000	Low	31	15	12	27	25	11	24	28	10
5,000,000	High	25	13	15	22	21	13	21	23	11
10,000,000	Low	42	17	14	31	28	12	30	31	11
10,000,000	High	30	15	19	25	24	15	25	26	13
20,000,000	Low	Not recommended			42	30	14.5	34	35	13
20,000,000	High	Not recommended			30	26	20	31	34	16

Note. For electrical heating 1 electric watt provides 3.41 Btu of heat, or, looking at it from another point of view, 1 kilowatt-hour on your electric bill has given you 3410 Btu of heat for 1 hour, whether you used it for heating or for light, television, or an electric toaster or blender.

[a] Gross area of residence itself, not including public spaces.

[b] Reduce length by 2 ft if furnace can be serviced through the door to the furnace closet.

The following illustration shows typical equipment-room layouts for a moderate-sized project and gives two of many possible arrangements, depending on space available. Note that tube servicing areas can be combined or "tranferred" by use of doors or removable panels. The illustration implies that the equipment is not at the top of the building. If it were, the boiler flues would probably go directly through the roof.

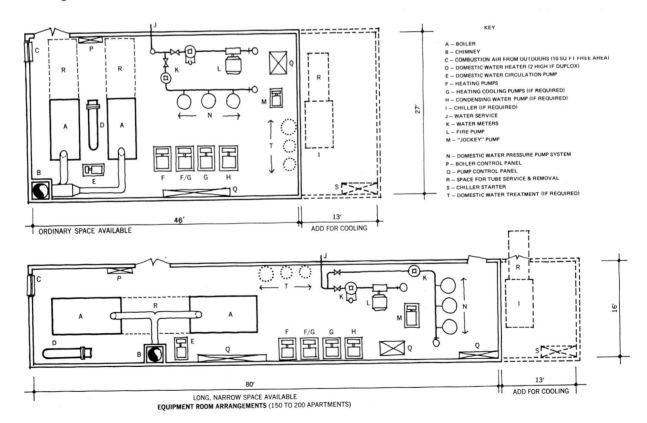

KEY
A – BOILER
B – CHIMNEY
C – COMBUSTION AIR FROM OUTDOORS (10 SQ FT FREE AREA)
D – DOMESTIC WATER HEATER (2 HIGH IF DUPLOX)
E – DOMESTIC WATER CIRCULATION PUMP
F – HEATING PUMPS
G – HEATING COOLING PUMPS (IF REQUIRED)
H – CONDENSING WATER PUMP (IF REQUIRED)
I – CHILLER (IF REQUIRED)
J – WATER SERVICE
K – WATER METERS
L – FIRE PUMP
M – "JOCKEY" PUMP

N – DOMESTIC WATER PRESSURE PUMP SYSTEM
P – BOILER CONTROL PANEL
Q – PUMP CONTROL PANEL
R – SPACE FOR TUBE SERVICE & REMOVAL
S – CHILLER STARTER
T – DOMESTIC WATER TREATMENT (IF REQUIRED)

ORDINARY SPACE AVAILABLE

ADD FOR COOLING

LONG, NARROW SPACE AVAILABLE
EQUIPMENT ROOM ARRANGEMENTS (150 TO 200 APARTMENTS)

BUILT-IN CONSERVATION

Building owners, architects, and designing engineers who have not yet expressed concern for the depletion of this planet's supply of energy will have to face reality, and soon. A few common-sense rules, observed wholly or even in part, can materially reduce the energy consumed for heating and cooling in the life of a building.

1. FENESTRATION. The glass worship characteristic of mid-twentieth-century architecture, whether for genuine design reasons or, covertly, for cheaper construction cost, has been an insatiable energy gobbler. The use of double- or triple-pane "insulating" glass is only a palliative, not a solution. Triple glazing will still conduct three to four times as much heat as a reasonably well-insulated wall.

2. ORIENTATION. If a choice is at all possible, face each building so that its major glass exposure is least exposed to sun and prevailing winds when cooling is involved. If, on the other hand, a building must be heated, judicious solar exposure is obviously a benefit in energy consumption. The compass direction of exposures is not the only way to employ orientation. The presence or absence of hills, trees, and other buildings are also factors to be considered.

3. SOLAR COMPENSATION. In cold and temperate latitudes, use of eaves, balconies, or similar overhangs is an ancient and effective device, if coupled with judicious orientation. For example, in the northern hemisphere south-facing glass with shading from an overhead will permit restricted solar radiation entrance in the summer when the sun is high, and much more desirable heat from the sun in winter, when the solar angle is low.

Other techniques are being explored. For example, reflective glass is an extremely effective agent to reduce the heat of solar radiation in the summer, but is counterproductive in the winter when that heat will be an economic bonanza. Pivoted sash is now being made, so the reflective surface will face out in summer, inside in winter, thus gaining the best of both worlds.

4. INSULATION. Insulation should be used both as an adjunct to the building's exposed surfaces and in consideration of the material of which those surfaces are made. Lightweight concretes and special mixes, including insulating substances, air spaces, insulating glass of the double-pane type, tinted glass that blocks out part of the solar input, prefabricated panels which include factory-installed insulation, and the use of wood in lowrise buildings are some of the design and construction decisions that will pay their way in fuel savings and, even more important, help to conserve a dwindling global supply.

5. REFLECTIVE SURFACES. Color and finish of surfaces, especially those directly exposed to the sun, are important. When cooling is the prime consideration, the roof and walls should be as light as possible to reflect solar radiation, and windows, too, should be tinted or coated for the same purpose, whenever feasible, as discussed above. Conversely, dark surfaces and clear glass are helpful when heating is the greater concern.

6. OVERHANGS. The perimeter wall of a ground floor is often set in for architectural reasons from the wall line of the building above. This creates an overhang at the second-floor level. If the overhung floor is occupied, that is, if it is not storage space, it can pose a critically important problem in a climate in which heating is required. A cold floor contributes to miserable living. Therefore a ceiling should be dropped over the

open area below the second floor to create a dead space which must be well insulated. In addition, the dead space should be warmed by the general heating system so that the second floor will benefit from the same temperature as every higher floor in the building. This policy applies, of course, wherever there are overhangs.

HEATING MEDIA

Fireplaces or stoves, which were fueled by wood, coal, oil, or gas, heated rooms in former days. Many up-to-the-minute electrical heating devices and methods have returned to this old principle of direct exposure. Otherwise, a medium must be provided through which heat will travel from the fuel source to the location of need. Our common media in buildings are steam, water, and air. Their various attributes and drawbacks should be compared for the project being served so a suitable selection can be made. A designer should not be typed as always choosing any one of them. Different problems do not necessarily call for different solutions but careful study will at least promote a logical solution.

In our consideration of steam, water, and air, noise is not discussed as a factor. A properly designed and constructed distribution system for any one of the three will be quiet. A badly conceived or built piping system can be noisy, whatever the medium. Furthermore, fuel efficiency should be comparable with any of them. Installation cost, oftener than not, will favor air; steam is more expensive and water frequently the highest in cost. Varying circumstances, however, may upset this order, and it behooves us to continue our examination of the merits of all three.

Steam releases approximately 960 Btu/lb of the medium, which compares with 10 to 50 Btu/lb of water and 5 to 15 Btu/lb of air. These figures also illustrate one of the two strong points of steam as a heat-conveying medium: its ability to heat quickly and raise a cold room to the comfort level in a hurry. This advantage is not so dramatic as the above numbers would seem to show, however, because there is a limiting factor in the ability of the heating device to transmit all of this sudden warmth.

The second attribute of steam is its rapid distribution without expenditure of mechanical energy. Little more fuel than that required to make steam in a boiler will raise its pressure to a level that will cause it to travel to the far reaches of a piping system in short order and with reasonably even distribution, so that all parts of the building will receive their share. The condensed steam may have to be pumped to force it back into the boiler or to expedite total circulation in a very large building, but the steam itself moves under the impetus of its own pressure.

Against these two advantages of steam are two drawbacks. The first, and most serious, has to do with its narrow temperature range. In small simple steam-heating systems the temperature of the medium is always within a degree or two of 215° F. Whether the temperature outside is 50° F and requires just a touch of heat, or −15° F and demands full throttle, the heating medium is the same—not a very satisfactory performance factor. In the most sophisticated systems there may be a range from 190 to 215° F, but it, too, does not begin to reflect the variation in requirements.

The second consideration against the use of steam is its somewhat corrosive effect on pipes and other vessels containing it and the comparative complexity of adjuncts to the system, such as traps and thermostatic vents, whose exact functions need not be discussed here.

Water has the great advantage of wide temperature variability. In 50° F weather the water temperature may be as low as 80° F, just enough to send up a little warmth. That temperature can readily be raised to 220° F, when it drops below zero outdoors, making water really responsive to load demands. The principal weakness in the use of water as a heating medium is its temperamental behavior in a pumped piping system. Most water systems are pumped, or "forced" in the trade expression, despite the fact that there are many highly successful gravity flow installations in single and duplex residences which balance themselves out quite well. Installations of any considerable size require pumped systems, and for many years the large pipe sizes required for good gravity flow have militated against gravity systems even in small buildings.

Forced water systems, no matter how carefully designed, can be difficult to balance correctly to give every space its intended share. Parallel to this problem in distribution is the surpassing importance of keeping water pipes free of air. Comparatively small air accumulations can impede or stop circulation in small or major parts of a building, with resultant failure to heat.

Unlike steam and air, water is virtually incompressible. When it is expanded by rising temperatures, as most substances are, a chamber called a compression tank, which allows the expanding water to compress a volume of entrapped air, is introduced into the system. Compression tanks are usually mounted on the ceiling or in an otherwise noncritical space. For small buildings and systems this tank will often be found on the boiler room ceiling. In tall buildings there is an advantage in locating the compression tank at or near the top of the system because a much smaller tank up high will do the work of a large tank located down below. Therefore, in highrise buildings the compression tank will often be found tucked away in the elevator machine penthouse or some other inconspicuous space in that area of the building.

Air offers the advantage of great flexibility of temperature, ranging from 75 to 130°F in forced systems and as high as 175°F in gravity systems. It has, by definition, a ventilating effect that changes the ambience and helps to create an atmosphere of comparative freshness, although it must be conceded that an air system can also spread unpleasant cooking odors to rooms remote from the kitchen. Another point for this medium is the ease with which it may be used to humidify by picking up moisture from the heating equipment and conveying it directly where it is needed. In addition, system leaks cause no damage, an advantage not enjoyed by steam or water.

Finally, a strong advantage is the ease with which cooling and summer dehumidification can be added to an air-heating system, whereas steam or water heating may require an entirely independent cooling system. We shall see that large building installations which combine central water distribution and local air supply can also offer heating and cooling in a single system, frequently without need for any distributing ductwork.

Mention has been made of gravity air systems, which are in the same category as gravity water systems, confined to small installations, and used decreasingly even there.

The disadvantage in the use of air is the space it requires. The ducts for air distribution are substantially larger than water or steam piping, and space must be arranged for them in the construction. To a somewhat lesser extent air heating equipment also requires more space than water or steam boilers of comparable capacity. In general, heating or heating-cooling air systems are practical only for single residences. Multiple dwellings can be served by multiple systems, but when the number of homes in one building exceeds six, air systems require too much space when centrally located outside the living areas. If, on the other hand, each system is installed in the residence it is to serve, there is no limit to the number per building. There are other considerations, however. If fuel is used for heating, flues become a difficult problem, and the space required for each piece of equipment subtracts from the rental or salable area.

Electricity is not really a medium for the transmission of heat; it is a fuellike source. Its direct use, however, makes any other medium unnecessary, and at this point it may logically be compared with steam, water, and air. On the favorable side its transmission requires the least space in the way of piping and may often be combined with electrical energy for other uses. It is easy to control and lends itself readily to room-by room thermostatic guidance. Often there are "no moving parts," a simplicity that results in minimal maintenance costs.

Disadvantages in electrical heat, in addition to the cost factor already cited, are found principally in temperature inflexibility; there is no way to get reduced electrical heat in mild weather. This is somewhat overcome by dividing the heating elements, particularly the large ones, into several separately controlled stages. The high temperature of electric heating elements, far above that associated with steam, water, or air, poses some hazard of fire or personal injury but safeguards built into equipment, and intelligent control of materials in environs of electric heaters make dangerous incidents quite infrequent.

COOLING EQUIPMENT

The temperature of Lake Superior, largest of the Great Lakes of the United States and Canada, is said never to rise above 52°F, even at the height of summer. A home or a residential complex built on the shore of that lake could be comfortably cooled by use of water drawn from the nearly inexhaustible source, passed through air cooling equipment, and returned to the lake slightly warmed by the experience. Some sort of societal control would have to be exercised so that this source of virtually free cooling could not be overexploited, thus raising the lake temperature and spoiling it for everyone. Because the water temperature is just as important as the quantity, a level is quickly reached at which the temperature is all-important. For comfort cooling in most of the world it is necessary to squeeze some moisture out of the air. Water temperature above 55°F is useless for dehumidifying air for almost all cases.

It follows, therefore, that, for any favored site that can boast an adequate supply of water from well, river, lake, or rain cistern colder than 55°F and whose availability can be predicted to last into the indefinite future, *natural water* is Nature's gift for cooling, and should be seized eagerly. Unfortunately there are not many areas in the planet whose air temperatures require cooling and which can boast of a supply of such cold water.

There is one other natural recourse for cooling, also applicable in limited areas only. It is called *evaporative cooling*, which can be successful in deserts or desert-like regions, whose outdoor relative humidities are extremely low, below 10%, specifically, even when the temperature is above 100°F. In these rare cases water at any ordinary temperature for domestic supply can be sprayed into this hungrily dry air. Some of the water will evaporate, thus raising the humidity but reducing the temperature. If the rate of evaporation is controlled, the result will be air cool enough and not too moist for a comfortable environment.

Mechanical refrigeration must be resorted to for cooling in the overwhelming majority of cases, when conditions for natural water cooling or evaporative cooling do not exist. The first half-century of air conditioning has produced three basic types of refrigerating machine, used in various situations according to their suitability. Before considering the comparative strengths and shortcomings of these machines, let us examine the mechanics of the refrigeration process as it applies to air cooling.

The purpose of refrigeration is to remove heat where it is not wanted. Heat is a form of energy that cannot be destroyed and, at the level at which it is extracted from the air, cannot be put to useful work. Consequently, the second function of the refrigeration plant is to dispose of this heat in a way that will not create a nuisance. If these two basic functions are kept in mind by nontechnical people, they will find much of the mystery of refrigeration cleared away. Now to translate the principles into machinery.

The medium that removes the unwanted heat is called a refrigerant, a substance chosen because it has the property of absorbing heat. Refrigerants are expensive, too expensive to discard when they have picked up their quota of heat. Thus the process is a continuous cycle, designed to use the same refrigerant over and over again. The following is the basic cycle and the refrigeration equipment that implements it:

1.   The refrigerant absorbs the unwanted heat from the space to be cooled.

2.   The refrigerant is placed into a state in which it can easily dispose of the heat it has absorbed. Changing its state requires mechanical work or more heat in a compressor or concentrator.

3.   The unwanted heat (plus heat added to the refrigerant in Step 2) is separated out of the system in a condenser.

4.   The condensed refrigerant is restored to a condition in which it can best absorb heat, through an expansion valve, orifice, or metering device. The cycle then goes back to Step 1 and repeats itself.

Basically, this is equipment for convenience, not efficiency. Work is expended just to move heat from one place to another.

Refrigeration systems are classified as direct or indirect. In direct systems, often called "direct expansion," air blows over finned tubes in which the ready-to-absorb-heat refrigerant is circulated. Indirect systems are those in which the refrigerant chills water; the water, in turn, circulates through finned tubes over which the air to be cooled is blown. Direct systems are confined to small-capacity installations such as room coolers and air conditioning systems for stores and offices of modest size and to larger installations in which the refrigeration plant is located close to the air processing unit (at most the plant may serve two units).

At this point let us insert a word about refrigeration capacity. The American industry is married to a term that goes back to the original mechanical cooling plants whose sole purpose was to make ice. The measure of capacity is the rate of cooling required to produce 1 ton of ice in 24 hours. It is called a "ton" of refrigeration and can be remembered as 12,000 Btu/hr. To be more specific, direct refrigeration systems range from ½ ton (6000 Btu/hr) room coolers to about 75 ton (900,000 Btu/hr) "packaged" rooftop units. Indirect systems may overlap at the lower end of their range, from 25 tons for a small office complex up to thousands of tons for a huge residential or office building or convention hall. Building codes often fix the size of direct refrigeration systems, particularly for residential use, far below the upper limit we have cited and should always be consulted on this point if direct systems are being contemplated. Most systems for multiple residential use are indirect, and those for single rooms or single residences may be one or the other.

Step 3 in the refrigeration cycle, as described a little way back, refers to the condenser. This does exactly what its name implies; it condenses the refrigerant from gaseous to liquid form, in which process the refrigerant releases all the heat. To do this the condenser uses a large quantity of coolant, of which the most readily available and least expensive is air. Next in line is water. These are the two condensing substances generally used. The reason for Step 2 can now be revealed. The refrigerant was put into its new state at that time in order that air or water at the actual available temperatures could condense it.

Air is free for the purpose, but it is a poor conductor of heat, and therefore large quantities of it must be moved over correspondingly large surfaces behind which the condensing takes place. Water, comparatively, is an excellent conductor of heat, thus more desirable but often expensive to use and becoming scarce and too precious for air cooling. Refrigeration technology has worked out a compromise.

Water is circulated as the condensing agent (this water having no direct connection whatsoever with the ultimate process of chilling the air in the residential area). The water thus circulated picks up the heat and, of course, becomes warmer. This water is then sprayed into an outdoor air stream, in which a small part of it evaporates into the air, cooling the remainder of the water, which is then recirculated through the condenser. The part that has evaporated must be constantly replaced with fresh water, but it amounts to only 2 to 4% of the total circulated. The equipment in which the condensing water is sprayed into the air stream is called a cooling tower. An alternate piece of equipment combines the "tower" and the condenser and is called an evaporative condenser. The functions of these items of machinery are identical. The cooling tower or evaporative condenser must be located where it can take in large quantities of outdoor air, used to evaporate the small amount of condensing water. Often the best place is the roof, remote from occupied areas, for some noise is associated with the movement of air and water and the moist air discharged is unpleasant. If the roof location is chosen, the equipment, which is quite large, should be architecturally integrated with the elevator penthouse. If a roof location is impractical, often for aesthetic reasons, an on-the-ground spot must be found at some distance from any building. The last alternative, location inside the building, is possible but quite expensive and with numerous possibilities for annoyance and damage.

Location of a condenser that uses air as its only condensing agent follows the same rules as those laid down for location of cooling towers and evaporative condensers.

Types of condensers usually applied to various sizes of refrigeration plants are listed as follows:

1. Water-coolled condensers, in which the condensing water is discharged to the sewer after having passed through the condenser once, are becoming rare as water supplies are threatened by rising population and proliferation of air conditioning. Their use now is virtually confined to 7½ tons and smaller and only when circumstances make installation of air-cooled condensers impossible.

2. Air-cooled condensers are widely used, ranging in capacity from the ½-ton familiar "window" room cooler to 75-ton plants and occasionally even larger.

3. The cooling tower or evaporative condenser equipment applies to the larger plants. Their sizes may drop into the air-cooled condenser range, but they are usually placed in the 100-ton and indefinitely upward capacities.

The three types of refrigeration machine referred to bear the formidable names of reciprocating, centrifugal, and absorption. Some strange facts of industrial life are illustrated in the use of these machines:

1. RECIPROCATING.   This is the most mechanically complex of the three kinds of equipment, the most subject to wear and the need for replacement of its multitude of moving parts. Yet it is by many hundredfold the most commonly used. Reciprocating machines have the field to themselves in sizes smaller than 25 tons and are virtually unopposed at 25 to 100 tons. The smallest units, 5 tons and smaller in capacity, sell in vast numbers for such applications as room and apartment coolers. Manufacturers have been motivated to build them to be quiet and with their normal vibration well contained. The larger machines, however, tend to be noisy and shaky and to require a comparatively high quantity of energy to operate. As a rule they are driven by electric motors, but occasionally gas engines or turbines serve the purpose.

2. CENTRIFUGAL.   This basically simple, turbinelike machine is built in capacities of 50 to 1000 tons, driven by electric motor or steam or gas turbine. Maintenance and replacement of parts should be minimal, noise level is moderate, and little vibration is apparent. The centrifugal compressor is not competitive in installation cost with reciprocating machines for capacities smaller than 200 tons; for example, two 75-ton reciprocating machines will usually be less expensive than one 150-ton centrifugal.

3. ABSORPTION. This type of equipment uses heat instead of the work of a motor or engine to power the refrigeration cycle. It is often selected when natural fuel is freely available and cheaper than electric energy. In some localities this is particularly true in summer; inducements are offered to encourage off-season use of fuels in order to smooth out the annual demand curve. Absorption machines offer the advantage of quiet vibration-free operation. The only moving parts are small auxiliary motor-driven pumps, one of which helps to maintain the extremely low vacuum that must be held inside. A small machine, of the 25-ton size, uses gas directly for its heating medium, but for many years the trend has been to large units, ranging from 100 to 1500 tons, with steam or high-temperature water (240°F or more) providing the heat. The principal disadvantages of absorption machines are the somewhat temperamental nature of the refrigeration cycle and the comparatively bulky size and weight of the unit. The "nature of the cycle" is such that a comparatively slight irregularity can put the machine out of commission and in such a way that it takes half a day or longer to get it working again.

Refrigeration plants can, of course, contain more than one machine. For machines of the same type it is an almost invariable rule that the overall installation cost of a single large machine is less than multiple units of the same aggregate capacity.

If the criterion is reliability rather than cost, the question must be viewed differently. For a critical industrial process requiring 1000 tons of cooling, the best solution might be three 500-ton machines; full capacity would be available even in the event of failure of one piece of equipment. For a residential installation, in which continuous cooling is desirable but not vital, a 1000-ton load might call for two 500-ton machines on the theory that if one broke down the other would be able to do at least part of the job and some cooling should be more palatable than none at all. In many cases, however, the lowest first cost determines the issue, and the single machine is installed with acceptance of the obvious risks of resident alienation.

Selection of cooling towers offers similar choices but different parameters. A tower or evaporative condenser is a comparatively uncomplicated piece of equipment, less likely to collapse in action. It is quite large in physical size, and two units might overflow the available space. On the other hand, this equipment costs much less, ton-for-ton, than refrigeration machinery, and duplicate units do not pose so severe an economic problem.

The following table offers minimum space requirements for refrigeration plants of various sizes:

Gross Living Area[a] (sf)	Tons Capacity	Number and Kind of Machine	Space Length, Including Servicing Area (ft)	Width (ft)	Height (ft)
110,000	200	2 reciprocating	25	17	7.5
110,000	200	1 centrifugal	32	13	7
110,000	200	1 absorption	34	12	8.5
275,000	500	1 centrifugal	33	16	8.5
275,000	500	1 absorption	45	14	10
275,000	500	2 centrifugal	32	22	7
550,000	1000	1 centrifugal	40	24	13
550,000	1000	1 absorption	61	16	12
550,000	1000	2 absorption	40	24	10

[a] The ratio used here of square feet of actual residential area (including closets, bathrooms, and interior halls, but excluding public corridors and stairwells) per ton of cooling is 550. This is a fair average but will obviously vary according to climate, building construction, direction of exposure, and similar factors.

The approximate space requirements predicted in this table are in addition to those approximated for a central heating plant. Occasionally the total can be reduced by combining servicing areas for the major items of equipment; that is, making the servicing lengths common. If this is possible, the length of the refrigeration plant space can be reduced by one-third. That reduction can also be realized sometimes by providing servicing doors at one end of each refrigeration machine, permitting its tubes to be removed to space outside the equipment room. With respect to space-saving in combining heating and cooling plants, however, one possible code restriction may govern. Some localities prohibit refrigeration and fuel-burning machinery to be operated in the same room. This must be ascertained before combined equipment rooms are arranged.

HEAT PUMPS

Refrigeration equipment has been defined as taking heat from where it is not wanted and disposing of it where it will cause no nuisance. A reversal of the refrigeration cycle permits the same machinery to perform the opposite function, to take heat from where it is not needed and transfer it to where it is; in short, to act as a heat pump. The reversal is not mechanically difficult to do. It is accomplished by operating appropriate valves in the refrigeration cycle piping. It happens that reciprocating machines operate in a range of pressures and with a refrigerant that makes heat pumping most feasible. Therefore this type of machinery is used for heat pumps. A striking heat pump advantage is that it has a coefficient of performance of 1.8 to 1 up to 2.8 to 1, which means that it will deliver that much more heat from the source than the heat equivalent of the electricity used.

What limits the use of this technique is convenient availability of heat. To illustrate, in a locality in which outside temperatures never fall below 35° F the outdoor air itself can serve as the heat source for the comparatively small heating requirement in such a climate, even though air is a poor conductor. Important impediments crop up in colder parts of the world, however. First, more heating is required and, second, heat becomes progressively more difficult to extract as the source air get colder. These facts have limited the widespread use of heat pumps.

There are, of course, other heat sources. The earth itself is one, but it, too, is not a good conductor of heat. This means that such a large tract of earth must be used for the source that the method is impractical. Another potential heat source is underground or surface water in large quantities and at moderate temperatures. The latter is a requisite, of course, because heat can be removed practically from water only down to its freezing point, and if the water is rather cold to begin with not a lot of heat is available. Water conducts heat well; it is comparatively noncorrosive, easy to pump, and altogether a desirable heat source.

SYSTEMS

There is no invariable rule of order in which decisions can be made to define the HVAC system for residential occupancy. Heating and cooling requirements, fuel and energy selections, heating and cooling media, and equipment types and locations have been touched on. Certainly no less important is the determination of the kind of distribution system to be used within each dwelling unit, a decision that might also fix the larger project distribution system, if one is required, to bring heating and cooling to each residence.

There is a fairly wide range of systems of heating, cooling, and combined heating and cooling from which to choose. The first guidepost to be fixed must be whether the overall plan is to make each residence independent, to design a complete central system to serve each dwelling unit in the project according to its needs, or to provide some combination of the two whereby each residence is served by its independently operated subsystem but draws some kind of basic central-plant service to make its subsystem operative. What factors decide which of these categories fits the project being planned?

INDEPENDENT SYSTEM.   There are two principal categories of multiple dwelling projects whose natures point to entirely separate heating and/or cooling plants for each residence. The first is the "tract home" project in which single units, attached in groups or completely detached, are scattered about a comparatively large site. Here the costs of central distribution are often prohibitive and the building for a central plant obtrusive and out of character.

The second is the condominium in which each dwelling unit is its owner's castle, and fewer shared services and expenses mean fewer opportunities for friction and misunderstanding. If the condominium is in a single large building or a number of smaller multistory buildings, it is often found that an electrical heating (and cooling) system answers the need, for there is no problem of fuel distribution or collection of flue gases. This does not always have to be the case, however. Gas-fired equipment has been developed which can vent its products of combustion through a wall. When local codes permit, single dwelling units in a multistory building can use this kind of furnace and/or cooling unit. Practical considerations confine this technique to lowrise buildings, perhaps up to six floors.

The independent system has a clear plus-minus standing on its mechanical merits. The plus factor is that is cannot totally break down. Complete failure of one system will have little or no effect on any other. The countervailing disadvantage is that there are many small pieces of equipment to be maintained and thus more numerous service calls to be contemplated. Whether the cost of these calls is to be borne by the user or by the project as a whole is a factor that enters into the making of the first decision on which system to use. A closely related question is that of length of equipment life and replacement cost. Perhaps it should not be so, but it is a fact of industrial life that mass-produced small heating and cooling units have predictable operating life spans one-half to one-quarter the length of more carefully made central machines. Over the long run, this usually balances out any first-cost advantage the individual furnaces, boilers, or compressors may have.

CENTRAL SYSTEM.   The central heating and/or cooling system is particularly attractive economically in a single large building or a group of large buildings. The "large" building might be a low- or midrise, seven floors or fewer, covering a great land area, or a highrise of eight floors or more. The highrise structures offer several factors that make central systems particularly advantageous, although when the height exceeds 30 stories certain drawbacks begin to appear.

One of the chief benefits of a central system lies in the minimal space needed for equipment in or adjacent to the residential areas. Because it is the highest value space in the building, it is well saved. Clearly, however, a major drawback in central systems lies in their interdependency. Trouble in Apartment 17-D may have repercussions in Apartment 18-D and above but even more often in Apartments 16-D and on down.

COMBINED SYSTEM.   The combined system offers some of the advantages of each of the others but it also contains some of their drawbacks. Its design usually contains the same kind of buildings that were proposed as good subjects for central systems, and its heating and/or cooling air supply units and distribution system serve one residence only. It receives some central service or services from a project plant which might eliminate fuel distribution, flues, refrigeration compressors, condensers, or heating units, or some combination of them, from the individual residences.

As in most compromises, the system combines some of the strengths and weaknesses of the two it amalgamates. There is comparatively little interdependence, but there is some, with the attendant risks, and there is little, if any, saving in space. On the other hand, the number and cost of service and replacement calls should be materially fewer than for the independent systems.

INDEPENDENT HEATING AND COOLING SYSTEMS

Electrical heating lends itself readily to independent, residence-by-residence heating. Fed by electrical energy from the dwelling unit's own power service, often metered and directly charged, the actual method of heating may take any one of several forms.

"Baseboard" electrical resistance heaters are designed to simulate ornamental baseboard trim. Their dimensions are not much greater than standard baseboard trim (generally two and a fraction inches maximum depth by six and a fraction inches high). These heaters provide a continuous curtain of low-level heating, preferably along the outside wall of each room. Controlled by their built-in thermostats or by a central thermostat mounted at a strategic location in the room, they offer a simple and effective means of heating. Their capacity per unit length is somewhat limited unless their physical size is so increased that they cannot pretend to look like baseboards. In a sense, however, this limitation is a healthy one. It dictates that attention be given to maintaining moderate heat losses, which means good insulation, reasonable glass areas, and control of air leakage from outdoors.

Electric convectors can be thought of as concentrated baseboard heaters. They are analogous to the old-fashioned steam or hot-water convectors or radiators and provide the total heat needed in a room in one or very few locations, preferably under a window or windows. Sizes vary greatly according to heating capacity, but an average dimension would be 25 in. high by 48 in. long by 6 in. deep. The device might be recessed or partly recessed into the wall construction, in which case particular care should be exercised that it is well insulated on the rear and exposed sides.

Electric radiant panel heating has proved successful in many residential applications. Like all radiant heating systems, it provides a large source of low-level heat which produces a comfortable environment. Like other radiant systems, however, it has the disadvantage of being unable to concentrate a proportional amount of its heat at the outside wall line of greatest heat loss, and there is likely to be a narrow uncomfortably cold zone in that part of the room. Electric radiant systems do boast one advantage over the wet systems. By their nature they have less construction bulk to warm up or cool down and are much more quickly responsive to changing load demands. It is in the nature of heating that loads do fluctuate, often very quickly. The sun swings around its daily course, outside temperatures change, lights go on and off, and people come in and out.

Electric radiant panels are invariably installed on the ceiling in one of two forms. The ceiling itself may be made up of factory-manufactured panels in which electrical conducting-resisting materials have been imbedded, each panel rated for its electric input and therefore heat output. The panels are heavily insulated on the up-facing side, so that nearly all the heat goes in the direction in which it is wanted. The other common method is the one usually applied to concrete slabs in multistory buildings. After the slab has set and the shoring has been cleared away, electric conducting-resisting cable is applied to the underside of the concrete in long serpentine loops in which adjacent lengths of cable may be 2 to 6 in. apart, depending on the room heating load. Cable is secured to the slab at intervals close enough to prevent its drooping, and the thinnest

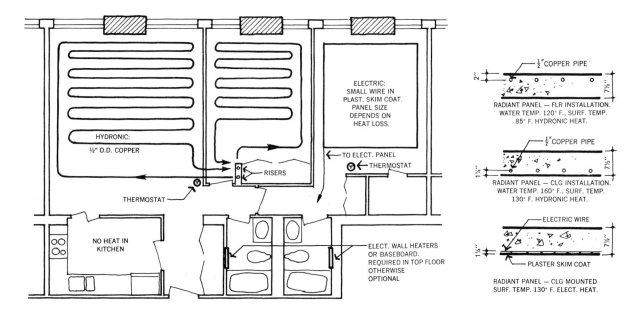

possible "skim" coating of plaster, usually ³⁄₁₆ to ¼-in. thick is applied to hide the cable, distribute its heat over the entire area, and give a finished ceiling appearance.

Electric furnaces fall into the category of residential fan-coil units, a prolific kind that is prevalent in the central and combined systems as well as in the independent systems now under discussion. The fan-coil unit description is similar to that of the heating furnace, and like the furnace the fan-coil unit may be horizontal or vertical in its major aspect. Briefly, then, it includes a small blower or tandem blowers, driven directly or by pulleys and belt from a fractional horsepower electric motor or motors, and assembled with filters and heating and/or cooling finned tube coils in a steel casing. If instead of coils there is an electrical resistance heating element, the unit is called an electric furnace.

Fan-coil units may be of such capacity that one unit will serve a single room, a group of rooms, or an entire residence. If the fan-coil is combined in a single housing with a refrigeration machine, it is called a self-contained unit. A well-known example of self-contained equipment which also includes the refrigeration condenser is the through-the-wall or "window" room cooler, which takes in outdoor air directly, uses and expels some of it for condensing purposes, and mixes a small amount of it with recirculated room air to help ventilate the room being cooled. This machine is sometimes furnished with a built-in electrical resistance heater and thus can cool, ventilate, or heat the space when required. Dimensions of an average unit are about 17 in. high by 16 in. deep and 25 to 42 in. long.

Similar self-contained fan-coil units are available in sizes to heat and cool an entire dwelling in conjunction with appropriate air distribution ductwork. These units are too large to be spotted casually in a wall or window opening and are usually floor mounted at an outside wall, where condensing air is readily available. This arrangement, however, uses up an appreciable amount of premium living space and has found little favor.

What has gained widespread use is the split independent system rather than the self-contained. Here the horizontal or vertical fan-coil unit is mounted or suspended in an interior closet, entrance hall, or similar living space of lower desirability, and the refrigeration compressor-condenser is mounted as a unit on the outside, thus moving a source of noise and vibration away from the dwelling quarters. In one- or two-story residential buildings space for the refrigeration machine can often be found on the

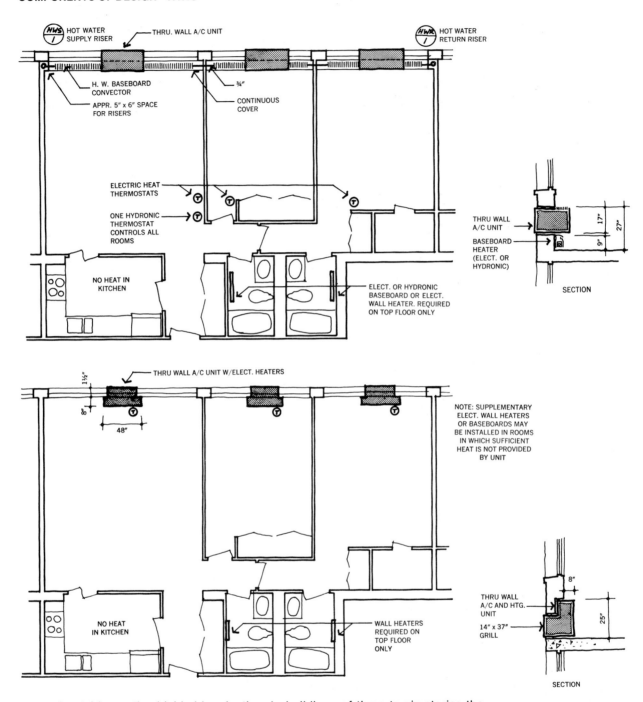

ground outside, partly shielded by planting. In buildings of three to six stories the refrigeration assemblies may be mounted on the roof with careful vibration isolation and structural provisions. If the method is at all practical in multiple-story buildings, it will be by the use of balconies, at least one for each dwelling unit, on which the refrigeration equipment can be located so as not to spoil the balcony entirely for recreational purposes.

In all these installations small copper refrigerant lines are run between the outside refrigeration machine and the inside coil, and in all cases this leaves the problem of heating to be solved. For one- or two-story residences a natural fuel furnace can be introduced as an adjunct to the fan-coil unit or a refrigeration coil can be installed in

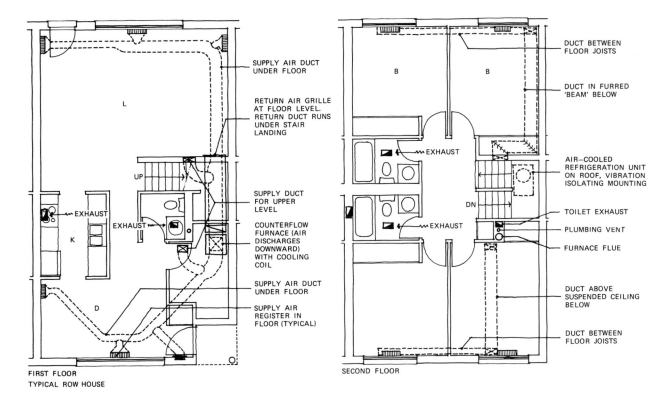

SUPPLY AIR DUCT
UNDER FLOOR

RETURN AIR GRILLE
AT FLOOR LEVEL.
RETURN DUCT RUNS
UNDER STAIR
LANDING

SUPPLY DUCT
FOR UPPER
LEVEL

COUNTERFLOW
FURNACE (AIR
DISCHARGES
DOWNWARD)
WITH COOLING
COIL

SUPPLY AIR DUCT
UNDER FLOOR

SUPPLY AIR
REGISTER IN
FLOOR (TYPICAL)

DUCT BETWEEN
FLOOR JOISTS

DUCT IN FURRED
'BEAM' BELOW

AIR—COOLED
REFRIGERATION UNIT
ON ROOF, VIBRATION
ISOLATING MOUNTING

TOILET EXHAUST

PLUMBING VENT

FURNACE FLUE

DUCT ABOVE
SUSPENDED CEILING
BELOW

DUCT BETWEEN
FLOOR JOISTS

FIRST FLOOR
TYPICAL ROW HOUSE

SECOND FLOOR

conjunction with a standard furnace. Although the flue problem becomes difficult, these arrangements can be used for buildings as high as five or six stories. For higher buildings the furnace problems become too serious to cope with and heating must be done electrically. This may be done by a resistance heater installed in the fan-coil unit or its ductwork or, if the climate is suitable, by the use of a heat pump as an embellishment of the refrigeration machine. Recall that if the heat pump can be used, it

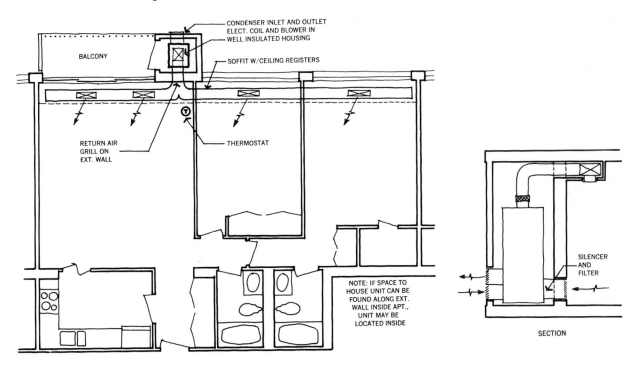

CONDENSER INLET AND OUTLET
ELECT. COIL AND BLOWER IN
WELL INSULATED HOUSING

SOFFIT W/CEILING REGISTERS

BALCONY

RETURN AIR
GRILL ON
EXT. WALL

THERMOSTAT

NOTE: IF SPACE TO
HOUSE UNIT CAN BE
FOUND ALONG EXT.
WALL INSIDE APT.,
UNIT MAY BE
LOCATED INSIDE

SILENCER
AND
FILTER

SECTION

127

will return about 1¾ times as much heat per electrical watt as the straight resistance heater.

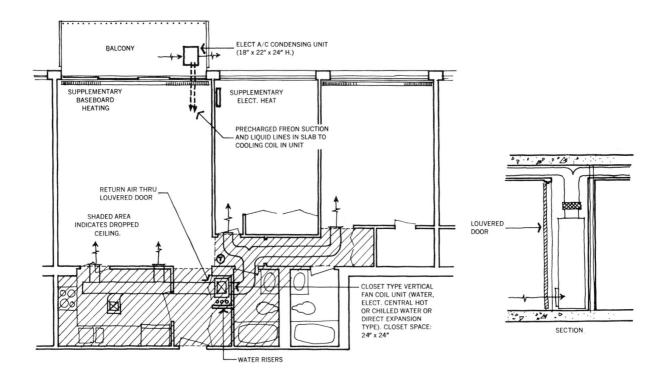

Two practical rules should be inserted here to govern the installation of these types of equipment. First, if the fan-coil unit is used for cooling, a drainpan must be incorporated in the unit to catch moisture condensed from the conditioned air by the coil and a drainpipe must be run from the pan to conduct the condensate to a sewer or drainage outlet. In "window" units this condition has been met in most units by draining the pan to the fan which moves the outside air used for condensing purposes. When enough condensate accumulates, the fan blades pick it up and fling it into the atmosphere with such velocity that it becomes mistlike and is absorbed into the air. Occasionally when the adjustment is not quite right, passers-by are made aware of it by what seems to be a light drizzle on a sunny day.

The second rule is that the cooling coil should be after, or downstream of, a fuel-burning furnace. If the coil is first in line, the chilled air off the cooling surface will pass through the furnace. In summer the products-of-combustion side of the furnace's heat exchanger is in direct contact through the flue with the hot, humid air from outdoors, and the cold on one side of the furnace metal will cause condensation of moisture in the hot weather air on the other side. That moisture will rust the heat exchanger. If it is impossible to avoid an arrangement of cooling coil first, the furnace must be made of stainless steel, which is expensive but will not rust.

There is a final word of caution regarding installation of fan-coil units serving more than one room, especially if the unit is mounted outside the house itself; for example, in a utility closet. Layout of supply ductwork conveying the warmed or cooled air is an obvious requirement in the design, but sometimes an unwary designer will forget that air must be recirculated from the living quarters back to the fan-coil device. If this calls for ductwork or for the use of construction space above suspended ceilings or soffits, it must be made certain that no other construction such as masonry fire-separation partitions shuts off the duct or passage. If there is an impediment of that nature, a legal way must be found to go through or around it.

CENTRAL HEATING AND COOLING SYSTEMS

The hallmarks of the central system are a mechanical plant in which heating and/or cooling capacity is sufficient to serve an entire building or project and a water piping distribution system that connects the plant with every part of the residential area. Elements of the heating and cooling plant have already been considered, and the piping systems are no less important. They must be designed with at least equal care. An understanding of their potentialities, problems, and comparative values reveals possibilities and requirements, particularly structural requirements, associated with the various piping arrangements.

Pipe systems for central residential heating and cooling are described as one-, two-, three-, and four-pipe. The two-pipe system is the most widely used. There is a further classification into direct and reversed return.

One-pipe systems are used only for heating. When they are feasible, they are favored for low-cost and minimal space requirements. Water is pumped through a single main which feeds a number of heating devices such as baseboard convectors or standard convectors. At each heating device a specially designed tee fitting whose size is selected for the particular application extracts as much water from the main as that device needs. That part of the water passes through the heater and then returns to the

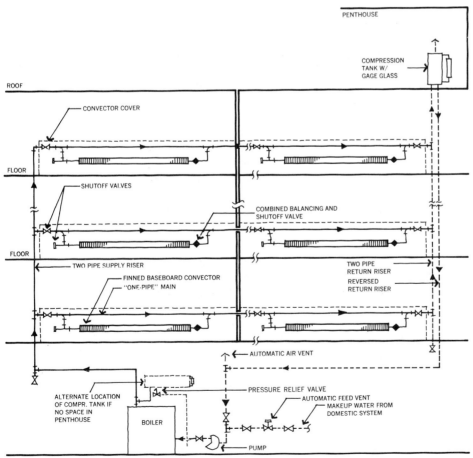

TYPICAL WATER HEATING PIPING DIAGRAM (SHOWING 1-PIPE AND 2-PIPE SYSTEMS)

main, downstream of where it was taken off. In multiple-story buildings one-pipe systems can often be mixed with two-pipe, which are reviewed next. Two-pipe (separate supply and return) vertical risers with one-pipe horizontal mains between them can serve a number of heating devices on the same floor level, a useful arrangement because it minimizes the locations in a building at which risers must be allowed for in the construction.

One-pipe systems also apply to steam heating, particularly in old buildings. The use of steam for heating, in residential applications particularly, has been reduced to the vanishing point in new building design, and new one-pipe systems are rare. They can work, however, in buildings of modest height. Steam is supplied to radiators or convectors in a vertical riser pipe, and after it has given up its heat in the heating device and condensed to liquid form the condensate water returns down the same pipe. That pipe must be large enough to permit simultaneous passage of steam and water. In three-story buildings the riser can even feed up from the lowest floor so that steam and water are traveling in opposite directions! In taller buildings, up to 10 floors, steam is piped under the roof, from which risers feed down, and steam and water move in the same direction. For taller buildings the one-pipe system is simply not practical. Too much steam and water are in the risers and the design becomes unmanageable. Economy of installation is the reason for one-pipe systems. Their great drawback is that the heating device must be all on or all off; throttling a valve will impede return of the condensate.

Two pipe systems provide separate channels for supply and return water, either or both for heating and cooling purposes. When applied to steam heating, the two-pipe system permits throttling of the steam supply when the heating load is light, for example, in mild weather, and only part of the heating device is supplied with steam, thus reducing its capacity commensurate with the demand on it.

Two-pipe water systems for heating and cooling have a serious drawback, best illustrated by an example that applies to the climate in large parts of the world. Early in the morning of a spring or autumn day the outdoor temperature may have fallen to 50° F and a little heat is needed. Water at 90° F may be circulated to meet this mild need. By noon of this sunny day it is 75° F outdoors, and cooling is being called for, particularly on the southern exposure (in the northern hemisphere) where the sun is streaming into the huge modern windows. Cooling needs water at about 50° F. The manufacturer of the equipment has probably warned that no water warmer than 80° F should ever be run into the machine, so the distraught building operator has had to run 90° F early-morning heating water through the building until it naturally cooled down to 80° F and then run that through the chiller until it dropped to 50° F. If the project is a large one, it is well on in the afternoon by the time all that has been accomplished and almost time to start heating again for the approaching cool evening.

This very real operating trial can be lessened by dividing the project piping and pumps into separate zones, so that the exposures that face the sun in the cool mornings may be supplied with chilled water much earlier than those that get no sunlight at all or get it later in the day. This piping is not easy to arrange in buildings of irregular or complex shape, and even in square or rectangular buildings perfectly compass-oriented the operator must respond to the weather, the cloudiness of the day, the actual temperature swing, and so on. Therefore the zoning method has its own pitfalls.

Even zoning in a two-pipe system cannot solve another common problem. Occupants of one dwelling expect a large group of friends in for Sunday afternoon cocktails and need cooling at once. Their elderly neighbors, occupying an identical apartment with the same exposure, are spending a quiet afternoon at home. Noting that the outside temperature is 50° F, they invoke the lease provision that entitles them to heat. There is no way in which a two-pipe central system can satisfy both sets of tenants or apartment owners, and someone must take on the unpleasant task of breaking the news to one or the other.

An obvious answer is the four-pipe system in which there are separate and independent piping systems and pumps for heating and cooling that make these services available simultaneously throughout a building or project, at least in intermediate weather when one or the other may be needed at any time. Equally clear is the drawback to the arrangement. It is an expensive installation that requires extra unusable space in the habitable areas. It is a luxury that is sometimes found in the highest room-rate hotels but much less often in residential buildings.

In an attempt to compromise between the inflexibility of two-pipe distribution and the high cost of the four-pipe arrangement, a three-pipe system has been introduced. Separate heating and cooling piping and pumps characterize it, and common return mains are associated with each pair of supply pipes. Used to its full potential generally in the intermediate seasons, its theory is that enough diverse calls will be made for heating and cooling simultaneously and that the mixture of return water will not be too warm for the chiller nor too cold for the boilers. Introduced with fanfare, the systems have met with some success, but they have proved to be temperamental in operation and conducive to problems in the central plant. Sales pressure for their use noticeably diminished a few years after their introduction.

Reference has been made to direct and reversed return piping systems which apply to water distribution and can be simply illustrated. Assume a central plant and pumps in the lowest floor of a building (the effect is exactly the same wherever the location and this assumption merely ties down the example). Warm or chilled water is distributed to this multiple-story building by a number of two-pipe risers. Consider one of these pairs of pipes—supply and return. The simplest way to run the piping would be floor by floor through a branch supply pipe at each level, diminishing the supply riser as it goes up because it carries less water floor by floor. The return would be the same, starting at the top with a minimum size riser from the uppermost floor, increasing as it gets down back to its source. The problem here is that water takes the easiest flow pattern it can find. The heating-cooling unit on the lowest floor offers the shortest path for its supply and return water and will tend to grab an undue share. The same pattern will exist all the way up, and the unit at the top, where the exposure is probably the worst, will get only the leavings.

One way to even things out is to provide easily adjustable indexed valves called balancing fittings, through which artificial resistance can be added to the nearest units' branch piping so that each will get a fair share. In a riser that feeds a large number of units the adjustment of these balancing devices becomes an extremely sensitive and time-consuming procedure. They can be manufactured and factory preset to allow a theoretically calculated flow of water through each one, but they are more suitable to laboratory control than to the uncertainties and irregularities of a construction project. If the job is to be done the right way, it will require considerable field time, which may cancel out the first-cost advantage of this piping method, known as "direct-return."

Its counterpart is the "reversed-return" piping method (see preceding illustration). To use the same illustration, the supply risers are identical, but the return risers start at the lowest floor of the building and pick up water, floor-by-floor, going up, as its companion supply riser is dropping it off. When the now full-size return riser reaches the top of the building, it joins all the other returns and goes back down in one large return main. The theory here is that the heating-cooling unit whose water has the shortest supply path has the longest return path, and vice versa; pressure losses through all the units are almost identical, and the system is substantially self-balancing. Balancing cocks are usually provided at each unit as a safety precaution, but the reversed-return system often requires no balancing whatever.

The additional cost in the reversed-return system is the cost of the one big vertical main, the height of the building, which is at least partly offset by the cost of sophisticated balancing devices and balancing time required in the direct-return arrangement. There is a warning here, however. If, for some architectural, structural, or aesthetic reason, the building design does not permit gathering the return risers at the top, then each pair of supply and return risers will have to have its own associated reversed-return riser running all the way down, to be gathered at the bottom in the space also used for the distribution of the supply risers. This means multiple reversed-return risers and more space at the riser locations. It may also be a serious cost impediment to the use of this relatively foolproof reversed-return system.

Engineers differ on the hazards of the direct-return arrangement. There is general agreement that for five-story structures the simplest direct-return system is not too hard to balance. For 6 to perhaps 16 stories many engineers will consider preset balancing fittings without too many misgivings. For taller buildings engineers will generally insist on reversed-return piping.

In any long piping runs, whether risers in tall buildings or horizontal mains in large lowrise buildings, the effects of pipe-length expansion and contraction must be allowed for. Such allowances may be in the form of pipe configuration, often a large "U" in the run of the pipe, of fabricated expansion joints constituting bellows that squeeze or relax to accommodate movement, or, when the general arrangement permits, provision for movement in branches taken off the main to compensate for movement in the parent pipe by controlled movement in the subordinate.

The "U" bends are often feasible in horizontal mains. The bellows expansion joint is most useful for risers. A serious cautionary note here is that this kind of device must be accessible for maintenance and replacement and that the necessary access panels may be aesthetically undesirable.

The branch takeoff flexibility serves both horizontal and vertical mains and is generally a well-advised piping design feature even if the other cited methods of expansion allowance are employed.

There is no sacred rule governing the length that the piping must be when special expansion provisions are necessary. It depends on the circumstances of each system. A fair estimate of a maximum length would be 75 ft.

When pipe risers are located close to columns, it is mandatory that mechanical and structural engineers coordinate their designs so that connections of horizontal structural members with the columns will not be endangered. In the following illustration arrangment (C) is usually preferable on that count.

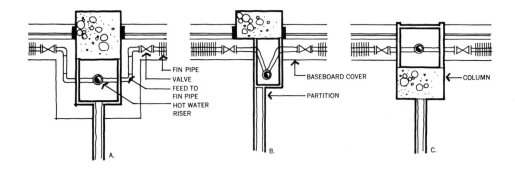

FIN PIPE
VALVE
FEED TO
FIN PIPE
HOT WATER
RISER

BASEBOARD COVER

PARTITION

COLUMN

A.   B.   C.

The heating and cooling devices used in conjunction with central systems are similar in type to those in independent systems. For heating only, there are radiators, convectors, and radiant panels. Radiators are usually cast iron and have comparatively large areas of exposed surface which approach the temperature of the water or steam contained within them. They emit heat by a combination of low-level radiation from these hot surfaces and convection, or continual rising of air warmed by direct contact with them, up through air spaces in the radiator. Old-fashioned cast-iron radiators put together in sections, with feet supporting the end sections, are still seen in many old buildings, but they are no longer made. Present-day radiators are still assembled in sections, but they offer a smooth front appearance with patterned designs for the convected air passages and are more pleasing aesthetically. They have much smaller dimensions than the old ones, particularly in depth, but correspondingly lack the enormous heating capacities boasted by the old monsters.

Convectors, both the baseboard and more concentrated types, are similar to those described under electrical heating for independent systems. Steam or water baseboard "wet heat" convectors are made in a larger range of sizes and output capacities. The smallest residential types are akin to the electrical baseboard described, but for severe load applications they may go to nearly 4 in. deep and 10 in. high. When baseboard convectors are used in conjunction with a one-pipe distribution system, as already described, their cabinet height can sometimes be increased to accommodate the one-pipe main concealed in the cabinet and feeding a series of baseboards. The designer must always remember that the last convector in line is getting the coolest water and its length must be increased to suit (see the illustration above).

When balconies are in the picture, baseboard convectors must be designed carefully to avoid an excessive step up at the balcony door.

Radiant panels, too, are similar to those described for electrical systems. Serpentine tubing, which carries warm water, can be laid directly in a concrete floor or ceiling slab or applied and covered with plaster after the slab or other flooring is completed. The tubing is usually copper, ⅜ in. in diameter, and requires cement plaster to a thickness of about 1 in. for adequate cover and distribution of heat. Plaster expands with heat at about the same rate as copper, and there is little cracking of plaster for this cause. It is essential that a new system be started with very slow increase of water temperature and with safeguards against drafts. Plaster which dries too quickly will crack.

Fan-coil units for central systems are fed with the project's warm and chilled water in season. For two-pipe distribution systems each unit will have one finned coil. For three-and four-pipe systems each unit may have one coil with appropriate valving in the pipe branches to select between warm and chilled water or two coils with separate supply (and return in four-pipe distribution) branches from the warm and chilled water risers. The fan-coil units differ primarily in shape, where and how they are to be mounted.

The first fan-coils developed simply copied the concept and appearance of the long familiar convector. Housed in a rectangular casing about the size of a convector, although a little deeper because of the dimensions of the fans, these units were intended to be mounted under windows and to discharge their air upward to blanket the area of greatest heat exchange with the outdoors. In multistory buildings, the only kind in which fan-coil units make economic sense, space is generally found for risers in partitions or walls running perpendicular to the outside walls, and branches from risers to fan-coil units are concealed in the outside wall construction or in special horizontal chases which are part of the designed wall elevation. It is also possible to leave the pipe branches exposed, as was often done with runouts to the old fashioned radiators, but this alternative finds little favor. The pipes are unsightly and subject to damage. If they are to be concealed in the outside wall construction, care must be taken to insulate them and ensure flow through them at all times, if subfreezing temperatures can occur.

The fan-coil system was found to be a quiet, readily controllable, and effective method of heating and cooling, and the under-the-window units were soon supple-

COMPONENTS OF DESIGN—HVAC

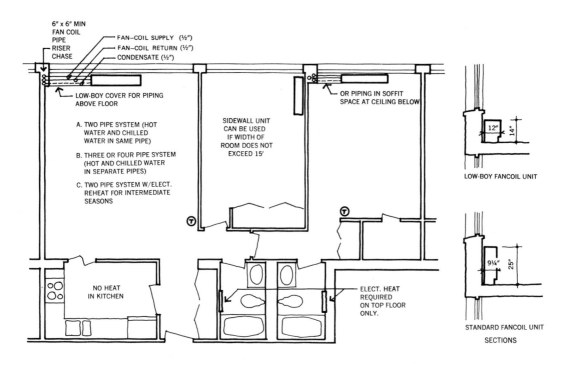

mented by larger, suspended units capable of supplying an entire apartment by ductwork or construction air passages, and by vertical, floor-to-ceiling units, which contain the entire riser systems by which they are fed. The latter found considerable favor soon after their introduction into the market because of the substantial labor savings that can be realized with them and their lower overall installation cost. The units themselves are comparatively expensive, but when wheeled into place, set up, and a few quick piping connections made at the top or bottom, the entire job is done. Their housings enclose not only filters, fan, coil, discharge and intake outlets, insulation, controls, and two-, three-, or four-pipe risers but cooling condensate drain risers as well. Their height of a little less than 8 ft is selected to fit the standard residential ceiling height, with enough margin to get them into place. Their location is, of course, of paramount importance. For most applications they should be at the perimeter of the building, where the heating or cooling load is greatest. If the planning is done properly and in advance, both the building elevation and room layout can be made to accommodate the necessary space. Frequently one vertical fan-coil unit can be made to serve two rooms if control is not needed in each. Conversely, if a room has a long perimeter with continuous glass, necessitating unit mounting at the outside corner, one fan-coil may not be able to distribute heat and cooling for the entire exposure length, and two units, one in each corner, may be required. Of course, they may be designed to supply the adjoining rooms as well.

When fan-coil risers are placed at a building perimeter, a high degree of design coordination must be observed. The pipe openings through the floor slabs must not in any way weaken the structure by interfering with beams or reinforcing bars.

Suspended fan-coil units are usually concealed above a lowered ceiling, located in a part of the residence in which a clear ceiling height of 7 ft or a little less is not objectionable. This may be in a bathroom, utility space, hall, or closet, and convenient access for servicing filters, motor, blowers and coil must be provided. Suspended units in particular, but even floor-mounted fan-coils which serve an entire residence or section, usually discharge air through ducts or construction spaces at ceiling level. In multistory buildings it is often not feasible to provide duct space outside the bounds of

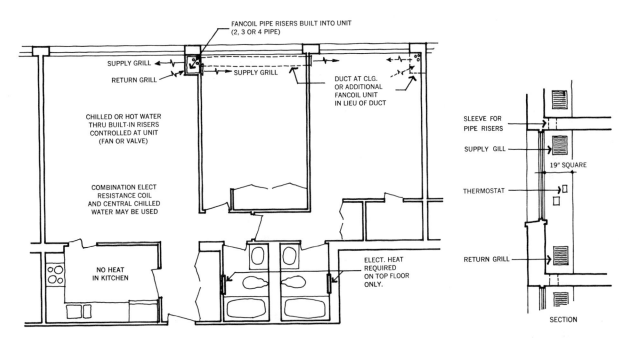

the floor and the structure at or above the ceiling. In such cases it may not be possible to supply air or to pull recirculated air at the critical locations for heat loss and heat gain (e.g., under windows or continuous glass area). It is particularly important that these places of maximum exposure be protected by heat in cold climates. Without that design precaution, convection of air cooled by contact with the frigid glass surface will cause that air to fall along the outside wall and sweep across the floor as a chilly draft, a source of major discomfort to occupants. There are cases in which the perimeter configuration of the building will simply not allow for fan-coils at the perimeter, and suspended units in the interior are the only solution. In such circumstances a split system in which baseboard radiation along the perimeter handles enough of the heat load to eliminate the cold draft curse may be necessary for comfort; the fan-coil will pick up the rest of the heating load and, of course, all the cooling requirements.

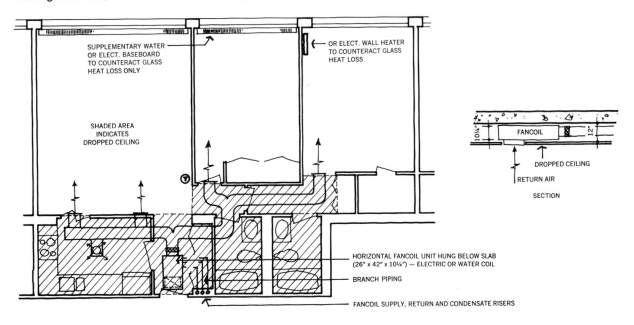

135

COMPONENTS OF DESIGN—HVAC

There are modifications of the fan-coil unit principle that find occasional use in residential buildings, particularly multistory structures of 6 to 20 stories. One is the induction unit, which uses the aspirating power of comparatively high pressure air, instead of a motor driven fan, to move room air to be heated or cooled across a finned coil. The high pressure air is produced in a central air conditioning unit in which it is warmed or cooled as the season demands, filtered, and sent through a system of round ducts and risers to the induction units mounted under the window in each room. An aspirating effect permits a quantity of high pressure air to induce a flow of room air several times its own volume through the heating-cooling coil in the unit. This induced air does a major part of the heating or cooling, which enables the designer to minimize the quantity of primary (high pressure) air and thus keep the duct riser sizes to a minimum as well. The induction unit system requires a primary air duct riser in addition to the pipe risers at every location. Condensate drain-riser pipes are sometimes omitted in this system because all the dehumidification is supposed to be accomplished in the primary air and there is no moisture left to be squeezed out in the occupied spaces. Accidents and malfunctions can occur, however; moist outdoor air can blow into a room through windows left open, and dehumidification can occur at induction units under particular circumstances. Some designers choose to avoid any possibility of grief by providing condensate piping against the remote danger. Others play the percentages and save the cost.

The primary air in induction systems is usually all taken from the outdoors, and no air is recirculated from dwelling to dwelling. This offers an advantage in the presence of constant fresh-air ventilation. An equal volume of air is removed from the premises by bathroom or kitchen exhaust ventiliation. All in all, the system is excellent, but expensive to install and consequently has found limited use in residential projects.

COMBINED HEATING AND COOLING SYSTEMS

A combined system, embodying individual operation and central services, usually entails the lowest first-cost installation of heating and cooling in a residential building. It is a central hot-water heating plant with baseboard convectors and through-the-wall room coolers operated by the residents (see the illustration on p. 126). The project pays for the heat, occupants pay only for the cooling in their apartments, and complications are minimal. The same division can be made by using standard convectors or radiant panel heating combined with through-the-wall coolers.

Particular circumstances can reverse this arrangement. If a highrise residential building is to be combined with commercial use, it may be advantageous to expand a central chilled-water plant to provide cooling for the residential section, perhaps through a fan-coil system, but then require each occupant to pay for electric heat in conjunction with each fan-coil unit.

An ingenious combined system has been developed which offers energy conservation and consequent low operating cost in multiple dwellings. The independent element is a self-contained unit for each residence, with blower, motor and drive, filters, coil, housing, and a heat pump refrigeration compressor. The central part of this system is a two-pipe water circulating system which can serve all self-contained units, and in whose supply main 85°F water circulates the year round. This water is used for condensing purposes in the cooling season and as the heat pump source in cold weather. In the intermediate seasons, houses requiring cooling at a given time will be putting heat into the circulating water, whereas houses whose exposure warrants heating would simultaneously be extracting heat from it. When everybody requires heat, a central boiler plant will replace the heat that has been extracted from the water by the heat pumps. When all residences are being cooled, a central cooling tower installation will remove all the heat from the water that has been added. Clearly, there can be times in spring and autumn when the demands for heat and cooling will balance one another. Refrigeration machinery in southern exposures puts as much heat into the water as northern exposures extract from it, and neither boilers nor cooling towers have to do any work at all.

CONTROLS

Heating systems are designed for the coldest expected day combined with an adverse wind. Cooling systems are sized for the hottest, most humid anticipated weather, with the sun shining brightly, at least normal occupany, and some use of indoor heat-producing functions such as lights, television sets, and cooking. Because these "design" conditions are rarely encountered, it follows that heating and cooling systems have more capacity than they need most of the time and would thus make a house warmer or colder than comfortable, all of which is a roundabout way of stating a rather evident truth—that HVAC systems must be controlled in order to function satisfactorily most of the time.

Controls can vary to a great extent, depending on the construction budget, the importance of operating cost, the sophistication of the occupants, and their likelihood to be demanding. Consider the following list of controls in rising order of complexity and cost.

1. MANUAL VALVES.   These reduce or shut off a flow of steam for heating or flow of water for heating or cooling to each radiator, convector, or fan-coil unit. Because every unit should be provided with a shutoff to permit its repair in any event, this primitive method of control adds no cost to the installation. It is a poor control, however, because it requires frequent attention and considerable skill on the part of the occupant.

2. WATER TEMPERATURE CONTROL.   Water temperature is adjusted automatically according to outside temperatures and wind conditions; the warmest water is supplied when it is coldest outside and vice versa. This system can be further refined if the water piping is arranged in zones so that different exposures will receive different water temperatures at any time, based on wind direction and solar exposure. The counterpart of this control in steam heating systems is one by which steam is supplied to the heating elements for a greater or lesser proportion of the time, based on the need dictated by outside conditions. In either case, if the system is well designed and the control well calibrated, the occupants will find that little or no adjustment of manual valves is necessary. Note that the principles and practice of water temperature control apply to both heating and cooling operations. Developed for heating originally, this control can effect substantial economy in the cooling season by holding water temperature at the highest level consistent with satisfactory cooling, which is dependent on outdoor and indoor load conditions.

3. FAN SPEED CONTROL FOR FAN-COIL UNITS.   Typically, each fan-coil is factory-provided with a motor that may operate at two or three speeds to produce variable volumes of air. High speed would answer the need for cooling and/or heating on the "design" day. The lower speeds might suffice for most of the rest of the time. The occupant learns what unit operation best fits the needs and sets the switch accordingly. The switch should also have an OFF position, but the danger in this should be cited. If an occupant leaves for a summer vacation and turns the switch off, normal leakage of outside air into the house may permit humidity to build up to outdoor levels. The fan-coil unit has the fan turned off, but chilled water is circulating steadily through the

coil. Soon the steel housing around the coil will become quite cold because there is no air passing through the unit it to prevent it. The moist room air strikes the cold metal surface and moisture condensed from the air runs down the housing onto the floor. The returning vacationer is greeted with a wet, stained, and moldy carpet. This is by no means a theoretical story. Enough water can be generated this way over a period of time to run along the floor until it finds a way to leak into the apartment below. To avoid this peril, prudence dictates that in addition to the fan speed switch there should be an electric valve on the chilled water supply line; when the fan is off, water flow will stop or very nearly stop because there can be another kind of danger (in horizontal fan-coil units). If the resident leaves for a long winter vacation and turns the fan off, thus closing the valve, a severe cold snap could conceivably cause the trapped water to freeze in the fan-coil unit. To circumvent this, a tiny hole can be drilled in the electric valve to permit a slight flow of water, enough to prevent freezing but not enough to chill the housing and cause condensation in summer. These little horror stories illustrate the importance of considering all the implications of whatever controls system is chosen.

4. FACTORY BUILT-IN THERMOSTATIC CONTROL FOR THROUGH-WALL ROOM COOLERS. This is the first mention of thermostatic controls, which sense the temperature in the room and operate the cooling system automatically to suit. If electric heat is built into the fan-coil unit, a room-heating thermostat should likewise be built in. In addition to room coolers cited in the preceding paragraph, simple fan-coil units can also be factory supplied with thermostats that sense room-air temperature and thereby actuate an electric valve that governs the water supply to the coil. This valve may be the ON-OFF type, two-position, either-or, or gradual acting, which regulates water flow in close accordance with the actual requirement at any time. The thermostat obviously must have characteristics suitable to operate the kind of valve selected.

5. SELF-ACTUATING VALVES FOR HEATING OR COOLING. Usually these valves are not factory-installed but rather are separately purchased and mounted in the field. They require no electric operation, sense room temperature at the heating or cooling unit itself, and take a position that permits a flow of water commensurate with the load.

6. REMOTE ROOM THERMOSTATS. A thermostat that is separated from the heating or cooling device can be mounted in any location in the room. Often careful consideration in the design stage will produce a location best suited to provide optimum comfort in the room, a location better than adjacent to the heating or cooling device, as described in (4) and (5) above. This remote thermostat can operate a fan-coil unit blower or a valve for a heating convector, fan-coil unit, or induction unit. It requires an electric box, wiring and, perhaps a conduit and thus requires a more expensive installation than those cited. It almost always does a better job of temperature controlling, which justifies the cost.

7. ZONE CONTROLS. Residences heated and cooled by ductwork in single HVAC units can enjoy separate zone control in at least two arrangements. One may be an independent coil in the duct to each room or group of rooms; the water flow to the coil is regulated by a room thermostat mounted in the area served. In this context one group includes the bedrooms and the other contains the living and dining areas. In a second and more common zoning method motor-driven air volume dampers, one in each zone duct, are operated by room thermostats. If an air unit provides both heating and cooling, there must be an automatic or manual method of reversal according to season. In summer high room temperatures call for more air, in winter, less, and the automatic volume dampers must operate with seasonal instructions. A third zone-control method is by multizone systems, much more common in office and commercial air conditioning

than in residences. In this system the volume of air circulated to each zone remains constant but its temperature is varied according to need. In summer this is done by mixing cooled and uncooled air for each zone; in winter, by mixing heated and unheated air.

VENTILATION

If the word "ventilation" conjures up visions of fans and intricate duct systems, that really is taking the long way around, at least for residential conceptual thinking. What should come to mind first is simply "windows."

Windowless buildings, which include those with perimeter glass that cannot be opened, have become a twentieth-century phenomenon which followed the development of air conditioning, but their use has not spread to residential projects, where codes require window areas that open in living spaces. With rare exceptions, even the most sophisticated heating and air conditioning systems anticipate some contribution by window ventilation.

One dictionary definition of the word "ventilate" is "to admit fresh air into." Under atmospheric conditions in some of the world's industrial societies, that adjective "fresh" is more than a little suspect. Nevertheless, the need for changes in air content in an enclosed space requires little explanation. Occupants reduce oxygen quantity by their physiological processes. Likewise, equipment that burns fuel extracts oxygen from the building's air to do it. Odors are created by food preparation and bodily functions. Humidity is increased by cooking and cleaning processes that release moisture. Without changes and replenishment of the air content, an enclosed space would very quickly become uninhabitable.

INFILTRATION

The simplest residence is one in which kitchen and bathrooms have windows to the outdoors. Thus exhaust fans to remove air from those spaces are not needed. Assume that a house is heated by electricity or by steam or water from a remote plant. In neither case does air needed for combustion purposes have to come from the residence. Finally, say that the day is cold and that the occupants do not choose to open the windows, even a crack. How then is any kind of ventilation to be achieved? The embarrassingly unscientific answer is that outdoor air must leak in—an effect called infiltration.

The mere fact that windows and doors must be movable in order to perform their functions creates junctions in the construction of a building. Construction processes and materials are not so perfect that these junctions are absolutely tight, for example, like two machine-polished surfaces in an engine. Their imperfections take the form of cracks through which outdoor air is forced. Moreoever, every time an outer door opens outside air mixes with room air right at the entrance by the very motion of the door. In these crude ways basic ventilation is achieved.

Complete reliance on leakage must, however, be accompanied by some warning. By the installation of storm windows and supercaulking, infiltration can be reduced to a dangerously low level. An invalid or recluse may use the door infrequently. Finally, windows and doors must face more than one exposure. If the wind blows from the north for a week and the only openings are on the south, what can leak in? This question brings to mind a typical apartment building in which there is a central corridor with apartments on both sides whose windows have only one exposure. In such a building the apartment doors to the corridor must not be tight fitting. In the example cited above air will leak into the north-facing apartments. The pressure of this air will be exerted through the building via the doors so that an equal volume will exit through the south windows. It may be contended that the south apartment is really not being ventilated; it is only getting used air from the north apartment through the corridor. The fact is that the life-and-death need for oxygen replacement calls for a really surprisingly small quantity of air, and leakage through the north apartment windows is far more than the vital needs of residents on both sides of the corridor. The explanation is that when we breathe we do not by any means use up all the oxygen in the air we have taken into our lungs. Actually, we reduce oxygen content by only about 4% in every breath. So it is only when people are literally packed together without significant ventilation, as in the infamous Black Hole of Calcutta, that oxygen deficiency can quickly become dangerous.

As well as being a positive good for ventilation, infiltration must be considered for all its effects. One is that it obviously imposes a load on the heating system of a building in winter and on the cooling system in summer. These loads are much harder to predict than the easily measurable loads of heat loss or gain through walls, windows, and roofs. The type of window (or door) and frame to be selected and the quality of workmanship in the construction are imponderables that the designer must estimate in planning a heating or cooling system. Prudence dictates that a dim view be taken, and that the design be based on a higher rate of leakage than the designer hopes will be obtained. The odds here are all in favor of reasonable conservatism. The factor is almost never a large proportion of the heating or cooling load and somewhat overestimating it adds comparatively little to the size of heating or cooling equipment. Underestimating it, on the other hand, can lead to extremely unhappy occupants and perhaps disastrously expensive corrective measures.

An aspect of infiltration not touched upon when considering it as ventilation is that it brings in outdoor air as is. If the atmosphere is dusty, dirty, or filled with industrial odors, that is the way the interior will be. Mechanical ventilation, it will be seen, can help correct some of those problems.

Finally, infiltration causes a phenomenon known as "stack effect" in tall buildings and can be an unpleasant feature. In planning a highrise building, the designer should be aware of the danger of stack effect and take precautions to minimize its nuisance value. There is no way to eliminate it entirely. Consider what makes it happen.

Think of a tall building on a cold day. Inside the air is warmed to comfort temperature. Outside is cold air which is heavier, volume for equal volume. The temperature variation is enough to create a noticeable difference in weights of the air, and the taller the building, the greater the total amount of that difference, called the stack effect.

This effect causes the outside air to try to enter the building at or near its bottom and escape at or near its top. Designers should discourage the process emphatically. Why? Because unless the stack effect is controlled the unbridled leakage of outside air in the lower part of the tall building will cause the first floor lobby and perhaps the lower floor apartments to be cold; it will produce a most unpleasant and unmelodious whistle caused by incoming air rushing through the entrance and elevator door cracks and may even be so strong that many people will be physically unable to open out-swinging doors at the lobby level. The problem occurs as long as it is colder outside than in, and the colder the weather, the worse the nuisance. Practically speaking, it is usually of little concern when the temperature is above freezing outside.

What can be done about it? Simply to impede vertical motion of free air up through the building in every way possible. It is not possible to close off the vertical passages in a building completely. There are elevator shafts, pipe and duct shafts, stairways, and, in some buildings, smoke towers, but attention to detail can minimize the chimney effect of these necessary vertical risers. Elevator doors can be of better than the cheapest construction, well-fitted and permanently well operating. They should be closed automatically when the elevator is at rest, waiting for a call signal. Pipe and duct entrances into mechanical shafts must be thoroughly and permanently sealed, and to secure them further the shafts themselves must be sealed securely at periodic intervals in the building's height. Doors on the various floors leading into the exit stairways must be kept closed and should be tight-fitting, weatherstripped, and with solid thresholds. These measures should not be considered an unnecessary or burdensome expense. They can reduce stack effect materially. Dampers that permit smoke towers to discharge their intended function of smoke removal must be well made, and close fitting, tightly sealed when closed. If permitted by code, the main entrance doors should be revolving, which work better against leakage and are easier to operate against whatever stack effect remains after all the precautions have been taken. Front entrance and rear service doors should open into vestibules whose depth is great enough that the likelihood of inner and outer doors being open at the same time is reduced, although this possibility, of course, can never be eliminated entirely.

If the designer has successfully completed these steps, stack effect will be at a minimum, and whatever remains will have to be accepted on the premise that the planner has done all that is reasonably possible.

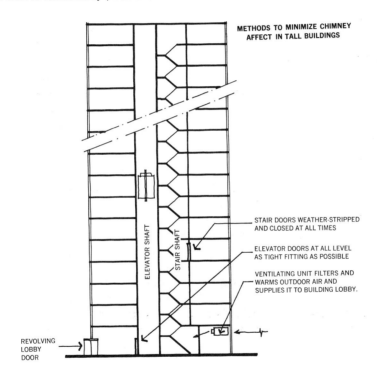

METHODS TO MINIMIZE CHIMNEY AFFECT IN TALL BUILDINGS

ELEVATOR SHAFT

STAIR SHAFT

STAIR DOORS WEATHER-STRIPPED AND CLOSED AT ALL TIMES

ELEVATOR DOORS AT ALL LEVEL AS TIGHT FITTING AS POSSIBLE

VENTILATING UNIT FILTERS AND WARMS OUTDOOR AIR AND SUPPLIES IT TO BUILDING LOBBY.

REVOLVING LOBBY DOOR

EXHAUST VENTILATION

Odors and excessive moisture generated in kitchens and bathrooms are best positively removed. In the preceding examination of infiltration the assumption was made that kitchens and baths had outside walls and windows and thus required no positive ventilation. The conclusion is valid according to most building codes but does not necessarily represent good practice. Even when there are bathroom windows, they will seldom be opened in cold weather, and if the wind is wrong, kitchen odors may be spread all over the house rather than evacuated through an open window.

If either of these rooms is interior, as they so often are, there is no question. Whatever the code, it will require positive exhaust ventilation.

Exhaust systems may be individual, central, or a combination of the two, a situation similar to that discussed for heating and cooling systems. First, individual systems call for an exhaust fan or blower for each kitchen and usually for each bathroom as well, although it is possible to combine exhausts from two or more bathrooms through ductwork to a single exhaust fan serving one dwelling unit. Kitchen and bathroom exhausts should never be combined. The kitchen exhaust fan is controlled by a switch of its own and is used as the occupant wishes. If each bathroom is served by its own fan, it may be controlled by a switch or wired to operate when the light is turned on. In interior bathrooms it is particularly important that the fan be built with motor overload protection, so that failure in the motor will be safeguarded electrically and will not cause coincident failure of the bathroom light. Bathroom exhaust fans discharge outdoors, probably through small ducts in the ceiling construction or directly through an outside wall. Each has a self-closing damper to permit air to flow out when the fan is running but to prevent outside air from blowing back in when it is not. Another desirable feature is a time delay relay that lets the fan run for a short time after the light is turned off. Kitchen exhausts usually discharge in the same way, with one exception. A kitchen exhaust system has been developed in which a hood, usually of finished and pleasing design, is mounted over the cooking range to entrap most of the fumes. The hood is an assembly that includes a blower and a combined filter and odor remover. The filter removes grease and dirt. The other component is activated charcoal or a similar substance which has the property of adsorbing minute particles that cause odors. The air thus treated is relatively clean and odor free and is discharged right back into the kitchen rather than outdoors. This process, of course, does nothing to remove kitchen heat, but it very materially reduces the need for makeup air in a multidwelling building. The savings in heating and cooling costs corresponds. The odor-removing substance will finally adsorb to its saturation and must be replaced or regenerated, an operation that is necessary, depending on the characteristics of the material used, once to four times a year.

Central systems are for multidwelling buildings and are particularly applicable to highrise concrete construction in which individual systems offer structural problems. Tiers of bathrooms or kitchens are served by duct risers, built with inlets from each bath or kitchen. Space must be found in the apartment plans for these duct risers, which usually increase in size as they near the central blower. Often these ducts can be located within the space that contains the plumbing riser pipes, especially since that space is always contiguous to the kitchen or bathroom. If the building is more than a few stories high, inclusion of duct risers will necessitate an increase in the size of the pipe shaft, which means loss of usable space in the dwellings, but the total shaft increase in actual area lost to the apartments is often more than justified by convenience, appearance, and construction cost.

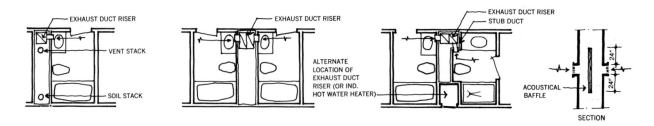

The central system duct risers may feed individual exhaust fans, usually roof-mounted directly above the riser. A number of risers may be grouped above the topmost ceiling to be served by one exhauster on the roof. If there is adequate space between the roof and the top-floor ceiling for plumbing, heating, and cooling pipes as well as exhaust ducts (usually 3 ft will do), all the risers may be picked up by ductwork mains running in that space and feeding central blowers, separate for kitchen and bathroom exhaust, mounted in the elevator machine penthouse. The decision will usually be based on cost preference, although other factors may enter. If a large part of a roof is used for recreational purposes, the individual exhausters cannot be used, and a single large blower hidden in the penthouse is preferred. One point should be clarified at this time. The exhaust risers do not have to move air to the top of the building. It is usually most practical to discharge it there, away from the likelihood of causing a nuisance, but sometimes it may be more convenient to move air downward to a point of discharge not far above the ground. This might apply in particular to a very tall building, more than 30 stories high. The size of riser ducts, and thus the shafts in which they are concealed, can be kept from growing out of hand by splitting them, taking the upper half of the building to the roof and the lower half down to an above-grade discharging blower.

An important caution in central systems is that noise from one dwelling must not be transmitted through the ducts to another. Carefully designed acoustical baffles at the register inlets in each apartment, and also in the riser itself, will eliminate this hazard. In fact, with proper precautions it is quite practical to serve back-to-back kitchens or bathrooms in separate residences with a single riser, thus saving space and cost. A last practical precaution is especially important in systems with individual roof fans for the risers. Here the fan is close above the exhaust register in the top-floor dwelling and must be selected carefully. The acoustical lining of the riser and the fan mounting curb provided will prevent the fan noise from being heard through the nearby register.

Central systems operate continuously or blowers are controlled by timers on a fixed schedule to operate certain hours of the day and night. If operation is continuous, heat and cooling are pulled out of the building, whether or not ventilation is needed in a particular room, an expensive waste of fuel and energy. If operation is timed, the waste is reduced, but will still exist, besides which exhaust may not be available when occupants with unusual hours need it most.

The combined exhaust system attempts to use the strength and discard the disadvantages of the individual and central systems. There are two principal types, both of which feature the common risers of the central system. In the first, each kitchen or bath is equipped with its small fan or blower, as in the individual system, but they discharge into the common riser, each through a self-closing damper that permits air to enter the riser but not to back up out of it when the fan is not running. The system has the advantage of controlling use when needed, with consequent energy savings and some saving in the size of the riser itself. In this system the direction of air in the common riser should always be upward.

In the second combined system each exhaust outlet is equipped with a motor-driven damper instead of a fan of its own. The light switch or ventilating switch in the bathroom or kitchen opens this damper and exhausts the room when needed. Otherwise the damper is tightly closed. This system requires an added area of sensitivity, which recommends the use of one large exhaust blower for the bathroom and one for the kitchen. If 19 out of 20 dampers are closed, the central blower must not be engaged in trying to pull the capacity for all 20 out of that one open damper. It must respond to the load. This response can be accomplished by pressure-sensing devices in the main air stream, which will close specially designed dampers at the blower itself or open them as necessary to maintain nearly constant pull throughout the system.

Either of the combined systems, but especially the second, will usually call for higher construction cost than the individual or central systems. When operating costs are considered, as they should be especially in these days of dizzying increases in energy fees, the payback will be rapid and the first investment more than justified. There is one advantage to be cited for the energy-wasteful central exhaust system, however. It has the minimum of moving equipment and will thus engender the lowest maintenance time and costs. By the same token, of course, if there is a breakdown in the central system or in the damper-type of combined system, all or a substantial number of dwellings will be without exhaust.

SUPPLY (MAKE-UP AIR) VENTILATION

For every cubic foot, inch, centimeter, or molecule of air exhausted from a building, an equal volume will enter. This can happen by leakage through cracks around windows and doors, one of the less desirable effects of which is the simultaneous entrance of dirt. Even beyond that, a high rate of suction through window cracks during a heavy rain can actually pull water into the rooms in sufficient volume to drench carpeting and damage furniture.

As long as windows and doors have to be opened and as long as winds blow, there will be air leakage, but it can be held under some control by the deliberate introduction of outside air into the building by some method of supply ventilation. Here are some of the options. In every case it is to be understood that the air introduced must be filtered and warmed or cooled to conform with building requirements.

1.   Individual room coolers are equipped with small openings to permit them to take in from the outdoors a portion of the total air circulated. They are usually fitted with manually controlled dampers, and the occupant can decide whether makeup air will be introduced—a rather haphazard method.

2.   The same kind of manually controllable outdoor air intake can be furnished with fan-coil units, either individual room or full residence type. In regions in which freezing temperatures are encountered it is unusual and dangerous to open to the outdoors fan-coil units that are centrally fed with warm and/or chilled water. No matter how carefully the controls are designed and installed, the dangers of freezing and bursting a pipe in any one of a great many units is too great a risk in view of the amount of damage than can be caused. If, however, an apartment unit has direct expansion cooling and electric heat, in which there is nothing to freeze, it may be a good way of bringing makeup air into the building. This reasoning does not hold only for multidwelling buildings. A residential furnace system with or without direct expansion cooling can be equipped with an outdoor air connection. All too few are.

3.   In multistory buildings an effective way to admit outdoor air is in a central supply system which draws it into all the public corridors of the structure. A way must then be found to direct the air from the corridors into the apartments, where it will make up their exhausted air. This can be done by deliberately creating gaps around the apartment doors and inserting rubber bumpers in the door frames to perform the dual function of permitting air to get in around them and at the same time decreasing the noise of closing doors. The bottom edges, however, should be sealed to prevent discoloration of carpets. Distribution of corridor supply air is not critical. Unless the corridor is unusually long, air supplied through a grille at one location will find its way to the points at which it is needed to make up exhaust. Besides apartment ventilation, an advantage of this system is that corridors are at a higher air pressure than the apartments, which helps to make corridors odor free and should eliminate the transmission of odors from one apartment to another. Even more important, smoke from a fire in one apartment will tend to be contained there if the public corridor is under pressure. If the building heating and cooling system features apartment fan-coil units in equipment rooms adjacent to the public corridor, they can take in corridor air for makeup purposes. It is possible also to introduce central supply air directly into the apartments through supply risers of the same nature as the exhaust risers, but this method is quite expensive to

construct and loses the advantage of pressurizing the corridor. If a central supply system has been installed in a building with variable exhaust, the supply blower(s) should be synchronized with the exhaust. If exhaust blowers operate on a timer, the supply blower should also be controlled in that way. If the system is the combined type with individual motorized kitchen and bathroom dampers and total volume control of the main exhaust blowers, the supply blower should be controlled in parallel. That parallel will usually be with the kitchen exhaust blower because it generally handles more air than the bathroom exhauster.

4.   Another good way of bringing ventilation and makeup air into a building is by an induction system, which has already been described. The primary air is 100% outdoor air.

5.   What quantity of makeup air should be introduced into a residential building by its supply ventilation system? There is a range of possibilities rather than firm rules.

    a.   Supply a volume exactly equal to the air exhausted to put the building in balance.

    b.   Supply 10 to 25% more than the exhaust quantity to pressurize the building and reduce (or eliminate) infiltration and stack effect.

    c.   Accept the fact that there will be some infiltration leakage due to wind, regardless of building pressure, and design the supply system to provide the difference between the total air exhausted and calculated normal leakage.

    d.   Arbitrarily select a proportion of the total air exhausted, between 40 and 75%, and let that be the capacity of the supply system(s).

Options (a) and (b) appear to be most logical, but experience tends to show otherwise. Winds are variable. On still, cold days (b) may pump in and heat far more air than is needed. On windy days there will probably be substantial leakage on the windward side in either case. Option (c) provides the designer with the comforting knowledge that the design is defensible, but (d) works just as well, especialy when used by engineers experienced in multidwelling planning.

In a discussion of air supply systems a word should be said about air filtering. On a rising scale of excellence we discuss first the filters provided by manufacturers in induction system units. They are thin fibrous screens, which can keep only the coarsest lint from getting to the induction unit's water coil. The primary air, however, has been thoroughly and effectively filtered in its central unit, where it was also warmed or heated and put under pressure.

Filters for apartment fan-coil units and for individual room coolers are also furnished by the manufacturer and are a small step above the quality of induction unit filters. Because a blower does move the air through them, they can offer a bit more resistance and do a little better filtering job.

Filters for entire residential units, such as apartment fan-coils or residential furnaces, are usually better quality and more effective in air cleaning. They may be the disposable type that uses fiberglass or a similar filtering medium, for single use only, or the cleanable type of steel fiber or like construction which can be washed clean and reused. At the highest level of filtering efficiency now available are the extremely effective units that attract dirt particles by electrostatic charging. They are particularly favored by sufferers from hay fever and other allergies because they free the air of tiny pollen particles that the ordinary filters cannot trap.

For large central air units, such as corridor supply or induction primary air supply, the disposable, permanent, washable or electrostatic filters described above are applicable. The favorite, probably, is still another type. This is a roll of fiberglass or similar filtering material that is motor driven to move slowly through the air stream. When the entire roll has unwound itself, it is discarded and a new one installed. The maintenance is much easier than is required to change a large number of filter cells.

VENTILATION SPACE REQUIREMENTS

Crucial in the planning of multistory residential buildings is the space that must be allocated to duct and pipe risers, lost space in the architect's view, but nonetheless necessary. Varying code and load requirements in different localities make it impossible to set hard and fast rules, but a few principles can be supplied, and an example or two may help to show how to apply them.

1. For each apartment bathroom air should be exhausted at a rate of 10 to 15 air changes per hour; that is, the volume of air exhausted in an hour should be 10 to 15 times the room volume. Assuming that the room height is 8 ft, this translates to an exhaust rate of 1.33 or 2.0 cubic feet of air per minute (cfm) for each square foot of floor area.

2. For each kitchen allow 12 to 18 changes per hour. With 8-ft ceilings, this equals 1.6 to 2.4 cfm per square foot of floor area.

3. For *individual* exhaust systems these quantities set the sizes of the small exhaust fans. For *central* systems the total of all bathroom quantities defines the required capacity of the bathroom exhaust fan (and the same for the kitchen), whereas the subtotals of the various tiers and collections of tiers determine the duct sizes to serve those subdivisions. The main ducts of the *combined* systems are sized like the central system ducts, except that use factors may be assumed because all apartments will certainly not be exhausted at any one time.

4. Duct sizes are determined by a simple formula:

Area (in square feet) is the air volume (cfm) divided by air velocity in feet per minute (fpm).

The smaller the air quantity, the lower the permissible velocity. This is a physical truth based on friction and noise levels, and, to avoid a lengthy excursion into physics, should be accepted on faith in this treatise. To be specific, for basic central systems the following rules can be used to give first approximations of duct sizes to aid a designer.

Air quantities up to 1500 cfm, velocity to 1000 fpm
Air quantity from 1500 to 2800 cfm, velocity to 1100 fpm
Air quantity from 2800 to 4000 cfm, velocity to 1200 fpm
Air quantity from 4000 to 7000 cfm, velocity to 1350 fpm
Air quantity above 7000 cfm, velocity to 1500 fpm

Having proposed some guiding rules, let us immediately list the exceptions. First, exhaust outlets whose design incorporates built-in acoustical treatment which effectively dampens air flow noise in ductwork have been developed. The outlets themselves are comparatively expensive but they save at least part of their cost by permitting higher riser air velocities and thus smaller duct sizes. They also save space. If these outlets are used, the recommended riser velocities may be increased 50%. Second, if the combined exhaust system is used, risers and collector mains should be sized to take advantage of their diversity at any given time. The first half of each riser, considered in the direction of air flow, should be sized for 100% use; the next quarter at 80%; the final quarter plus collector mains and blower itself at 70% of the total capacity of all the inlets. Finally, corridor supply risers can be greatly reduced by going to high velocity with acoustical air valves to control noise.

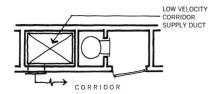

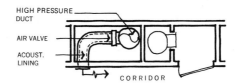

MISCELLANEOUS VENTILATION

The discussion on ventilation has centered around the residential units themselves, as the most important. Only mention need be given to miscellaneous requirements, some or all of which may be found in any project.

1.   Indoor automobile parking facilities. Removal of engine exhaust fumes, with provision for makeup air, warmed or unwarmed, depending on whether the garage is heated.

2.   Commercial areas, such as shops, restaurants, and grocery stores require their own complete HVAC systems, which may or may not be served, fully or in part, by the apartment building system. See the following section for further discussion of these options.

3.   Building service areas. Typical are the rubbish room, where garbage and trash are accumulated before being burned or baled, the elevator machine penthouse and electrical transformer rooms, where excess heat must be removed, repair shops, service shops (such as valet services), and the manager's office, all needing some combination of cooling, heating, air supply, and air exhaust.

MAINTENANCE AND OPERATION OF HVAC EQUIPMENT

In concluding this section on heating, ventilating, and air conditioning, let us give consideration to important factors in design and planning that concern the ultimate success and economical use of whatever systems have been chosen. The purpose here is not to remind the user that motors must be lubricated and filters cleaned or changed. Nor is it to estimate actual operating costs of a project. There are too many variable factors to make a general estimate practical. What is intended is to bring out factors that an owner or developer forgets only at great peril to the project.

First it is vital that all equipment be placed in such a way that every part of it can be reached and serviced. This may be self-evident, but in their zeal to make maximum living use of space all too many planners crowd equipment so unmercifully that it is dangerous or even impossible to maintain and operate properly.

Next are general considerations of operating costs. Who pays for what? Fan-coil systems have proved their worth, yet there is a small motor in every fan-coil unit which may run all or nearly all of the time. It is a small cost per hour, but over thousands of hours each year that cost is significant. Does the occupant pay this cost on the comparatively high individual electric rate or does the project pay on its much lower bulk rate? If the occupant pays, has that fact been made clear? Has the kind of small motor in these units been carefully considered in the light of its electrical efficiency? Specifically, one type of motor may cost $10 more than another. In a building with a thousand fan-coil units that means an initial expenditure $10,000 greater, a sum of money nobody gives away. The efficiency of the more expensive motor, however, may be such that the initial cost will be paid back in a year or less in lower bills for electricity.

Another electrical bill item that should be weighed in the planning process is the

COMPONENTS OF DESIGN—HVAC

"demand charge." Prudent equipment planning may provide a small refrigeration unit, for example, for mild weather use, saving hundreds of dollars in electrical bills for such months as April, May, and October. Higher installation cost may thus be returned in a few years. Such a unit might serve commercial areas only.

The use of various fuels for heating and different motive powers for cooling have been discussed as alternatives. Each project deserves a careful analysis of initial installation and long-range operating costs for each fuel and each method of powering refrigeration. There is no set answer that suits all cases. This year's project may show results quite different from last year's. Only after such an analysis can a fair opinion be reached and implemented.

FUEL AND ENERGY CONSERVATION

Consistent with sound engineering practice, conservation has been discussed in relation to design and operation of HVAC systems. But in view of the ever-more crucial importance of energy saving it is appropriate to bring various facts and suggestions together in a composite easy-to-locate list:

1. INSULATION. Not only do the gross areas of wall, window, and roof need to be considered, but also bothersome details such as edges of floors at or below grade, eaves and other overhangs, spandrel beams, and pipe spaces.

2. CONSTRUCTION. Parts of a building must fit together tightly, both when the building is new and when it is old. Here again attention to detail is of paramount importance. Joinings must be designed and sealed in a way that will prevent leakage of air or water from outside.

3. ORIENTATION. When feasible, take advantage of the sun's path, of trees and hills. Use the sun when it is needed; exclude it when it is troublesome.

4. PASSIVE SOLAR HEAT. Free use of the sun for heating depends on orientation. Other factors to be considered are use of glass, types of materials inside a building which can absorb and even store heat, solar angles to aid heating but permit cooling in its season, even the homely truth that bare branched trees will let sunlight through in winter whereas full leafing holds it out in summer. Passive solar heat depends on common sense.

5. ACTIVE SOLAR HEAT. Growing use of manufactured and catalogued equipment signals important advances in conservation through immediate use of our world's major source of energy. Home-made solar collectors are not to be excluded, but the growing market for solar products presages lower costs which, in turn, will encourage the upward spiral of use. Wholesale collection through use of satellites will have to be very carefully studied for effects on weather, crop growth, and similar vital factors.

6. COMBUSTION EFFICIENCY. Manufacturers will be motivated by competition to at least produce furnaces and boilers of maximum efficiency. As energy costs continue to rise, they will justify higher equipment costs first. A word of caution is appropriate for "retrofitting" existing furnaces and boilers to improve operating efficiency. There are numerous devices manufactured to improve combustion, and there undoubtedly will be many more. They promote better heat exchange by promoting action of flue gases, provide improved union of fuel and air molecules, and correct poorly designed chimneys, hold heat in the boiler or furnace when the burner has stopped rather than let it escape uselessly. Every idea has merit, but the sales promotions tend to make extravagant promises. "We will save 15% of your fuel bill." This is very possible, but such blanket statements are suspect because of the great variety of heating plants and situations.

148

7. OPERATING SCHEDULES. Let us consider two examples:

a. In a single-family residence, should the garage be heated through the winter? In most cases lack of heat will not injure the automobile, but are there any other stored materials which might be damaged? Do adjoining rooms have sufficient heat if the garage wall is cold? How about heating only on Saturdays, when the homeowner is using the garage workshop? If heating is still deemed desirable after considering all these factors, will a controlled temperature just above freezing be satisfactory?

b. In a highrise building, can bathroom and kitchen exhausts be turned off at certain hours, along with the associated make-up air system for the corridors? An example, of course, is the block of hours from midnight to 6 A.M. in most residential buildings. But kitchen exhausts might well be off from 9A.M. to 11:30A.M. and from 2P.M. to 5P.M. on weekdays. Will residents permit this? Will building codes permit it? It may well be that economic pressures are going to demand "yes" answers to both those questions.

8. AIR PURIFYING. Must bathroom and kitchen exhaust air be expelled from a building? Existing odor- and grease-removing devices, plus future improvements in this kind of equipment, might mean that the only replacement air needed will be the very small amount required to carry replenishment oxygen and prevent buildup of excessive humidity. This can provide tremendous fuel savings.

9. TEMPERATURE CONTROLS. Design *and maintain* controls which will prevent overheating or overcooling. The emphasis is not frivolous. Too often controls are neglected for years, cease to function, and waste prodigious amounts of energy as a result. No matter how simple or sophisticated they may be, controls require attention like any other moving equipment. Failure to give that attention can be expensive indeed.

10. HEAT PUMPS. These have been dealt with at p. 122. Although limited in usefulness in cold climates, their contribution to conservation during mild weather becomes more and more important as energy costs increase. The initial investment payback is hastened, and the heat pump should now be more seriously considered though once it seemed infeasible.

11. HEAT EXCHANGE. This concept applies to multiple-family housing in which bathroom and kitchen exhaust have been found necessary and in which there is outdoor make-up air to compensate partially for the exhaust. In winter, some of the heat from the exhaust air can be extracted and transferred to the make-up air. Exhaust is at space temperature, approximately 70° F, and the make-up air in winter is usually much colder. By passing the two streams of air through a properly designed heat exchanger the transfer can be effected.

This kind of air-to-air heat exchanger is very bulky, and, in an original design, space may not be found for it. A much more compact although less direct and less efficient heat transfer method is that of circulating a nonfreeze liquid through coils in exhaust and makeup air streams. The pumped liquid picks up heat from the exhaust air and surrenders it to the makeup air. In analyzing the gains from these conservators, one must remember to add to the debit side the extra power needed to force air and/or pump liquid through the heat exchangers. And on the credit side, add the energy saved for cooling in summer if the building is air conditioned.

COMPONENTS OF DESIGN—PLUMBING   5

Harry S. Nachman

Water is a necessity of life. In the design of buildings, particularly of residential buildings, we expect without possibility of exception that all residents will have free access to a water supply adequate to their basic needs. In fact, our laws make this mandatory.

"Basic needs" have expanded beyond the use of water to sustain life, to encompass sanitation and frequently fire control. That sentence just about provides a definition of plumbing as applied to buildings. Somewhat incidentally the distribution of fuel gas is often included in the plumbing trade but merely because of custom and some resemblance in appearance rather than because of any relationship.

The quest for water has determined the location of camps, settlements, and cities throughout human history and is the first problem to be disposed of in the planning of a housing project, whether a single residence or a tract of thousands. There are two categories of water source, individual and communal, and at least one must be available before any further planning can take place.

Individual sources of water may be subterranean streams or strata tapped by wells, a nearby river or lake, or rainfall which is collected and saved. Surface water is becoming more generally polluted and rainfall is usually not reliable.

For the most part, therefore, individual sources of water are sought in wells. There is no known rule predicting the depth or potential yield of an underground stratum of water to be tapped. The best guide is experience in the area. The more wells drilled, the better the chance of locating an additional adequate source. By the same token, the more wells drilled, the more water extracted from the stratum, and the greater the danger of exhaustion or serious depletion. Occasionally a stratum is under sufficient pressure to force its water to the surface with enough pressure left to allow it to flow in volume. The well that taps this kind of source is called artesian, but most wells require pumps to lift the water to the surface and to add enough pressure to make it flow.

A well is dug by drilling a circular hole in the earth to whatever depth is required to find an adequate supply. A pipe of material impervious to corrosion is forced into the hole to provide a permanent channel for the upflow. The bottom sections of this pipe constitute a perforated circular screen, usually of brass, which is imbedded in the water-bearing stratum. Its perforations permit water to flow into the pipe and are designed to exclude as much clay, sand, and gravel as possible. For most residential projects the well pipe will range between 4 and 8 in., although larger developments may require larger pipe sizes. The well pump is built to fit into the well pipe. The pump shaft is driven by an electric motor or gas engine at the top of the well and must be protected from the weather or other harm by an adequate enclosure. Depending on the location of the pump house, heat may be required in a climate in which subfreezing temperatures occur. The water will not freeze when it is flowing from underground, but overnight or at any time when there is no flow the danger exists.

The second water-source category is municipal. One of the first services that identifies a hamlet, village, town or city as a viable community is a water distribution system consisting of a network of corrosion-resistant pipes called water mains. The network is generally located under or adjacent to streets and public alleys; it is well-mapped and can be tapped by users under conditions controlled by the municipality. "Municipality" in this sense may be misleading. The control of a water system is often vested in a private, profit-making water company operating under a municipal franchise. In any case, the user expects a reliable flow of pure water whenever it is needed.

WATER QUALITY

Purity with respect to organisms dangerous or deleterious to human and animal life is the first criterion of water quality. In municipal systems this purity is part of the agreement, expressed or implied, between the supplier and the user. In private systems safety is the responsibility of the user, whose purification treatment is administered according to official regulations and regularly and frequently monitored by the supervising authority. The basic treatment generally consists of adding small quantities of chlorine sufficient to kill harmful organisms, but limited to minimize the unpleasant taste associated with this gas.

Another chemical additive is fluorine. Discovery of a phenomenally low incidence of tooth decay in a particular area of the Southwest led to an analysis of the local water supply and the discovery of an unusually high (although still miniscule) concentration of fluorides. Further testing convinced many dental authorities that a definite relation-ship existed, and many communities have begun to introduce this compound into their water supplies. There has been some objection to this practice on socioreligious grounds and some questioning of the long-range side effects that still remain uncharted.

Certain chemicals and compounds found naturally in water contribute to a quality called "hardness." The property of hardness is not a threat to life or health, but "hard" water becomes undesirable on two counts. First, it is difficult to use soap effectively, for hardness inhibits the formation of lather. Second, when water is heated, the com-pounds it contains are rapidly driven out and deposited on the heating surfaces. This deposit builds up until it forms a highly effective insulating layer, which at best will impair the effectiveness of the heater and at worst destroy it. Not all of this deposit remains in the heater. Some will build up in the pipes until, after the passage of years, they may be completely clogged.

Water hardness is expressed in the proportion of the hardness-producing com-pounds in a volume of water. A conventional scale is parts per million (ppm), that is, molecules or grams of compounds per million molecules or grams of water. On this scale water will usually range between 75 and 700 ppm.

A process predictably called "softening" is used to treat water whose hardness is high enough to endanger heaters and piping and to make soap ineffectual. How hard is too hard? A reasonable rule is that water whose hardness is measured at less than 140 ppm needs no softening for ordinary use; between 140 and 350 ppm at least that portion of it to be heated should be treated; at more than 350 ppm all the water should be softened. The process of softening is a chemical treatment in which the addition of certain salts will hold the hardness-causing compounds in solution and prevent their precipitation, thus neutralizing their ill effects. Tanks and vessels to contain the salts require space and maintenance, and the planning of equipment rooms must be done with the knowledge that treatment will be required. The hardness of water to be used can be determined from data available at the community water source or, in the case of private supplies, by testing first samples of the well water found.

The softening process must be controlled, preferably limited, to maintain hardness in the 50- to 75-ppm range. Soap lathers so well in soft water that removing it becomes difficult, and water with zero hardness can become corrosive to certain kinds of pipe.

In the foregoing discussion of water quality two assumptions have been made. When purity is the issue, it is assumed that the water is to be used for direct consumption. When the issue is hardness, it is assumed that cleaning is the primary consideration, either for hot or cold water. In residential buildings these are the major uses of water, but there is at least one more common need and that is for irrigation, generally lawn sprinkling. A cleaning chore in which hardness is unimportant and in which the water quality is usually of no consequence is the hosing down of stairs, walks, or windows. The cost of softening and/or purifying it is wasted, and it should be removed from the general water service upstream of such processes. A warning to remember here is that no unpurified water be permitted to mix with that certified for drinking purposes. To carry that precept one more step, it is even more important that water that has been used for sanitary purposes by no mischance be allowed to re-enter the water supply system.

WATER PRESSURE

The planner must investigate not only the quality of the water to be received but also the pressure at which it will be delivered. Pressure is needed for three purposes. First, for convenience. Pressure at the last point of use must be strong enough to provide a brisk flow of water in order, for example, to fill a bathtub in less than an hour. Second, the pressure must be sufficient to overcome flow friction encountered by the water as it passes through water meter, pipes, heater, faucets, and any other fittings in the plumbing system. Anything moving has to fight friction, and water is no exception. Pressure is also needed to carry water up the height of a building. Water has substantial weight, and in order to lift it to its highest point of use there must be enough pressure at the bottom to hold its weight in the vertical pipe.

Water pressure is expressed in pounds per square inch (psi). For each additional floor of an ordinary residential building there must be about 4 additional psi just to lift the water to that level.

Let us use these principles in a practical example—a 13-story apartment building. For proper action in the showers and waterclosets on the top floor the manufacturer of plumbing fixtures recommends a pressure of 15 psi. After the piping system has been designed we are able to estimate pressure loss due to friction on the meter, pipes, and fittings at 10 psi. The calculation for total pressure required is simple:

Factor	Pressure Required
Pressure at top of system	15 psi
Allowance for friction	10
Thirteen-story height	52
Total	77 psi

Few public systems maintain pressures at so high a level. Therefore the available pressure must be supplemented by a pressure-increasing system.

Let us consider a typical municipal water system in which the delivery pressure at a given location does not fall below 50 psi. How much pressure will the interior booster system have to add to the main pressure?

Pressure required	77 psi
Pressure available in the main	50
Necessary addition by booster system	27 psi

To provide this pressure boost, mechanical pumps, usually driven by electric motors, must be employed, although gas engines or turbines or steam engines may fill the need in rare cases. Three systems are found in common use:

1. OVERHEAD STORAGE TANKS.   One or more tanks, of a capacity that approximates the building's estimated full-day water supply, are located high enough above the top floor to produce, by the weight of the water, the pressure required at the top-floor fixtures. Pumps of comparatively small volume which fill these tanks throughout the night and during the midday low-use hours keep the tank level high enough to serve early morning and evening peaks. Steel tanks should be lined with a corrosion-resistant substance and checked periodically to ensure the integrity of the lining. Tanks also are often made of wood, which is impervious to water corrosion, but which can entail leaking joints.

The advantages of this system are counted in the small pump size and correspondingly small maximum demand for electricity and in the storage capacity of a day's supply in the event of pump or power failure. The disadvantages are spatial and structural. The tanks are large and, to produce the needed pressure at the top of the system, must stand high above the top floor. Using the figures developed before, 15 psi at top-floor fixtures require that the lowest operating level of the tank be about 34 ft higher, necessitating a penthouse structure substantially taller than that usually required for elevator machinery and override. The structural consideration concerns the larger penthouse and the weight of the filled tanks, a load that must be carried down the height of the building into the foundations.

2. THE HYDROPNEUMATIC TANK SYSTEM.   This approach was developed to avoid the added penthouse requirements described above. Intermittently operating pumps, sized to deliver the maximum flow of water anticipated, pump into a tank of moderate size, kept about half full of water and half of air under pressure equal to that needed to serve the building. The air "cushion" permits a part of the tank's water to be drawn off for use before the air pressure drops low enough to start the water pumps. The cushion and tank dimensions are selected so that the pumps will not run oftener than 12 times an hour during peak use and may mean only a few operations in six hours at night. Over a period of time the air cushion is slowly absorbed into the water; therefore a small air compressor must be part of the installation.

In both systems two pumps should be considered a necessity, each large enough to assume the entire load. Water supply is too important to entrust to a single mechanical device. The pumps should be used alternately to keep them in running condition and the wear equal.

3. PUMPING SYSTEM.   Begrudging even the reduced space required by the hydropneumatic tank, engineers have developed improved valves, controls, and pumps to produce the constant pumping system. In apartment buildings it contains three pumps.

One small one, called the "lead" pump, is sized for about 25% of the maximum expected demand and is on the line constantly or nearly so. The other two, equal in size, may be planned to serve 55 to 75% of the anticipated demand. Automatic controls shift the pumps into and out of action as dictated by load requirements, and control valves regulate output between the capacity steps represented by the pumps; for example, if the actual demand is 10% capacity, the lead pump will operate alone and its control valve will throttle its output from its 25% potential to the 10% demand. For periods of zero demand, such as the night hours, the system may be able to shut down entirely.

The great advantage of the constant pumping arrangement, known as the instantaneous system, lies in its saving of space and tank costs. These savings may be accentuated if the lead pump is eliminated and a two-pump system is installed. Less sensitive to fluctuating demands, this even more simplified system subjects the two pumps to much more operation at low capacity against heavily throttled control valves and is widely used when construction first-costs completely outweigh longer-range operating costs and problems.

Drawbacks in the instantaneous system are higher electrical costs because of the constant or nearly constant operation and greater maintenance costs consequent to the comparatively complex and fine-tuned controls.

In a very tall building a serious pressure problem of which planners should be aware is created by the very nature of the structure. Note in the foregoing example of the 13 story building that a pressure of 77 psi is required at its base. This approaches the 80 psi maximum safe pressure rating of standard fittings and faucets assembled in plumbing fixtures. The latter are critical. Whereas extras strong pipe fittings and general service valves are commercially available at premium prices that are not punitive, special fittings for mass-produced plumbing fixtures would, if available at all, be prohibitively expensive. Therefore, if the height of a building exceeds 13 living floors above the lowest living floor (often the second floor of the building), steps must be taken to protect the fixtures on the lower floors.

If the building height is only a few floors more than the safe maximum, these provisions may take the form of pressure-reducing valves in hot- and cold-water lines which serve the endangered lower floors to keep their supply within the safe limit. If the number of stories greatly exceeds the safe maximum, the number and arrangement of reducing valves will become awkwardly large and difficult to locate and service, and a "zoned" system is used in preference; for example, in a 25-story building the top 12 floors will be served by one pressure-boosting system, the lower 13 by a second. If overhead tanks are used, one set will be located in the penthouse as usual and will feed down only to the fourteenth floor. Space will have to be found at about the eighteenth floor for a lower zone tank system to supply the lower floors. If hydropneumatic tanks or the instantaneous system are used, the lower zone will be fed by one system in the basement, the upper zone by a second system operating at the required high pressure. The pipes distributing water from the high-zone pump system pass through the lower 13 floors without any connections made to them. The pipes and fittings, and any valves required, are selected for the pressure encountered and are commercially available, as mentioned before. By the time these "express" risers reach the fourteenth living floor the pressure due to height will have been sufficiently reduced to suit the fixture fittings.

In tall residential buildings particular care must be exercised to control water pressure in public laundries. Washing machines are manufacturer-rated for quite low pressures, compared with sanitary fixtures, and no matter whether or not the system is zoned, the laundries will require pressure-reducing valves unless they are at the top of the building or at the top of a pressure zone.

Another consideration in tall buildings is the pressure required on the ground floor. Often substantial water is needed for lawn sprinkling and car washing, and sometimes the laundry is located on that floor. To avoid the energy expense of pumping this water up to the pressure required to reach the top of the building (and then possibly reducing the pressure again for the laundry) it may be worthwhile to use direct main pressure, even though this method may require additional piping. Water is taken off the building service line before it goes to the booster pump and used for first-floor needs at main pressure. If this is done, however, the technique must be carried through into the hot-water system as well.

WATER HEATING

A good rule for domestic water heating keeps it at the lowest temperature acceptable to the residents. It has been noted that corrosion and mineral deposits are both accelerated with rising temperatures. A temperature of 140°F is considered maximum for general use to avoid discomfort or scalding. If residents will accept temperatures 10 to 15°F below that level, so much the better. For special uses that require hotter water, such as apartment dishwashers in a residential building or large commercial dishwashers in a public restaurant located in the building, local booster heaters must be provided with the machines. It is not advisable to operate an entire domestic hot-water system at 160°F simply because apartment dishwashers need that temperature to operate safely and are not equipped with booster heaters by the manufacturer.

Boosters in private dishwashers should be electrically heated. For general purposes domestic water heating follows the pattern of the comfort heating plant. If, for example, individual heating-cooling plants "fueled" by electricity are decided on, apartment water heaters are often consistent with the purposes of the individual heating-cooling plant; that is , the operating expense is allocated to the user's direct account.

If, on the other hand, a project has a central heating plant, domestic hot water will most frequently be generated as part of that plant, usually, although not invariably, using the same fuel. Then there is the matter of deciding whether domestic water is to be heated by the heating plant boilers, by independent heaters, or by a combination of the two. If a project maintains only one heating boiler, the domestic water should be heated independently. A boiler should be taken out of service for thorough inspection and refurbishing once a year; therefore a single-unit plant would have this done only at the expense of occupants who would be deprived of hot water for a few days each summer, an unnecessary annoyance.

In a plant of two or more boilers advantages of heating domestic water in common with the space heating may be found in saving boiler room space and, quite probably, in a lower initial installation cost. It must be emphasized, however, that water heating does not come free. There is the idea that heat is being generated in winter anyhow, so why not use some of it for heating domestic water? The fact is, of course, that the more work done, the more fuel needed to do it, and that heating boilers must be increased in size if they are to heat domestic water as well. The size increase index given in the following table is subject to considerable variation, depending on building exposure, entering cold water temperature, and similar factors.

Outside Design Temperature (°F)	Percent of Boiler Load Required for Domestic Water Heating
−10	20
+10	25
+30	33

The more boilers in the plant, the more efficient the summer operation for heating domestic water. If there are two boilers of equal size, both will be much larger than required by the summer load, except in very mild climates. If there are five, one will be efficient for summer water heating in a rather cold part of the world.

The mechanics of heating domestic water from boilers are simple. The most popular heat exchanger is a steel shell that encloses a bundle of small-diameter copper tubes. Steam or hot water from the boiler passes over the tubes, and the water to be heated passes through them. The heating medium is controlled by the temperature of the heated water to maintain a reasonably uniform output regardless of the demand. The great advantage in the use of this heater is the small space it requires. As an example, a 200-unit project's hot water needs would be met by a steam-fed exchanger a little more than 8 in. in diameter and 7 ft long. This device can be tucked away conveniently in a boiler room. If the project can afford the moderate additional expense, it is always advisable to install two exchangers on a full standby basis, alternate them in operation, and have one ready at all times to take over when the other requires service. This amenity is sometimes omitted in the interest of first-cost economy on the premise that short-term lack of hot water is not a disaster. Even then it is well to have a spare copper tube "bundle" on hand for quick installation. Several days or weeks of delay in getting replacement parts for a single heater are hard on owner-occupant relations.

Separate domestic water heating may take the form of a boiler and heat exchanger used only for that purpose. More often, the process is combined into one vessel, or a battery of vessels, in which the fuel heats the domestic water directly, without an intermediate exchanger. The fuel may be gas, oil, or electricity, and the heater may contain some storage capacity for heater water. The subject of hot-water storage is further explored after a brief mention of combining boiler-powered heat exchangers and independent heaters in a single plant, a combination that can sometimes be justified as an economical means of standby availability. If, for example, gas is used for domestic water heating, but not for space heating, a project may be equipped with one gas-fired hot-water heater for normal use and a standby heat exchanger off the oil- or coal-fired boiler.

Hot-water storage capacity acts as a bank in which deposits are made in times of surplus to be drawn on in times of need. This reasoning stems from the fact that the use of water is far from uniform during a day. Peaks occur in the early morning and evening hours. A simplified example illustrates the point. Suppose that the total use of hot water in a day is calculated at 4800 gallons, an estimate based on published studies which have proved over many years to be accurate, though leaning toward the conservative side. Furthermore, the maximum consumption is expected to be 900 gallons between 7 and 8 A.M. Two extreme positions may be taken. In one position heating capacity is selected for the maximum hour's use, that is, sufficient to heat 900 gallons per hour from the entering temperature of the domestic cold-water service to the utilization temperature of 125 to 140° F. The other extreme provides just enough heating capacity to make up the full day's use by working through the full day. That would be 4800 gallons divided by 24 hours or 200 gallons per hour. The storage bank would have to be large enough to make up the greater requirements during the peak hours. The most demanding hour requires 900 gallons, during which the heater will produce its regular 200 gallons. The bank, therefore, must be able to disgorge the balance of 700 gallons.

One last proviso completes this example. The "bank" referred to is almost always a cylindrical steel storage tank. As hot water is drawn off during the tank's contribution periods, that water is replaced by cold makeup water. About 75% of the contents of a properly piped hot-water storage tank can be drawn off before the colder mixture begins to affect the temperature of the draw-off. Therefore the tank must be sized so that the calculated contribution is only 75% of the full tank capacity. In the above example that means that the full size of the tank would be 930 gallons.

There is a substantial advantage in the use of a storage tank for a central plant system. The smaller heater means a smaller boiler, a smaller chimney, and more efficient operation because the heater is in full use for a high proportion of each day. There are important disadvantages also. The tank is space consuming and expensive. Its installation cost is often considerably higher than the incremental cost of the larger heater needed for a no-storage system against the heater calculated for a full storage system. The tank will, in time, become corroded, need repairs and, finally, replacement. There is no universal rule for choosing between the two extreme systems or any compromise position (larger heater, smaller tank) between. Each project must be examined on its own merits.

HOT WATER CIRCULATION AND PROTECTION

During the late night hours, when there may be little or no need for hot water in a residential building, the temperature of the water lying dormant in the distribution system will fall to nearly that of the building, some 60°F below its desirable delivery temperature. The first resident looking for hot water in the morning will be faced with a pipeful of cool water to be drawn off before the hot water arrives.

The solution to this problem is the installation of a secondary piping system that will permit water to return to the heater from the farthest point of utilization at a flow rate rapid enough to prevent the water from cooling in the pipes. The circulation may be by gravity, produced by the difference in weight between the warmest water and the slightly cooled water which has traveled through the pipes, just as the gravity water-heating systems operate, described in an earlier chapter. Frequently, the circulation is urged along by the installation of a pump at the gathering point of all circulating lines.

Circulating systems are highly desirable in almost every kind of residential building. Small single-family or two-family residences with one bathroom per apartment or two back-to-back and not far from the kitchen may have so little hot water piping that a circulating system is unnecessary.

A final note on water heating is concerned with safety. As water is heated above 39°F it expands. Air chambers in the system provide a means of cushioning this expansion, but if there is excessive expansion or the air chambers are filled with water, it will be necessary to provide a pressure relief valve that will open automatically and without fail to expel enough water to prevent unsafe pressures from building up. Usually the release of a small quantity of water will lower system pressure. A second danger is in the failure of the heater controls, which could permit water temperature buildup to scalding levels. This, too, can be met by the installation of a relief valve that will permit the escape of the excessively hot water before it reaches the users.

The two functions are usually combined in one valve, called a pressure and thermal relief valve. If the valve discharges at all, it may do so unexpectedly at any time, and for protection of personnel the discharge outlet should be piped to a safe point of disposal, preferably immediately above a drain. This is a point to be remembered particularly when individual water heaters are installed in single dwelling units. The relief valve discharge must be directed to a place where it cannot hurt anyone nor do any damage by releasing water where it will not be disposed of quickly and safely.

WATER PIPING

Water piping must resist erosion and corrosion, erosion caused by the flow of the liquid and corrosion by chemical action. For example, when air is also present—and all water supplies contain some entrained air—water reacts with iron to form iron oxide compounds called rust. Thus, when used for water distribution, steel pipe is protected by the application of an electroplated zinc coat (zinc has high corrosion resistance) in a process called galvanizing.

Other common materials used for the purpose are copper and brass, cast iron, an asbestos-cement compound, and a number of plastic compounds. Copper is expensive but easily handled and joined. When available, it is a great favorite for the manufacture of water pipes. Despite the tendency of its base to rust, cast iron undergoes changes in the casting process that make the material resistant to corrosion, and it is frequently used for underground water piping, particularly in 3-in. sizes and larger, for which copper is expensive. The great weight of cast iron makes it less useful inside buildings, in which its support becomes a serious problem.

Asbestos-cement pipe, too, is heavy and not easy to work. It has also been most useful in underground applications. Plastic pipe materials have gained rapid popularity in recent years because of their moderate cost and ease of joining; they resist not only corrosion but also the flow of electrical currents that can sometimes cause problems in metallic pipes. One serious limitation of plastic pipes, which are readily available on the market, is their unsuitability to high temperatures. They must not be located near a boiler or flue which could produce a temperature above 160°F in the material. Thus their use for ordinary domestic hot-water conveyance is cause for some nervousness, for if the water temperature controls fail and permit water temperature to rise unduly, to the danger of scalding users is added the peril of serious damage to the piping system!

The arrangement of water piping in a building has a familiar treelike pattern. An entering service is analogous to the tree trunk, and branches and twigs spread out to the various points of use. In large buildings especially, the branches should be disconnectable by valves, so that repairs can be made in any part of the system with a minimum of interruption in the rest. If water pipes are concealed, as they often are in residential construction, it is mandatory that access be provided to the valves by suitable panels or openings and that the valves be well identified with the part of the piping system they serve.

The general distribution of a piping system is categorized as upfeed or downfeed, the importance of which is that space must be allowed accordingly in the building for distribution either (or both) at the top or bottom. In a building whose height permits the use of available water pressure without pumping, the cold water will almost always be fed up, with a distributing main at the low level and risers feeding the plumbing fixtures above. If an overhead tank is used for pressure boosting, the cold water will be downfed from the tank, and a pipe attic or similar space must be provided under the roof to accommodate the distributing main.

Hot water can also be upfed or downfed. In a building six stories high the water is often upfed in each tier of plumbing fixtures. At the top of each hot-water riser a return circulating line is connected and brought down alongside. The circulating lines are connected by a collector main running parallel to the hot-water distribution main and returning to the heater. If the building is taller than six stories, the length of the doubled riser piping becomes a serious expense, and it is sometimes possible to extend each riser a few feet into the pipe attic or top ceiling space, collect these extensions at that level, and return in a single circulating riser to the heater, an arrangement that can be reversed. A single hot-water supply riser may be brought up to the top of the building, distributed at that level, the individual risers downfed and extended a short distance downward to the ceiling of the lowest level, where the collector main picks them up and returns them to the heater. In all cases each return riser should be fitted with a manually adjustable balancing valve to make the circulation flow reasonably consistent throughout the system. These balancing valves, as well as the riser shutoff valves, must be accessible wherever they are located, and for this reason it may be necessary to run longer piping than would be needed only for distribution.

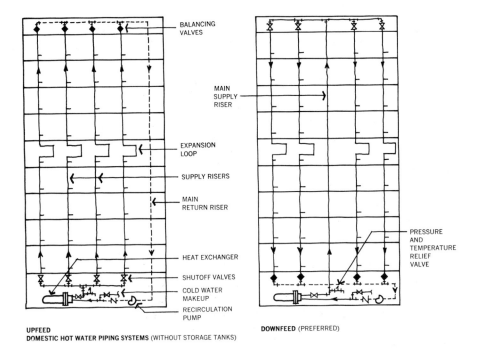

BALANCING VALVES

MAIN SUPPLY RISER

EXPANSION LOOP

SUPPLY RISERS

MAIN RETURN RISER

HEAT EXCHANGER

SHUTOFF VALVES

COLD WATER MAKEUP

RECIRCULATION PUMP

PRESSURE AND TEMPERATURE RELIEF VALVE

UPFEED

DOWNFEED (PREFERRED)

DOMESTIC HOT WATER PIPING SYSTEMS (WITHOUT STORAGE TANKS)

Sizing of hot-water recirculation pipes and pumps should be calculated, not just relegated to a rule-of-thumb treatment. Circulation problems are often due to undersized pipes or pumps. Obviously oversizing is undesirable, too, as a waste of money and energy.

Two dangers of damage to water pipes must be guarded against. The first is in the expansion and contraction of long runs, particularly in hot-water pipes. Expansion provisions for heating water pipes as previously described must be made, and all branches must be taken off mains and risers with a configuration of turns and bends that permits the branches to "give" as the main moves. This takes extra space, but it is absolutely essential disaster insurance.

The second peril is "water hammering." When a user opens the faucet of a plumbing fixture, water flows out and sets in motion an entire column of water in the branch, riser, and main. When the faucet is closed, usually abruptly, the momentum of the moving column must stop just as abruptly. Water is incompressible, as anyone can attest who has landed flat while diving, and reacts to the sudden flow interruption by slamming against the closed end of the pipe with destructive force. Not only does this produce an alarming noise, but it can cause damage to the pipe or adjoining portions of the construction. The cure for this hammering is to create air pockets in the piping system so that the water momentum can be spent by compressing air rather than by banging solid pipe. Every riser should be extended as much as possible beyond its highest branchoff, up to 2 ft, a dead length that remains as it was when installed, full of air. This air chamber serves as the needed cushion. Similarly, every branch should have its air chamber, perhaps half the length of the riser chamber. Some plumbing codes require that every plumbing fixture pipe connection be fitted with its own air chamber.

Hot-water piping should be insulated to minimize waste of heat. In cold weather, of course, the heat may not be wasted because it supplements what the heating system puts into the building, but in warm weather the loss of heat is a waste and possibly an annoyance. If the building is cooled, it adds to the cooling load and expense. Sometimes, parts of the hot-water piping system are left uncovered, but this "economy" is a first-cost saving only and will ultimately be lost in operating cost. Cold-water piping may have to be insulated for a different reason. If the water-supply temperature ever falls below the "dew point," condensation will appear on the exterior of the pipes (this is inelegantly called "sweating") and drip off and cause annoyance or damage to whatever or whomever is below. Thus, unless the water-supply temperature is certain to be high enough that sweating will never occur, insulation must be applied in a thickness sufficient to prevent it. Dew point of pipe surfaces is that temperature at which the air surrounding the pipes can no longer hold all the moisture it contains. So, as it is cooled by contact with the pipes, it deposits the excess moisture onto the cold surfaces as "dew." The insulation simply presents much warmer surfaces to the surrounding air.

BACK SIPHONAGE

If in extreme need or merely in a larcenous mood you want to siphon gasoline out of your neighbor's automobile, you set a pail below the gas tank level, insert a tube into the tank, suck sharply on the other end of the tube until gasoline begins to flow, and then drop that end into the pail. Flow will continue as long as there is liquid in the tank or until the pail is full and you pull the tube out. The pressure phenomenon that causes the flow to continue is called siphonage.

There is a parallel plumbing situation. I am washing the windows in my house. My pail of dirty water is half empty and I drop the hose into it and walk over to turn on the hose cock at the side of the house. The pail begins to fill when suddenly, down the street, a fire truck that has just arrived opens a fire hydrant wide. The enormous outflow of water at the hydrant causes the pressure at my end of the water main to drop suddenly to nothing. The disappearance of pressure causes the water in the pipes in my house to begin to flow backward down to the main that is below the level of my basement floor. This reversed flow starts a siphon from the pail through the open hose cock, and before I realize what is happening the dirty water has been siphoned out of the pail and into the water system, perhaps clear down into the main. When water pressure is restored, my neighbor (whose gasoline I have already stolen) may be drinking the water used for washing windows! The possibility may seem so far-fetched that it could not happen. Nevertheless, there have been occurrences of this kind, the liquid siphoned has been much more toxic than dirty window water, and in documented instances serious illness has resulted. It is imperative therefore that siphonage be prevented.

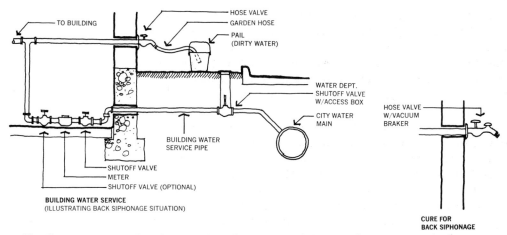

TO BUILDING

HOSE VALVE
GARDEN HOSE
PAIL
(DIRTY WATER)

WATER DEPT.
SHUTOFF VALVE
W/ACCESS BOX

CITY WATER
MAIN

BUILDING WATER
SERVICE PIPE

SHUTOFF VALVE
METER
SHUTOFF VALVE (OPTIONAL)

BUILDING WATER SERVICE
(ILLUSTRATING BACK SIPHONAGE SITUATION)

HOSE VALVE
W/VACUUM
BRAKER

**CURE FOR
BACK SIPHONAGE**

The first easy answer is to be sure that wherever possible water faucets run water from above the fixture; for example, some old-fashioned bathtubs and lavatories had spouts that admitted water low in the body of the fixture. The foregoing example of siphonage could then occur while the tub or basin was being filled if the water level was above the submerged spout. In tubs, lavatories, and sinks this possibility can be circumvented by placing the spout safely above the fixture's rim so that the water level cannot engulf it.

For washing machines, hose cocks, and toilets with flush valves the water cannot be introduced by free fall from above the fixture, and "vacuum breakers" must be installed. These devices are simple valves kept tightly closed by water pressure. When that pressure is released the device opens to permit air to enter, and air is the natural enemy of siphons. The siphoning cannot begin and there is no back flow. Plumbing codes now require vacuum breakers for use whenever over-rim supplies are not possible.

Antisiphon protection is required not only to protect the water supply from wastes, but from mixing with "process" water as well. Codes consider water used for heating, cooling, or refrigeration condensing as process water, which must be separated by an air gap from the domestic water.

WASTE DISPOSAL

For disposal purposes plumbing wastes are classified as storm and sanitary. Stormwater waste is rainfall or melted snow from building roofs and adjoining paved areas such as driveways, walks, and recreation pads. Sometimes the stormwater classification also includes moisture that seeps into the ground and collects under foundations and subgrade floors, where it can do damage. Sanitary drainage may be defined as everything else.

The purpose of stormwater disposal is to direct these wastes into natural watercourses without damage to land or construction. The purpose of sanitary disposal is to separate out the toxic and offensive solid or liquid matter and direct the remaining cleaned water into the natural watercourses. This definition is really quite modern and reflects growing awareness and concern for the pollution of natural water supplies. It was not so long ago that sanitary wastes were channeled directly into the nearest lake, river, or ocean, a practice by no means universally ended, but time is beginning to run out, especially as world population continues to rise.

Akin to water supply, waste disposal may be private or communal. An important consideration in property selection is the presence of public sewer facilities. Private means of sanitary waste disposal are expensive in installation cost and require maintenance attention throughout the life of a housing project, whether residence for one or thousands. Stormwater drainage may require great lengths of large disposal pipe and, if property is not markedly higher than the watercourse, expensive pumping equipment will be needed to lift the rainwater. A careful appraisal, including a survey when necessary, should be made of this situation for every piece of property, preferably before a purchase is made. In developed nations private storm and sanitary waste disposal systems are usually under rigorous state control for adherence to legal standards.

Private sanitary sewage disposal in residential projects containing only a few dwelling units may often be accomplished by simple seepage systems called tile fields. The sanitary wastes are first carried to a relatively large buried container called a septic tank. Because of its size, the tank retains incoming waste material so long and it moves through so slowly that solid matter drops out and sinks to the bottom. There is another and even more important effect. Certain kinds of bacteria thrive in these wastes and multiply by absorbing components toxic to higher forms of life. So thoroughly do these minute creatures do their feeding job in a properly designed tank that the liquid leaving the other end is nearly free of toxicity and actually contains some nutrients for soil.

From the tank it passes through a charging device called a dosing tank which, operating on a siphon principle, discharges intermittently to the tile field. The field consists of a grid of pipes laid in such a way that the water seeps out into the ground and finally finds its way to the surface, where it evaporates, or goes down into the subterranean water table. The tile pipes are generally laid about 30 in. below the surface, and their number and length depends on the character of the earth itself in the location of the field. If it is sandy, seepage will be quite rapid, and the length of pipe will be comparatively short. If the ground is dense clay through which water seepage is difficult and slow, the pipe length will be correspondingly great. A careful analysis of the ground, called a percolation test, must be made before a system is designed. The number of dwelling units that can be served by the simple tile field system depends on the area of property devoted to the field and the results of the percolation test. It may also depend on the local situation as a whole. In some rapidly developed areas, particularly in suburbs, in which unlimited use of tile fields finally overloaded the seepage abilities of the ground, irrespective of percolation tests, backyards became marshes in rainy weather.

When the size of the project or local conditions preclude the use of tile fields, a private sewage disposal plant is the alternative. This may require a major investment, allocation of space at a place in which sewage flow can be conducted with the least pumping or other difficulty, and careful design so that odors accruing from the process of separation do not become a nuisance or a hazard. The last step in private disposal systems, from the simplest septic tank and tile field to the most elaborate plant, is removal of the accumulated solid sludge that is resistant to bacterial action in the tank or chemical attack in the plant. This sludge may sometimes be sold as fertilizer material.

Municipal or other communal sewers offer great convenience for the owner of a project. By their purpose sewers are classified as storm or sanitary sewers. In some localities a single system, called a combined sewer, is provided for both purposes. In others only sanitary sewers are offered, and storm drainage runs into and over the ground as it would if there were no buildings. Still others modify that arrangement. A storm sewer is provided for streets and paved walks and driveways. It is not large enough, however, for building roof drainage, which must be permitted to spill on the ground and be soaked up. Under that kind of system a minimum unpaved ground area may be required in relation to the roof area that spills onto it. In any event, the planner must make the building and project design conform to the sewer system in the locality. Some localities, concerned by the ever increasing load imposed on their storm sewers as buildings and paving multiply, require retention ponds as part of major construction projects. These accumulate rainwater and release it slowly to the storm sewer after the major part of the rain has ended.

Materials commonly used for underground sewers are cast iron, vitrified clay tile, reinforced concrete, and asbestos-cement. There is some use of plastic piping which may well increase as it becomes more familiar and more widely accepted in plumbing codes. Because of its great strength and corrosion resistance, cast iron is favored in unstable ground or where heavy loads can be imposed. Tile and concrete pipe are much cheaper and entirely satisfactory for most applications that are not underneath buildings or other great weights. Their limitation is that they do break under stress, particularly at joints. The pressure of tree roots will sometimes crack a tile pipe joint so that the root can grow right into the pipe. There, nurtured by the passing sewage and moisture, the root may thrive until its growth blocks the pipe entirely and the result is a backup of sewage until the trouble can be cleared.

All sewers are subject to clogging over a period of time. Even storm sewers may carry a load of rain-borne dust, roof surface dirt, and leaves from trees. So every sewer installation must have cleanout provisions that allow access to every portion of the pipe. This "access" may be obtained through vaults called manholes that permit personnel to get right down to sewer level and work, through small pipe extensions to grade called cleanouts, or by a combination of the two. Manholes are both more expensive and more satisfactory for the purpose. In either case, access permits insertion into the pipe of an extensible tool designed to clear obstructions.

BUILDING DRAINAGE

The simple task of conducting sewage through pipes is complicated by one fact. The pipe is large enough to carry the maximum volume of waste expected at any time, but most of the time it will be empty or nearly empty. Ultimately it connects to a sewer in which there is, has been, and will be waste material that at best emits unpleasant odors and at worst dangerous organisms. The empty pipe is a direct conduit between the sewer and the inside of the residence through the drain openings in the plumbing fixtures.

The protection, of course, is in the familiar trap, which holds a plug of water in the drain pipe just below the fixture. That water shields the interior of the building from the sewer and must be inviolate at all times. There is a danger, however, of loss of entrapped water, and against this possibility the entire system of auxiliary piping called the venting system is employed in all buildings.

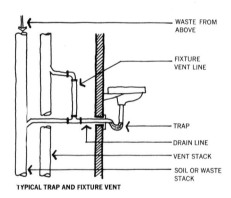

WASTE FROM ABOVE

FIXTURE VENT LINE

TRAP

DRAIN LINE

VENT STACK

SOIL OR WASTE STACK

TYPICAL TRAP AND FIXTURE VENT

Consider a trap, with its proper complement of water, that connects into a drain pipe into which other plumbing fixtures drain. Somewhere up the line a toilet is flushed or a bathtub is opened and a rush of liquid comes along the common pipe, pushing air before it, building up air pressure in its path. That pressure pushes the water up on one side of the trap. No great peril there, but now the big volume of water passes the point at which the fixture branch connects to the main pipe and the air pressure is reversed; air is now being sucked after the departing mass. The reversal pulls the water up the other leg of the trap and its momentum may carry it beyond the crown to start flowing toward the main pipe. This can set up the siphon situation already described. Once the flow begins the rest of the trap will be siphoned out and the protection is lost. The living areas may then have direct contact with foul-smelling and possibly toxic sewer gases.

The enemy here has been air pressure, and the venting system is designed to prevent important changes in air pressure from occurring in the pipes. Air balancing connections are made at each fixture or each group of fixtures, the practice depending somewhat on local code requirements. The individual vent pipes are connected to provide an integrated pressure balancing system. The major vent pipes finally connect with the atmosphere by extension through the roof. The major waste pipes are connected to the main vents at sufficient intervals to ensure no undue pressure changes; for example, in a tall building each main waste riser will be connected to its companion vent riser at the top and bottom and at intervals of five or six stories between.

Cast iron, galvanized steel, copper, and plastic pipes are common materials for waste and vent pipes. Cast iron and copper are expensive but virtually permanent. Galvanized steel seems to have a life-span of perhaps 40 years when used in vent piping in which, interestingly enough, corrosion seems to be worse than in drainage piping. Because the first points of failure in steel piping with screwed joints are usually at the threads, where the metal is thinnest, a combination of steel pipe lengths and cast iron fittings into which the pipe is caulked is an effective compromise. The use of plastic piping is still somewhat new at this writing, but signs point to its increasing adoption unless presently unsuspected defects are discovered after years of use.

The observations on pipe material apply in equal measure to sanitary pipe and to interior rainwater conductors from the roof, called downspouts. For buildings whose roof drainage descends on the exterior, the collection gutters and vertical leaders to the ground are usually sheet metal—galvanized steel, aluminum, or copper—the first two lower in cost and the third much longer in life. It has been implied before that the rainwater conductors may spill onto the ground, which should be protected at the point of spillage by a splash block or gravel bed to avoid erosion, or they may empty into underground sewers leading to a stormwater or combined disposal system.

Sizes of drain and vent pipes are predicted on the number of fixtures they serve and the maximum flow expected at any time. Sizes of downspouts and rain leaders are chosen by the maximum rate of rainfall expected in the area, based on records kept. Pipe sizes are codified in plumbing drainage practice to the extent that it is usually necessary only to count fixtures and to measure roof areas to select the pipe from the governing code tables. The tables show the minimum allowable sizes, used in all but rare cases and with uniform success. The following illustration shows typical dimensions of horizontal cross-section pipe spaces that serve fixtures in a variety of circumstances. Included here are allowances for venting, water risers, necessary expansion, and cases in which toilet room exhaust ducts are enclosed in the same shafts as the plumbing risers. From a piping standpoint it is advantageous to place the

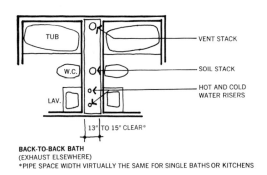

BACK-TO-BACK BATH
(EXHAUST ELSEWHERE)
*PIPE SPACE WIDTH VIRTUALLY THE SAME FOR SINGLE BATHS OR KITCHENS

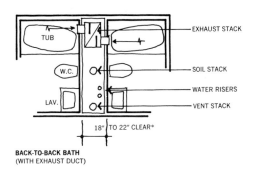

BACK-TO-BACK BATH
(WITH EXHAUST DUCT)

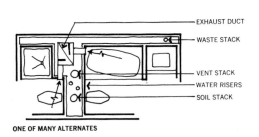

ONE OF MANY ALTERNATES

BACK-TO-BACK KITCHEN
(EXHAUST DUCT ELSEWHERE)

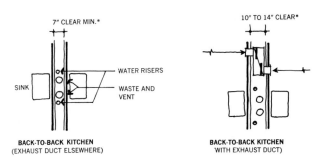

BACK-TO-BACK KITCHEN
(WITH EXHAUST DUCT)

lavatory between toilet and tub if all three are in the same room, but the arrangement of the toilet in the center is often better for design. Interior downspouts can sometimes be accommodated in sanitary riser pipe shafts. In other designs the downspouts may be taken down independently. In multiple-residence buildings there are usually fewer downspouts than plumbing pipe shafts.

Kitchen wastes require a separate word. Cooking grease and food wastes must be disposed of. The latter may be in ground-up form, the result of the work of garbage disposal units installed as part of the kitchen sink assembly. The grease may be dissolved in hot water only to solidify as the water cools and be deposited in the piping system. Grease can be removed in a fairly effective fashion in specially designed traps, fittingly named grease traps, installed in conjunction with each kitchen sink. Codes in different localities take varying views of this problem, some seeing none at all. The individual grease traps keep plumbing lines comparatively clean, but they must be treated periodically, an unpleasant task in a private kitchen or anywhere else for that matter. Some codes require that the kitchen waste lines be separated from all other wastes in the building, gathered and run through a central grease separation vault called a grease basin, and then joined with other sewage. Under this code, when a kitchen and bathroom share the same plumbing stack, there must be two separate waste pipes, although a common vent is permitted.

Another special provision affecting kitchen waste stacks in tall buildings must be mentioned. When detergents were first introduced for dishwashing, they created a volatile foam in the waste pipes. By the time this waste reached the base of the riser in a 10-story or taller building, it was so frisky that the turn in the riser to join the horizontal sewer running out of the building created an almost explosive foaming. Frequently the foam would back up right through the trap water below the sinks of a floor or two, and their occupants had sinkfuls of someone else's foam. The most satisfactory solution to this distressing situation was quickly found to be a second waste riser, which received the discharge of two or three lower floor sinks and joined the main riser only after they had both run parallel for perhaps 10 ft. The main stack still created foam when it turned, but the foam did not back up to the fourth or fifth floor, where the lowest sink was connected. The second stack, aptly called a "detergent stack," was not high enough to produce a serious foaming situation. In the years that followed, detergents were

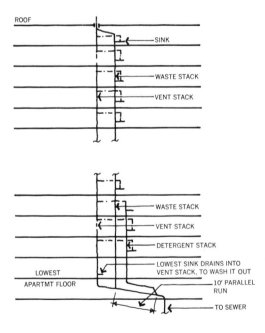

improved by their manufacturers to reduce the amount of foaming and materially lessen the problem. Some plumbing contractors report that it is now safe to omit the detergent stack and simply waste the very lowest sink into the bottom of the vent stack (which is legal). Others continue to prefer a detergent stack as a comparatively inexpensive insurance feature. Under some up-to-date plumbing codes, the choice has been removed. Detergent stacks are required.

GROUND WATER

If the usual level of ground water is high enough to pose any danger to the stability of building foundations or below-grade floors, or even if this level is reached only during a rainy season, a system of subsurface drainage should be installed. Borings into the soil and any other available data should be studied to determine the necessity for this precaution. When a basement floor is well below ground, and data are incomplete for any reason, it is well to provide drainage for safety's sake, since the cost is comparatively low.

Tile piping similar to that described for small private sewage disposal tile fields is used, in this case to admit seepage rather than to discharge it. The tile leads to a gravel settling basin to prevent sand, gravel, or dirt that may become entrained by the water seepage from entering the sewer. The water discharge from the basin is conducted logically to a storm sewer, although some code jurisdictions prohibit any connection other than direct rainwater drainage to their storm sewers.

The location usually preferred for drain tile is just outside the foundation walls, slightly above the level of the bottom of the footing. If the system becomes clogged, it is comparatively easy to dig in that location. There are three instances in which a location just inside the foundation walls may be selected. In the first, when one or more of the foundation walls are at the property line, pipe cannot be installed on the property of another. In the second, when excavation discloses a water spring beneath the lowest floor slab, the water must be drained off before it reaches the underslab level. The third might be in a building of large ground-floor area, in which some engineers prefer to supplement perimeter drain tile with interior laterals connected to the perimeter drains at fairly wide intervals. In the last two cases it is well, if feasible, to have both exterior and interior perimeter tile lines.

BELOW—SEWER DRAINAGE

If the elevation of subgrade plumbing fixtures or subfloor drainage tile is such that they cannot drain by gravity, allowing for a flow grade in the building drain line of at least 1% and for an additional reasonable margin of safety, such drainage must be pumped into the sewer. First it is collected in a large underfloor tank, called a sump. A float switch in the tank starts a lift pump when the tank capacity is approached. If toilets or other fixtures discharging solid materials are handled, the pumps and/or their piping must be large enough that the solids will not clog them. This type of pump is called an ejector and is not required if only clear liquid is to be lifted. The piping is arranged so that the pump cannot place the receiving sewer under pressure but lifts the discharge high enough to allow it to flow by gravity into the sewer.

If removal of drainage is in any respect critical, alternative (duplex) pumps should be installed for maximum protection against pump failure and with suitable automatic alarms to signal high-water level or pump outage.

Sumps are made of cast iron, cast fiberglass, or concrete, with tight fitting steel covers and access provisions to permit cleaning.

COMPONENTS OF DESIGN—PLUMBING

PLUMBING FIXTURES

Selection of plumbing fixtures for residential use is based on considerations of first cost, longevity, maintenance and operating costs, and aesthetics. The latter includes the selection of color, usually at a small addition to the cost of the standard white fixtures.

TOILETS (WATERCLOSETS).   The principal choice here is between flush-valve and flush-tank operation. A flush valve is a large orifice valve that passes enough water in a short time to cleanse the bowl thoroughly and refill the built-in trap. A flush tank is a storage device that accumulates enough water between flushes to achieve the same result. As a rule, the flush valve produces more water-movement sound than the tank. It requires larger water connections and larger main water pipes because of the greater instantaneous rate of flow. With fewer moving parts, it needs less maintenance. If exposed, it is unsightly, but if concealed, its maintenance becomes difficult.

In localities with cold service water, moisture can condense on a tank's exterior and antisweat provisions must be made. On the other hand, the top surface of a tank can act as a convenient shelf while the bathroom is in use, although it must never be considered a permanent counter; it must always be removable for servicing the working parts inside.

If flush valves are installed, it is wise to oversize the cold water risers and even wiser to run an entirely independent riser for each bank of valves. The reason for these precautions is that the high rate of water drawn tends to drop pressure in other fixtures in simultaneous use, thus reducing the flow of cold water in them and, changing the temperature of the hot-cold water mixture. These effects can be eliminated by correct pipe sizing and arrangement. All in all, the use of flush tanks has been preferred in most residential projects.

LAVATORIES (WASHBOWLS).   Will the lavatory be free standing or will it become part of a counter-bowl-cabinet assembly? Will it be made of china, impervious to corrosion but subject to possible (although unlikely) breakage, or steel or cast iron with hard-baked enamel coating, much lower in first cost but limited in life-span, for eventually the protective coating must chip and expose the metal? Should the faucet have a single handle, two handles and spout combined in one fitting, or the somewhat more elegant separated handles and spout? In any event, the fitting should include a lever-operated lift connected with the drain plug by which the entire action is controlled. The old-fashioned rubber drain stopper with chain is no longer in favor.

BATHTUBS.   The style, length, and material are at issue here. Style is a subjective matter of personal selection. Tubs too large to be cast successfully in china are made of metal. The better tubs are enameled cast iron, the cheaper ones enameled steel. The comparison is the usual story: the battle between low first cost and longer life. In tubs, as in lavatories, the drain operator should be combined with the faucet controls. The most widely used tub length is 5 ft, which often determines the width of the bathroom. Luxurious installations may call for tubs 6 in. longer, but bare-bones minimum housing may dictate the same amount shorter than the norm.

SHOWERS.   The primary choice here is whether the shower will have its own stall or be combined with the bathtub. In multibathroom houses there may be a combination, one bathroom boasting a tub with shower, the other only a shower stall, or perhaps the master bathroom may contain a tub and separate shower stall. Another consideration is water control. A simple two-valve hot- and cold-water mixer, manually controlled, may be adequate, but in the event of its use the general water-piping system should be generously sized. Otherwise simultaneous use of hot or cold water in neighboring fixtures can alter the mixture to the shower, with accompanying annoyance or possibly even danger to the user. Thermostatic mixing valves, although rather expensive, automatically maintain a set temperature, regardless of changes in supply, and thus provide security against scalding or chilling. Pressure-balancing valves are considerably less sensitive but also cost less. They are made safe against scalding or chilling by balancing a change in pressure on one side (hot or cold) with a corresponding change on the other by action in the valve.

KITCHEN SINKS. Few free-standing sinks are installed in present-day housing. A sink that becomes part of the kitchen counter, with the space below it arranged for storage, makes good planning sense. As noted before, the sink may be fitted with a garbage disposal unit, and a dishwasher mounted alongside can use the same water and waste connections that serve the sink. Single-handled faucets are a great convenience in this application, because hands are usually well occupied in the kitchen. The sink material itself can be stainless steel, enameled cast iron, or enameled steel. The stainless steel is virtually corrosionproof and should last indefinitely. The other finishes have the familiar possibility of ultimate chipping and corrosion of the exposed metal. Stainless steel has one disadvantage in appearance, however. It is difficult to keep it clean looking, no matter how clean it actually is. Water leaves spots on the surface which take work to remove.

LOCATION OF FIXTURES

One dictum in building design is so well-known and well-understood that it needs to be mentioned here only as a reminder of its universality. Whenever a floor plan can possibly accommodate them, plumbing facilities should be "backed up" to one another so that a minimum number of drainage and water mains can serve a maximum number of fixtures. This is especially important in multiple-story buildings, in which the length of duplicate risers makes the cost so much the greater, but the rule is still applicable in one-story buildings. Even though some pipe sizes may increase for multiple service, that cost is inconsequential in comparison with duplication of the pipes. Obviously, the workability, rentability, or salability of the residences is more important than piping economy, and no floor plan should be compromised. If bathrooms or bathroom and kitchen can be arranged to share common pipe space without such a compromise, there is no reason that it should not be done.

In the same line of thinking, it is desirable to locate and face fixtures to allow their water and drain branches to be served from the same pipe space. It is occasionally convenient that a lavatory, for example, occupy another wall than the toilet and tub. If this must be, it is not a disastrous expense, since it involves only an additional set of waste, vent, and water risers or branches. But if extra care and ingenuity in space layout can avoid that expense, they should be exercised.

FIRE PROTECTION

The fundamentals of fire protection lie in the materials of construction, divisions of the building, and access to and number of exits. These rules are discussed in earlier chapters. Fire warning equipment is described in a later delineation of electrical systems in residential buildings. Within the context of plumbing, fire protection has to do with the preparation of the project's water supply system for availability in emergencies merely for the reason that water is an effective fire-extinguishing agent.

The most useful "tool" for fire fighting is the local fire department. Every building project, residential or otherwise, must plan for fire hydrants to be connected to the water supply system, located so that the pumping and hose equipment can reach every part of the building or buildings. Therefore one of the earliest planning steps must be taken with the local fire authorities so that all regulations can be followed, that available hoses will fit the hydrants, and that the flow of water will be sufficient. Without this cooperation the project cannot and should not be built at all.

In two general areas the fire department's facilities may have to be supplemented by permanent fire-fighting installations in the project itself. First is that of instantaneous response—that is, when the time needed to summon the fire trucks and for them to arrive is deemed longer than minimum safety dictates; second, when the height of the building is beyond the reach of the department's pumping equipment.

LOCAL HOSES. One quick response agent is in hoses permanently connected to the water supply system, mounted in strategic locations. In buildings of more than one story the "strategic location" should be in or immediately adjacent to a stairway; for example, in the event of a fire near the stairway at one floor level a hose from the floor above or below can be used to work on it. The hoses must be fed by a system of water piping that is independent of the domestic water system, at least back to the building's water service entrance; thus fire-fighting pressure will not be influenced by the number of people who happen to be taking showers at the time the water is needed. Pipes that feed the hoses are called standpipes, and more particularly wet standpipes, because they are filled with water at all times. Many building codes require that a second valve be at each hose connection to each standpipe to which the fire department can attach its own hoses. Whether or not the code demands it, this provision should be made.

Wet standpipes must be terminated on the outside of the building at a place readily accessible to fire department pumpers and with protected threaded inlets to which their hoses can be connected. To minimize the possibility of loss of this vital fire-fighting feature by damage to hose threads or similar mischance, duplicate inlets, the familiar "Siamese" twin fitting, should be installed and protected by threaded caps. At each fire department connection it is necessary that a check valve be provided as well so that water can be pumped into the building but will not come pouring out. This is mentioned to point up the need for space inside the building wall for the pipe and valve, both of which are of substantial size and need room.

SPRINKLERS. The quickest response to a fire can be an automatic sprinkler system. The standard sprinkler is a fused valve connected to a well-supplied water source. Fire adjacent to the sprinkler will melt the fuse to release the valve and douse the flames. Sprinklers are spaced 9 to 13 ft apart in both directions; this spacing is intended to blanket an entire area and provide quick action before a fire can spread. It should always be remembered, however, that nothing is foolproof. Valves can be left closed, sprinkler heads painted shut, or pumps may fail to function. Call the fire department for every fire.

In residential buildings areas that have long been protected by sprinklers are rubbish/garbage collection rooms, rubbish chutes, garages and parking facilities, workshops such as carpenter shops, paint-storage areas, and restaurant kitchens. There has been some restiveness among fire-prevention officials and experts concerning fire and smoke hazards that can endanger the occupants of highrise buildings, whose means of escape, especially from the upper stories, may be arduous and slow. Construction provisions such as compartmentation and self-closing doors have been discussed in earlier chapters. In addition, pressure has been brought to add residential area sprinklering as a code requirement in certain circumstances. This may range from a single sprinkler inside the apartment door to prevent spread of fire into the public corridor, to full coverage of the entire area, or to sprinklers only in the public corridors and stairways. Developments are unfolding rapidly and every local change should be followed closely by planners and designers.

Another factor affecting the decision whether to provide sprinklers may be economic. A reduction in the annual cost of fire insurance may pay for a sprinkler installation in very few years. Accurate data should be secured in advance of planning and the decision made on the basis of complete understanding.

Sprinkler piping is subjected to little interior corrosion because the water inside seldom if ever flows. Ordinary steel pipe, without galvanizing or other particular protection against corrosion, is generally used because of its comparatively low cost. Plastic pipe is not likely to become a substitute because in its present stage of development it cannot withstand temperatures likely to be present even in the early stages of a fire. Space requirements for sprinkler piping have to do with headroom and, to some extent, appearance; for example, if dwelling spaces are to be sprinklered, public acceptance will dictate concealed piping with only the sprinkler heads visible. The means of concealment would depend on the method of construction, and it is even possible in some cases for the reverse to occur. Floor construction might be designed to accommodate the sprinklers, by use of steel construction rather than concrete, especially in buildings of moderate height.

On the other hand, in portions of the building that don't "show," such as workshops, parking areas, and rubbish rooms, where sprinklers may be required, the piping is usually best left exposed and clear headroom below it becomes important. Requirements for clearance between the head and the ceiling above, in order to distribute the water evenly throughout the area served by the head, the height of the head, its connection to the main pipe, and the diameter of the pipe itself add to a total of 10 to 12 in. which impact on the clear usable headroom in a sprinklered space.

DRY STANDPIPES.   In some jurisdictions the fire department requires the installation of standpipes that are not attached to any water system. They are empty risers in the usual standpipe locations, with hose valves and/or hoses at each floor level. The lower end of this "dry" standpipe is extended through an outside wall above grade, with a Siamese fitting for connection to the fire department's pumper. The dry standpipes may be in place of or in addition to the wet.

FIRE PUMPS.   When the height of a building requires pressure greater than that made available by the fire department's equipment to serve the top floor's hose, the building must have its own pressure-boosting system. This is exactly analogous to the need for pressure-boosting pumps already discussed in connection with domestic water systems. Fire pumps must be completely independent of the pumps for domestic water in some jurisdictions. In others the same pumps may be used for both purposes, with appropriate automatic valve operation to close off domestic water use during a fire. When fire pumps are separate, buildings of extraordinary height require zones for the fire system like those for the domestic water, so that excessive pressures are not encountered at the lower floor hose outlets.

Buildings of such great height are built of noncombustible materials and only the contents can burn. Smoke can spread readily through such a building, but fire itself is contained in limited areas. For this reason the fire pumps are designed with the expectation that they will have to supply water for only a few hoses at a time. In a building more than one zone high the lower zone pumps will usually supply water not only for the hoses in their own zones but also for the intakes of the upper zone pumps. Thus the upper zones need pressure-boosting capacity only for their own zone's height, not for the entire height of the building up to the top of that zone.

The fire department connection on the outside wall of the building permits the department's pumper to help supply water to the fire pumps. It is often extended and adapted by arrangement of the piping to achieve the opposite effect; that is, the fire pumps in a building may be used to augment fire department equipment in fighting a fire in a nearby building or in a hard-to-reach area of the protected building itself.

Fire pumps are controlled automatically by pressure in their discharge lines held high enough to operate the topmost hose. As soon as a hose valve is opened and water rushes out, the line pressure drops and the pump starts. By the same token, if there is a leak in a standpipe or other fire line, the pump, sensing only loss of pressure, will start. If the leak is tiny, oozing a spoonful of water a month at one joint in a farflung piping system, it may be impossible to locate it because that amount will evaporate as quickly as it leaks. Nevertheless, when a couple of spoonsful have been lost, the fire pump senses a drop in pressure and on it goes, alarms sound and a full-scale production takes place just as if there were a fire. Because fire pumps operate only in emergencies, they are not selected for quiet operation, and if all this excitement occurs in the middle of a night it becomes a decidedly unpleasant experience for the residents.

To combat this by no means unusual chain of events a tiny booster pump called a "jockey" is installed in conjunction with each fire pump. It is set to operate at a pressure a little higher than that which will start the fire pump. Then, if there is a small leak in the system, the jockey pump will replace the miniscule amount of lost water to maintain system pressure and prevent the big pump from running.

Fire pumps must be as reliable as it is humanly possible to make any mechanical device. If the pump is driven by an electric motor, as it frequently is, the electrical service for the pump must be independent of any other electrical service and should run underground from outside the building directly to the pump and its control. Sometimes fires start in the electrical service area, and it would be disastrous to have fire-pump service vulnerable to a fire! It is also feasible to make fire pumps completely independent not only of damaged building electrical service but also of electrical power failure in the entire area by driving the pumps with gas engines or turbines or gasoline or Diesel engines. Needless to say, special caution must be taken in piping the gas or storing liquid fuel for such a purpose.

Fire pumps should be tested regularly by running them to make sure that they are always in condition to operate in case of need.

FIRE EXTINGUISHERS. Fire hoses and sprinklers throw an enormous quantity of water and are intended for fires of serious magnitude. For wastebasket fires, fires in appliance motors, or similar limited blazes, the water thrown by a hose might do considerably more damage than the fire could. In such cases it is convenient to employ small portable extinguishers, mounted in a prominent and accessible location. There should be at least two on every residential level, or more if the building is large. Extinguishers should also be hung in the elevator machine room, workshops, mechanical and electrical equipment rooms, and parking facilities. Great care must be exercised in the selection of extinguishers for a given location. On residential floors probably the best kind is one charged with water under pressure. When a fire is likely to be electrical in nature, such as in an elevator machine or electrical service room, a carbon dioxide fog or dry chemical spray, which are agents that cannot conduct current back to the handler, should be used. Water cannot be applied, of course, when there is any danger of freezing.

Like fire pumps, extinguishers must be checked frequently to ensure their constant good operating condition.

PLUMBING SPACE REQUIREMENTS AND COSTS

Various illustrations show typical space requirements for pipe riser and connection areas, heaters, and pumping equipment.

Typical in multiple-residential projects is an arrangement by which the project as a whole has only one water service and the total consumption is measured by one meter for payment by the single owner or combine of residents. Depending on local water department rules, the meter may be located in a vault outside the building or mounted inside. The vault location is more expensive, but the other requires valuable space in the mechanical equipment room. In either case there must be an accessible valve outside the building so that the water department can remove the meter in the event of malfunction or in the unlikely case of nonpayment of the water bill. If the water supply stems from a private well, meter requirements are, of course, nonexistent unless for any reason it is desirable to determine the water consumption.

Water provided for fire fighting is usually not metered directly because the meter introduces noticeable resistance in the service pipe, and every bit of available pressure is needed when a fire breaks out. To protect against unauthorized use of water from the fire system for other purposes, however, a detector meter is often installed in the fire service. Mounted in a small line piped alongside the fire service line, it senses flow in the main line and records the flow.

In projecting operating costs for a proposed (or actual) residential building project, plumbing charges must be considered by the planner as part of the building's total burden. These charges will include some or all of the following, which can be measured directly or estimated with reasonable accuracy by the designing engineer:

1. Domestic water consumption.
2. Sewer tax. When imposed, it is often equated to domestic water consumption.
3. Cost of heating domestic water.
4. Fire department connection tax.
5. Cost of operating pumps for domestic water supply, hot-water heating, hot-water circulation, sewage, and groundwater ejection.
6. Maintenance costs for pumps, charging fire extinguishers, and so on.

COMPONENTS OF DESIGN—ELECTRICAL 6

Harry S. Nachman

Inspection of a luxurious home built in the 1920s might well reveal construction quality, details, and finishes superior to anything that could be found today. Fifty-year-old plumbing could still fall in the same category. If warm-air heating had been designed, a replacement heat exchanger might have been installed in the furnace over the years, but the system would probably be functioning as well as ever and with plenty of excess capacity built in. There would have been no cooling, but that could have been added without too much difficulty. All in all, the old home would still be more than a suitable place for gracious living, except for one thing.

By present-day standards the electrical installation would be a disaster. The number of receptacles (people often call them "outlets") in each room would be completely inadequate for the number of lamps and appliances now deemed necessary to everyday living. The size of the electrical service would be between one-half and one-third of that required in the last half of the twentieth century. Facilities for communication, security, and auditory recreation would be absent, at least in the sense of having been built into the structure. As a final damning blow, a 50-year-old residence subject to building code inspection based on the present-day code in its area would probably pass with flying colors in every category except the electrical!

What is demanded by electrical codes in today's residential construction? First, a minimum size of entering service to accommodate not just the electrical load when the building is new but to anticipate reasonable future trends that will increase it. It costs comparatively little to increase service size when a house is built but a great deal more to rip it out and replace it with a larger service when a few years' experience has proved it to be inadequate.

What happens when electrical service, or any part of the electrical distribution system, is too small? First, it must be understood that electricity is different in its behavior under stress from the other major services we bring into residential buildings—water and gas. When the load gets too heavy, the last two just give up. You can push just so much water or gas through a pipe with a given pressure and, if more is needed, it simply will not come. Electricity is suicidal. The more asked for, the more will flow until the conductors carrying it become so overloaded that the heat due to their

175

condition consumes them by burning or melting. Only then, when there is nothing left to carry it, does the electrical flow stop.

Now, of course, human ingenuity has found a way to prevent electrical systems from destroying themselves by overloading, whether careless, thoughtless, or accidental. Weak links are deliberately placed in the distribution chain in readily accessible locations. Before an overload approaches the point of danger, the weak link breaks and protects the rest of the chain. There are two types of "weak links" in common use—fuses and circuit breakers. A fuse contains a compound with comparatively low melting point which actually destroys itself when overloaded. A circuit breaker is an automatic switch which opens and interrupts its electrical circuit when its temperature rise indicates an overload. Fuses, or at least the melting compound in the fuse, can be used only once and must be replaced after every overloaded condition. Circuit breakers can be manually restored to operating position. Of course, neither should the fuse be replaced nor the circuit breaker restored until the condition that caused the interruption in the first place has been located and corrected.

Circuit breakers are favored in present-day electrical construction, both residential and other, because they make it unnecessary to carry a stock on hand. They are also easier to work with, although fuses have one important technical advantage, of which the building planner should be aware. It sometimes happens that an accident occurs which produces an enormous surge of electrical power in the lines. This may be caused by lightning striking the lines, by two major conductors touching each other as the result of a storm, or of insulation wearing through. The magnitude of the current in such an event may be so great and the time in which it builds up so unimaginably quick that the "switching" action of a circuit breaker is overwhelmed, and before the breaker can open, its parts melt together to form a channel through which the current continues to pass until something else melts that was not intended to and a fire results. Fuses can be constructed to operate under these major "short-circuit" load conditions; that is, to melt and vaporize as intended and not to melt into a mass that keeps the circuit intact. These are standard, readily obtainable fuses, and it is good practice to use them at the point at which service enters a building even if circuit breakers protect every point thereafter. The enormous overloads can come only from power company lines, and only the power company can tell the designer how much the worst surge of current from its equipment can possibly be. Fuses at the point at which that surge would enter the building are then selected to match the heaviest possible current.

The assumption in the preceding paragraph should be examined promptly; that is, that building electrical service comes from a power company, either publicly or privately owned and franchised to operate in a given area by the government's representatives. In the vast majority of cases this is true, but there are exceptions. Let us consider them.

TOTAL ENERGY PLANTS

A power company usually has an exclusive franchise for selling electricity in its area but it has no monopoly on the technology of generating its product. The developer of a thousand-unit tract housing site or of a huge highrise apartment-complex might find it feasible to build a generating plant for that project. To make such an owner-built generating station pay, every possible bit of heat from the generator engines must be used for other purposes. In residential buildings the "other purposes" are heating and cooling of the spaces and heating of domestic water. The reclamation consists of passing the exhaust gases from the generator engines through heat exchangers, which may take the form of boilers, furnaces, or some combination of the two.

The more electricity generated at any time, the more hot gases discharged from the generator engines, and the more heat available for other uses. For residential work this offers certain problems because the maximum or minimum use of electrical power does not necessarily coincide with the greatest need for heating, cooling, or domestic hot water; for example, on a cold winter night the lowest outside temperatures often occur in the early morning hours when people are asleep; minimum electricity is required but enough heat should be supplied to obviate waking in frigid rooms. For this kind of contingency the owner-operated plant must be equipped with auxiliary fuel burners to help out when the generator exhaust gases are not sufficient to do the job.

The owner-operated generating plant is often called a "total energy" plant because it serves all the energy needs of the project. Needless to say, it represents a major investment and should never be undertaken without a painstaking, comprehensive, and wise analysis of the economics involved.

PURCHASED ELECTRICITY

Most residential projects purchase electricity from franchised power companies. A discussion of the company's equipment which most bears on the planner of a residential project requires, first, a brief review of some simple electrical facts.

The measure of electricity we care about is power. Power lights the lights and drives the appliance motors. Power is measured in watts. Electric power is produced by the quantity of current flowing, measured in amperes, multiplied by the pressure that causes it to flow, measured in volts. Finally, resistance to electrical flow, discussed below, is measured in ohms. Now this is a simplified statement. Other factors enter, but these salient points are sufficient for our purposes.

It follows that for a given quantity of power the larger the pressure (voltage), the smaller the current (amperes). It is not difficult to see that the size of electric conductors is determined chiefly by the current flow (amperes). It is like a water pipe in this respect. The size of the water pipe is measured by the maximum volume of water expected to flow at any time, and the water pressure determines the thickness of the pipe wall. Similarly, electrical pressure determines certain properties of the material to withstand the pressure, whereas the size of the conductor depends on the current flow. There is a second factor as well. As in water, there is electrical friction or resistance to flow. The longer the conductor, the greater the friction; therefore in long distances of conductor run it is necessary to increase the size in order to reduce total friction.

An electric power company transmits large quantities of power over long distances. In order to keep the transmission cables to a reasonable size and cost, the transmission voltages range from 2400 volts for overhead lines in residential areas to as much as 300,000 volts in cross-country major lines. Voltages entering our homes must be at a level that is not lethal in the event of accident. Early in the age of electricity it was found that the maximum pressure at which shocks would be only unpleasant but seldom worse than that is 100 to 150 volts. For standardization electric lights and small motors have consequently been made to operate at approximately 115 volts in some parts of the world and 230 volts in other. Most of the current available in places of habitation today is at one of those voltages. As explained later, the 230-volt systems usually expose occupants to no more than 115-volt shocks.

So we have thousands of volts in the power lines outside and one or two hundred volts inside our dwellings. The device that makes the reduction is called a transformer. The power company generally furnishes the transformer or transformers for a residential project. If the power transmission cables run overhead on poles, it is likely that the transformers will be pole-mounted as well, which is both unsightly and unwelcome.

COMPONENTS OF DESIGN—ELECTRICAL

Many power company distribution systems have gone underground in recent years, and even when most of the mains are overhead, it is often possible to pay a fairly modest premium to have them run underground in a residential property. Power-company requirements that transformers fed by underground mains be in underground vaults outside or inside the buildings served inhibited the development of underground service for years. The vaults were large and expensive to construct outside or wasteful of space inside. Recent improvements in transformer design have seen the development of compact, steel-housed units which are safe to mount on small protective concrete pads at ground level and whose size is such that the transformers can often be hidden by bushes and other plantings. They must, of course, be accessible. For large projects it is often economical to scatter several rather small units in key locations rather than to concentrate the service in one place. In very large highrise apartment buildings in crowded city areas an underground or in-building vault may still be necessary.

The use of transformers is not restricted to electric company installations. In total energy plants it is usually practical to generate and distribute at voltages higher than the 120 volts finally utilized; 480 volts is common for this purpose. Standard commercial motors built for this voltage are fed directly by service at that level, and the power needed for lighting and small appliances is taken from small transformers distributed throughout the buildings.

This practice is also widespread in utility-company-served highrise buildings in which low voltages would require large distributing conductors. Power is taken from the company transformers at 480 volts and used and transformed as described above.

Our discussion of electrical systems centers on alternating current (ac) only. The only present-day use of direct current (dc) is for speed and smooth acceleration control of high-grade elevators, for which the direct current is generated within the elevator equipment itself, using ac power from the building service.

ELECTRICAL PROVISIONS WITHIN A RESIDENCE

Practice and code requirements governing electrical construction are aimed at safety against shocks suffered by contact with current carriers and safety against fires, a danger already discussed in the use of electricity. First, of course, is that conductors must be insulated. Most conductors in residential work are cables, either copper or aluminum, insulated with a tightly adhering nonconducting covering based on plastic or rubber. For large-scale distribution, particularly in highrise buildings, the major carriers may be copper or aluminum bus bars, insulated by sheet-steel housing. The housing and bus-bar assembly is called a bus duct. Copper conductors have a higher current-carrying capacity per unit of area than aluminum and maintain better and tighter connections than aluminum conductors. Nevertheless, aluminum is becoming more widely used because of the higher cost and growing scarcity of copper. Aluminum is finding favor in bus-duct applications and in the larger sizes of wire conductors rated above 40 amperes. Most of the wiring in residences is in smaller conductors, rated at 20 or 15 amperes, and in these sizes copper is still the favorite because it holds the pressure of screw-type connections better than aluminum.

Insulated wires are further protected against rubbing or other damage to the extent that the insulation could be broken. Electrical codes are unanimous in their regulation of this protection for service conductors in garages, basements, on the outside of buildings, or in similar exposed areas. These conductors are enclosed in steel or aluminum pipe called conduit, which differs from pipe used for most other mechanical services in its malleability, and can be easily and neatly bent on location into turns and offsets required to clear obstructions. Because of its light weight and consequent ease of handling, aluminum conduit is gaining great favor, especially in the larger sizes. One caution must be observed, however. Aluminum conduit should never be imbedded in concrete because a reaction set up while the concrete is setting causes it to deteriorate.

Electrical codes differ regarding the protection of wires other than service conductors in residential work. Some codes require that all wires be in conduit. Other codes permit the use of flexible cable consisting of two or more insulated conductors with an outer sheath of moisture-resistant, flame-retardant nonmetallic material. This cable is not to be embedded in masonry or slabs, but it can be run through hollow construction, such as stud walls or partitions, at much lower overall cost than conduit and wire. Armored cable, in which the insulated conductors are run in a flexible metallic sheath rather than the nonmetallic cover, is also available, but it is more expensive. If the governing code allows conduit to be omitted, the nonmetallic sheath is favored due to its lower cost and greater flexibility.

A word must be inserted here about grounding electrical systems. If the insulation on a wire in a lamp or appliance rubs through or if a defect develops in a terminal connection, "leakage" of current will result. This condition may go undetected until someone touches the lamp or appliance, and at the same time has contact with a radiator or plumbing fixture. The current will then pass through the body of the toucher (a shocking experience) and the heating or plumbing system all the way to the point at which the water service pipe enters the building before running to earth. In this way the leakage will have been "grounded" to the detriment of the intervening body. To avoid this hazard, which can be lethal or merely annoying, electrical systems are artificially grounded, and leaking currents can take a route other than the human body to dissipate. Grounding consists of providing a path from the farthest end of the system to the ground by way of the water service pipe or, if that is inconvenient, through copper rods driven 10 ft or so into the earth. The terminal grounding connection is made right at the entering electrical service equipment to water main or ground rods. From the ends of the electrical system to the service equipment the path is kept continuous by uninterrupted conducting metal. If the entire system is run in conduit or in armored cable, the conduit pipe or metal armor sleeve will serve as a satisfactory grounding conductor, provided that connections are made and kept tight throughout. If nonmetallic sheathed cable is used, an extra conductor must be run inside the sheath, to serve as the continuous grounding conductor. Even so, this installation is lower in cost than conduit or armored cable.

In addition to insulation, wire protection, and grounding, the chief safety device in wiring practice is the electric box. The final connections to every lighting fixture and every receptacle or other convenience device must be protected in a sturdy box, usually of steel rustproof construction. The box has five solid faces, but the sixth is open to permit access to the wiring connections. The open side is ultimately covered with a finished plate which faces the living area. Some or all of the five sides are punched with easily detached caps called knockouts to provide passage for incoming and outgoing conductors. The size and depth of the box are determined by the number of conductors entering it.

Boxes mounted in masonry require that it be cut out to accommodate them unless the wall is finished with furring strips and plaster or wallboard. The furring should be designed to allow for the depth of the boxes, thus avoiding the expense of cutting the masonry. Boxes mounted in concrete columns or slabs must be set in the forms and cast into the concrete. They must also be of heavier construction suitable for that service.

Wherever possible, wires should be run without breaks between their points of origin and the box in which they terminate. When the length is so great that this cannot be done and the wires must be extended by splicing, a box must be provided where the splice is made.

Unflagging care must be used in mounting boxes straight and true and the wall opening must be large enough only to accommodate the box. Boxes on opposite sides of the same wall should be at least 6 in. apart, measured along the wall length, if the wall is in a single residence, 12 in. if it separates two dwellings. The penalties for failure to observe these precepts are the ugly appearance of crooked cover plates, dirt streaks set up by air currents from loose-fitting openings, and sound transmission from room to room or, even worse, apartment to apartment.

Returning for a moment to the high-quality residence of the twenties, whose electrical failings led off this section, we would find one element of electrical construction more strongly represented than in present-day practice. There would probably be ceiling lights in each bedroom and bathroom, ceiling fixtures and bracket lights in the living room, and an imposing chandelier in the dining room. Taste 50 years later favors individual selection in lighting by much greater use of floor and table lamps. There will still be ceiling lights in the dining area and kitchen, inside each entrance, and in every major closet. Unless the bathroom is quite large, a light over or flanking the mirror will meet the need. A light directly above the kitchen sink often supplements the kitchen ceiling light. Utility rooms, garages, basements, and hallways must have service lights. Balconies, outside entrances, public areas, and walkways all require lighting consonant with their uses and with the general tone of the environment.

It is often preferable that the builder provide light outlet boxes and leave the selection and purchase of the fixtures to the occupants. If this meets renter or buyer resistance, a reasonable allowance can be made for their cost, beyond which the occupants will pay for their own taste. Even when this option is elected, the designer and builder should retain control of exterior entrance and balcony lighting and of all the other exterior fixtures that affect the visual aspect of the buildings.

All lights should be operated by switches located at the door to each room. This may sound like an obvious statement, but sometimes cost corners are cut by using pull-chain switches for closet lights, a nuisance in all respects. Occupants are much better served by door switches, which turn on the light whenever the door is opened. Another convenience to be commended is the installation of multiple switches for rooms in which there is more than one entrance.

The paucity of electrical outlets in our home of the twenties has been corrected by modern codes. The old order of only one or two outlets in a room gave rise to the "octopus" effect of plugs on adapters connected to those outlets and spawning a growth of cords draped around the room, to be tripped over, to be subject to insulation damage, and to be a general nuisance. The new codes require receptacle boxes at frequent intervals, usually no farther apart than 12 ft measured on the room's perimeter, thus leaving no more than 6 ft to reach any point with a cord. The general thrust is to have unused receptacles rather than a lot of cords.

The receptacles themselves are familiar. Despite the comparatively large number required by present-day codes, each almost always has two distinct points of attachment and costs no more than single outlets. All receptacles must be the grounded type identifiable by the small third opening, centered between and slightly set off from the two prong openings.

In rooms that are not equipped with fixed ceiling or bracket lighting fixtures at least one receptacle must be switched from the door to permit safe entrance in the dark. It behooves the occupant to connect a lamp to a switched outlet and it is likewise incumbent on the designer and builder to switch an outlet to which a lamp will logically be connected. Sometimes only half a duplex receptacle is switched to permit a clock or other device requiring constant power to be connected to the other half.

Receptacles, like switches, should be mounted at a convenient height for normal use. Sometimes they are set into the base of the wall to make them as inconspicuous as possible, but this necessitates cutting the trim. They are usually mounted 8 to 12 in. above the floor. However, there are at least two important exceptions to this practice. In housing for the elderly, receptacles are mounted at twice that height to minimize stooping, and wherever there is baseboard heating they should be carefully located, of course, to avoid placement behind the heating element. In addition to that obvious precaution, they should also be placed so that cords will not come in contact with the convectors, the heat of which will dry out and embrittle the insulation.

DISTRIBUTION AND SERVICE

Some discussion is needed of electrical distribution in residential buildings, not in the way of a treatise, but to clarify space and access requirements for this vital facet of building construction. First, electrical distribution shows much of the treelike pattern already alluded to in water distribution. The main trunk is the incoming service, large and strong enough to support and nourish all its branches, but not so big as all of them added together. What should its size be?

Sizing the service required in a factory is easy. Add the requirements of all the motors that will be running at the same time, the lights that will be in use, plus any special electrical processes known in advance, put in a safety factor for the new and unforeseen, and there you have it. A residence is another matter. How many lights and appliances will be in use at one time? Will a load be plugged into every receptacle, all going merrily or madly at once? Is there an electric range and, if so, will it ever be in use when the air conditioner is turned on (the answer is yes)? Even more difficult, if a hundred identical residences are connected to the same service, must it be a hundred times as large as the service to one residence (the answer is no)?

The best answer to these questions lies in experience. Over the years experience has been codified into minimum standards published for virtually all localities. This is not to say that an experienced designer cannot select larger service and distribution sizes than the code standards. Codes are based on a vast storehouse of records and observations and incorporate more than adequate safety factors to minimize the likelihood of a service being undersized. Therefore their minimum standards are usually selected as actual service sizes.

Let us look at the service selection for a typical residence from a typical electrical code (the National Electrical Code, published by the National Fire Protection Association of the United States and widely used throughout the States). First a little about voltage. It was stated earlier that a common domestic pressure is 115 volts. The most economical method of providing this voltage is by three conductors, two of which are traced all the way back to the electrical generator, and the third grounded in the earth. The electrical pressure, or voltage, between the two "live" conductors is 230 volts. By a phenomenon whose explanation is beyond the scope of this discussion the voltage between either of the live wires and the grounded wire is exactly half that, or 115 volts. This procedure is relatively safe because accidental contact between a person and the electrical system will almost always involve one wire, one loose connection, or one side of a receptacle, and the worst shock that a person can get is by acting to ground that one live wire. That puts 115 volts through the body. The only way the much more dangerous 230 volts can be experienced occurs when the victim deliberately makes himself a conductor between the two live wires. With this in mind, choose the service size for a 2500 sf residence from the National Electrical Code.

ESTIMATED LOAD

2500 ft @ 3 watts/sf	7,500 watts
Two kitchen appliance circuits @ 1500 watts each	3,000 watts
	10,500 watts

Actual use estimate:

First 3000 watts @ 100% use	3,000 watts
Remaining 7500 watts @ 35% use	2,625

FIXED LOAD

Electric range, total capacity, 12,000 watts; maximum use predicted at any moment	8,000 watts
Electric clothes dryer	4,600
Electric heat, 25,000 watts	
Air conditioning, 15,000 watts	
Control these appliances so that they cannot operate simultaneously; use the larger figure only	25,000 _____
Total load	43,225 watts

Harking back to the earlier formula that volts times amperes equals watts, we find our service size in amperes:

$$\text{amperes} + \frac{\text{watts}}{\text{volts}} = \frac{43,225}{230} = 188 \text{ amperes}$$

In a final bow to conservatism and safety in choosing a service, the code says that no service switch may be loaded to more than 80% of its rated capacity. In our example that means that the switch size would be 188 ÷ 0.80, or 235 amperes. Unfortunately, there is no commercially made switch rated between 200 and 400 amperes, and we should have to choose a 400-ampere switch, protected by 250-ampere fuses. for that is the nearest size above our 235-ampere calculation. The service conductors would accordingly be sized for 250 amperes.

The service size for a large building or complex follows the same pattern, with appropriate variations. The "use estimate" factor, which simply reflects the expectation that everything will not be running at once, becomes lower the more residents served. The electrical loads for motor-driven elevators, pumps, ventilating fans, and cooling towers must be added, together with public corridor, lobby, and outdoor lighting. The service voltage may well be 460 instead of 230, and the service will undoubtedly be "three-phase" instead of the "single-phase" we have used in the example without talking about it. Use of three-phase current is much more economical in service size and in any event is virtually mandatory for large motors. To complete the picture let us say that in the final ampere calculation of three-phase service the voltage in the denominator is multiplied by 1.732. Therefore, if our residence in the example were operated with three-phase 230-volt service, the calculation would have read

$$\text{amperes} = \frac{43,225}{230 \times 1.732} = 109 \text{ amperes}$$

which requires a 200-ampere switch only. However, technical complications dictate that a single-residence service will usually be single-phase. This follows through in multiple-residence buildings, in which the total service is three-phase but the branch service to each dwelling is still single-phase. The various dwelling services are balanced among the three available phases.

Now we know the size of the tree trunk. We have, incidentally, already mentioned that every service entering a building must have a main switch (or a group of switches totaling at least the calculated amperes) where the service conductors enter the building. The remaining distribution consists of filling in the rest of the tree. In a residence of modest size there may be only a few branches.

For safety and convenience, outlets are combined in groups called branch circuits, fed by a pair of conductors and protected by a single circuit breaker or fuse. The groups are arranged so that no circuit is expected to carry more than 1400 watts, at worst loading conditions. A moment's reflection shows that this is a respectable load. A television set pulling 550 watts, a 300-watt lamp, and five 100-watt lamps can live happily on one circuit. On the other hand, a typical room air conditioner at 1300 watts must have a circuit of its own, and a large air conditioner, pulling 2100 watts, needs a special oversized circuit breaker and larger wires to suit.

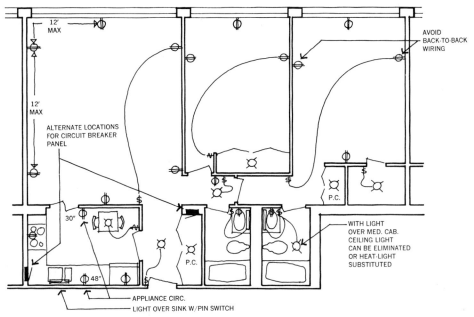

TYPICAL APARTMENT LIGHTING AND WIRING

All these circuits with their attendant circuit breakers are brought together in a distribution panel, which is just an oversized electrical box containing the necessary bus bars, circuit breakers, and wire connection terminals in a neat, easily serviceable arrangement. In a residence of moderate size the box may contain the main service switch as well. The entire distribution center is in one place, where the electric service enters the dwelling; the main switch and the circuits for lights, receptacles, kitchen appliances, air conditioners, electric range, clothes dryer, and electric heat. The total may vary from four circuits in an apartment for the elderly to 24 in a large house. It may be convenient and economical to divide the circuits into two or more small distribution panels, one perhaps to serve the bedroom wing and another, the living area. The main switch feeds a main distribution panel adjacent to or combined with it. The main distribution panel, in this example, contains two circuit breakers large enough to protect the wires called feeders, and has a capacity large enough to serve the distribution panels. The panels themselves are mounted in inconspicuous but readily accessible locations and are recessed in hollow partitions in order to conceal the conduits or sheathed cable leading to and from them. Panel boxes have a depth of about 4 in. and the thickness of the partition must be made to cover them completely, leaving only their fronts accessible and visible.

On a larger scale this kind of division of distribution serves highrise buildings as well. The details differ but the pattern remains. There is the incoming service from the transformers and one or more service switches. The main distribution panel, which

COMPONENTS OF DESIGN—ELECTRICAL

contains breakers or fused switches for large pump and fan motors, public lighting, elevators, and bus duct risers which in turn feed the apartments, now becomes quite large. The main distribution panel may feed, in addition to the bus duct risers, subdistribution panels scattered through the building. They, in turn, serve the various public motor and lighting loads.

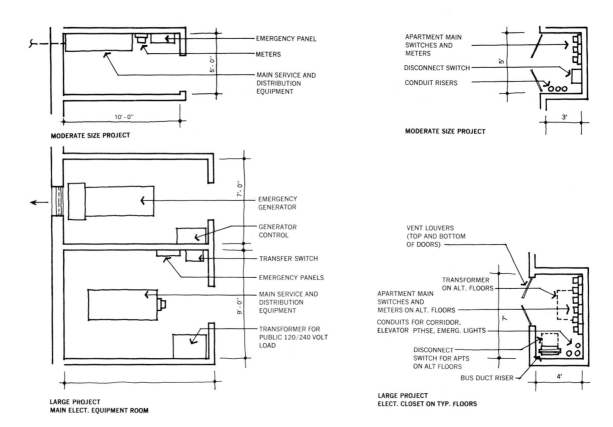

Arrangement of service to the individual residences in multistory buildings depends on the aspect of the building. Up to six stories it is often found economical to feed tiers of apartments with a vertical distribution pattern. Each apartment's distribution panel is located in a closet, kitchen, or passageway, one above the other. The lower panels are built to permit the feeders for the upper apartments to pass directly through. There are as many conduit risers as there are apartments.

In taller buildings a more economical solution involves a single-bus-duct riser which passes through an electrical closet off the public corridor on every floor. In the buildings that are very large in area as well as tall, there may be more than one bus riser, each serving 8 to 12 apartments per floor, this requiring as many electric closets as there are risers. In buildings that combine separate apartment towers in one structure, it is impossible to reach all public corridors from one bank of elevators, and a riser is required for each tower, even though it may serve only one or two apartments per floor. In such cases, depending on the total load size, there may be a cost advantage in choosing wire in conduit rather than bus duct. Electrical closet arrangements have numerous possibilities. In general, the elements included are the riser, a submain switch or circuit breaker for the feeder which, tapped off the riser, serves the apartments on a given level, and an apartment main switch to protect each apartment feeder. The apartment feeders are concealed in the construction, from the electrical closet to the apartment circuit breaker panels. One closet arrangement finds all of these elements on

184

each floor. In a building with 460-volt distribution, transformers are needed for the apartment circuit breaker panels. One closet arrangement places all of these elements on each floor. In a building with 460-volt distribution, transformers are needed for the and all even-numbered floors transformers large enough to serve every two floors may be mounted in the electrical closets. Correspondingly, on the third, fifth, seventh, and all odd-numbered floors assemblies of main switches will be located to serve the apartments on the two floors. Other arrangements are feasible, depending on the number of apartments, closet sizes, and similar factors. In some electrically heated buildings the main risers carry as many as 12,000 volts. These and the accompanying transformers will be housed not in the same closets as the apartment switches because of the hazard of the high voltages but rather in an adjoining locked closet, to which only authorized personnel has access.

In the descriptions of distribution systems no mention has yet been made of measuring the quantity of electricity used by the occupants. That may or may not be necessary.

If the project produces its own electricity and charges each occupant for its use or if it is served by a power company and residents pay the project owner or the power company for the amount consumed, the distribution system must include a meter for each dwelling. The meters are usually mounted in factory-fabricated assemblies along with the apartment main switches and require little, if any, more space than the main switch assemblies. Public light and power must be separately metered, generally at the main distribution center, where public and residential services are separated. If current is to be resold to the occupants, the main meter will measure the entire input, and the difference between this total and the consumption in all the individual dwelling units is the public use. If the project is a condominium or cooperative, the cost of public electricity will be shared by agreement.

The computation of electrical charges can be a most interesting task. It is possible that the dawning era of energy restrictions will change the practice, but until now it has been accepted that the large users pay lower average rates. This encourages use and, in a sense, makes the small user the subsidizer of the large. However, it is not all gravy for the latter, for that rate includes not only the direct cost of the energy used but another factor called "demand charge," which reflects peak usage. Its philosophic base is that the power company must provide enough plant capacity to serve this maximum load, even if it is seldom reached.

Special rates have been offered by electric companies to promote and encourage electric heating, which often requires separate meters, and appreciable additional initial cost of installation. Before that extra cost is undertaken the load should be thoroughly analyzed. It may be that another rate, even without the bonus for heating, may actually be cheaper, in which case use it!

EMERGENCY LIGHT AND POWER

In the event of failure of electric power occupants of one- or two-story buildings will be inconvenienced. People living above the second floor of midrise buildings will be seriously inconvenienced, and anyone living above the fourth-floor level of a highrise will be threatened. If the power interruption is due to fire, the two last categories of occupants will be *seriously* endangered.

To lessen the peril, most codes require at least minimal emergency lighting in mid- and highrise residences. This lighting is supposed to remain on during service failure and thus must be independent of other services. Minimum emergency lighting usually includes illuminated signs clearly marking stairways, visible from all parts of the public corridors, and exit signs on the ground level from the stairways to the outside. It further includes enough lights in the public corridors and stairwells to enable people to use them safely when all other light has failed.

Many codes have permitted the use of separate services on the same electric power company lines that provide the main service on the theory that major problems will occur within the building confines and not in the electric company's system. The companies have set up admirable networks for distribution, and failure in one part of a system will often be corrected almost immediately by transferring the load to another. That word "often" is looming larger and larger as complexity of systems increases and perhaps quality of maintenance and workmanship in the manufacture of components deteriorates. Whatever the reason, power failures seem to be more and more frequent, and there is no noticeable likelihood of a reversal of this trend. What that means, of course, is that an electrical outage in the main service of a project, if it stems from a larger failure in the power company network, will also knock out the emergency service derived from the same lines.

One cure for that problem is in the use of phosphorescent lights, which continue to glow for a time after the electric lamp has failed. This is useful for exit signs, whose glow in the dark acts as a guide to stair doors and outside exits and lasts long enough to permit evacuation of almost any building. The intensity of glow is faint, however, not nearly enough for illumination of halls and stairs, a function of emergency lights.

So an answer must be found for emergency lighting needs. One is available in the form of the battery-switch lamp pack. A storage battery is connected to the regular building source of power by a standard receptacle. This power keeps the battery charged and also registers at the "brain" of the pack. If the regular power source is interrupted for any reason, the brains operates a switch in the assembly, which turns on a low-wattage, high-intensity lamp (or lamps) that will illuminate a considerable stretch of corridor or stairway—that is, enough to permit safe passage of personnel even under panic conditions. For the sake of appearance and avoidance of the possibility of vandalism the packs may be remote from the lamps, locked in a closet or behind a locked panel. The batteries do wear out in time, with or without use, and must be checked and replaced periodically. There are three common types of batteries available, and, needless to say, the lowest cost unit lasts the shortest time. The best batteries are expected to last 8 to 10 years between replacements.

Exit signs and emergency lights are not the only potential needs in the event of power failure. Fire-alarm systems and firestation communication systems, discussed later, should be powered at all times. Power failures may not go back to the supplying utility. There may be a burnout in a transformer that supplies all or an important part of a project's service. Replacement of a transformer may take many days. (If this should happen in winter in a cold climate (and it usually does!), must the residents move out and all the water in the pipes be drained to prevent them from freezing? More and more pressure is being exerted to provide emergency generating plants at least for major housing projects. If the project has its own total energy generating station, it would be a small auxiliary plant. When power is purchased from an electric utility company, the plant would be independent and project-operated, fueled by gas, gasoline, or Diesel oil, the latter two safely stored on the premises. Local code requirements must be ascertained before a fuel is selected. Such a plant would be sized to perform some or all of the following functions.

1. Operate exit signs.
2. Operate emergency lights.
3. Operate one domestic water pressure pump.
4. Operate a fire pump or pumps.

5. Operate one or more boilers and heating pumps.

6. Provide power for at least one elevator. This has several values:

    a. An elevator is available for fire-fighters if the interruption is caused by fire.

    b. An elevator is available for upper floor residents if the outage is of long duration.

    c. If a sudden power failure leaves one or more elevators stranded between floors, there will be power to move them, one at a time, to a floor landing, where the occupants can be taken off.

7. Operate a fire alarm system.

8. Operate communication systems for fire-fighters, from elevators, and for residents in general (especially in housing for the elderly).

Items 7 and 8 can be served by their own storage battery systems if there is no emergency generator or if it is deemed preferable to separate them from the emergency generating system.

    Emergency generators sufficient to these needs are available commercially. They require space, ventilation, and sometimes water for cooling and should be tested regularly under load to ensure their readiness at all times. They are expensive and noisy, but as more and more people move to tall buildings and more ugly incidents are recorded there is less excuse to build without this kind of vital precaution for the safety and well-being of the occupants.

AUXILIARY ELECTRICAL SYSTEMS

Light and power are the primary electrical systems. Ancillary systems are required for safety, security, communication, and pleasure. The explosive advance in electronic technology by which today's marvels are superseded by tomorrow's miracles makes the listing of techniques or facilities out-of-date before a manuscript can go to press. Thus, much of the discussion of security and communications is of a general nature that suggests the kinds of information that might be transmitted without detailing all the potentialities.

SAFETY

Structural design and site planning address themselves to the safety of residents against such natural hazards as earthquakes, high winds, and floods. Safety in the electrical context protects against fire or smoke inhalation, which can be as lethal as fire. The subject was opened in the discussion of fire protection, which has to do with extinguishing fires underway. Here we consider methods by which firefighting personnel and building occupants can be informed of danger in its early stages. The first order of business, of course, is to determine the minimum requirements of governing codes. Beyond that base, additional precautions may be deemed well worth their cost.

1. FIRE ALARM SYSTEMS

    a. The alarm can be transmitted in one or more ways:

    By direct electrical connection to the local fire department, by all odds the best, applicable only when the department has the electronic gear necessary to receive and identify the signals.

    By connection to an independent security agency, which will relay the message to the fire department.

By an audible alarm in a location in the building that is within earshot at all times.

By an audible alarm outside the building.

By a general alarm audible inside the building. A drawback is the possibility of disturbing residents (possibly to the point of panic) for a minor incident in the middle of the night. A two-stage alarm, first sounding a limited warning and only after sufficient time for exploration going to a general alarm, is sometimes a good answer to that problem.

By a zoned alarm, audible only in the threatened area.

b.   The alarm can be initiated by various agents:

By a water flow alarm. If an automatic sprinkler goes off anywhere in the building or if someone uses a standpipe hose, the alarm is energized.

By a smoke detector. This is a sensitive electronic device which detects smoke of greater intensity than that caused by a cigar or pipe and often before smoldering rags or paper burst into flame will send out a warning of impending danger. Detectors can be placed in unattended areas like equipment rooms, electrical closets, storage rooms, and stairways. One or more detectors can also be placed in every residence.

By a heat detector. Operating like smoke detectors, these devices send out signals in the event of abnormal temperatures or of a sudden abnormal rise in temperature, which will be picked up before it reaches a dangerous level. These detectors are less sensitive then smoke detectors.

By manual "pull" stations, the familiar fire alarm boxes mounted in public exits. Their use with a general or local alarm system should be viewed with caution. They offer too tempting an outlet for creating a nuisance.

Signal systems should always contain a trouble circuit, which automatically sends out a special trouble signal, distinguishable from an alarm signal, when any break or other electrical interruption occurs anywhere in the system. In buildings of any great size or complexity the signal system should also contain an annunciator board, which will identify the area from which the signal emanates. Alarm systems must always be powered by the best in emergency circuitry in order to function under any circumstances.

2.   FIRE-FIGHTER'S SAFETY SYSTEM

In highrise buildings in particular an auxiliary voice communication system physically parallel to the standpipe water installation enables fire-fighters to communicate from various levels of the building. This system must extend to the fire department's Siamese connection on the outside.

3.   OCCUPANTS DISABILITY

A pushbutton system, by which occupants of a multiresidential project can signal for help when illness or other incapacity strikes, is a valuable adjunct particularly in housing for the elderly. It is vital that the signal be transmitted to an annunciator board that gives both audible and visual notice monitored at all times. Signal buttons which will register on the annunciator board should be located in each bathroom and each bedroom. This system is valuable in multidwelling buildings and in single-dwelling tract-type housing.

4.   ELEVATOR TROUBLE

In the event of elevator failure, the elevator installation includes an emergency button the sounds an alarm bell in the building. In addition, each elevator cab should carry a telephone on a special line. Occupants in a stalled elevator may tend to panic, and a reassuring voice that will give instructions of procedure and reports of repair progress can ward off serious consequences.

SECURITY

In a perfect world doors would serve only to keep the weather out. In our much less than perfect society not even door and window locks are enough to make us feel safe, and we are forced to go to electric and electronic systems of varying sophistication to help protect our homes and persons.

1. DOOR SIGNAL AND RELEASE SYSTEMS

    a. Pushbutton and buzzer, bell or chimes. The button is located at the front and rear doors. The rear signal is sometimes omitted in multiple-occupancy buildings, in which the buttons are grouped in a lobby inside the entrance and usually require an accompanying directory for identification. Often the buttons and directory are combined with mailboxes, as assembly usually purchased and installed by the electrical contractor.

    b. In multiple residences there will be an independent voice communication system in conjunction with the signal system to permit an occupant to identify the button pusher. Each occupant controls a release button in conjunction with the speaker, which opens the main door if the identification is satisfactory. If a building has 24-hr service, the door release is unnecessary, and the signal and voice communication are taken care of by the doorman.

    c. Television surveillance of the entrance areas on a closed circuit has proved to be a valuable security tool. A specific channel is set aside which permits each occupant and/or the building staff to check the identity of everyone who signals. It may also give the building manager an opportunity to monitor the entrance areas against loiterers.

    d. Electronic burglar alarm systems further protect residents. Windows and doors are protected by wiring, such that forcible entry sends a signal to a central watch station or trips an audible alarm. In highrise buildings, in which the only point of entry to an apartment is the door to the corridor, the system can be arranged so that the resident sets a key when leaving. If the door is subsequently opened in any unauthorized manner, an alarm sounds and an annunciator shows at a central watch point, usually in the building. In all burglar alarm systems it is important that the occupant be taught to "unset" the alarm on returning home to avoid sending out signals when someone admits a neighbor or opens a window for air.

COMMUNICATION

1. First in electronic communications is the telephone. Telephone companies, operating as a franchised public utility, usually provide the instruments and the cable that connects them to the central system. In single residences of days gone by all the cable ran exposed along the basement ceiling, turning up into walls to reach the boxes that served the instruments. This method is still practiced in lowcost housing, but concealed conduit through which the cable can be pulled has become much more common, especially since basements have been eliminated in so many houses. The conduits from all telephone outlets are gathered together at a terminal cabinet or box in a closet or utility area, from which they are fed by the outside service cable. In multiple-occupancy and highrise buildings, the arrangement is merely enlarged. A terminal cabinet feeds an entire building. Two to six apartments may be fed by a single cable in a riser conduit, which returns either directly to the terminal cabinet or to a central telephone major cable riser that leads from the terminal cabinet. The cabinets themselves are easy to locate because they are only about 4 in. deep. A cabinet of that depth, 2 ft wide by 4 ft high, will serve quite a large building. In concrete slab buildings a

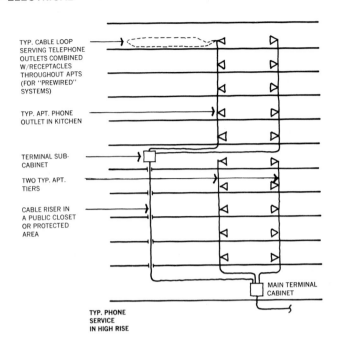

TYP. CABLE LOOP
SERVING TELEPHONE
OUTLETS COMBINED
W/RECEPTACLES
THROUGHOUT APTS
(FOR "PREWIRED"
SYSTEMS)

TYP. APT. PHONE
OUTLET IN KITCHEN

TERMINAL SUB-
CABINET

TWO TYP. APT.
TIERS

CABLE RISER IN
A PUBLIC CLOSET
OR PROTECTED
AREA

MAIN TERMINAL
CABINET

TYP. PHONE
SERVICE
IN HIGH RISE

system of prewiring which has found favor eliminates the larger part of the conduit but conceals the cable. Cable is laid in the concrete forms, starting from a steel telephone box located as a rule in the apartment kitchen, and looped around the apartment to possible points of connection in boxes combined with electrical receptacles in most or all of the rooms. An entire loop is made back to the box in the kitchen. Therefore a single break in the cable which could occur while the concrete was poured would still leave both halves of the line alive. The advantage is in the large number of locations at which telephone extensions may be attached, depending on the resident's needs and furniture layout. This flexibility is gained at absolutely minimal cost, because the telephone company provides the cable and the boxes and the only cost of the building is the comparatively small labor charge to loop the cable around the forms.

2. Private voice communication systems can also be provided. Front and rear entrance talk-and-listen systems, already described, can be extended so that residents can call the project's central office, the garage, the commissary, the swimming pool or gymnasium, or one another, if the system is extended to that degree. Called intercommunication, or "intercom," systems, they may be completely private or adjunctive to the outside telephone system. Many telephone companies make an earnest effort to sell these systems to housing developers because they are attractive rental or selling features. Obviously they must also be profitable to the company. A private system generally represents a substantially higher first cost and requires that the maintenance expense be borne by the project, but unless the housing is designed with the idea of a quick sale in mind the greater investment and maintenance costs will be paid back in a few years by operating cost savings, especially if good equipment is selected and well installed.

3. A continually expanding field that embraces communications of a sort, along with safety and security in an integrated package, is the electronic marvel that gathers and disseminates data. The possibilities are many. A system may communicate the results of monitoring many factors of building operation, along with all the alarms for fire, smoke, personal distress, and security. What kinds of "factors of building operation"? Fuel and electrical consumption, temperatures of cooling water, outside temperatures, temperature of elevator motors and generators, temperatures of boiler flue gases,

domestic water pressure, fire-pump operation, and timed operation of corridor supply and kitchen and toilet exhaust systems. The possibilities are as broad as the imagination. The data can be recorded, or they can be used to sound an alarm when some operation departs from the normal. Use of electricity can be automatically measured and invoiced for a large number of residents. The installation costs of these wonders fall as the techniques are improved and expanded, and the future probably offers developments we cannot even imagine at this time.

ENJOYMENT

Central systems for the improvement of radio and television signals are the principal electronic methods that enhance recreational facilities.

1. Underground cable companies, franchised as public utilities, serve buildings by bringing in a multitude of channels for commercial television, public and educational television, local and community programming, and FM and AM radio. The cable is carried through the buildings in a system of conduit risers (if preparations are made when the building is planned) to feed boxes in all apartments. Occupants decide individually whether to tap the cable passing through their boxes and pay a fee if the decision is affirmative. Boxes are located at key places in each residence, one in the living room and at least one in the bedroom. If there are multiple bedrooms, boxes should be located in partitions between them, in order that one cable can serve two locations.

2. In areas in which cable utilities are not available, multistory buildings still provide central systems to eliminate an unsightly forest of television antennas on the roof. A single mast, designed to receive all locally available channels, serves a private cable which is distributed through the building in much the same way as the public cable. An electric power outlet from the building system, at 120 volts, is needed to energize the system. Often the building owner or a licensee will make this private service available for a fee. In other cases, a fee is charged for the initial connection to the private cable, but no rent is levied thereafter.

3. The use of centrally distributed music in public areas of a residential project, such as the elevators, lobby, swimming pool, and commissary, must be listed under the heading of enjoyment for those who like it. To me it is a sour way to conclude the section on electrical installations because I hold strongly to the opinion that this is one of the minor curses of twentieth-century life. However, even the most unwilling member of the captive audience must acknowledge that this "pleasure" exists, and that it must be listed as available, either from a commercial source at a fee or over the private inter-communication system.

COMPONENTS OF DESIGN—SOCIAL AND BEHAVIORAL

7

James R. Anderson

The social and behavioral components of the design of housing are essential to the overall success of any final residential environment. This chapter will present social and behavior components of design that must be considered in the design of housing. Knowledge of these aspects has come from such sources as the social sciences as well as architectural research and experience. Such diversity in information sources is sought because it is important to obtain as much information as possible about how residents use and perceive their residential environments. Such diversity in information sources is useful because it is important to validate the information from any single source.

PARTICIPATION

One way to obtain information about the social and behavioral components of design is to involve the ultimate occupants and users in the design process. This is almost always what occurs when an architect designs a single-family house. The architect tries to establish a personal communication with the client. If the architect is sensitive about the needs of the client, there will be few social and behavioral issues that will not be discussed. When the design is completed and constructed, the architect's awareness of the client will have focused the priorities of the solution and the client's participation will have strengthened the sense of ownership and control.

It is difficult to obtain a high level of participation when designing multifamily housing. Quite often the identity of the residents will not be known until after construction of the housing is complete. However, user participation is still important and should occur because it can lead to a more successful design.

There are several ways in which user participation can occur, even in the design of multifamily housing, including activities such as group meetings and discussions, as well as more formal and systematic activities such as interviewing and survey work.

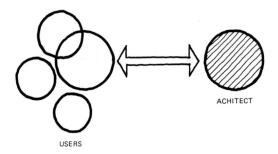

ACHITECT

USERS

There are a number of good books listed in the bibliography that discuss the characteristics of these activities and the differences between them.

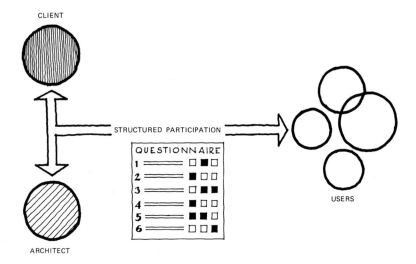

CLIENT

STRUCTURED PARTICIPATION

QUESTIONNAIRE

USERS

ARCHITECT

One source of participants that should be considered is the community surrounding the site of the future housing development. The participation of this group can reduce the anxiety and animosity which neighborhood residents may feel toward the proposed multifamily housing development. It is as important for housing to be designed to fit the existing social and behavior context of the neighborhood as it is that it fit the existing visual context of the neighborhood. Second, neighborhood residents may become residents of the proposed development or may be similar to the residents. Knowing their perceptions and their lifestyles would be very useful information for the design process.

SATISFACTION

Concern for the social and behavioral aspect of design represents a concern for residents' satisfaction with where they live. Francescato, Weidemann, Anderson, and Chenoweth,[22] after examining the responses of residents in 37 multifamily housing developments, developed a conceptual model of residential satisfaction. The model indicates not only that physical design contributes to residential satisfaction, but also that residential satisfaction is directly affected by factors outside of the architect's control: residents' perceptions of their neighbors and of the economic value of where they live. Also, good management and maintenance are seen to be extremely important in the success of multi-family housing. Architects must realize that it is possible that even the best design will fail because of aspects outside of their control.

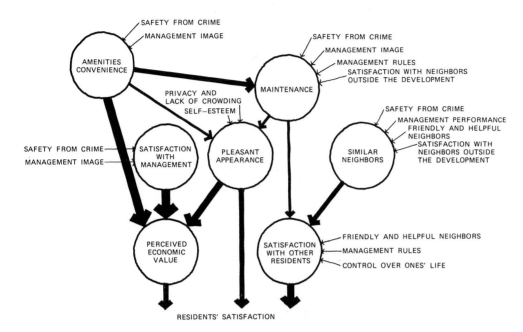

While Francescato *et al.* thoroughly discuss the model, the remainder of this chapter is primarily a discussion of design matters that they, and others, have found to contribute, in a social or behavioral sense, to the success of multifamily housing, as residents perceive it. First, important social and behavioral issues are examined, then important characteristics of the physical environment.

SOCIAL AND BEHAVIORAL ISSUES

TERRITORIAL DEFINITION

From a social and behavioral standpoint, exterior spaces should be well-defined and well-articulated. Having well-defined exterior spaces, or territories, has been found by Newman[23,24] to curb crime and vandalism. A clear definition of exterior spaces also encourages residents to use those spaces in such activities as gardening while they respect the spaces of other residents.

Although managers of housing often worry that territorial definition can make site maintenance (such as lawn mowing) more difficult, they should realize that it can also have a positive benefit for management. When residents are responsible for defined exterior spaces surrounding their units, it is easier for management to identify which residents are creating maintenance problems. In row houses low barriers and elevation changes are used to distinguish boundaries, and gated fences allow greater resident control of spaces.

EXTERIOR PERSONALIZATION

Residents often like to alter their environments to reflect their own individuality. They plant flowers and shrubs, add decorative elements to facades, paint doors and other

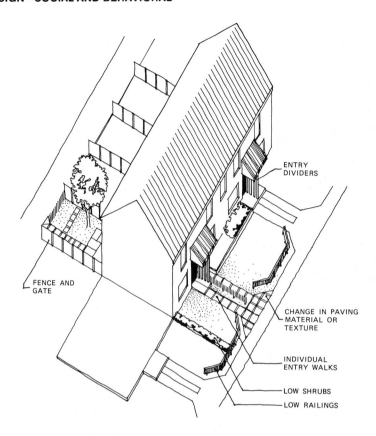

surfaces, and develop specific activity areas, such as patios. While personalization can disrupt the design of the housing environment, more often it provides a visual richness to the housing site which the original developer is not able to provide. The architect should stimulate personalization by providing residents the opportunity to express their own individuality. For example, by physically defining areas for planting flowers residents with this inclination have a place for this activity, while the architect promotes a visual harmony that might not otherwise occur if the residents were to choose their own locations for planting.

Encouraging personalization in highrise housing is more difficult than in lowrise housing, but the experience of Lewis[25] in several public housing developments indicates that even in highrises exterior spaces can be personalized.

INTERIOR PERSONALIZATION

Personalization is more apt to occur in the interior of dwellings than in exterior spaces. This is partly a function of management; rules governing interiors are more lenient than those regulating the exterior. Also it is a function of security; the interior is where residents have the ability to exercise control to ensure that personalization items are not vandalized or destroyed. Designers need to keep in mind that dwellings must accommodate a large variety of individuals with a large variety of furnishings and other means of expressing personal experiences and preferences.

A number of studies have focused on furnishings in multifamily housing. Comparisons have been made between the predicted placement of furniture by architects and the actual placement of furniture by the residents. It has been found that the variety and amount of furnishings that residents have often exceeds what the designer expects. This is especially true after a resident has lived in the same apartment for a number of years, and accumulated more and more furniture and other objects. Room designs must allow for flexibility in furniture placement. Residents seldom place furniture in the arrangement expected. Designers should avoid elements, such as vertical strip

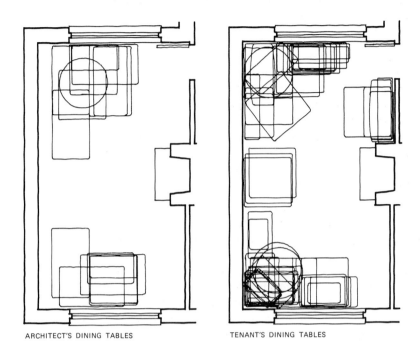

ARCHITECT'S DINING TABLES   TENANT'S DINING TABLES

windows, that can disrupt the usable floor space. Generally, no furniture can be placed in front of such a window. Of course, an alternative would be to allow the architects and designers to illustrate to residents, either by written document or in person, how they intend furnishings to be arranged and why these arrangements are most desirable. Even then, because it is unlikely that all residents would want to arrange their furniture in exactly the same way, a more appropriate alternative would be the provision of spaces that allow variety in furniture placement.

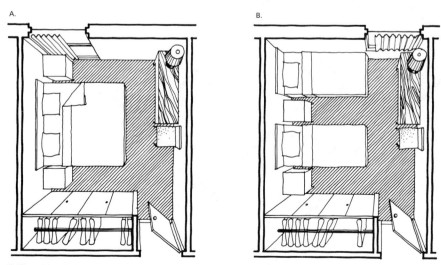

ON 'A' IMPROPER WINDOW PROHIBITS THE USE OF TWO TWIN BEDS AND LIMITS OPTIONS
(DOUBLE BED OR PUSHED—TOGETHER TWIN BEDS HAVE TO BE USED UNLESS BED IS PUSHED
AGAINST WINDOW).

197

COMPONENTS OF DESIGN—SOCIAL AND BEHAVIORAL

PRIVACY

Privacy does not mean isolation. Rather, it is the ability to control when and where an individual will be faced with neighbors or their sounds and activities. Designers should provide both visual privacy and privacy from the sounds of neighbors.

EXTERIOR PRIVACY.   In the exterior spaces of the site, controlling sound can be difficult. A barrier must be placed between the dwelling and sources of unwanted sound. Vegetation can be used to reduce the noise from high activity areas. For example, evergreen shrubs and low trees might be planted between a play area for older children and residences. Although vegetation will not eliminate the noise, if properly selected, it can make the level more tolerable.

Residents should also have visual privacy from certain areas of high or objectionable activity, for example, recreation areas and trash storage areas. Again, evergreen shrubs and low trees planted between a play area for older children and residences would provide visual privacy, as well as a barrier for noise.

INTERIOR PRIVACY.   Two privacy issues must be addressed when designing housing interiors. First, both visual and sound privacy from other residents must be established. Residents should be able to control the amount of sound that comes into their units and the extent to which others can see into their units. Particularly troublesome is the elimination of the sound from adjacent dwelling units. Kuper[26] in 1953 studied units whose floor plans essentially required that the heads of the beds in adjacent apartments would be against the party wall. Residents were found to be troubled and embarrassed by the noises from their neighbors. Francescato et al.[27] found complaints of this type still existed in 1973. Acoustic privacy from adjacent units can be established in a number

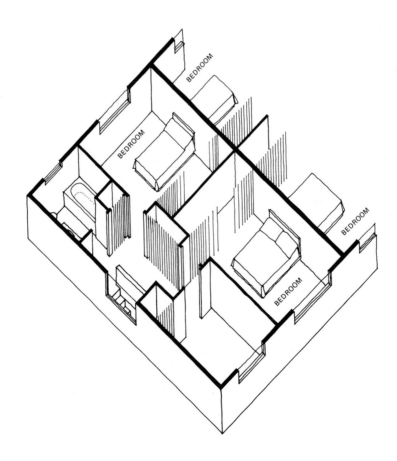

of ways, including the placement of sound absorbing spaces, for example, closets and storage cabinets, as well as by use of sound-absorbing material.

To promote privacy within the dwelling some spatial relationships help, for example, placing entrances to bathrooms in nonpublic areas and bedrooms in the least accessible areas. Other, subtle, issues are involved, such as the ability of several members of a household to be within the same dwelling and yet separate from each other. Francescato et al.[28] indicated that being able to get away from other household members is important to people. Privacy within the home can be augmented by providing one or more semiprivate spaces, such as a loft or study alcove.

SOCIAL INTERACTION

There is ample evidence from the social sciences that the design of housing developments, both highrise and lowrise, can inhibit or encourage casual social interaction among the residents. Moller[29] suggests that the physical environment of housing affects the mental health of people by the way that it fosters or inhibits casual meetings and the formation of friendships. Thus the designer must promote opportunities for residents to encounter their neighbors casually. In such casual meetings friendships are developed. The shared physical environment of two strangers can provide the opportunity for friendship, if that friendship is desired.

However, casual interactions must be kept within the public and semipublic spaces of the development. If they impinge upon individuals, or their dwelling units, the positive value declines and the negative value as an infringement on privacy increases. Architects must balance the need for individual privacy with the need for corporate community.

The designer can provide opportunities for casual social interaction by clustering public facilities: laundry rooms, parking lots, mail boxes. These areas will be much more successful in facilitating social interaction than a more explicit social area. An area set aside especially for sitting, chatting, and casual socializing is all right if friendships exist, but without an existing fabric of friendships these areas will usually be unused.

PHYSICAL CHARACTERISTICS OF RESIDENTIAL ENVIRONMENTS

SIZE AND DENSITY

The sizes of housing developments that architects are asked to design vary from a minimum of one to over a thousand dwelling units. Also, for any given number of units, there is a wide range in the possible density of those units.

Francescato et al.[30] found that, in the subsidized housing which they studied residents were often as satisfied in high-density developments as in low-density developments. Lansing et al.[31] found that, in the middle-income housing that they studied, densities greater than 12 dwelling units per acre were associated with decreased residential satisfaction. Baldassare[32] examined the relationship between neighborhood density (in terms of census tract density) and responses to two national surveys. He found a clear relationship between high neighborhood satisfaction and low density.

It is clear that designing often becomes more difficult in high-density situations. The provision of amenities such as adequate visual and auditory privacy becomes more difficult as densities increase. Therefore, it seems that providing good housing becomes more difficult as density increases. However, it is also clear that if attention is paid to aspects such as privacy, maintenance, and territorial control, residents can be satisfied with housing at high densities.

The size of a multifamily housing development, in number of dwelling units, can affect the success of the development. Francescato et al.[33] found that the greater the number of dwelling units in a development, the lower, the degree of satisfaction with living there. They concluded that developments of relatively small size are easier to design and manage. However, small size alone will not be of much help when other aspects of the designed environment are negative.

SITE LAYOUT

A large variety of site layouts can be successful in multifamily housing. While some architects believe that certain types of layout are intrinsically better than others (for example, Frampton,[34] who sees inherent virtures of livability in a lowrise high-density type of layout known as "carpet" or "matrix" housing), there is no indisputable evidence that there is only one successful layout type. In fact, Francescato et al.[35] found relatively low levels of resident satisfaction in an example of carpet housing. Residents cited problems with privacy from neighbors and the inconvenient location of common facilities such as parking and recreation. Again, as with density, a particular layout type can make specific problems, such as parking, recreation, or privacy easier or more difficult to deal with. As Francescato et al. point out, no matter what type of layout is chosen, the specific way in which it is detailed will lead to its ultimate success or failure.

RECREATION FACILITIES

Adequate recreation facilities in multifamily housing developments should provide recreation opportunities for specific groups of individuals: preschoolers, grade school children, teenagers, and young adults. Each of these groups has particular needs and interests which influence both the location and the type of facilities provided.

The youngest group, preschoolers, needs to have facilities close to the dwelling unit. An enclosed, secure outdoor yard space adjacent to each dwelling unit may often be sufficient. If the outdoor space is of sufficient size (probably 100 sf or more) and if it can be easily observed from the interior of the dwelling unit, then adults can allow the youngest children to play outside and still supervise them from the home (see illustration on top p. 201).

In common recreation areas provided for the youngest children facilities must be of such a scale and type that they will not attract older children. Often 80-100 sf will provide sufficient space. Large preschool tot-lots may be taken over by grade school children or teenagers, and become unavailable to the group for which they were intended. Also, tot-lots must be located in close proximity to the dwelling units since their use often depends upon the child being accompanied by a parent or an older

sibling. Therefore, a number of small tot-lots placed around a housing development is apt to be more desirable than a single large tot-lot in a central location.

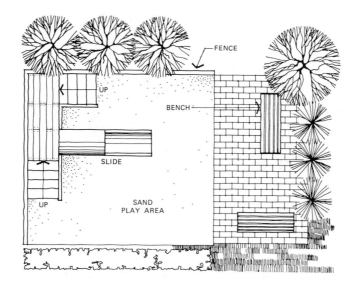

Separate recreation areas must usually be designated for grade school children and teenagers. The interests, needs, and abilities of these two groups are vastly different. Grade school areas should probably be kept within the residential area of a development, where there is the potential for casual adult supervision. Teenage facilities might better be placed on the periphery, where teens can feel more independent. Grade school children will want facilities which challenge the imagination and motor skills. Sculptural elements will usually prove to be nothing but unused sculpture. Facilities that have been successful for this group include items like cable slides and bike trails (see illustration on p. 202).

Teenagers will need facilities that support their interests in sports, socializing, and automobiles. Basketball areas (with adjacent sitting areas and water fountains) and car wash areas are among the facilities that will be used by this group.

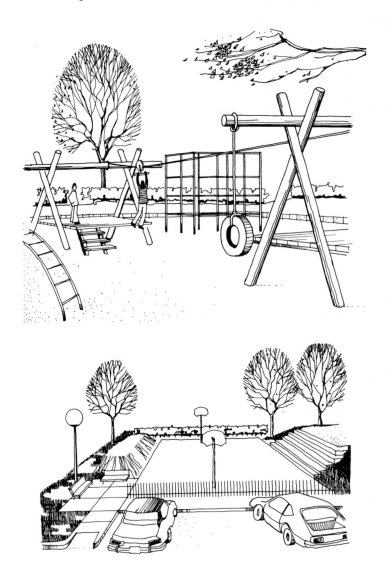

PARKING

The provision of adequate parking in multifamily housing often accounts for a major portion of the land use. No doubt the ideal solution for the automobile is an attached garage for every unit (indeed a two-car garage); unfortunately, this is generally impossible to achieve. There remains, however, a large variety of solutions for automobile parking. Francescato et al.[39] when they examined 37 multifamily developments found some parking solutions more satisfactory to residents than others. Shown here is a site plan they found to have satisfactory parking arrangements and the site plan of a development where parking was less than satisfactory. Obviously, one distinction between these plans is that the less satisfactory parking arrangement consists of large parking lots at the periphery of the dwelling units. This separation of parking from residences has the theoretical benefit that it separates pedestrians and vehicles. However, it entails some practical problems which residents seem to feel outweigh the potential theoretical benefits. Those problems include an inability to observe and protect the automobile from vandalism and theft. A second difficulty is the distance between an individual's car and dwelling unit. In inclement weather, ordinary tasks such as bringing home groceries can become quite unpleasant or even impossible as the distance between car and dwelling unit is increased.

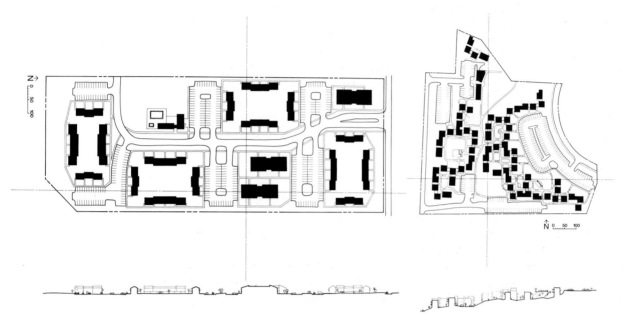

Designers should be aware of the tendency of residents to assume ownership of specific parking spaces. Residents generally feel that the parking spaces directly in front of their units are their own. When neighbors or outsiders park in spaces which the residents claim as their own, antagonism and, in fact, physical violence can occur. Thus, although four parking spaces may be provided for a building of four dwelling units, their location directly in front of only one unit may lead to conflict among the neighbors.

The emphasis on bringing the automobile close to the dwelling unit does not mean that all attempts to do this will be successful. The designer must be aware of, and

sensitive to, certain undesirable associations. For example, parking should not be arranged such that headlights shine into bedroom windows. Also, parking should not be arranged so that the primary view from a living room consists of the grill work of automobiles.

It should be noted that one possible solution to some of the parking problems, a solution often suggested by multifamily housing residents, is the assignment of spaces to individual units. This is, of course, more than a design solution since it requires the commitment of housing management to undertake the assignment and to enforce it.

There is a tendency for a parking area to become recreational. Without other appropriate facilities, much of the recreational activity of grade school children and teens will occur in and adjacent to the parking areas. Bicycling, ball games, and "hanging out," in parking areas, can threaten the safety of the children and teens as well as the security of the automobiles left there. These problems can be alleviated by providing other facilities, locating parking so that adult resident surveillance can occur naturally, and using configurations that reduce the area of any single parking area.

STORAGE

Storage is often neglected in the design of housing. The lack of sufficient storage has been observed to be a significant problem for the functioning of family life. In multifamily housing it is not uncommon to find objects such as bicycles, snow tires, and lawn mowers stored in hallways, kitchens, balconies and furnace rooms which militates against the original function of these spaces and provides a constant source of aggravation to the residents. It is important to remember to provide easily accessible storage specifically for outdoor furnishings and equipment.

APPEARANCE

The appearance of housing, along with such aspects of the housing environment as management and other residents, has been found by Francescato, et al.[37] to be a major determinant of satisfaction with where one lives. Their research indicates that satisfaction with appearance depends less on using a specific style than it does on the presence of a complex visual image, with a variety of shapes, sizes, and colors. Apparently in considering their own residential environment, people are more apt to agree with Venturi[38] that "less is a bore" than they are with more common doctrine that "less is more." Becker,[39] Hesselgren,[40] and Francescato et al.[41] all confirm the need for visual complexity in the exterior forms and spaces of a residential environment. Of course, this should not be interpreted as license for design that is chaotic. Basic principles of visual design must be adhered to: rhythm, balance, and proportion.

The use of a substantial amount of plant materials has been found important by a number of researchers (Anderson and Butterfield,[42] Becker,[43] and Peterson,[44]). As Becker[45] points out, the careful placement of plant materials can make a development composed of rather ordinary buildings attractive. The designer must remember, however, that immature shrubs and trees are apt to have minimal impact upon the appearance of a development, and unless they are properly maintained, they can often be a negative factor.

Attention to detail is important. The care, selection, and placement of exterior lighting fixtures, the location and concealment of utility meters and boxes, the location and concealment of garbage storage areas are among specific details that must be dealt with, to achieve overall attractiveness.

The geometry of interior spaces can be used to vary their formality. Canter and Wools,[46] studying the effects of room configuration, found that a rectangular interior space was felt to be formal while the same interior with a sloped ceiling was felt to be informal.

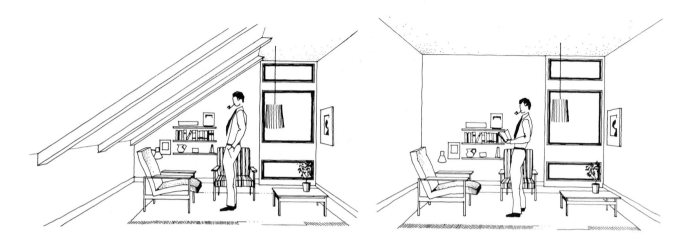

In the long run, the continued attractiveness of a multifamily housing development will depend upon the way in which it is maintained by residents and management. To the extent that the architect makes a development easy to maintain, long-run attractiveness will be positively influenced. However, ease of maintenance accomplished at the expense of variety in materials, colors, and shapes will merely result in efficiency, not attractiveness.

ANTHROPOMETRICS

The architect must remember that variety in people is great: height, weight, and strength vary among individuals. Yet different people are often expected to use a similar environment. The kitchen counters in residences are often placed 36 in. from the floor both in housing for the elderly and housing for young singles. However, the heights of elderly women can be expected to be several inches less than those of young women, who are probably several inches shorter than young men. How can the same counter height be expected to be comfortable for all?

The answer, of course, is that the same counter height will not be equally comfortable for people of different heights. The study of anthropometrics has determined that, in order to maximize comfort, the physical environment should fit the physical dimensions of the user. Thus, what is needed is a range of counter heights, chair seat heights, etc., that will fit the variety of body sizes that the architect can expect will use the environment. For example, the average seating height information from *Graphic Standards*, is usually the only one used for design. Neglect of this issue can result in discomfort and irritation to the user. For example, an elderly woman of 5 ft 2 in. sitting on a concrete bench in front of her apartment building can expect her feet to go to sleep if the seat height is greater than 16 in.

One practice that can help designers to develop plans that are more practical is to include the plan view of a person, as well as furniture when showing the plan of a room. Simply drawing a room with its required furnishings does not prove that it will work. The remaining spaces must be sufficient for people who are standing, walking, bending over, and otherwise occupying space (see illustration on p. 206).

In designing housing, the architect must consider how to make the environment accessible and usable to the disabled. This requires an initial recognition of the variety

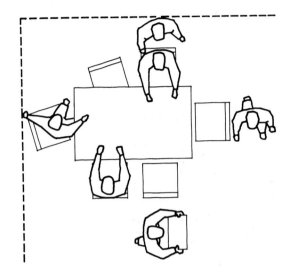

of disabilities and the way that the physical environment can handicap a disabled person. Local and federal government agencies often require a portion of new housing to be accessible to disabled persons, particularly those confined to wheelchairs. This requires a thorough understanding of the anthropometrics of the person in a wheelchair.

GENERAL CONCERNS

ENVIRONMENTAL DETERMINISM

All architects must consider their individual positions on the question of environmental determinism. Under what conditions, if any, can the physical environment cause people to behave, think, or feel in a particular way.

Rather than holding a strict view of environmental determinism, the architect probably needs to adopt a view of environmental facilitation, that the environment can provide support for a range of behaviors that depend on *individual choices* of persons using that environment.

It is obvious that the physical environment does determine certain behaviors in extreme cases. For example, a refrigerator and range in a room certainly determine that meals will be prepared there. However, other behaviors not related to food preparation are not excluded. The environment usually permits a range of behaviors, rather than only a specific behavior. For example, the same room used for food preparation might also be used for informal social gatherings, but socializing is not determined by the presence of a refrigerator and range in the same way that food preparation is.

QUALITY OF SOCIAL AND BEHAVIORAL INFORMATION

Both architects and social scientists need accurate information about the social and behavioral components of the housing environment. Architects must make immediate decisions about the designs of specific environments. On the other hand, social scientists caution against immediate use of such information. They want to improve the quality of the current information. Those two viewpoints may seem in conflict, but in reality are simply two equally legitimate concerns.

It must also be remembered that the nature of information about the social and behavioral components of housing design is different from the information about some other components of design. Some items of social and behavioral information may be unstable, over time or over geographic areas. This is not to say that social and behavioral information is therefore not useful to the designer; designers must use the best information available to them. Rather, the implication is that closer attention will need to be paid to the quality and source of this type of information than is paid to information about other components, such as structure.

AVAILABILITY OF SOCIAL AND BEHAVIORAL INFORMATION

Attention will also have to be paid to judging systematically the success of specific design decisions based upon social and behavioral information. The emerging concept of post-occupancy evaluation seeks to do this. Such evaluation will allow designers to increase their confidence in specific social and behavorial concepts. It will allow clients to increase their confidence in designer's decisions. Also, evaluations will allow designers to direct social scientists toward correcting deficiencies in the existing knowledge of environment-behavior interactions.

Obviously, this chapter has not identified all available information about specific social and behavioral components of design. That is beyond the scope of an individual chapter; examination of material such as that listed in the bibliography will provide additional information. However, the preceding does indicate that information about the social and behavioral components of the design of housing is available. While this information may often be incomplete, it can contribute to the design of successful housing.

COMPONENTS OF DESIGN— DEVELOPMENT AND FINANCING   8

Jared Shlaes

ASSESSING THE SITUATION

Housing development involves large capital commitments, several levels of government, a wide variety of businesses and individuals, and long periods of time, in the course of which a great many things can go wrong. Murphy's Law works just as efficiently in this field as in others. As a result, successful development requires drive, alertness, and careful planning.

It helps to study the situation carefully before a development is undertaken. The first step is ordinarily an evaluation of market conditions. The developer and the lenders will want to know how great is the market potential of the development, how well the development concept meets the apparent desires of the market, who the likely customers will be, and how strongly they will be drawn to the project.

A massive literature exists on this subject, and a number of firms specialize in the necessary research. Professional market and feasibility analysts have skills and knowledge to contribute as do real estate counselors and appraisers. Many developers, however, choose to rely on their own observations and instincts. In an active marketplace, where there are many comparable developments which can be observed and copied or modified as needed, or in the case of an isolated and unique development not susceptible to the usual kinds of market analysis technique, this approach may be entirely adequate. Where conditions are less clear and research can yield needed information, though, the relatively small investment required is more than justified. A properly conducted market analysis yields precious information regarding the size and characteristics of the demand pool from which tenants or buyers must be attracted, gives a good indication of the rents or prices that can be charged, provides a realistic projection of the time required to fill or sell the project, and helps the architect and the developer design accommodations that will be attractive to the desired prospects. Such things as floor plans, unit equipment and finishes, parking arrangements, and project amenities should answer the needs and wishes of the desired occupants rather than the prejudices of the architect or developer. While it is not necessary to follow market research slavishly, one should know about the indications it can provide.

Knowledge of existing demand has little value if it is not accompanied by knowledge of available and prospective supply. A careful investigation of competing developments and of those that may be in the pipeline will provide a good indication of the market in which a project will have to survive. Building permit data, architects' and contractors' scuttlebutt, media announcements, and other sources can give at least an approximate picture of the amounts, characteristics, and locations of other projects likely to be competing with yours for the available demand. Equally important is a close analysis of competing developments to see how they stack up and to learn how serious the threats they may offer are.

Once demand and supply conditions are at least roughly known, it is possible to consider the financial feasibility of the project. With preliminary plans drawn to reflect market research findings or the developer's estimates, preliminary cost estimating follows. Using rules of thumb or experience in comparable developments, developers and their financing advisors can usually project with a reasonable degree of accuracy what total project costs are likely to be. These will incorporate not only land and construction costs, but also the full array of so-called soft costs: points paid to lenders and mortgage brokers, interest on funds borrowed during construction, architectural and engineering fees, prints of drawings and specifications, property surveys, soils tests and borings, carrying costs on unoccupied units, and marketing costs including model apartment furnishings, leasing or sales personnel, brochures, advertising, public relations, commissions to outside brokers, and custodial costs. Cost estimates should also include appropriate allowances for anticipated price escalations and an ample allowance to cover contingencies.

With the preliminary overall cost budget in hand, the economic potential of the project can be measured against estimated costs to arrive at a judgment of feasibility. Rental projects are of course treated differently from sales projects such as condominium and row house developments. For a rental project, the developer will estimate rents for each unit, by square footage or any other yardstick adjusted as necessary, and will add up the rents to arrive at an estimate of gross possible rental income. From this may be deducted a vacancy and rent loss allowance based upon the experience of other developments in the area. To the rental income projection may be added any rents expected from commercial space and allowances for incidental income from parking, laundry, and other services sold to tenants. The resulting adjusted total is the estimated effective gross income of the project.

From this estimate operating costs are then deducted. These include janitorial and ground services, supplies, fuel, electricity for common areas, water and sewer charges, allowances for repairs and periodic redecorating and painting, any charges for special items such as television antenna service, casualty and liability insurance premiums, and taxes including property taxes. Subtracting these items yields the estimated net operating income (NOI), which is the basis of most appraisal and financing calculations.

Rental projects have ordinarily been funded with borrowed money repaid over a long term on a level payment basis. Money market conditions have changed so dramatically in recent years that this may no longer be the case except for projects developed under government loan programs. Privately funded conventional long-term self-amortizing mortgages, long the mainstay of real estate finance, are well understood by lenders and developers and permit rapid calculation of debt service requirements, which are based on formulae that provide for the periodic repayment of the loan in equal installments, usually monthly. Each such installment incorporates a payment for interest on the amount of the loan still outstanding at the payment date, plus a contribution towards the eventual retirement of the loan. Such loans may either be self-liquidating or partially self-liquidating, with an unsatisfied portion of the loan, known as a balloon, left unpaid at the time of maturity. By means of mortgage payment books available from many lending institutions and financial pocket calculators payment schedules can be determined. (See the following page for examples.)

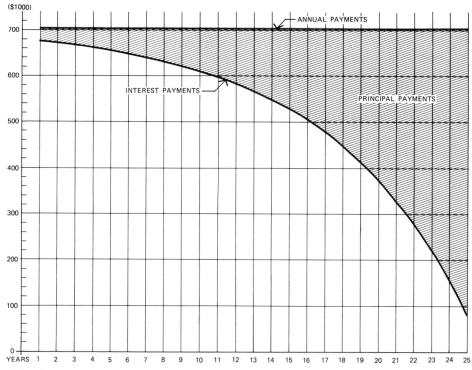

SELF—AMORTIZING LEVEL PAYMENT LOAN:
ANNUAL LOAN PAYMENT SCHEDULE

SELF-AMORTIZING LEVEL PAYMENT LOAN: ANNUAL PAYMENT SCHEDULE[a]

Year	Principal	Interest	Total
1	$ 29,725	$675,000	$704,725
2	33,738	670,987	704,725
3	38,293	666,432	704.725
4	43,462	661,263	704,725
5	49,330	655,395	704,725
6	55,989	648,736	704,725
7	63,547	641,178	704,725
8	72,126	632,599	704,725
9	81,863	622,862	704,725
10	92,915	611,810	704,725
11	105,459	599,266	704,725
12	119,695	585,030	704,725
13	135,854	568,871	704,725
14	154,195	550,530	704,725
15	175,011	529,714	704,725
16	198,637	506,088	704,725
17	225,454	479,271	704,725
18	255,890	448,835	704,725
19	290,435	414,290	704,725
20	329,644	375,081	704,725
21	374,146	330,579	704,725
22	424,655	280,070	704,725
23	481,984	222,741	704,725
24	547,051	157,674	704,725
25	620,903	83,822	704,725

[a] The diagram and the annual loan payment schedule are based upon a 25-year self-amortizing level payment loan of $5,000,000 borrowed at an interest rate of 13.5%. For purposes of this illustration, payments are made annually, with each payment equal to 14.095% of the original loan value; in practice, payments would be made monthly and the annual payment total would be slightly lower because of more frequent compounding.

In the case of government-funded or guaranteed mortgage programs such as those of the U.S. Department of Housing and Urban Development's Federal Housing Authority, the Government National Mortgage Association's tandem program, or the various programs made available by state housing finance authorities, debt service schedules may stretch out over longer periods than in conventional mortgages, often reaching 40 years rather than the 25 or 30 years common in conventional mortgage practice. These government programs typically require additional periodic payments in the form of mortgage insurance or other charges intended to help fund the operations of the agency. The longer repayment period, which reduces periodic debt service requirements, will usually more than compensate for these additional charges, and may, under certain programs such as the FHA Section 236 low- and moderate-income rental housing program and GNMA's tandem program, provide the needed funds at below-market interest rates, perhaps in exchange for an agreement to offer the resulting dwelling units at below-market rents and other concessions. Whether the mortgage is conventional or government-aided, the most important test of feasibility is the ability of the project to meet its debt service requirements out of NOI with enough left over to provide an operating cushion and some sort of return on the owner's investment. Although tax benefits can be an important and even a determining factor in feasibility calculations, the developer must be able to show the lender that NOI is sufficient for debt service or the lender will not ordinarily accept the risk and the project will not be built.

The calculation for sales projects is basically similar, but simpler. Anticipated selling prices of the individual units are summed to arrive at the estimated gross sales potential. From this amount the costs of sale are deducted. These are essentially the same as the hard and soft costs associated with a rental project, except that carrying and selling costs tend to be much heavier when units must be sold instead of rented. The amount left over after these costs are deducted is the anticipated profit before income taxes; it must be sufficiently large to offer an inducement to the developer for the risks being undertaken and a reassurance to the lender that an ample cushion is available to cover any problems during development. While developers often base preliminary calculations on the assumption of a quick sell-out that will require no allowances for carrying unsold units during the marketing period, in real life sales programs can stretch over several years, so it is prudent to prepare a detailed schedule that sets forth anticipated sales, costs and profits over the entire anticipated marketing period (Tables 3, 4, and 5 give examples).

Just as construction dollars are laid out as work is completed, soft costs and at times land costs can be paid out over time. The details will vary from one project to the next and will depend to some degree upon market conditions and the policies of the lender, but it is usually possible to persuade at least some purveyors of construction and other services to wait for their compensation until the rental or sales program is far advanced, thus minimizing the developer's cash requirements and interest costs. This practice may, of course, entail inferior work.

Because a dollar in the future is worth less than a dollar today, and indeed much less in times of high interest rates, it is necessary to translate anticipated future dollars into current terms in making feasibility calculations. This is done by a process known as discounting, which is based upon the rules of compound interest. Because compound interest theory and discounting techniques are beyond the scope of this work, the reader is referred to any of the standard texts on the subject. Those familiar with pocket financial calculators will be able to carry out the needed procedures in most cases; if not, professional help must be sought.

Careful feasibility analysis requires the consideration of other possible outcomes. Some developments can more easily stand a longer rent-up or sell-out period than others, or a misjudgment in rent or pricing. A 10% error in rental projections may wipe out a heavily subsidized housing project, but may do little harm to a luxury rental. Because different levels of risk are associated with different kinds of projects, the prudent investor will be careful to match project risk against personal investment standards.

Income tax factors can make an immense difference. Because under existing laws improved real estate is treated differently from most other investments for income tax purposes and because those laws were in part calculated to encourage new rental housing development, special benefits are available to the rental apartment developer. These take the form of allowable depreciation rates that range up to twice the appropriate straight-line depreciation rate (see the diagram and table below) and permission to depreciate the entire cost of the improvements even though they may be financed with the help of nonrecourse debt. It is often possible, or at least has often been possible in the past, to fund large apartment developments with relatively small amounts of equity capital, particularly under government-aided housing programs which offer mortgages based upon 90% of cost, where cost is defined to include an allowance for the builder-sponsor's profit and risk which tends to approach 10% of total value, thus obviating any substantial capital contribution by the developer. The tax shelter opportunities created by such highly leveraged financing and by the rules applicable to improved real estate are useful in raising any needed capital and in enhancing the overall feasibility of the project. While changes in the laws affecting tax shelter are always to be expected, housing should continue to enjoy favored treatment compared to most other forms of investment (see illustrations below and on p. 214).

While a detailed discussion of income taxes would be out of place here, two important principles should be noted: First and most important is the rule that where level-

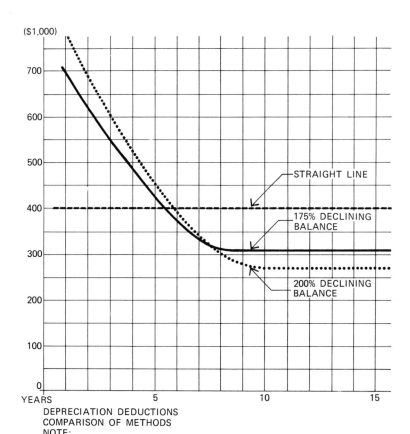

DEPRECIATION DEDUCTIONS
COMPARISON OF METHODS
NOTE:
Method shifts from declining balance to straight-line at point calculated to produce best results for taxpayer.

DEPRECIATION SCHEDULES: COMPARISON OF METHODS[a]

Depreciable Basis: $6,000,000

Life: 15 years

Method

Year	Straight Line	175% Declining Balance	200% Declining Balance
1	$400,000	$700,000	$800,000
2	400,000	618,333	693,333
3	400,000	546,194	600,888
4	400,000	482,471	520,770
5	400,000	426,183	451,334
6	400,000	376,461	391,156
7	400,000	332,541	339,002
8	400,000	314,726	293,801
9	400,000	314,726	272,816
10	400,000	314,726	272,816
11	400,000	314,726	272,816
12	400,000	314,726	272,816
13	400,000	314,726	272,816
14	400,000	314,726	272,816
15	400,000	314,726	272,816

[a]Method shifts from declining balance to straight-line at point calculated to produce best results for taxpayer.

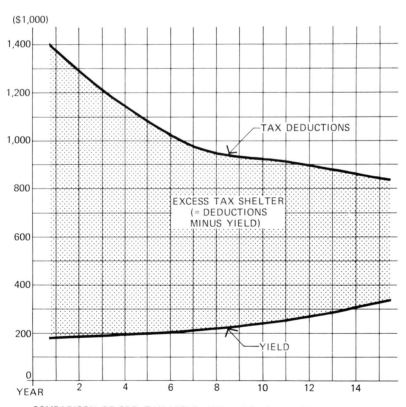

COMPARISON OF PRE—TAX YIELD AND INCOME TAX SHELTER (YIELD=CASH RETURN TO EQUITY PLUS AMORTIZATION PAYMENTS)

payment long-term mortgage financing is used, the deduction from ordinary income provided by mortgage interest payments will decrease over time as the mortgage is paid down and as that portion of the mortgage payment attributable to debt reduction increases. This decline in interest payments starts slowly and then increases at an increasing rate (see diagram on page 211). As a result, tax shelter associated with mortgage interest payments under these conditions will shrink rapidly, and at times catastrophically, after a certain number of years. This shrinkage must be planned for.

Second, it is important to remember that where accelerated depreciation methods such as double declining balance or 175% declining balance are used, depreciation deductions will *also* tend to decline, but at a decreasing rate. The resulting depreciation curve (see diagram on page 213) makes this clear. When the level-payment mortgage is combined with an accelerated depreciation method, the result is massive deductions from income in the early years followed by a rapidly deteriorating income-tax position, often at a time when income from operations is also declining because of the aging of the improvements. Recapture rules can create an income tax trap in which the unhappy owner, who no longer has available the hefty deductions of the early years to offset income from other sources, is now in the position of either using other funds to keep the project afloat, or letting it go under and thereby incurring the immense income tax penalties associated with recapture. These can very nearly wipe out the accumulated value of all the tax savings of the project during its early years, as the Internal Revenue Service considers abandonment or foreclosure to be the equivalent of a sale for tax purposes, and the sale is deemed to relieve the taxpayer of the liability represented by the unpaid balance of any existing mortgages, whether or not the taxpayer is personally liable for its repayment. Many sophisticated developers avoid accelerated depreciation for this reason, instead they use straight-line methods which create much less of a recapture problem in the event of premature sale or project insolvency.

Once the preliminary calculations have been completed and the project has been determined feasible on a preliminary basis, costs can be refined as project design advances and further information comes to light. After planning and design have been completed, final construction costs ascertained to the extent possible, and financing arrangements made, all figures are reviewed so that financing, accounting, and income tax forecasts can be prepared with confidence. The development is then in a position to move forward.

Not only income tax effects, but also the anticipation of further inflation can influence feasibility calculations and developers' thinking. Particularly where fixed-dollar mortgage financing is available, developers and investors alike will look forward to an inflationary future in which current dollars can be repaid later using inflated dollars thrown off by the project. If the investor can look forward to massive tax shelter in the early years, followed by equity growth far in excess of loan amortization payments because of inflation, a venture which may at first seem only marginally worthwhile may appear much more profitable. This kind of thinking has greatly influenced developer decisions in markets where conversion of rental apartments to condominium at some future date is a realistic possibility. Other effects of inflation may be less desirable: high interest rates, new mortgage loan formats often involving lender participation in the profits of a venture, variable interest rates, and the like.

Returns on investment as calculated by equity investors may vary greatly between investors and compared to the returns expected from other forms of investment. High-bracket taxpayers will look upon housing development ventures very differently from the way that lower-bracket institutional investors will, and the returns required by both may include explicit or implicit components reflecting inflation and income-tax considerations. The mortgage interest rate, long a yardstick in the analysis of real estate development, is no longer a reliable indicator of the equity returns desired by investors, nor are available interest rates considered adequate returns by most long-term rental apartment lenders unless accompanied by some participation in venture profits.

SELECTING THE PROJECT AND THE SITE

Not every kind of housing development is suited to every developer or investor. Sophisticated developers with strong tax shelter orientation will be interested in and profit from large-scale rental developments, particularly if they are financed under one or another government-aided programs intended to maximize investment leverage and tax shelter. More conservative or less sophisticated builders and investors may prefer conventional loan programs if they are available on feasible terms, or sales programs for condominiums and row houses which are essentially manufacturing operations and require manufacturing and marketing skills rather than financial sophistication.

The selection of the project also involves consideration of size and location. The size desired may be a function of the available capital, of market availability, of lender attitudes, of site limitations, or of the developer's own willingness to accept risk and handle operations at various project sizes. Many developers are prisoners of their own organizations and must build almost regardless of cost and demand considerations if they can find the money; others are far more cautious and will move only when they see a clear opportunity for substantial profit.

Project location may be a question of opportunity or of comparative judgment. Quite often developers will seize upon an available option if the terms are right and the location appears practicable. Where there is an opportunity to choose, though, it pays to consider the alternatives before selecting a site.

Other things being equal, the preferred site will be large enough to accommodate a project of the desired size, located in an area or neighborhood that will be attractive to customers able to pay the price, have high visibility, adequate soil conditions, good drainage, sufficient utilities, pleasant surroundings, suitable access, pleasant contours not requiring expensive rearrangement, and perhaps such distinguishing amenities as a good view or a desirable microclimate. Needed zoning must be in place or available within a reasonable period of time. Environmental or other constraints limiting development must not be unduly restrictive, and the site should be available on terms which leave the developer maximum freedom to investigate the site before committing large amounts of money, usually under an option agreement which can be extended if necessary.

Some developers are large enough to operate in a number of market areas and to select their sites in terms of long-range marketing objectives rather than the immediate attractiveness of the site itself. For most developers, though, a key question is operating convenience, which ordinarily dictates a site in or near the developer's primary area of operations.

GETTING PERMISSION

Zoning and other legal constraints upon development are of primary importance in site selection and development planning. Occasionally a project can be forced upon an unwilling community through the courts or by political maneuver, but a price will be paid—and not only in dollars. The delays accompanying such efforts will drive up costs by increasing interest charges on borrowed funds, and will also increase the uncertainties and risks which accompany any real estate development. A site already zoned, located in an area where other similar developments have been built or are currently underway, not subject to any unusual environmental or other restrictions, is preferable unless there is some compelling reason to choose otherwise.

Whether or not the needed zoning appears to be in place, it is advisable to meet and confer with key community leaders to test attitudes and establish procedures at an early stage. A degree of candor is necessitated. Preliminary plans and renderings, estimates of the tax revenues likely to be generated by the project, projections of school demand and other requirements for public services are helpful, if not essential. It is important to establish confidence as soon as possible, and equally important not to abuse that confidence by consciously misleading local officials, with whom you will be dealing as the project goes forward and who well know how to repay any abuse of confidence.

It is important that zoning and any other needed approvals such as environmental rulings be clearly established at an early stage, and that they not be modified later in ways that might harm the project. First-rate legal and professional consultants, who can minimize the risks of change, are well worth their cost.

PLANNING THE DEVELOPMENT

Financial and loan program limitations are the first consideration in planning the development. If rents and prices must be at minimum levels, there is no reason to develop elaborate and costly building concepts; if loan program requirements are designed for standard building types, originality may be too costly to be practical. Federal and state loan programs may also require specific building characteristics that will govern, at least to some extent, the form of the development: barrier-free design, presence or absence of specific amenities, minimum floor area requirements (which tend to become maximums in practice).

Once mandatory development characteristics have been taken into account, creative planning can begin. The site itself will dictate the massing and general form of buildings and landscaping. Local market conditions may suggest a preferred building format. In some areas, for example, eight-unit buildings are commonly accepted and can readily and profitably be resold by the developer, while in others larger or smaller groups of units may be preferred. The units themselves must be planned in terms of local needs and preferences, not solely in terms of the architect's or the developer's ideas. These can be established through market research or through a careful comparison of the performance of competing units in the same market area.

Increasingly important in both siting and building design are energy concerns. Correct building orientation, careful window placement, heavy insulation, double glazing, and the use of earth-moving and solar-collection techniques to reduce energy consumption may be necessary or desirable for legal, social, or economic reasons. The costs of such features can be weighed against the benefits to be anticipated over the life of the projects, using established discounting techniques. Even where high first costs may not be clearly offset by anticipated benefits in the form of energy savings, a reasonable expectation of further energy cost increases may encourage the use of all available conservation devices.

Throughout the planning process, of course, costs and benefits must be constantly traded off. More space, more light, higher energy efficiency, better views, and greater sound resistance are almost always desirable, but they may bring with them excessive costs. A balance must be struck between desired qualities and available funds.

An essential aspect of development planning is staging: how will the project be phased? If it is judged that the market can absorb, say, 100 units per year, then overall financial and development planning should reflect that level of demand while it retains some flexibilitiy in case things go faster or more slowly than anticipated. Phases should be reasonably self-contained so that deferring a phase will not render already completed phases unattractive or uninhabitable.

COMPONENTS OF DESIGN—DEVELOPMENT AND FINANCING

Once the general form, massing, and staging of the project are known, it becomes possible to prepare a preliminary schedule and draft a critical path diagram setting forth key sequences and events which must occur if the project is to be completed on time. Any such schedule or diagram must allow enough flexibility to handle the many crises and unanticipated occurrences which will inevitably arise. The experienced development manager will know how to minimize their impact and get the job done if scheduling is thorough and realistic.

FINDING THE MONEY AND PLANNING THE FINANCING

Real estate financing falls loosely into three categories: end or permanent loans, interim or construction loans, and equity funds.

The end loan is the permanent mortgage which will be placed on the property when the project is finished. It may be in the form of an overall loan covering an entire rental apartment complex or some building or combination of buildings within it, or it may be an individual loan on a condominium apartment or an individual row house.

It is the end loan which serve as the ultimate source of the bulk of the money needed to build most projects. Unless the developer is very certain of end loan availability, it will be wise to seek, at an early stage, commitments for such loans from responsible lenders before proceeding with construction. The cost of such commitments, ordinarily a small percentage of the amount committed, can be an excellent investment in times of rising interest rates or tightening money markets. Interim lenders, who want to make sure that the money will be there to repay them when the building is finished, will ordinarily insist that such commitments be made available as take-outs.

The interim loan or construction loan, usually provided by a bank, savings and loan association, real estate investment trust, mortgage banker, or other short-term loan source, is intended to cover all or most of the cost of acquiring the land and building the buildings. It may also include an allowance for the cost of carrying the project through to completion, including interest charges and other soft costs and a contingency reserve. Interest rates usually fluctuate with the prime rate, and the loan is for a relatively short term in anticipation of project completion and the take-out by the end lender. Like the end lender, the interim lender is ordinarily secured by a first mortgage or its equivalent on the property, so that in the event of default it can step in to take over and complete the project. Borrower guarantees are also frequently required. Realistic budgeting and scheduling are important in negotiating both end and interim loans to minimize the risk that delays or sudden escalations in interest rates will force cash requirements beyond available resources.

In addition to the funds made available by the end and interim lenders, cash may be required from the developers for project completion, carrying, and marketing. Lenders may require this as a way of assuring the developer's interest in the project, or money market conditions may be such that adequate borrowed funds are simply not available. In either event, the developers will use their own cash and lines of credit or those of their equity partners or investors to fill the gap and meet project needs. A recent development, seen before during the credit pinches of 1969 to 1970 and 1973 to 1974, is the increasing participation of insurance companies and other long-term lenders in equity investments, often in the form of equity participations supplementary to the basic loan agreement or in the form of direct joint venture and partnership arrangements in which the lender puts up all or a portion of the required funds in exchange for a share in project ownership.

From the viewpoint of the developer, who wants to retain as much as possible of the benefits of ownership while minimizing the risk to assets and maximizing chances of successful completion, such arrangements may be quite helpful. Instead of appearing as an entrepreneur tapping loan sources for needed capital, the developer becomes, in effect, a paid associate or agent of the capital source, receiving compensation in the form of earned construction profits plus a major participation in any profits of the venture. The financial leverage ordinarily sought in a development venture by maximizing the ratio of borrowed funds to equity capital is in effect handed over by the institutional lender in exchange for willingness to undertake the deal and share the profits.

A wide variety of government-aided mortgage programs exists to encourage developers in producing rental housing. The purposes and costs of these programs vary widely. Many of them require rents controlled tightly at levels far below market, which may be adequate to allow satisfaction of debt service requirements and payment of a modest dividend, but which can be adjusted only with extreme difficulty to reflect increasing operating costs. Others are more lenient. The programs are constantly in flux. Detailed discussion is beyond the scope of this work; a mortgage banker or attorney familiar with the programs available in the project area should be consulted. Because subsidy programs of this nature may soon constitute almost the only sources of funds for rental apartment development, individuals and communities interested in facilitating such development should be familiar with them.

In approaching prospective lenders, it is important to provide documentation as complete as possible, showing the scope of the project, preliminary physical plans (including at a minimum a site plan, typical floor plans, and typical elevations, plus, if possible, a rendering showing the overall concept, supplemented by sketches of

COMPARISON OF PRETAX YIELD AND INCOME TAX SHELTER [a]

Year	Amortization Payments	Cash Return to Equity	Total	Depreciation (175%)[b]	Interest Deductions	Total Tax Deductions
1	$ 29,275	$150,000	$179,275	$700,000	$675,000	$1,375,000
2	33,738	150,000	183,738	618,333	670,987	1,289,320
3	38,293	150,000	188,293	546,194	666,432	1,212,626
4	43,462	150,000	193,462	482,471	661,263	1,143,734
5	49,329	150,000	199,329	426,183	655,396	1,081,579
6	55,989	150,000	205,989	376,461	648,736	1,025,197
7	63,548	150,000	213,548	332,541	641,176	973,717
8	72,126	150,000	222,126	314,726	632,599	947,325
9	81,863	150,000	231,863	314,726	622,862	937,588
10	92,915	150,000	242,915	314,726	611,810	926,536
11	105,459	150,000	255,459	314,726	599,267	913,993
12	119,696	150,000	269,696	314,726	585,030	899,756
13	135,854	150,000	285,854	314,726	568,871	883,597
14	154,195	150,000	304,195	314,726	550,530	865,256
15	175,011	150,000	325,011	314,726	529,714	844,440

[a]This example is provided for illustrative purposes only. Actual tax shelter benefits will vary greatly, depending upon the impact of the minimum tax and other provisions of the tax law upon particular investors.
[b]Method shifts from declining balance to straight-line at point calculated to produce best results for taxpayer.

significant details), market analysis reports, a survey, results of any soils tests and borings, evidence of the proposed borrower's qualifications and capacity to repay, appraisals, and *pro forma* statements showing the economic characteristics of the project. These may be worked up in some detail to show anticipated costs, revenues and cash flows over the duration of the project. Lenders will be interested in the developer's qualifications and track record as well as in the specifics of the project.

RENTAL APARTMENT BUILDING DEVELOPMENT PRELIMINARY PRO FORMA[a]

DEVELOPMENT COSTS

HARD COSTS

Land acquisition	$ 2,200,000
Construction: building I (110 units; 116,000 sf @ $45/sf)	5,220,000
building II (same)	5,220,000
Site work	300,000
	$12,940,000
Contingency allowance (10%)	1,294,000
Total construction/hard costs	$14,234,000

FINANCING, SERVICE FEES, AND RELATED SOFT COSTS

Construction loan interest (15% × 75% × $17,500,000 × av. ½ year)	$ 984,000
Points on construction loan	328,000
Fees (legal, brokerage, etc.)	175,000
Miscellaneous	175,000
Marketing (advertising, models, staff)	400,000
Carrying cost of vacant units and other operating losses during rent-up	600,000
Total soft costs	$ 2,662,00
Total development costs	$16,896,000
rounded to	$16,900,000

PERMANENT FINANCING

Mortgage: 75% of $17,500,000 for 25 years @ 13.5% interest (annual constant 14%)	$13,125,000
Equity: 25%	$ 4,375,000
Annual mortgage expense (annual payments = 14% of $13,125,000)	$ 1,838,000

PRO FORMA INCOME AND EXPENSE

INCOME

Apartment rents: 220 @ $1200/month average	$ 3,168,000
Store/office rents	50,000
Other income (recreation fees, parking fees, etc.)	72,000
Total	$ 3,290,000
Less: vacancy and collection loss (5%)	−165,000
Estimated gross income	$ 3,125,000

EXPENSES

Management	$ 160,000
Fuel/heat	100,000
Electricity	38,000
Water/sewer	11,000
Payroll	65,000
Services	6,000
Maintenance, repairs	90,000
Decorating, painting	66,000
Real estate taxes, insurance	494,000
Miscellaneous	10,000
TOTAL	$ 1,040,000
Net operating income	$ 2,085,000
Less: mortgage payments	1,838,000
NET CASH FLOW	$ 247,000
Return on equity	5.65%[b]

[a] Figures are purely illustrative and should not be used as guides.

[b] This return would be considered inadequate by most developers. Even at the relatively high rents and low expenses projected, the project doesn't work, nor do most others under current conditions.

DEVELOPMENT COSTS AND INCOME OVER TIME: SALES PROJECT

	Year				
	1	2	3	4	Total
DEVELOPMENT COSTS					
Land acquisition	$ 7,800	$ 70,200	$ 0	$ 0	$ 78,000
Planning & engineering	24,000	24,000	0	0	48,000
Site work	0	112,000	80,000	0	192,000
House construction	0	36,000	462,000	198,000	696,000
Financing	8,440	23,440	58,500	17,060	107,440
Administrative and other	20,000	34,000	48,000	27,600	129,600
Commissions	0	0	21,600	21,600	43,200
Total costs	$ 60,240	$299,640	$670,100	$264,260	$1,294,240
INCOME					
Sales (@ $60,000)	$ 0	$ 0	$720,000	$720,000	$1,440,000
Net cash flow	$(60,240)	$(299,640)	$ 49,900	$455,740	$ 145,760

Source: Urban Land Institute, Residential Development Handbook (1978), and Shlaes & Co.

Emphasis will be on favorable previous experience and on the financial capability of the borrower. They will be particularly interested in the details of project funding, seeking to assure that the funds to be provided under the loan agreement will be sufficient, together with the borrower's available resources, to complete the project.

MINIMIZING THE TAX BITE

Because real estate, and in particular multifamily residential real estate, is among the few surviving escapes from the relentless escalation in the real income tax rate allowed by Congress, tax-conscious investors and developers pursue development ventures that from any other viewpoint would be beneath their attention. Few if any of these benefits attach to the development of housing for sale, which is treated like any other manufacturing operation and produces fully taxable ordinary income after deductions for costs of sale and other usual items. Trusts and elaborate corporate structures may be used to distribute the burden, defer it, or in other ways minimize it, but in the end the tax must ordinarily be paid.

Rental housing development, though, remains another ballgame. Interest paid and depreciation taken on new buildings are still fully deductible from income even though the buildings may have been largely funded with nonrecourse debt and so may have cost several times the actual cash outlay of the equity owner who gets the full benefit of that deductibility. In addition, new rental apartments are still eligible for favored depreciation treatment: sum-of-the-years-digits or declining-balance methods (up to a 200% declining balance rate may be used). These depreciation deductions, coupled with the high interest deductions that result from the customary level payment mortgage plan, produce tax shelter in the early years of the project's life far in excess of any cash dividends likely to be thrown off by the equity. This shelter can be applied within limits to other income, and produces salable equity values far greater than a simple capitalization of anticipated cash returns might suggest (see diagram on page 214).

Developers are familiar with this opportunity for gain and often sell or syndicate their equities to high-bracket investors, who become limited partners and share in the tax shelter and other benefits in exchange for a substantial cash commitment. Recent income tax reforms have modified the real impact of these concessions, and many investors continue to seek out and buy tax shelters of this type in apparent disregard of the eventual consequences, which usually include full payment of any taxes deferred. In times of sharp inflation, of course, any heavily leveraged investment that increases in value at the same pace as the general level of price increases will multiply the value of the equity through the effects of leverage. It is important to remember, though, that movements in the other direction are also possible, and that leverage works both ways.

Because the share of the profits in a typical real estate development taken by federal and state income taxes is so great, careful tax planning is important. Qualified professionals should be retained at an early stage, and their thinking should be incorporated in the overall financial and development plan.

SUPERVISING THE PROJECT

While the architect and the construction manager or contractor may be primarily responsible for completing the physical aspects of the development in a timely fashion, the developer exercises a supervisory role, to protect the investment made and to help the architectural and construction bosses meet their respective objectives without impairing the overall purposes of the development. The time lines laid down by the developer, often to reflect the seasonality of the market for the finished product or the requirements of the loan agreement, must be respected by all parties, and the developer will move rapidly to correct any apparent slippages in the construction schedule if they threaten that time line.

The project budget also requires careful watching. Changes in scheduling required by circumstances may force adjustments in the cash budgeting of the project. If these in turn result in increased interest or construction costs, provision must be made for them. The contractor will often have priorities quite different from those of the project, and may need to be forcefully reminded of its obligations to maintain the project schedule.

In addition to overall scheduling and budgeting responsibilities, the developer will be called upon for many small decisions as the project moves forward. Final adjustments to unit and building designs, appliance and color selections, and the approval of minor code compliance and other changes may be required. It is the market sense and marketing orientation of the developer that should govern in these matters if they do not interfere unreasonably with the architect's design concept and the builder's working requirements.

The developer will also be interested in providing intelligible and reasonable guarantee packages for purchasers of sales units, in preplanning an intelligent marketing effort, and in laying the groundwork for a rational management program after the building is completed and occupied. This can become particularly important in the case of condominiums and other developments requiring collective decisions by the occupants after the project is complete. Minor builder decisions can often have major impact on the maintenance costs and problems to be encountered later when the occupants take over, and should be responsibly considered by the developer.

In establishing a condominium or other form of collective ownership it is extremely important to draft the bylaws and the legal structure in such a way as to minimize friction and possible blowups later on. Careful and experienced counsel should be employed. The Community Associations Institute and the Urban Land Institute, both Washington-based, can provide model bylaws and guidance; also worth consulting is the Institute of Real Estate Management, an affiliate of the National Association of Realtors.

MARKETING THE PROJECT

A valid concept and a physical program which reflects that concept are not sufficient to assure project success. The units must be marketed—promptly, smoothly, and at sufficient prices. This will have required careful planning, recruitment of a competent staff, and development of suitable marketing materials. Professional marketing organizations exist, often as teams or departments within established real estate firms, but many developers prefer to form their own, recruiting and training personnel according to their own standards and practices. Adequate and sometimes outstanding training aids are available from the Realtors' National Marketing Institute, the National Association of Home Builders, and other sources.

The selection and furnishing of model units is an important aspect of the total effort. Requirements will differ in different markets, but it is ordinarily a good idea to furnish at least one model of each unit type. While furnishings in some markets must be eye catching to attract the attention of browsers, serious prospects will be more interested in an interior which reflects their own aspirations, and should be offered furnishings at least conceivably within their means. While some decorators try for minimum cash outlays, an investment in furnishing of reasonable quality can usually be recovered by selling the completed apartment or its furnishings to a customer in a hurry. The location of the models and the project office should be planned in such a manner as to force prospects through the sales office as they leave, where they can be spoken to and where staff can be available to answer questions.

Advertising and public relations programs must be crafted to fit the needs of the project. Sometimes a theme or image can be developed which will attract more than ordinary attention and expedite the marketing effort. Advertising budgets and planning should be worked on in consultation with competent marketing professionals, and an organized public relations campaign mounted to maximize exposure of the project through the media during the marketing period. It is important, though, not to oversell the project and thereby create unrealizable expectations.

Leasing policies and lease forms in subsidized rental projects may be essentially dictated by the government agency responsible for the program. Where they are not, local practice and the experience of major developers can be good guides.

Customer service is a vital aspect of marketing. Careful and respectful handling of customers and their complaints pays dividends as the project moves forward and helps to prevent repercussions later. Personnel who are sincerely motivated to be helpful can be of greater value than those interested only in closing sales or leases.

All marketing efforts should reflect the market information garnered in the course of feasibility analysis and from periodic visits to competing developments. The results of advertising and public relations campaigns should be continuously monitored so that lessons gathered from experience can be used to modify promotional efforts as needed. Market research techniques including depth interviews of those who have chosen the project as their home may yield valuable additional information.

PLANNING FOR TOMORROW

The business of housing production has changed radically in recent years and is evolving in new, still unclear directions. The conventional rental apartment may well be a thing of the past. Pressures for rent control in many communities, coupled with the high cost of money and the unwillingness of lenders to commit large sums for long terms without provision for protection against inflation or participation in owners' rewards, make it unlikely that the financial structures long associated with rental apartments will survive in anything like their traditional form. Subsidy programs, however, will probably be increased to take up some of the slack, if only in response to pressures from tenant groups and cities anxious to maintain a reasonable proportion of rental units in their housing stock. Developers able to use these programs to full advantage will continue to survive and thrive.

The drop in real income which Americans have had to face during the recent inflationary period suggests that despite recent surges in property values, capital for new housing will be in short supply in the years to come. Some shrinkage in unit sizes and some reduction in the amenities associated with multiple-family dwellings can therefore be expected. As family sizes continue to shrink, the number of households to grow, and the number of elderly to increase, apartments and other attached dwelling units should increase their share of the total housing market, creating new opportunities for apartment planners and developers.

Still to be measured is the impact of lifestyle adjustments which became noticeable in the 1960s and are becoming institutionalized. New forms of households, probably including various collective lifestyles, may well lead to changes in standard unit patterns to accommodate households with multiple heads. Projects which allow relatively modest individual accommodations in attractive settings with ample accommodation for collective recreation and socializing, perhaps on the model of the better singles complexes and resort hotels, will become more common. Rising energy costs will encourage this trend, and may also sustain the present relatively high level of reurbanization as working adults strive to bring home and workplace closer together.

If high interest rates continue, as now seems likely, income available for uses other than housing will represent a smaller share of total expenditures. This makes it all the more important that designers and developers strive for new and attractive housing formats at an affordable cost.

DESIGN METHODOLOGY

9

John Macsai

Although gathering data or programming and becoming familiar with and sorting out components is an orderly process, putting it all together, the design phase, is hardly ever orderly.

The best program, the most thorough knowledge of components, will not ensure good design. Good architecture will depend on the designer's talent, ability to respond to the challenge, and unrelenting, patient search for a solution. A multitude of avenues will have to be traveled. Many will turn out to be deadends before the answer is found. The designer works simultaneously on many levels: to consider plan, structure, mechanical system, exterior form, and the urban or suburban context into which the buildings will fit, to mention only the main categories. These categories influence one another; the limitations of one open new options in the others and vice versa. Design is a complex process.

Design seems altogether too mysterious to be rationally analyzed, which is the stated purpose of this book. Design methodology is the rationalization of the design procedure. It does not eliminate the "mystery" that makes a building good architecture. On the contrary, our purpose is to cast light on the inherent possibilities of each housing type, therefore to help the "mystery" to happen.

The chapters in this section deal with the design methodology of housing types that are grouped under the headings of high-, mid-, and lowrise. There is no generally accepted definition of these categories. In this book lowrise is a walk-up without elevators (two to three stories, maximum four); midrise is defined as a building that uses hydraulic elevators and consequently is limited in height (four to six or seven stories); highrise starts when electric elevators must be substituted for hydraulic ones and the maximum number of floors is limited only by current technology.

To develop the analysis from small toward large, from lowrise toward highrise, seems logical at first glance. A different approach was elected, however; highrise apartment buildings are discussed first. The highrise, because of its vertical repetitiveness, requires the strongest restraint and discipline; therefore it serves as an ideal introduction to design methodology by pointing the way from the most limited (highrise) toward the most permutable (lowrise) with an intermediate range (midrise) which can have the characteristics of both. Many issues and problems occur in all three categories. Because highrise is the first to be discussed, the issues already covered are only alluded to under lowrise or midrise.

Each category is considered as a solution of a housing problem. Currently fashionable social judgments are avoided as much as possible; for example, studies indicate that the highrise as a housing type creates more problems than it solves for low-income families. The studies deal with highrises built in the last 25 years, built without our present awareness of the need for "defensible space" so lucidly advocated by Oscar Newman. The fact is that these highrises, so justly criticized, were badly designed. Further, in most cases—however well designed—they would have been doomed to fail, due to the crowding together of broken families with large numbers of children, with a minimum of money and an even less than minimum of social institutions to serve them. In the belief that cures for our social ills can be found, without blaming them on highrises, these housing types are discussed as workable options under the proper circumstances for all social groups.

In each category apartment prototypes are illustrated. These prototypes are not necessarily usable under all circumstances; however, their introduction, to quote from Roger Sherwood's excellent book,

> is especially useful in the design of housing because housing lends itself readily to systematic, typological study. Most building types, such as theaters, schools, factories, or even office buildings, have to respond to different programs and are rarely consistent and repetitive. Housing, because it consists of repeating units with a constant relation to vertical and horizontal circulation, can more logically be studied in terms of its typological variations. Although housing would seem to embrace almost unlimited possible variations, in fact there are not many basic organizational possibilities and each housing type can be categorized fairly easily.[47]

HIGHRISE

The vertical repetitiveness of the highrise demands considerable design discipline, which means, naturally with exceptions, that all apartment floors are identical (typical) and that the mix of apartments on a typical floor is in proportion to the total mix of the program.

Because it repeats so often, the shape of the typical floor has significant influence on cost. Exterior walls are expensive. Every break in the floor configuration not only increases the perimeter of the building but multiplies this increase by the number of floors. Consequently the advantages gained from varied configuration should be carefully weighed against added cost.

Not only is the shape of the typical floor significant economically but so is its size.

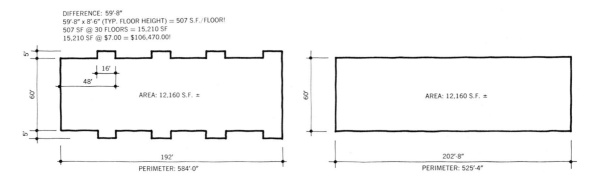

DIFFERENCE: 59'-8"
59'-8" x 8'-6" (TYP. FLOOR HEIGHT) = 507 S.F./FLOOR!
507 SF @ 30 FLOORS = 15,210 SF
15,210 SF @ $7.00 = $106,470.00!

AREA: 12,160 S.F. ±   16'   48'   5'   60'   5'   192'   PERIMETER: 584'-0"

AREA: 12,160 S.F. ±   60'   202'-8"   PERIMETER: 525'-4"

This is especially true in relation to reinforced concrete framing which is the most commonly used structural system for highrise apartment buildings today. Because building codes require heavy fireproofing of the structural frame, concrete—particularly flat plate with randomly placed interior columns—has many advantages over steel, which have been discussed in detail in the structural chapter. Briefly, flat plate provides a ready ceiling surface, whereas steel construction, unless it is a combination of steel beams with concrete slabs, often requires suspended ceilings without any mechanical need for the space created by the suspension; floor thickness, less in concrete, results in a lower building, less exterior wall, and shorter stairs; random column spacing is adaptable to good apartment layout and liberates the plan from the restrictions of the column grid; columns and beams once poured are finished, whereas in steel they must be covered and fire protected. Because there are enough advantages to concrete framing to make it a prevalent construction type, the typical floor of a highrise should be such (or it should be subdividable into such areas) that it most efficiently utilizes the daily productive capacity of the concrete framing and pouring crew. Pouring sequence and "ideal" floor size, as described under structural framing, must be taken into account.

The maximum length and configuration of the typical floor is also influenced by the available construction technology (crane reach, material handling, and so on). Current technology, together with the structural system, limits the building height as well. As the building gets taller and the distance between the ground and the top of the building increases, the longer it will take to transport workers and materials and pump water. As the building becomes very tall, the more likely it is, depending on when construction started, that it will run into below-freezing weather and costly winter protection will be required.

Elevators also influence height. Sometimes it makes good economic sense to stay below the maximum height if an added floor or two would necessitate a more expensive elevator system or an additional elevator.

Smokeproof towers are also a factor. The building height or the number of floors at which code requires the introduction of smokeproof towers should be watched. Smokeproof towers mean added cost, nonutilized floor area, and larger, consequently harder to plan, stair shafts. If increasing the typical floor is possible on the site and will result in a building under the height necessitating smokeproof towers, much will be gained economically.

All the caveats about floor size and building height indicate that the higher the highrise, the costlier it becomes, or conversely, savings occur when the number of floors is smaller and the typical floor plan is larger because more apartments share the costly vertical elements such as stairs and elevators.

To these general rules must be added the efficiency ratio of typical floors which is also valid for all highrises with the exception of the exterior corridor types. The nonrental area of a typical floor is generally between 10 and 15% of the gross floor area. When the total of nonrental spaces (public corridor, stairs, elevators, refuse chute, stack, electrical room, and corridor air supply ducts) is more than 15% of the gross floor area, not including balconies, the plan should be seriously re-examined!

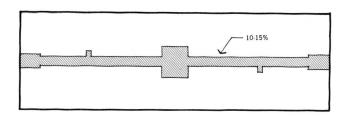

DESIGN METHODOLOGY

Knowing this efficiency ratio will help the designer to do some fast calculations before drawing a single line.

Example

The clients mix calls for

$2/3$—2-BR apartments @ 1200 sf
$1/3$—1-BR apartments @ 900 sf

The smallest group that reflects this ratio

2—2-BR @ 1200 sf = 2400 sf	
1—1-BR @ 900 sf = 900 sf	
Total net	3300 sf

Add for nonrental space

13% of 3300	=	430 sf
Total		3730 sf

For concrete-pouring economy 3700 sf is obviously not a viable area. Double 3730, or 7460 sf, is better but still under the approximately 9000 sf ideal minimum. Triple 3730, or 11,190 sf, will suffice for concrete pouring, but one hopes for—if possible—an even-number multiplier. Therefore four times 3730, or 14,920 sf, appears to be ideal, and the typical floors would then have four 2-BR–1-BR groups, or 12 apartments per floor. This figure should be tested against a variety of criteria.

Zoning. Is 14,920 sf of ground coverage allowed? The total number of apartments permitted by zoning density should be divided by 12 to determine the number of floors needed; if this number is multiplied by 14,920 sf and the common area (lobby, recreation, and so on) are added to the result, is this above or below the total floor area permitted by zoning?

Site conditions. 14,920 sf divided by the average apartment building width of 60 ft will result in a building 250 ft long; will this fit on the site with all the required setbacks?

Code. Is 14,920 sf below the maximum permitted for the construction type already determined by the number of floors? Within allowed travel distances, will two exits be adequate?

Aesthetic. What is the proportion of the volume, the length of which is 250 ft and the heights as calculated above? What is the impact of this volume on adjacent open space and buildings?

Problems of height, floor area, and floor efficiency occur for every highrise. Beyond them, however, each building type has its own logic. Many approaches have been used to group highrise apartment buildings into prototypes. Perhaps the most universally accepted approach is the grouping by apartment access and vertical and horizontal distribution systems (see illustration on p. 229).

CENTRAL-CORRIDOR SYSTEM

The central-corridor system (also called "inner corridor" or "double-loaded corridor") is considered the most economical highrise apartment building (**1–12**).* This is easy to understand when we consider that every square foot of public corridor serves two apartments instead of one, as in the case of exterior corridors. It becomes even more obvious when we compare central corridor to point block. In the first maximum gross

*Bold face numbers in parentheses refer to the projects at the end of the book.

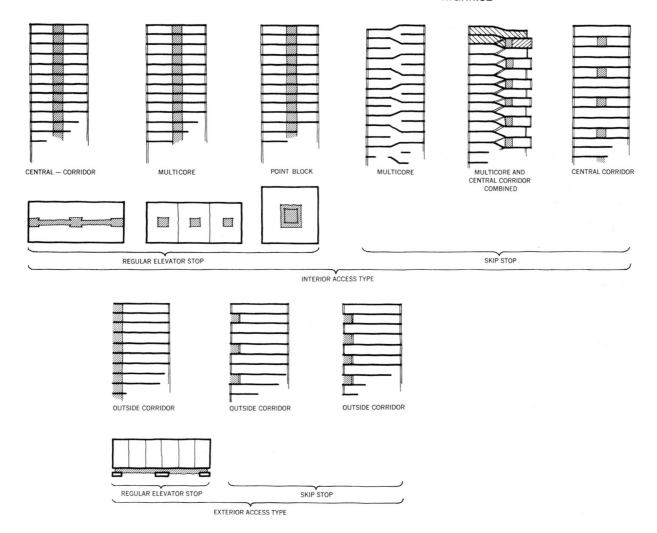

CENTRAL — CORRIDOR MULTICORE POINT BLOCK MULTICORE MULTICORE AND CENTRAL CORRIDOR COMBINED CENTRAL CORRIDOR

REGULAR ELEVATOR STOP SKIP STOP

INTERIOR ACCESS TYPE

OUTSIDE CORRIDOR OUTSIDE CORRIDOR OUTSIDE CORRIDOR

REGULAR ELEVATOR STOP SKIP STOP

EXTERIOR ACCESS TYPE

floor area is possible with a minimum number of stairs and elevators; in the second the floor area is limited by the core size. The comparison is even more favorable in the multicore type, with its large number of elevators and stairs.

The economic advantage is not without concomitant problems. A central-corridor system results in a long corridor which, unless broken up or daylighted, if not at the elevators, at least on the ends, can be barren and inhuman (**6, 7, 11, 12**). Very long corridors militate against a feeling of community or "knowing your neighbors." Surveillance, a deterrent to crime, is extremely difficult in long corridors.

When a preferred view occurs on one side of the building, almost half the apartments cannot enjoy it in a central corridor type. The situation is somewhat improved when the building is parallel to the view direction; an angled view is an acceptable substitute for a direct view and the living rooms could project out of the main volume to improve the angle.

When budget prohibits the use of air conditioning, environmental comfort is reduced by the loss of highly desirable cross ventilation in the central-corridor building.

Orientation poses difficult decisions for the architect when the design is a central-corridor scheme with only two main elevations. Air conditioning and indifference to heating costs pushed this problem into the background for many years; however, the current energy shortage is forcing us to face it today. There are no clear answers. A southern orientation is ideal (low, penetrating sun angle in the winter when sunshine is

229

needed, high angle in the summer when solar heat is not desirable), but means that half of the apartments face north without any sunshine at all. An east-west orientation is better because all units enjoy sunshine, but worse if one wants to save in cooling energy.

The central-corridor building which is only two-directional (has solid end walls) grew out of tightly built-in urban conditions when the building was fitted between two adjacent structures. Its use on large sites in which such restraints do not exist is the result of structural considerations (**15, 20**). For many years it was common practice to utilize the end walls as wind-resisting shear walls that at best could be penetrated by small "punched" openings. It was found that these end shear walls are hard to form; consequently they are rather costly. The use of interior shear walls or shear cores and the increased use of scattered shear panels allows the designer to open up the end walls completely. The resulting four-directional central corridor building is the most common type today unless site conditions prevent its use.

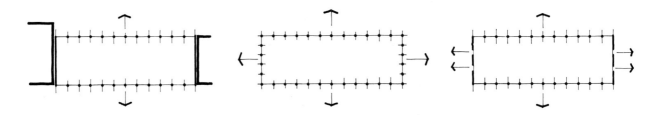

CENTRAL-CORRIDOR SYSTEM: APARTMENT

Each building type modifies the apartments placed within its confines. The central-corridor type, once its other limitations are accepted, restricts the apartment minimally. What determines the kind of apartment the designer is able to work out is the total building length and depth.

In order to be economically feasible the typical floor should contain a maximum number of apartments. Given the minimum room widths determined by the program,

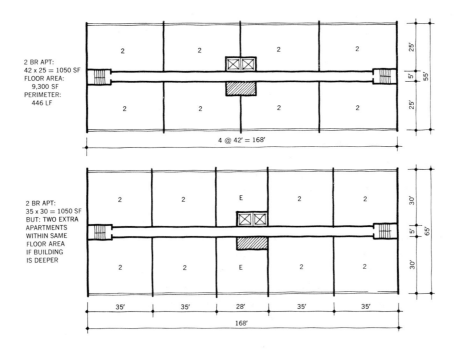

just so many apartments can fit into the available building length. The number of apartments in this length can be improved on if each apartment is arranged—keeping the gross area constant—with shorter exterior exposure and increased depth. Naturally, this will put constraints on the apartment. Dining space along the exterior wall is out of the question. Bedrooms become so narrow that dressers and desks must be placed along the exterior wall, thus eliminating the option of floor-to-ceiling fenestration. The inner ends of the rooms become darker. In spite of all this, buildings with narrow, deep apartments tend to be more economical: using the same gross square foot area, they have smaller perimeters, which minimizes the costly exterior wall, and conserves energy (see illustration on bottom p. 230).

The apartment plan is not independent of the other elements of planning: the vertical cores, elevators, and stairs. It is possible to plan these vertical core elements independently when site conditions and economy permit more than simple building configurations (**4–7, 9–12**). In tight, compact, economical plans the core elements have to bite into the apartment space proper or, to use another term, borrow space from the apartment (**1–3, 8**). About 60 to 70 sf is as much borrowing as any apartment plan can take easily. This area equals about half the area of an average stair, a single elevator shaft, or electric room and refuse chute.

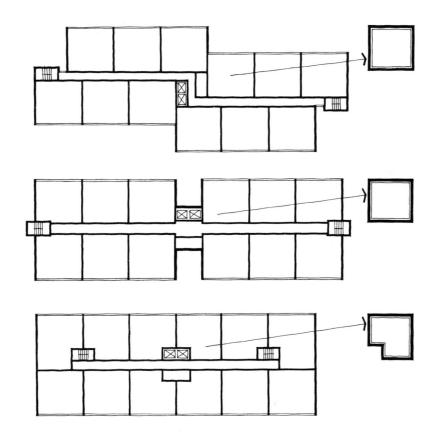

The illustrations show one-bedroom, two-bedroom, three-bedroom, and efficiency apartments with average depth and exterior exposure as well as with increased depth and reduced exterior exposure. They show the consequences of using some of the apartment space ("borrowing") to fit elevators, stairs, and other core elements along the central corridor (see illustrations on p. 232–234).

It is important to be aware that the apartments illustrated above are averages reflecting more the marketing conditions than living styles. As these conditions change,

DESIGN METHODOLOGY

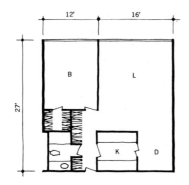

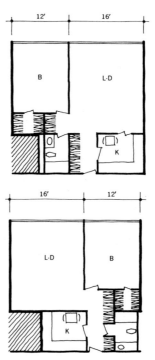

AVERAGE DEPTH — ONE BEDROOM APARTMENTS

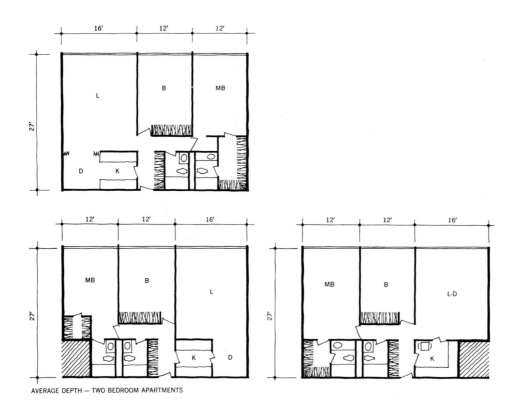

AVERAGE DEPTH — TWO BEDROOM APARTMENTS

232

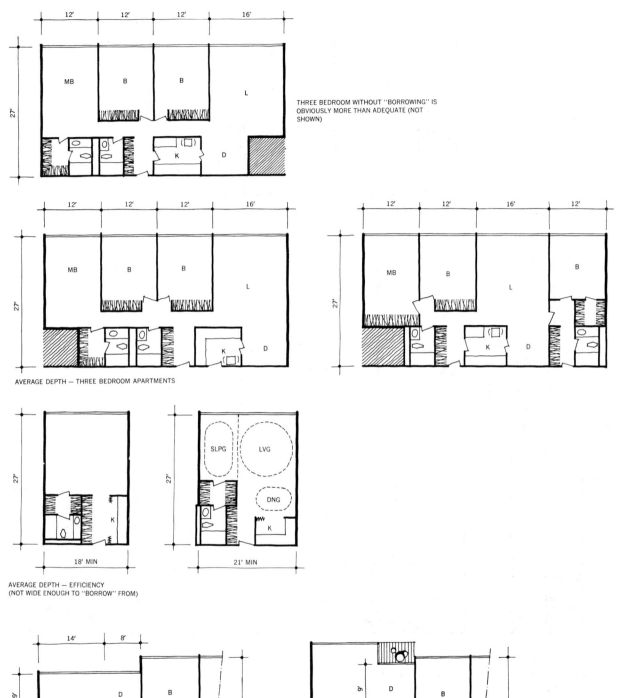

THREE BEDROOM WITHOUT "BORROWING" IS
OBVIOUSLY MORE THAN ADEQUATE (NOT
SHOWN)

AVERAGE DEPTH — THREE BEDROOM APARTMENTS

AVERAGE DEPTH — EFFICIENCY
(NOT WIDE ENOUGH TO "BORROW" FROM)

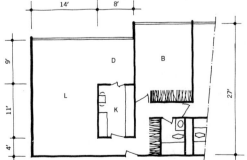

AVERAGE DEPTH — OUTSIDE DINING

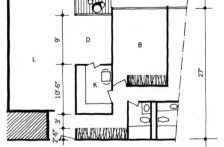

233

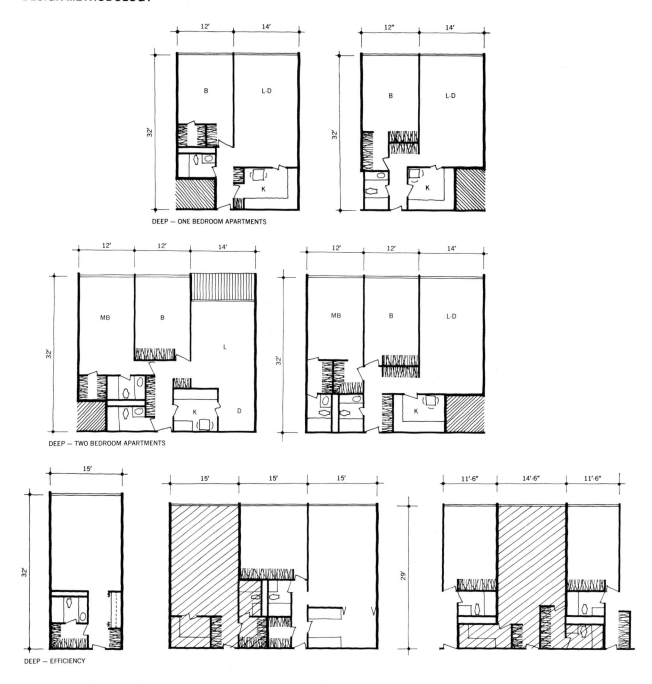

DEEP — ONE BEDROOM APARTMENTS

DEEP — TWO BEDROOM APARTMENTS

DEEP — EFFICIENCY

as the users' living style is more and more recognized, prototype plans must undergo a metamorphosis.

Even before that, the prototypes themselves—the results of economic equation, of emulating past successes, and lack of experimentation—should be recognized as laden with shortcomings. Bedrooms, attempting to use minimum exterior wall, when occupied by two children cannot be subdivided to provide privacy; therefore the apartment is not flexible enough to accommodate family growth. One wonders if sleeping has to take place in a room along the exterior wall. With advancement in mechanical ventilation a change in our building codes might liberate the exterior zone for activities that need daylight instead of using it as bed containers. Dining rooms in most prototypes can be used only for small formal meals and are not adaptable as family

HIGHRISE

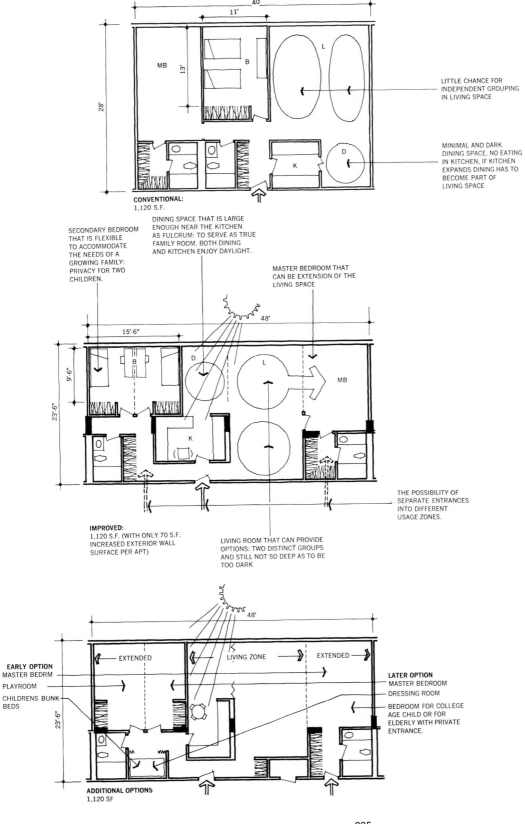

LITTLE CHANCE FOR
INDEPENDENT GROUPING
IN LIVING SPACE

MINIMAL AND DARK
DINING SPACE, NO EATING
IN KITCHEN, IF KITCHEN
EXPANDS DINING HAS TO
BECOME PART OF
LIVING SPACE

CONVENTIONAL:
1,120 S.F.

SECONDARY BEDROOM
THAT IS FLEXIBLE
TO ACCOMMODATE
THE NEEDS OF A
GROWING FAMILY:
PRIVACY FOR TWO
CHILDREN.

DINING SPACE THAT IS LARGE
ENOUGH NEAR THE KITCHEN
AS FULCRUM: TO SERVE AS TRUE
FAMILY ROOM. BOTH DINING
AND KITCHEN ENJOY DAYLIGHT.

MASTER BEDROOM THAT
CAN BE EXTENSION OF THE
LIVING SPACE

THE POSSIBILITY OF
SEPARATE ENTRANCES
INTO DIFFERENT
USAGE ZONES.

IMPROVED:
1,120 S.F. (WITH ONLY 70 S.F.
INCREASED EXTERIOR WALL
SURFACE PER APT)

LIVING ROOM THAT CAN PROVIDE
OPTIONS: TWO DISTINCT GROUPS
AND STILL NOT SO DEEP AS TO BE
TOO DARK

EXTENDED   LIVING ZONE   EXTENDED

EARLY OPTION
MASTER BEDRM
PLAYROOM
CHILDRENS BUNK
BEDS

LATER OPTION
MASTER BEDROOM
DRESSING ROOM
BEDROOM FOR COLLEGE
AGE CHILD OR FOR
ELDERLY WITH PRIVATE
ENTRANCE.

ADDITIONAL OPTIONS
1,120 SF

rooms, although it has been proved that family activities such as young children playing, studying, or watching television tend to take place near that great family magnet, the kitchen. Master bedrooms do not get multiple use in most current arrangements, and their location adjacent to the living room, instead of in the far corner, could open up the living space for large parties or varied activities in defined but not completely isolated groups when not in use as a bedroom. The more frequent splitting of one bedroom from the others would allow a separate exit and would permit the use of this room for young adults or for the elderly living with the family. The improvements are many. Their concomitant economic consequences, in most cases increased building perimeter, could be balanced by other savings.

Ultimately plans could be conceived in which only the perimeter walls of the apartment, bathrooms, kitchen plumbing, exhausts, structural columns, and certain electric risers are fixed. This arrangement would permit the long-term lessee and certainly the condominium owner to place walls, with limitations obviously, to fit needs and lifestyle.

Naturally, flexibility is not without problems. As Brolin points out:

> Smaller-scale ways of achieving flexibility, like movable interior walls, are not much more flexible than the mega-structure in practice. A young couple needing a one-bedroom apartment now but a nursery in two years must rent enough space for the nursery from the beginning. Otherwise they must take away from the existing space to get the extra room when they need it.[48]

CENTRAL-CORRIDOR SYSTEM: RHYTHM

The moment apartments are placed next to each other a major design decision is in the making, one that will have unalterable consequences for the total design of the building. Regardless of whether the architect opts for a grid of exposed structural framing, for a masonry-clad exterior with punched openings, or even for such a homogeneous and anonymous exterior surface as a curtain wall, the apartments placed along the exterior will form a definite pattern or rhythm.

When it is the architect's intention to express on the exterior, the distinctions between living spaces and the bedrooms (with different fenestration, projections, and indentations or by the use of balconies) and to create a differentiated elevation that at least symbolizes, if not clearly states, the presence of human habitation, the rhythm of living rooms and bedrooms is self-evident (**8–10, 32, 35**).

Even if such intention does not exist, even if living rooms and bedrooms are identical in width, even if their differing widths could somehow be hidden behind identical column bays, the rhythm of living rooms and bedrooms is not to be neglected. To begin with, the architect might change the design. The client might also change the program and suddenly call for balconies in front of all living rooms. When something like this occurs and the placement of living rooms and bedrooms is not in a recognizable rhythm, a kind of disorder will result that no "exterior design" can camouflage.

Exterior rhythm means the recognizable regularity of different elements (in this case living rooms and bedrooms) and consequently must be intentional—ordered. Even irregularity as a rhythm—as unintentional and accidental as it may seem—is planned. Ultimately, even if the architect opted for ambiguity, for contradictions, or "circumstantial complexities," so well understood by Venturi, "order must exist before it can be broken."[49]

Rudolph Armheim describes disorder slightly differently. He says that while

> an orderly arrangement is governed by an overall principle, a disorderly one is not.

However, the components of a disorderly arrangement must be orderly within themselves, or the lack of controlled relations between them would disrupt nothing, frustrate nobody. You cannot sabotage a melody unless there is one, and one melody cannot be incompatible with another unless each of them possesses a structure of its own. I therefore define disorder as a clash of uncoordinated orders.[50]

Nobody described rhythm in architecture more poetically than Rasmussen.

The architect is usually forced to create a regular method of subdivision in his composition on which many building artisans will have to work together. The simplest method, for both the architect and the artisans, is the absolutely regular repetition of the same elements, for example solid, void, solid, void, just as you count one, two, one, two. It is a rhythm every one can grasp. Many people find it entirely too simple to mean anything at all. It says nothing to them and yet it is a classic example of man's special contribution to orderliness. It represents a regularity and precision found nowhere in Nature but only in the order man seeks to create.

When a number of one-family houses are built at the same time according to a single plan, the rhythm is often more complicated. The ordinary London terraced house from the eighteenth century has three bays with the entrance door at one side. There they stand, in waltz measure: one, two, three, one, two, three.

The term rhythm is borrowed from other arts involving a time element and based on movement, such as music and dancing.

Architecture itself has no time dimension, no movement, and therefore cannot be rhythmic in the same way as music and dancing are. But to experience architecture demands time; it also demands work—though mental, not physical, work. The person who hears music or watches dancing does none of the physical work himself but in perceiving the performance he experiences the rhythm of it as though it were in his own body. In much the same way you can experience architecture rhythmically—that is, by the process of re-creation already described. If you feel that a line is rhythmic it means that by following it with your eyes you have an experience that can be compared with the experience of rhythmic ice-skating, for instance.[51]

The importance of rhythm in planning can be best illustrated by example. The exercise that follows is in a sense restricted; the site is bordered on adjacent property lines by existing structures with solid end walls. Zoning is such that there is really only one logical way to position the building. Although this type of situation is not the most common, it was selected to highlight the issue and not further complicate it by options of varied configurations or by the possibilities of four directionality. The principles of rhythm arrived at in this example are applicable on any site and building with any program mix.

Example

Program Mix

25%—1-BR apartments @ 700 sf
50%—2-BR apartments @ 1000 sf
25%—3-BR apartments @ 1400 sf

DESIGN METHODOLOGY

SITE CONDITIONS

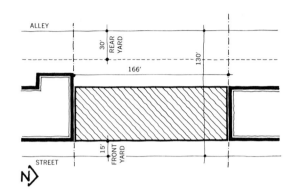

PRELIMINARY CONSIDERATIONS, ZONING CHECK.   Based on front and rear yards required by zoning and no side yard requirements, the only viable option is a building 166 ft long. Thus site and zoning determines the typical floor volume. (This restricted condition was selected for our example because it helps to focus attention on procedure rather than providing a wide range of options in which other factors—not yet discussed—would come into play.) Assuming an average building width of 60 ft, the typical floor area becomes 9360 sf, a reasonable size for concrete pour.

The smallest group that reflects the program mix

1 (25%)—1 BR @ 700 sf	= 700 sf	
2 (50%)—2 BR @ 1000 sf	= 2000 sf	
1 (25%)—3 BR @ 1400 sf	= 1400 sf	
Four apartments	4100 sf	
Add for nonrental 13%	533 sf	

Gross floor area for 4 apartments 4633 sf
9360 sf ÷ 4633 sf = approximately 2

Therefore on a typical floor

$$2 \times 1 = (2) \ 1 \ BR; \ 2 \times 2 = (4) \ 2 \ BR; \ 2 \times 1 = (2) \ 3 \ BR$$

Based on the above, the number of spaces that require exterior exposure is as follows:

(2) 1 BR × 2 (1 living room + 1 bedroom) = 4 rooms	
(4) 2 BR × 3 (1 living room + 2 bedrooms) = 12 rooms	
(2) 3 BR × 4 (1 living room + 3 bedrooms) = 8 rooms	
Total	24 rooms

The building has two exposed faces; therefore 24 ÷ 2 = 12 rooms on each face; 166 ft length minus 1 ft for end walls equals 165 feet; 165 ÷ 12 = 13 ft 9 in. Before any further steps can be taken exterior options and their consequences on room sizes must be kept in mind.

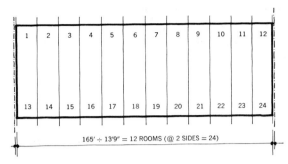

165' ÷ 13'9" = 12 ROOMS (@ 2 SIDES = 24)

The 13 ft 9 in. module can be accepted as an expression of equal column bays, provided the columns are wide enough so that by shifting partitions behind the columns the living room width can be increased and the bedroom width can be reduced because 13 ft 9 in. (less partitions) is too much for a bedroom when the extra space can be better used in the living room.

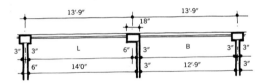

The columns can be rearranged to reflect the wider living room and the narrower bedroom, presuming that an acceptable rhythm of "L" bays and "B" bays can be found. In this case a two bedroom apartment has three rooms @ 13 ft 9 in., or 41 ft 3 in. However, 41 ft 3 in. also equals one living room @ 16 ft and two bedrooms @ 12 ft 1½ in.

A masonry clad exterior with punched window openings, if that is the designer's choice, allows an even rhythm of windows on the exterior, whereas in the interior the living rooms are wider and the bedrooms are narrower. Fenestration that expresses this room width differentiation is certainly no problem at all.

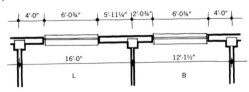

With curtain wall or load-bearing concrete mullions a grid can be found that consists of modules, four of which make up a living room and three, a bedroom. Using the 41 ft 3 in. two-bedroom apartment, 41 ft 3 in. ÷ 10 = 4 ft 1½ in. module; 4 × 4 ft 1½ in. = 16 ft 6 in. living room, 3 × 4 ft 1½ in. = 12 ft 4½ in. bedroom. (Another possible grid that would work is three modules for the living room and two modules for the bedroom.)

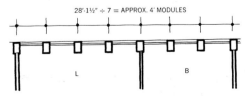

28'-1½" ÷ 7 = APPROX. 4' MODULES

DESIGN METHODOLOGY

Using longer spans (20 ft 7½ in. that are conducive to dividing the width of the building into three bays) in which a bay equals one living room or two bedrooms a system invariably used by Mies van der Rohe, has its problems because the bedrooms are too narrow compared with the living room size. Cutting the span in half provides no added flexibility.

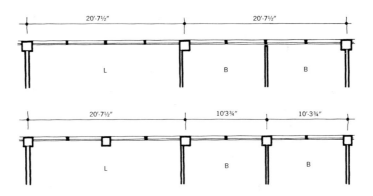

Disregarding their effect on parking, any of the above options—at least at this point—are possible and for the sake of early studies we are safe to use the 13 ft 9 in. module as a grid until a basic scheme is achieved when we start differentiating between living room and bedroom bays.

What are the possible layouts? (Balconies are shown in front of all living rooms to emphasize the question of rhythm.)

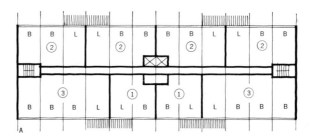

SCHEME A.   Core elements are borrowed from the sleeping zone; since two elements are not sufficient to create rhythm in this case we have simple symmetry instead.

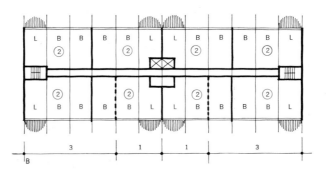

SCHEME B.   The core elements are borrowed from the living zone; the rhythm is poor (pairs of balconies are fighting with single balconies; a pair is not simply the sum of its components and becomes a new phenomenon, or mathematically $a + a$ is not equal to $2a$, but to b!) the pairing of apartments along their sleeping zones provides built-in flexibility: out of 2 two-bedroom apartments a one-bedroom and a three-bedroom apartment can be created.

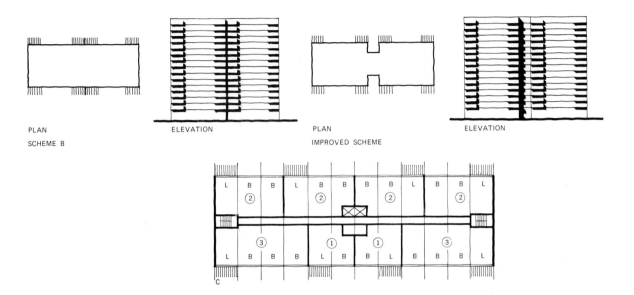

PLAN

ELEVATION

PLAN

ELEVATION

SCHEME B

IMPROVED SCHEME

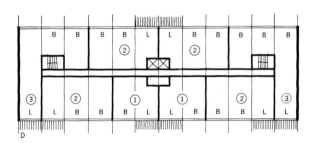

SCHEME C.   The core elements are borrowed from both zones; this scheme tries to remedy the rhythm problem by using all single balconies; the rhythm is good. Assuming that there is a preferred view toward the east, the number of apartments facing the view—at least from their living rooms—can be increased by having end apartments occupy both sides of the building ("wrapping them around").

SCHEME D.   Six out of eight apartments face the preferred view; the core elements are borrowed from the living zone; the balcony rhythm on the west elevation is poor; symmetry is not rhythm. If two elements cannot, one element will not create rhythm.

DESIGN METHODOLOGY

SCHEME E.   Rectifies the rhythm problem; borrowing the entire stair from the "wrap-around" three-bedroom apartment poses unique problems on this scheme as well as on the preceding one.

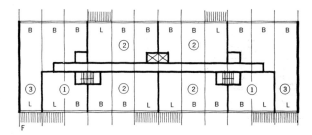

SCHEME F.   Eliminates the difficulties of the three-bedroom apartment, but a price must be paid; the core elements that would function better in the center are dispersed because it is exceedingly difficult to borrow from both zones of a two-bedroom apartment of average depth.

The program mix and apartment sizes fit rather easily without leftover space in the 166 by 60 ft floor area dictated by site conditions and zoning. If the property were 180 ft long and the program stayed the same, 180 ft − 1 ft for end walls = 179 ft; 179 ÷ 12 = approximately 15 for each room. This is obviously adequate for living rooms but far too large for bedrooms. Shifting partitions behind columns will not reduce the bedroom width sufficiently. Three times 15 ft makes up a two-bedroom apartment equaling 45 ft. This is just about what is needed for a two-bedroom apartment with dining along the exterior wall (14 ft living room, 8 ft dining alcove, 11 ft 6 in. bedroom, 11 ft 6 in. master bedroom). Presuming that these improved apartments (a two-bedroom becomes 1180 sf) can be marketed; this is an acceptable alternate.

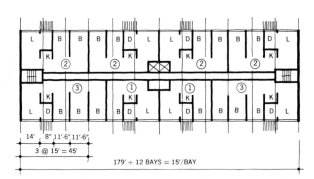

What if 1180 sf (two-bedroom) with exterior dining is too luxurious? The options on the new property using the preceding module of 13 ft 9 in. are 179 ÷ 13 ft 9 in. = 13 modules on each side of the building; 13 × 2 = 26, but the eight apartments on the floor need only 24 modules! There is an excess of two modules that equals a one-bedroom apartment, making a total of nine apartments per floor and changing the mix to 2 three-bedroom (22.5%), 4 two-bedroom (44.5%) and 3 one-bedroom (33.25%) apartments. Even if the client were to agree to this modified mix, the odd number of modules (13) and the odd number of one-bedroom apartments do not lead to an orderly disciplined solution as long as there is an intent to express living rooms differently from bedrooms. There is, however, a way out, if a uniform, undifferentiated exterior is desirable.

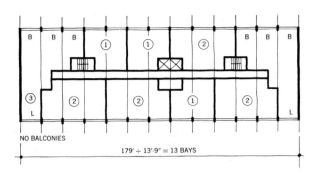

NO BALCONIES

179′ ÷ 13′-9″ = 13 BAYS

If 13 ft 9 in. results in an odd number of modules, what happens to the room sizes with the next even number? 179 ÷ 14 = 12 ft 10 in. per module. This means, approximately, a 14-ft living room and 12-ft bedrooms and is acceptable. However, with 28 modules the mix changes substantially from the one given in the program: 2 three-bedroom (20%), 4 two-bedroom (40%), and 4 one-bedroom (40%) apartments.

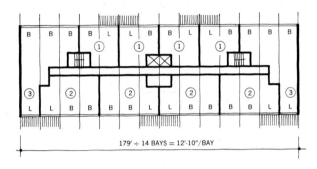

179′ ÷ 14 BAYS = 12′-10″/BAY

Is it possible to stick to the original mix and the 13 ft 9 in. module on the 180-ft property?

Assuming that the issue of the preferred view is not an important one, the simple way to handle the extra two modules is not to use them at all or to use the extra modules for the vertical core elements in the center, strongly articulated.

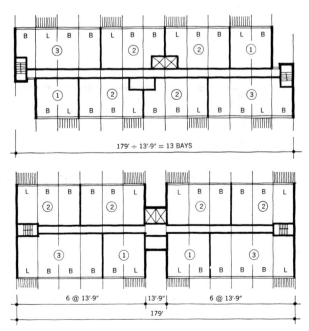

179′ ÷ 13′-9″ = 13 BAYS

6 @ 13′-9″   13′-9″   6 @ 13′-9″

179′

DESIGN METHODOLOGY

If the preferred view cannot be neglected, the preceding scheme can be modified. The price is poor balcony rhythm or no balcony for the one-bedroom apartment.

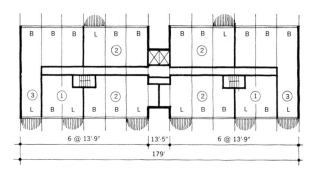

If the wrap-around three-bedroom apartments can take some added luxury (approximately 300 sf), the extra modules can be split between them.

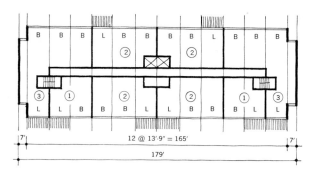

Finally, the increased property size does not necessarily require a new floor plan. The building can stay as it was, leaving a 14-ft voluntary yard on one side (assuming that it is in accord with the zoning laws) that can be used ideally as a loading dock.

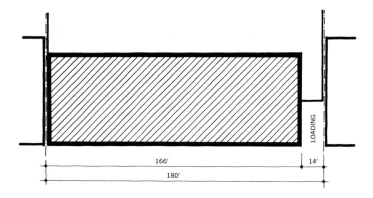

Throughout this example a small-span concrete framing was used. A large (20 ft 7½ in.) grid poses different problems. As long as the view issue can be disregarded, the system works well. Wrap-around apartments at the ends to increase the number of those who can enjoy the view create considerable difficulty because of the inflexibility of the large-span grid system on a restricted lot.

244

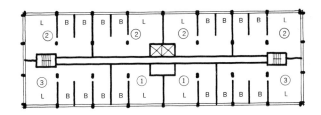

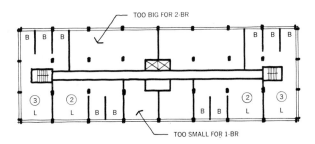

CENTRAL-CORRIDOR SYSTEM: END APARTMENTS

When dealing with the end apartments of a central-corridor building, the designer is faced with a set of special conditions.

Unless the stair shaft is pulled out of the main building volume (when, in fact, the end apartment is not different from any of the typical apartments) or the stair is positioned at the very end of the building centered on the public corridor (when the end apartment is minimally altered), the typical unit undergoes a serious metamorphosis when it becomes an end apartment.

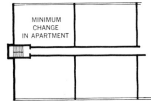

It is always advisable to reduce the travel distance and minimize the length of the corridor. When the stairs are pulled in from the end of the building to achieve this, part of the corridor (now behind the stair) can be added to the end apartments. In this manner, by decreasing the nonrental space the efficiency of the floor plan is increased.

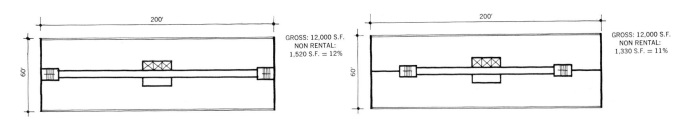

The part of the corridor that now becomes part of the apartments permits larger kitchens and/or dining spaces. When the building is free standing (in contrast to the example in the preceding chapter), fenestration of these dining areas will improve the apartments considerably (**7, 15, 20**).

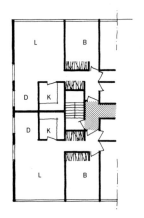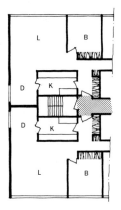

Wrap-around apartments open up a completely new set of possibilities; however, when the building has solid ends due to the restrictions of the site, options are limited (**15, 20**).

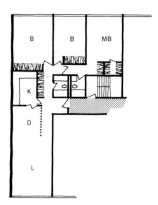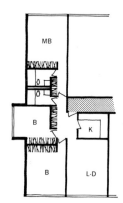

When site conditions permit the structure to open up on its ends, it becomes a four-directional building and it is possible to place one of the bedrooms instead of the kitchen along the end wall assuming that the building is deep enough (**1, 5**).

A three-bedroom apartment must have a minimum of four exterior spaces (living room plus three bedrooms) occupying four modules. When one of these rooms is along the end, the module requirements of a three-bedroom apartment are reduced to three. The chances to increase the number of apartments on the typical floor, within the same length but with a slightly increased depth, have improved (**1, 5, 8, 38, 48**).

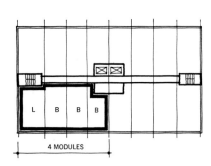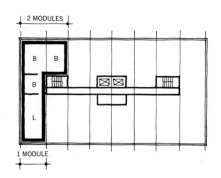

Depending on the depth of the building and on the bedroom-size requirements, it is possible to plan two, three, or even four bedrooms that front exclusively on the end wall (**3, 8**).

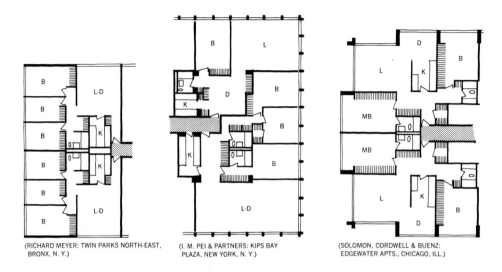

(RICHARD MEYER: TWIN PARKS NORTH-EAST, BRONX, N. Y.) (I. M. PEI & PARTNERS: KIPS BAY PLAZA, NEW YORK, N. Y.) (SOLOMON, CORDWELL & BUENZ: EDGEWATER APTS., CHICAGO, ILL.)

More than accommodating an extra bedroom or two, a complete efficiency apartment—or if the depth is adequate, even an entire one-bedroom unit—can face the end of the building without using any of the modules along the building length (**1, 2, 4**).

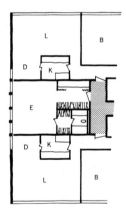

The economy of deep buildings (with narrow but deep apartments) becomes quite obvious when the possibilities inherent in the use of the ends of the building are also exploited.

CENTRAL-CORRIDOR SYSTEM: SYMMETRY—SEQUENCE

The location of vertical core elements influences the typical floor significantly and could limit its options severely. The most critical factor is the elevator. Logically the elevator is located in the center of the building, equidistant from apartments on each side. The result is a strong central element from which planning proceeds to the right and left (**1–4, 8**). Apartments are arranged in symmetrical pairs: to increase the chance of switching a bedroom from one apartment to the other (two 2 BR = one 3 BR + one 1 BR); to back up, when possible, the kitchens or bathrooms of adjacent apartments.

As the example in the preceding chapter illustrates, symmetry is not rhythm.

247

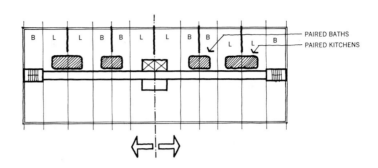

Sometimes the articulated core will solve the rhythm problem by splitting the building into two entities (**5, 7, 10**).

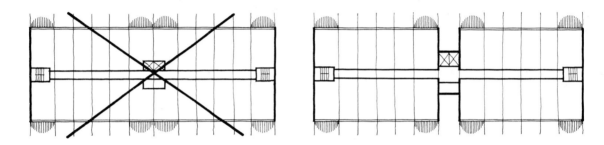

Site limitations, traffic conditions, or program considerations on the ground level may dictate the noncentral location of passenger elevators or, if there is a separate one, the service elevator. The total of vertical core elements may still be symmetrical.

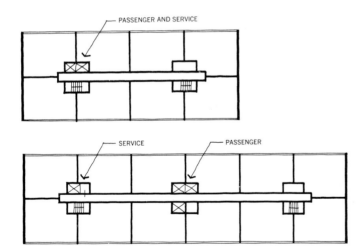

Core elements may become so large that the space for them cannot be comfortably borrowed from two adjacent apartments. This is common when three or four elevators are in a group and with smokeproof towers that have a gravity-type exhaust shaft of considerable size. In order to arrange the apartments around these large cores, part of each apartment may have to protrude beyond the simple oblong of the plan. In such a plan protrusions should occur rhythmically, whether or not all of them are justified by enlarged cores (see illustration on top p. 249).

When the central vertical core elements are handled so that no borrowing from the

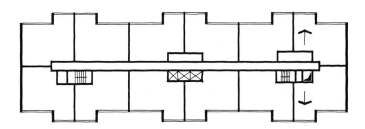

apartments is necessary, the restraint of planning from the central axis has been eliminated, which opens up the possibility of sequence instead of symmetrical planning (**9, 39**).

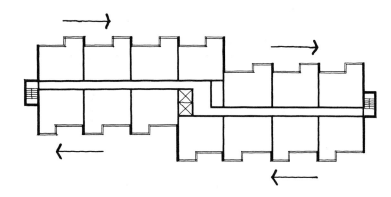

There are other circumstances that generate sequence planning of apartments. One is simply the architect's desire to get away from symmetry. Since most apartment buildings are symmetrical, sequence is a refreshing change. It might also make it easier to locate an asymmetrical entrance canopy on the first floor when site conditions dictate it.

Providing a view from each, protruded, living room is another way to generate sequence planning. Only sequence arrangement will prevent a tenant from looking into a neighbor's bedroom from this pulled-out living space. Planning in sequence works best when all apartments are identical or when not more than two different apartment types occur.

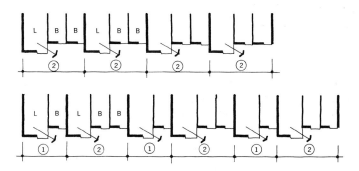

CENTRAL-CORRIDOR SYSTEM: CORRIDORS

Public corridors are the elements of central-corridor apartment buildings that are most difficult to design and most neglected. The best apartment will be degraded in the minds of the occupants who, on entering the lavish lobby and ascending in a plush elevator cab—perhaps with piped-in music to enhance the illusion further—will step out into the long, narrow, grim corridor.

Buildings with broken volumes solve these problems by cutting the visual length of the corridor in half. Widening the waiting space is easily possible with this scheme, and a small increase in the perimeter and the building length can give the corridor adequate light, a view during the day and perhaps at night (7).

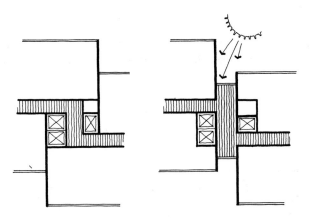

The customary unbroken-volume, central-corridor scheme must provide at least a wider space in front of the elevators than the standard 5-ft corridor width (1, 4, 8, 10). Not only will this widening make waiting for the elevators pleasanter, but it will suggest a different visual treatment (carpeting, ceiling, and lighting) to emphasize this as a central element of the corridor. Although the actual length of the corridor is not changed, its effect will be minimized by this widening (See also chapter on fire safety: how compartmentation necessitated by new highrise fire codes influences elevator vestibules.)

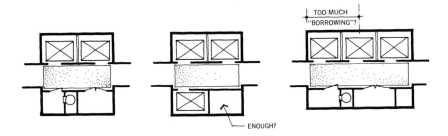

The vertical core itself can also be utilized to block the long corridor view, at least in part. This works best with two elevators (or with three when the other core elements are located elsewhere). If the core is too long, it will result in excessive borrowing from the adjacent apartments.

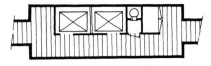

In extremely long buildings it is not unusual to have two independent elevator cores. A pair of doors in the center, working in both travel directions, will cut the corridor length effectively. When the building is so long that the maximum travel distance permitted by code necessitates a third means of egress, this third stair can act as a corridor break.

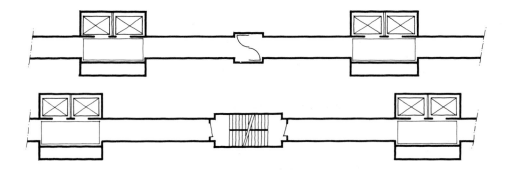

The part of the corridor in front of the elevators offers many possibilities, which is not the case with the rest of the corridor. When the apartments are not laid out symmetrically around the corridor center line as an axis, there is no rhythm of apartment doors. The regularly spaced corridor lighting relates poorly to these irregular door locations. When doors are regularly opposite each other, indenting them and treating the floor differently will help to ameliorate the effect of the long corridor (**5**). If the indentations are made wide enough, it is possible to reduce the width of the public corridor.

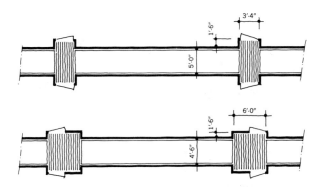

Under any conditions the corridor as the major horizontal channel of distribution merits close attention. It involves the waiting area in front of the elevators, corridor length, door rhythm, and lighting. For the elderly handrails should be provided at a 2 ft 9 in. height.

CENTRAL-CORRIDOR SYSTEM: FRAMING

Framing options have been discussed in detail under the chapters of structural components. Exchange of ideas and exploration of possibilities with the structural engineer cannot take place soon enough. Nevertheless, the designer, though no structural engineer, needs to have enough structural sense to recognize the applicable framing principles at the moment solutions are first considered even before meetings with the engineer.

The program conditions and the architect's own desires at this point have already started the selection process. The major masses of the project have been studied and the relation of the garage to the apartment tower has been established. The placement of columns in relation to or independent of parking has been set. Soil conditions and the need for caissons have been investigated. Exterior form has suggested exposed frame, complete coverup, or partial cladding (with masonry or curtain wall). All the variables of the typical floor plan have led to a determination of the possible exterior rhythm of form, framing, and fenestration.

Each framing system, with its own inherent limitations, will leave its stamp on the molding of the typical floor plan. Only understanding the consequences of each on planning and on economy permits a selection to be made. Prevailing practice and the limitations or desires of the contractor—if at this stage a contractor already has been selected—will make the decision easier.

Concrete framing, for a variety of reasons already discussed, is the most common of structural systems for highrises. When used with large (up to 22 ft) spans, it closely approximates steel framing (**1, 2**) except that it provides more liberties than steel in adapting column shapes to floor plans. Interior columns are not on an absolutely rigid grid (**5, 8**), and even if "flying forms" are used, adaptation is possible. The large span system, resulting in a slab 7 in. or thicker, is more expensive than the small. It has its advantages, however. Standard plumbing traps can be buried in a 7½-in. slab, whereas thin slab requires other provisions such as special traps, furred ceiling in bathrooms, or thickened slab in limited areas. Large span is more adaptable to a good parking layout, and column transfer is less likely to be needed. The tripartite division of the tower width makes the outer bays useful as driving aisles on the garage floors.

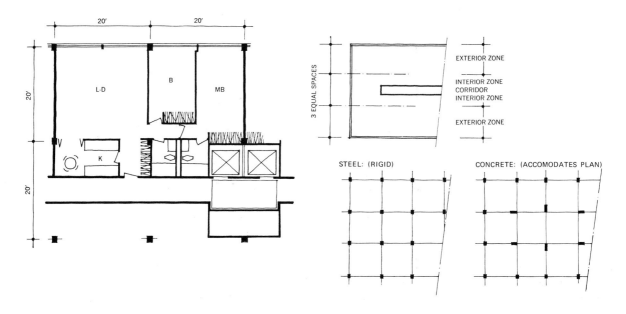

The small span system (maximum 15 or 16 ft) is quite economical because of the resulting thin slab (5 to 5½ in.) and the reduced floor reinforcing. The cost of the increased number of columns is outweighed by the savings in slabs. Its disadvantage is the increased number of caissons needed, unless pairs of columns can be easily supported on a caisson or spread footing can be used. This is a system that is not ideal when parking is directly below the apartment tower. The small bay can accommodate only one automobile with a lot of space left over and can be remedied only by costly column transfer. As costly as this is, it should be weighed against the savings gained by thin slabs on a large number of typical floors (see illustration on top p. 253).

The great planning advantage of concrete framing is its complete flexibility in column placement. In fact, instead of establishing a grid around which the plan must be molded,

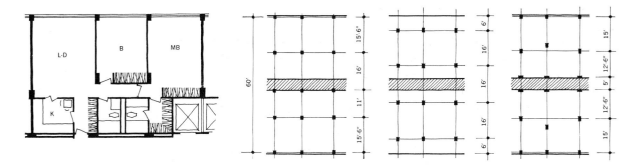

columns can be located even after a preliminary plan has been worked out, presuming, however, that the widest room, the living room, does not exceed the span maximum selected for reasons of economy.

Load-bearing walls, masonry or precast concrete, with cast-in-place or precast concrete slabs, can be used for highrises up to a limited number of floors. Spans pose no particular problem with either slab type. Walls can be accommodated within the plan, although a certain discipline in planning is required. The drawback of load-bearing walls is not only the limited height (because of which it is best suited for midrises) but the inflexibility of planning the parking and common areas on the ground level.

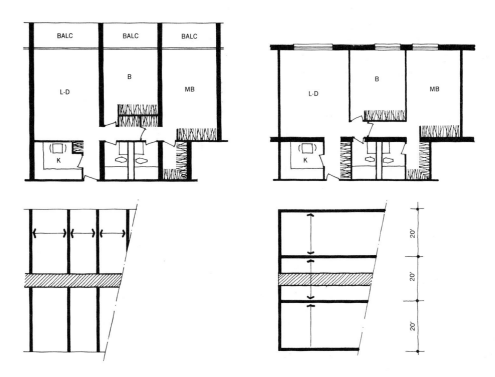

MULTICORE SYSTEM

The multicore apartment building can be used to satisfy a variety of factors. Site conditions are the primary: the presence of a significant view and the requirement on the developer's part that a maximum number of apartments should enjoy it (**15, 16**). The multicore type, answers the desire for short corridors, provides a sense of seclusion, a feeling of community and improved surveillance. The multicore type exhibits a very human approach but is undeniably costlier than a central-corridor building.

DESIGN METHODOLOGY

To illustrate the evolution of this building type, it is best to return to the hypothetical example with a preferred view toward the east.

It was found in the example that when wrap-around end apartments—or through apartments—were introduced, the number of units that could take advantage of the view increased. Through apartments are possible only at the ends of a center-corridor scheme. If the building could be cut up into several short central-corridor buildings, each with its own vertical core, the chances for through apartments would multiply.

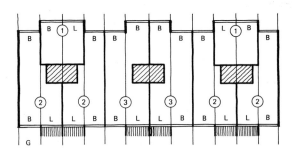

SCHEME G: The majority of the apartments, six out of eight, face the preferred view. Rhythm is excellent. Because each segment of the multicore needs two means of egress, two elevators, refuse chute, electrical room, and corridor air supply duct, this scheme is very costly. It would be less so if it were a midrise project with hydraulic elevators and scissor stairs instead of two regular stairs as required by the highrise fire-code. One could get by with one elevator per segment because hydraulic elevators need less servicing and tend to break down less often; when they do, the 5- to 6-story climb in an emergency would still be manageable compared with highrises.

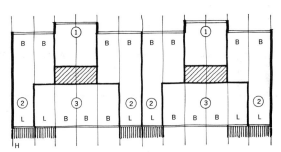

SCHEME H.   Helps to reduce the number of cores without changing the number of apartments with preferred view. Rhythm is equally good. It still has more core elements than the central-corridor scheme and for the same mix and size of apartments requires a larger floor area (10,690 sf) than the equivalent central-corridor building (9960 sf). It is important to realize that although the size and cost did increase, so did the efficiency ratio of the plan because the long corridor had been shortened. In the central-corridor type with through apartments at the ends there is 1100 sf of nonrental space (11%); in the multicore, 910 sf of nonrental space (8½%).

The concentration of all the vertical core elements results in an area too large to be easily borrowed from the adjacent apartments. Consequently parts of the apartments, or entire apartments, might protrude from the building envelope (**15, 51**). Arrangement of the core elements depends on the number of apartments around the core (see illustration on top p. 255).

Because the multicore type consists of independent building segments, it lends itself to architectural forms not easily achieved with a central corridor. The independent

254

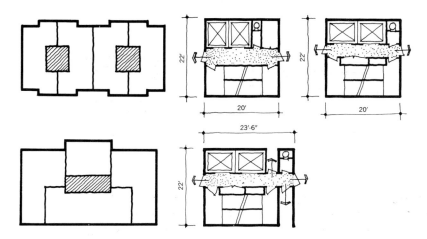

segments, site conditions permitting, can be clearly articulated by a variety of means, even by sliding the segments along their common wall. Similar sliding, so often desired to reduce long corridors or to break up the volume, requires additional building length in central-corridor types to solve the "break" of the corridor at the sliding axis.

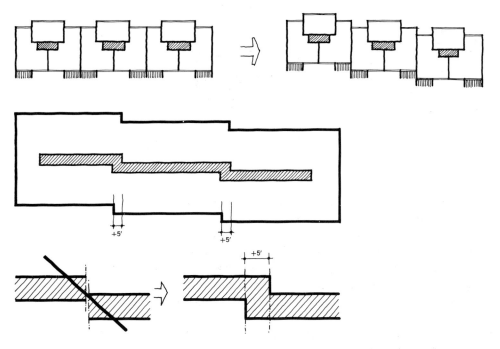

POINT-BLOCK SYSTEM

The borderline between a central-corridor apartment building and the one commonly called point block is sometimes hard to define. A short but deep central-corridor scheme actually could be considered as a point block (**3, 4, 20, 23**) (see illustration on top p. 256).

Most point blocks in contrast to the central corridor scheme face at least four (or more directions (**17–31**). Whether the end is open or not, a central-corridor scheme is planned linearly, parallel to the long sides. The point block is schematically a square (or near square), and the apartments are planned along all sides in a ring pattern around the core. The limits of a point block lie in this circular planning. The central-corridor

255

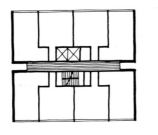 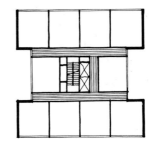

scheme can be extended almost endlessly (except that stairs must be introduced because of travel distance restrictions) and its number of apartments per floor is theoretically unlimited. The point block expands radially. Assuming a maximum useful depth for any apartment, the radial expansion is limited: as more apartments are placed along the circumference, the radius will grow, and at one point the space inside of the apartment ring will be more than is necessary for the vertical core elements and the corridor.

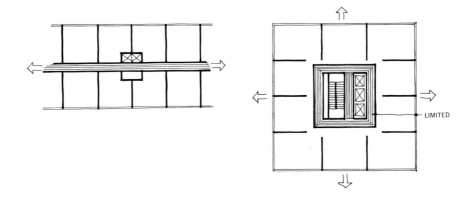

Because the efficiency ratio of 15% maximum nonrental space has to be kept for the point blocks as well, we could say that the maximum useful core will determine the maximum size of the point block. If the core (vertical core elements plus corridor) is equal to 15% of the gross floor area, the rental portion can be calculated readily. This also means that the taller the point-block building, the larger it can become because its core will be larger (more elevators and smokeproof tower instead of regular stairs).

How the core relates to rental space in the point block plan is best illustrated with an example.

We assume a core containing two elevators and a scissor stair in a 30 by 30 ft grid. (See the chapter on fire safety, how new highrise fire codes will influence the use of scissor stairs.)

Each 900 sf square of the grid is adequate for a one-bedroom apartment. The core

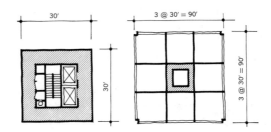

(900 sf) to gross floor area (8100 sf) ratio is excellent: 11.3%. The difficulty lies in the corner apartments, which are hard if not impossible to enter.

To remedy the tricky entrance problem branch corridors have been added in a pinwheel pattern. This not only helps to solve the apartment entry but provides the corridor with light and view. It has, however, proved to be too luxurious:

Original gross floor area	8100 sf
Increase	+600 sf
Total gross	8700 sf
Original core area	900 sf
Increase	+600 sf
Total core:	1500 sf = 17.24% of gross!

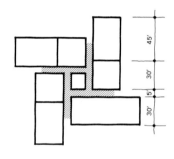

The apartment entry problem could be solved without the luxurious corridor system, thus considerably improving the floor efficiency:

Gross floor area	8200 sf
Core area	1000 sf = 12.2% of gross

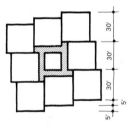

Returning to the original grid, half of the one-bedroom apartments could theoretically turn into two-bedroom units by simple extension. The core (900 sf) to gross floor area (9900 sf) ratio is too good to be true: 9.1%. The problem is that the plan hardly functions due to the difficulties of entering the two-bedroom units.

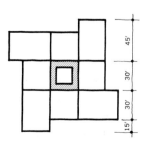

Again, branch corridors can remedy the situation by adding light and view to the core:

Original gross floor area	9900 sf
Increase	+600 sf
Total gross	10,500 sf
Original core area	900 sf
Increase	+600 sf
	1500 sf = 14.3% of gross

There is no need to eliminate the light and view created by the extended corridor as it was necessary to do in the one-bedroom plan. The increased gross floor area can take an increased core without losing efficiency.

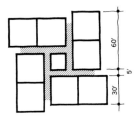

With a given core size, determined by the height of the building, the more rental square footage surrounding the core, the more economically efficient the plan will become. Deep plans with narrow exterior exposure can maximize this efficiency.

It is not necessary that the public corridor form a ring around the vertical core elements (**17, 30**). Depending on where the surrounding apartments can be entered, the amount of corridor, and consequently the total core area, can be reduced. Splitting the vertical core elements and using an "H"-shaped corridor is more efficient than the ring (**21–23, 28, 31**). To serve more than six apartments the wings can be extended, but the maximum dead-end corridor permitted by code must be kept in mind. When no dead-end is allowed, a ring corridor is the only answer.

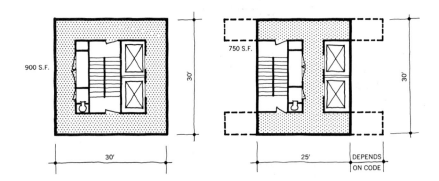

When there are a large number of apartments on the typical floor and the core becomes bigger than needed for stairs, elevators, refuse chute and so on, the extra space can be filled with tenant lockers (**21**). This is well justified when no other inexpensive space is available in the building for these lockers or when the proximity of lockers to apartments results in major marketing advantages. Otherwise, locating the lockers on expensive floor space makes little sense.

Point blocks can take many shapes, each of which has its own inherent limitations. The classic pinwheel is a sequential dynamic shape, most conducive to experimentation and invention (**28, 30, 31**). Less dynamic but still quite free is the "inverted symmetry" type. Axial plans can be symmetrical around a single axis, double axis, or four axes, leading to the circle, with its unlimited number of axes and the difficulties of pie-shaped apartments (**17–19**). Very tall buildings with considerably increased cores can be well fitted into triaxial arrangements and triangle- or tripod-shaped plans (**24**).

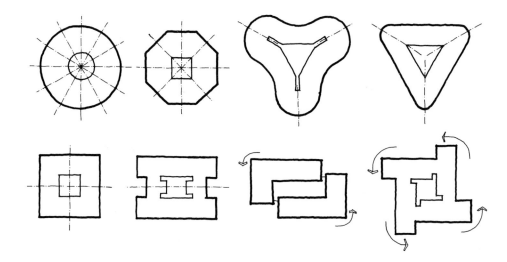

An interesting form of point block is the linked tower: two point blocks form a multicore plan (Davis Brody & Associates), or the link is used to house the elevator core (Hoberman & Wasserman). Sizable savings can be realized. In fact, a complete circle will have been traveled: point blocks linked by an elevator core are nothing but central-corridor buildings with bold articulation (**25, 27**).

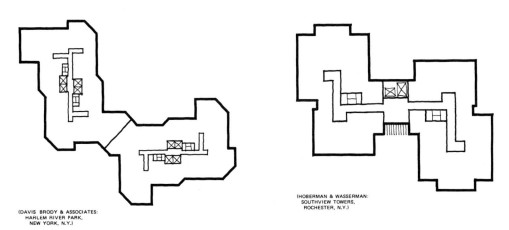

(DAVIS BRODY & ASSOCIATES: HARLEM RIVER PARK, NEW YORK, N.Y.)

(HOBERMAN & WASSERMAN: SOUTHVIEW TOWERS, ROCHESTER, N.Y.)

The principles of apartment planning described for the central-corridor scheme are valid for point blocks as well. While a point block maximizes the use of 90 degree double-exposure (corner) apartments, it also presents some unique problems. Unless the corridor is extended, which greatly increases the nonrental space, these apartments are hard to enter, especially when corner living rooms with maximum light and wide-angle views are most marketable. The passage from entrance to living room inevitably bypasses the sleeping area. Imaginative planning should make this passage as direct and bright as possible. When the living room is pulled away from the corner, the problem will have been eliminated.

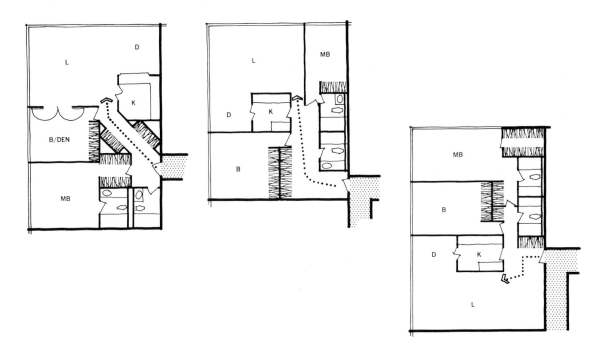

Structural principles already discussed do not change when a point block is planned. What happens, however, is that the vertical core elements concentrated in the center can act as a structural core, and the corridor, plus the normal apartment depth, creates two manageable bays in which the column line coincides with the line between inner and outer zones.

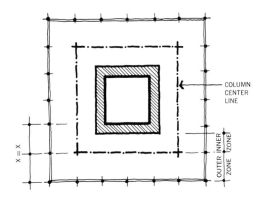

Why a point-block instead of a central-corridor building? Obviously, the first generator of this type of building is ground-level conditions (setbacks, maximum allowable ground coverage of the tower, parking layout, etc.). Marketing might be a generator (need for more corner apartments) and so might the architect's sense of form. This slender articulated shape offers more exciting possibilities than the large slab that often results from the central-corridor plan. On sites that have several towers the advantage of point block is that it minimizes building overlap and provides unblocked views from a maximum number of apartments.

EXTERIOR-CORRIDOR SYSTEM

The major advantage of the exterior-corridor scheme is that all apartments can have two exterior zones because of this form of access (**13, 14, 27, 33, 35, 37**). Its logical use is in moderate climates, in which advantage can be taken of the double exposure for cross ventilation. In northern latitudes the corridor exposed to the elements is far from ideal; it becomes icy, windswept, and snowpacked. The use of the exterior-corridor scheme for low-cost housing, regardless of the climate, has been justified by some because of the outdoor area it can provide adjacent to the dwelling and because the open corridor is easily observable, at least up to a reasonable number of floors (**33**).

It is not an economical type of housing. Each of its apartments carries twice the amount of corridor cost of the central-corridor scheme. What is true about the cost of the corridor is also true about the vertical core elements; compared with the central-corridor solution, their cost is absorbed by half the number of units. To accommodate the same number of families as a central-corridor apartment building on the same area of ground, the outside-corridor building will be twice as tall and less wind resistant as a result of its narrowness.

Aside from the question of wind resistance, the same structural principles apply as they do to the central-corridor building. The ubiquitous outside corridor is generally handled as a cantilevered slab, although when the corridor is long columns along its edge can create added scale and articulation.

The same apartment types can be used with this scheme as in the inner corridor, except that the principle of borrowing is seldom applicable, for the vertical cores can be separated easily and handled as independent elements.

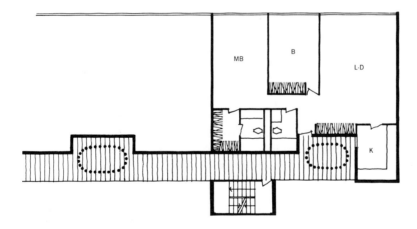

When the apartment types of the central-corridor scheme are applied to an outside gallery, the real significance of the exterior-corridor system is lost. The double exposure of this scheme demands a different approach to apartment planning, one that takes advantage of the fact that rooms can face in two directions. Naturally, this is not quite true. The gallery side of the apartments—except that of the last one—really faces a public walk, which presents serious limitations. Bedrooms cannot face this way unless they have clerestory windows which, with the gallery overhanging, provide poor light. Again there is the question of climate; it may be a good solution in extremely bright semitropical regions. On the other hand, living rooms, dining spaces, and kitchens can get by with less privacy. Placed along the corridor they provide an added degree of surveillance that may be desirable.

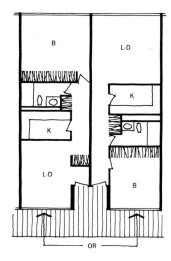 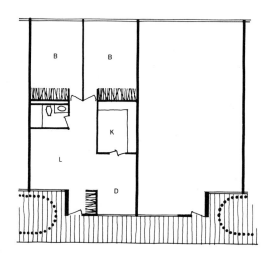

When significant indentations are called for in the plan or when the entire gallery is made considerably wider than necessary for mere passage (sometimes to accommodate out-swinging screen doors), well-observed play areas for small children and sitting areas for adults can be created. Some kind of symbolic separation, however—level change or low fencing—is necessary between the passage and these areas if they are to serve as porches or verandas and to create a sense of private territory and "ownership" by the occupant (**33**).

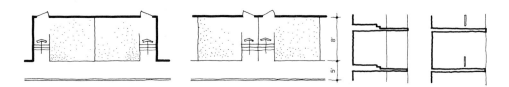

The vertical core elements provide the designer with a variety of options in exterior-corridor buildings. To begin with, they can be borrowed from the apartment and handled as part of the building volume. The result is long, powerful galleries. They can be handled also as independent elements, strong vertical towers, juxtaposed to the horizontality of the gallery.

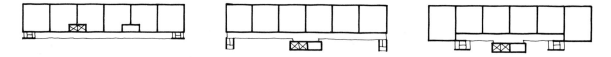

It has been advocated that galleries, especially when they serve as major traffic channels between buildings, be considered as "streets in the sky." This concept will remain an unrealized dream, for without shops and community spaces—which are costly and in the case of shops, need to be self-supporting—there are no viable streets. "It seems that once . . . shops, views of outside community life, and the automobile have all been taken away, the thing that remains is only a corridor."[52]

SKIP-STOP SYSTEM

Central-corridor, multicore, point-block, exterior-corridor types—all are generated by differing horizontal distribution channels. These terms, in their common use, suggest elevator stops at every floor. However, when the plan is such that only every second or third elevator stop is necessary, we are talking about a completely new category, the skip-stop system (**16, 32–37**), which can also be central corridor, exterior corridor, multicore, and, very rarely, point block.

What is even more important than the alternating elevator stops in this system is the fact that most or all apartments are on more than one level; hence the name "multilevel apartment scheme" often used for skip-stop.

In addition to regular (one-level) apartments, skip-stop schemes generate three basic multilevel apartment types:

1. Regular apartments that are entered on the floor above or below by way of a two-story interior stair hall.
2. Apartments on two or three levels. The levels have half-floor differences.
3. Truly two-story apartments with interior stairs.

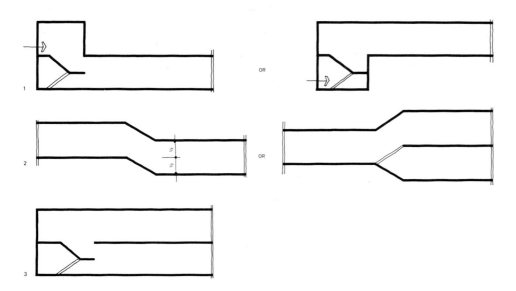

Stairs, the connectors between the various levels, play a relatively minor role as an aesthetic element in the first two types. They are not free standing and are surrounded by walls on two or three sides. In the third type the stairs can become the major element of spatial excitement when carefully handled and displayed. To gain maximum aesthetic pleasure not only from the stairs but from the interrelation of the two levels, this is possible only when the living space becomes truly two stories high and when the upper space appears as a mezzanine within the high space.

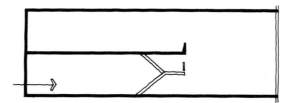

DESIGN METHODOLOGY

Combining the three basic types with regular apartments permits almost unlimited combinations.

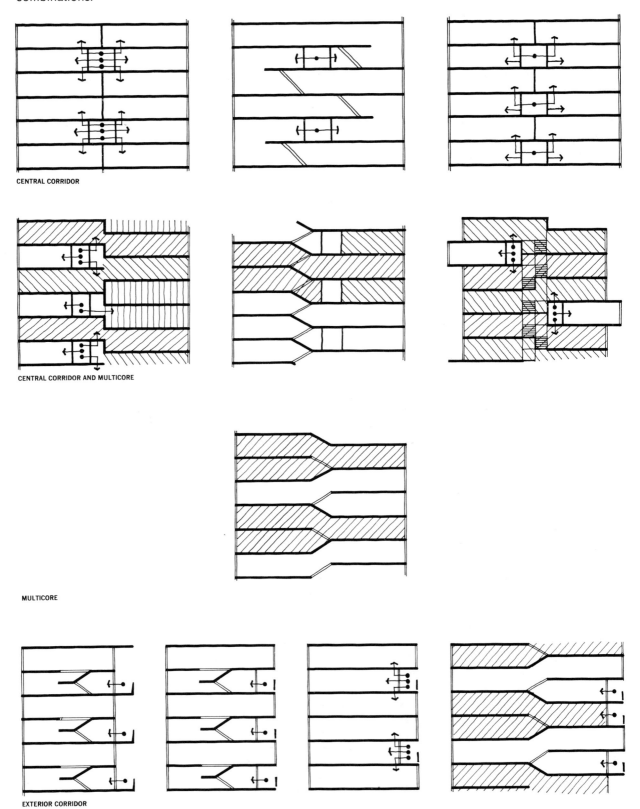

CENTRAL CORRIDOR

CENTRAL CORRIDOR AND MULTICORE

MULTICORE

EXTERIOR CORRIDOR

Multilevel apartment schemes require careful analysis of the building code. Does the code require a separate exit into a public corridor for each floor of a two-story apartment? What about the exits for a trilevel scheme? Careful attention must be paid to framing the breaks in the floors and to the vertical alignment of plumbing shafts and exhaust ducts. When the kitchen occurs above the living space of the floor below, there is no kitchen carpeting that would help to minimize impact noises; a special liner must be used under resilient flooring.

These are just some of the major difficulties and caveats. Spaces on more than one level are obviously unfeasible for the elderly. Multilevel apartments are costly and their design must be justified. The justifications are varied: view problems, market requirements for unusual interior spaces, space for simultaneous but conflicting activities, maximum separation between sleeping and living zones, and so on, not to mention the variety that can be introduced on the exterior. Admittedly every designer is challenged by the idea, and, if it can be worked out within the budget, why not?

In weighing costs it should not be overlooked that, as in multicore schemes, the elimination of corridors on alternating floors will increase the rentable space. According to a study by the Urban Design Group of the New York City Planning Department (*Architectural Record*, April 1971), in a skip-stop prototype worked out by the group "the total structure creates about 25 percent less gross cubic feet of building than do 'normal' corridor-every-floor projects having the same number and size of apartments."

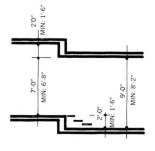

It is also possible to create two-story apartments or level changes in apartments without a skip-stop elevator scheme (**11, 15**). In the same way that a plan can be shifted horizontally, portions of an apartment can be slid along a vertical axis to introduce more than a one-floor elevation. It is costly compared with the level slab and is usually warranted only in high-rent housing. The increased cost is primarily in the special framing around the depressed portions of the floor.

The simplest form of level break is the depressed living-dining-kitchen complex. In another form the living room alone is depressed, which gives the dining space an elevated appearance. In this way, although it is in the interior zone, it is well defined (**15**).

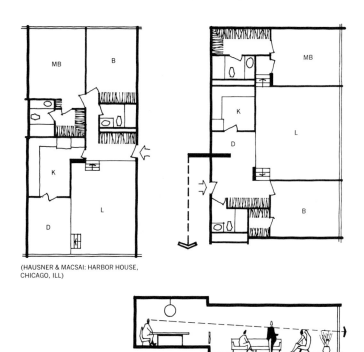

(HAUSNER & MACSAI: HARBOR HOUSE, CHICAGO, ILL)

DESIGN METHODOLOGY

To break the level between living and dining space the dining area must be more than adequate in size, for level breaks eliminate the possibility of expansion. The break itself can be handled with a railing or simply an open step.

In addition to the spatial variety created in the interior, the change of floor levels opens up exciting new possibilities on the exterior of the building when properly expressed.

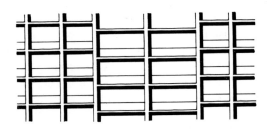

SYNTHESIS

Having discussed the components of the highrise apartment building and the basic systems of organizing the units into a vertical container, we are faced with the question of whether there is a way of putting it all together in logical progression.

Needless to say, the number of variables is so immense that there is no foolproof formula, one that would cover all cases, for no two problems have identical conditions. Nevertheless, some broad directions suggest themselves.

Again an example will best illuminate the issue. There is a client who wants to build a middle- to upper-income condominium containing two-bedroom units of approximately 1050 to 1100 sf. The typical user is middle aged with grown children. The location is a midwestern urban site, one with a definite view that not only will help to market the units but also will raise sales prices. Setbacks and density, determined by zoning, allow 240 dwellings (about 170 units per acre, or 265 sf of land per dwelling unit).

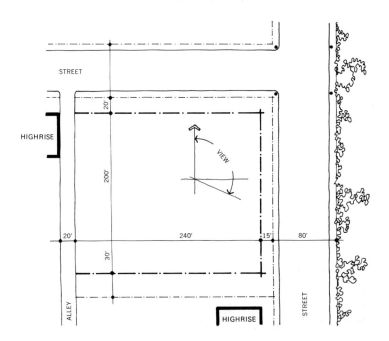

Lot dimensions and view will strongly influence the system of apartment organization. Even before considering the site, however, two of the possible systems (central corridor, multicore, point block, exterior corridor, and skip-stop) can be eliminated immediately—the exterior corridor because of climate and cost, the skip-stop because of cost and user resistance to stairs within the apartment. This leaves central corridor, multicore, and point block.

What are the possibilities of this site? Scheme A is a central-corridor solution far enough from the highrise to the south to allow good angled views even from the farthest apartment. It has a large number of units, 12 per floor, and uses concrete construction

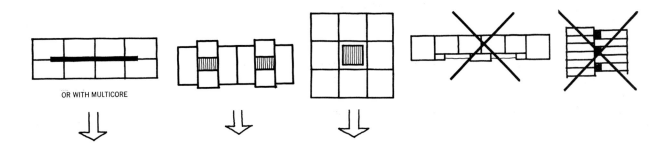

OR WITH MULTICORE

economically. Scheme B is also a central-corridor solution but solves the view problem unsatisfactorily and can be discarded. Scheme C, a multicore that requires a fourth elevator, is a modification of B that would improve the view. There are 10 units on a floor. Scheme D is a point block with 8 units on a floor and a good view from most. Because of the small number of units per floor, it is taller than the others and requires a smokeproof tower (at least under our hypothetical code).

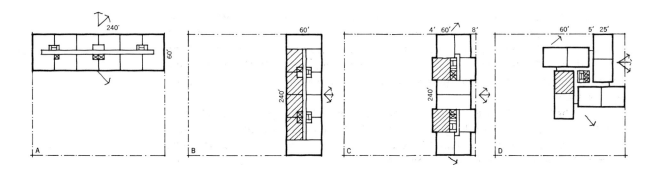

A comparative analysis of these schemes should help deciding on one of them, at least until the next step. Which has the smallest area for 240 apartments? Which has the least exterior skin? Which has the smallest nonrental-to-gross ratio? Which has the maximum number of apartments with view? At least two of the schemes score acceptably in some of the categories.

Category	Scheme A	Scheme B	Scheme C	Scheme D
Size of floor in sf (and number of units) × number of floors = gross tower area in square feet for 240 units	14,400 (12) × 20 = 288,000[b]	12,000 (10) × 24 = 288,000[b]	12,960 (10) × 24 = 311,000	10,880 (8) × 30[a] = 326,400
Perimeter per floor × floor height × number of floors = skin in square feet	600 × 8.5 = 5100 × 20 = 102,000[b]	520 × 8.5 = 4420 × 24 = 106,000[b]	570 × 8.5 = 4845 × 24 = 116,280	550 × 8.5 = 4675 × 30 = 140,250
Nonrental sf per floor; percent of gross	1640 11.4%[b]	1360 11.3%[b]	1540 11.8%[b]	1530 14%
Percentage of apartments with view	100%[b]	60%	80%[b]	87.5%[b]

[a] Added cost of smokeproof tower.
[b] Acceptable scores.

Scheme A seems to score well from every point of view except for one major drawback—the long corridor that will have to be dealt with. Scheme B is equally economical; its corridor is shorter but it does not solve the view problem. Scheme C costs more but has unique advantages in its muticore setup. Scheme D is obviously uneconomical. On another site for another market scheme D could still be the answer (in any case it should be kept, at least for the sake of comparison, through the next step). Each scheme has its own exterior possibilities and limitations. Regardless of all the rational comparisons, the impact of the tower mass, so different in each scheme, should be studied; the way in which each scheme lends itself to the designer's intent on the exterior should be considered at this point.

It should be noted that one of the major drawbacks of this kind of exercise is the elimination of contextual design. Building height, mass, and shape—not to mention exterior material, fenestration and details—should be studied in the context of the surroundings. "Contrasting" or "fitting-in" are fundamental considerations and if the last one is chosen, it must start quite early, when the tower location and volume are being selected.

How do the towers relate to the common elements of the building—parking, storage, laundry, and recreation? Parking, the largest of all common elements, with strong functional requirements that cannot be easily disposed of, should be the first to be examined. The type of ownership (condominium) necessitates one-to-one parking regardless of zoning requirements. In this case the sponsor's program calls for self-parking.

Among the remaining three solutions D cannot accommodate the required 240 cars on two levels as the others can. The third parking floor is a problem: with one parking level in the basement, the two-story bulk covering practically the entire site forms an unfriendly barrier to the neighborhood. Although two parking levels below grade would lower the bulk, let us assume now that a high water table on the site prohibits a subbasement. This would eliminate scheme D. Had we not set the above conditions, D would remain a viable option for further analysis. Both A and C have more than 240 stalls in this schematic study. Considering that parking spaces will be eaten up by the swimming pool—if it is on the deck—and that the loading dock and stairs will further cut into them, scheme C is tight, whereas A presents an easy parking solution.

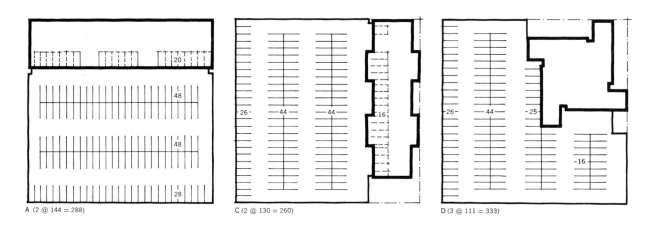

A (2 @ 144 = 288)   C (2 @ 130 = 260)   D (3 @ 111 = 333)

Traffic conditions around the site also favor scheme A. Because of the heavy traffic on the north-south street and the possibility of a pile-up at the traffic light, entry and exit appear to be easier on the less traveled east-west street. Loading from the alley, possible only in scheme A, is also preferred. Loading for scheme C—regardless of the street—is rather cumbersome because this scheme has two vertical cores and the loading path must reach both.

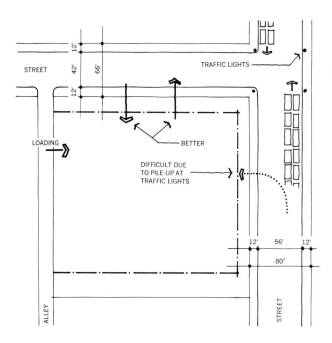

Further testing—in scheme A—of the interrelations of parking, loading, exit, and entrance seems to present no difficulties. Considering the possibilities of integrating the vertical tower and the horizontal parking volume, this scheme lends itself to a number of options that should be studied at this time, though for the sake of continuity in this illustration they can be deferred for the moment. There is adequate length for the ramps under the tower and the entire lower parking level can be located in the basement. Half-level depression of the parking volume to reduce ramp length is without advantage in this case (a higher water table could alter this decision).

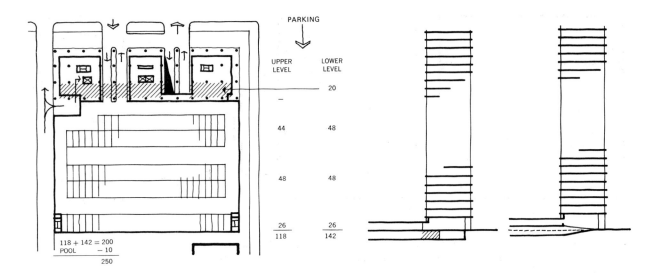

The next step in the investigation concerns the common spaces. Using criteria discussed in Chapter 2 and making some assumptions, we can establish space requirements for each need.

MECHANICAL AND STORAGE AREAS

Electric gear and transformer	800 sf
Pumps and hotwater heater	500 sf
Building storage	300 sf
Refuse room	300 sf
Receiving room	400 sf
Tenant lockers (240 @ 25)	6000 sf

LOBBY AREA

Lobby and mail room	1500 sf
Pram room	150 sf

RECREATION AREAS

Pool (open) with deck area	6000 sf
Tennis courts	6200 sf
Sauna (and pool toilets)	1200 sf
Meeting room (and storage, kitchenette)	3000 sf
Game rooms	600 sf
Laundry	500 sf

Examination of the spaces that are left after solving parking and loading will indicate that the center area B (approximately 1700 sf net) is about right for lobby and pram

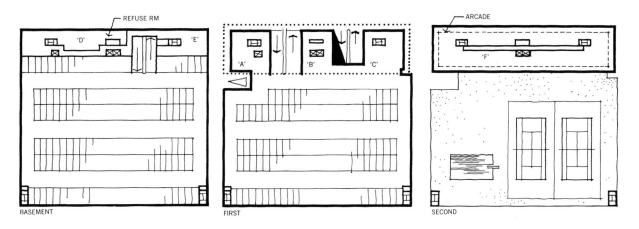

BASEMENT   FIRST   SECOND

room in the proper location. Area A (approximately 2300 sf net) next to the service elevator is ideal for receiving room and building storage, with the leftover space used for some of the tenant lockers. Area C (approximately 2400 sf net) is cut off from the service elevator and is not useful for tenant lockers; it is excellent, though, for electrical gear and transformer (with good access), for pump and hotwater heater, as well as for building storage. The spaces left in the basement, areas D and E (approximately 6000 sf net), are useful for the balance of the tenant lockers and refuse room.

The deck of the garage can comfortably accommodate tennis courts and open swimming pool with adequate space left for a sundeck. The indoor recreation spaces called for under the arbitrary program add up to about 5300 sf and the lowest typical floor provides 12,700 sf of useful area (area F), more than twice the amount needed. It is ideally located for recreational purposes near the pool and tennis courts.

Even if this floor were cut back to the arcade line of the first floor—assuming this is wanted for architectural form—it would still have a useful area of 9200 sf, more than is needed for the program. The surplus space can be utilized for tenant lockers, thus eliminating the need for space in the basement.

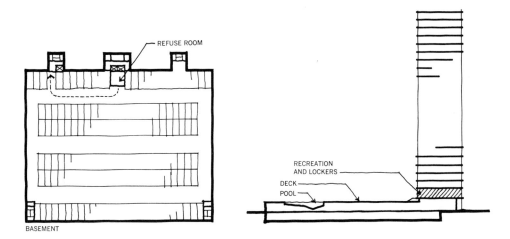

BASEMENT

A similar investigation should be made for every possible scheme that answers the program's requirements. Only after the designer has been assured of the general allocation of spaces and the working interrelations of volumes can detailed planning of the typical floors be more than wasted exercise.

DESIGN METHODOLOGY

EXTERIOR

The previous example was analyzed to cast light on synthesis. Each step was taken with a warning about exterior consequences, although these exterior issues were delayed for the convenience of illustrating a procedure. In reality, the effect on exterior form is kept in mind as each step is analyzed.

The chart that compares the economic benefits derived from each of the four possible schemes would be a meaningless exercise without a simultaneous comparison of volumes. The question must be asked: is this the volume the designer wants? On multitower sites, when the designer's options are not so limited, the issue of the volume becomes even more crucial.

It is obvious that, even within the limitations of rational design, and generators such as site, zoning, program, and mix, the designer must make some basic decisions about the building volume. The building—in this case the tower—might be predominantly vertical or horizontal, tall or squat, thin or fat. Arnheim analyzes this problem extensively. According to him, though a horizontal (parallel to the ground) building fits into the landscape easily, it "tends to float on the surface of the ground because parallels do not interlock. Contact is all the more tenuous because the shape of such a building undercuts the vertical dimension of the gravitational pull. The building has little weight; it does not press down."[53] This is hardly the case with residential "towers." There is little question that a vertical building "stands." In fact here the gravitational forces and the building shape coincide so that the building tends to sink into the earth unless the ground floor of the building is treated as a base. Most highrise apartment buildings require considerable public space and parking that tend to form such bases under the vertical tower. Inbetween shapes, ones that are neither explicitly horizontal or vertical require a great deal of attention. These shapes can be made to "appear" either horizontal or vertical by the articulation of the facade, by the strong horizontals of spandrels, ribbon windows, or galleries, or by the strong verticals of volume breaks, balconies, and bay windows.

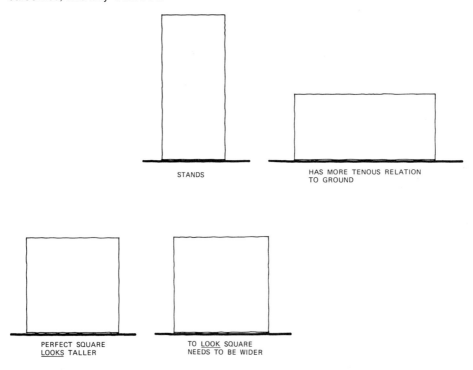

STANDS

HAS MORE TENOUS RELATION TO GROUND

PERFECT SQUARE LOOKS TALLER

TO LOOK SQUARE NEEDS TO BE WIDER

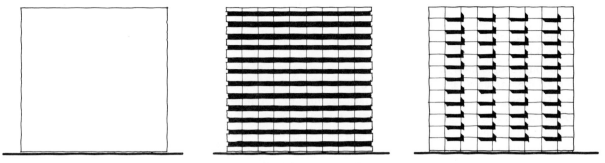

INBETWEEN SHAPES CAN BE ACCENTED (HORIZONTALLY OR VERTICALLY) BY FACADE ARTICULATION

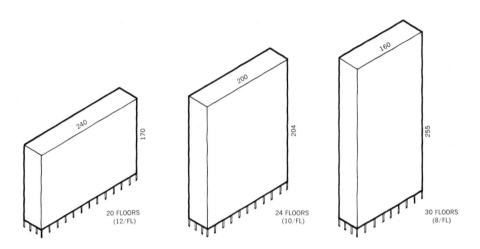

20 FLOORS
(12/FL)

24 FLOORS
(10/FL)

30 FLOORS
(8/FL)

Once the mass is tentatively decided on—tentatively because every decision must be subject to reevaluation as its effects are further realized—the most soul searching question faces the designer: the building exterior. Naturally, it was brought up earlier at the time the plan was conceived, but now it must be solved.

Budget, climate, and the availability of construction technology and materials affect the exterior, as does the architect's theory of form. Although philosophical approaches to exteriors can be discussed, it must be conceded that many, or even all, may be appropriate under certain conditions.

On the one hand, we find the designer whose goal is to give clear exterior presence to the structure. The Chicago group—if such gross oversimplification is permitted—under the influence of Mies van der Rohe's early highrises and of the strong buildings by members of the Chicago School, has been the main advocate of the expressed frame. The New York group—another oversimplification—heir to a long tradition of brick-clad highrises, deals with large masonry surfaces where the graphics of the punched openings and sculpturing of brick volumes are the dominant aim, and exterior rhythm does not necessarily require structural purity.

Expressing the structure is not limited to exposed frame. Cladding—brick or other—

273

will also suggest structure but less explicitly. In any case, "a structure makes us uncomfortable if we can't somehow see or sense what supports it. Expressing the structure is by no means an architectural whim but, I believe, a psychological necessity of good design."[54]

Paul Rudolph's statement that architects wish to build "dominant buildings" and to maintain "intimate scale" points out one of the difficulties in designing highrise housing. The designer strives for the human, residential, or "intimate scale"[56] against many odds, one of which is the sheer volume of the tower. We do not need to strive for dominance in highrises; it is there whether we want it or not. The difficulty of highrise residential exteriors lies in just this: the higher the rise, the more dominant the mass, and the harder it is to achieve intimate scale. Intimate scale in this case means residential scale—to express what the building really is, a hive of human habitation. The designer has the option to deny that individual dwellings exist by using completely anonymous curtain walls or by superimposing a structural grid. However, there is always an alternate option, giving "tangible presence to people," to use the phrase coined by Donlyn Lyndon. Whatever the means, particularized rhythm, balconies, or bays, the intent is to suggest the existence of someone in the rooms. The tendency is from the general to the particular or, as Charles Jencks said, "the general, repetitive geometry is made more particularized by being changed where a bedroom differs in size."[56] Proceeding from inside out, from plan to exterior form, the plan is organized to take advantage of every expressible particularity within economic realities.

What Arnheim calls for is a "readable relationship" between the interior and the exterior of a building. This relationship is one of the fundamental difficulties in architectural design. Again, according to Arnheim, "whether such a correspondence between outside and inside is desirable depends on stylistic preference." Nor is such correspondence easy to achieve. What happens inside cannot be completely expressed on the exterior. Even if it could, one would have to question it, as Arnheim does:

> The frankly informative appearance of buildings whose inside holds few spatial secrets offers little of the teasing richness and sophisticated complexity found in architectural styles that deviate from such elementary parallelism. Simple parallelism also reflects little of the dramatic struggle by which the architect must plan from the inside and from the outside at the same time—two kinds of planning that typically involve quite different considerations and accordingly different shapes.[57]

Thus there is the structure that wants to dominate and there is the human dwelling that wants to be recognizable. It is the exterior wall that will hide or express, emphasize or quietly deny one or the other of these aspects. The wall, in fact, to quote Venturi, "becomes the spatial record of this resolution and its drama," or, differently stated by him in the same book.

> Louis Kahn has referred to "what a thing wants to be," but implicit in this statement is its opposite: what the architect wants the thing to be. In the tension and balance between these two lie many of the architect's decisions.[58]

Decisions on volume and exterior expression must not be made out of context, in disregard of the building's environment. To quote Arnheim again:

> From the outside, architecture is never alone. Surrounded by other buildings, by landscape, or by unoccupied space, a work of architecture

depends in all its visual dimensions—size, shape, texture, color, spatial orientation, etc.—upon its environment. The surroundings decide whether a building appears as a pinnacle or an inconspicuous attendant, whether it is large or small, harmonious or out of step.[59]

EXPOSED FRAME: COLUMN BAYS.   The importance of the rhythm created by bay sizes and by the order of living rooms and bedrooms cannot be overemphasized. Though this issue has already been amply covered in earlier chapters, no discussion of exposed frame would be complete without it (**1–3, 5, 15–17, 19, 22, 23, 26**).

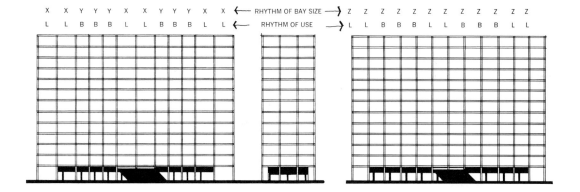

Beyond rhythm, the issue *par excellence* is proportion: the proportions of the negative spaces or voids between slabs and columns; the proportions of the framing members themselves; the proportions of the slab thickness to the column widths.

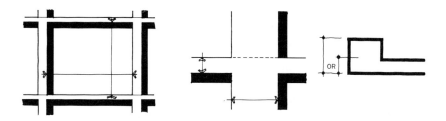

When the required structural slab is thin, the issue of real versus apparent structure emerges and the slab edge must often be made heavier than needed to achieve proper proportions at a cost that should be taken into consideration. To quote Rudolph:

> The actual structural members of this tower are so small that they would never read from a distance. . . . If you should expose the actual structural members, you would not have the apparent sense of structure.[60]

Or Scott:

> In the first place, it is clear that the vivid constructive properties of a building, insofar as they are effectively constructive, must exist as *facts*. The security of the building and hence also of any artistic value it may possess, depends on this; and a support which seemed to be adequate to its load, but actually was not, would, as construction, be wrong. But insofar as they are vivid, they must exist *as appearances.* It is the effect which the constructive

properties make on the eye, and not the scientific facts that may be intellectually discoverable about them, which alone can determine their vividness.[61]

To achieve the desired proportions columns can be molded according to the architect's design: square, broad, narrow, and deep (**5, 15, 22, 23**). The designer's ability to mold columns, however, will be affected by the mechanical system of the building, by pipe risers, vertical fan-coil units, and so on.

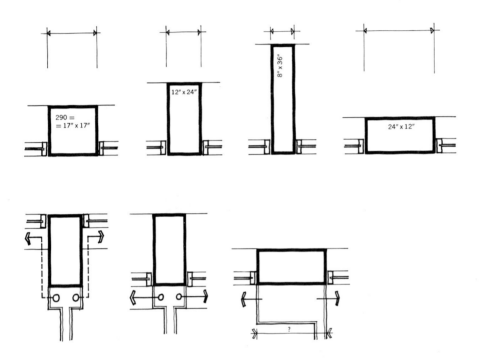

The concrete frame can be thought of as continuous and flowing, in which necessary joints are de-emphasized or as elements erected one after the other in a series of pours in which pour joints are deliberately expressed. These rustications are especially helpful in identifying main frame from secondary-pour spandrels. When rustication deteriorates into decoration, when pouring sequence is disregarded, "joints" are self-willed.

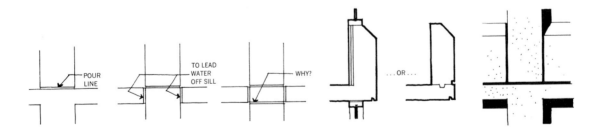

Spandrels can be made of a variety of materials in addition to poured concrete and expressed, such as with precast concrete panels and masonry infill, or camouflaged, such as with masonry behind structural glass or porcelain-enameled/metal panels that simulate the fenestration above (**19**). The height of the spandrel can be determined by several factors besides the sense of proportion: factors such as the furniture to be placed against it in bedrooms and the dimensions of the horizontal heating/cooling element. Fire codes may also determine spandrel height to minimize potential flame spread.

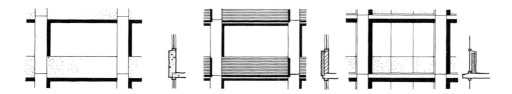

In addition to spandrels, solid elements can be used within the structural frame not only to cut down on the glass area but to accommodate partitions. Partitions that do not occur on column line can be lined up with mullions. Far more leeway in locating partitions is provided by solid vertical panels that also create a secondary rhythm on the elevation. Recent attempts to deal with energy conservation by increasing the insulating properties of the building envelope are likely to lead to the introduction of more and more solid panels within the structural frame.

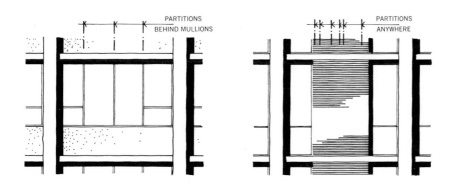

There is a complex relation between solid and glass infill panels within an expressed structural frame. Each is an "infill" of the frame. When the glass is a "hole" in the solid infill, however, it has lost its relation to the frame proper and conveyed a mixed, aesthetically confusing message. In a typical bay, when the glass does not touch at least three of its sides, such aesthetic confusion occurs.

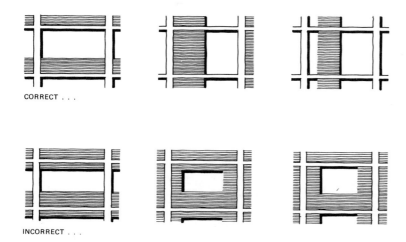

DESIGN METHODOLOGY

In the ideal sense and in disregard of energy conservation the structural frame ought to be filled with glass to express that indeed it surrounds a void. The use of dark anodized aluminum, tinted glass, and toned window shades or curtain liners helps to heighten this effect. The more the glass wall recedes in relation to the column and slab edge, the more voidlike the fenestration appears. This relation of glass to frame edge is a critical one and the accumulated dirt on horizontal surfaces should be spilled or lead off in such a way that it does not dirty the frame.

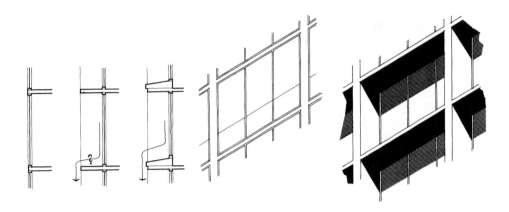

When heating and cooling elements require it, exterior air intake grills can be integrated into the skin. Otherwise, they may lead to further articulation of the exterior (**3, 16, 20**).

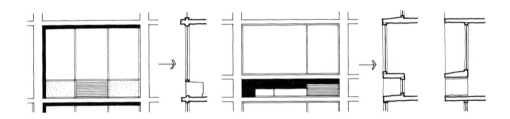

Ultimately the glass area itself, in spite of dark anodized aluminum frames, becomes a network of horizontal and vertical mullions, the proportion of which critically affects the exterior. Other issues must also be faced: the amount of light and natural ventilation required by code, the method of exterior window washing (the window washer climbs out of the apartment or is raised on the outside in a scaffold or the window can be

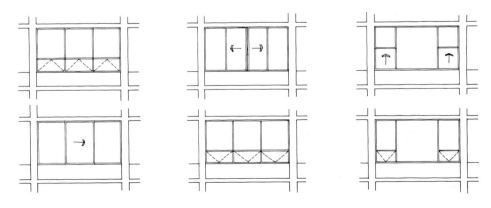

washed from the inside using removable sashes), possibilities of draping (will operating sash interfere with drape?), screens (if on the exterior, the screens will create a rhythm that must be planned).

Three special parts of the apartment tower need additional attention: the corner, the top, and the bottom.

It has been said that one of the most difficult issues facing the architect is the turning of the corner on a building. Here the "facades" meet and become volume or three-dimensional reality. In a four-directional tower, when adjoining walls are similarly fenestrated, the issue revolves around the articulation of the corner column (**1, 2, 4, 5, 21, 26**). In a perspective view it appears heavier than the rest, though in truth it carries less load.

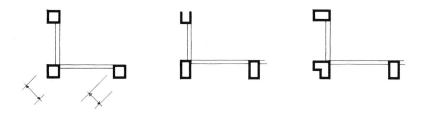

When the tower is two-directional the end wall may be a concrete shear wall with a pattern that expresses the floor slabs behind, thus providing continuity with the expressed frame on the main elevation (**3, 15, 16, 19, 20, 23**). (The cost problem of end shear walls and their contribution to the racking action due to exposure to low temperatures has already been covered in Chapter 3.) The end wall may also be filled, completely or partially, preferably with the same material that served as filler for the spandrels.

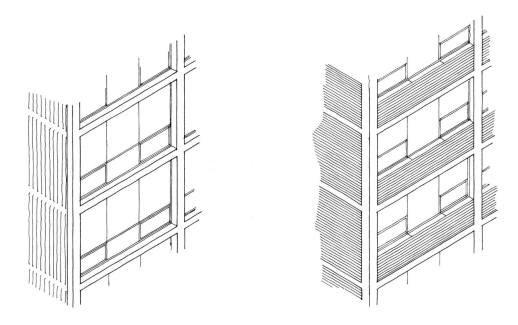

The bottom floor of the tower, whether on grade or on top of the "parking box," usually houses different functions than the typical floors and consequently is treated differently. The bays are filled—glass or solid—or indented to form an arcade. The floor above the arcade requires insulation which is achieved by a furred-down volume that also serves as a gathering space for plumbing stacks and heating risers. The articulation of this furred element needs sensitive handling (**19**), as do canopies, in their relation to columns and arcade.

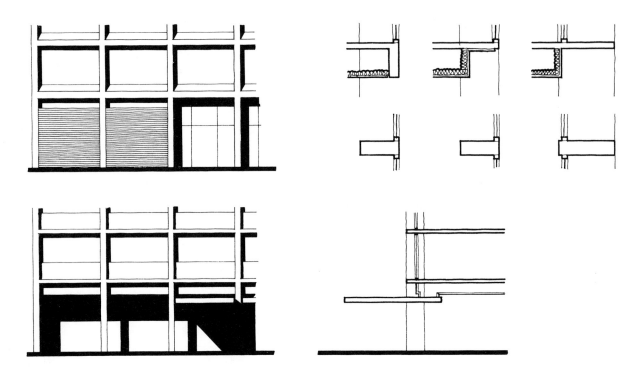

A more fundamental issue concerning columns on the first floor is their dynamics: the relation of the column height to the height of the typical floor and the total building. Arnheim classifies columns as short, passively bearing pressures, or long, in which case the vectors push up against the supported elements and down against the base.

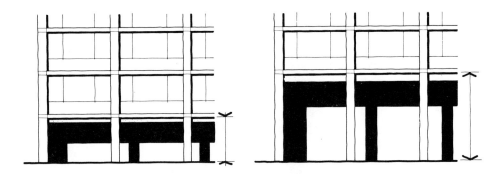

In a manner similar to gathering pipes in a space below the tower, a space is required above the top floor of the building, where bathroom and kitchen exhaust ducts and corridor air supply ducts can turn horizontal to reach the proper location of the fan equipment. This space is generally located above the inner zone. It may also be carried to the edge of the tower, especially when a heavy horizontal element is needed aesthetically or to repeat at the top the rhythm of spandrels (**2–4, 21, 26**). The handling of the roof flashing detail may result in an added closure element over the top slab and will require careful articulation.

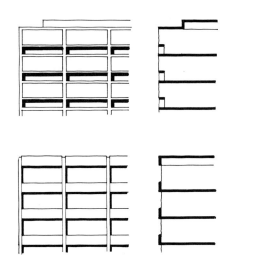
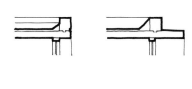

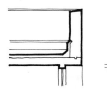
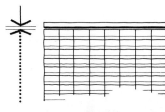

To put it in aesthetic terms, if the tower appears to be solidly anchored to the ground and soars upward, it is desirable to weigh down this vertical thrust. A heavy element—parapet or duct gathering space—might do the job (**2, 4, 21**). Occasionally a heavier crowning belt is needed and a floor with different functions—lockers, community space—and therefore with different fenestration might be used (**5, 20, 22**). A high screen wall, to wind-shield a roof-level pool or hide mechanical penthouses, is another device (**15**).

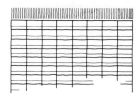

EXPOSED FRAME: LOAD-BEARING MULLIONS.   The discipline imposed on the designer by the exterior columns is not an easy one, though it is most satisfying when successfully adhered to. This discipline demands that rooms do not straddle column lines. When the columns are replaced with load-bearing mullions (a series of small columns), almost unlimited flexibility of planning is attained (**4, 20, 21**).

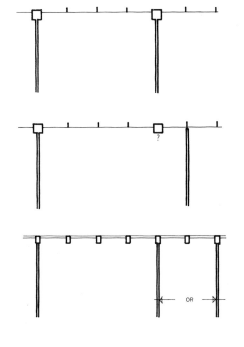
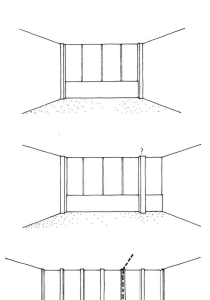

DESIGN METHODOLOGY

The grid system has its shortcomings. If the exterior column bay is considered less than ideal to express the individuality of a particular habitation, the grid system is completely unconducive for bays, balconies, or any kind of expression of different spaces. It camouflages instead of expresses the particular.

If this hindrance is accepted, it can be handled elegantly. Much of its elegance lies in details and proportions, in the articulation of its elements. The space between the load-bearing mullions and the slabs wants to be a void, far more than in bay system structures. Therefore, if a spandrel is required, it is either a concrete extension of the slab or is made to look like glass being faced by some kind of glassy material and not a new material, like brick.

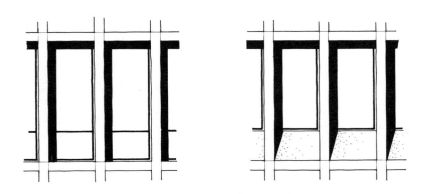

When the load-bearing mullion system is used on a four-directional structure, the handling of the corner detail demands acute sensitivity. Unless the corner is liberated from the mullion (glass butts glass) or the building is "soft cornered" (in fact has no corners), the corner mullion will appear to be clumsy and heavy, regardless of its articulation.

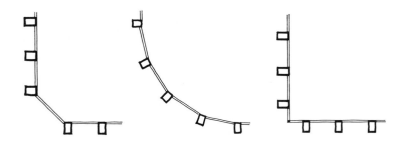

In most cases, either for the sake of openness or because it would otherwise interfere with parking, the load-bearing mullions cannot run down to the ground. They will have to be supported on girders, whose articulation is a challenging problem. The height required for these girders can easily accommodate the furred space needed above arcades. When the height of the girder is increased because of the span, it can accommodate a complete floor behind it. The relation of column height to girder depth and total building volume is even more critical here than on buildings with exposed column bays. Arnheim's observations of column dynamics should be kept in mind (see illustration on p. 283).

CLASSING: CURTAIN WALL.   Curtain-wall cladding of the structural frame provides the designer—by its relatively small modules of vertical elements—with planning

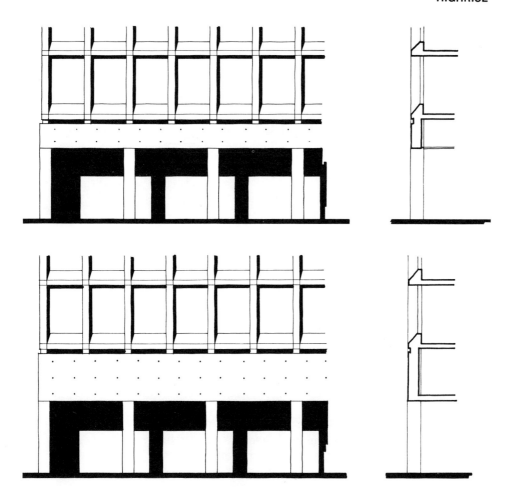

flexibility similar to what the load-bearing mullion system provides (**1, 24**). However, although the load-bearing mullion system is still a structural grid, the cladding by curtain wall completely covers the structural frame; at best, when well handled, it "suggests" the frame. In losing much of the strength of the exposed framing, nothing is gained in expressiveness of human habitation. If there is anything that neglects the variable, the particular, it is the curtain wall.

The punched window in masonry cladding carries a clear message: it is a particular window with people behind it. An exposed frame with its overall grid subdues the window; it is hard to recognize and distinguish it from spandrels. When the building is clad by a curtain wall, windows are lost. They melt into ribbons (vertical or horizontal). "The suggestion of window is gone, and so is the suggestion of people."[62]

The beauty of a curtain wall is in its uninterrupted reflective quality, which mirrors the intricate, varied, and often bizarre silhouettes of old buildings and the simple geometry of the new. The reflections of sky and clouds, of sunshine and storm, make it an everchanging prism of atmospheric conditions. Strong, curving shapes—like the Lake Point Tower by Schipporeit & Heinrich in Chicago—change the reflected image as the observer travels around the building and lend the structure a kaleidoscopic, dynamic quality.

Curtain walls of precast concrete are used less often in the United States than those of steel or aluminum framing. The easy availability of metal and the high development of the metal industry make this so. In contrast is the infant status of concrete prefabrication for exterior wall elements.

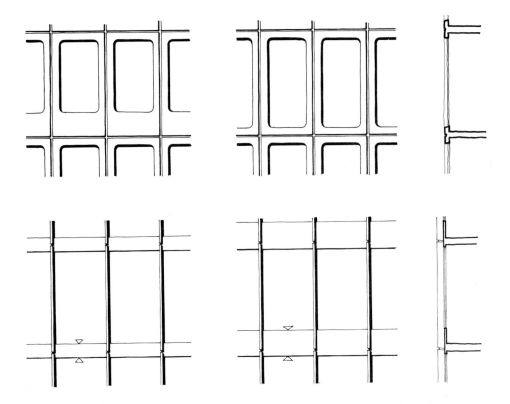

Curtain walls rely on refinement of detail in their aesthetic appeal. Some of the key factors are the thickness and articulation of members and the shadows they cast, or conversely the smooth, flush, skinlike quality of new high-tech systems. Other factors are the proportions of the module to floor height and of the glazed area to the cladded slab edge, especially when this edge is a heavy element that combines the cladding of slab and spandrel.

Curtain walls are particularly accommodated to mechanical systems. Vertical pipe risers do not have to be on the inside faces of columns in which column-to-slab connection is most critical and in which horizontal piping must make tortuous turns around the columns. The space between exterior column face and curtain wall is ideal for risers and straightforward horizontal connections. The grills of horizontal heating/cooling elements can be made to fit in the grid of the curtain wall and will melt into the total pattern.

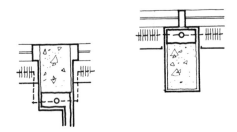

If "turning of the corner" was difficult with exposed frame and especially with load-bearing mullions, it is almost an insurmountable aesthetic task with curtain walls. The curtain wall can cover all the columns except the corner one, and although Mies refined wrestling with this insoluble detail to an art, even he never succeeded. The corner column—which for load-carrying quality is the least important—is exposed not because the designer wants it to be, but because nobody has figured out a way to handle it. The best solution to the problem is to avoid it by cantilevering the corner—in fact, divorcing the curtain wall corner from the column.

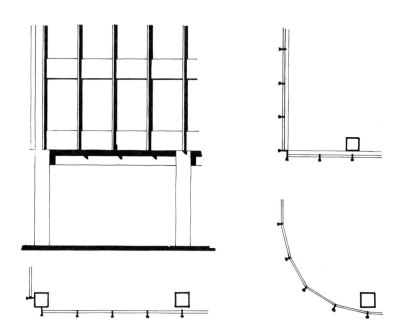

CLADDING: MASONRY.   Masonry cladding liberates the inherent possibilities of the exterior wall from the limiting presence of the structural frame (**6–12, 14, 27–32, 34–41**). The breaking up of overwhelming surfaces, the interruption of the repetitive grid, all that is considered "human" in highrises, are readily achievable with masonry cladding. Cladding, however, is no license for undisciplined, nonrhythmic planning. Poor rhythm in living and sleeping spaces will show up on a masonry-clad structure too. If a masonry exterior skin gives the designer a broader scope to shape openings freely to reflect the spaces behind it, the rhythm of these spaces becomes even more important.

When openings and solids are identical (vertically as well as horizontally), the repetition produces unrelieved boredom. The choice of size and shape is almost unlimited because the number of openings in a highrise will permit custom-made rather than stock sashes without economic disadvantage. However, because of this freedom of choice, brick exteriors require sensitive treatment. Gone is the superimposed grid of the structural frame, which in no way ensures good architecture but provides the unimaginative architect with a more or less acceptable crutch. The selection of masonry (most often brick, sometimes structural clay tile or even patterned concrete block) is important; so is the color, texture, size, and pattern of the masonry. However, the main issue is the window, the hole cut into the masonry surface.

Arnheim talks about the rivalry that takes place between the wall (skin) and the window (hole):

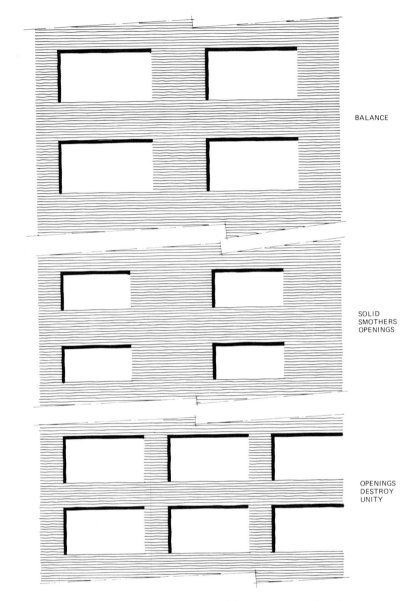

BALANCE

SOLID
SMOTHERS
OPENINGS

OPENINGS
DESTROY
UNITY

Masonry cladding lends itself to varied shapes and sizes of fenestration not only reflecting the character of the interior space (a solid spandrel for furniture placement in a bedroom, more glass in a living room, and so on) but also providing interrelations and juxtapositions of strong graphic quality (**8, 27, 28**).

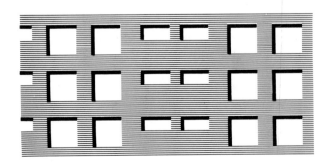
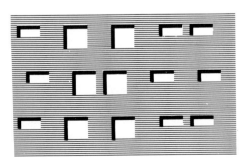

The chances of expressing specific spaces differently—and thus creating rhythm—is considerably enhanced in skip-stop highrises with their multilevel apartments (**32, 35**). The vertical alternation of living and sleeping spaces adds a unique rhythm to the exterior.

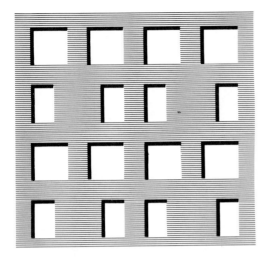 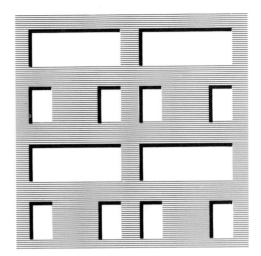

What is also possible on masonry-clad exteriors is the actual molding of openings for a variety of possible reasons: to integrate the grills of heating/air conditioning units; to combine regular windows (vision) with clerestories (light) in bedrooms that are short of furniture space.

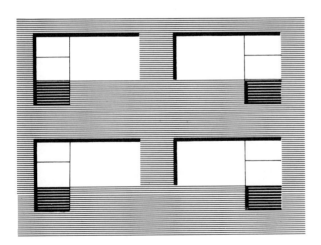 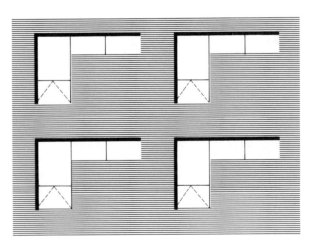

Cladding does not necessarily hide the structural frame that exists behind it. With enlarged openings, the masonry cladding can reflect the structural framework quite strongly. It is also possible to express the structure more explicitly by exposing the actual concrete members, at least in part (**10, 37, 38**). Periodically exposed structural elements (columns or slabs) overlay a secondary pattern on the pattern of openings. Completely exposed horizontal slabs not only cut the cost of shelf angles, but also tend to minimize the effect of bulk on a masonry-clad building volume (**37**).

287

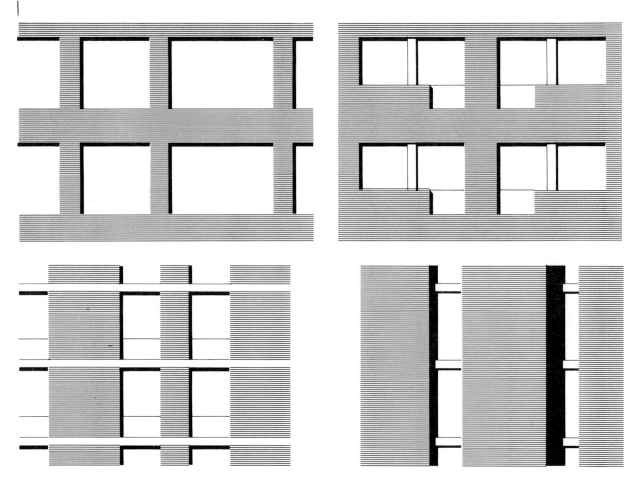

The corners of masonry-clad buildings present no problem compared to those with exposed frame. The volume is generally continuous around the corner. However, open corners are possible in a variety of ways:

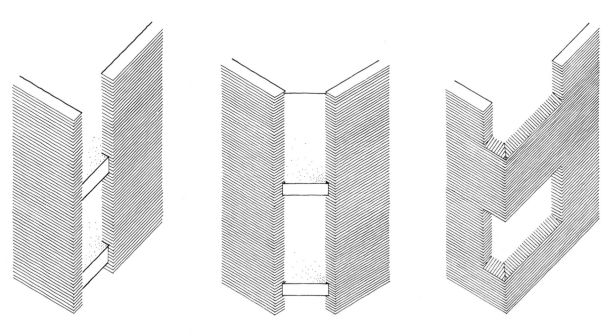

One of the most difficult issues the designer faces when choosing masonry cladding for the exterior of a highrise is the bottom of the building, the way it rests on the ground. The problem is minimized when ground-level functions do not require opening up the volume at this level, when the entire masonry mass grows out of the ground (**31, 39 41**).

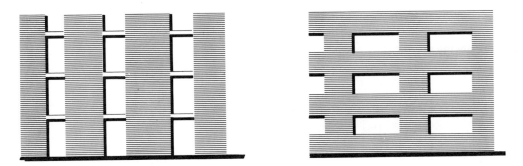

If an open ground floor becomes a necessity, cladding the supporting elements seems a more satisfactory solution than exposing them. The "resting" of the heavy masonry mass on seemingly spindly supports has the appearance of structural unstability, although in fact the cladding masonry is supported at each or every other

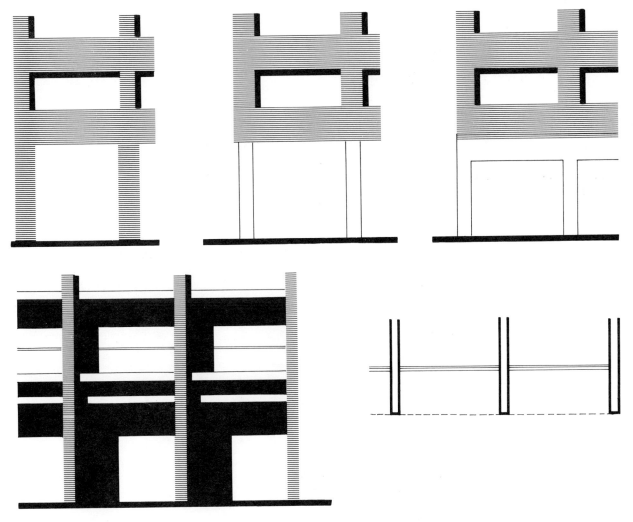

floor level by shelf angles. Attempts to solve this problem by exposing the floor above the arcade—to give the impression of a single concrete slab supporting the entire masonry mass—is equally incongruous. Truly load-bearing masonry wall construction obviously does not present a problem at its base.

Arnheim's analysis of this problem mentions the "visual weight of the fully enclosed cube of the building" that tends to crush the slender columns. Exposing the frame, on the other hand, transforming the solid of the building into a skeleton, reduces the visual weight and tends to "eliminate the discrepancy between load and support."[63]

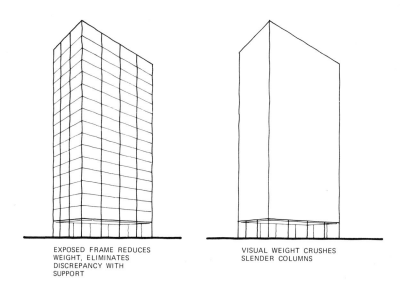

EXPOSED FRAME REDUCES
WEIGHT, ELIMINATES
DISCREPANCY WITH
SUPPORT

VISUAL WEIGHT CRUSHES
SLENDER COLUMNS

Unless the building has exposed concrete slabs on which the entire masonry wall rests, shelf angles will be attached to the slab edge to support the skin of face brick at each floor level while the concrete block or metal stud backup rests on the slab itself. Unless a special and costlier detail is used, the joint at the shelf angle is wider than the other joints and it will be visible. This situation is even worse when, to economize, the

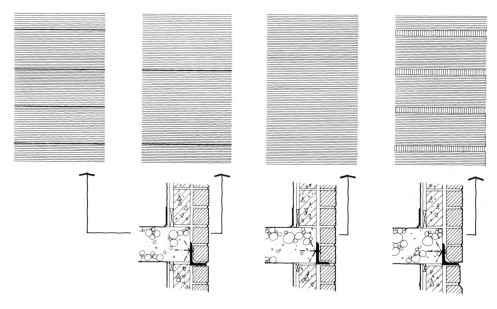

shelf angle is eliminated on every second floor. When budget permits and shelf angles are used at each floor they can be emphasized by special detailing and can become a secondary linear pattern on the building.

BALCONIES.   The human desire to decorate the box is ancient, and no design philosophy of the machine age has succeeded in killing it. The major change is that today the designer looks for functional or technical requirements to achieve visual excitement. Inasmuch as an apartment building is a "box," structural frame, fenestration, volume breaks, and other devices are used to "decorate" it.

When the program calls for balconies, the desire to decorate is easily satisfied. Balconies and the shadows they cast can break up the monotony of the facade. Dressed with furniture and plants, they add life and color to the appearance of the building, and an excellent opportunity for individual human expression (**6, 9, 10, 12–18, 21–23, 27, 33, 37–41**).

A balcony can fit into the indentation of the building volume, can project from the exterior wall, or can be a combination of both. In any case to be usable it should be not less than 5 ft deep, preferably 6. The dimensional prerequisite is the small conversation group, a table with chairs around it. The indented balcony has several advantages. It is wind protected and offers more privacy and security at highrise height. Being indented, it helps to break up the volume of the box. It also provides access from more than one room. With certain mechanical systems it can serve to locate the air-cooled condenser or even larger equipment if the equipment casing and the balcony are designed in an integrated manner.

The rhythm of living and sleeping spaces is further emphasized by a balcony in front of the living room. It is important to realize that when two balconies are paired, the sum takes on a quality different from that of the parts, regardless of how unobtrusively the high divider, necessary for privacy, is handled. Emphasizing their individuality by slight separation helps but does not answer the need for privacy. When the balconies are indented, however, the problem is removed because the rhythm created by the volumes between the recesses becomes more dominant.

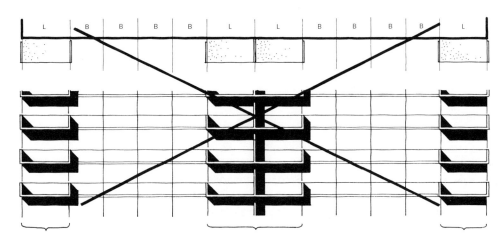

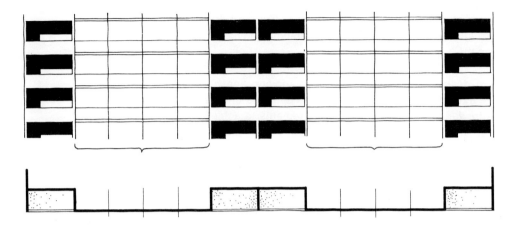

The question of rhythm cannot be avoided with continuous balconies. The dividers between apartments, no matter how thin and de-emphasized, will be apparent. Now, instead of just the living rooms, entire apartments will have to produce rhythm.

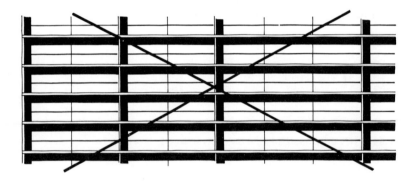

One of the problems created by sequence planning occurs when balconies are required. When the living room in one apartment is adjacent to the bedroom in the next, privacy is seriously jeopardized unless balconies are designed to discourage peepers.

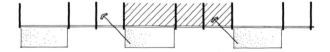

Because balconies have a strong impact on the design of the building, the decision to create lacy openness or sculptural solid forms must be carefully weighed. Building code requirements in regard to railing height must be checked; the tenant's sense of security and privacy should be considered; the view is another deciding factor; and the draining of the balcony must be studied. Once these basic issues have been disposed of, the options are many, not only in shape but also in railing.

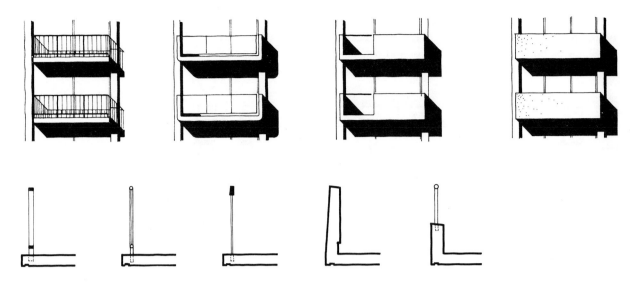

Because economy prohibits the installation of interior downspouts, balconies are generally drained outward. When the railing is open at the bottom and the balcony slab is not turned up at its outside edges, the chances are good that dirt will wash off and discolor the slab at unexpected spots. A solid balcony rail or upturned slab edges can provide the location for drain spouts that, when well planned, can become design elements.

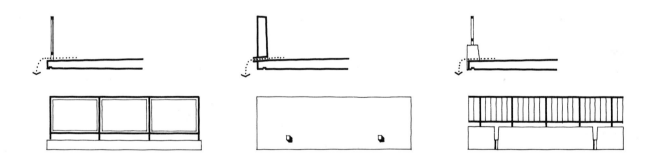

Doors to the balcony can be swinging or the more popular sliding. A 7- or 8-in. curb under the door, contrary to expectations, is accepted by most users who do not mind stepping over it. The curb gives protection against snow pile-up and an opportunity to place a heating element under the door. One of the advantages of continuous balconies is that sliding doors can be used as operating sashes to permit the occupant to wash the windows.

Balconies create a pattern. Quietly overall or dynamically moving, the reasons for the variation are many. A pattern may develop from the program that does not require a balcony for each apartment. A building type such as the skip-stop may have an inherent pattern. Using alternating balcony sizes and locations may not have functional

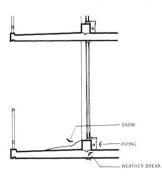

293

justification; it may be done simply to create visual variety or to strengthen and underline the designer's intent, as in Rudolph's Crawford Manor in New Haven, Conn., in which balconies do not line up one above the other on one side because they "otherwise would appear from a distance as a shaft vertically" (**6**).

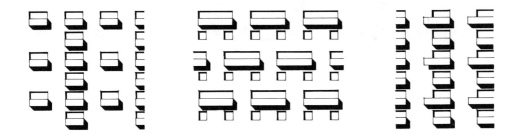

VOLUME BREAKS. Structural grid, fenestration, and balconies all give scale to the large masses of highrises. Except for the purest of purists, who seem to be satisfied with the strength of the expressed frame and the monumentality of the simple volume, architects have been seeking logical reasons to articulate and break up the overwhelming mass of apartment buildings. The increased perimeter and cost do not seem to be enough of a deterrent to stifle this urge.

Several of the features that generate breaks in the building volume have been discussed under various headings, such as indented balconies, pulled-out living rooms, protrusions in the volume to accommodate vertical core elements, and breaks to introduce light into inside corridors (**6, 7, 9–12, 16, 17, 18, 22, 23, 31, 36–41, 44, 48, 51**).

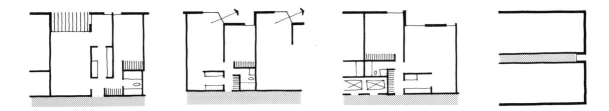

Link-generated volume breaks used to interrupt very long corridors and to utilize vertical core elements in more than one building have also been mentioned (**5, 7, 10, 23, 25, 34, 47, 48**).

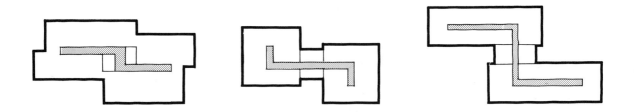

Additional molding of the building volume may be the result of various planning problems. Bay windows not only add space to the living room in relatively narrow building volumes but also help to improve the view and catch sunlight on north elevations. Conversely, in deep buildings indentations bring daylight to interior spaces. In tight plans, in which storage requirements cannot be satisfied within their confines, closets projecting beyond the exterior walls may provide a solution in addition to helping modulate the volume (**6, 16, 22, 31, 51**).

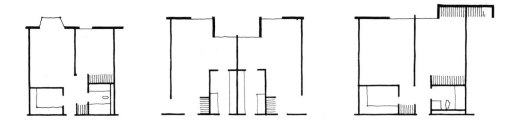

Site conditions also may generate volume breaks. Adaptation to diagonal property lines is the most obvious. Limitations in the length of the lot can be overcome by overlapping.

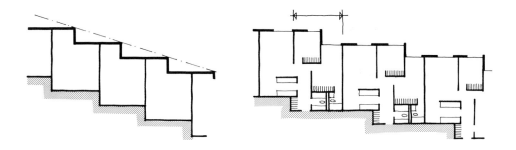

Major volume breaks in complex buildings of L, T, or other shapes present a special problem at the inside corner where the wings meet. Interior spaces created at the intersection are not easy to utilize and the possibility of cross view must be avoided (**12, 24, 25, 27, 29, 42, 43, 46**).

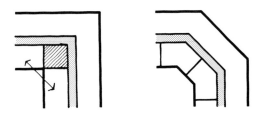

All the volume breaks mentioned have one thing in common: they occur on every floor and create continuous vertical elements. Volume breaks, however, can also be horizontal.

The main generator of these breaks is the need for increased floor area in a particular group of apartments or increased space for corridor in skip-stop schemes (**9, 11, 14, 34, 36, 37, 45, 46**).

The projecting and recessed forms, angled at the corners and overhung at the top, both reflect and make possible a greater variety of apartment plans and sizes. The diagonal corners open vistas and rooms; the thrusting overhangs mean larger apartments. (Ada Louise Huxtable on the Waterside Apartments in New York, by Davis Brody & Associates *The New York Times*, February 10, 1974) (**29**).

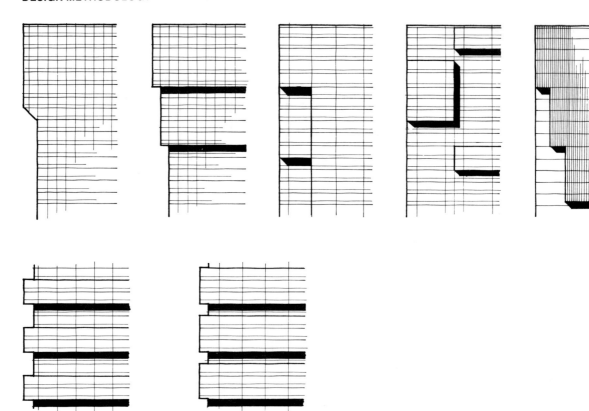

Terrace housing at the bases of highrises, integrating lowrise and apartment towers by gradually receding volumes, and introducing terraces at the tops of buildings or even continually from top to bottom, are other forms of vertical volume breaks which utilize these breaks for outdoor extension of the living space (**14, 35, 36, 42, 43**).

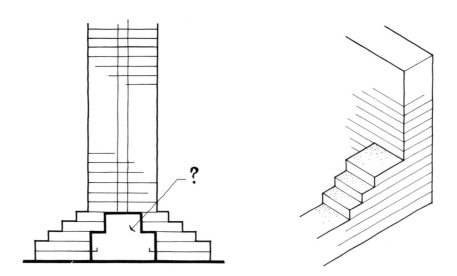

Because of the inherent cost problem, horizontal volume breaks do not occur with great frequency. The underside of a volume projection requires thermal insulation. The top, in addition to being thermally insulated, will have to be roofed, and if it is used as a terrace, membrane waterproofing and wearing slab or paving material will be required above the concrete slab. All this has to be done with high-quality materials and work, for it occurs above living spaces. The result is considerable cost, which explains the caution with which such volume breaks are handled.

TOP AND BOTTOM.   Most highrise apartment buildings (except those with on-grade open parking, and minimal amenities) consist of two distinct volumes: the vertical tower and the horizontal base. Functionally these two are quite distinct, one for dwellings, the other for parking, commercial, storage, mechanical, and other spaces. When merged, however, there is a functional ambiguity—part of the vertical may be devoted to parking and part of the horizontal to apartments—and the articulation of the two is more of an aesthetic issue than is functionally self-evident.

On closely built-in, tight sites without side yards there is little or no option for articulation because the merging of the two volumes stays unresolved, hidden behind adjoining structures.

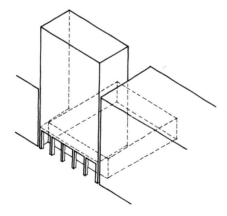

Larger sites present a multitude of options. The simplest, naturally, is presented when the property is large enough to handle the horizontal volume completely or in part as a separate element, and with the tower "resting" on grade the issue is purely that of linkage. The articulation occurs in plan, in the horizontal plane.

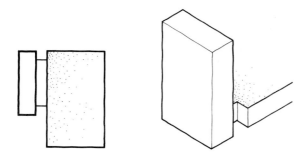

When the two volumes merge, the tower may still appear to be growing out of the ground, surrounded on two or three sides by the base; it might also become completely one with the base except on its end, where articulation by having the tower overlap the base is still possible.

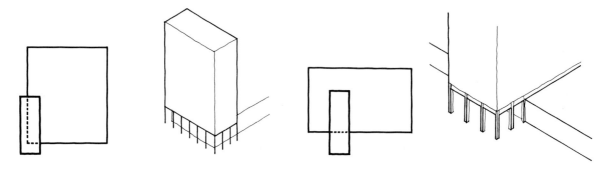

When the base is so large that the tower is set back a considerable distance from its edge it rests on the base as if it were sitting on the ground and there is no aesthetic question of intersection. The articulation occurs in section, in the vertical plane.

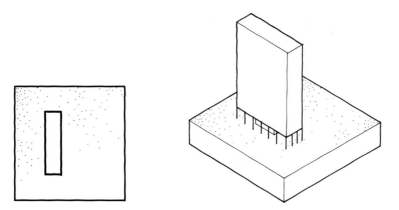

The most critical condition presents itself when the tower ends on the same plane as the base. Distinct separation can be achieved either vertically, suggesting a tower growing out of the ground surrounded by its base, or horizontally, suggesting a tower sitting on top of its base, by a reveal or preferably by a functionally justifiable separator such as differently expressed intermediary floor which houses a different function. Distinct articulation, however, is not the only option the architect has. Ambiguity where the two volumes intersect may be accepted or even exploited. Fusion of the two volumes can be achieved by using elements that make the transfer from horizontal to vertical a gradual one.

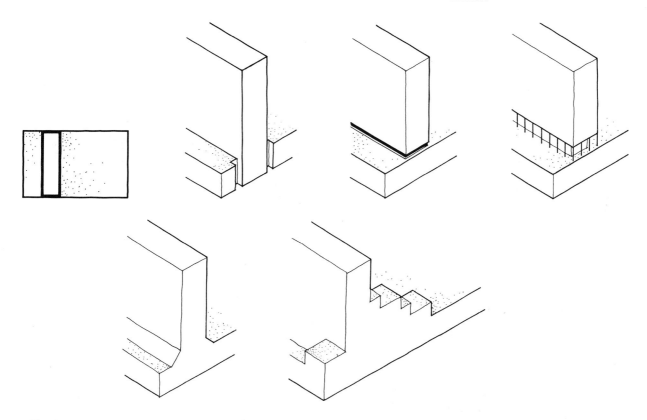

The base proper, an architectural problem that presents an unlimited number of choices, depends on issues such as whether the exterior expression should be different from or continuing that of the tower, the amount of penetration required for the lobby, arcade, or vehicular access, the amount and kind of glazed area needed for the lobby, and commercial and recreational facilities. One of the difficulties is the way the base, most commonly a heavy masonry-clad box, grows out of the ground. Occurring at pedestrian level, its immediately visible presence has a forbidding quality and should be softened, by being lifted, lowered, and screened through landscaping.

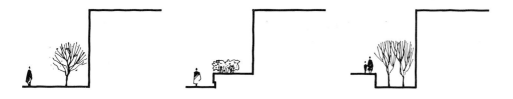

The first floor, whether of the base on which the tower stands or of the tower proper when the tower has contact with the ground, is especially important from the point of view of the human environment. Very few highrise buildings can be seen from a far enough distance to be visible in their entirety. The top is easily seen from any distance; the bottom only from so close that significant interaction occurs and materials, details, and scale need great care and attention. As Arnheim puts it:

> If human beings are to interact with a building functionally, they must be united with it by visual continuity. Huge though a building may be as a whole, it can make contact with the visitor by providing a range of sizes, some small enough to be directly relatable to the human body. These

human-sized architectural elements serve as connecting links between the organic inhabitant and the inorganic habitation.[64]

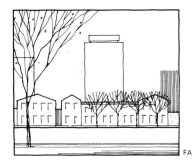

FAR

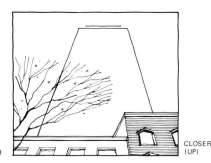

CLOSER (UP)

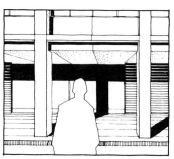

NEAR (STRAIGHT)

Somewhat less visible at the opposite pole—and therefore generally neglected—is the way the tower ends at the top. It is only less visible from ground level, however. From the upper floors of adjacent highrises it is quite significant. In the long vistas of the city it is an important element of the skyline.

Only thorough cooperation between the architect and the mechanical engineer and an awareness of the problem as soon as the typical floor is being planned will eliminate the incredible chaos occurring on our rooftops. The roof elements are admittedly not easy to organize. Some, like the elevator penthouse, the stair penthouse, and the boiler stack are tied to the location of the vertical core, others like fan housings, cooling towers, or mechanical rooms can be located with more freedom. All require different heights: 9 ft is enough for a stair penthouse, 11 to 12 ft for a fan housing or mechanical room; the elevator penthouse should be 17 to 18 ft above the roof and the boiler stack must rise above that. If it is impossible to organize these elements into a well-conceived volume, it is at least possible to screen them from view with a fence or shield that shows as a simple mass on the roof.

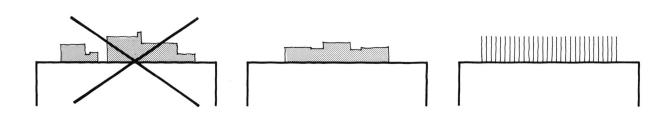

LOWRISE

The design of highrise apartment buildings is related to the limitations of the structural system, mainly concrete, and the vertical core elements among which the elevators play a major role. Entering the world of lowrise, the designer is in an entirely different atmosphere. Gone are the restraints of the structural frame. There are no elevators at all.

This is not to say that lowrise design is devoid of structural discipline. Within the limit of four floors, however, building codes are far more liberal, particularly in regard to fireproofing. A wide range of structural options is permitted: wood frame; load-bearing masonry walls with wood, bar joist, or precast concrete floor framing; and such hybrids as poured-in-place concrete slab resting on steel pipe columns.

In selecting a structural system, the maximum floor area permitted by the code for a particular construction type is the first consideration. This is followed by the skill limitations of local contractors or the available materials in the locality. Magnitude or volume also becomes a consideration, in contrast to highrise design, in which height alone ensures a large enough volume. As the building volume increases, so does the likelihood that the budget will afford a more sophisticated construction type. Small jobs are likely to be built more simply of the well-tried exterior-protected wood frame, but, under any conditions, the designer has more options than on the design of highrises.

Exterior walls, which need a lesser degree of fireproofing, can also be more varied. Although masonry or stucco is the usual answer under more stringent city codes, a variety of wood sidings can be used in areas of lower density.

Greater options, however, do not negate the principles of the dwelling unit planning that we have discussed. Good function, circulation with a minimum amount of wasted space, and adequate room size are equally desirable for dwellings in lowrises as are the other components of design previously covered.

The major difference is that the 15% maximum nonrental space is reduced in lowrises because elevators, stacks, or refuse chutes are not required and, in limited types, even one staircase is permitted. Obviously there is no nonrental space at all in single-family attached types. In core type duplex and quadruplex walk-ups with one staircase nonrental space may be as low as 5 to 6%; when there are two stairs, it may go up to 8 to 9%. In central-corridor lowrises the nonrental space should not exceed 12 to 14%.

Naturally the most significant difference between highrise and lowrise buildings is their scale due to the reduced distance from which the lowrise is observed. Configuration and articulation become more important, detail is brought closer, and texture is magnified. Parts can be touched—or they produce the feeling that they can be—and, therefore, must be handled with increased attention. The interaction of building and ground is immediately visible; the way the building is seen in silhouette against the sky is apparent; and more important is that both can be seen together because the lowrise, due to its shortness, is perceived as a total image, which seldom occurs with highrises.

Lowrise construction starts with the single-family house, which not only is felt to best accommodate family needs, but also to fulfill the user's dream of privacy, security, and identity. The variables of the single-family house are so numerous, however, and have been so intensely covered by a volume of literature, that the discussion of them in this study was decided against.

Housing—in contrast to the house—is the result of economic constraints. Its vertical and horizontal grouping of dwelling units allows for higher densities, and therefore, lower land cost per unit, which saves material as well as energy. As Sam Davis defines it in his excellent study, "a new goal for housing may be to maintain the features and amenities of the single-family house while aggregating many more units on a single site for economy's sake."[65]

The various lowrise prototypes, not unlike highrise prototypes, can be grouped by horizontal and vertical distribution systems into distinct categories. While one occasionally finds—especially among single-family attached types—one-story solutions, from the point of view of land use these are not economical and are the exception rather than the norm (see illustrations on p. 302).

Each lowrise prototype can be defined by its characteristic density, which will be analyzed in detail later in this book.

SINGLE FAMILY ATTACHED HOUSING

The single-family attached type, as its name suggests, comes closest to the individual house. Obviously, it still preserves many advantages of the house—privacy, security, and identity, as well as immediacy to the ground and access to the automobile—while it provides the benefits of grouping. It starts with the so-called zero lot line concept of clustered single-family homes and goes all the way to the fully attached row houses. This sequence has a parallel in the historic development of land preservation.

DESIGN METHODOLOGY

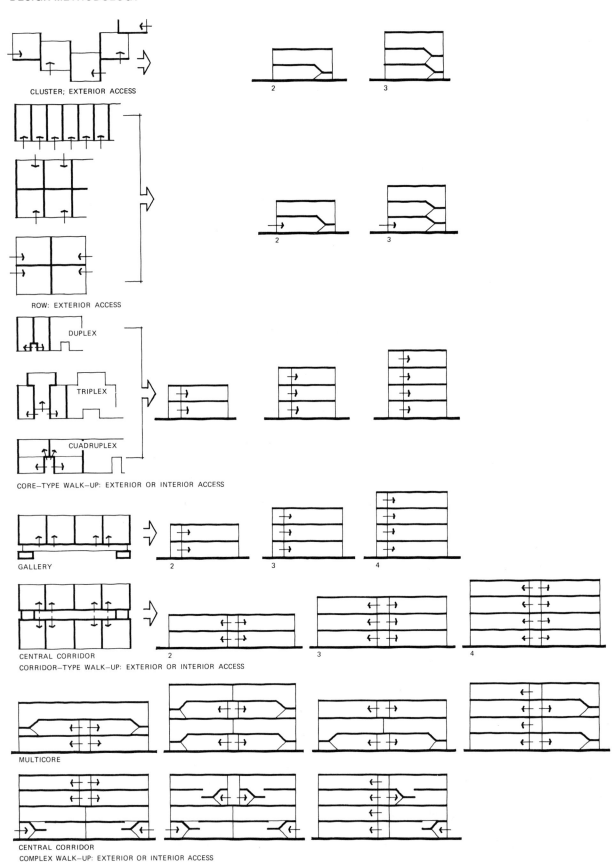

CLUSTER; EXTERIOR ACCESS

ROW: EXTERIOR ACCESS

DUPLEX

TRIPLEX

CUADRUPLEX

CORE—TYPE WALK—UP: EXTERIOR OR INTERIOR ACCESS

GALLERY

CENTRAL CORRIDOR

CORRIDOR—TYPE WALK—UP: EXTERIOR OR INTERIOR ACCESS

MULTICORE

CENTRAL CORRIDOR

COMPLEX WALK—UP: EXTERIOR OR INTERIOR ACCESS

The earliest single-family housing found on the tells of Mesopotamia were attached dwellings that made use of common walls. This was necessary because of the limited space on the walled plateau of the tell. The "row house" continued in use in the densely built Greek and Roman cities and was neglected only in the rural, feudal, world of the Middle Ages, with its agricultural economy and lack of city life. The row house was reintroduced when cities were reborn in the commercially developing countries of northern Europe. A city dwelling (town house) *par excellence*: shop on the ground level, the apartment of the burgher above.

CLUSTER HOUSING.   The clustered single-family house results from site planning or newer zoning techniques (**53–56**). As Sam Davis describes it:

> . . . this zoning technique means that the dwellings can be clustered into relatively high density units (perhaps up to 20 to the acre). Cost savings can be considerable since fewer roads and utilities must be employed, and since the houses are made more efficient by the sharing of walls. This feature reduces materials and energy consumption. Reduction in cleared land as well as planning for communal amenities not otherwise affordable by individual households has resulted in a high degree of user satisfaction with cluster housing. In terms of the dwelling units, the strength of the cluster concept is that the single family house and its domain may still be distinguishable at increased densities.[66]

A recent headline in a builders' magazine, "Detached Look in Attached Units" indicates that this type is generally perceived by the user as an individual house. The clustered unit looses few of the advantages of the house. The major disadvantage is the loss of four-directionality. Grouping generally makes these units two-directional though three-sided exposure is also possible with clever siting. The other disadvantage concerns the automobile. While generally speaking, access to one's car is still immediate, remote parking sometimes is unavoidable.

Untermann and Small[67] distinguish two fundamental conceptual cluster arrangements: one around the entrance court and the other around the garden court.

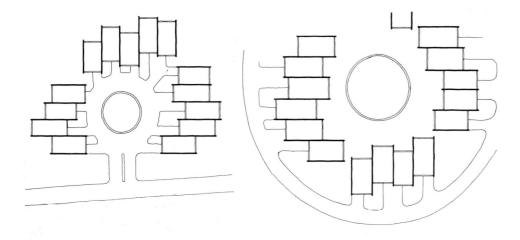

ROW HOUSES.   Compared to this clustering, the row house, on the other end of the single-family attached type, forms a linear pattern with a maximum of shared walls. (Groups of row houses can also be arranged in clusters, as we shall observe.)

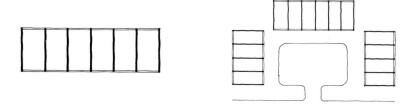

The most common two-story row house places living zones on grade level and sleeping zones on the upper floors, though such clear demarcation is not always possible and bedrooms can be found on the first floor as well. On sloping sites, when both levels are grade-connected, the subdivision can be reversed if the entrance is on the upper level. Although the bedrooms are generally located on the second floor, bathrooms—when more than one is called for—can be split between the two. The lower level bathroom then serves the living zone and guests and can be used also for the bedrooms above as long as it can be reached without crossing the living space.

In most row houses the number of bedrooms will determine the width of the structure, though the stair also plays a significant role. Two- or four-bedroom row houses have simple designs. Three-bedroom layouts pose problems. The third bedroom, because it occupies the same building width as the two bedrooms on the other side, has to be

large, with its own bathroom and walk-through closet (**58–60**). When the program calls for three bedrooms of equal size, taut planning can be achieved by overlapping of the second floor. This overlap requires the careful study of fire and sound separation. When the site is narrow, the third bedroom (or fourth) can be provided by the addition of a full or partial third floor on top of a two-bedroom row house (**61–63**).

The double-run stair, located in a central zone, allows maximum utilization of the two outer zones for bedrooms. What works so simply on the second floor, however, creates circulation problems on the first (**57, 64**). When the stair—the vertical connector—is in the center zone, the passage leading to it from the entrance bisects one of the living zones. If the row house is wide enough, this cut-off space can serve as a study or library. If it is narrow, the results are wasted space and traffic through the living zone. One way to eliminate the problem and still keep central, double-run stairs is to enter the row house in the middle, near the stairs (**59**). This, however, is possible only in end row houses and staggered rows. A better way to alleviate the problem, to shorten the distance from the entry to the stair, is to slide the two halves of the row house along the long axis to bring the entrance nearer to the stair. This sliding can occur on both floors or on the ground floor only.

FIRST FLOOR   SECOND FLOOR   SECOND FLOOR ALTERNATE

The single-run stair, which originates on the first floor near the entrance and leads to the second-floor landing in the central zone, seemingly eliminates these problems (**57**). Naturally it helps when the third bedroom is large enough to provide space for it. Otherwise, the row house—especially the two- and four-bedroom one—will have to be made wider to accommodate the stair. Nor is the first floor problem-free. It is most difficult to create ideal circulation—from kitchen or backyard to basement—without

DESIGN METHODOLOGY

having to cross the living space, and a well defined entry hall with guest closet is hard to achieve. The problem is somewhat similar with pulled-out stairs handled as an independent volume.

These difficulties encountered in connection with the single-run stair bring into focus some of the basic problems of the single-family attached type, both cluster and row: the linkage to various exterior functions. The solution to all or some of the following linkages will profoundly influence the first-floor plan.

1. GARBAGE COLLECTION.   Is it on the same side or on the opposite side of the main entrance? The kitchen should be on the garbage-collection side.

2. VISUAL SURVEILLANCE.   This can be best achieved from the busiest part of the living zone, the kitchen or the family room. Where is surveillance important? On the yard side? (When the yard is fenced in, less surveillance is needed.) On the entry side where parking is generally located? Is there a common outdoor area that needs to be observed?

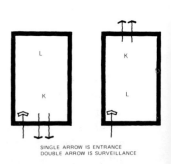

SINGLE ARROW IS ENTRANCE
DOUBLE ARROW IS SURVEILLANCE

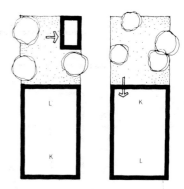

3. GARDEN MAINTENANCE. Is there a tool shed in the yard? If tools are in the basement, is there an areaway stair directly to the basement, or will passage with tools have to be made through the living zone? If there is a solution that works for the backyard, what happens in the front yard when garden tools are needed?

4. PARKING. Is there a lot on the entrance side for both guest and occupant parking? If only guest parking is on the entrance side, where is occupant parking: in a separate garage behind the unit, in an attached garage, or, on sloping sites, below the unit (Attached **55**; sloping **56**; common covered **62**)?

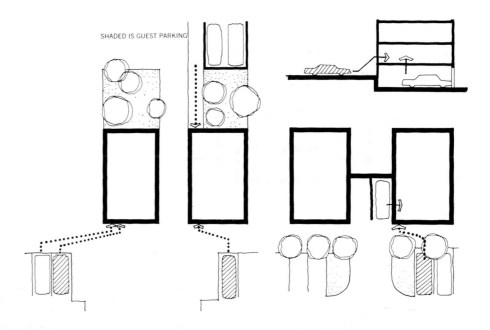

SHADED IS GUEST PARKING

The row house clusters (on p. 308) illustrate how under various site conditions these criteria will influence the location of the entrance, kitchen, and living room on the first floor.

Adaptation to significantly sloping terrain, unless avoided, will influence single-family attached units more than other multifamily housing types. Sliding the floors along a horizontal axis will result in terrace housing, and sliding the elements along a vertical axis will lead to the split-level. To use the split-level units on a level site may seem incongruous, but it does provide daylight for the basement (**57**). It works especially well with the adjacent ground depressed; that is, by adapting the terrain to the split-level unit. Another advantage of this scheme is its ability to create space a story and a half high in the living room while maintaining the regular ceiling height in the kitchen and other rooms.

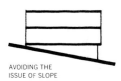

AVOIDING THE
ISSUE OF SLOPE

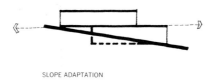

SLOPE ADAPTATION

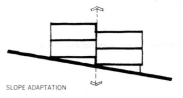

SLOPE ADAPTATION

DESIGN METHODOLOGY

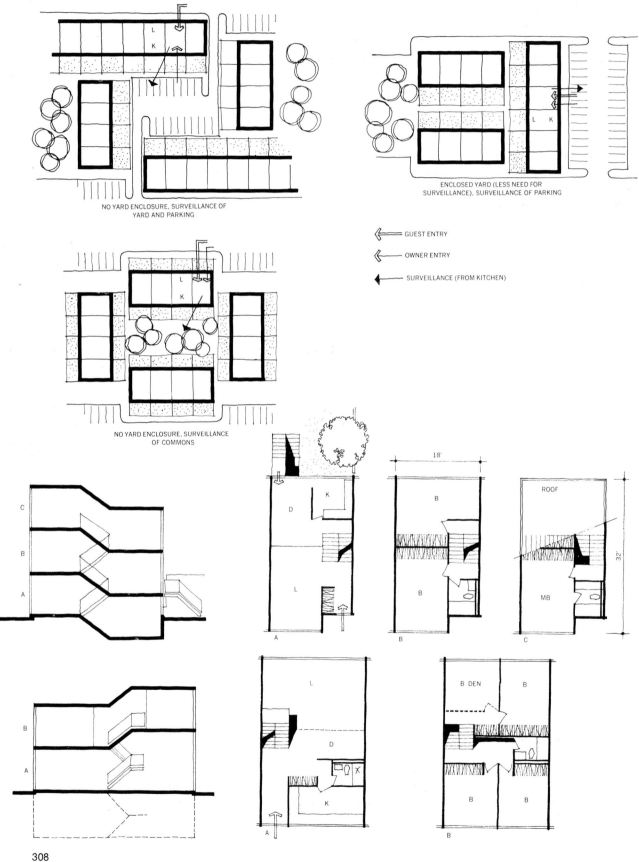

NO YARD ENCLOSURE, SURVEILLANCE OF
YARD AND PARKING

ENCLOSED YARD (LESS NEED FOR
SURVEILLANCE), SURVEILLANCE OF PARKING

NO YARD ENCLOSURE, SURVEILLANCE
OF COMMONS

GUEST ENTRY

OWNER ENTRY

SURVEILLANCE (FROM KITCHEN)

The most important advantage of the split-level is that it can halve the vertical walking distance between floors. Interconnections between garage and living levels or between living and sleeping levels are thus made easier. Traffic conditions and proper site planning will put the garage on grade. Pedestrian entrance and the living room still can be raised by half a level if one uses exterior stairs, or preferably, terraces to get up to the entrance. Flat sites adapted to the split-level concept by mounding will gain a visual variety, the benefits of which—for both user and marketer—will outweigh the cost of moving earth.

LEVEL 1   LEVEL 2   LEVEL 3

Terrace housing, as has been mentioned, is another form of adaptation to the sloping site by level splitting, this time along a horizontal axis. Its classic prototype is the historic hill town, and a more recent example is Siedlung Halen in Switzerland. It has a delightfully strong visual form, but the waterproofing of the roofs that are used as private outdoor space poses difficult and costly technical problems. Another drawback is automobile access. Remote parking is almost inevitable with this type of housing. When tried on a flat terrain—to quote Sam Davis "the underside or 'belly' of the structure becomes a problem. In the urban setting, the underside can become commercial space while the artificial hill surface, open to the sunlight and air, remains housing."[68]

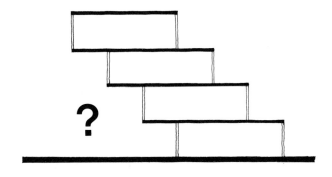

DESIGN METHODOLOGY

When the row house, due to urban site constraints, must be narrow, but the program calls for a large number of bedrooms, the solution is often a full or at least partial third floor as was previously discussed. Without increasing the number of floors and vertical travel, the extra bedroom, or bedrooms, can also be accommodated by the introduction of inner courts which increase the amount of exposed building surface and therefore the possible number of bedrooms (**65**).

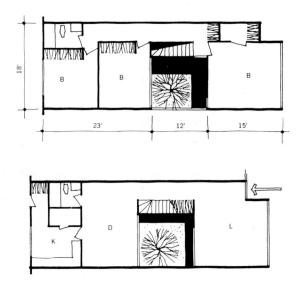

The back-to-back rowhouse is not used as an independent building type except on the ground level of complex walk-ups and is discussed under that heading. A form of backing up rowhouses is the recently popular arrangement of "quads" or "fourplexes" in suburban developments which result in economies in construction and land and higher densities.

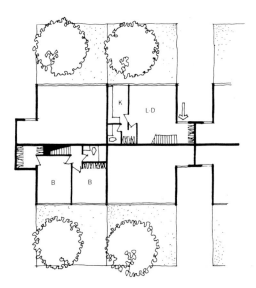

In addition to the plan of the individual unit, the real issue of row houses is their attachment. The fundamental attachment methods are pairing and planning in sequence. Planning in pairs limits the rows to an even number. Except in condominiums, pairing permits backing up bathrooms and kitchens of rental units on common stacks. Walks to the entrances can also be paired, thus reducing the amount of pavement. When the number of units is uneven or a larger degree of articulation is desired, planning in sequence is the answer. In either case, end row houses with their added exposure lend themselves to treatment different from that received by those in the row. Neither pairing nor sequence planning is limited to straight-line demarcation between units (**64**). A wide variety of overlaps and interlocks is possible. Staggering opens up unlimited possibilities to mold the row in order to meet site conditions or architectural preferences (**53, 55, 56**).

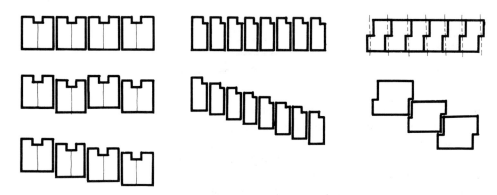

The row house, as the purest individual-access housing, poses special problems in the relation of the unit's ground level to public or semipublic spaces.

Open front yards can be defined and separated from public areas by a variety of means: hedges, fences, or a level change that provides, if not a physical, at least a psychological barrier. When the row house directly adjoins public space, at least a minimal definition and separation is desired.

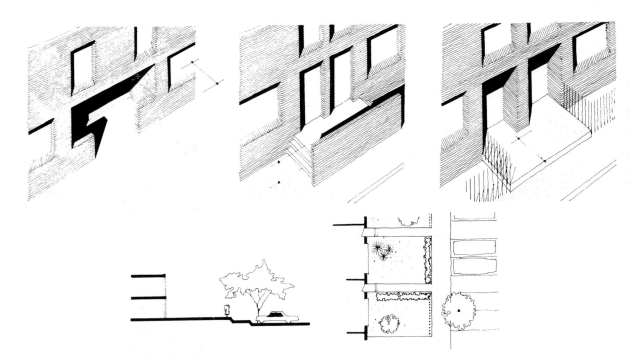

DESIGN METHODOLOGY

Rear yards can be fully private and completely fenced in. They can be semiprivate, separated from adjacent yards, but open or partly open to common areas. When they are fully open, at least some grade separation will define the private from the public.

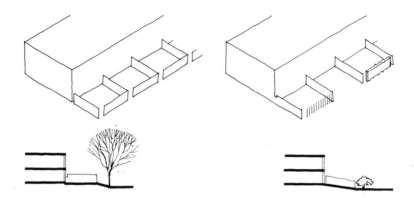

MATRIX HOUSING. A most interesting application of the attached dwelling with private court is found in the matrix systems (**65, 66**). The dwelling is arranged around an inner court or courts, and maximum daylight penetration can be achieved for a one-story type. Two-story units tend to cut off sunlight and can be used only in bright, sunny climates. A good compromise is the partial two-story unit. Privacy in the relatively small court is essential and only one unit should face it. At first glance one would think that the matrix provides a higher density than the ordinary row house. This, however, is not the case except on sloping terrain when "access from above" becomes possible and walking passage, created on the tops of units stacked on the hillside obviates the provision of space-consuming "streets." (See density analysis in the chapter on Sites.) The great attraction of the matrix lies in the unlimited combinations that are possible and the fascination of the resulting geometry, or carpet pattern which accounts for this arrangement being sometimes called carpet housing.

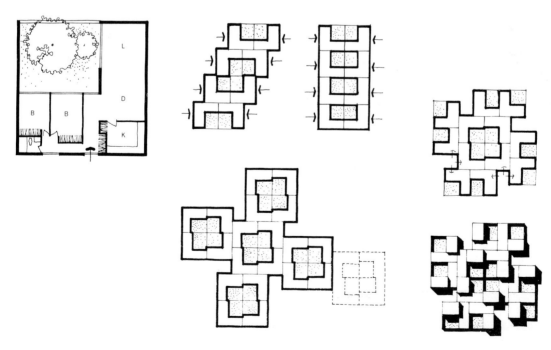

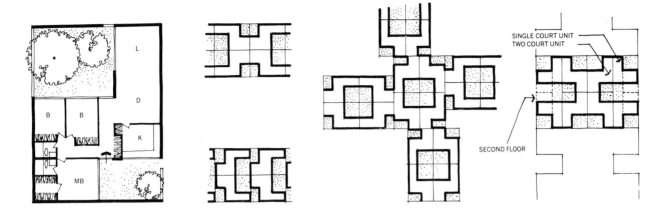

WALK-UPS

Single-family attached housing, even when it is three stories high and covers relatively little ground, has grade-level access and thereby can achieve only limited densities.

When dwelling units are stacked above each other and the upper ones have upper level access, the maximum comfortable vertical walk determines the height and the densities possible.

Alternatively, moving dwelling units off the ground will help create a site plan with more open public space available for a variety of activity areas while row house densities are maintained.

Because the sole means of access to an apartment—except on the ground floor—is by the stairs, the walk-up building is limited in height. Obviously, comfort is the factor. The need for density and economy generally does not permit the ideal of only two stories. Walk-ups are usually three stories high and, if the slight discomfort of climbing the stairs is accepted, the height can be stretched to four stories but no higher. Because of this discomfort, however, an attempt is made to reduce the climb. The building is often depressed by half a story in relation to the entrance elevation. Although this provides some amelioration of the climbing distance, the concomitant problems of depressed yards, snow removal, retaining walls, and lack of visual privacy on the depressed floor are self-evident.

Occasionally the building is depressed to overcome strict zoning regulations of height. When this happens it is prudent to inquire whether habitable space is permitted by code when it is below grade, how far below, and what exactly is meant by "grade."

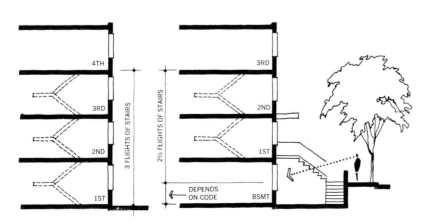

DESIGN METHODOLOGY

CORE-TYPE WALK-UPS.   Core-type walk-up buildings consist of a stair core (one or two stairs as required by code) serving a limited number of apartments on each floor (**67–71**). Depending on whether there are two, three, or four apartments around the stair, this type is called duplex, triplex, or quadruplex. The triplex is uncommon in the United States, though in Europe it is often seen. A series of cores forms a multicore walk-up, an economical option, in contrast with highrises in which multicore means an increased number of elevators.

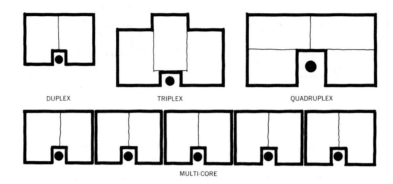

DUPLEX   TRIPLEX   QUADRUPLEX

MULTI-CORE

Exit requirements for core-type walk-ups vary all over the map, and familiarity with the local code is essential. Some codes, depending on construction type, number of units served by a stair, and the size of the units, will allow a single means of egress in buildings of limited stories. A single stair is desirable not only because of economy but also for better chances of surveillance and less opportunity for prowlers. When codes permit a single stair to serve a limited number of floors, this number can be stretched by depressing the building, provided, however, that the code considers it a basement and thus it does not count as a floor when stair requirements are considered. Some building codes will permit a single stair for four-story or even taller buildings of duplex or quadruplex types as long as there is access to the roof from the apartments and the next stair—within permitted travel distance—can be reached via the roof.

Stairs play an important role in core-type walk-ups. How the problem is solved will have significant consequences for the apartment plan itself. In duplexes the stairs may force the location of the apartment entry to be near the end of the apartment oblong, thus creating internal traffic problems (**67, 68**). Ideally, the stair should function so that the apartment entry is near the center of the apartment oblong, approximately between the living and sleeping zone to prevent any difficult traffic patterns (**69, 70**) (see illustrations on p. 316).

The stair is only one of the plan generators of duplexes. Bathrooms and kitchens also serve as generators of the plan. How they will be paired will determine whether the stair

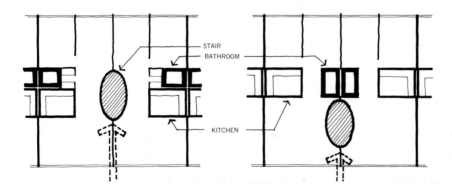

STAIR
BATHROOM

KITCHEN

core can be moved to the center. Centrally located stairs will result in modification of the ground floor because passage to them will have to be borrowed from ground-level apartments (**69, 70**).

The number of bedrooms and the kind of dining space obviously influence basic duplex arrangments. The number of bedrooms determines the width of the units. Dining space and its relation to kitchen and living room will also affect the internal traffic pattern.

Quadruplexes, when the building code permits a single exit, must have the kind of stair arrangement that provides access to all four apartments from a single landing (**71**). When two means of egress—two stairs—are required, many arrangements are possible In all cases it is important to determine whether the code requires the stairs—one or both—to be in a 2-hour or 1-hour enclosure. Entry into the apartment oblong is preferred near the center rather than at the edge.

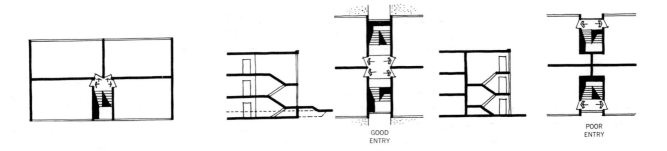

The stair core that consists of two stairs and a short corridor can be used to articulate the building volumes, to generate form in a large variety of ways, including staggering of units.

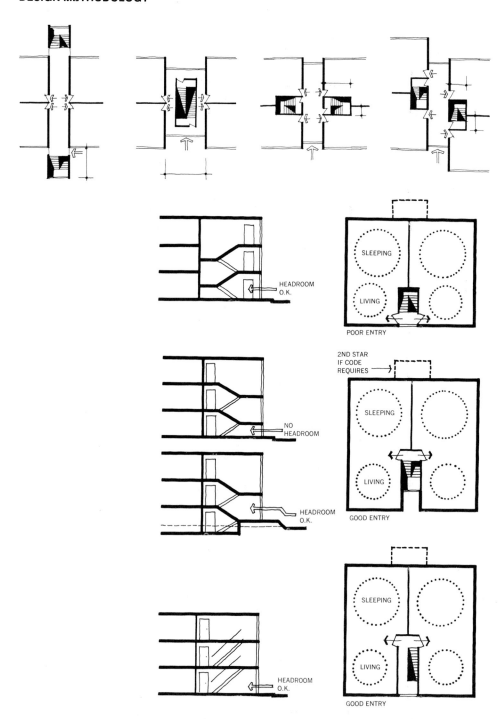

In contrast to the duplex, the quadruplex by its very nature forces placement of the entrance at one end of the apartment oblong instead of in the middle (between living and sleeping zones). This can be avoided only by the addition of spur corridors which may increase the nonrental area unnecessarily and result in a longer dead-end corridor than allowed by code.

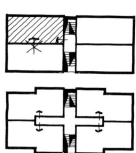

Entrance to the apartment oblong at its end creates problems that are unavoidable in this building type (**71**). To get to the bedrooms from the front door, the living space will have to be crossed, or in a reversed arrangement the passage from entry to living room becomes a long corridor without daylight as it bypasses the bedrooms. In spite of these imperfections in circulation, this building type enjoys a great market popularity under the misnomer "garden apartments."

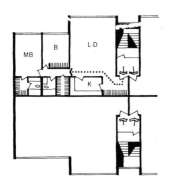 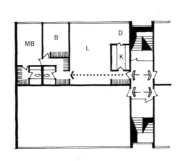 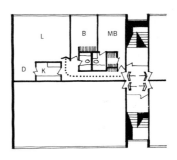

The possibilities of grouping duplexes or quadruplexes are similar to those of symmetrically planned row houses. Straight-line, alternatingly recessed pairs, and diagonal staggering are all variations of attachment.

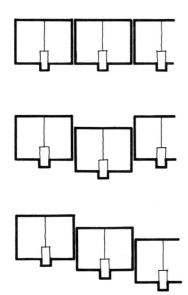 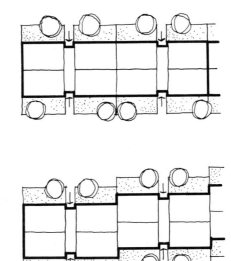

Quadruplexes with one means of egress can generate a variety of imaginative linkages, depending on site constraints and the acceptability of higher costs due to considerably increased building perimeters (see illustrations on top p. 318).

Core-type walk-ups, in contrast to single-family attached dwellings whose laundry, tenant storage, and heating facilities are included in the unit, may need basements for the location of these common elements, though locating them within the dwelling unit is also possible.

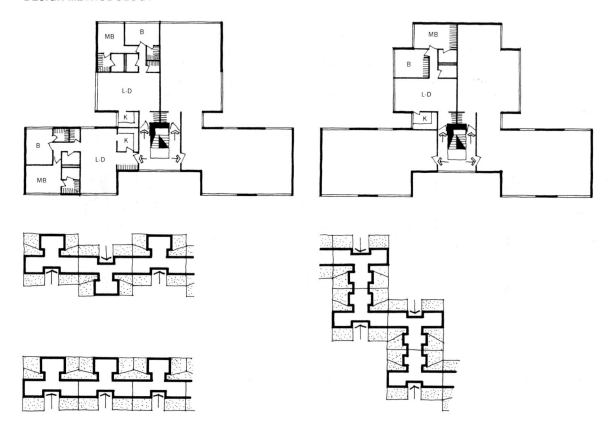

In spite of the popular term "garden apartments," only the ground floor units can be directly connected to private yards; apartments on the upper floors are generally compensated with balconies or terraces, another strong form generator of this building type.

CORRIDOR-TYPE WALK-UPS.   The desire to maximize the number of units served by the stair core leads directly from the core-type walk-up to the corridor type (**72–77**). Four units are about as many as a stair core can handle; six units result in an excessive dead-end corridor, unacceptable by most codes, and eight are possible only with a central-corridor scheme.

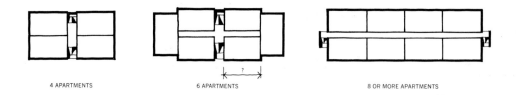

4 APARTMENTS   6 APARTMENTS   8 OR MORE APARTMENTS

The outside-corridor type, which also can increase the number of units, has a low efficiency in regard to nonrental space and has limited climatic use. At this point a comparison between core-type, central-corridor, and outside-corridor designs will highlight the differences in efficiency (see illustration on top p. 314).

Building codes permit a lower rate of fire protection for lowrises. This low-rated construction type, however, has floor area limits, a problem that does not apply to core-type buildings, which have inherently limited floor areas. When the corridor-type walk-up has a larger floor area than permitted by code, a firewall of prescribed rating

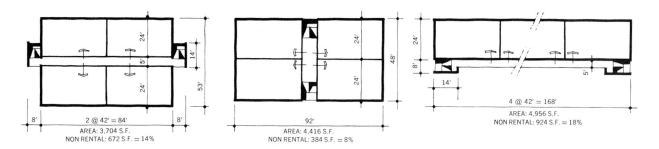

must subdivide it into sections, none of which may exceed the code-allowed maximum. Depending on the local regulations, a simple set of smoke-stop doors may be acceptable when the firewall bisects the corridor; otherwise a double set of rated fire doors may be required. In either case doors must swing in both directions to prevent obstruction of travel toward the fire exit.

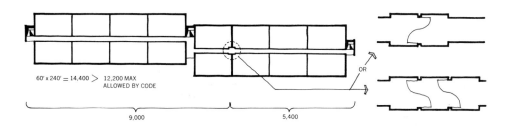

If the end stairs (required by code) are the sole means of vertical circulation, doubling of lobby-vestibules, no matter how small, splitting of mailboxes, and lessening of security may be required. When a centrally located stair is added, it is used mainly for circulation. The end stairs then become the fire stairs. A break in the building volume at this central staircase provides space for a small lobby on the first floor. Otherwise apartment space will have to be sacrificed, and the window rhythm on the elevation will have to be interrupted.

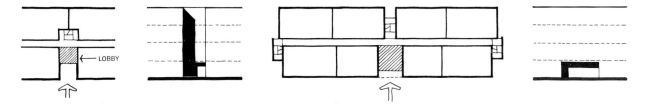

The central-corridor walk-up is used less often than the exterior-access type with its attached or bridgelike detached corridors. The advantages of the exterior corridor walk-up, especially under favorable climatic conditions, are obvious. The most significant is the double exposure of each dwelling unit. Because the framing system of lowrises is so much more economical than highrises, the large portion of nonrental space is acceptable.

An increasingly common type of exterior-corridor walk-up is the "piggy-back," in which row houses are stacked one above the other (**72, 74**). Exit requirements of the building code must be carefully analyzed to ascertain whether direct egress is required from the bedroom level of the upper row house.

When the exterior- and interior-corridor systems are combined in clusters of interior-corridor buildings connected with open galleries or in interior-corridor building segments alternating with exterior-corridor types, strongly articulated building volumes result (**75, 77**).

Another interesting application is the clusters of back-to-back units partly surrounded by and connected with an exterior gallery system that is greatly enhanced by varied handling of exterior stairs (**73, 76**).

In contrast to the highly clustered sculptured appearance of the preceding grouping, the corridor-type walk-up can have its aesthetic appeal in the low, long volume that results when a large number of apartments have to be contained (**74**). This powerful volume lends itself to periodic articulation that occurs at the stair cores. It can be adapted to sloping terrain, which will shift half a floor at the stairs.

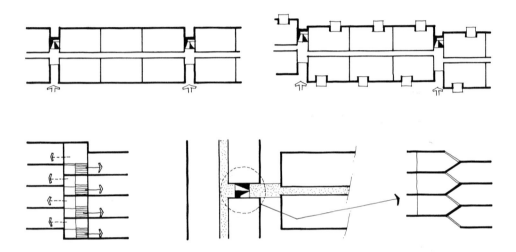

MIXED WALK-UPS.   The walk-ups discussed up to this point stack identical units above one another. To accommodate a complex mix of the client's program, to place family-oriented units with large numbers of bedrooms on the ground level and units for smaller households above, or to eliminate the necessity for the elderly to climb stairs in a walk-up, vertical stacking of like units can be avoided. Instead of pure types, we are talking about mixed walk-ups containing core-type units and exterior- or central-corridor apartments in various combinations (**78–87**).

The first group consists of all exterior-access dwelling units. Row houses and regular exterior-corridor apartments can be combined in a variety of ways; the row house is usually on the top to minimize exterior stair heights (**78**).

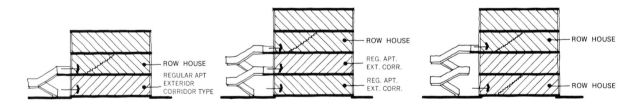

Core-type access characterizes the second group of combinations. Row house on row house can fall into this group as well, when the upper row house is reached by an inside stair. This is possible only when the building code does not require a second means of egress for the upper unit. The more common combination in this group consists of row houses and duplexes.

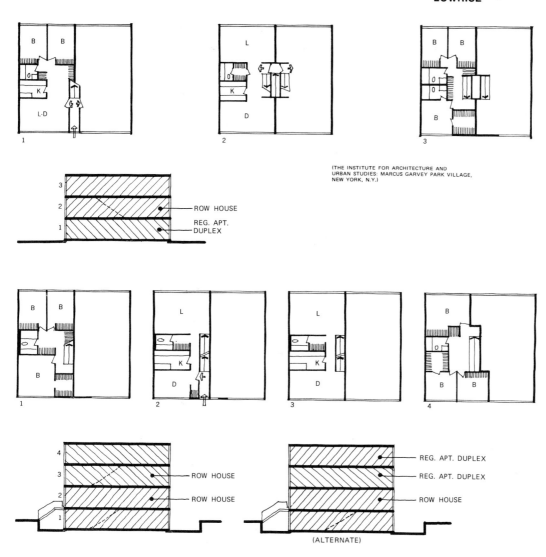

(THE INSTITUTE FOR ARCHITECTURE AND
URBAN STUDIES: MARCUS GARVEY PARK VILLAGE,
NEW YORK, N.Y.)

Combinations of exterior and interior access are also possible. To mention only the simplest form, back-to-back row houses with ground-level entry can be placed on the lower level of central-corridor lowrises.

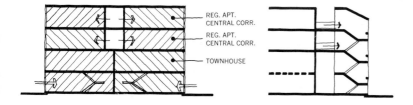

The possibilities inherent in stacking and attaching walk-ups are almost unlimited if structural framing, plumbing, and ventilation ducts can be properly aligned. Stairs pose a special challenge. Whether they are exterior or interior, a thorough understanding of the building code is necessary not only for compliance but because code provisions may generate novel solutions for stairs and exterior corridors or unusual combinations of dwelling units to solve exit problems.

Mixed walk-ups fascinate designers because their planning becomes truly three-dimensional. Planning not only horizontally but vertically adds the challenge the ordinary lowrise often lacks. The opportunity to change fenestration from floor to floor, completely logical because the apartment type itself changes, makes mixed walk-ups even more favored by the designer, for it allows the manipulation of the exterior not easily possible with pure types. Because the stacking of different units one above the other is likely to result in recesses for terraces, in projections of units, or in other volume breaks, the opportunities to mold the building form are further enhanced.

MIDRISE

Midrises start where walk-ups stop, at five stories. (**41–52**). Where the miderise ends is hard to agree on. According to the definition used in this book, the height of a midrise depends on how far a hydraulic elevator can be put to practical use. Not all will agree. Some consider an eight-story building midrise, while there are five-story buildings that have electric elevators.

Obviously, as the number of dwelling levels increases to four, five, or six compared to the lower numbers in walk-ups, the density increases too. Midrises can reach a density of 60 to 80 units per acre.

According to planning principles, there is little difference between highrise and midrise. All building types (central corridor, exterior corridor, multicore, and so on) can be adapted to midrises, and all highrise apartment types can be applied.

Structurally, midrises are truly on the borderline. In some locations five- or six-story midrises can have wood framing with masonry exteriors. As the fireproofing requirements of the local building code increase, the framing system of the midrise changes from exterior-protected wood to poured-in-place concrete with all the possibilities between. When considering the structural options of midrises, the designer, accustomed to the simplicity of the highrise concrete frame, has to keep more hybrid systems in mind. The most commonly used ones are steel framing, load-bearing masonry, or a combination of the two. The floor system is generally steel bar joists with metal deck and poured concrete on top or precast concrete floor elements. The first one necessitates suspended ceilings, which are not required with precast concrete floors unless the visible joints in the ceiling become objectionable. It is important to keep in mind that bar joist floor framing due to the increased floor-to-floor height will make the stair runs longer than usual with either concrete or even wood floors.

Underground parking serving midrises is not uncommon when the cost of parking can be absorbed by the limited number of the units in the midrise. When the parking is under the building, the floor separating parking from dwelling units must be carefully considered in view of fire separation requirements of building codes. Wood is out, and concrete or fireproofed steel has to be used.

Since midrises include only a limited number of apartments, they cannot easily absorb the cost of parking garages and are therefore often provided with open on-grade parking. When common elements are minimal or are located in a separate building, when the lobby is small and lockers and mechanical space are in the basement or on the roof, the ground floor of the midrise can be used for open but sheltered parking. Depending on the number of floors and apartment sizes, a good percentage, if not all, of the parking can be taken care of in this way.

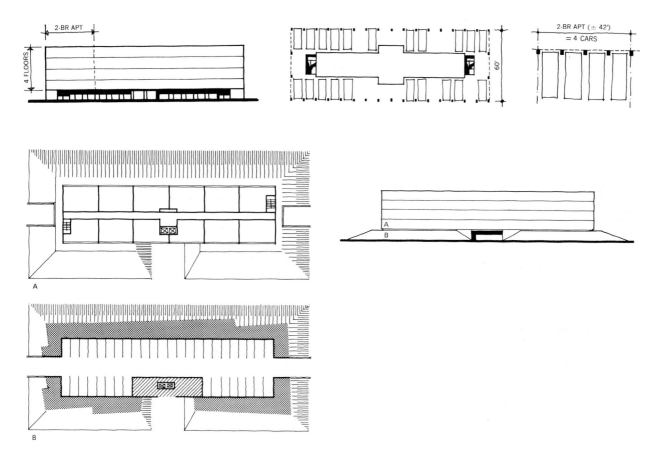

When the ground floor is used for lobby, lockers, and mechanical space, and the apartments start on the second floor, access to the elevator is simple. When the first floor is utilized for apartments, the more indirect access necessitates borrowing apartment space for lobby and loading and results in difficult volume penetration. In addition, the greater ceiling height required by lobbies must be considered.

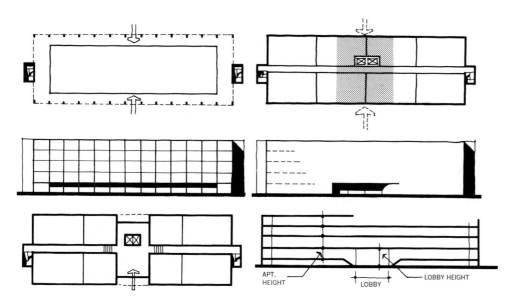

323

DESIGN METHODOLOGY

Midrises, like walk-ups, lend themselves to a wider range of linkage possibilities than highrises. Because they are low, complete or almost complete rings are possible as long as the sunlight can penetrate the court. Covering this court with a heavily glazed roof system will result in a year-round communal space, the atrium (**52**). Sometimes, to introduce more light and air, the exterior corridor is detached from the building itself to form a network of bridges.

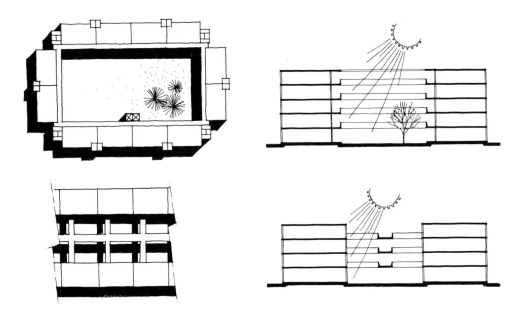

A logical use of the midrise is in low-income public housing. Compared with lowrises, it permits considerable density; compared with highrises, it is economical to build. In its exterior corridor or multicore form it provides a high degree of surveillance.

LOW- AND MIDRISE EXTERIORS

Lowrises and midrises, like highrise apartment buildings, reflect their particular structural systems on their exteriors. Economy seldom permits—and the height of the building certainly does not warrant—pure skeletal structure for lowrises. Mies' row houses in Detroit are the exception rather than the norm. Structural framing of lowrises is usually hybrid. The combinations and variations are many and complex, so that simple categorizations that are possible in highrise construction cannot be made here.

The large majority of lowrises are exterior-clad structures—wood, stucco, and masonry—that emphasize the articulation of the building volume and the pattern of fenestration rather than the structural frame with any measure of purity (**40, 41, 44, 63, 72, 84, 87**).

This is not to say that the lowrise structure cannot be expressed. When it is the intention of the designer, a degree of structural expressiveness can be achieved. If function and energy cost permit large glass areas, the load-bearing masonry walls can be shown and further emphasized by extending them beyond the glass line. If floors are poured or precast concrete, they are readily expressible (**38, 39, 45, 47, 57**).

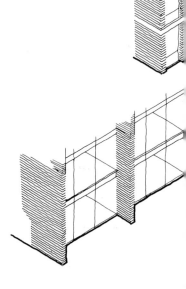

When floor framing is wood or steel bar joist, expressing the floor is not so easy. Both wood and steel require fireproofing on the exterior. In spite of this, the masonry cladding that acts as fire protection can suggest the floors. This is a good example of apparent structure instead of actual.

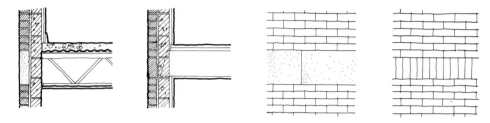

In the case of low- and midrises, the structural grid cannot be used as an exterior design crutch. The clad exterior wall and the penetration of window openings become the dominant elements of exterior design. The issues that were covered under masonry cladding of highrises apply here also: pattern and rhythm of openings; shape of windows; relation of window shapes to each other; the relation of fenestration to solid wall.

These basic aesthetic issues also apply when the exterior is not masonry clad, but is sheathed with wood or covered with stucco.

Lowrises with the potential of different floor plans at different levels permit window variation from floor to floor, a variation that is only possible on a highrise when it contains two-story apartments. Two-story row houses with their living rooms on the first floor and their bedrooms on the second, mixed walk-ups, and piggybacks lend themselves to a variety of window juxtaposition or alignment.

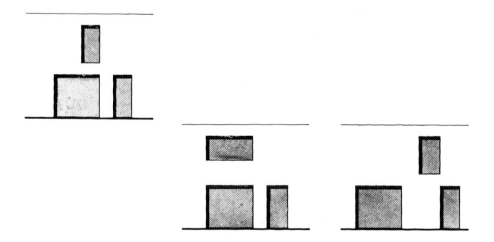

Whether the wall is load-bearing masonry or a clad balloon frame, the thing to watch for is the structural integrity and stiffness of the wall, which can easily be undermined when only "graphic play" motivates the arrrangement of openings. Energy conservation is another issue that is increasingly in the way of indiscriminate selection of window sizes. Lowrise projects often do not have the number of repetitive dwellings found in highrise and, consequently, custom-made windows become so costly that the designer is limited to manufacturers' standard sizes. When the exterior material is masonry, the length of lintel (and code requirement of fireproofing it) is another economic problem.

DESIGN METHODOLOGY

As far as window types are concerned, the reduced wind problem easily permits casements, which were not used in highrises. Ground relatedness and the frequent use of terraces and balconies often lead to sliding doors. Since the basic framing system and other factors make the lowrise cheaper than the highrise, better windows—wood, plastic-cladded wood—may be affordable.

Because they don't have to occur twenty or thirty times above each other as on highrises, odd shapes—circles, triangles—are occasionally possible on lowrises. Similarly, because of reduced frequency, projecting window boxes or bay windows occur more often.

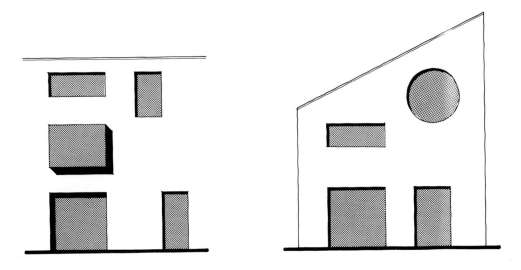

The fenestration can significantly alter the perceived proportions of the building volume. In the section on highrises, it was shown how the apparent proportions of a square facade change with vertically grouped balconies or with horizontally banded windows. Generally speaking, highrises are high and lowrises are low, regardless of

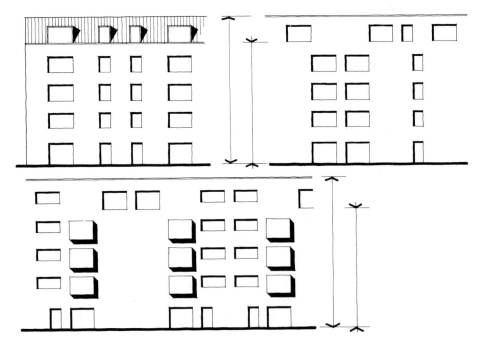

how we use windows. Midrises, however, depending on their length, frequently present odd proportions, neither soaring, nor hugging the ground. It is almost impossible to make these low—but not low enough—volumes appear tall. To make them appear lower, on the other hand, is possible. This is especially desirable on mixed-use sites when midrises occur together with row houses and lowering their apparent height helps them relate to the row houses better. To change fenestration or even the shape of the building on the top floor of a midrise tends to achieve this effect (**38, 41, 42, 44–46, 51**). (See illustrations on bottom p. 326.)

Regardless of fenestration pattern, the key issue is scale, closeness to the observer. Textures and details are experienced by the viewer as part of the visual environment instead of as abstract patterns on a tower. Nuances are spotlighted. Even such small items as the placement of a gas meter or a through-wall bathroom exhaust become extremely important.

The walls of lowrises, as the bordering and enclosing elements of an exterior space, are much more a part of that space than highrises, which are obelisks standing inside the space. The walls of the lowrise form the backdrop for the human interaction that takes place in the exterior space.

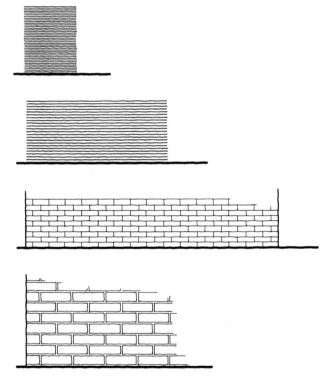

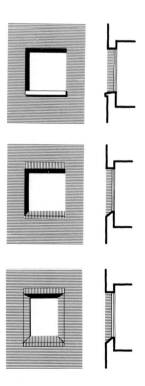

Closeness makes the fenestration more important too—the material of the window sill, its relation to the wall plane, its angle, and the way it ends at the jamb; the shape of the window jamb and its depth; the lintel, its material, its weight, its apparent ability to span and support—these are only some of the issues that we perceive on the lowrise while we overlook their significance on the twenty-fifth floor of a highrise.

DESIGN METHODOLOGY

Because of this intimacy vis-a-vis the observer, not only windows and walls, but also the building has a more significant relation to the ground and to the sky. In referring to lowrises, Paul Rudolph once said (to paraphrase) that no one ever wrote a sonnet to the silhouette of a flat-roofed building.

Lowrises with their easily articulated volumes already tend to break up the straight-line intersection of building and sky and create a silhouette of interest, even with a flat roof. Two-story dwelling units extending above the roof line, mansards, and indentations for terraces are elements that can help to vary, intensify, and enhance the contour against the sky.

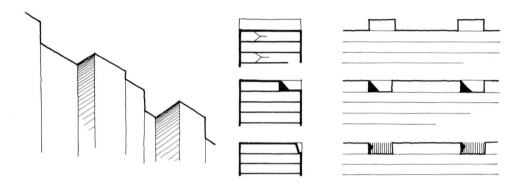

The termination of the wall, the edge detail, is so visible in lowrises that the various options demand far more scrutiny and sensitivity than in highrises (**40, 41, 58, 61–63, 84**).

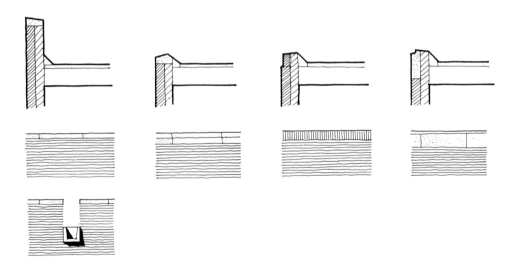

A unique problem is encountered when lowrises are part of a mixed development containing buildings of various heights. The view of the lowrise from the upper floor of a midrise or highrise is also an important one. The flat roofs of lowrises with vents, stacks, and condensing units scattered around do not present a pleasing picture. Unfortunately these tar-and-gravel flat roofs are still the most economical. When budget permits, however, the view from above can be improved with partial or full sloping roofs, which provide a rich vocabulary for varied volumes and silhouettes, not to mention the "residential character" they help conjure in the mind of the user (**49, 50, 53–56, 69, 71, 76, 78, 80–83, 85, 86**).

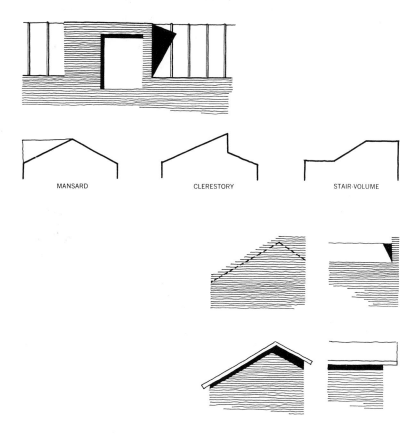

The linkage with the ground is just as important as the contour against the sky. Though often covered by planting, it is the most closely observed border of the building. Whether the building sits on grade, is lifted up on a plinth, or is depressed, the meeting of wall and ground is a delicate problem (**45, 59, 62, 65**).

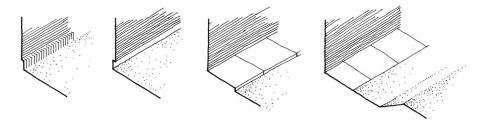

All other elements that serve as transition between the ground and the structure—stoops, steps, terrace platforms, stairs—are important. Similar sensitivity is needed for yard-enclosing structures—fences, garden walls, wing walls—in their method of attachment to the building (**40, 46, 50, 51, 67, 71, 72, 76, 78–80, 84–87**). (See illustrations on p. 330.)

The less restrictive structural system and zoning envelope allow the designer of midrise and especially lowrise housing a large degree of freedom in varying the building volume. While the utility of balconies 200 ft above grade can be questioned, the delight

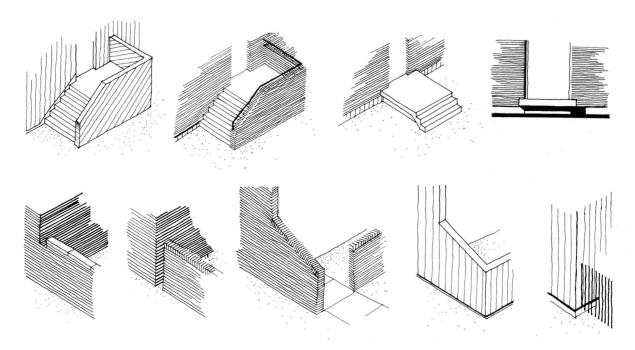

of having terraces three or four floors above grade, still in visual and audio contact with nature, is obvious. The desire for such "outdoor" spaces has led, particularly in pleasant climates, to volume breaks that greatly enhance the residential quality of many walk-up projects. The visual play of these volumes together with varied and sloping roofs and with intimate relation to the ground suggest housing quality that is rarely achieved in highrises (**49, 50, 75, 80–82, 85, 86**).

SITES

Site planning, though an essential component of housing design, is an independent discipline with extensive literature that contains so much information that no attempt could be made to cover it in a brief chapter of this book. Topography, drainage, vehicular movement systems, road network, and other topics not only require detailed treatment that is beyond the scope of this study, but also have been covered in specialized literature to which the reader is referred in the bibliography. For the practitioner seeking a brief library of references, Kevin Lynch's *Site Planning* is an old classic. *Site Planning for Cluster Housing* by Richard Untermann and Robert Small and *Site Planning Standards* by Joseph DeChiara and Lee Koppelman are equally useful. Valuable information is also found in the site planning section of *Time Saver Standards* and in HUD *Minimum Property Standards* as well as in the publications of the Urban Land Institute. Here these topics are simply called to the designer's attention.

Two issues that, though part of the specialized site planning literature, demand more thorough discussion in a book on housing are density and context; the first because it is a prime determiner of what type of housing can be built on a particular site; the second because it has been sadly neglected.

DENSITY

It is not an exaggeration to say that the zoning ordinances that set density for a site in fact determine the form of housing. Short of one's disregarding economy and grossly underutilizing the site, density dictates the housing type. It is important therefore to understand density terminology and to be able to judge and "feel" density figures.

Density can be given in terms of *floor area ratio* (FAR), *minimum lot area per dwelling* (MLA), or, most commonly, *dwelling unit per acre* (DUA). It is important to differentiate between *net density* (the number of dwelling units on the housing site proper exclusive of streets) and *neighborhood density* (including streets, roads, and possibly other community facilities). Because of the variation in the areas of roads and community facilities the densities used in most studies, as well as in this book, usually refer to net density.

Except for the very experienced in the field of housing it is hard to "feel" the consequences of a given density figure because comparison of projects is so difficult. Two projects are seldom identical. When one compares density data found by such reliable sources as Lynch, Diamond, or the Urban Land Institute one finds variations that can only be explained by the fact that the projects studied varied in dwelling size, parking ratio, and amount of open space.

| | DUA | | | FAR | |
Building Type	Lynch	Diamond	ULA	Lynch	Diamond
Single family	1–7	1–8	1–65	up to 0.2	up to 0.24
Two family	10–12	14–16	8–10	0.3	0.44
Row house	16–20	19	16–20	0.5	0.56
Three-story walk-up (garden apartment)	40–45	52	25–35	1.0	1.06
Six-story elevator	67–75	84		1.8	1.92

Density numbers should always be used with caution. Not only are apartment sizes different in each project, but also the mix of apartment types varies. Parking ratios and the kind of parking required (open vs. enclosed, adjacent vs. clustered) differ. Open space varies, as does the kind of open space (private vs. public, sideyard vs. no setback).

The situation is further complicated by the fact that many projects do not use only one housing type. One might consist of row houses and midrises while another uses a mixture of walk-ups. In addition, the individual designer's skill in creative manipulation can always increase the given density slightly.

Density figures are obviously most reliable when a large number of possibilities have been charted—using identical criteria—by the same designer. The most thorough and usable study of this kind has been prepared by Jack Diamond in Toronto.

What becomes obvious from this chart, as well as from the comparative site plans at the end of this chapter, is that density not only suggests the arrangements of the buildings on the ground, but also implies a building type and such living qualities as ground-relatedness or proximity to one's automobile.

Diamond's studies show that above 35 dwelling units per acre (DUA) the number of ground-related dwellings is never more than one-third of the total units; above 75 DUA the drop is serious, and the ground-related units decrease to 25% or less. Densities of 8 to 20 DUA allow private parking, with a close relation of automobile to dwelling; above this number common or clustered parking is required but still can be on-grade; above a density of 40 or 50, most of the open space of the site is absorbed by on-grade parking and an enclosed garage is required (the top of which can be used for dwellings and recreation); densities over 100 require multilevel garages.

The most serious shortcoming of density charts is that they deal with housing as so many distinct segregated types. They seldom show a mix of housing. Most charts— Jack Diamond's is an exception—reflect the idea that while maximum housing quality can be achieved with ground-related low-density types, when land is scarce or

DESIGN METHODOLOGY

Dwelling Type	1 Single detached	2 Semi detached	3 Joined court	4 Duplex	5 Row house	6 Triplex	7 Quadruplex	8 Back to back Semi detached
Isometric								
Plot Plan								
Dwelling units/acre (dwelling units/hectare)	8 (20)	14 (35)	16 (40)	17 (42)	19 (47)	21 (52)	23 (57)	24 (59)
Floor area ratio % open space	0.24 76%	0.38 81%	0.44 56%	0.48 88%	0.56 72%	0.60 80%	0.66 67%	0.66 67%
Unit relationship to grade	on grade	on grade	on grade	50% on grade 50% gr. related	on grade	33% on grade 66% gr.unrelated	50% on grade 50% gr. related	on grade
Access to unit	private on grade	private on grade	private on grade	50% priv. on gr. 50% priv. stair	private on grade	33% priv. on gr. 66% common stair	50% priv. on gr. 50% priv. stair	private on grade
Unit aspect	quadruple	triple	triple	quadruple	double (opposite)	quadruple	triple	double (adjacent)
Private outdoor space	on grade	on grade	on grade	50% on grade 50% gr. related	on grade	33% on grade 66% gr.unrelated	50% on grade 50% gr. related	on grade
Parking	private on grade	private on grade	private on grade	common on grade	private or com. on grade or u/g	common on grade	common on grade	private on grade

Dwelling Type	9 Stacked row house (1½ / bay)	10 Stacked row house (2/bay)	11 Garden apartment	12 3 - storey walkup apartment	13 Medium rise stacked units	14 Combined apartments & row houses	15 Slab block apartment	16 High rise point block apartment
Isometric								
Plot Plan								
Dwelling units/acre (dwelling units/hectare)	31 (77)	35 (86)	52 (128)	65 (160)	71 (175)	84 (207)	90 (222)	120 (296)
Floor area ratio % open space	0.86 72%	1.14 72%	1.06 62%	1 36 55%	1.95 68%	1.92 62%	1.78 82%	2.62 87%
Unit relationship to grade	33% on grade 66% gr. related	50% on grade 50% gr.unrelated	33% on grade 66% gr.unrelated	33% on grade 66% gr.unrelated	33% on grade 33% gr. related 33% gr.unrelated	25% on grade 75% gr.unrelated	small % on grade majority ground unrelated	small % on grade majority ground unrelated
Access to unit	33% priv. at gr. 66% priv. stair	50% priv. at gr. 50% com. stair	common stair	common stair	common elevator	25% priv. at gr. 75% com. elev.	common elevator	common elevator
Unit aspect	double (opposite)	double (opposite)	double (opposite)	single	double (opposite)	double (opposite)	single (and double adj.)	single (and double adj.)
Private Outdoor space	33% on grade 66% gr. related	50% on grade 50% gr.unrelated	33% on grade 66% gr.unrelated	33% on grade 66% gr.unrelated	33% on grade 33% gr. related 33% gr.unrelated	25% on grade 75% gr.unrelated	small % on grade majority ground unrelated	small % on grade majority ground unrelated
Parking	common underground	common underground	common underground	common underground	common underground	common underground	common on grade or u/g	common on grade or u/g

Assumptions For Calculations

Dwelling Type	Unit Area in SF	No. of Floors per Unit	Lot Size in Ft.						
1	1200	1 or 2	50 × 100	6	1200	1	60 × 100	13	800	2	consolidated
2	1200	1 or 2	30 × 100	7	1200	1	60 × 100	14	800 & 1200	1 and 2	consolidated
3	1200	1 or 2	25 × 100	8	1200	2	30 × 65	15	800	1	consolidated
4	1200	1	50 × 100	9	1200	1 and 2	consolidated	16	800	1	consolidated
5	1200	2	21 × 100	10	1200	2	consolidated				
				11	800	1	consolidated				
				12	800	1	consolidated				

Note: 10% circulation space added for dwelling types 11 through 16.

expensive the only solution is a slab-midrise or ultimately a highrise. More recently an alternate has been provided by the "high-density lowrise" (really a misnomer because often it uses elevators). This combines a variety of housing types at densities up to 40 or even 60 DUA. It improves on land cost efficiency when compared to the pure lowrise and in construction costs and social benefits, such as extent of ground-related units, compares well to the highrise.

CONTEXT

Though the issue of contextual design has been mentioned throughout this book, it is especially relevant when site is discussed as the relation of a building to the surroundings. Regardless of other qualities, an apartment building is ill fitting if it is not appropriate to the environment. Sensitivity to context must underlie the entire design process. However, it is in discussing housing sites that context becomes most crucial.

Merrill C. Gaines[69] describes contextual issues as formal patterns, activity patterns, and climatic patterns and deals predominantly with the first two (the third being extensively covered in specialized literature). He defines a pattern as a set of repeating elements or a total configuration, be it building shapes or human circulation routes. The designer's response to this pattern is "to replicate the pattern elements or continue the overall order; for instance, using the same shapes or adding to the circulation network."

> The *formal contextual patterns* are the most commonly observed, and in some ways the most obvious means architects have of relating their buildings to locale. Specifically, these patterns are *space, shape, scale, mass and proportion, pieces and details, and material, texture and color*. They constitute indentifiable micro and macro physical characteristics within the environment—the elements of buildings, sites, and settings. It is through the continuation of one or more of these variables that designers seek visually to unite their work with the surroundings.
>
> In replying to observed formal patterns, architects have a *geographic* as well as a *temporal* range from which to draw inspiration. The geographic component suggests that influences can come from near or far; from *immediate* sources, *local* sources or *regional* sources. The time component implies that the *past*, the *present*, and even the *future* can provide vehicles for contextual relationships.
>
> Immediate geographic sources are those 'next door.' Understandably, this is an often recognized pattern when the setting is comprised of major physical elements in nearby proximity.
>
> In the case of *activity patterns*, the sources of inspiration are not built form, but rather observations about human behavior. Also, intent is again important. The recognition and response within this pattern group over formal issues clearly implies priorities on the part of the designer.
>
> Three activity patterns are identified: *circulation, individual behavior*, and *group behavior*. In each instance, the pattern is established by some type of human activity within the contextual setting such as movement, socialization, territoriality, and so on. Circulation is treated as a distinct category due to the considerable influence it can exert as a contextual pattern. Individual versus group behavior obviously distinguishes between those activities performed singularly or in a collective manner.

The most important criteria of contextually responsive design are "appropriateness, reinforcement-amplification, and ambiance" according to Gaines, the first of these being primary. Since contextual patterns vary, overlap, and differ in significance, no checklist is possible. "The questions to be asked are what patterns, singularly or in total, constitute the most significant aspects of the defined environment? And, how can these patterns, in specific architectural terms, best be extended?"

For the most cohesive and lucid discussion of contextual design, the reader is referred to Brent C. Brolin's *Architecture in Context/fitting new buildings with old*. Brolin's statement that respect for the spirit of the times is less valuable as an architectural concept "than respecting the spirit of the place" should be the motto of any designer who intends to create meaningful housing.

Contextual awareness is obviously an issue of overwhelming importance on small urban sites where various elements are physically close. As the size of the site increases and reaches large exurban acreage, the importance of context diminishes.

SINGLE-BUILDING URBAN SITES

The fundamental problems on a single-building urban site have been highlighted in the section on synthesis. The issues are similar in the case of high-low-, or midrise apartment buildings. The building program and the zoning envelope tend to define the design. Locale-related problems, traffic patterns, movement systems, topography, etc., clearly play a lesser role.

Responding to a context provided by close-by buildings is particularly important. Not only is there a strong relationship between the new building and its environment, in fact, the two frequently *join*, as in the case of base volumes of adjacent highrises. The problem of "touching" is critical on sites without side yard requirements because here the housing is infill in its true sense. This requires responding to the adjacent formal pattern with building height, roof, or eave line, exterior material and color, and, foremost, with rhythm of fenestration.

MULTIBUILDING URBAN SITE

The issue of context sensitivity here is slightly less compelling. Now several buildings on the site must interrelate. High- or midrises sitting on a parking base and low-, mid-, or highrises with ground-level open space between them, present somewhat different problems.

ON PARKING BASE

1.   The apartment building volumes enter into a more complicated relationship with the lower volume, the garage. Placement of the buildings often depends on the most efficient parking layout below. If there is a single entrance control for the security of an entire project, connection of the main lobby with the elevator lobbies of the individual buildings becomes a complex problem.

Similarly, if there is a single loading area, its connection with the service elevators of the individual buildings is also complex and so, in reverse, is the hook-up between the individual refuse rooms and the loading dock.

2.   The relationship of the apartment volume to the environment can now be planned instead of dictated by zoning and setbacks as was the case on single-building sites.

The apartment volumes relate to an existing structure or group of structures to form continuity or contrast, to open up space or close it.

The shadows cast by the volumes on the neighborhood—their effects on parks, vegetation, and play areas at particular times of day—are to be considered.

Orientation, for view, sun, wind, becomes a factor in siting the buildings.

The views of or from existing structures and public spaces should, when possible, be respected.

3. Apartment volumes within the project gain another dimension in their relation to one another.

The aesthetic relation is a constantly changing one, depending on the observer's viewpoint, on the changing surfaces in sunlight or shade, and on the shadows cast by the buildings. They overlap one another or open up unexpected vistas. They also reflect one another in their glass surfaces.

The positions of buildings should be considered with an intent to provide views and light for a majority of units. The distances between them depends on the amount of overlap, and both are related to height. From the point of view of minimum overlap and maximum view the advantages of the point block become obvious.

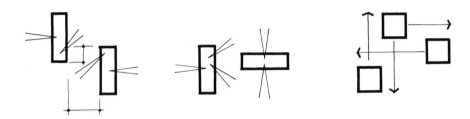

Minimizing views from apartment to apartment is equally important to ensure privacy.

Individual buildings may also be linked together. They can be joined at end walls or by the vertical transportation core. Either way, especially when the site is large enough to provide multiple links, new possibilities open up for meandering volumes and exciting spaces created between them.

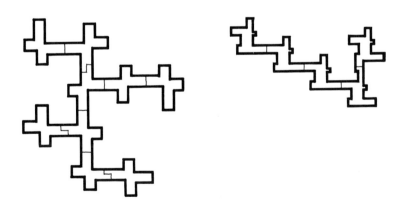

ON GRADE.   When density is lower and there are fewer cars, when there is no parking garage volume, and buildings are farther apart, movement systems (pedestrian and vehicular) and the social hierarchy of open spaces emerge as generators of the site plan in addition to the interrelation among building volumes.

One of the movement systems is pedestrian: the movement of the user—resident or guest—across the property. The other movement system deals with vehicles and involves not only movement, but storage. Garages that are attached or under buildings entail fewer problems than does clustered open parking, which needs to be screened to reduce visual blight. Movement of vehicular services also must be considered: delivery and pick-up of mail, refuse removal, fire fighting, and ambulance calls.

DESIGN METHODOLOGY

Exterior space can be public, semipublic, semiprivate, or completely private. The arrangement and treatment of spaces can provide privacy and security when needed or foster social interaction when desired. Clear definition of use of outdoor space will eliminate user dissatisfaction. The distances between balconies, terraces, or windows and adjacent buildings should be studied with privacy in mind. Pedestrian or vehicular traffic should not approach a building, window, balcony, or private open yard too closely. Otherwise, vehicular noise or light will create a disturbance, and pedestrian proximity will intrude on one's privacy. Eye-level windows facing each other should not be closer than 75 ft, and principal windows should be at least 20 ft from any public way unless that way is well below the sill (Lynch). Private outdoor space is predominantly used by adults. Common outdoor areas are chiefly for children. Security is a user concern under all conditions. Oscar Newman[70] discussed a variety of ways to achieve security (social contact, observation, surveillance opportunities). The distinct demarcation of use areas, to separate one's own turf, is felt to be primary. Housing sites open to the public or accessible to outsiders lead to discontent. Successful site plans lack ambiguity.

> The site must be designed so that there is a clear delineation between private outdoor spaces and communal outdoor spaces as well as a clear delineation between space "belonging" to the housing development itself, and that "belonging" to the adjacent neighborhood. Clarity about which portions of the site are available for play and which are not and an understanding between residents and management about territorial control are likewise very important. Residents in many evaluation studies of housing developments report that problems occur where there is a misunderstanding between management and residents regarding delimitation of territory or maintenance responsibilities; between adults and children when there is a misunderstanding about where the latter are expected to play; and between residents and nonresidents regarding use of facilities and space which the former group believe is their particular right. Residents have frequently had no previous experience of living in an arrangement whereby they share interior access space and exterior recreation space with their neighbors. Most of us 'act' in a certain space with reference to previous comparable spaces we have been in or lived in. But, if you have only lived in a single family house or a sterile apartment building, there is no prior experience to understanding how one should view or use common landscaped areas and communal facilities. Lack of ambiguity in the site plan, management sensitivity, and the provision of resident manuals can alleviate these problems.[71]

An issue often neglected on multibuilding urban sites is orientation. Every dwelling needs to enjoy sunlight. Buildings should be oriented so that their windows and outdoor recreation areas are not "in the shadow of another structure more than fifty percent of the time they can be reached by sunlight."[72] The debate of east-west v. north-south orientation is almost meaningless on these urban sites however, since site constraints, the visual need for a variety in building orientations, the relation to the surroundings generally take precedence over orientation toward any particular direction even if that direction would be preferable for wind, sun, or energy saving. These preferences can be more easily responded to on large sites, mostly exurban.

> If structures are too close to each other, especially if they surround a space, noises will resonate within them. Every room should have adequate light and air: a substantial piece of sky should be visible through the windows from normal standing positions in the room to ensure good daylight and

prevent claustrophobia. A minimum standard may be that from each window, in principal rooms, the major part of the forward 60 degree cone of vision should be unobstructed by anything that is more than half as high above the sill as its distance from the window. This minimum is assured by spacing buildings at more than twice their height, but other, denser arrangements will also pass this test.[73]

Sensitivity to context is still very important on multibuilding sites. While the inner open spaces and views on these sites can be somewhat separated from the surroundings, the periphery is still in contact with it, and there is a psychological, if not physical, linkage throughout. Architectural response can be achieved by using sympathetic color, texture, massing; employing allusions to the style of the surrounds, such as arches, gables, bay windows. These can integrate elements of the past into the modern design, which has the effect of restating with modern means the visual experience of the old.

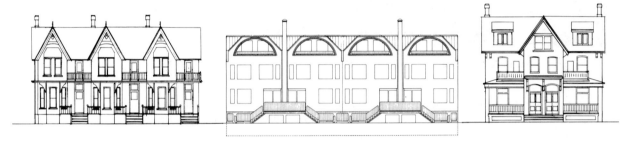

A. J. DIAMOND ASSOC: QUEENS UNIV. HOUSING, KINGSTON, TORONTO

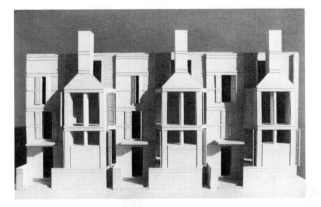

BARTON MEYERS ASSOC: GHENT SQUARE, NORFOLK, VIRGINIA

Another response is to set the new within or behind the old, so it is seen through or in conjunction with the old, linked by properly scaled open space.

In dealing with an urban context, new housing must respond to the existing scale. High-density housing in its pure highrise form, properly set back or not, has been mostly unsuccessful in this respect. One means is using a variety of housing forms within a project, such as Sert did in Peabody Terrace in Cambridge, which "incorporates high elements to achieve density, but lower ones to meet the scale of the

337

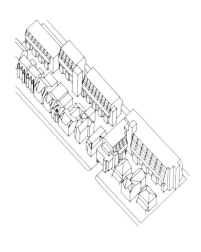

BARTON MEYERS ASSOC: DUNDAS SHERBOURNE, TORONTO, ONTARIO

existing Cambridge neighborhood."[74] Mixed housing form does not necessarily mean separate buildings. Stepping down to the river edge (Roosevelt Island housing by Sert; Plaza 1199 in New York by Hodne and Stageberg) or to the lower-scaled neighborhood (Coney Island housing by Hoberman and Wasserman) can be solved by one building taking on varied configurations.

The bordering of highrise projects with terrace housing to hide the bulk of the parking

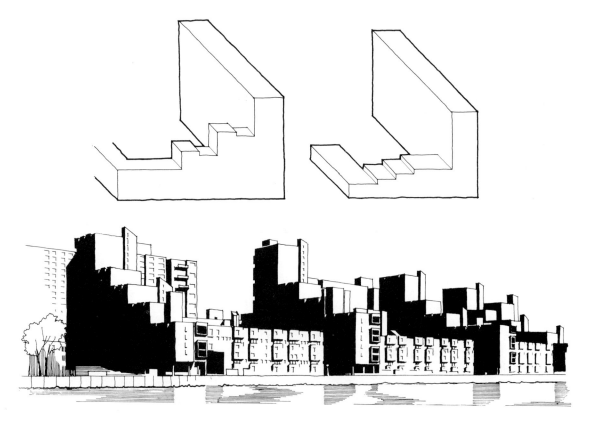

garage is another method of meeting neighborhood scale. Housing, instead of a forbidding blank wall of a garage, meets the user.

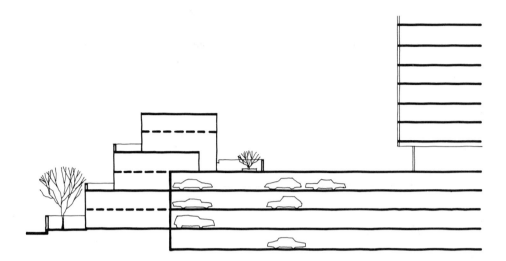

Mixed-use zoning, besides its other human benefits, helps achieve neighborhood scale. The bordering stores, with their arcades, shop windows, displays, and signs create a scale buffer between the street and the tall housing volumes.

MULTIBUILDING EXURBAN SITES

When multibuilding, usually large, exurban sites are discussed, the density referred to is quite often "neighborhood density," which includes roads, open recreation areas, etc., within the total boundary of the site. The term "gross density," which includes half of the bounding streets as well, is sometimes used as a description.

The issues of contextual design are minimally important in these developments. However, needs already discussed, such as movement systems, privacy, security, and territoriality, still must be fulfilled on these sites. Orientation for energy conservation, sunlight, or ventilation can be achieved more easily here than in urban locations.

Those technical issues of site planning that are well covered in the extensive specialized literature will only be referred to at this time.

Streets are to discourage through traffic. Their width, grade, surfacing, radii, right-of-way, and methods of dead-ending are determined by local ordinance. Road pattern, especially that of secondary roads, should be designed in conjunction with building groupings. Cul-de-sac or loop streets are the principal alternatives to the so-called access streets that parallel main roads.

Sidewalks are also locally regulated in surfacing, width, slope, and curbing. Local regulations also determine whether they are needed on one or both sides of a road or not at all, if pathways through the project do not parallel vehicular access.

Topography will affect not only the road pattern and drainage, but the building type proper. Steep grades and excessive cut and fill are to be avoided wherever possible.

Drainage must be carefully coordinated with local authorities in matters such as direction of flow and methods of acceptable water detention.

Landscaping can include earth mounding where the terrain is flat. Besides visual pleasure, landscape can help control sun, wind, and noise.

Contextual sensitivity on these sites is replaced by ecological awareness, the preservation of existing features such as terrain, flora, drainage, lakes.

DESIGN METHODOLOGY

EXTERIOR SPACES

Whether the site is small or large, urban or exurban, once it contains more than one building, a dynamic relation is created between those buildings and the exterior space. Even the single building on a small site enters into similar space-defining relation with the other buildings around it. Site planning, in addition to solving problems of movement, orientation, linkage to cars or common facilities and other functional requirements, is the design of spaces between buildings.

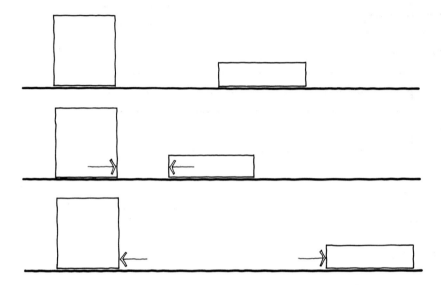

Are there distances that foster a sensation of equilibrium between buildings, where relations feel proper, and where the sense of space is strongest? According to Robert M. Beckley[75] "at a ratio of 1:4 (height: width), enclosure is barely perceived. At a ratio of 1:3, the feeling of enclosure is stronger, but a sense of an outdoor room has not yet been created. A ratio of 1:2 produces a definite visual enclosure, and a 1:1 ratio produces a very strong visual enclosure." According to Lynch,[76] to use another measurement, we can detect a person 4000 ft away, recognize him/her at 80 ft, see the face clearly at 45 ft, and enter into direct relationship between 3 and 10 ft. Or to describe it differently, outdoor dimensions of 40 ft appear intimate, 80 ft is still human scale, and 450 ft is about the maximum dimension which successful outdoor spaces in the past have. Ashihara[77] relates distance to building height:

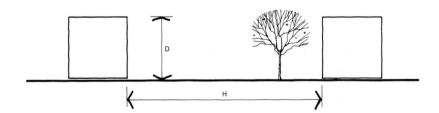

If D/H becomes larger than 3, distance is too great.
If D/H becomes smaller than 1, distance is too small.
If D/H = 2 to 3, distance is comfortable.

FHA guidelines are more specific about distances between buildings and also take into consideration windows.

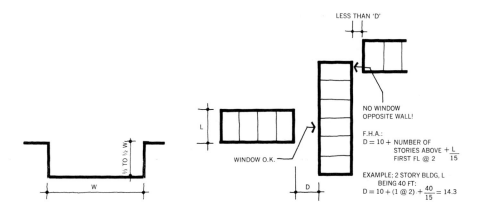

Forces are set up not only between buildings, but between buildings and various objects—sculpture, trees, signposts—anchored in the exterior space. In fact, "not only does the setting determine the place of the object, but inversely the object also modifies the structure of the setting."[78]

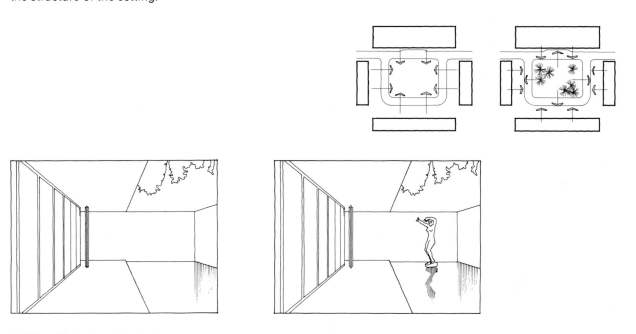

Ashihara[79] deals with similar phenomena, but expressed in terms of centrifugal or centripetal forces.

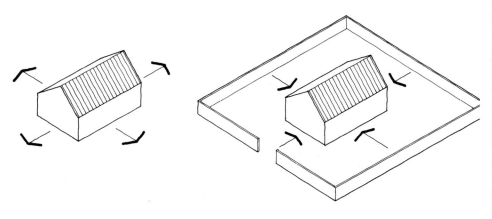

341

DESIGN METHODOLOGY

Once dynamic interrelations between buildings acting through the open space are recognized, it becomes clear that exterior space can be modified by changing these forces. Arnheim's analysis suggests a variety of spatial manipulations:

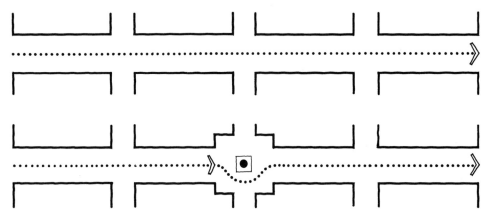

A SHORT TERM GOAL SUGGESTS THAT A STRETCH OF THE JOURNEY HAS BEEN COMPLETED

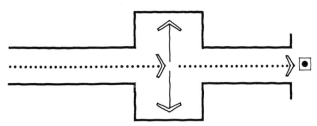

OPPOSING FORCES TO THE MAIN AXIS GIVE OPTIONS FOR DECISION, FREEDOM TO CONTINUE OR NOT

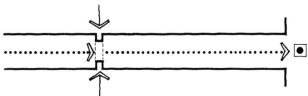

TEMPORARY RETARDATION IS AN INCENTIVE FOR FORWARD MOVEMENT.

Open space is perceived by all the senses: kinetic, as one walks through; audio, as one hears children at play, the rustle of leaves, or the gushing of water; tactile, as a bench is touched; olfactory, as the fragrance of flowering shrubs is smelled; but primarily through a special kind of vision. Space is seen, not as a single view, but in sequence over an extended period of time while the observer is in motion. The eye, like a motion picture camera, registers a series of images. This serial vision, which requires the study of outdoor space to be at human eye level, makes the customary bird's eye view of architectural site studies inadequate.

Gordon Cullen's[80] study of exterior space through sequential views is a fundamental way to look at any site design though, unfortunately, it is seldom done. It sensitizes us to differentiate between foreground, middleground, and background. Cullen deals with techniques and devices such as change, enclosure, modulation, deflection, linkage, juxtaposition, that determine how we move through and how we sense space and feel a variety of meanings and moods, such as anticipation, mystery, prediction, surprise, and

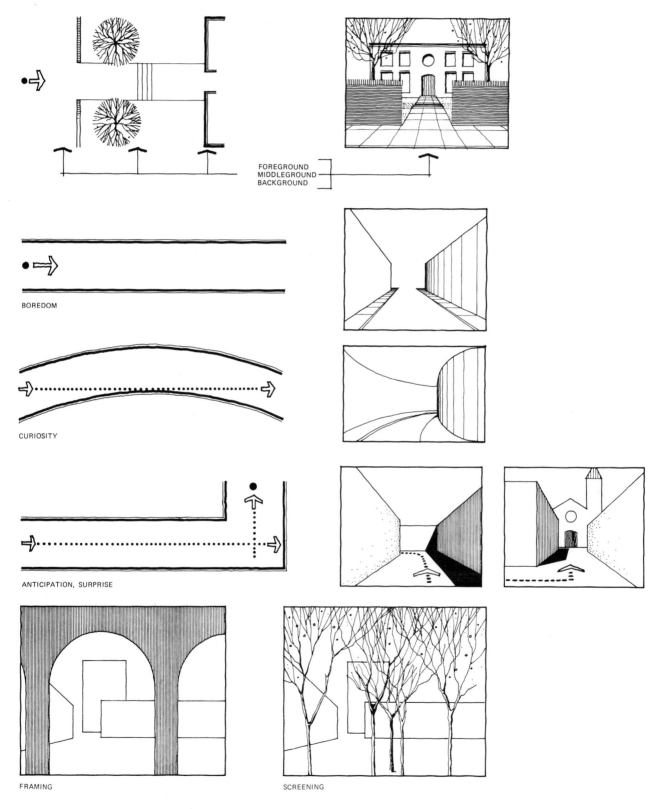

FOREGROUND
MIDDLEGROUND
BACKGROUND

BOREDOM

CURIOSITY

ANTICIPATION, SURPRISE

FRAMING

SCREENING

teasing. Our image of the exterior is modified by screening, framing, punctuation, foiling, and countless other devices.

Exterior places (using Lynch's criteria for sensuous space) should

> be within the range of comfort: not too hot, too noisy, too bright, too cold, too silent, too loaded or empty of information, too steep, too dirty, too clean.
>
> …have diversity, giving the inhabitant a choice of the environment he/she prefers at any time.
>
> …support the action that people want to engage in there.
>
> …have a clear perceptual identity: recognizable, memorable, vivid, engaging of attention, differentiated from other locations. The 'sense of place' is the cornerstone of a handsome and meaningful environment.
>
> …have their identifiable parts so arranged that a normal observer can relate them to each other and can understand their pattern in time and space."
>
> …be perceived as meaningful, its visible parts not only related to each other in time and space, but related to other aspects of life: functional activity, social structure, economic and political patterns, human values and aspirations, even individual idiosyncrasies and character.
>
> …play a part in the intellectual, emotional, and physical development of the individual, particularly, in childhood, but perhaps also in later years.

DENSITY STUDIES

On the following pages a variety of density studies are presented using the most common housing types. For each type the density is analyzed with similar criteria: outdoor recreation space is the same; parking is 1.25 cars/unit in each case and is open parking; all building types contain 12300 sf 2-BR apartments, the only exception is the row house which is 1400 sf. The site that is being used in the analysis is a 535 ft. × 270 ft. urban block with optional setback requirements. This 3.3 acres site is the basis for calculating net density. When neighborhood density is shown, it refers to the site plus half of the 66 ft. wide streets around it (4.5 acres).

The results of the studies are tabulated below. Low or extremely high densities were avoided. The densities shown both for Net and Neighborhood Density are average to high. They seem to be slightly lower than the figures arrived at by Lynch or Diamond; however, as cautioned before, density numbers arrived at by different authors cannot possibly match since, if not the criteria, certainly the planning methodology will always differ.

Housing Type	Net Density	Neighborhood Density
Row house (2 story)	17	12
with partial-deck parking	20	15
with full-deck parking	22	16
Patio house/matrix (1-story)	18	13
Same on sloping site	20	15
3-story walk-up (quadruplex units)	36	26
Same with underground parking	60	44
3-story walk-up (duplex units)	32	24
4-story walk-up (duplex units)	38	28
Same with underground parking	58	42
5-story midrise	60	44
Same with underground parking	72	53
6-story midrise	75	55
Same with underground parking	84	62

ROW HOUSE (1400 sf)

Assumed net density: 20 units/acre
Lot area: 535 × 270 ft = 144,450 sf = 3.3 acres
Number of units: 3.3 acres @ 20 = 66 units
Parking: 66 @ 1.25 = 83 cars

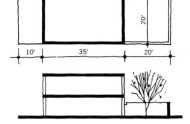

Ground utilization

66 row houses @ 700 sf =		46,200 sf
66 yards @ 600 sf	=	39,600 sf
83 cars @ 300 sf	=	24,900 sf
		110,700 sf

144,450 sf − 110,700 sf = 33,750 sf (25%)
Open area left for circulation and outdoor recreation (approximately half for recreation)

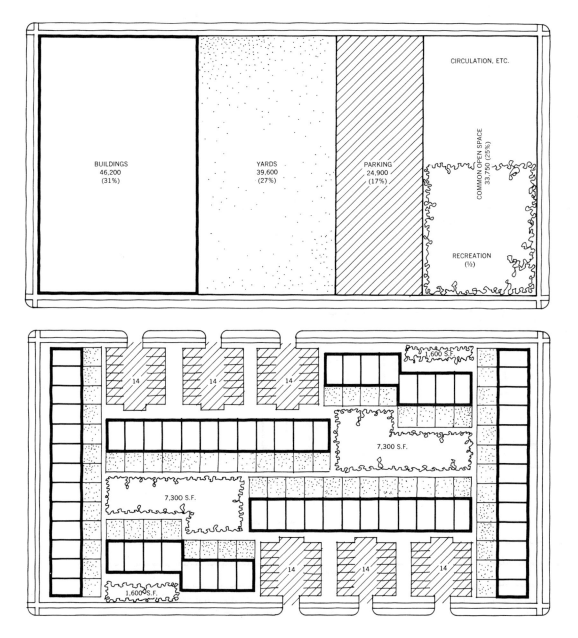

345

DESIGN METHODOLOGY

ROW HOUSE (1400 sf)

Lot area: 535 × 270 ft   = 144,450 sf
    Less 35% of the lot to improve outdoor recreation space to be left open)   = −50,000 sf
                                                                                                            94,000 sf

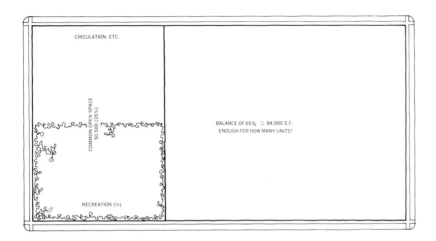

A single unit requires
   Row house proper   = 700 sf
   Yard   = 600 sf
   Parking 1.25 @ 300 sf = 375 sf
                  1675 sf

94,000 sf ÷ 1675 sf = 56 units
56 ÷ 3.3 acres = **17 units/acre net density**
(for suburban sites with roads 56 ÷ 4.5 acres = **12 units/acre neighborhood density**)

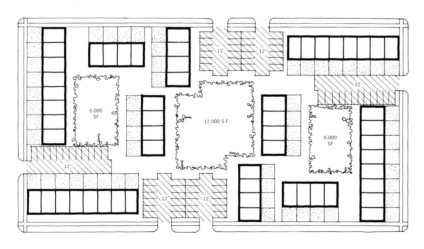

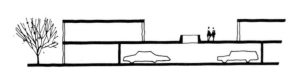

Partial decking of parking can increase **net density to 20 units/acre.**

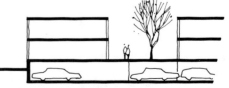

Full decking of parking can increase **net density to 22 units/acre.**

PATIO HOUSE IN MATRIX (1200 sf)

Lot area: 535 × 270 ft	=	144,450 sf
Less 15% of lot for circulation and recreation	=	−21,600 sf
Left for units and parking		122,850 sf

A single unit requires

House proper	=	1200 sf
Yard	=	400 sf
Parking 1.25 @ 300 sf	=	375 sf
		1975 sf

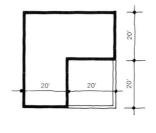

122,850 sf ÷ 1975 sf = 62 units
Say 60 ÷ 3.3 acres = **18 units/acre net density**
(**neighborhood density:**
60 ÷ 4.5 acres = **13 units/acre**)

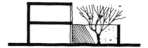

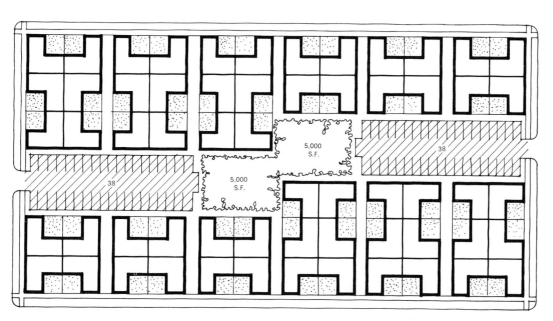

On sloping sites where units can slide above one another and patios or even walkways can occur above units (costly!) **net density** can be increased to **20 units/acre.**

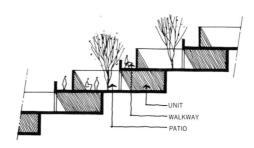

DESIGN METHODOLOGY

THREE-STORY WALK-UP/QUADRUPLEX (average two-bedroom = 1200 sf)

Lot area: 535 × 270 ft   = 144,450 sf
    Less 25% of lot for circulation and recreation   = −33,750 sf

Left for units and parking   110,700 sf

Each apartment needs for ground
coverage
    (90 × 55 ft) ÷ 12 (units per building)   =   416 sf

Each apartment "carries" part of yards
    belonging to first floor apartments
    (90 × 30 ft) ÷ 12 (units per building)   =   225 sf
Parking 1.25 @ 300 sf   =   375 sf

                                 1016 sf

110,700 sf ÷ 1016 sf = 108 units
Because there are 12 units/building
    108 ÷ 12 = 9 buildings
Try 10 buildings @ 12 = 120
120 ÷ 3.3 acres = **36 units/acre net density**
(neighborhood density:
120 ÷ 4.5 acres = **26 units/acre)**

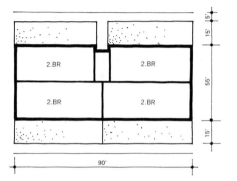

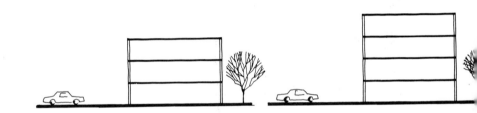

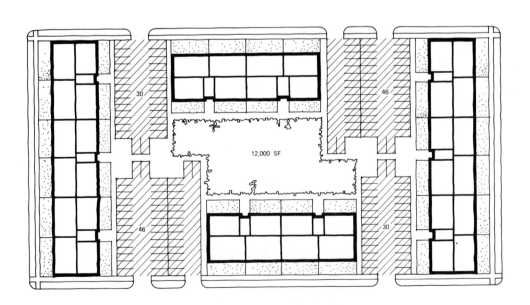

Underground parking will permit 12, four-story buildings @ 16 units or 196 total;
196 ÷ 3.3 acres = **60 units/acre net density**

THREE-STORY WALK-UP/DUPLEX (average two-bedroom = 1200 sf)

Lot area: 535 × 270 ft   = 144,450 sf
   Less 25% of lot for circulation and recreation = −33,750 sf

Left for units and parking   110,700 sf

A single building requires:
   Building proper: 50 × 52 ft   =   2600 sf
   Yards: 30 × 50 ft   =   1500 sf
   Parking (1.25 @ 300 sf) × 6 units/building =   2250 sf
                                       6350 sf

110,700 sf ÷ 6350 sf = 18 buildings
18 @ 6 apartments = 108 units
108 ÷ 3.3 acres = **32 units/acre net density**
(**neighborhood density**:
108 ÷ 4.5 acres = **24 units/acre**)

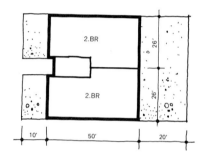

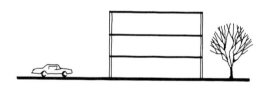

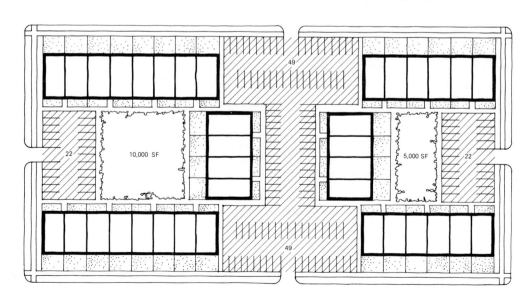

DESIGN METHODOLOGY

FOUR-STORY WALK-UP/DUPLEX (average two-bedroom = 1200 sf)

Lot area: 535 × 270 ft	=	144,450 sf
Less 25% of lot for circulation and recreation		−33,750 sf
Left for units and parking	=	110,700 sf

Land required by each building:

Building proper: 50 × 52 ft	=	2600 sf
Yards: 30 × 50 ft	=	1500 sf
Parking (1.25 @ 300 sf) @ 8 units/building	=	3000 sf
		7,100 sf

110,700 sf ÷ 7,100 sf = 15.59 say 16 buildings
16 @ 8 apartments = 128 units
128 ÷ 3.3 acres = **38 units/acre net density.**
(**neighborhood density:**
128 ÷ 4.5 acres = **28 units/acre**)

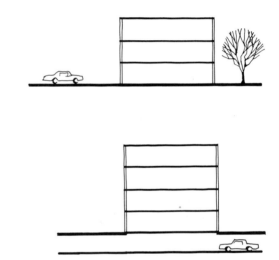

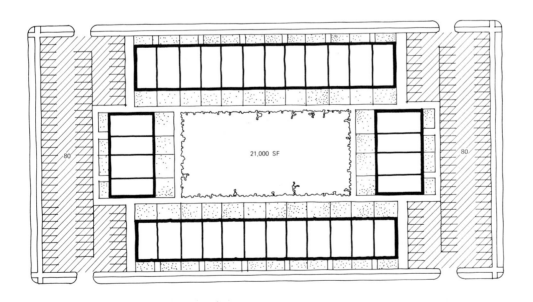

21,000 SF

Underground parking will permit 24 buildings @ 8 units or
192 units total; 192 ÷ 3.3 acres = **58 units/acre net density.**

FIVE-STORY MIDRISE (average two-bedroom = 1200 sf)

Land required for building per unit:
  (42 × 62 ft) ÷ 10 (units per building segment) = 260 sf per unit

Land required for parking per unit:

Parking (12.5 @ 300 sf) @ 10	=	3750 sf
Less parking under building		
8 cars @ 200 sf	=	−1600 sf
		2150 sf
2150 sf ÷ 10 units	=	215 sf/unit

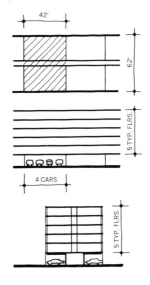

Recreation
  Assumed criteria: all 2-BR units with 2 adults + 1 child

Child recreation: 1 @ 20 sf	=	20 sf
Adult recreation: 2 @ 100 sf	=	200 sf
Mixed recreation: 3 @ 25 sf	=	75 sf
		295 sf, say 300 sf

Less:			
	Balcony 6 × 15 ft	=	−90 sf
	Laundry	=	−10 sf
	Roof deck	=	−40 sf
			160 sf/unit

Land for building	= 260 sf
Land for parking	= 215 sf
Land for recreation	= 160 sf
Total per unit	= 635 sf

Lot area: 535 × 270 ft	= 144,450 sf
Less setbacks	= −14,450 sf
Left for units, parking, and recreation	130,000 sf

130,000 sf ÷ 635 sf = 204, say 200
200 ÷ 3.3 = **60 units/acre net density**
(**neighborhood density:**
200 ÷ 4.5 acres = **44 units/acre**)

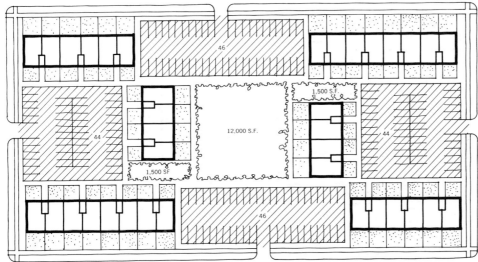

The 14,600 sf of outdoor recreation space is considerably less than called for by the criteria (200 units @ 160 sf = 32,000 sf) beause much of the parking is on single-loaded driving aisles and carries disproportionate amount of aisle space (car + aisle: 400 sf instead of 300 sf).

Underground parking will increase **net density** to **72 units/acre.**

DESIGN METHODOLOGY

SIX-STORY MIDRISE (average two-bedroom = 1200 sf)

To increase the outdoor recreation space that was lacking in the preceding study and to reduce "sea of asphalt" appearance, assume parking in two-level structure, the top of which is developed for recreation. Eliminating parking under the buildings, leaves six typical apartment floors.

Unit:

6 apartment floors @ 40 units	=	240 units
Less 2 units per building for lobbies	=	−8 units
		232 units

232 ÷ 3.3 acres = **70 units/acre net density**

Parking:
2 parking levels in each garage = 4 levels
4 @ 72 cars = ±290 cars = 232 apartments @ 1.25

Recreation:

2 decks @ 21,000 sf	=	42,000 sf
On grade	=	11,000 sf
		53,000 sf

Required as per preceding study criteria

232 units @ 160 sf	=	−37,120 sf
Overage		15,880 sf

If the 15,880 sf overage is used for 16 row houses with private yards on top of the parking deck,
232 units + 16 units = 248 units
248 ÷ 3.3 acres = **75 units/acre net density.**
(neighborhood density:
248 ÷ 4.5 acres = **55 units/acre)**

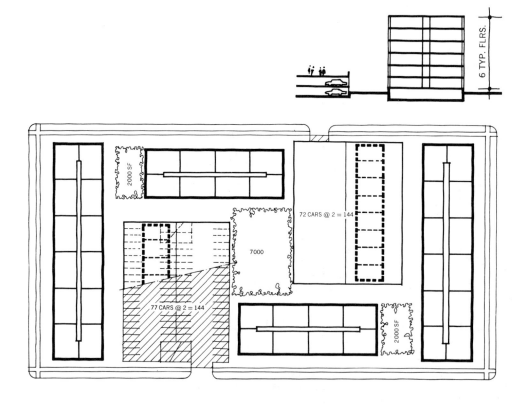

Underground parking will increase **net density** to **84 units/acre.**

HIGHRISE

Using parking as a determiner of ultimate net density on the site

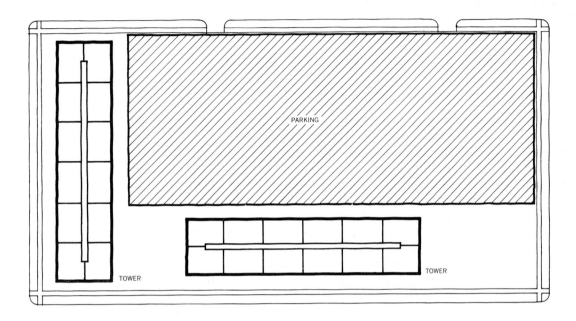

One-level parking in area shaded: 300 cars
   Using 1:1.25 ratio, 300 cars serve 240 units
   240 units ÷ 2 buildings = 120 units/building
   120 units ÷ 12 units/floor = **10 floors**

   240 ÷ 3.3 acres = **72 units/acre net density**

Two-level parking in area shaded: 2 @ 260 = 520 cars
   Using 1:1.25 parking ratio, 520 cars serve 416 units
   416 units ÷ 2 buildings = 208 units/building
   208 units ÷ 12 units/floor = 17.33, say **17 floors**
   (17 @ 12 = 204 units/building
   204 @ 2 = 408 units)

   408 ÷ 3.3 acres = **123 units/acre net density**

Two-level parking over the entire site: 2 @ 400 = 800 cars
   Using 1:1.25 parking ratio, 800 cars serve 640 units
   640 units ÷ 2 buildings = 320 units/building
   320 units ÷ 12 units/floor = 26.66, say **27 floors**
   (27 @ 12 = 324 units/building
   324 @ 2 = 648 units)

   648 ÷ 3.3 acres = **200 units/acre net density**

. . . and so on upward depending on parking volume capacity.

SPECIAL USERS

What has been said so far in this book applies to housing that serves the general public. There is, of course, no such thing as "the general public." As the architect learns about the peculiarities of the user for whom the building is planned, adjustments will be made in the design approach. To accommodate a specific market, the mix might change: the number of three- and four-bedroom units will increase if there are a large number of

DESIGN METHODOLOGY

families with children; there will be more one- and two-bedroom units for empty-
nesters; more studios for singles. Other changes will also be made if one knows about
the user. Within the apartment, a dining-kitchen area might be preferable for a given
clientele. Providing for another type of user might dictate large bedrooms for alternate
activities. The kind of common facilities offered will also alter if one is aware of user
idiosyncracies. All of these changes are relatively minor compared to the adjustments
required for elderly or handicapped persons in mix, apartment layout and community
facility design.

ELDERLY

Housing for the elderly constitutes the largest unmet housing market today in spite of
the growing number of HUD-subsidized projects and the spreading "elderly communities" in the Sun Belt, mainly in Arizona, Florida, and California. Senior citizens (over 65)
comprise the fastest-growing segment of U.S. population. Presently, there are
approximately 23 million persons over 65 in this country, more than 10% of the citizenry.
In addition, the life expectancy today is well over 70, and it is estimated that by the end of
the century, the number of elderly will have increased to 30 million. Architects should
also take into account the passing of the three-generation household. Enlightened
social agencies make every effort to ensure that those elderly who only a few years ago
were institutionalized, today, with home-delivery services, day care, and other assistance, function outside of nursing homes. They therefore need residential options.

The U.S. Census Bureau estimates that 15.8 million households are headed by
persons 65 or over. Of this group, 11.1 million are homeowners, but it is predicted that
about one million will move to apartments in a year. The reasons are various, but mainly
economic. Many are unable to maintain their homes without expensive household help.
They have relatively fixed incomes and are more susceptible to rising taxes and utility
costs, shrinking real income, and all other expenses associated with homeownership.
They need less space. Home maintenance with reduced stamina is a burden. Often
neighborhood changes require adaptation difficult for old persons; often these
changes mean security problems. The number in need of rental units is further
increased by those who are displaced through condominium conversion.

Design for the elderly must start with the understanding of what it means to grow old.
Through the work of behavioral scientists, especially such pioneers in the field of
environment and aging as Leon A. Pastalan and M. Powell Lawton, the architect can
learn a great deal about how the process of aging might affect the physical environment.
While it is true that the circumstances and needs of elderly people vary considerably,
which makes effective housing design difficult, Pastalan concludes that the negative
changes experienced in aging, described by him as a "loss continuum," can be
abstracted. Between ages 50 and 65: children leave home; 65 and 75: loss of
occupational roles, loss of income, death of spouse and friends; 75 and 85: increased
loss of sensory acuity (especially visual and audio), loss of health (including energy
level and physical mobility), diminished independence; above age 85: serious loss of
health, independence, and sensory acuity.[82] Both Pastalan and Lawton point out that
just as the adaptive capacities of older people are diminished, a poorly designed
environment requires them to make major adaptations.

As the older person's competence level decreases in relation to the norm, his or her
behavior will be increasingly affected by the environment. A physical setting which a
person of average competence may deal with by adaptive behavior may be too taxing
for those with a low level of competence. Lawton's studies call for a supportive
environment, which will help maintain adaptive behavior in the less competent elderly
though it will not be so supportive that it leads to boredom.

Challenge and support have been suggested as equally appropriate, depending on the need and capacity of the individual and the amount of challenge or support involved. How does the person become matched with the environment, or environmental aspects, that can give him the most satisfying life?

The most important aspect of the answer is that most people, if given the appropriate range of choice, will themselves choose what is most consistent with their needs.[83]

Clearly, designers should keep in mind that the older person must be provided with the widest range of environmental options, with increased opportunities for individual choice.

In order to respond to the changing needs of the elderly, facilities should range from totally independent to totally dependent housing, such as long-term care facilities (nursing homes) with various levels of nursing care. Facilities with nursing, which really are health care facilities, cannot be covered within the confines of this book. Those that will be discussed as forms of housing can be grouped under three types:

1. INDEPENDENT. A multifamily housing development for self-sufficient residents with minimum communal social facilities. Other services if and when needed, can be provided home-delivered.

2. CONGREGATE. A service-intensive setting. For those with increased needs, housekeeping, food, and other services are provided "in-house."

3. COMMUNAL. A pioneering group-living arrangement of a limited number of elderly with food facilities on the premises and other services (health, social, etc.) delivered when needed by a sponsoring social agency. In fact, this is less service-intensive than the congregate type.

The location for any housing for elderly people should be secure and crime-free, especially in large urban areas. Obviously, design can compensate for lack of neighborhood security, but such measures are at best compromises. Second in importance is "neighborhood quality," the proximity to and availability of grocery and other retail stores, banks, or check-cashing agencies, religious institutions, health services, movie houses, coffee shops, restaurants, libraries; all the activities that cover daily needs and add vitality to surroundings. The proximity to public transportation, unless private minibus service is provided, is a must; nearness to a park is a definite asset. Being close to younger people in the surrounding neighborhood or in mixed-age complexes is an advantage. Proximity to the sponsoring social agency makes receiving its home-delivered services (meals-on-wheels, volunteers, shopping-bus, etc.) easier.

In arguments about housing type for the elderly, the most frequently discussed topic is highrise v. lowrise. Studies conducted with the elderly indicate no clear choice. Responses depend on a person's background and previous housing experience. The location, size of a project, site conditions, and local zoning will naturally suggest a particular housing type.

Approximately 60 units is considered a minimum size to justify the development cost and needed community facilities. Aside from economic considerations, the other disadvantage of very small projects according to some planners, is that inhabitants cannot have active social lives. Of course, this is not true for residents of group-living arrangements that provide small social groups. On the other hand, projects with over 300 apartments tend to have institutional characteristics. Proper planning can break up such projects into series of 80- or 100-unit neighborhoods.

DESIGN METHODOLOGY

The mix of apartments is largely determined by demography and the profile of the potential user; therefore, it is likely to change in time. Currently, since most apartments for the elderly are occupied by singles a large majority of apartments (around 90 to 95%) have one bedroom. Separate living room and bedroom are held to be minimal requirements by occupants; studios or efficiencies are considered undesirable. A good percentage of the one-bedroom units should be able to accommodate two persons. HUD or local agencies require a certain small number of units to be designed for the physically handicapped, though experience shows that these are often not filled by wheelchair-bound residents.

Especially in the field of housing for the elderly designers should understand the various forms of sponsorship and their historic developments. Historically, congregate housing has had no government subsidy, though funding for this housing type started recently on a very limited basis. This implies, therefore, that congregate housing usually serves higher-income people. Most of these facilities have been sponsored by religious institutions, which are often located nearby as part of a "campus" complex. The overwhelming number of projects of independent housing for the elderly are government assisted (HUD). While in the 1960s the majority of sponsors were public housing authorities or nonprofit organizations, during the 1970s an increasing number of profit-motivated private developments were built.

Because of the number of participants in the decision-making process, the architect's role is a difficult one.

> The designer of a building for older people has two clients—the sponsor or housing authority and the older person himself. We can assume that most housing for the elderly is being built by sponsors who have the genuine best interest of the older person in mind. In subsidized housing we are less likely to have the developer-consumer conflict of economic interest that charac-terizes much open-market housing. However, the communication gap is at least as bad when we consider that for open-market building, consumer behavior provides reasonably adequate feedback to the designers as to what kinds of dwellings sell easily and are thus assumed to be satisfying the user's needs. In the case of the elderly, only the well-to-do have the freedom to choose among many alternative forms of living situations. There is a long waiting list for just about every kind of housing for the elderly, and there is very little opportunity for the consumer to do anything but grab fast for the first available living quarters that he is lucky enough to encounter, and never mind the luxury of being able to choose what he really wants.

> Thus, the sponsoring organization must be the advocate for the consumer whether the older person wishes it to be or not, and whether anyone in the organization knows anything about building for the elderly or not.

> The older person is thus, except under very unusual circumstances, com-pletely bypassed in the decisions regarding the kind of building he will have to use. Understandably, asking the potential consumer what he would like is a difficult task.[84]

Since so much housing for the elderly is government assisted, the architect will have to closely follow HUD minimum property standards, fundamentally a good guide as long as the designer and sponsor do not let minimum standards become maxima.

INDEPENDENT HOUSING. All housing for the elderly, even for the most inde-pendently functioning, must provide environmental support, especially for sensory losses and losses in mobility. Various spaces of the dwelling unit will be described with a view to creating such supportive environments. However, some general recommendations can be made for all spaces:

Flooring should be nonslip, have minimum changes in elevation and material, and avoid thresholds. Tubs should be nonskid.

Lighting level should be efficient to compensate for eyesight problems. On shiny floor surfaces, glare should be avoided. Ceiling fixtures that tempt risky bulb change are dangerous.

Signage should be large, readable (preferably widely spaced, light-colored letters on dark background), clear.

Visual clues which help avoid confusion and hazard should be used (colored switch plates instead of those melting into the wall, colored stair nosing that stands out, etc.). Different color schemes in the public areas of each floor help eliminate disorientation.

The anthropometric data of the elderly (they are shorter) and their limited reach (due to arthritis) should be kept in mind when locating switches, outlets, elevator buttons, shelves, clothes rods, etc.

Hardware selection should take into account weaker limbs and arthritic hands (balanced, easy-to-operate main doors, lever handle instead of door knob, kind of faucets, window operation, etc.).

Safety should always be uppermost: proper fire protection, water temperature controls, gas shutoffs, front stove controls, burn-shields, emergency signals in bedrooms and baths, etc.

Security should be carefully studied: entrance/apartment intercom, phone jacks, visual surveillance of entrance, single entrance if possible, quality hardware, etc.

All design should encourage social interaction and stimulate participation in group activities while it provides spaces for those who want complete privacy or more intimate socializing in smaller groups.

The guiding principle in designing for a population deprived of many choices should be to provide as many options as possible.

Dwelling Unit. The issue of how large the dwelling unit ought to be to serve the elderly comfortably has been much argued and is best summarized by Lawton:

> There is no magic formula for size, nor any reliable research data yet on tenant satisfaction as a function of domicile size. HUD's property standards will allow an efficiency (kitchenette, with combination dining-living-sleeping area) apartment with as little as 255 sf and a one-bedroom unit 350 sf in size (plus closets and bathroom). British standards suggest, but do not require, 320 and 480 sf, respectively.
>
> There seems to be general agreement among advocates for the elderly that new specially built housing for the elderly provides too little living space. Most people who move into such housing are, if anything, oversupplied with furniture. Moving too much into a small area will make living difficult and even unsafe, but the alternative is to part with personally meaningful possessions. Professionals in service to the elderly become irate at the imposition of such low minimum-space requirements on federally assisted housing. Our data are not yet complete in this area. However, very few tenants spontaneously complain of their units being too small.[85]

Isaac Green[86] calls for considerably larger sizes, averaging 670 sf for single-occupancy one-bedroom units, 730 sf for double-occupancy one-bedroom units, and 870 sf for two-bedroom apartments serving independent elderly; the averages are slightly higher in congregate housing. The fact is that almost no units for the elderly are built this large currently. One-bedroom apartments generally range between 500 and 600 sf in assisted housing.

Whatever has been said in this book about the various components, and their interconnections, of a typical dwelling unit by and large holds true for elderly occupants. This discussion will mainly point out where housing for the elderly is different.

Entrance. The entry should have a direct connection to closet and living space and as direct a connection as possible to the kitchen. It should be slightly wider than in ordinary dwellings, to provide a chair to sit on for putting on snowboots, for instance. Visual privacy is equally important for the elderly, but is often sacrificed in order to "minimize circulation space" in an already small apartment. This is a mistake.

Living/Dining Space. Since living/dining rooms in dwellings for the elderly are usually small, careful location of doors, windows, and circulation space is essential for maximum utility of the space. Orientation is specially important for the elderly, who spend considerably more time in an apartment than other users. North orientation with lack of sunlight should be avoided if possible. Windows should be lower to provide even wheelchair-bound elderly with an easy view out. Window sills of proper width and of proper impervious material are ideal for plants. The need for balconies is still much debated. The results of studies are unclear. Many of the elderly use the balconies infrequently, but those who use them do so often. To provide options, Lawton argues for balconies in at least 20 to 25% of the apartments. Use of balconies will depend on the location of the project, its climate, view, etc. Naturally, curbs under the balcony doors are unacceptable for the elderly. A high (42 in.) railing should be provided, and lighting or at least a waterproof outlet is highly desirable.

Kitchen. In addition to good overall illumination and strong light over the sink, daylight for and view from the kitchen are especially needed for the elderly occupant, who tends to spend a good deal of time there. This has led to such solutions as open kitchens, semiclosed kitchens with borrowed daylight, and kitchens at exterior walls with windows.

However, as Lawton warns, daylit kitchens should not be achieved "at the expense of daylight to cheer up a living area." One must also be aware of the fact that kitchens, at the exterior wall, except in corner apartments and dual-exposure units such as row houses or units in gallery-access buildings, will increase the length of the apartment and, consequently, the cost of the job. This increased length is difficult to achieve with minimum square footage units. The open kitchen in the inner zone of the apartments calls to mind another of Lawton's observations:

> Many tenants express the wish for a way to close off a dirty kitchen from view. On the other hand, there is great convenience in being able to put food directly on a table close to where the food is prepared. One might try for a solution that would allow room for a table very close to the food preparation area with a sliding door or divider that could close off the area once the table is served. Of course, many people will prefer to carry their food, perhaps to a table on the distant side from the kitchen near a window. Our research has told us that elderly tenants prepare and serve meals to others relatively infrequently. However, this occasion is an extremely important one for those who do so.[87]

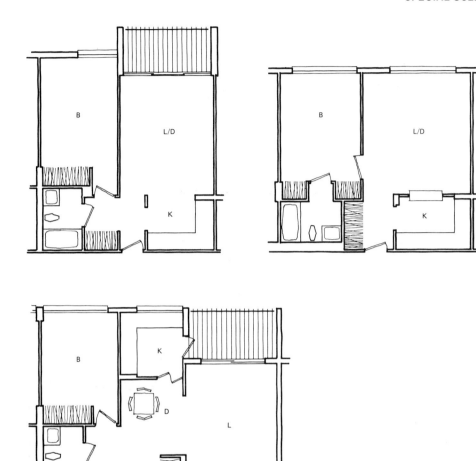

Ideally a kitchen should include space for a small table to function as a good work place or as an additional eating spot besides the dining area in the living/dining room.

Storage space and appliances must take into consideration the physical limitations of the many elderly who suffer from arthritis. Reaching high or stooping low is difficult. Reduced stamina necessitates periodic sitting down. A full-height pantry with bifold doors is a desirable amenity in addition to wall cabinets. Wall cabinets should not be located over stoves and refrigerators. Swinging doors of wall cabinets should be narrow. Sinks should have knee space under them to allow the use of stools (hot water lines and traps should be insulated to avoid burning). Electric stoves with front controls are considered safest. Undercounter ovens pose a problem, but one seldom has the luxury of a separate wall-oven of proper height. Undercounter refrigerators are obviously to be avoided. A vertically divided two-door refrigerator/freezer is obviously the best because it allows for variation in areas of reach. If this is—and it is in subsidized housing—too costly, a standard one-door refrigerator is used, the freezer should be on top for the ambulant elderly (on bottom for the wheelchair bound). Subsidized units seldom can afford dishwashers; they are more common for market-rent apartments. Garbage disposals present a special problem: although their number is increasing in elderly units, they can clearly be a hazard.

Bedroom. In dwellings for the elderly, the bedroom is used extensively, partially because older people need more frequent rest periods, partly because they are more

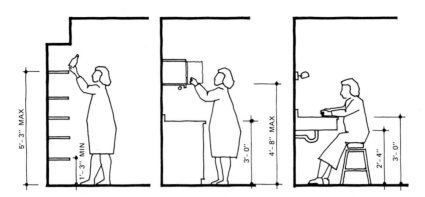

frequently bedridden. Bedrooms should be designed to accommodate twin-beds, though currently 80% of the units are singly occupied. In single-occupancy bedrooms, HUD requires, in addiion to furniture listed in the chapter on dwelling units, a 1 ft 8 in. by 3 ft 6 in. desk. All beds should be accessible on three sides. An emergency signal should be within reach of each bed. Bedrooms should have phone jacks and TV outlets.

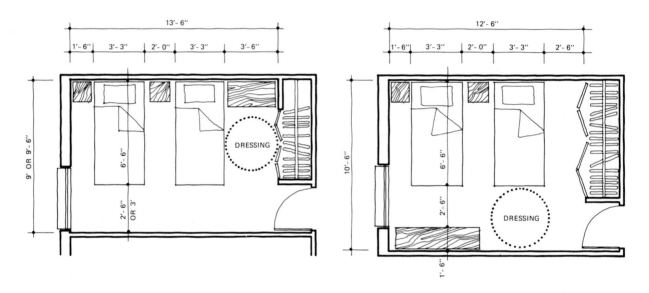

Bathroom. Both for safety and convenience, this must be a very carefully designed space in dwellings for the elderly. The need for a direct route between bedroom and bathroom is essential, especially during the night when illumination is poor. The door of the bathroom should be at least 2 ft 8 in. (similar to all other intra-apartment doors according to HUD), and it should swing out. If there is a lock, it must be operable from the outside. Grab bars are required both at the toilet and at the tub/shower. The location of the toilet next to a wall will not only accommodate a grab bar, but also a toilet-paper holder and an emergency signal. Much has been said about the relative merits of tubs or showers. Both pose hazards, the tub probably more so because it requires a step. When showers are used, one should discuss with the sponsor the desirability of shower seats (a requirement by HUD) and the use of a flexible shower nozzle. Also, if all units are designed with showers, there should be a public bath with tub at least on alternate floors. Tubs should always be nonskid, and shower heads scaldproof.

General Storage. In addition to the usual closet spaces, the elderly need some special consideration. Though they accept reduced apartment size as they move into senior

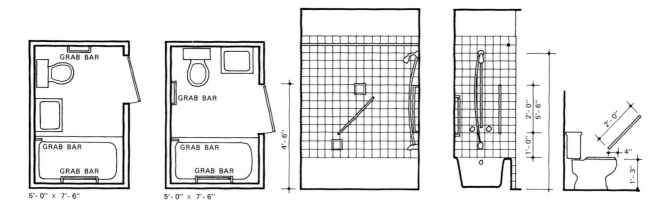

5'-0" X 7'-6"   5'-0" X 7'-6"

housing, they often would like to bring with them mementos. Adequate storage should be provided for these, preferably within the apartment.

Corridors, Elevators, Stairs. Although daylight is desirable in corridors, when a window is placed at the end it often produces glare, hurts the eye, and tends to disorient the elderly. Corridors should promote easy orientation; the corridor configuration should not be confusing. Distinct identification of floors or wings through color or graphics is suggested. Recessed apartment entry doors relieve the monotony of long

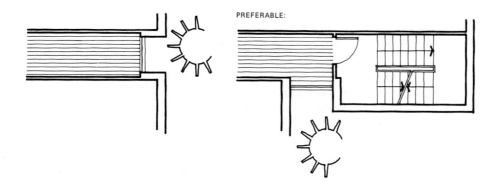

PREFERABLE:

corridors; however, the recess should not be more than 18 in. Deep recesses or sharp turns in the corridor could provide hiding places for prowlers and increase the anxiety of residents, especially in urban areas.

Daylit lounges near the elevator have been advocated by planners though they are seldom used. A small place to sit down while waiting for the elevator, however, is highly desirable. Where budgets prohibit individual balconies, Lawton recommends a shared balcony near the elevators, especially when it is shaded from the hot afternoon sun.

HUD requires handrails on at least one side of all public corridors. At least one of the elevators must be large enough for a wheelchair, and one must be a 2500-lb service type suitable for handling ambulance stretchers. There should be two-way intercoms between elevator cabs and an office or manager's apartment. Elevators should have railings. Stairs rising more than 24 in. and wider than 4 ft according to HUD requirements must have railings on both sides; risers cannot exceed 7½ in.

Entrance/Lobby/Outdoor Space. Besides being an entrance, the vestibule-lobby and/or lounge is a natural social space. It is advisable to locate the administrative space adjacent to this area, where interaction between residents and management can be fostered. Here while the mail is awaited, while the goings on of the outside world are observed, social interaction can take place. Adequate seating is essential here as well as in the covered and open sitting area in front of the entrance ("front porch"), a favorite outdoor place of the residents. Public toilets should be nearby. An entrance canopy under which residents can be dropped off is of utmost importance. Security devices are especially important for the elderly. The best, a 24-hour switchboard receptionist in the lobby, is only found in congregate housing. Otherwise, for independent housing, an intercom entrance control system is generally used. Visibility and surveillance of all entry points, advocated by Oscar Newman, is also recommended here.

In addition to the "front porch," other outdoor areas should provide a variety of options for the resident: sit in the sun or shade; sit in seclusion or in a group; play outdoor games such as shuffleboard or chess; have barbecues; do gardening; walk without barriers on well illuminated walkways without excessive slopes (HUD maximum 5%, or 1:20) and with rails when encountering steps; enjoy greenery. For sitting activity, benches should be carefully selected. They must have backs. A two-seater is preferable to a long bench. If social interaction is desired, benches should face each other or be at 90° so people can easily converse. Light but sturdy portable furniture gives maximum options in arrangement. Private outdoor places and patios should be properly defined at least by shrubbery to give a sense of territoriality.

Parking should be designed so that it allows easy circulation and prevents confusion. Both stalls and driving aisles need to be wider than usual, certainly no less than 9 ft for stalls. No parking used by the elderly should be further than 150 ft from the main entrance (or in case of enclosed parking garage from the elevator). Parking spaces should be provided for 25 to 50% of the units and should include parking for residents, employees, and visitors, the total depending on location (urban-suburban), access to shopping and to public transportation, and the economic profile of residents.

Social/Recreational. The most important place for recreation is the multipurpose room for unprogrammed socializing and programmed activities such as movies, cards, bingo, lectures, parties, pot luck meals. Its basic requirements (kitchen, storage, etc.) are not dissimilar from the community rooms for regular apartment buildings described already in this book. If it is visible through glass partition from the lobby/lounge, it can encourage participation. With movable dividers, it can also provide opportunities for individual or small group activities in relative privacy. Furnishing in a noninstitutional manner will further increase the use of this space.

A craft or hobby room, properly equipped, can serve for activities that could not take place in the multipurpose room because of the mess they create or the fixed and heavy equipment they need. Greenhouses when provided are much used.

Lastly, the laundry can be considered social space. While some planners advocate laundries on each floor to act as social magnets, Lawton's observations do not bear this out. A central laundry is indicated (using the same design criteria as those of regular housing), with comfortable seating, toilets nearby, with not only adequate daylight, but direct access to a clothesline outdoors.

In large developments one often finds other amenities (beauty salon, medical examination room, library, etc.) generally associated with congregate housing.

CONGREGATE HOUSING. Much that has been said in connection with independent housing for the elderly applies to congregate housing. Here only the differences will be pointed out.

Congregate housing serves a less independent population, one that is in need of some special services. These services might be meals and housekeeping generally provided on the premises; shopping, dressing, grooming provided in-house or by visiting aids. They generally do not include medical services except those that are of a first-aid nature or occasionally an out-patient clinic. Naturally, in communities where health or social service personnel are not available these services must be provided within the premises. Residents impaired enough to require nursing care are not part of the congregate housing population; they are served by nursing homes.

Housekeeping service means for the designer a linen room on every floor with linen shelving and cart storage in addition to a central supply room and employee facilities. Laundry is generally picked up and delivered by commercial services.

The availability of food service does not mean the elimination of kitchens in the dwelling units since not all the residents will take advantage of it. It might mean, however, reduced-size kitchens or even kitchenettes.

The central food service area consists of dining room; kitchen including food storage, preparation, dishwashing and refuse storage areas; and food service employees' facilities (lunch area, locker room, and toilets).

The dining room should be a sunny, cheerful space with the minimum institutional atmosphere. Mealtime is the height of the social day. Comfortable lounge space for the residents who anticipate the meal and come early should provide a background for socializing. Decor, not unlike that in a popular restaurant, should be stimulating, with an atmosphere (perhaps a bar with subdued lighting) that suggests an "event," not a daily chore. Seating around four-person tables should provide the majority of accommodation, with some six-person tables for larger groups. Aisle space should be larger than usual for those with canes or walkers. In the case of wheelchair-bound users, especially wide side aisles and chair-to-chair distances should be used.

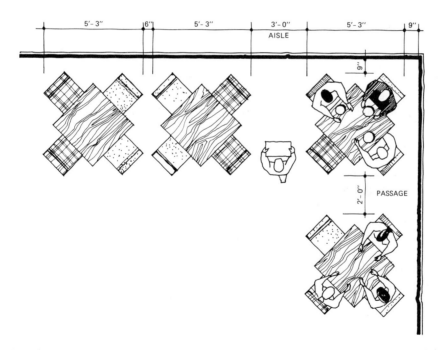

Outpatient clinics minimally consist of several examination/treatment rooms and waiting areas with adequate privacy and toilet access.

Social services, counseling, and delivery of other supports to the residents usually occur in office spaces that are part of an enlarged administration area consisting of receptionist (facing the lobby and providing an added sense of security), waiting space, manager's office, and office(s) for social worker(s), visiting psychiatrist(s), or agency personnel; a small conference room to discuss cases is most useful.

Some congregate housing projects for the elderly provide specialized social spaces

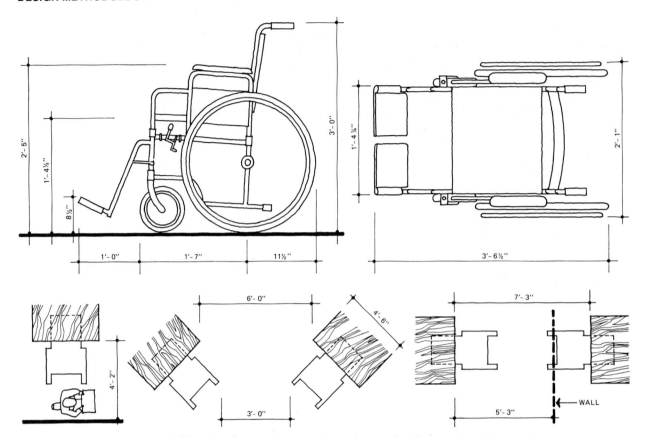

not generally found in independent housing: card and game rooms, library, music room. Some provide gift shop/commissary spaces, often run by the residents themselves. One facility in Canada has not only a resident-run commissary, but also tailor shop, cleaner, coffee shop, satellite post office, and small branch bank, all managed by the elderly residents themselves.

COMMUNAL HOUSING.   A new concept in housing for the aged pioneered by the Council for Jewish Elderly in Chicago is a small communal facility where a limited—up to 24—number of senior citizens share household chores. Each person has an individual bedroom and bath (arranged in clusters of four around common living rooms and snack kitchens) and is expected to participate in cooking, housekeeping, and group planning activities. Common facilities such as communal living room, laundry, craft room, greenhouse, conference room form the core of the building and are shared by all residents. The entire group prepares and eats lunch and dinner together in the central dining area, served by a large kitchen. Staffing is minimal, the idea being to promote self-help and independence with group support for elderly who otherwise could not function independently or perhaps not even in a congregate setting (see illustration on page 265).

HANDICAPPED

Progress in medical science not only expanded the average life span, but also increased the survival rate of wounded soldiers and victims of accident or disease. Many of these survivors are disabled or physically handicapped and are able with current technology to live productive lives. The increased number of the handicapped during the past decade has spotlighted the shortcomings of our environment in accommodating them.

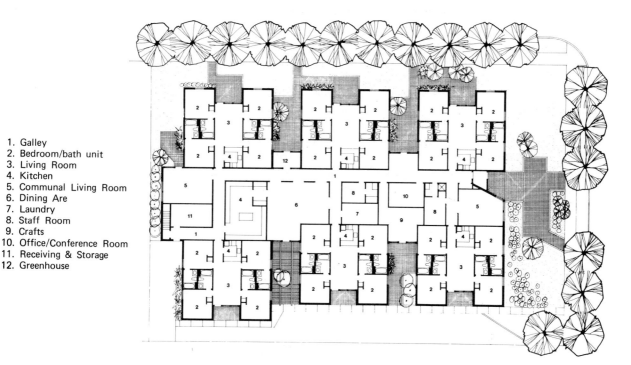

1. Galley
2. Bedroom/bath unit
3. Living Room
4. Kitchen
5. Communal Living Room
6. Dining Are
7. Laundry
8. Staff Room
9. Crafts
10. Office/Conference Room
11. Receiving & Storage
12. Greenhouse

Of the various kinds of handicapped people, blind and the deaf need less adjustment in their physical environments, those suffering from locomotion difficulties and especially those temporarily or permanently in wheelchairs have space needs that make the greatest demands on the designer. Since the problems of the handicapped have only recently been properly identified, regulations governing design are new and sometimes untried. Furthermore, federal (HUD, ANSI*), state and local codes not only overlap, but also differ. It is, therefore, essential that the architect become thoroughly familiar with the standards for the handicapped governing the building to be designed.

The first step of such familiarity is to know what are the public areas of the building that must be accessible to the handicapped and what number of dwelling units are to be designed for handicapped occupancy. Most local, state, and federal regulations agree on public areas; where they differ is the number of dwelling units to be available for the handicapped. HUD requires public space accessibility (using ANSI standards) in all housing for the elderly and in all other housing with 25 or more dwelling units. HUD sets the number of dwellings to be suitable for the handicapped at 10% of each dwelling unit type in buildings designed for the elderly. Half of these units must have kitchens accessible for the handicapped. Naturally, one could ask why all public spaces and all apartments should not be available for the handicapped? The current answer is obviously cost.

Accessibility standards do not ditinguish between the young war veteran and the arthritic elderly in wheelchairs. When providing a barrier-free environment for the elderly handicapped, one should keep in mind that the majority of older people do not operate wheelchairs with the facility of younger persons; wheeling strokes are short; the movement of the chair is wobbly; the turning radius is larger; elbows are more extended. If there is a conflict in the standards to be followed, it is well to use the strictest when designing for the elderly.

Occasionally, codes and well-meaning proposed standards conflict. A refrigerator should have its freezer compartment on the top for the ambulatory elderly; this cannot

*American National Standards Institute, New York

365

DESIGN METHODOLOGY

be reached from a wheelchair! HUD requires the bathroom door to swing out, a security measure in case the older persons faints and collapses against the door and would otherwise block help from entering; for the younger person in a wheelchair, it is much easier to enter a bathroom if the door swings in, presuming there is a 5-ft radius space in the bathroom to get out of the way of the door swing. Should the door viewer be placed for the wheelchair-bound so the ambulant elderly has to bend down? In such cases, special foresight is required of the designer as well as of the sponsor.

Five percent of the required parking should be for the handicapped (HUD), stalls should be at least 12 ft 6 in. wide. Walks from a parking area to the main entrance should be as short and direct as possible, with a maximum gradient of 5% (1:20) and a width of 5 ft to accommodate two wheelchairs passing. Joints in walks should be narrow, grating hole widths minimum, and curb cuts should slope no more than 1:12 (8.33%).

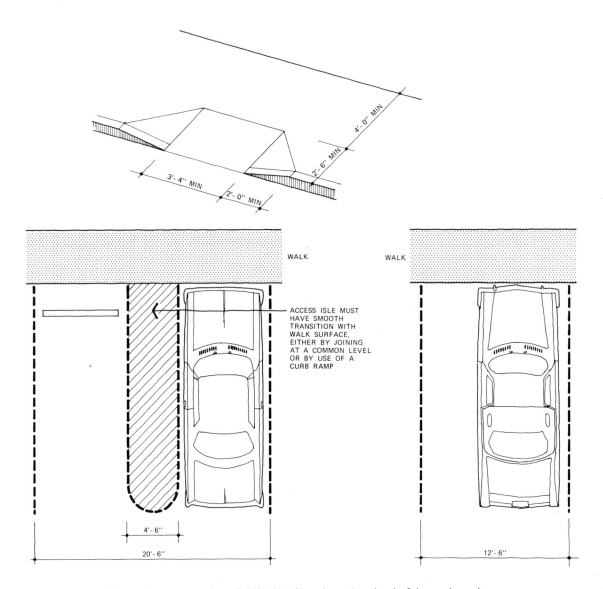

Ramps should not slope more than 8.33% (1:12) unless the rise is 3 in. or less, in which case 1:8 is acceptable; ramps should be 4 ft wide with adequate horizontal clearance both at top and at bottom. Because handrails are used by some wheelchair-bound persons to pull themselves up a ramp, an additional lower handrail should be provided. Even ramps of 3-ft width are acceptable except when the ramp changes direction; with a 180° turn there should be a platform at least 8 ft by 5 ft; with a 90° turn, one 5 ft by 4 ft. Entrance vestibules must be deep enough for a wheelchair. Thresholds are to be avoided or should have feathered edges. Elevators should be sized for wheelchair users (minimum 4 ft 3 in. by 5 ft 8 in. clear inside). Elevator controls, indicators, apartment door handles, all should be planned to be within the reach of the wheelchair-bound. Elevator door timing should be slowed down. Corridors must be 5 ft

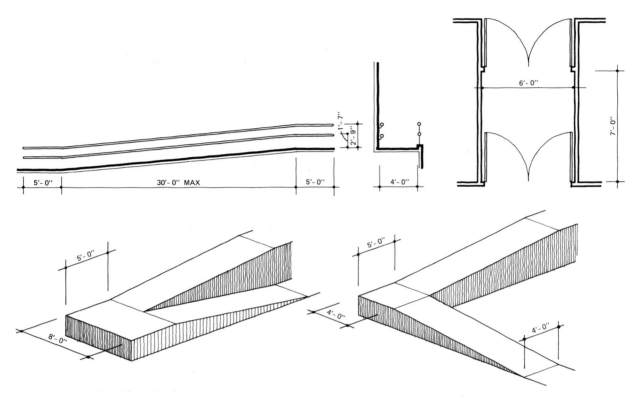

wide to allow passage and proper turning space. In stairs HUD sets maximum riser at 7½ in. and prohibits open risers. Square nosings should also be avoided for the handicapped; bevelled or rounded nosings are acceptable.

Within the apartment, HUD calls for a 3 ft 4 in. minimum corridor width and for all doors to have at least 2 ft 8 in. clear opening (which means 2 ft 10 in. door). Experiments indicate that with 2 ft 8 in. clear opening the corridor should be 3 ft 6 in.; however, if the clear door opening could be increased to 3 ft, the corridor could be reduced to a 3-ft width, and the wheelchair would have adequate space for a 90° turn.

One of the most important requirements (not covered by HUD, but by other agencies) is the space needed for the occupant of a wheelchair to open a door when the door opens toward the wheelchair.

This permits the person using the wheelchair to pull open the door without the need to roll backward. The level difference between floors is critical. If the difference is more than ½ in., or if the level change is not at least 45° beveled, manipulating the wheelchair is extremely difficult. The type of flooring is also important. Deeppile carpets and soft padding are obstacles for the wheelchair-bound person.

Needless to say, all controls (switches, thermostats, call buttons, air conditioner controls, window hardware, etc.) must be within easy reach from the wheelchair; a 3 ft 6 in. height is ideal although 4 ft is acceptable 1 ft 6 in. above the floor is best though 12 in. is still reachable.

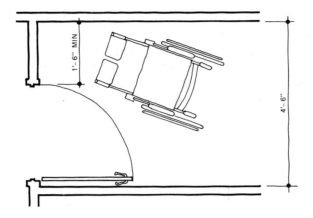

In bedrooms, since it is essential that the long side of each bed can be approached by a wheelchair, aisles must be 3 ft. Space in front of chests of drawers should be 3 ft 6 in. Space between closets (especially those with bifold doors) and beds should ideally be 5 ft to allow the wheelchair to turn around. HUD requires that one clothes rod in a closet should be adjustable to 48 in.

Bathrooms pose a complex set of problems. In addition to the grab bars required for the elderly, HUD calls for the bathtub to be accessible along its entire length. When showers are used, they cannot have a curb and must have a minimum dimension of 4 ft by 4 ft. HUD also calls for shower seats. Other authorities on the subject go even further than HUD on barrier-free design for bathrooms. They pay special attention to the space requirements of various transfer methods from wheelchair to toilet. There is no complete agreement on just how far one should go in this regard. Experience indicates that the 5-ft radius for turning around is not necessary when the bathroom is properly arranged: the water closet parallel to a wall long enough to install a grab bar; water

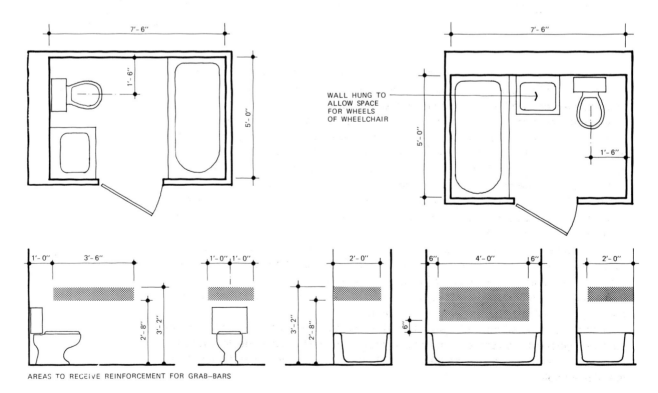

AREAS TO RECEIVE REINFORCEMENT FOR GRAB-BARS

closet center line 18 in from the wall; wall-hung lavatory between tub and toilet; tub located so that a person can pull up parallel to it; and tub controls on the wall the person is facing. When lavatory counters are used, they should be high enough to allow wheelchairs to roll under. The edge of the counter should have a rail for the wheelchair-bound to hold for getting up from the chair. A medicine cabinet is preferable on the side, or the handicapped may not be able to reach it across the counter.

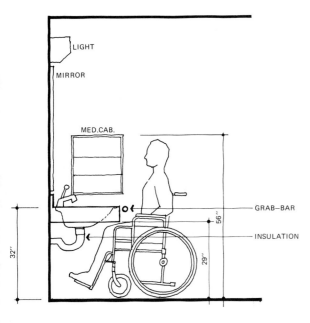

Kitchens, in addition to the features suggested for the elderly, should have adequate floor space for the wheelchair, and eating-kitchens should be sized accordingly.

Special consideration should be given to the type of refrigerator, counter open space (wheelchair clearance under the counter), and stove, oven, and storage space to be provided.

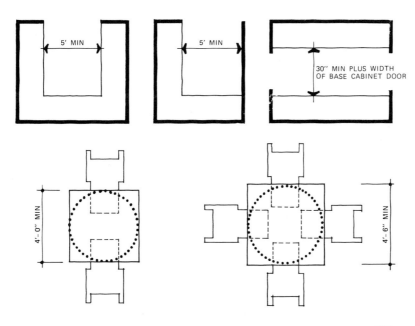

DESIGN METHODOLOGY

In public areas, all authorities require at least one lavatory and one water closet for each sex to be suitable for the wheelchair user according to ANSI (adequate manuvering space; one stall 5 ft wide). If there are public phones and drinking fountains, HUD requires one of them to be a height accessible for people in wheelchairs. In laundries, at least one washer and one dryer should be front-loading with front coin slots.

NOTES

1. *Form in Civilization*, W. R. Lethaby, Oxford University Press, London, 1957.

2. *Conversations with Architects*, J. W. Cook and H. Klotz, Praeger, New York, 1973.

3. "Theory in Practice," Robert Geddes, *Architectural Forum*, September 1972.

4. "Architecture, Psychology: The Passion Has Passed," Robert Sommer, *A.I.A. Journal*, April 1980.

5. *The Failure of Modern Architecture*, Brent C. Brolin, Van Nostrand Reinhold, New York, 1976.

6. *Apartments, Their Design and Development*, Samuel Paul, Reinhold, New York, 1967.

7. "Zoning Laws: The Case for Repeal," David J. Mandel, *Architectural Forum*, December 1971.

8. *The Zoning Game*, Richard F. Babcock, University of Wisconsin Press, Madison, 1969.

9. *Housing Quality, A Program for Zoning Reform*, Urban Design Council of the City of New York, 1973.

10. *Death and Life of Great American Cities*, Jane Jacobs, Random House, New York, 1961.

11. *The Zoning Game*, op. cit.

12. *The Zoning Game*, op. cit.

13. *Housing Quality, A Program for Zoning Reform*, op. cit.

14. *Housing Quality, A Program for Zoning Reform*, op. cit.

15. *Apartments, Their Design and Development*, op. cit.

16. *Modern Housing Prototypes*, Roger Sherwood, Harvard University Press, Cambridge, Mass. 1978.

17. *Experiencing Architecture*, Steen Eiler Rasmussen, M.I.T. Press, Cambridge, Mass., 1959.

18. *Multistory Housing*, Karl Wilhelm Schmitt, Praeger, New York, 1966.

19. "What Should Chicago Do About High-rise Fires," Nory Miller, *Inland Architect*, August 1974.

20. *Defensible Space*, Oscar Newman, Macmillan, New York, 1972.

21. *Defensible Space*, op. cit.

22. *Residents' Satisfaction in HUD Assisted Housing: Design and Management Factors*, R. Francescato, S. Weideman, J. Anderson, and R. Chenoweth, U.S. Department of Housing and Urban Development, Washington, D.C., 1979.

23. *Defensible Space*, op. cit.

24. *Community of Interest*, Oscar Newman, Anchor/Doubleday, New York, 1980.

25. "People/Plant Proxemics: A Concept for Humane Design," P. Snedfeld and J. Russel, eds., *The Behavioral Basis of Design*, Dowden, Hutchinson & Ross, Stroudsburg, Pa., 1976.

26. *Living in Towns*, L. Kuper, ed., Cresset, London, 1953.

NOTES

27. *Residents' Satisfaction in HUD Assisted Housing: Design and Management Factors*, op. cit.

28. *Residents' Satisfaction in HUD Assisted Housing: Design and Management Factors*, op. cit.

29. *Architectural Environment and Our Mental Health*, C. Moller, Horgen, New York, 1968.

30. *Residents' Satisfaction in HUD Assisted Housing: Design and Management Factors*, op. cit.

31. *Planned Residential Environments*, J. Lansing, R. Marans, and R. Zehner, Institute for Social Research, Ann Arbor, Mich., 1970.

32. *Residential Crowding in Urban America*, M. Baldassare, University of California Press, Berkeley, 1979.

33. *Residents' Satisfaction in HUD Assisted Housing: Design and Management Factors*, op. cit.

34. "The Evolution of Housing Concepts 1870–1970," K. Frampton, *Lotus International* Vol. 10, No. 2.

35. *Residents' Satisfaction in HUD Assisted Housing: Design and Management Factors*, op. cit.

36. *Residents' Satisfaction in HUD Assisted Housing: Design and Management Factors*, op. cit.

37. *Residents' Satisfaction in HUD Assisted Housing: Design and Management Factors*, op. cit.

38. *Complexity and Contradiction in Architecture*, Robert Venturi, Museum of Modern Art, New York, 1966.

39. *Housing Messages*, F. Becker, Dowden, Hutchinson and Ross, Stroudsburg, Pa., 1977.

40. *Men's Perception of Man-made Environment—an Architectural Theory*, Sven Hesselgren, Dowden, Hutchinson and Ross, Stroudsburg, Pa., 1975.

41. *Residents' Satisfaction in HUD Assisted Housing: Design and Management Factors*, op. cit.

42. *Understanding the Causes of Appreciation of Outdoor Spaces in Multifamily Housing* (working paper), J. Anderson and D. Butterfield, Housing Research and Development, Urbana, Ill. 1980.

43. *Housing Messages*, op. cit.

44. "A Model of Preference: Quantitative Analysis of the Perception of the Visual Appearance of Residential Neighborhoods," G. Peterson, *Journal of Regional Science*, Summer, 1967.

45. *Housing Messages*, op. cit.

46. "A Technique for the Subjective Appraisal of Buildings," D. Cantor and R. Wools, *Building Science*, December, 1970.

47. *Modern Housing Prototypes*, op. cit.

48. *The Failure of Modern Architecture*, op. cit.

49. *Complexity and Contradiction in Architecture*, op. cit.

50. *The Dynamics of Architectural Form*, Rudolf Arnheim, University of California Press, Berkeley, 1977.

51. *Experiencing Architecture*, op. cit.

52. "Beyond Golden Lane, Robin Hood Gardens," Anthony Pangaro, *Architecture Plus*, June 1973.

53. *The Dynamics of Architectural Form*, op. cit.

54. *A Place to Live*, Wolf von Eckardt, Dell, New York, 1967.

55. *Conversations with Architects*, op. cit.

56. *Modern Movements in Architecture*, Charles Jencks, Anchor/Doubleday, New York, 1973.

57. *The Dynamics of Architectural Form*, op. cit.

58. *Complexity and Contradiction in Architecture*, op. cit.

59. *The Dynamics of Architectural Form*. op. cit.

60. *Conversations with Architects*, op. cit.

61. *Architecture of Humanism*, Geoffrey Scott, Doubleday, New York, 1924.

62. *Dimensions*, Charles Moore and Gerald Allen, Architectural Record Books, New York, 1976.

63. *The Dynamics of Architectural Form*, op. cit.

64. *The Dynamics of Architectural Form*, op. cit.

65. *The Form of Housing*, Sam Davis, ed., Van Nostrand Reinhold, New York, 1977.

66. *The Form of Housing*, op. cit.

67. *Site Planning for Cluster Housing*, Richard Untermann and Robert Small, Van Nostrand Reinhold, New York, 1977.

68. *The Form of Housing*, op. cit.

69. "Teaching a Contextual Architecture," Merrill C. Gaines, *Journal of Architectural Education*, Spring 1980.

70. *Defensible Space*, *op. cit.*

71. *The Form of Housing*, *op. cit.*

72. *Site Planning*, Kevin Lynch, M.I.T. Press, Cambridge, Mass., 1971.

73. *Site Planning*, *op. cit.*

74. *The Form of Housing*, *op. cit.*

75. *Introduction to Urban Planning*, Anthony J. Catanese and James C. Snyder, eds., McGraw-Hill, New York, 1979.

76. *Site Planning*, *op.cit.*

77. *Exterior Design in Architecture*, Yoshinobu Ashihara, Van Nostrand Reinhold, New York, 1970.

78. *The Dynamics of Architectural Form*, *op. cit.*

79. *Exterior Design in Architecture*, *op. cit.*

80. *Townscape*, Gordon Cullen, Reinhold, New York, 1961.

81. *Site Planning*, *op. cit.*

82. *Spatial Behavior of Older People*, Leon A. Pastalan and Daniel H. Carson, eds., University of Michigan, Ann Arbor, 1970.

83. *Planning and Managing Housing for the Elderly*, M. Powell Lawton, John Wiley, New York, 1975.

84. *Planning and Managing Housing for the Elderly*, *op. cit.*

85. *Planning and Managing Housing for the Elderly*, *op. cit.*

86. *Housing for the Elderly*, Isaac Green et al., Van Nostrand Reinhold, New York, 1975.

87. *Planning and Managing Housing for the Elderly*, *op. cit.*

PROJECTS

Highrise—Central Corridor

1. Ludwig Mies van der Rohe: Lafayette Towers, Detroit, Michigan
2. Stanley Tigerman: Boardwalk, Chicago, Illinois
3. I. M. Pei & Partners: University Plaza, New York, New York
4. I. M. Pei & Partners: Washington Square East, Philadelphia, Pennsylvania
5. Solomon, Cordwell, Buenz & Associates: Hawthorn House, Chicago, Illinois
6. Paul Rudolph: Crawford Manor, New Haven, Connecticut
7. Davis Brody & Associates: 2440 Boston Road, Bronx, New York
8. Gruzen & Partners: Arthur Schomburg Plaza, New York, New York
9. Gilbert Switzer & Associates: Sbona Towers & Senior Center, Middletown, Connecticut
10. Keyes, Lethbridge & Condon: Tiber Island, Washington, D.C.
11. Backen Arrigoni & Ross: 2000 Broadway, San Francisco, California
12. John Sharratt Associates: Villa Victoria/Torre Unidad Elderly, Boston, Massachusetts

Highrise—Exterior Corridor

13. William Morgan: Oceanfront Condominium, Ocean City, Maryland
14. The Hodne/Stageberg Partners: 1199 Plaza, New York, New York

Highrise—Multicore

15. Hausner & Macsai: Harbor House, Chicago, Illinois
16. Hausner & Macsai: 1500 Sheridan Road, Wilmette, Illinois

Highrise—Point block

17. Bertrand Goldberg Associates: Marina City, Chicago, Illinois
18. Gruzen & Partners: Arthur Schomburg Plaza, New York, New York
19. Skidmore, Owings & Merrill: Dorchester Apartments, Chicago, Illinois
20. Hausner & Macsai: 1110 Lake Shore Drive, Chicago, Illinois
21. Ezra Gordon—Jack Levin: Newberry Plaza, Chicago, Illinois
22. Thorsen & Thorshov Associates: Ebenezer Towers, Minneapolis, Minnesota
23. Freerks/Sperl/Flynn: 727 Front Avenue, St. Paul, Minnesota
24. Schipporeit & Heinrich: Lake Point Tower, Chicago, Illinois

PROJECTS

25. Hoberman & Wasserman: Southview Towers, Rochester, New York
26. Solomon, Cordwell, Buenz & Associates: 1555 N. Astor, Chicago, Illinois
27. Conklin & Rossant: Monument East, Baltimore, Maryland
28. Barber & McMurry: Rokeby Condominiums, Nashville, Tennessee
29. Davis Brody & Associates: Waterside, New York, New York
30. Conklin & Rossant: Two Charles Center, Baltimore, Maryland
31. Harry Weese & Associates and Ezra Gordon–Jack Levin: Lake Village, Chicago, Illinois

Highrise—Skip stop

32. Prentice & Chan, Ohlhausen: Twin Park Northwest Site 4, Bronx, New York
33. Davis Brody & Associates: Riverbend, New York, New York
34. Giovanni Pasanella Associates: Twin Parks West Sites 10–12, Bronx, New York
35. Hoberman & Wasserman: Coney Island Site 5/6, Brooklyn, New York
36. Sert, Jackson and Associates: Roosevelt Island, Parcel 3, New York, New York
37. Davis Brody & Associates: East Midtown Plaza, New York, New York

Midrise

38. Ezra Gordon-Jack Levin: South Commons, Chicago, Illinois
39. Solomon, Cordwell, Buenz & Associates: 1555 Sandburg Terrace, Chicago, Illinois
40. John Sharratt Associates: James Cleveland Building, Keene, New Hampshire
41. John Macsai & Associates: Triumvera Midrises, Chicago, Illinois
42. Booth/Hansen Associates: Dearborn Park Midrises, Chicago, Illinois
43. Gruzen & Partners: Maple Knoll Village, Springdale, Ohio
44. Nagle, Hartray & Associates: Highland Park Housing for the Elderly, Highland Park, Illinois
45. Diamond & Myers: Dundas/Sherbourne Housing, Toronto, Ontario
46. Diamond & Myers: Hydro Block, Toronto, Ontario
47. Freedman/Clements/Rumpel: Florida Christian Home Apartments, Jacksonville, Florida
48. Aubrey J. Greenberg & Associates: Four Lake Village Apartments, Lisle, Illinois
49. Donald Sandy Jr./James A. Babcock: Portobella, Oakland, California
50. R. E. Hulbert and Partners: The Fairways, Coquitlan, British Columbia
51. Hausner & Macsai: Winnetka House, Winnetka, Illinois
52. Schipporeit, Inc: Garden House, Maywood, Illinois

Lowrise—Cluster

53. William Morgan Associates: Sea Gardens, Seminole Beach, Florida
54. R. H. Hulbert and Partners: Greenside, Surrey, British Columbia
55. The Mithun Associates: Sammamish Shores Condominiums, Bellevue, Washington
56. The Mithun Associates: Sahalee Village Condominiums, Redmond, Washington

Lowrise—Row house

57. Keyes, Lethbridge & Condon: Tiber Island, Washington, D.C.
58. Booth & Nagle: Atrium, Elmhurst, Illinois
59. Harry Weese & Associates and Ezra Gordon–Jack Levin: Lake Village, Chicago, Illinois
60. Booth/Hansen & Associates: Briar/Orchard Townhouses, Chicago, Illinois
61. Louis Sauer Associates: Second Street Townhouses, Philadelphia, Pennsylvania
62. Barton Myers Associates: Ghent Square, Norfolk, Virginia
63. Nagle, Hartray & Associates: Davids' Plaza, Chicago, Illinois
64. Louis Sauer Associates: Canterbury Garden Co-op, New Haven, Connecticut

Lowrise—Matrix

65. Backen Arrigoni & Ross: Tustin Apartments, Tustin, California
66. Werner Seligman and Associates: Elm Street Housing, Ithaca, New York

Lowrise—Walk-up/Core Type

67. Joe J. Jordan: Reno Street Public Housing, Philadelphia, Pennsylvania
68. Harry Weese & Associates and Ezra Gordon–Jack Levin: Lake Village, Chicago, Illinois
69. Esherick Homsey Dodge and Davis: Banneker Homes, San Francisco, California
70. Marquis & Stroller: St. Francis Square, San Francisco, California
71. Paul Rudolph: Buffalo Waterfront Housing, Buffalo, New York

Lowrise—Walk-up/Corridor Type

72. Booth & Nagle: Portals, Chicago, Illinois
73. Donald Sandy Jr./James A. Babcock: University Park, Ithaca, New York
74. Werner Seligman and Associates: Elm Street Housing, Ithaca, New York
75. Brent Goldman Robbins & Brown: Esplanade Village, Redondo Beach, California
76. Martin/Soderstrom/Matteson: East Burnside, Portland, Oregon
77. Antoine Predock: The Citadel, Alburquerque, New Mexico

Lowrise—Walk-up/Mixed

78. Collins & Kronstadt: Sursum Corda, Washington, D.C.
79. Charles W. Moore Associates: Church Street South, New Haven, Connecticut
80. William T. Cannady & Associates: Lovett Square, Houston, Texas
81. Fisher-Friedman-Associates: Promontory Point, Newport Beach, California
82. Fisher-Friedman-Associates: The Islands, Foster City, California
83. Louis Sauer Associates: Penn's Landing Square, Philadelphia, Pennsylvania
84. Louis Sauer Associates: Lombard Condo's, Philadelphia, Pennsylvania
85. Henriquez & Partners: False Creek Cooperative, Vancouver, British Columbia
86. Moshe Safdie and Associates: Coldspring New Town, Baltimore, Maryland
87. The Institute for Architecture and Urban Studies/David Todd & Associates: Marcus Garvey Park Village, Brownsville, New York

PROJECTS

1

LAFAYETTE TOWERS
Detroit, Michigan

Architect:
LUDWIG MIES VAN DER ROHE
Chicago, Illinois

Number of dwelling units: 292 @2 buildings
  94—Efficiency @2
  118—one bedroom @2
  74—two bedroom @2
  6—three bedroom @2
 Gross floor area: 594,000 sf (including garage)
 Construction cost: $8,000,000 approximately (including garage)
       $13.47/sf
       $13,700/unit
 Year of bid: 1961
 Site area: 9.5 acres
      30.5 units/acre
 User: middle income
 Financing: FHA 220

Photo credit: Baltazar Korab

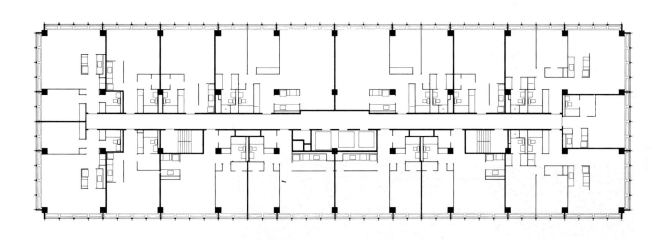

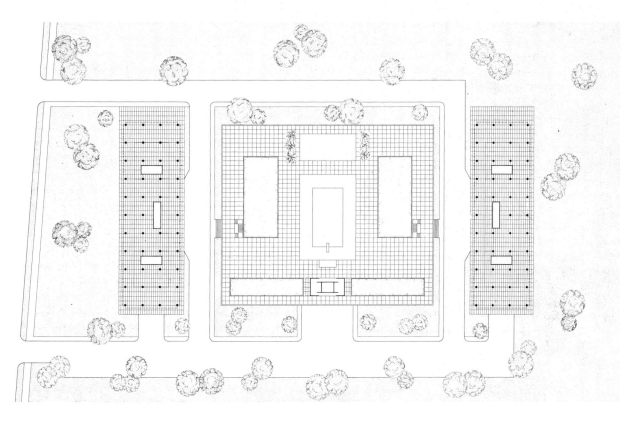

2 BOARDWALK
Chicago, Illinois

Architect:
STANLEY TIGERMAN
Chicago, Illinois

Number of dwelling units: 450
    150—Efficiency
    200—one bedroom
    100—two bedroom
  Gross floor area: 526,000 sf (including garage)
Construction cost: $8,500,000
                $16.15/sf
                $18,889/unit
    Year of bid: 1972
      Site area: 1.35 acres
              333.5 units/acre
         User: Middle income
    Financing: FHA 221 (d) 4

Photo credit: Ruyell Ho

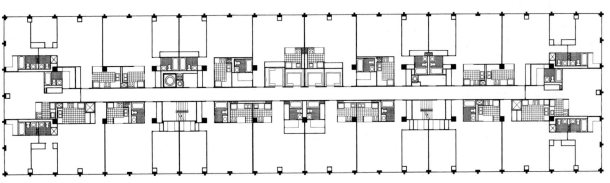

BOARDWALK 383

3

UNIVERSITY PLAZA
New York, New York

Architect:
I. M. PEI & PARTNERS
New York, New York

Number of dwelling units: 177 @3
    2—efficiency @3
    58—one bedroom @3
    59—two bedroom @3
    58—three bedroom @3
  Gross floor area: 795,000 sf (including garage)
Construction cost: $11,367,000
    $14.29/sf
    $21,407/unit
    Year of bid: 1964
    Site area: 4.86 acres
    109 units/acre
    User: middle income
    Financing: 2 towers—New York State Dormitory Authority
    1 tower—New York City Mitchell-Lama

Photo credit: George Cserna

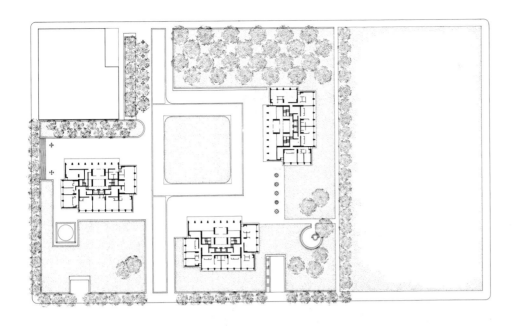

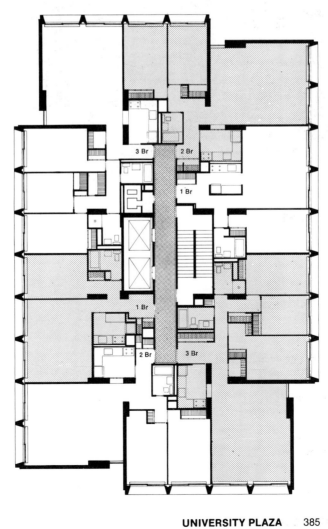

3 Br

2 Br

1 Br

1 Br

2 Br

3 Br

4

WASHINGTON SQUARE EAST
Philadelphia, Pennsylvania

Architect:
I. M. PEI & PARTNERS
New York, New York

Number of dwelling units: 240 @3 buildings
      30—efficiency @3
    150—one bedroom @3
     60—two bedroom @3
  Gross floor area: 937,350 sf (including garage)
Construction cost: $12,659,000
                $13.50/sf
                $17,582/unit
     Year of bid: 1962
       Site area: 4.2 acres
                170 units/acre
          User: middle income
    Financing: FHA

Photo credit: George Cserna

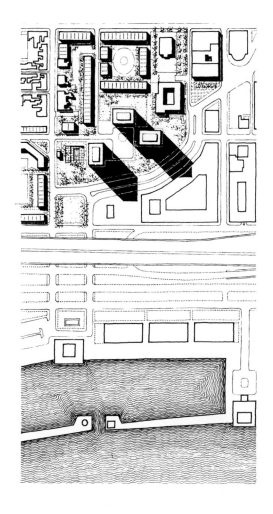

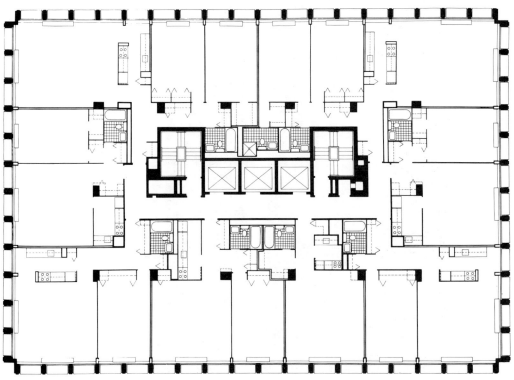

5   HAWTHORNE HOUSE
Chicago, Illinois

Architect:
SOLOMON, CORDWELL, BUENZ & ASSOCIATES
Chicago, Illinois

Number of dwelling units: 456
    108—efficiency
    240—one bedroom
    108—two bedroom
Gross floor area: 508,700 sf (including garage)
Construction cost: $9,363,000
                $18.40/sf
                $20,533/unit
Year of bid: 1966
Site area: 1.28 acres
                356 units/acre
User: middle to upper income
Financing: conventional

Photo credit: Orlando Cabanban

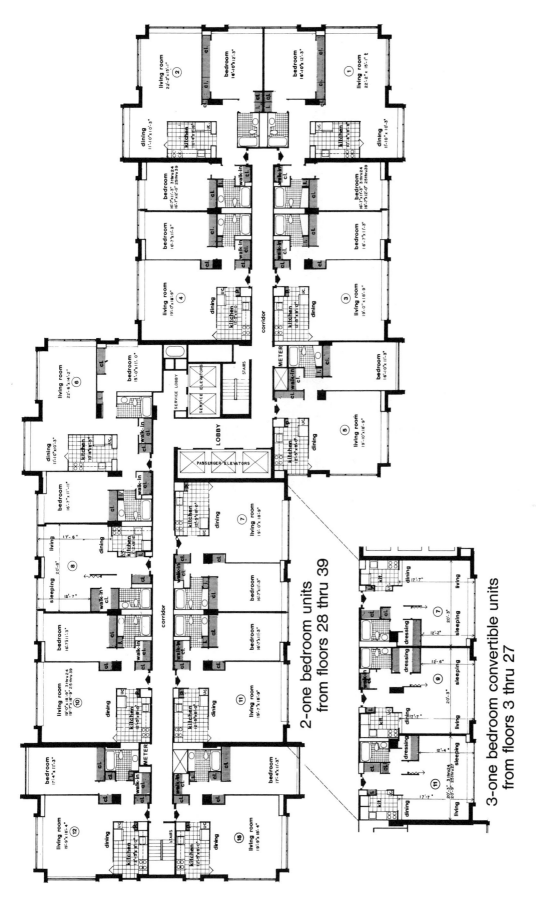

2-one bedroom units from floors 28 thru 39

3-one bedroom convertible units from floors 3 thru 27

6

CRAWFORD MANOR
New Haven, Connecticut

Architect:
PAUL RUDOLPH
New York, New York

Number of dwelling units: 109
    52—efficiency
    52—one bedroom
     5—two bedroom
  Gross floor area: 60,615 (open, on grade parking)
Construction cost: $1,003,000 (+ approximately $383,000 site work)
                 $16.55/sf (not including site work)
                 $9200/unit (not including site work)
    Year of bid: 1964
      Site area: 0.75 acres
               145 units/acre
         User: elderly
    Financing: public housing

Photo credit: Robert Perron

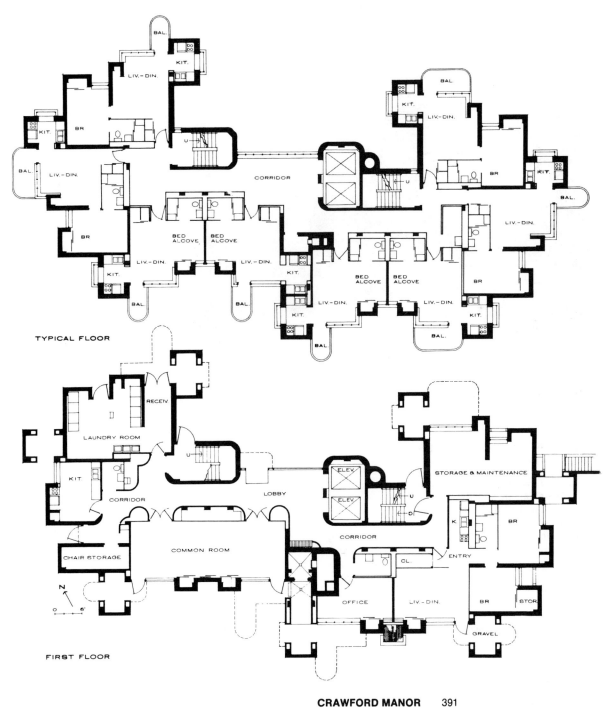

TYPICAL FLOOR

FIRST FLOOR

N

0   6'

CRAWFORD MANOR   391

7

2440 BOSTON ROAD
Bronx, New York

Architect:
DAVIS BRODY & ASSOCIATES
New York, New York

Number of dwelling units: 235
  39—efficency (elderly)
  156—one bedroom (elderly)
  40—two bedroom
 Gross floor area: 175,390 sf (on grade, open parking)
Construction cost: $5,200,000 (+ $400,000 site development)
       $29.64/sf (+ site development)
       $22,128/unit (+ site development)
  Year of bid: 1970
   Site area: 1.95 acres
       120.5 units/acre
     User: low income—elderly
   Financing: state financed

Photo credit: Norman McGrath

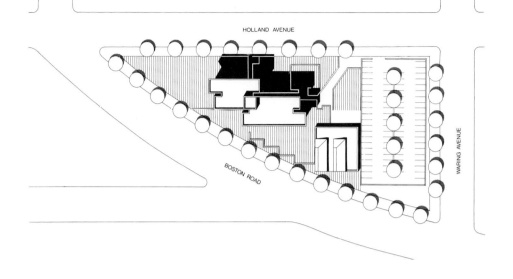

TYPICAL UPPER FLOOR

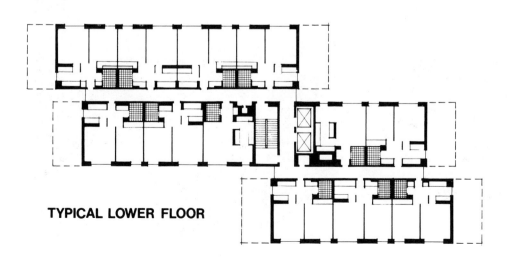

TYPICAL LOWER FLOOR

8 ARTHUR SCHOMBURG PLAZA
New York, New York

Architect:
GRUZEN & PARTNERS
New York, New York

Number of dwelling units: 600
      Towers: 17—efficiency @2
               68—one bedroom @2
            102—two bedroom @2
     Central   85—three bedroom @2
   Corridor: 28—four bedroom
            28—five bedroom
  Cross floor area: 585,530 sf
              462,000 sf towers
               85,460 sf central corridor
               31,600 sf community
                6,470 sf retail
Construction cost: $23,000,000 (including garage, community and retail)
              $39.28 sf
              $38,333/unit
    Year of bid: 1971
     Site area: 1.83 acres
              328 units/acre
         User: 60% moderate income
              30% low income
              10% elderly
     Financing: New York State Urban Development Corporation

Photo credit: David Hirsch

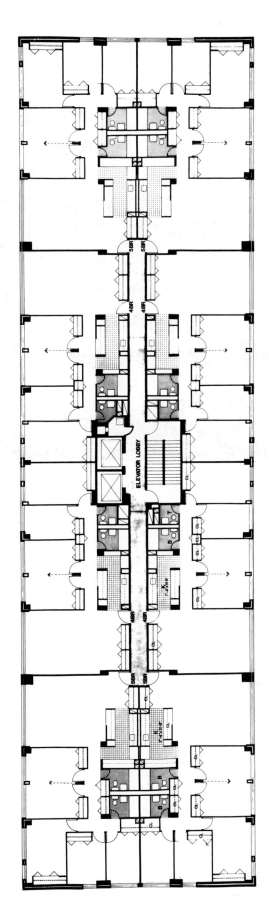

SBONA TOWER AND SENIOR CENTER
Middletown, Connecticut

Architect:
GILBERT SWITZER & ASSOCIATES
New Haven, Connecticut

Number of dwelling units: 129
    82—efficiency
    47—one bedroom
  Gross floor area: 95,730 sf (including Senior Center)
Construction cost: $2,132,000 (including Senior Center)
                  $22.27/sf
                  $16,527/unit
    Year of bid: 1970
      Site area: 2.23 acres
                58 units/acre
         User: elderly: low, middle, upper
    Financing: HUD Turnkey

Photo credit: Thomas A. Brown

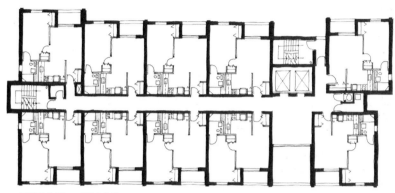

TYPICAL FLOOR

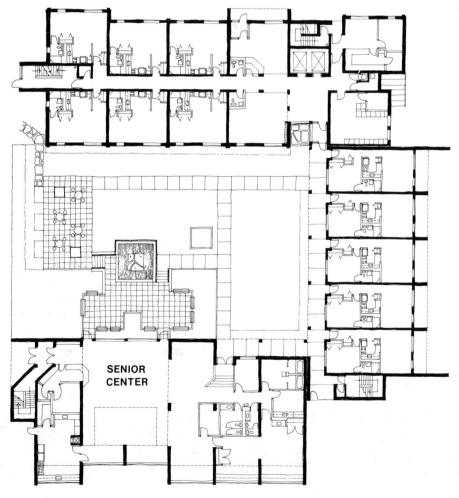

SENIOR
CENTER

FIRST FLOOR

10　TIBER ISLAND
Washington, D.C.

Architect:
KEYS, LETHBRIDGE & CONDON
Washington, D.C.

Number of dwelling units:　453
　　　　　Highrise:　160—efficiency
　　　　　　　　　　120—one bedroom
　　　　　　　　　　 80—two bedroom
　　　Townhouses:　 60—two bedroom
　　　　　　　　　　 25—four bedroom
　Gross floor area:　446,000 sf highrises
　　　　　　　　　　186,000 sf townhouses
　　　　　　　　　　103,000 sf garage
Construction cost:　$8,508,000
　　　　　　　　　　$5,670,000 highrise
　　　　　　　　　　$11.35 sf (including garage and half site development)
　　　　　　　　　　$16,937/unit (including garage and half site development)
　　　　　　　　　　$2,161,000 townhouses
　　　　　　　　　　$12.22 sf (including half site development)
　　　　　　　　　　$26,753/unit (including half site development)
　　　　　　　　　　$450,000 garage
　　　　　　　　　　$227,000 site development
　　　Year of bid:　1963
　　　　Site area:　8.12 acres
　　　　　　　　　　56 units/acre
　　　　　　User:　middle to upper income
　　　Financing:　FHA

Photo credit:　J. Alexander

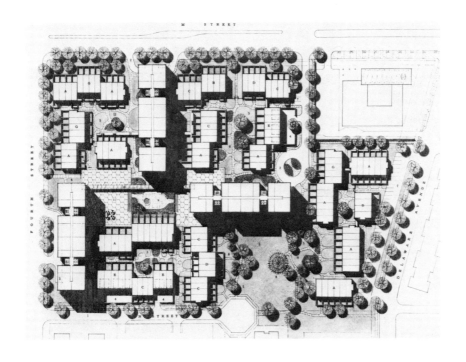

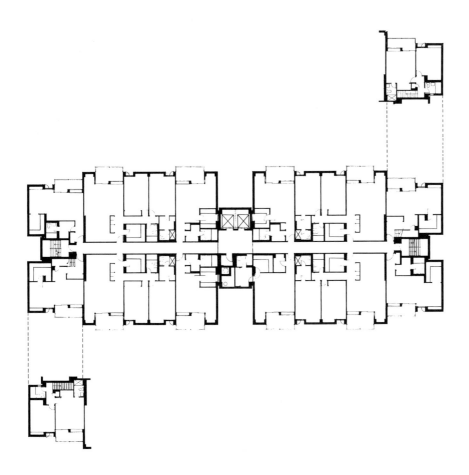

11

2000 BROADWAY
San Francisco, California

Architect:
BACKEN, ARRIGONI & ROSS, INC.
San Francisco, California

Number of dwelling units: 221
    203—efficiency
      6—two bedroom
      6—two bedroom (two story)
      6—three bedroom (two story)
  Gross floor area: 245,180 sf (including garage)
Construction cost: $4,750,000 (including garage)
                  $19.37sf
                  $21,493/unit
     Year of bid: 1969
       Site area: 0.51 acres
                  433 units/acre
           User: middle income
     Financing: FHA

Photo credit: Ed Stoecklein

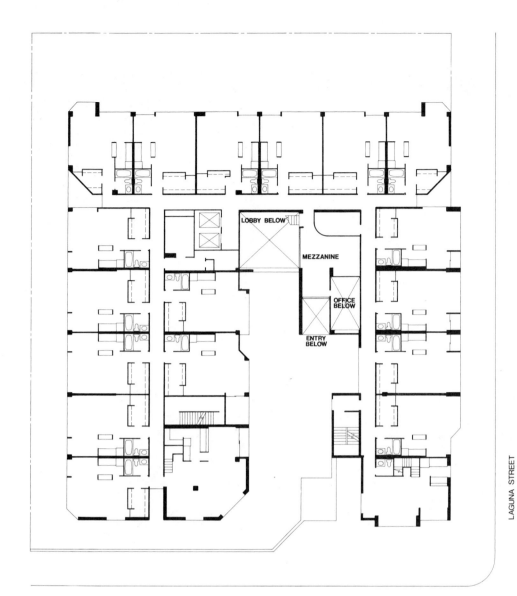

LOBBY BELOW

MEZZANINE

OFFICE
BELOW

ENTRY
BELOW

LAGUNA STREET

BROADWAY

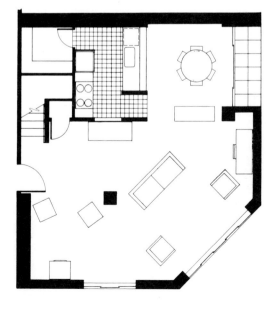

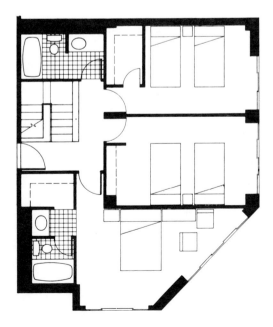

2000 BROADWAY 401

VILLA VICTORIA/TORRE UNIDAD ELDERLY
Boston, Massachusetts

Architect:
JOHN SHARRATT ASSOCIATES, INC.
Boston, Massachusetts

Number of dwelling units: 204
     177—efficiency
      86—one bedroom
       1—two bedroom
Gross floor area: 127,260 sf
Construction cost: $3,774,840
              $29.66/sf
              $18,500/unit
Year of bid: 1973
Site area: 1.42 acres
              144 units/acre
User: elderly
Financing: HUD turnkey

Photo credit: Steve Rosenthal

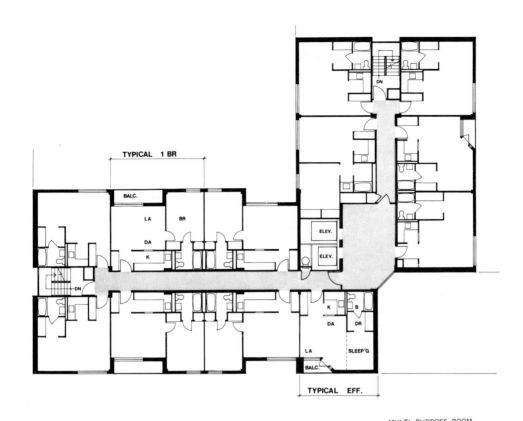

TYPICAL 1 BR

BALC.

LA   BR

DA

K

DN

ELEV.

ELEV.

K   B

DA   DR

LA   SLEEP'G

BALC.

TYPICAL EFF.

MULTI—PURPOSE ROOM
ABOVE COMMERCIAL,
TOILETS ABOVE LOBBY.

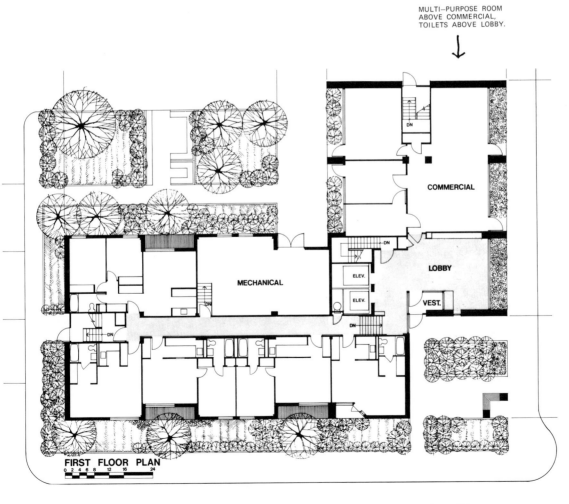

DN

COMMERCIAL

MECHANICAL

DN

ELEV.

ELEV.

DN

LOBBY

VEST.

DN

DN

FIRST FLOOR PLAN

0 2 4 6 8   12   16   24

VILLA VICTORIA/TORRE UNIDAD ELDERLY   403

13

OCEANFRONT CONDOMINIUM
Ocean City, Maryland

Architect:
WILLIAM MORGAN ARCHITECTS, P.A.
Jacksonville, Florida

Number of dwelling units: 170
    84—one bedroom
    86—two bedroom
  Gross floor area: 235,530 sf
                (including garages and terraces)
Construction cost: $5,600,000 (approx.)
                $23.68/sf
                $32,840/unit
    Year of bid: 1973
      Site area: 2.5 acres
                68 units/acre
         User: upper/middle income
    Financing: conventional

Photo credit: Lautman Photography

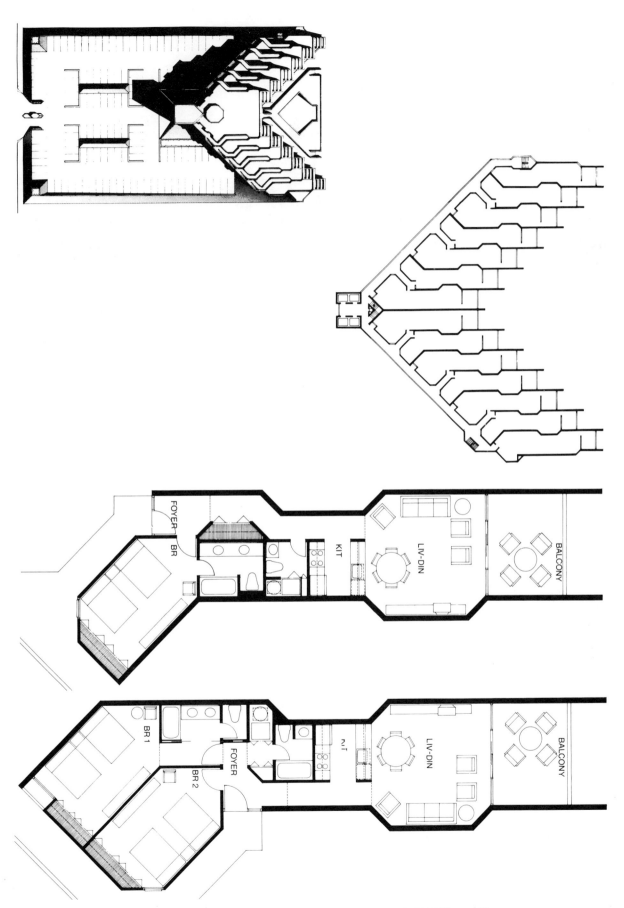

14

1199 PLAZA
New York, New York

Architect:
THE HODNE/STAGEBERG PARTNERS, INC.
Minneapolis, Minnesota

Number of dwelling units: 1518
  Highrise: 1124
    162—efficiency
    554—one bedroom
    408—two bedroom
  Midrise: 394
    125—two bedroom
    197—three bedroom
    72—four bedroom
Gross floor area: 1,604,690 sf (including garage)
Construction cost: $65,500,000
    $40.82/sf
    $43,150/unit
Year of bid: 1973
Site area: 12 acres
    127 units/acre
User: low to moderate income
Financing: 236 Mitchell/Lama

Photo credit: Norman McGrath

FLOORS 3-10

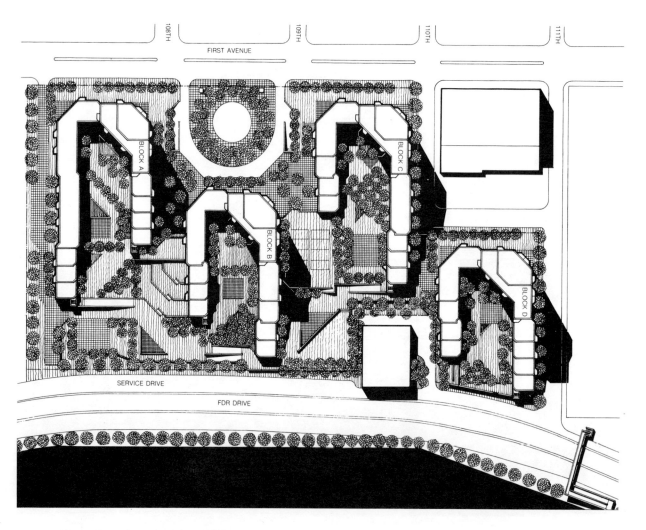

FLOORS 11-29

36'-0"

balcony below

br 1 br 1 br 2 live live br 1 br 2 br 2 br 1

2 BR 2 BR 2 BR

1 BR live e b kt kt b kt live

1 BR live k k

br 1 live j c e live

0 BR b b 1 BR kt

live kt b 1 BR kt

live kt b br 1

BR b b br 1

kt e live kt

r 1 BR

br 1 br 2 live

UPPER LEVEL

br 2 br 1 br 1 br 2 br 1 br 1 br 2 br 1 br 1 br 2

br 2 b b b b b

a p c down down down down down

UP br 3 br 3 br 2 br 3 br 2 br 3

escape balcony

LOWER LEVEL

13'-0"

4 BR 3 BR 3 BR 3 BR

2 BR 2 BR 2 BR

br 4 live live live live live live

a p c g k k g k k g k k g

down UP UP UP

j c

15

HARBOR HOUSE
Chicago, Illinois

Architect:
HAUSNER & MACSAI
Chicago, Illinois

Number of dwelling units: 278
    50—one bedroom
   175—two bedroom
    53—three bedroom
  Gross floor area: 488,000 sf (including garage)
Construction cost: $6,856,000
             $14.00/sf
             $24,662/unit
    Year of bid: 1965
      Site area: 1.08 acres
             257.5 units/acre
         User: middle to upper income
    Financing: conventional

Photo credit: Bill Engdahl/Hedrich-Blessing

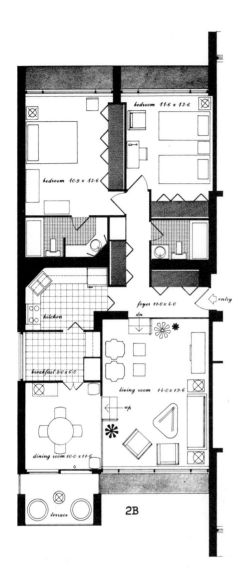

bedroom 11·6 x 13·6

bedroom 10·9 x 15·6

kitchen

breakfast 8·0 x 6·0

foyer 11·0 x 4·0

dn

living room 14·0 x 19·6

up

dining room 10·0 x 11·6

terrace

2B

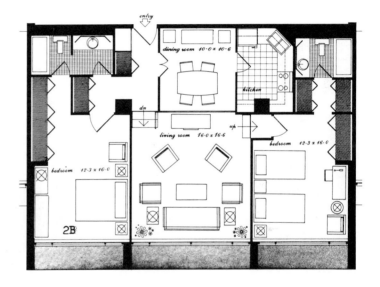

entry

dining room 10·0 x 10·6

kitchen

dn

living room 16·0 x 16·6

up

bedroom 12·3 x 16·0

bedroom 12·3 x 16·0

2B

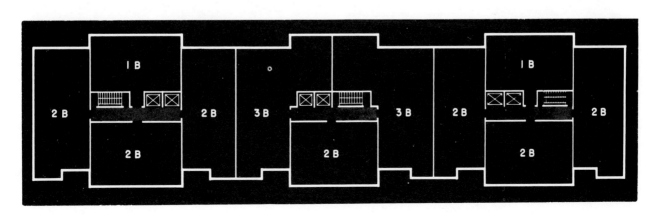

1 B

2 B

2 B

2 B

3 B

3 B

2 B

1 B

2 B

2 B

16   1500 SHERIDAN ROAD
Wilmette, Illinois

Architect:
HAUSNER & MACSAI
Chicago, Illinois

Number of dwelling units: 111 (condominium)
    1—efficiency
    1—one bedroom
   38—two bedroom
   40—three bedroom
   21—four bedroom
Gross floor area: 326,500 sf (including garage)
Construction cost: $4,770,00 (including garage)
                 $14.63/sf
                 $42,973/unit
Year of bid: 1968
Site area: 3.37 acres
                 33 units/acre
User: upper income
Financing: conventional

Photo credit: Orlando Cabanban

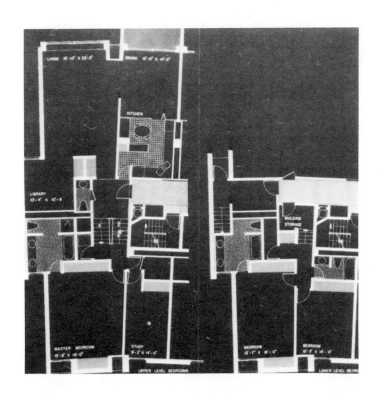

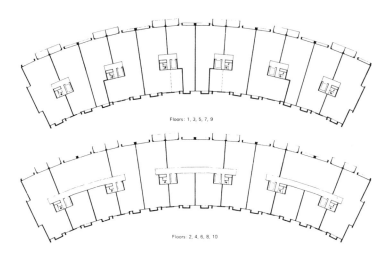

Floors: 1, 3, 5, 7, 9

Floors: 2, 4, 6, 8, 10

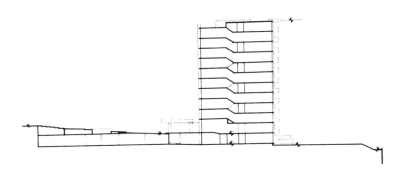

17

MARINA CITY
Chicago, Illinois

Architect:
BERTRAND GOLDBERG ASSOCIATES
Chicago, Illinois

Number of dwelling units: 896
     128—efficiency @2—256
     288—one bedroom @2—576
      32—two bedroom @2—64
  Gross floor area: 1,192,000 sf (towers only include parking and balconies @½)
Construction cost: approximately $11 to $13/sf
     Year of bid: 1960
       Site area: part of complex development
           User: middle to upper income
      Financing: FHA

Photo credit: Suter/Hedrich-Blessing

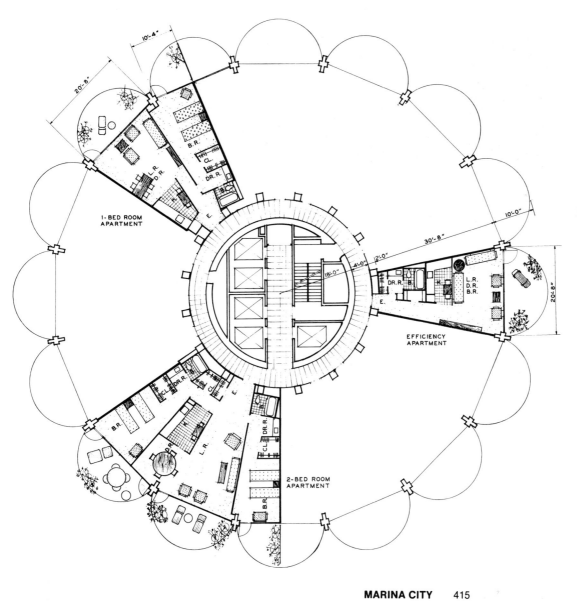

1-BED ROOM
APARTMENT

EFFICIENCY
APARTMENT

2-BED ROOM
APARTMENT

B.R.

CL.

DR.R.

L.R.

E.

K.

D.R.

DR.R.

B.R.

DR.R.

L.R.
D.R.
B.R.

10'-4"

20'-8"

10'-0"

30'-8"

20'-8"

18'-0"

4'-0"

2'-0"

18

ARTHUR SCHOMBURG PLAZA
New York, New York

Architect:
GRUZEN & PARTNERS
New York, New York

Number of dwelling units: 600
      Towers: 17—efficiency @2
               68—one bedroom @2
              102—two bedroom @2
               85—three bedroom @2
Central Corridor: 28—four bedroom
               28—five bedroom
Gross floor area: 585,530 sf
      462,000 sf towers
      85,460 sf central corridor
      31,600 sf community
      6,470 sf retail

Construction cost: $23,000,000 (including garage, community, and retail)
      $39.28 sf
      $38,333/unit
Year of bid: 1971
Site area: 1.83 acres
      328 units/acre
User: 60% moderate income
      30% low income
      10% elderly
Financing: New York State Urban Development Corporation

Photo credit: David Hirsch

416   **HIGHRISE—POINTBLOCK**

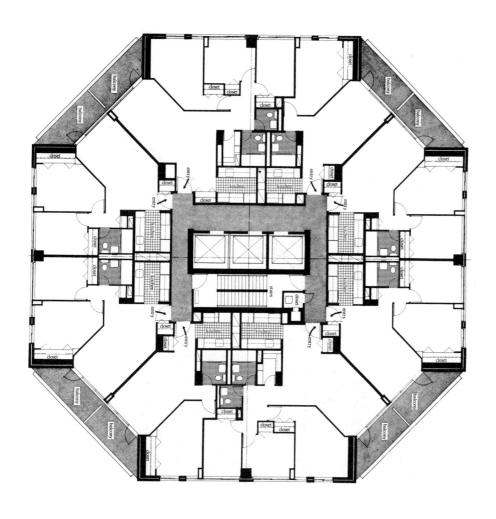

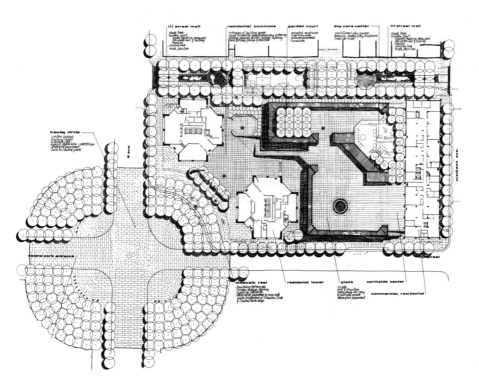

19 DORCHESTER APARTMENTS
Chicago, Illinois

Architect:
SKIDMORE, OWINGS & MERRILL
Chicago, Illinois

Number of dwelling units: 35
      14—two bedroom
      14—three bedroom
      7—two bedroom townhouses
  Gross floor area: 96,200 sf (including parking)
Construction cost: $1,300,000
               $13.50/sf
               $37,140/unit
     Year of bid: 1966
       Site area: 0.51 acres
               69 units/acre
          User: upper income
     Financing: conventional

Photo credit: Ezra Stoller

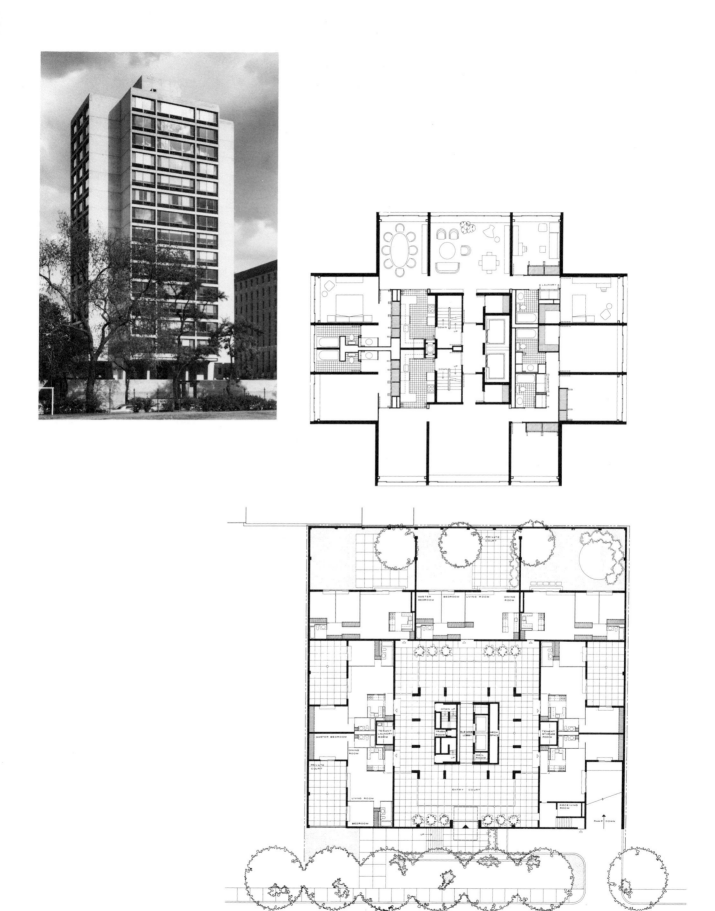

20

1110 LAKE SHORE DRIVE
Chicago, Illinois

Architect:
HAUSNER & MACSAI
Chicago, Illinois

Number of dwelling units: 74 two bedroom apartments (condominium)
Gross floor area: 166,000 sf (including garage)
Construction cost: $3,070,000
$18.49/sf
$41,496/unit
Year of bid: 1968
Site area: 0.25 acres
296 units/acre
User: upper income
Financing: conventional

Photo credit: Hedrich-Blessing

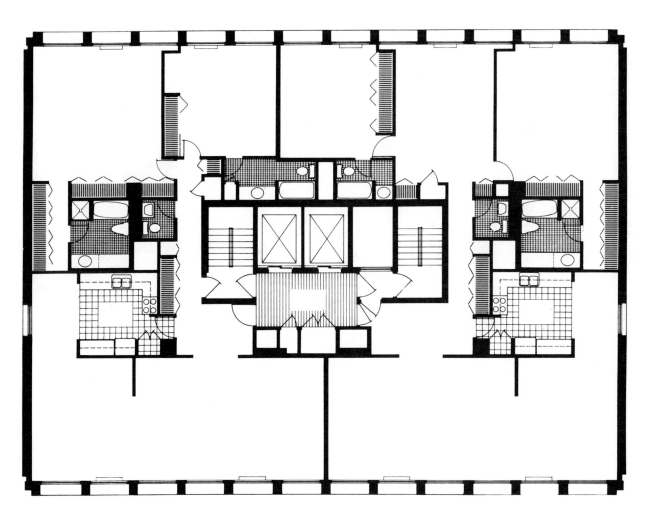

21 NEWBERRY PLAZA
Chicago, Illinois

Architects:
EZRA GORDON—JACK LEVIN
Chicago, Illinois

Number of dwelling units: 624 apartments (+ 15 townhouses)
  221—efficiency
  234—one bedroom
  143—two bedroom
  26—three bedroom
Gross floor area: 930,000 ft (including garage + 80,000 commercial, not including
  townhouses)
Construction cost: $13,661,000 (not including townhouses)
  $14.68/sf
  $21,893/unit
Year of bid: 1971
Site area: 1.63 acres
  392 units/acre
User: upper to middle income
Financing: FHA 207

Photo credit: Orlando Cabanban

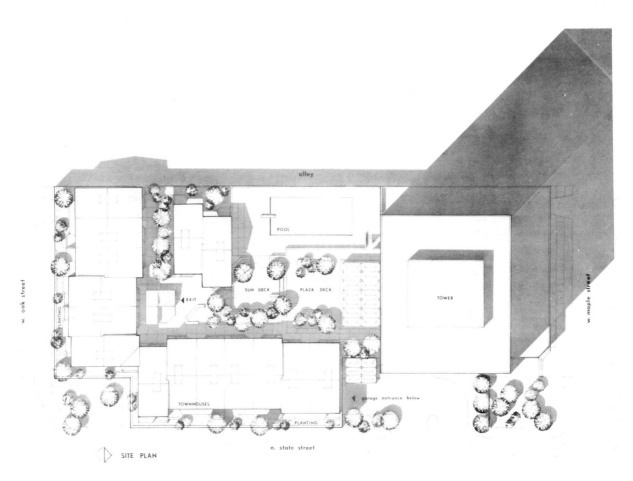

SITE PLAN

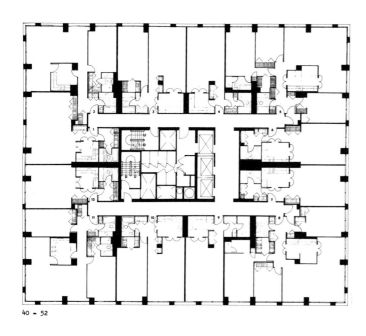

40 - 52

1 - 39

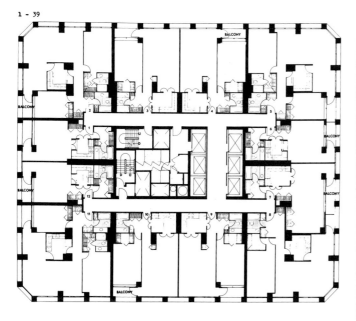

NEWBERRY PLAZA 423

22

EBENEZER TOWER
Minneapolis, Minnesota

Architect:
THORSEN & THORSHOV ASSOCIATES, INC.
Minneapolis, Minnesota

Number of dwelling units: 200
      84—efficiency
    114—one bedroom
      2—two bedroom
  Gross floor area: 141,240 sf (open, on grade parking)
Construction cost: $2,739,000
             $19.39/sf
             $13,695/unit
      Year of bid: 1969
       Site area: 0.92 acres
             217.5 units/acre
          User: elderly
    Financing: HUD Program No. 202

Photo credit: G. Edwards

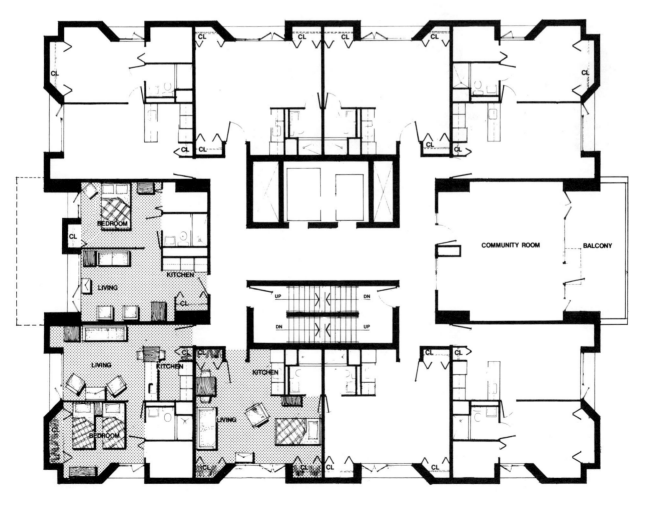

EBENEZER TOWER 425

23

727 FRONT AVENUE
St. Paul, Minnesota

Architect:
FREERKS/SPERL/FLYNN
St. Paul, Minnesota

Number of dwelling units: 151
     150—one bedroom
      1—two bedroom
  Gross floor area: 117,420 sf (open, on grade parking)
Construction cost: $1,954,000
             $16.64/sf
             $12,940/unit
     Year of bid: 1967
         User: low income (elderly)

Photo credit: Robert Sperl

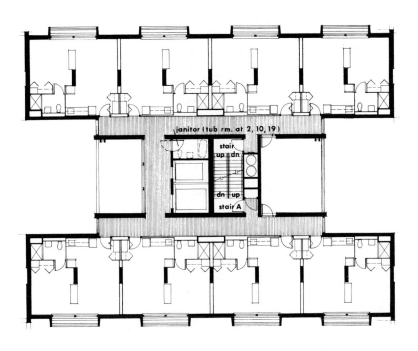

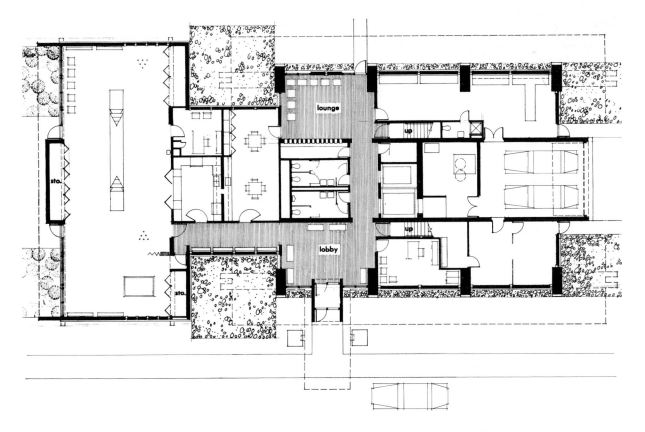

24

LAKE POINT TOWER
Chicago, Illinois

Architect:
SCHIPPOREIT & HEINRICH
Chicago, Illinois

Number of dwelling units: 900
    120—efficiency
    360—one bedroom
    300—two bedroom
    120—three bedroom
  Gross floor area: 1,732,000 sf (including garage)
Construction cost: not available
    Year of bid: 1965
      Site area: 2.92 acres
           308 units/acre
        User: upper income
    Financing: conventional

Photo credit: Hedrich-Blessing

428   **HIGHRISE—POINTBLOCK**

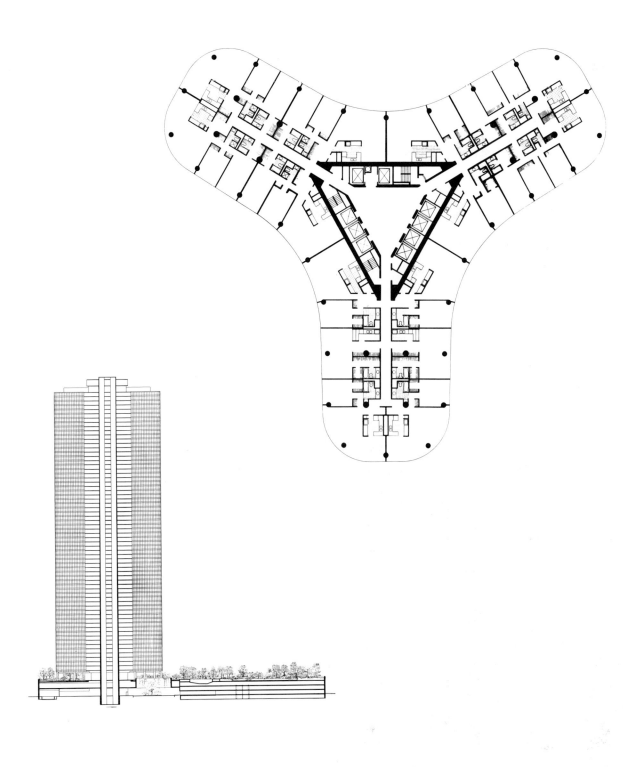

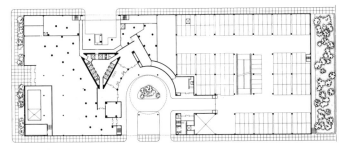

25 SOUTHVIEW TOWERS
Rochester, New York

Architect:
HOBERMAN & WASSERMAN
New York, New York

Number of dwelling units: 193—one bedroom apartments
Gross floor area: 145,000 sf (open, on grade parking)
Construction cost: $3,756,000
$25.00/sf
$19,461/unit
Year of bid: 1971
Site area: 1.6 acres
120 units/acre
User: low to moderate income
Financing: UDC, FHA 236

Photo credit: Norman Hoberman

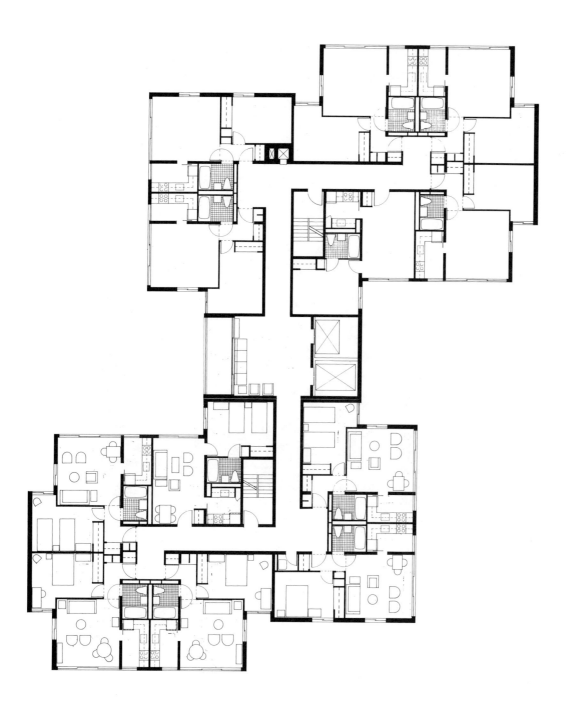

1555 N. ASTOR
Chicago, Illinois

Architect:
SOLOMON, CORDWELL, BUENZ & ASSOCIATES
Chicago, Illinois

Number of dwelling units: 113
    46—two bedroom
    45—three bedroom
    22—four bedroom
  Gross floor area: 388,350 sf (including garage)
Construction cost: $8,800,000
                $22.66/sf
                $77,880/unit
Year of bid: 1972
Site area: 0.72 acre
                157 units/acre
User: upper income
Financing: conventional

Photo credit: Hedrich–Blessing

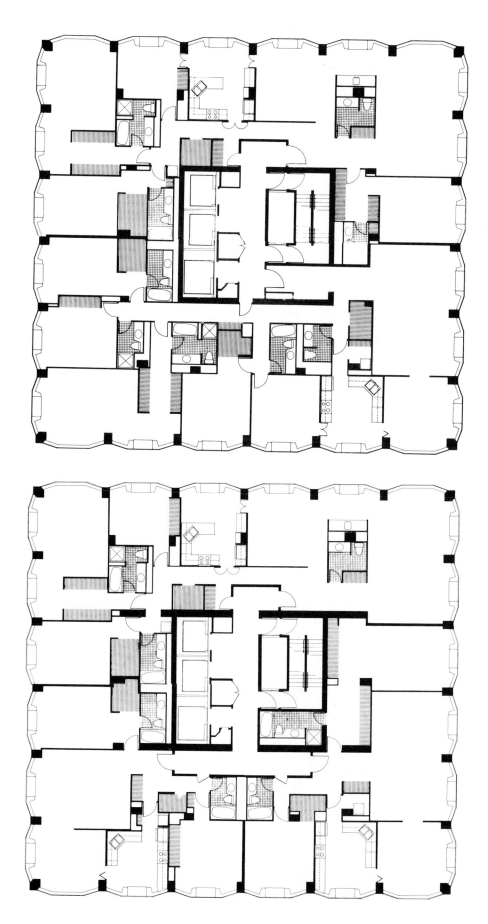

27

HIGHRISE—POINTBLOCK

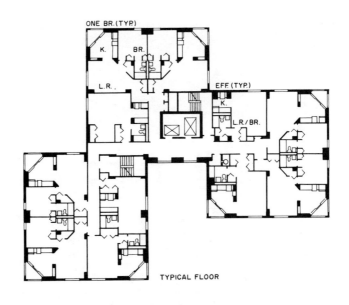

ONE BR.(TYP.)

K.

BR.

L.R.

EFF.(TYP.)

K.

L.R./BR.

TYPICAL FLOOR

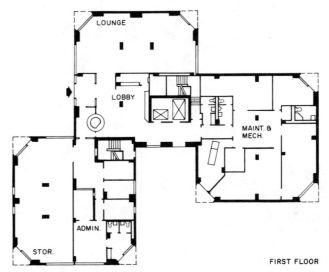

LOUNGE

LOBBY

MAINT. &
MECH.

ADMIN.

STOR.

FIRST FLOOR

MONUMENT EAST
Baltimore, Maryland

Architect:
CONKLIN & ROSSANT
New York, New York

Number of dwelling units: 187
  85—efficiency
  102—one bedroom
  Gross floor area: 136,000 sf
  Construction cost: $4,826,000
    $35.48/sf
    $25,807/unit
  Year of bid: 1973
  Site area: 0.75 acre
    249 units/acre
  User: elderly
  Financing: HUD Turnkey

Photo credit: Norman McGrath

28

ROKEBY CONDOMINIUMS
Nashville, Tennessee

Architect:
BARBER & McMURRAY INCORPORATED
Knoxville, Tennessee
(Design consultant: Martin Holub A.I.A.)

Number of dwelling units: 72
    8—one bedroom
   31—two bedroom
   33—three bedroom
Gross floor area: 161,000 sf (including garage)
Construction cost: $6,200,000
                $38.50/sf
                $86,110/unit
Year of bid: 1974
Site area: 2.94 acres
                24.5 units/acre
User: upper income
Financing: conventional

Photo credit: Larry Taylor/Format

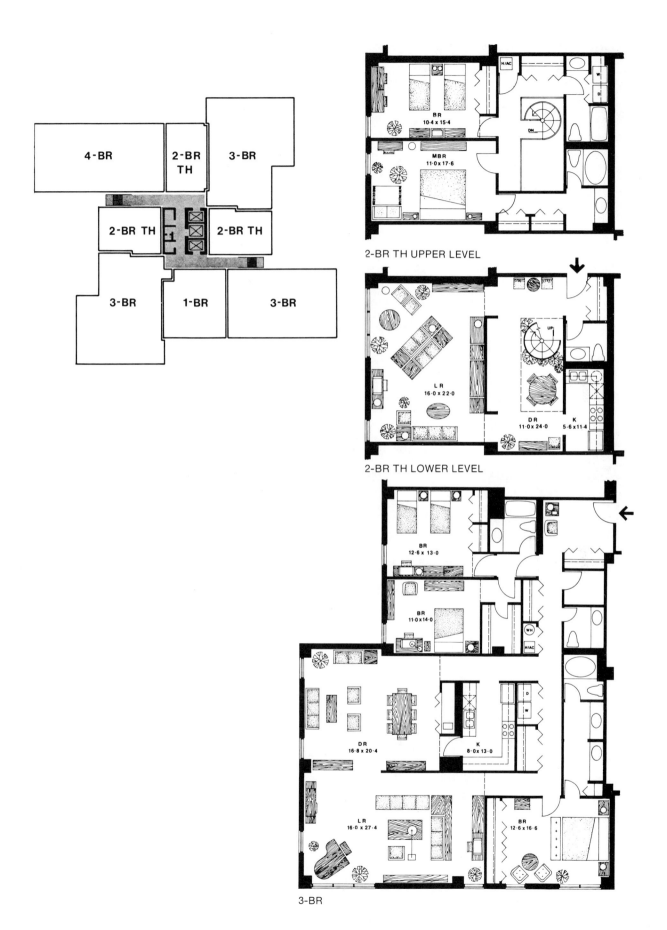

4-BR

2-BR TH

3-BR

2-BR TH

2-BR TH

3-BR

1-BR

3-BR

BR
10·4 x 15·4

MBR
11·0 x 17·6

H/AC

DN

W

D

2-BR TH UPPER LEVEL

LR
16·0 x 22·0

UP

DR
11·0 x 24·0

K
5·6 x 11·4

2-BR TH LOWER LEVEL

BR
12·6 x 13·0

BR
11·0 x 14·0

WH

H/AC

DR
16·8 x 20·4

K
8·0 x 13·0

D

W

LR
16·0 x 27·4

BR
12·6 x 16·6

3-BR

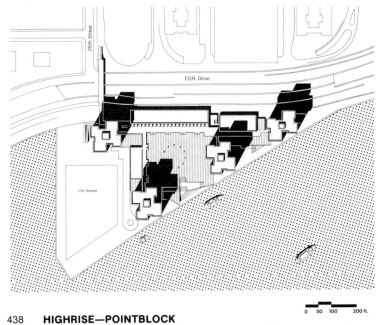

29

438 **HIGHRISE—POINTBLOCK**

UPPER FLOORS

MIDDLE FLOORS

WATERSIDE
New York, New York

Architect:
DAVIS BRODY & ASSOCIATES
New York, New York

Number of dwelling units: 1470 (breakdown unavailable)
Gross floor area: 2,269,500 sf (including garage)
Construction cost: $54,800,000 (including garage)
$24.00/sf
$32,278/unit
Year of bid: 1971
Site area: 6 acres
245 units/acre
User: middle income
Financing: UDC—Mitchell-Lama

Photo credit: Robert Gray

LOWER FLOORS

WATERSIDE 439

30 TWO CHARLES CENTER
Baltimore, Maryland

Architect:
CONKLIN & ROSSANT
New York, New York

Number of dwelling units: 410
    102—efficiency
    308—one bedroom
Gross floor area: 717,852 sf (including 254,000 sf garage and 80,000 sf stores)
Construction cost: $8,513,000 (including garage and stores)
    $11.85 sf
    $20,763/unit
Year of bid: 1964
Site area: 1.9 acres
    210.5 units/acre
User: middle income
Financing: conventional

Photo credit: J. Alexander

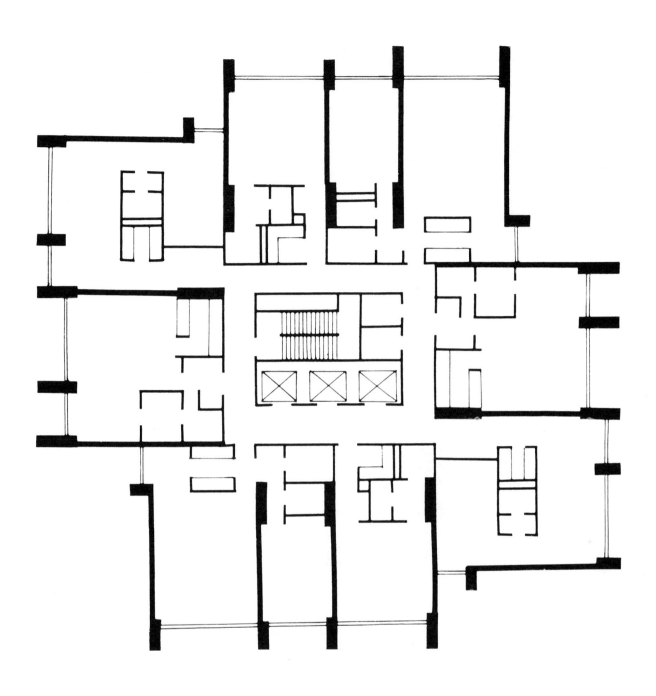

31

LAKE VILLAGE (highrise)
Chicago, Illinois

Architect:
HARRY WEESE & ASSOCIATES
EZRA GORDON—JACK LEVIN
Chicago, Illinois

Number of dwelling units: 200
      50—efficiency
      75—one bedroom
      75—two bedroom
  Gross floor area: 182,700 sf (open, on grade parking)
Construction cost: $3,091,000
                  $16.91/sf
                  $15,455/unit
    Year of bid: 1971
     Site area: part of large complex
         User: moderate income
    Financing: FHA 236

Photo credit: Philip Turner

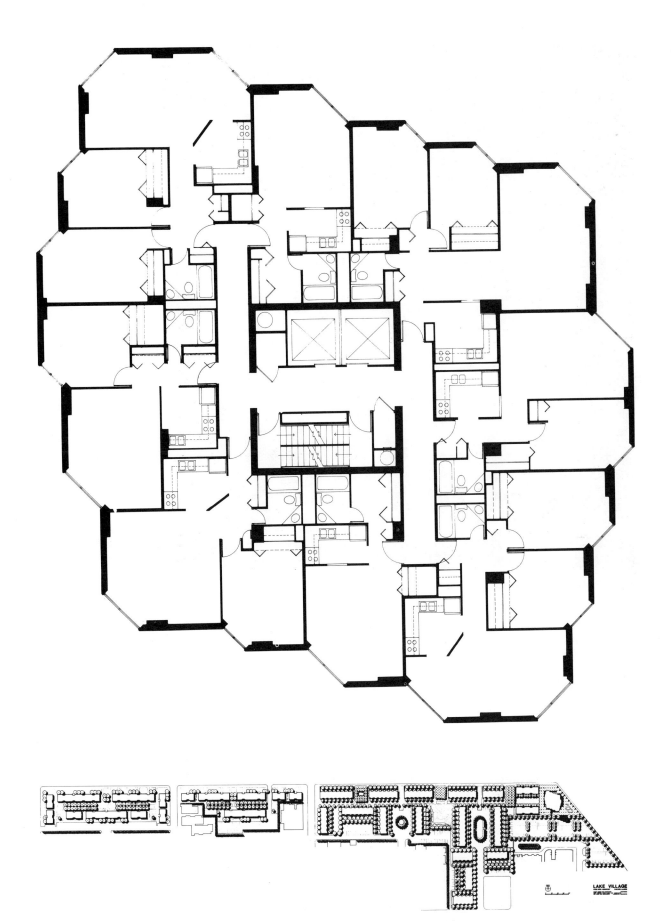

LAKE VILLAGE 443

32

TWIN PARKS NORTHWEST—SITE 4
Bronx, New York

Architect:
PRENTICE & CHAN, OHLHAUSEN
New York, New York

Number of dwelling units: 120
    6—efficiency
   30—one bedroom
   36—two bedroom
   36—three bedroom
    6—four bedroom
    6—five bedroom
  Gross floor area: 114,680 sf (open, on grade parking)
Construction cost: $4,047,000
               $35.28/sf
               $33,725/unit
   Year of bid: 1970
     Site area: 1.24 acres
              96 units/acre
        User: low and moderate income
  Financing: FHA 236

Photo credit: Elliot Fine

TYPICAL FLOOR PLAN
FLOORS 2,5,8,11,14 & 17

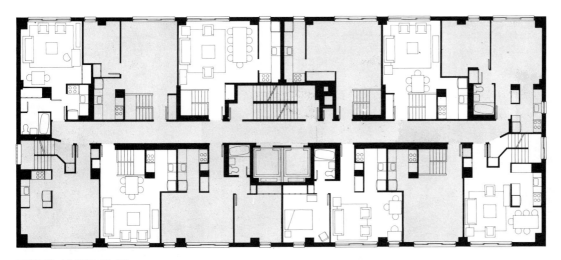

TYPICAL FLOOR PLAN
FLOORS 3,6,9,12,15 & 18

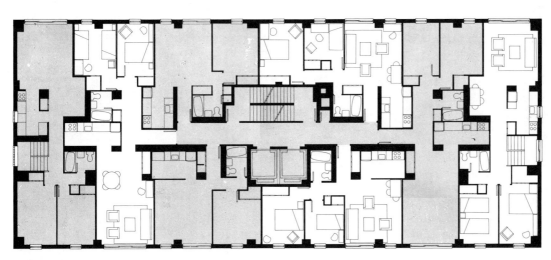

TYPICAL FLOOR PLAN
FLOORS 4,7,10,13,16 & 19

33   RIVERBEND
New York, New York

Architect:
DAVIS BRODY & ASSOCIATES
New York, New York

Number of dwelling units: 625
        32—efficiency
       280—one bedroom
       263—two bedroom
        50—three bedroom
    Gross floor area: 787,000 sf (including parking)
    Construction cost: $11,900,000
                         $15.12/sf
                         $19,040/unit
       Year of bid: 1966
        Site area: 3.7 acres
                     169 units/acre
             User: middle income
       Financing: Mitchell-Lama

Photo credit: David Hirsch
               Norman McGrath

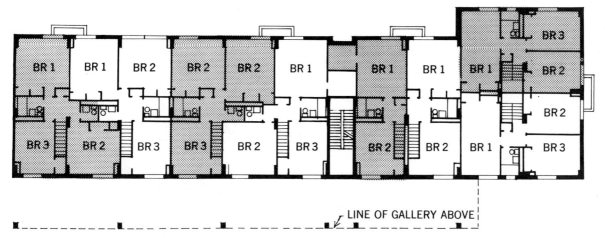

LINE OF GALLERY ABOVE

UPPER LEVEL

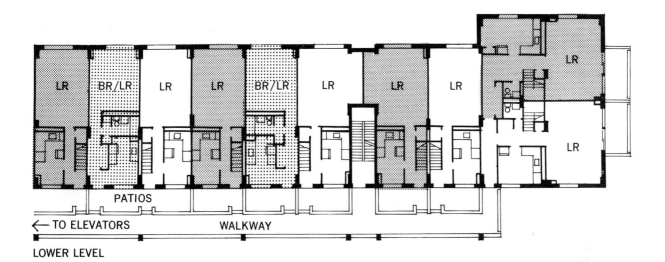

PATIOS

← TO ELEVATORS   WALKWAY

LOWER LEVEL

34 TWIN PARKS WEST—SITE 10–12
Bronx, New York

Architects:
GIOVANNI PASANELLA ASSOCIATES
New York, New York

Number of dwelling units: 186
    5—efficiency
    28—one bedroom
    53—two bedroom
    64—three bedroom
    12—four bedroom
    24—five bedroom
Gross floor area: 237,500 sf (not including parking)
Construction cost: $6,320,000
    $26.61/sf (not including parking)
    $33,978/unit (not including parking)
Year of bid: 1971
Site area: 1.5 acres
    124 units/acre
User: low income
Financing: FHA 236

Photo credit: Giovanni Pasanella Associates

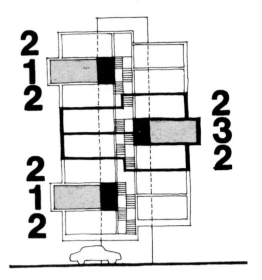

KEY SECTION

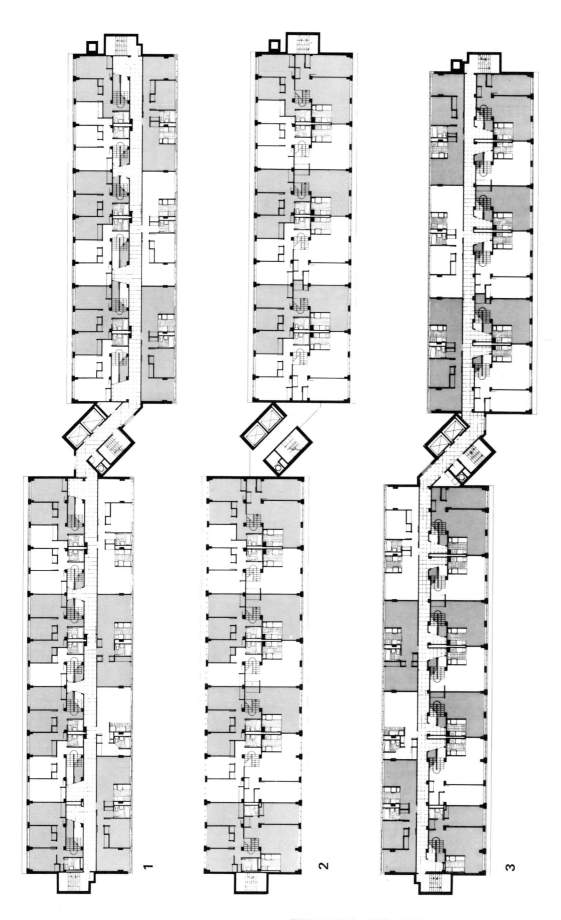

1

2

3

CONEY ISLAND—SITE 5/6
Brooklyn, New York

Architect:
HOBERMAN & WASSERMAN
New York, New York

Number of dwelling units: 334
     19—efficiency
     45—one bedroom
   132—two bedroom
   105—three bedroom
     22—four bedroom
     11—five bedroom
  Gross floor area: 379,650 sf (including garage)
Construction cost: $11,000,000
                 $28.97/sf
                 $32,934/unit
     Year of bid: 1970
       Site area: 3.5 acres
                 95.5 units/acre
          User: low to moderate income
     Financing: FHA 236

Photo credit: Norman Hoberman

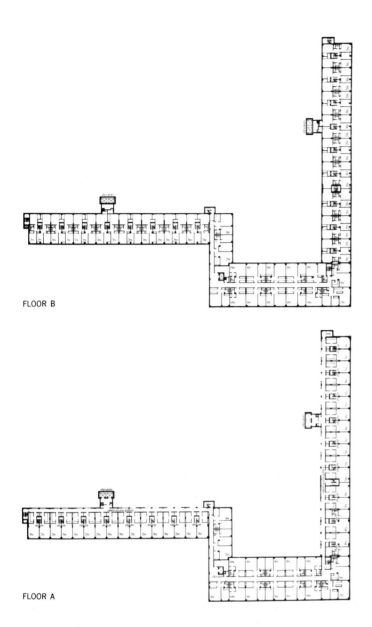

FLOOR B

FLOOR A

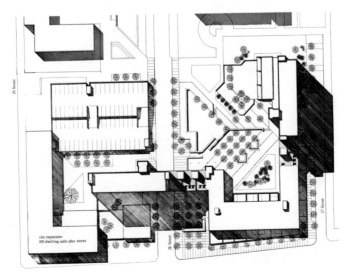

site expansion—
100 dwelling units plus stores

36 ROOSEVELT ISLAND, PARCEL 3
New York, New York

Architect:
SERT, JACKSON AND ASSOCIATES
Cambridge, Massachusetts

Number of dwelling units: 361
     4%—efficiency
   26%—one bedroom
   45%—two bedroom
   19%—three bedroom
    6%—four bedroom
  Gross floor area: 520,000 sf (including garage, 13,800 sf commercial, 17,300 sf school)
Construction cost: $15,000,000
                $28.83/sf
                $41,551/unit
    Year of bid: 1972
      Site area: 2.85 acres
                126.5 units/acre
          User: low to middle income
    Financing: UDC and Mitchell-Lama

Photo credit: Steve Rosenthal

3 BEDROOM UNIT

2 BEDROOM UNIT SOUTH

2 BEDROOM UNIT NORTH

1 BEDROOM UNITS NORTH

3 BEDROOM CORE UNIT

corridor level   noncorridor level

4 BEDROOM DUPLEX UNIT

3 BEDROOM CORE UNIT

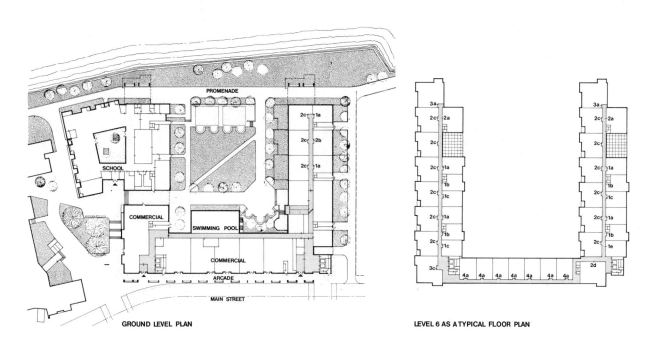

GROUND LEVEL PLAN

LEVEL 6 AS A TYPICAL FLOOR PLAN

ROOSEVELT ISLAND, PARCEL 3   453

37 EAST MIDTOWN PLAZA
New York, New York

Architect:
DAVIS BRODY & ASSOCIATES
New York, New York

Number of dwelling units: 737 (breakdown unavailable)
Gross floor area: 1,075,500 sf (including parking)
Construction cost: $22,685,000 (including parking)
$21.00/sf
$30,780/unit
Year of bid: 1969
Site area: 3.5 acres
210 units/acre
User: middle income
Financing: Mitchell-Lama

Photo credit: Robert Gray

Typical duplex floors

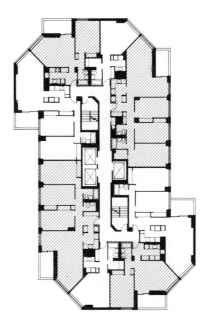

Typical tower floor

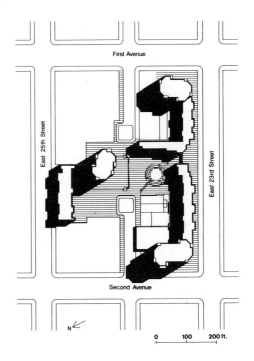

EAST MIDTOWN PLAZA　455

38

SOUTH COMMONS (midrise)
Chicago, Illinois

Architect:
EZRA GORDON—JACK LEVIN
Chicago, Illinois

Number of dwelling units: 68
     25—efficiency
     28—one bedroom
     11—two bedroom
      4—three bedroom (two story)
  Gross floor area: 70,942 sf (open, on grade parking)
Construction cost: $1,017,000
                   $14.33/sf
                   $14,956/unit
     Year of bid: 1966
       Site area: part of large complex
           User: middle income
     Financing: FHA 220

Photo credit: Orlando Cabanban

6TH.

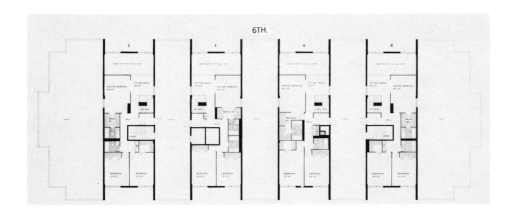

5TH.

2ND, 3RD, 4TH.

1ST.

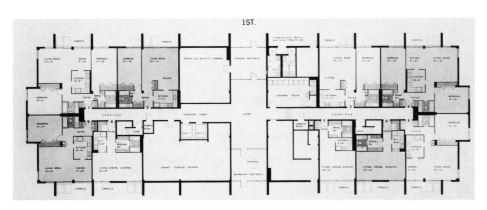

39

1555 SANDBURG TERRACE
Chicago, Illinois

Architect:
SOLOMON, CORDWELL, BUENZ & ASSOCIATES
Chicago, Illinois

Number of dwelling units: 96
    48—one bedroom
    36—two bedroom
    12—three bedroom
    Gross floor area: 158,100 sf (not including parking)
Construction cost: $1,617,000 (not including parking)
                 $10.22/sf (not including parking)
                 $16,844/unit (not including parking)
      Year of bid: 1969
        Site area: part of large complex
             User: middle income
      Financing: FHA 207

Photo credit: Henry Kluck

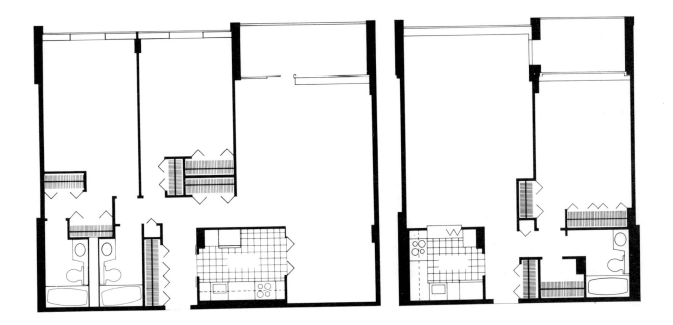

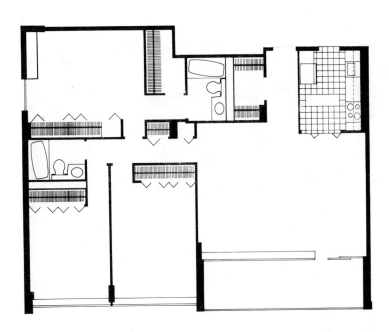

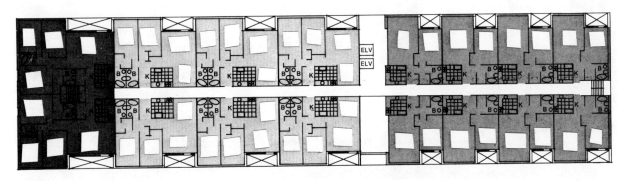

1555 SANDBURG TERRACE   459

40 JAMES CLEVELAND BUILDING
Keene, New Hampshire

Architect:
JOHN SHARRATT ASSOCIATES INC.
Boston, Massachusetts

Number of dwelling units: 75
    All one bedroom
Gross floor area: 62,700 sf
Construction cost: $1,420,600
    $22.66/sf
    $18,940/unit
Year of bid: 1976
Site area: 1.03 acres
    72.8 units/acre
User: elderly
Financing: HUD 221d-4 and HUD section 8

Photo credit: Steve Rosenthal

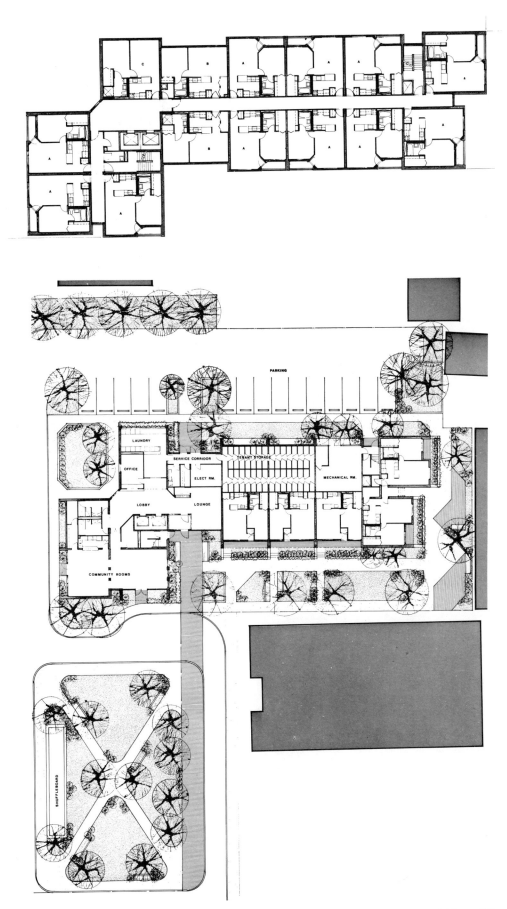

LAUNDRY

SERVICE CORRIDOR

OFFICE

ELECT. RM.

TENANT STORAGE

MECHANICAL RM.

LOBBY

LOUNGE

COMMUNITY ROOMS

PARKING

SHUFFLEBOARD

JAMES CLEVELAND BUILDING 461

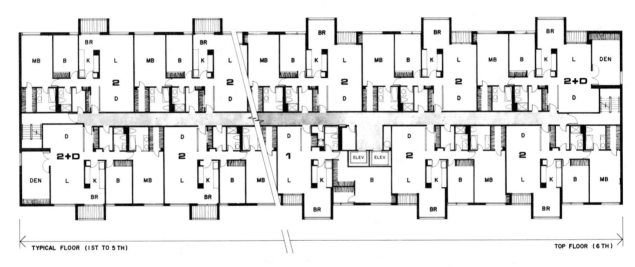

TYPICAL FLOOR (1ST TO 5TH)   TOP FLOOR (6TH)

TRIUMVERA MIDRISES
Glenview, Illinois

Architect:
JOHN MACSAI & ASSOCIATES
Chicago, Illinois

Number of dwelling units: 60
     7—one bedroom
    41—two bedroom
    12—two bedroom plus den
  Gross floor area: 112,500 sf
Construction cost: $2,470,000 (without site work)
                $21.95/sf
                $41,166/unit
     Year of bid: 1977
Site area (typical cluster including midrise and 20 row houses):
          2.8 acres
          28.6 units/acre
        User: middle-upper income
    Financing: conventional

Photo credit: Howard N. Kaplan

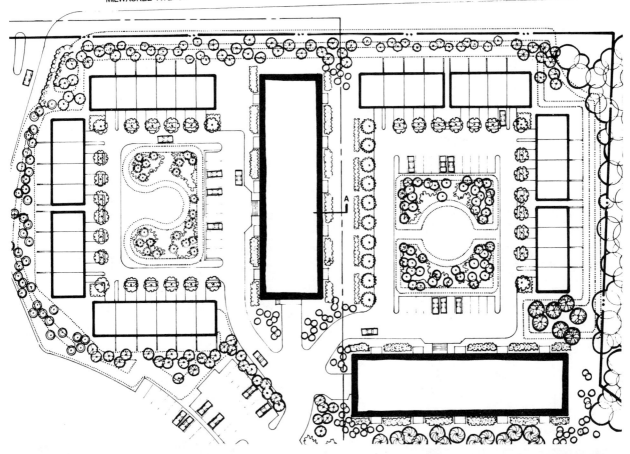

MILWAUKEE AVENUE

TRIUMVERA MIDRISES 463

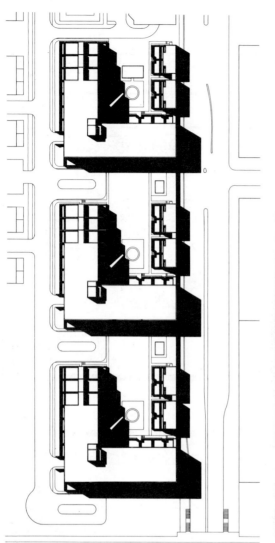

42

DEARBORN PARK MIDRISES
Chicago, Illinois

Architect:
BOOTH/HANSEN & ASSOCIATES
Chicago, Illinois

Number of dwelling units: 235
In midrises: 8—one bedroom
                144—two bedroom
                 69—three bedroom
                  2—four bedroom
In row houses: 8—three bedroom
                  4—four bedroom
Gross floor area: 447,252 sf
Construction cost: $13,250,000
                    $29.62/sf
                    $56,383/unit
Year of bid: 1977
Site area: 4.29 acres
            54.7 units/acre
User: upper income
Financing: conventional

Photo credits: Hedrich Blessing

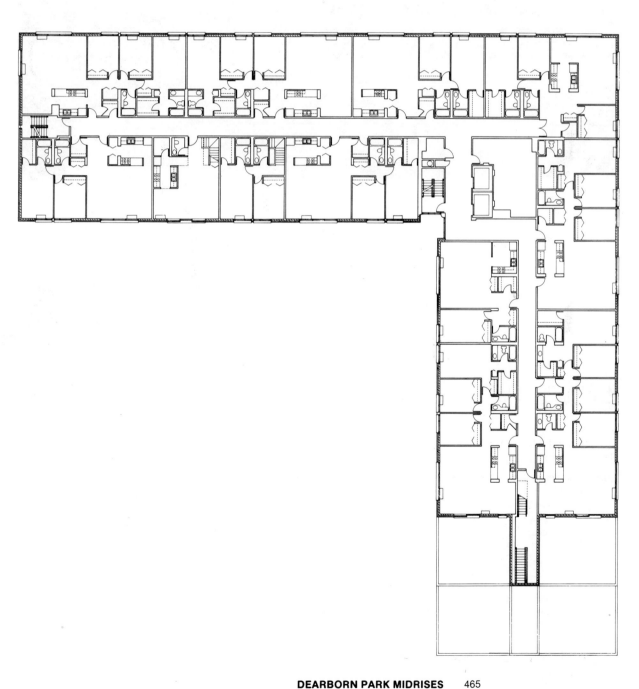

43

MAPLE KNOLL VILLAGE
Springdale, Ohio

Architect:
GRUZEN & PARTNERS
New York, New York

Number of dwelling units (in the independent housing wing):   121
        13—efficiency
      108—one bedroom
   Gross floor area: 110,000 sf
Construction cost
   (this wing only): $4,200,000
                       $38.18/sf
                       $34,710/unit
        Year of bid: 1975
          Site area: Not separable for this wing
               User: low- to upper-income elderly
          Financing: conventional

Photo credits: Bo Parker

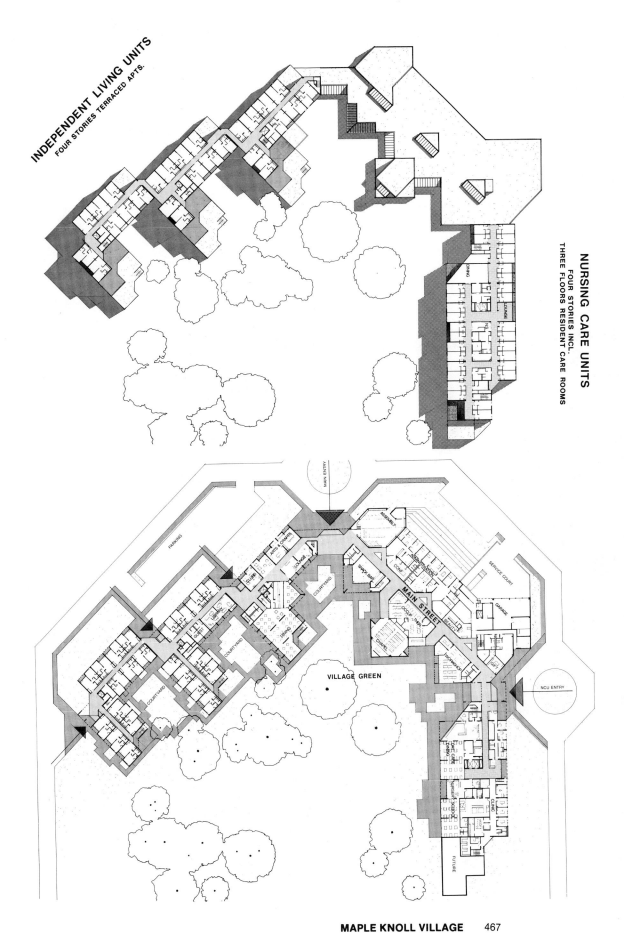

INDEPENDENT LIVING UNITS
FOUR STORIES TERRACED APTS.

NURSING CARE UNITS
FOUR STORIES INCL.
THREE FLOORS RESIDENT CARE ROOMS

MAPLE KNOLL VILLAGE 467

44 HIGHLAND PARK HOUSING FOR THE ELDERLY
Highland Park, Illinois

Architect:
NAGLE, HARTRAY & ASSOCIATES, LTD.
(Formerly Booth Nagle & Hartray/Ltd.)
Chicago, Illinois

Number of dwelling units: 69
     6—efficiency
    63—one bedroom
  Gross floor area: 50,000 sf
Construction cost: $1,400,000
                 $28.00/sf
                 $20,290/unit
     Year of bid: 1976
       Site area: 1.37 acres
                 50.4 units/acre
         User: elderly
     Financing: IHDA

Photo credit: Philip Turner

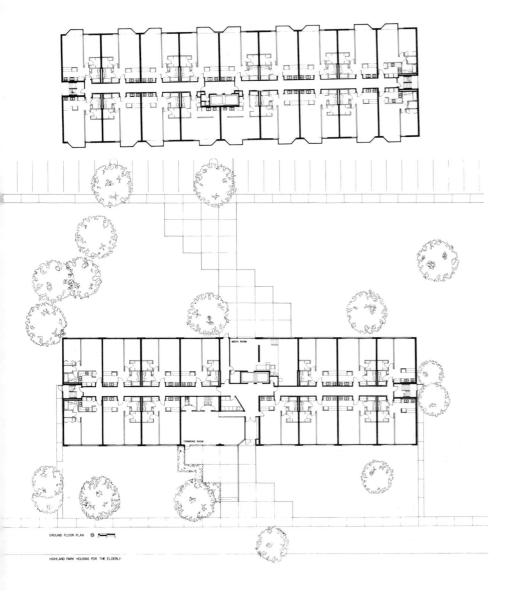

GROUND FLOOR PLAN

HIGHLAND PARK HOUSING FOR THE ELDERLY

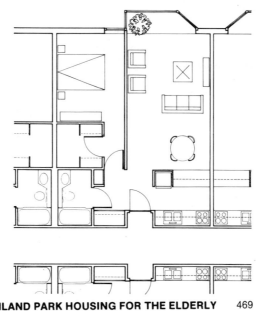

HIGHLAND PARK HOUSING FOR THE ELDERLY 469

45

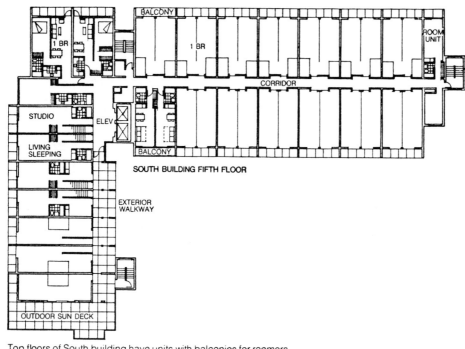

SOUTH BUILDING FIFTH FLOOR

Top floors of South building have units with balconies for roomers.

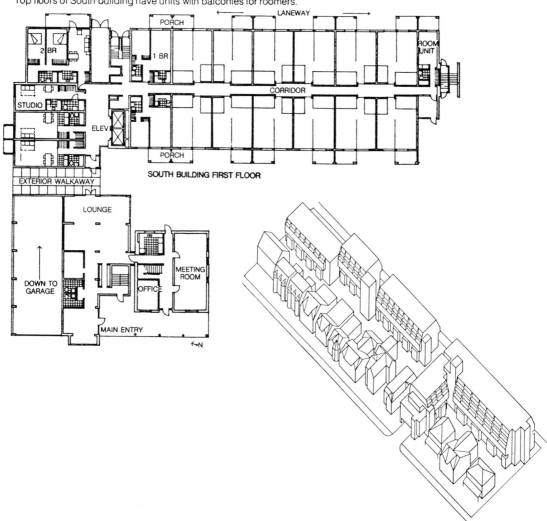

SOUTH BUILDING FIRST FLOOR

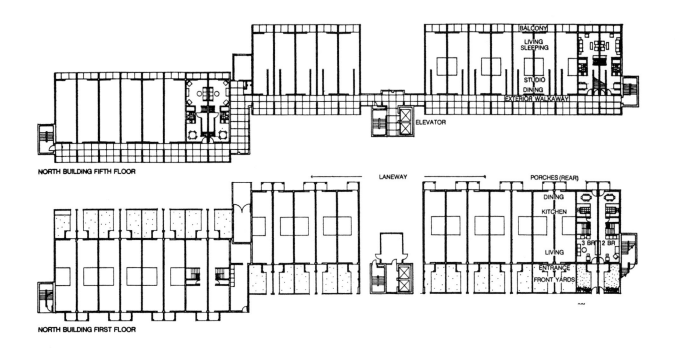

NORTH BUILDING FIFTH FLOOR

NORTH BUILDING FIRST FLOOR

DUNDAS/SHERBOURNE HOUSING
Toronto, Ontario

Architect:
DIAMOND & MYERS
(Barton Myers, Partner-In-Charge)
Toronto, Ontario

Number of dwelling units: 302
    81—efficiency
    97—mini one bedroom
  101—one bedroom
    13—two bedroom
    10—three bedroom
Gross floor area: 169,330 sf
Construction cost: $5,300,000
             $31.30/sf
             $17,550/unit
Year of bid: 1974
Site area: 1.27 acres
          238 units/acre
User: 75% low income, 25% middle income
Financing: CMHC

Photo credit: Ian Samson

46 HYDRO BLOCK
Toronto, Ontario

Architect:
DIAMOND & MYERS
(A. J. Diamond, Partner-in-Charge)
Toronto, Ontario

Number of dwelling units: 113
    38—efficiency
    46—one bedroom
    16—two bedroom
    13—three bedroom

  Gross floor area: 99,120 sf
Construction cost: $3,300,000
                $33.29/sf
                $29,200/unit
    Year of bid: 1977
      Site area: 1.09 acres
                103.7 units/acre
         User: low to moderate income
    Financing: CMHC financing for subsidized housing

Photo credit: Nir Baraket

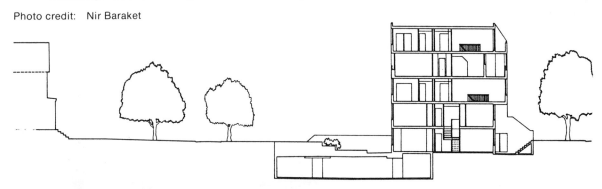

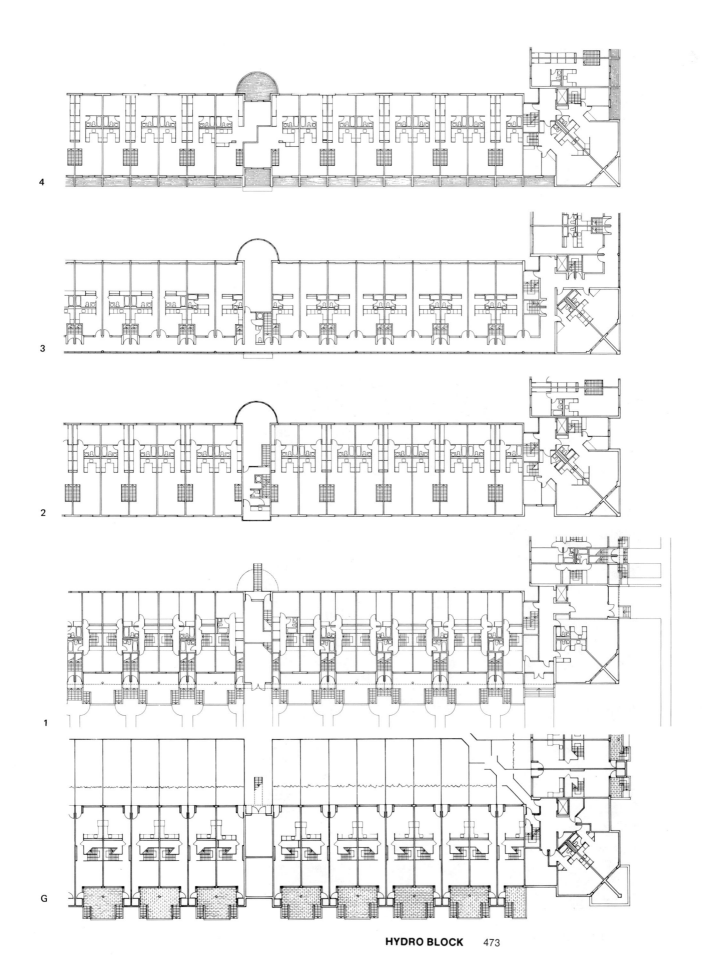

HYDRO BLOCK 473

47 FLORIDA CHRISTIAN HOME APARTMENTS
Jacksonville, Florida

Architect:
FREEDMAN/CLEMENTS/RUMPEL Architects/Planners Inc.
Jacksonville, Florida

Number of dwelling units: 180
    60—efficiency
    120—one bedroom
Gross floor area: 120,620 sf
Construction cost: $2,100,000
    $17.40/sf
    $11,666/unit
Year of bid: 1970
Site area: 4 acres
    45 units/acre
User: low- to middle-income elderly
Financing: FHA-236

Photo credit: Belton Wall

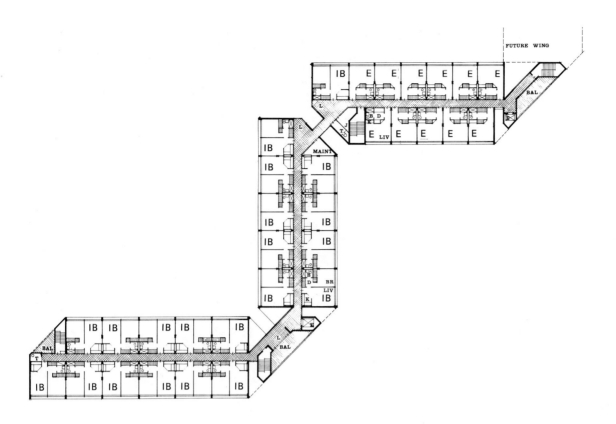

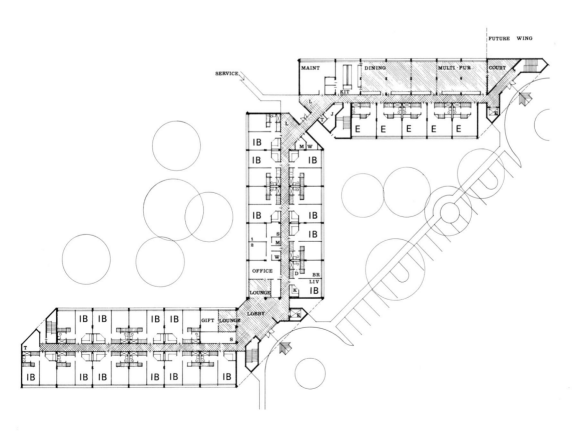

48

FOUR LAKES VILLAGE APARTMENTS
Lisle, Illinois

Architect:
AUBREY J. GREENBERG & ASSOCIATES, Inc.
Chicago, Illinois

Number of dwelling units: 60
     40—one bedroom
     20—two bedroom
  Gross floor area: 73,390 sf
Construction cost: $847,660
              $11.55/sf
              $14,130/unit
    Year of bid: 1969
      Site area: 19.3 acres for midrises
             15.6/units/acre
         User: middle to upper income
    Financing: conventional

Photo credit: Linda Reed

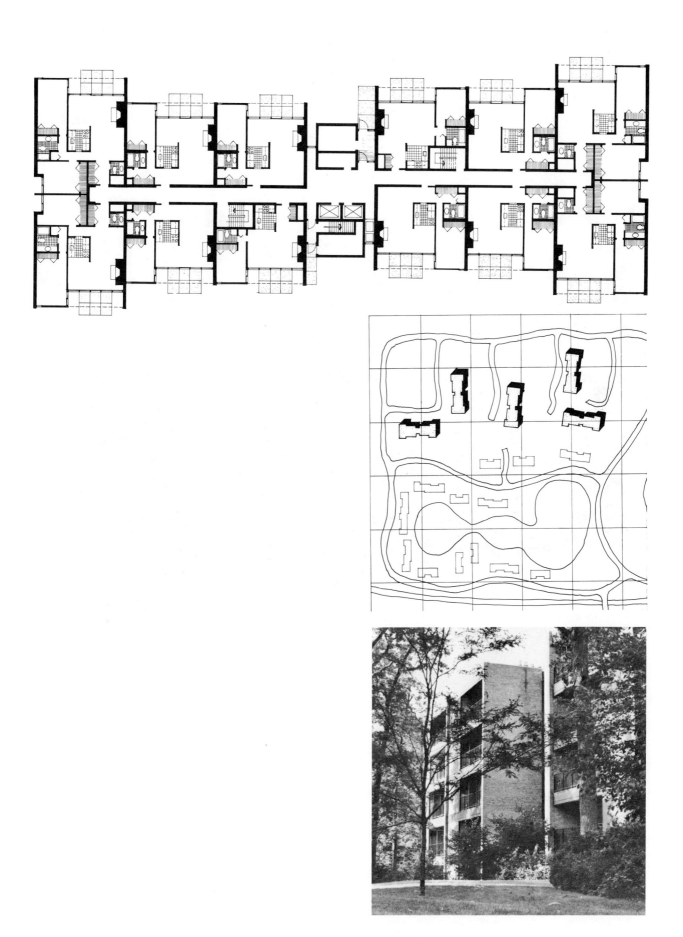

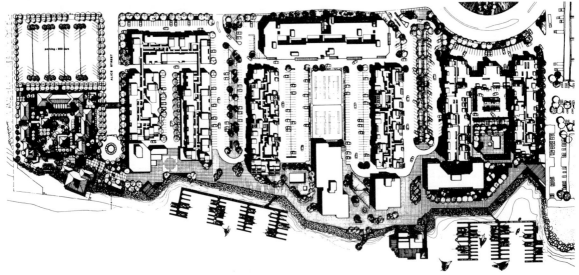

49

PORTOBELLO
Oakland, California

Architect:
DONALD SANDY JR./JAMES A. BABCOCK
San Francisco, California

Number of dwelling units: 200 (+400 future)
  Gross floor area: 250,000 sf
  (incl. 50,000-sf commercial)
Construction cost: $4,000,000
                $16.00/sf
Year of bid: 1972
Site area: 30 acres
         20 units/acre (including future)
User: middle income
Financing: conventional

Photo credit: Jeremiah O. Bragstad
             Lance Gardner Biesele

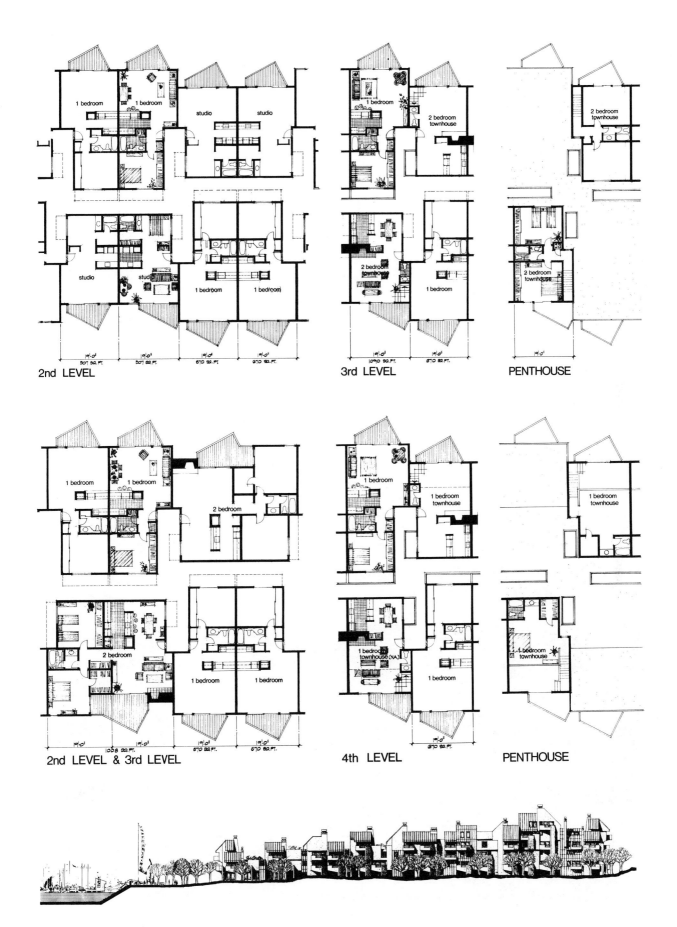

2nd LEVEL

3rd LEVEL

PENTHOUSE

2nd LEVEL & 3rd LEVEL

4th LEVEL

PENTHOUSE

50 THE FAIRWAYS
Coquitlam, British Columbia

Architect:
R. E. HULBERT AND PARTNERS
West Vancouver, British Columbia

Number of dwellings: 58
      8—one bedroom plus den
   30—two bedroom
   20—two bedroom plus loft
Gross floor area: 98,600 sf
Construction cost: $4,500,000
                $45.64/sf
                $77,590/unit
Year of bid: 1976
Site area: 1.8 acres
                32.2 units/acre
User: upper income
Financing: conventional

Photo credit: Simon Scott

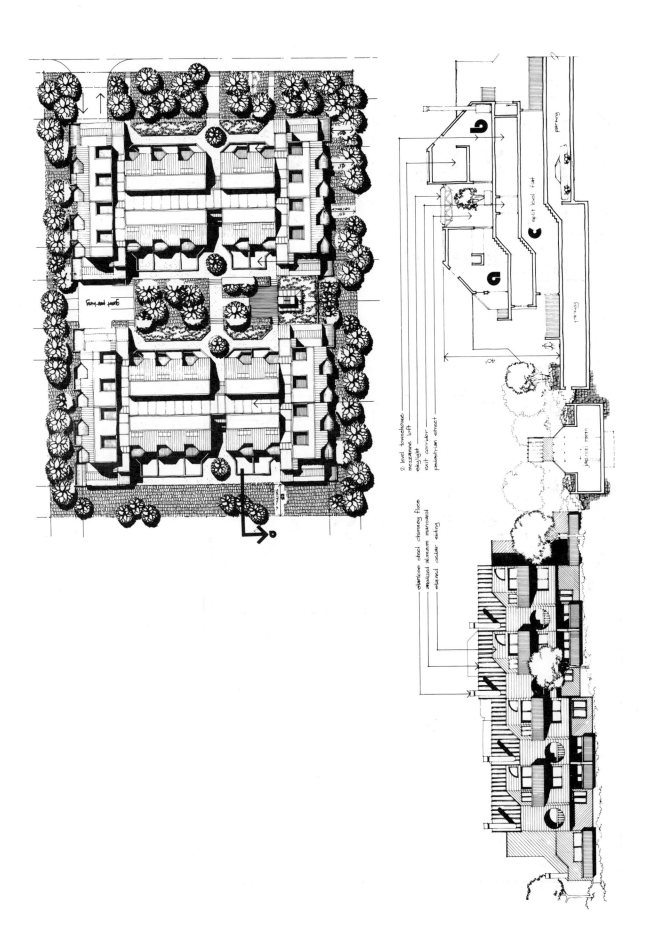

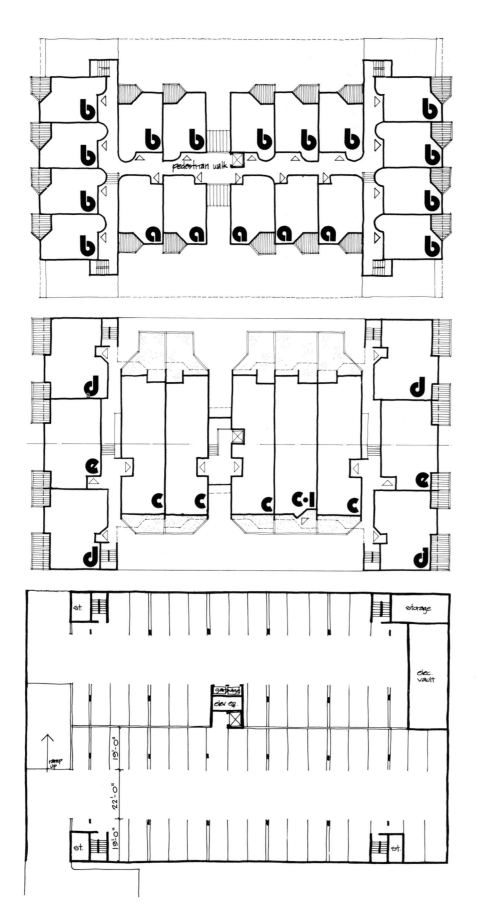

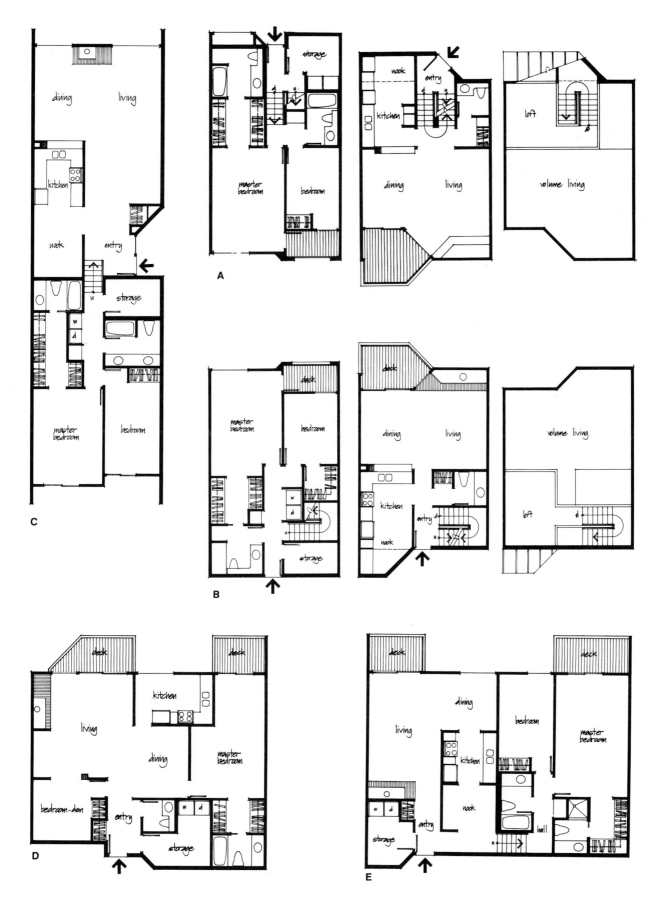

A

B

C

D

E

WINNETKA HOUSE
Winnetka, Illinois

Architect:
HAUSNER & MACSAI
Chicago, Illinois

Number of dwelling units: 64
    12—two bedroom
    40—three bedroom
    12—four bedroom
  Gross floor area: 177,300 sf (including garage)
Construction cost: $3,050,000
                    $17.20/sf
                    $47,656/unit
    Year of bid: 1970
      Site area: 1.76 acres
                    36.5 units/acre
         User: upper income
    Financing: conventional

Photo credit: John Macsai, Howard N. Kaplan

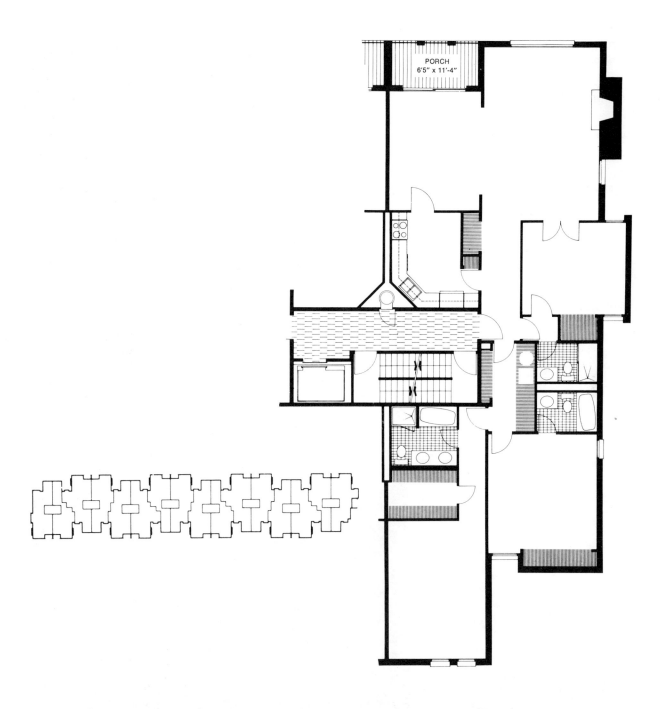

PORCH
6'5" x 11'-4"

WINNETKA HOUSE   485

52 GARDEN HOUSE
Maywood, Illinois

Architect:
SCHIPPOREIT INC.
Evanston, Illinois

Number of dwelling units: 145
    144—one bedroom
      1—two bedroom
Gross floor area: 133,500 sf
Construction cost: $3,332,160
                $24.96/sf
                $22,980/unit
Year of bid: 1977
Site area: 1.6 acres
           90 units/acre
User: low- to middle-income elderly
Financing: IHDA

Photo credit: James L. Spacek

GARDEN HOUSE 487

53 SEA GARDENS
Seminole Beach, Florida

WILLIAM MORGAN ARCHITECTS, P.A.
Jacksonville, Florida

Number of dwelling units: 15
    All two bedroom plus loft
Gross floor area: 23,940 sf
Construction cost: $649,000
    $27.10/sf
    $43,270/unit
Year of bid: 1977
Site area: 1.85 acres
    8.1 units/acre
User: middle income
Financing: conventional

Photo credit: Otto Baitz

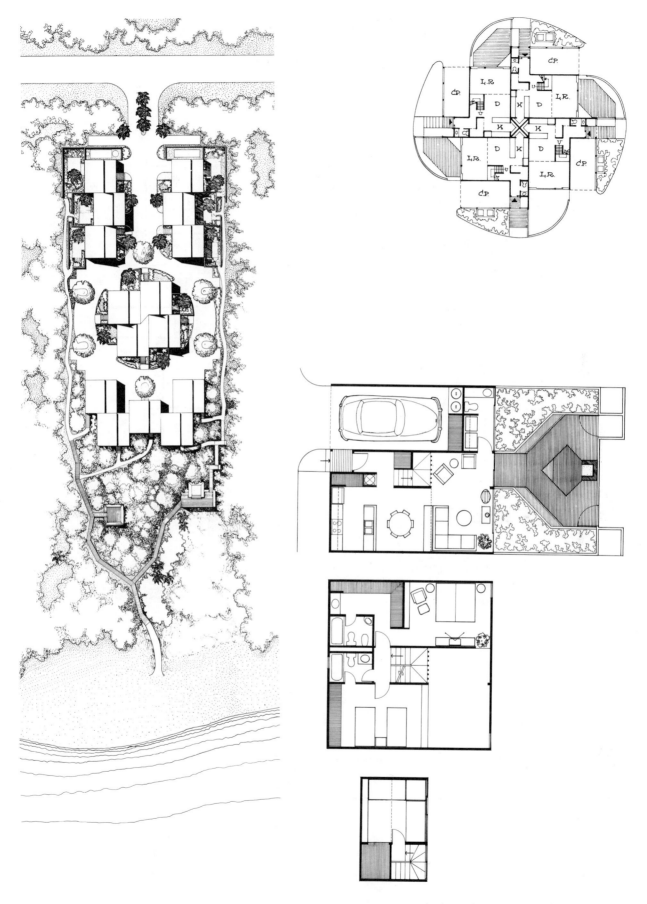

SEA GARDENS   489

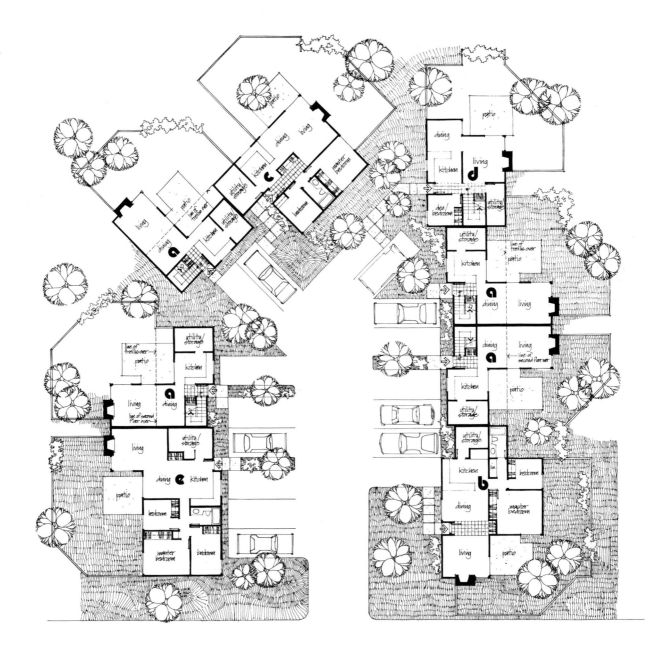

54

GREENSIDE
Surrey, British Columbia

Architect:
R. E. HULBERT AND PARTNERS
West Vancouver, British Columbia

Number of dwelling units: 276
    221—two bedroom
     55—three bedroom
Gross floor area: 260,000 sf

Construction cost: $5,200,000
                 $20.00/sf
                 $18,800/unit
Year of bid: 1977
Site area: 46 acres
           6.5 units/acre
User: middle income
Financing: federal assisted rental program

Photo credit: Simon Scott

SAMMAMISH SHORES CONDOMINIUMS
Bellevue, Washington

Architect:
THE MITHUN ASSOCIATES
Bellevue, Washington

Number of dwelling units: 29
        14—two bedroom row houses
        15—two bedroom apartments
Gross floor area: 75,950 sf
Construction cost: $1,900,000
                   $25.00/sf
                   $65,520/unit
Year of bid: 1973
Site area: 2.4 acres
           12 units/acre
User: upper income
Financing: conventional

Photo credit: James K. M. Cheng

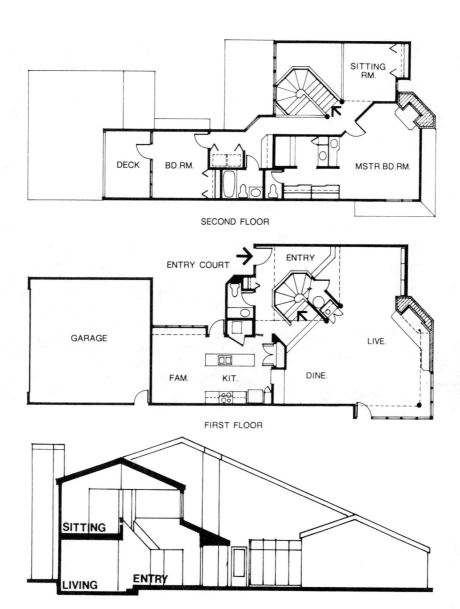

SECOND FLOOR

FIRST FLOOR

SAMMAMISH SHORES CONDOMINIUMS   493

56

SAHALEE VILLAGE CONDOMINIUMS
Redmond, Washington

Architect:
THE MITHUN ASSOCIATES
Bellevue, Washington

Number of dwelling units: 25
    12—two bedroom
    13—three bedroom
  Gross floor area: 45,000 sf
Construction cost: $945,000
              $21.00/sf
              $37,800/unit
    Year of bid: 1970
      Site area: 5 acres
            5 units/acre
         User: upper income
   Financing: conventional

Photo credit: James K. M. Cheng

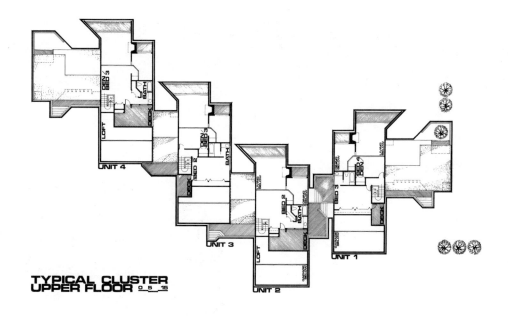

TYPICAL CLUSTER UPPER FLOOR 0 5 15

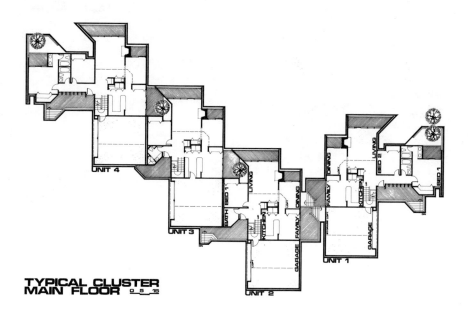

TYPICAL CLUSTER MAIN FLOOR 0 5 15

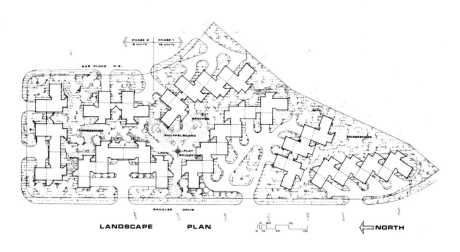

LANDSCAPE PLAN ⟸ NORTH

SAHALEE VILLAGE CONDOMINIUMS 495

57

TIBER ISLAND
Washington, D.C.

Architect:
KEYES, LETHBRIDGE & CONDON
Washington, D.C.

Number of dwelling units: 453
     Highrise: 160—efficiency
            120—one bedroom
  Townhouses: 60—two bedroom
            25—four bedroom
Gross floor area: 446,000 sf highrises
      186,000 sf row houses
      103,000 sf garage
Construction cost: $8,508,000
      $5,670,000 highrise
      $11.35 sf (including garage
      and half site development)
      $16,937/unit (including
      garage and half site
      development)
      $2,161,000 row houses
      $12.22 sf (including
      half site development)

$26,753/unit (including
half site development)
$450,000 garage
$227,000 site development
Year of bid: 1963
Site area: 8.12 acres
      56 units/acre
User: middle to upper income
Financing: FHA

Photo credit: J. Alexander

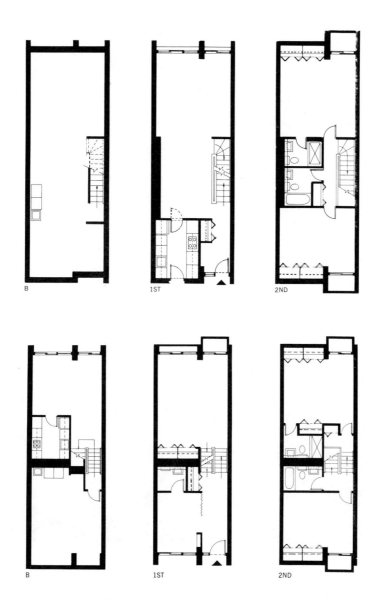

B   1ST   2ND

B   1ST   2ND

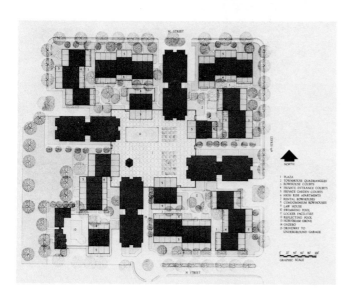

NORTH

1 PLAZA
2 TOWNHOUSE QUADRANGLES
3 ROWHOUSE COURTS
4 PRIVATE ENTRANCE COURTS
5 PRIVATE GARDEN COURTS
6 HIGH RISE APARTMENTS
7 RENTAL ROWHOUSES
8 CONDOMINIUM ROWHOUSES
9 LAW HOUSE
10 SWIMMING POOL
11 LOCKER FACILITIES
12 REFLECTING POOL
13 HORNBEAM GROVE
14 GAZEBO
15 DRIVEWAY TO
UNDERGROUND GARAGE

GRAPHIC SCALE

TIBER ISLAND   497

58 ATRIUM
Elmhurst, Illinois

Architect:
BOOTH & NAGLE
Chicago, Illinois

Number of dwelling units: 210 (+240 in midrises, not completed)
          10—two bedroom
         150—three bedroom
          50—four bedroom
Construction cost: $19.00/sf (on grade, open parking)
    Year of bid: 1972
      Site area: 17 acres
                   12.5 units/acre
          User: upper to middle income
     Financing: conventional

Photo credit: Philip Turner

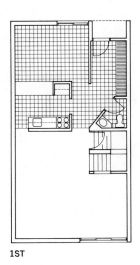

1ST

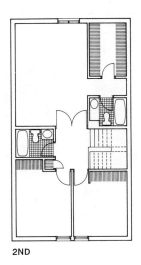

2ND

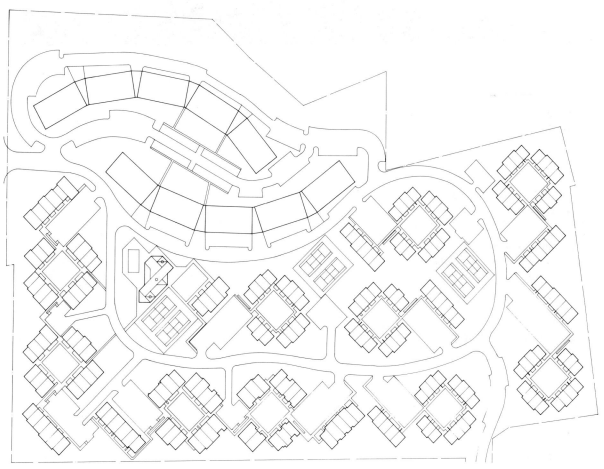

59

LAKE VILLAGE (row houses)
Chicago, Illinois

Architect:
HARRY WEESE & ASSOCIATES
EZRA GORDON–JACK LEVIN
Chicago, Illinois

Number of dwelling units: 18
     6—three bedroom
    12—four bedroom
  Gross floor area: 43,920 sf
Construction cost: $746,640
                $17.00/sf
                $41,480/unit
    Year of bid: 1968
      Site area: Part of large complex
         User: upper income
   Financing: conventional

Photo credit: Orlando Cabanban

2ND   1ST   BSMT

2ND   1ST   BSMT

LAKE VILLAGE   501

60

BRIAR/ORCHARD TOWNHOUSES
Chicago, Illinois

Architect:
BOOTH/HANSEN & ASSOCIATES
Chicago, Illinois

Number of dwelling units: 4
    4—3 bedroom row houses
Gross floor area: 10,320 sf
Construction cost: $560,000
          $54.26/sf
          $140,000/unit
Year of bid: 1979
Site area: 17 acre
          23.5 units/acre
User: upper income
Financing: conventional

Photo credit: Sandin/Karant

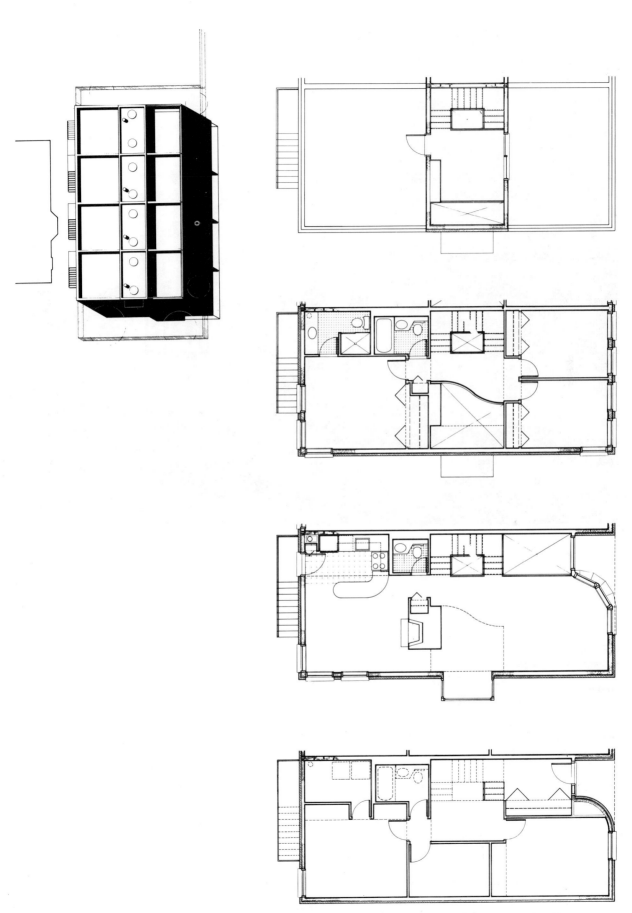

BRIAR/ORCHARD TOWNHOUSES   503

61

SECOND STREET TOWNHOUSES
Philadelphia, Pennsylvania

Architect:
LOUIS SAUER ASSOCIATES
Philadelphia, Pennsylvania

Number of dwelling units: 8
    8—three bedroom
  Gross floor area: 18,080 sf
  (parking off-site)
Construction cost: unavailable
      Year of bid: 1971
        Site area: 0.18 acre
              44.4 units/acre
           User: middle to upper income
    Financing: conventional

Photo credit: David Hirsch

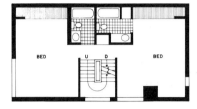

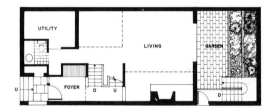

SECOND STREET TOWNHOUSES 505

62 GHENT SQUARE
Norfolk, Virginia

Architect:
BARTON MYERS ASSOCIATES
Toronto, Ontario

Number of dwelling units: 11
   All three bedroom
Gross floor area: 36,040 sf
Construction cost: unavailable
Year of bid: 1978
Site area: 0.69 acre
   16 units/acre
User: upper income
Financing: conventional

Photo credit: Lautman Photography

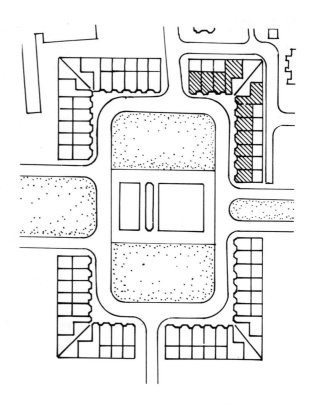

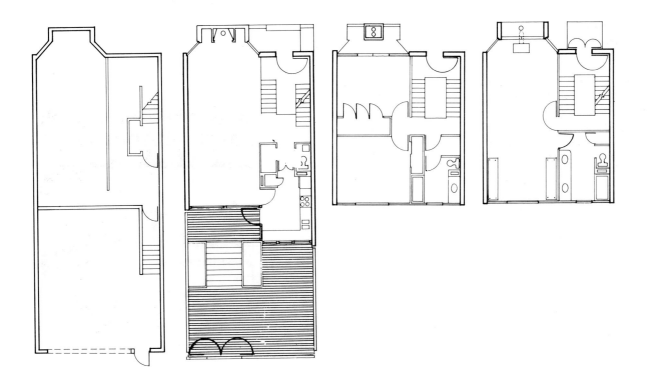

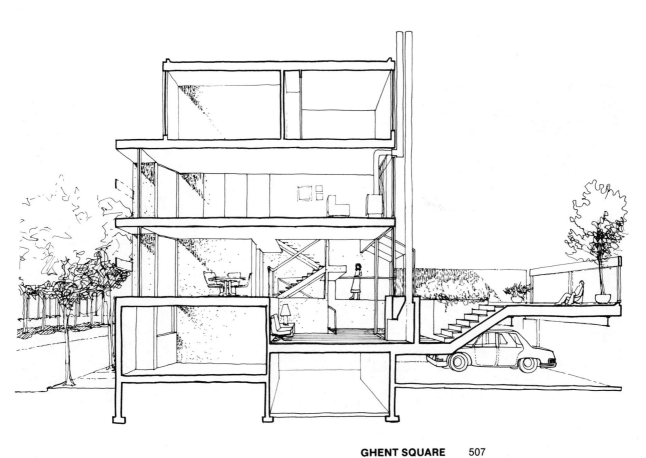

63 DAVIDS' PLAZA
Chicago, Illinois

Architect:
NAGLE, HARTRAY & ASSOCIATES, LTD.
(formerly Booth Nagle & Hartray/Ltd.)
Chicago, Illinois

Number of dwelling units: 10
        All two bedroom plus den
    Gross floor area: 24,000 sf
        (including 9000 sf commercial)
Construction cost: $800,000
                     $33.33/sf
                     $80,000/unit
     Year of bid: 1977
       Site area: 0.25 acre
                    40 units/acre
            User: middle income
       Financing: conventional

Photo credit: Orlando Cabanban

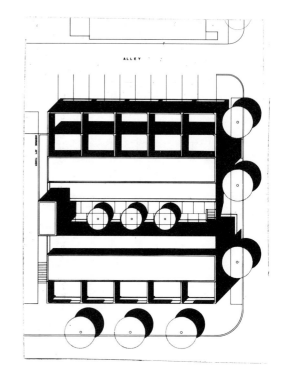

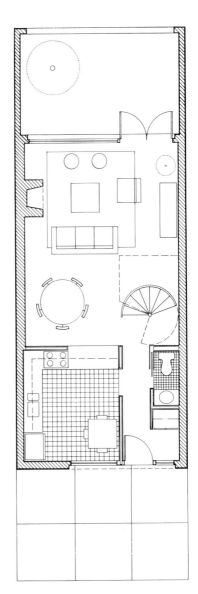

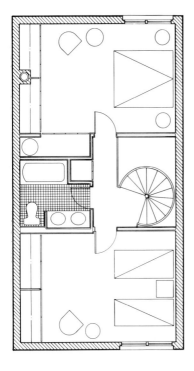

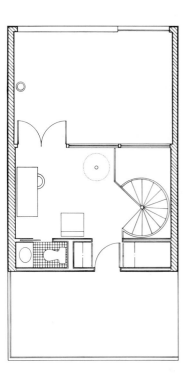

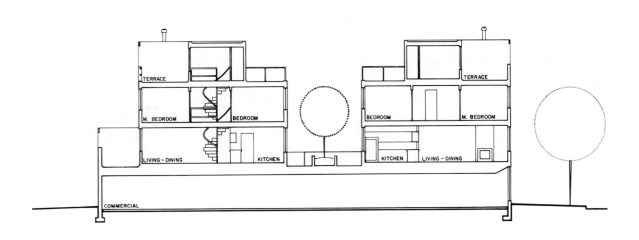

64 CANTERBURY GARDEN CO-OP
New Haven, Connecticut

Architect:
LOUIS SAUER ASSOCIATES
Philadelphia, Pennsylvania

Number of dwelling units: 34
    16—four bedroom row houses
    12—one bedroom walk-ups
    6—two bedroom walk-ups
    Gross floor area: 38,000 sf (open, on grade parking)
Construction cost: $850,000
                    $22.36/sf
                    $25,000/unit
    Year of bid: 1970
    Site area: 1.56 acres
                    22 units/acre
    User: low income
    Financing: FHA 235

Photo credit: Otto Baitz

3RD

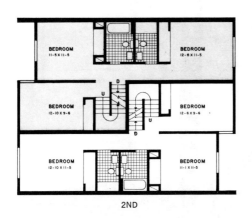

2ND

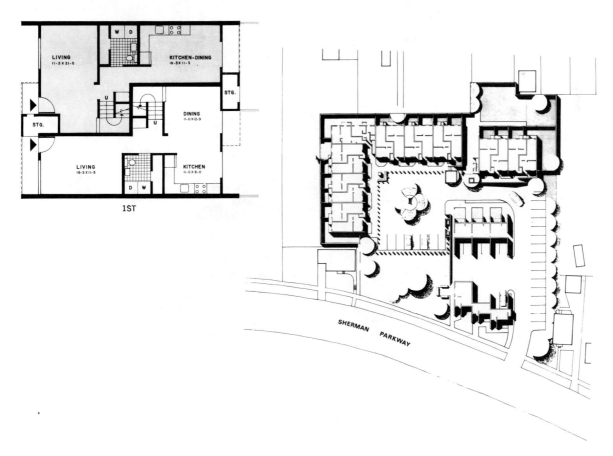

1ST

SHERMAN PARKWAY

65

TUSTIN APARTMENTS
Tustin, California

Architect:
BACKEN ARRIGONI & ROSS, INC.
San Francisco, California

Number of dwelling units: 296
　　57—two bedroom (patio)
　　167—one bedroom (patio)
　　72—two bedroom (flats)
Gross floor area: 258,450 sf (open,
　　　　　　　　　　on grade parking)
Construction cost: $2,580,400
　　　　　　　　　　$9.98/sf
　　　　　　　　　　$8,718/unit
Year of bid: 1968
Site area: 11.89 acres
　　　　　　25 units/acre
User: low to middle income
Financing: private

Photo credit: Ed Stoecklein

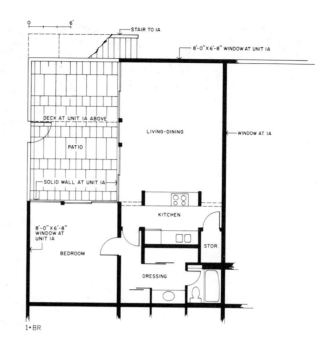

0   6'

STAIR TO IA

8'-0" X 6'-8" WINDOW AT UNIT IA

DECK AT UNIT IA ABOVE

LIVING-DINING

WINDOW AT IA

PATIO

SOLID WALL AT UNIT IA

8'-0" X 6'-8"
WINDOW AT
UNIT IA

KITCHEN

STOR

BEDROOM

DRESSING

1•BR

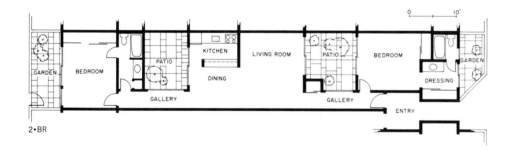

0   10'

GARDEN

BEDROOM

KITCHEN

LIVING ROOM

PATIO

BEDROOM

GARDEN

PATIO

DINING

DRESSING

GALLERY

GALLERY

ENTRY

2•BR

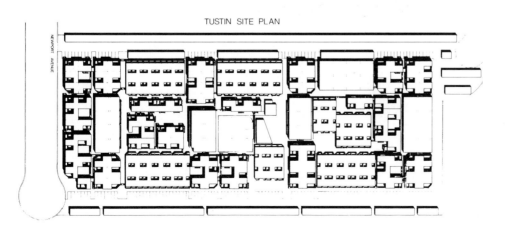

TUSTIN SITE PLAN

NEWPORT AVENUE

TUSTIN APARTMENTS   513

66

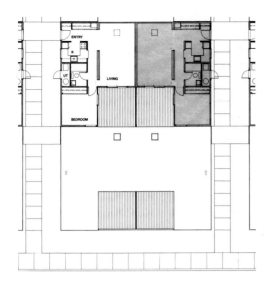

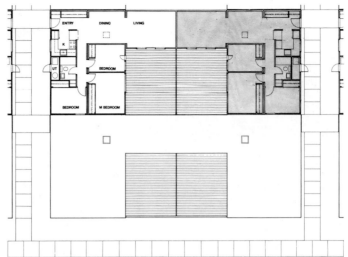

1 BR ATRIUM PLAN

3 BR ATRIUM PLAN

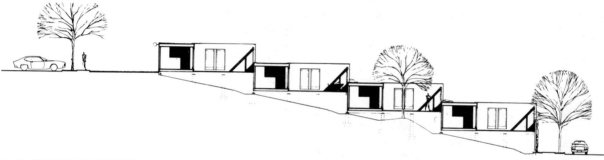

ELM STREET HOUSING
Ithaca, New York

Architect:
WERNER SELIGMAN AND ASSOCIATES
Cortland, New York

Number of dwelling units: 235
    28—one bedroom atriums
    72—three bedroom atriums
    80—two bedroom in row house
       on row house walk-up
    20—one bedroom in row house
       on row house walk-up
    17—one bedroom in duplex walk-up
    18—four bedroom in duplex walk-up

Gross floor area: 211,770 sf (on grade,
                      open parking)
Construction cost: $5,173,000
                $24.42 sf
                $22,013/unit
Year of bid: 1970
Site area: 17.63 acres
            13.5 units/acre
User: 70% middle income
        20% low income
        10% elderly
Financing: UDC (FHA 236)

Photo credit: Nathaniel Lieberman

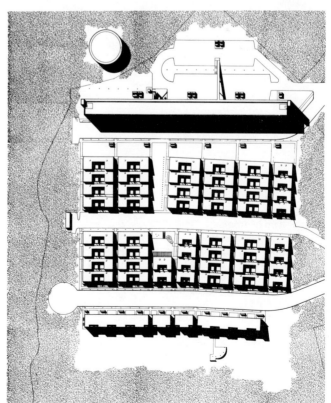

ELM STREET HOUSING   515

67

RENO STREET PUBLIC HOUSING
Philadelphia, Pennsylvania

Architect:
JOE J. JORDAN
Philadelphia, Pennsylvania

Number of dwelling units: 33
    24—two bedroom
     9—three bedroom
  Gross floor area: 53,200 (open, on grade parking)
Construction cost: $478,500 (including land and architect fee)
                 $8.99/sf
                 $14,500/unit
      Year of bid: 1965
       Site area: 0.92 acres
                 36 units/acre
          User: low income
     Financing: HUD Turnkey

Photo credit: Lawrence S. Williams

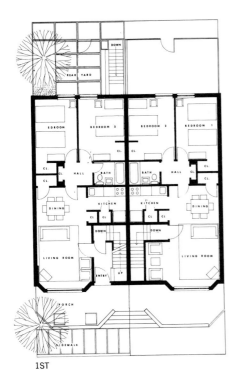

1ST

2ND

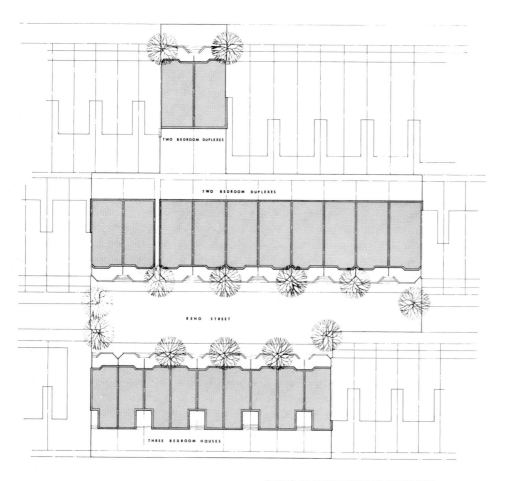

TWO BEDROOM DUPLEXES

TWO BEDROOM DUPLEXES

RENO STREET

THREE BEDROOM HOUSES

RENO STREET PUBLIC HOUSING   517

68 LAKE VILLAGE (walk-up)
Chicago, Illinois

Architect:
HARRY WEESE & ASSOCIATES
EZRA GORDON–JACK LEVIN
Chicago, Illinois

Number of dwelling units: 122
    24—one bedroom
    70—two bedroom
    28—three bedroom
  Gross floor area: 120,070 sf (open, on grade parking)
Construction cost: $1,615,550
                $13.45/sf
                $13,242/unit
    Year of bid: 1968
      Site area: part of large complex
          User: moderate income
    Financing: FHA 236

Photo credit: Philip Turner

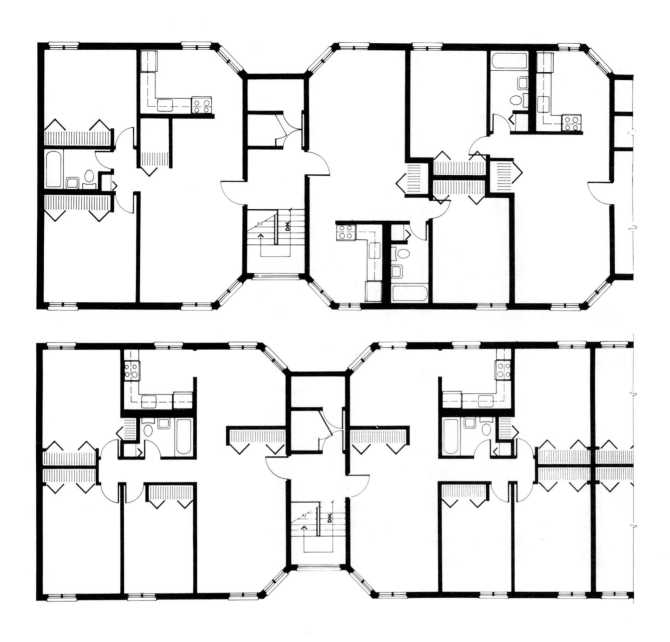

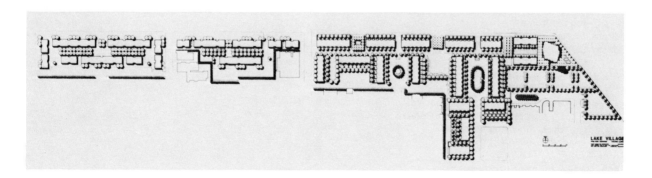

69

BANNEKER HOMES
San Francisco, California

Architect:
ESHERICK HOMSEY DODGE AND DAVIS
San Francisco, California

Number of dwelling units: 108
     12—one bedroom
     40—two bedroom
     35—three bedroom
     21—four bedroom
  Gross floor area: 168,000 sf
Construction cost: $1,790,000
                $10.65/sf
                $16,574/unit
    Year of bid: 1967
      Site area: approximately 2.45 acres
                approximately 45 units/acre
         User: low income
    Financing: FHA 221 (d) 3

Photo credit: Kathleen Kershaw

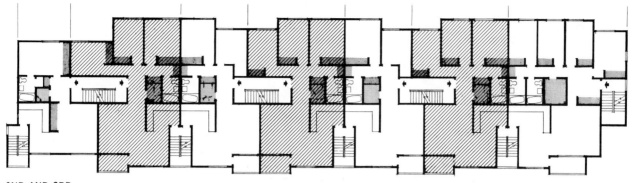

2ND AND 3RD

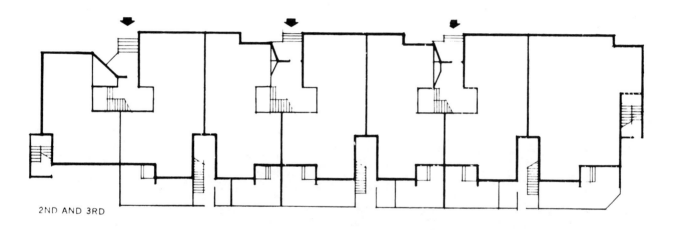

2ND AND 3RD

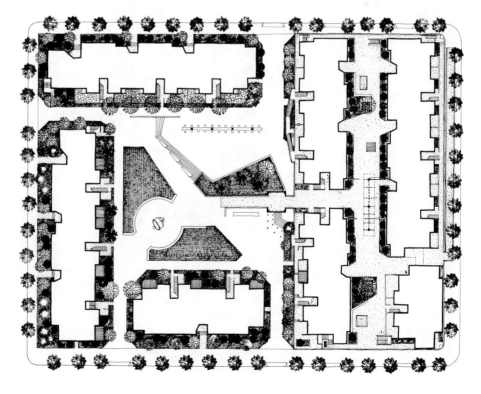

BANNEKER HOMES   521

70 ST. FRANCIS SQUARE
San Francisco, California

Architect:
MARQUIS & STOLLER
San Francisco, California

Number of dwelling units: 299
      14—one bedroom
    107—two bedroom
    178—three bedroom
    Gross floor area: 305,600 sf (including approximately 20,000 sf parking structures)
    Construction cost: $3,497,000 (including parking structures and site work)
                    $10.74/sf
                    $11,696/unit
           Year of bid: 1962
            Site area: 8.15 acres
                    36.5 units/acre
                User: low income
          Financing: FHA 221 (d) 3

Photo credit: Karl H. Riek

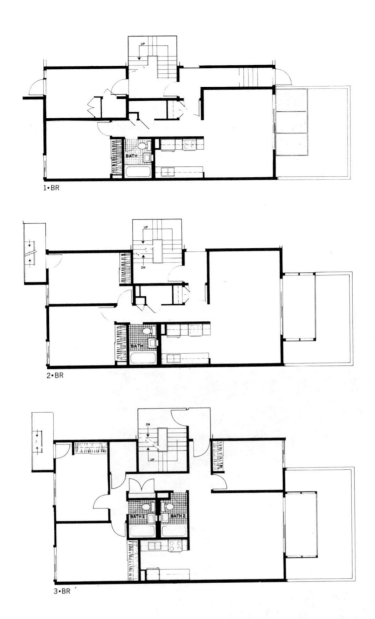

1•BR

2•BR

3•BR

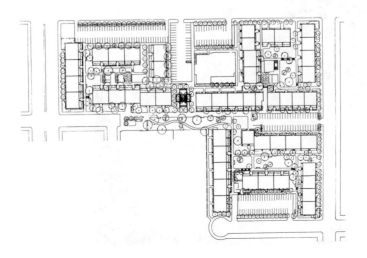

71 BUFFALO WATERFRONT HOUSING
Buffalo, New York

Architect:
PAUL RUDOLPH
New York, New York

The project, in addition to the walk-ups illustrated here, contains midrises and the data refer to the total project.
Number of dwelling units: 814
     178—efficiency
     197—one bedroom
     287—two bedroom
     152—three bedroom
     Construction cost: $20,790,000
     Year of bid: 1970–1972
    Site area and density: not available
Square feet of buildings: not available
            User: low income
      Financing: U.D.C.

Photo credit: Donald Luckenbill

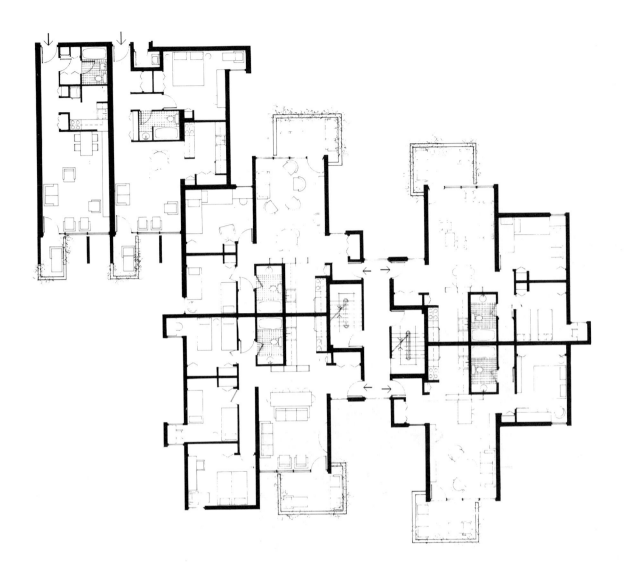

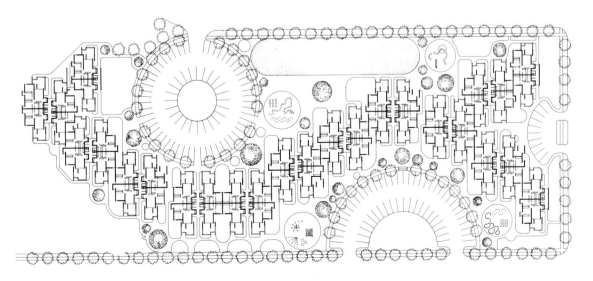

BUFFALO WATERFRONT HOUSING 525

72

PORTALS
Chicago, Illinois

Architect:
BOOTH & NAGLE
Chicago, Illinois

Number of dwelling units: 50 three bedroom apartments
  Gross floor area: 75,000 sf
Construction cost: $1,350,000 (open, on grade parking)
                     $18.00/sf
                     $27,000/unit
      Year of bid: 1971
        Site area: 0.94 acres
                     53 units/acre
             User: middle income
        Financing: conventional

Photo credit: Philip Turner

A

A

B

B

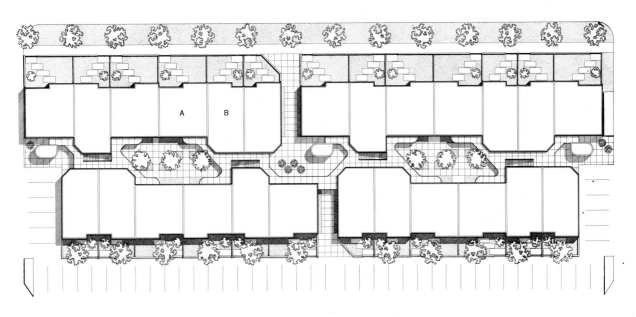

A   B

73

UNIVERSITY PARK
Ithaca, New York

Architect:
DONALD SANDY JR./JAMES A. BABCOCK
San Francisco, California

Number of dwelling units: 300
      117—one bedroom
       83—two bedroom
  Gross floor area: 160,000 sf
Construction cost: $3,600,000
              $22.50/sf
              $12,000/unit
     Year of bid: 1971
       Site area: 10.9 acres
              27.5 units/acre
           User: low income
     Financing: conventional

Photo credit: Lance Gardner Biesele

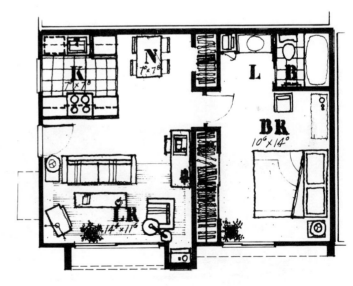

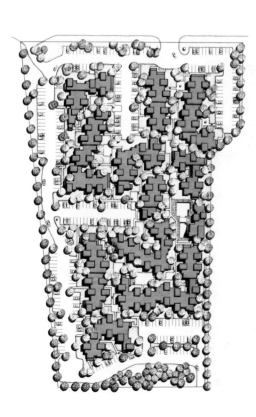

74 ELM STREET HOUSING
Ithaca, New York

Architect:
WERNER SELIGMAN AND ASSOCIATES
Cortland, New York

Number of dwelling units: 235
    28—one bedroom atriums
    72—three bedroom atriums
    80—two bedroom in townhouse on townhouse walk-up
    20—one bedroom in townhouse on townhouse walk-up
    17—one bedroom in duplex walk-up
    18—four bedroom in duplex walk-up
  Gross floor area: 211,770 sf (on grade, open parking)
Construction cost: $5,173,000
                $24.42 sf
                $22,013/unit
      Year of bid: 1970
        Site area: 17.63 acres
                13.5 units/acre
           User: 70% middle income
                20% low income
                10% elderly
      Financing: UDC (FHA 236)

Photo credits: Nathaniel Lieberman; aerial: C. Hadley Smith

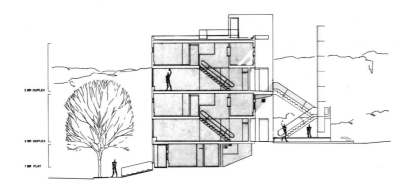

2 BR DUPLEX

2 BR DUPLEX

1 BR FLAT

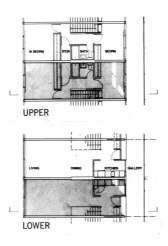

M BEDRM | STOR | BATH | BEDRM

UPPER

LIVING | DINING | KITCHEN | GALLERY

LOWER

ELM STREET HOUSING 531

ESPLANADE VILLAGE
Redondo Beach, California

Architect:
BRENT GOLDMAN ROBBINS & BROWN
West Los Angeles, California

Number of dwelling units: 105
    29—efficiency
     9—one bedroom
    22—two bedroom
    45—three bedroom
  Gross floor area: 156,000 sf (including parking garage)
Construction cost: $1,400,000
              $8.97/sf
              $13,333/unit
     Year of bid: 1971
       Site area: 1.2 acres
             87 units/acre
           User: upper to middle income
     Financing: conventional

Photo credit: Chuck Crandall

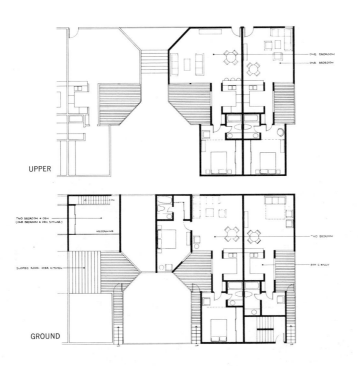

UPPER

ONE BEDROOM
ONE BEDROOM

TWO BEDROOM & DEN
(ONE BEDROOM & DEN SIMILAR)

MEZZANINE

SLOPED ROOF OVER KITCHEN

GROUND

TWO BEDROOM

SEA C ENCY

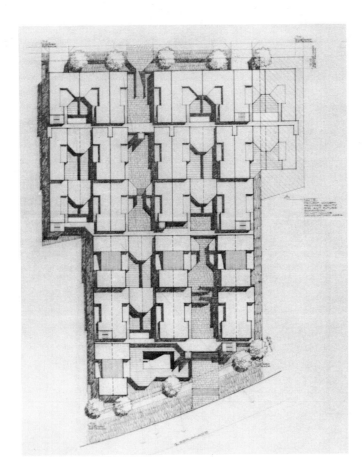

ESPLANADE VILLAGE   533

76

2·BR

deck

deck

fireplace

deck

1·BR

534   **LOWRISE—WALKUP/CORRIDOR TYPE**

EAST BURNSIDE
Portland, Oregon

Architect:
MARTIN/SODERSTROM/MATTESON
Portland, Oregon

Number of dwelling units: 26
    10—one bedroom
    16—two bedroom
Construction cost: $10.00 sf
    Year of bid: 1967
    Site area: 0.78 acres
               33.5 units/acre
    User: middle income
    Financing: conventional

Photo credit: Edmund Y. Lee

77

THE CITADEL
Albuquerque, New Mexico

Architect:
ANTOINE PREDOCK
Albuquerque, New Mexico

Number of dwelling units: 232
    102—efficiency
    128—one bedroom
      2—guest units
Gross floor area: 123,160 sf (open, on grade parking)
Construction cost: $2,000,000
              $16.23/sf
              $8,621/unit
Year of bid: 1972
Site area: 5.43 acres
           43 units/acre
User: middle income
Financing: conventional

Photo credit: Joshua Freiwald

E

1•BR

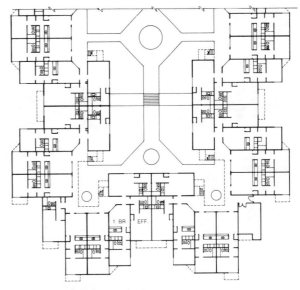

1 BR   EFF

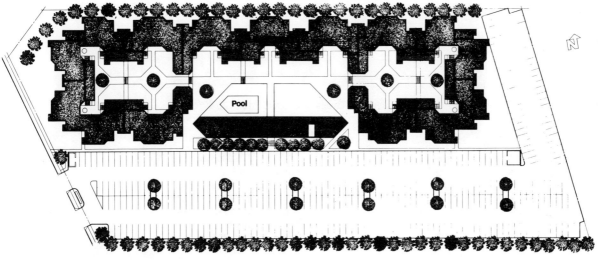

Pool

N

Site Plan

78

SURSUM CORDA
Washington, D.C.

Architect:
COLLINS & KRONSTAD
Silver Springs, Maryland

Number of dwelling units: 199
  Apartments
    30—efficiency
    14—one bedroom
    30—two bedroom
    14—three bedroom
  Row houses
    25—three bedroom
    46—four bedroom
    20—five bedroom
    20—six bedroom

Gross floor area: 193,000 sf (open, on grade parking)
Construction cost: $3,000,000
  $15.53/sf
  $15,075/unit
Year of bid: 1968
Site area: 5.63 acres
  35.5/units acre
User: low to moderate income
Financing: FHA 221 (d) 3

Photo credit: Mark G. Farris

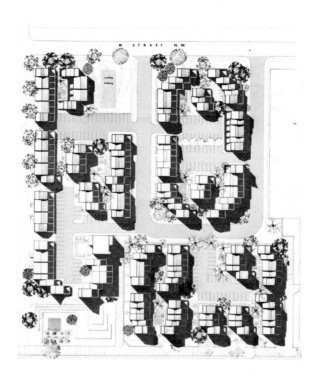

3RD

2ND

1ST

79 CHURCH STREET SOUTH
New Haven, Connecticut

Architect:
CHARLES W. MOORE ASSOCIATES
Essex, Connecticut

Number of dwelling units: 301
     5—one bedroom
  102—two bedroom
  151—three bedroom
     9—four bedroom
   34—five bedroom
Gross floor area: 335,300 sf + 13,400 commercial (parking mostly open, on grade, some under building)
Construction cost: $5,887,000 sf (including commercial)
                  $16.88/sf (including commercial)
                  $19,558/unit (including commercial)
Year of bid: 1970
Site area: 8.26 acres
           36.5 units/acre
User: low income
Financing: FHA 221 (d) 3

Photo credit: Sharon Lee Ryder

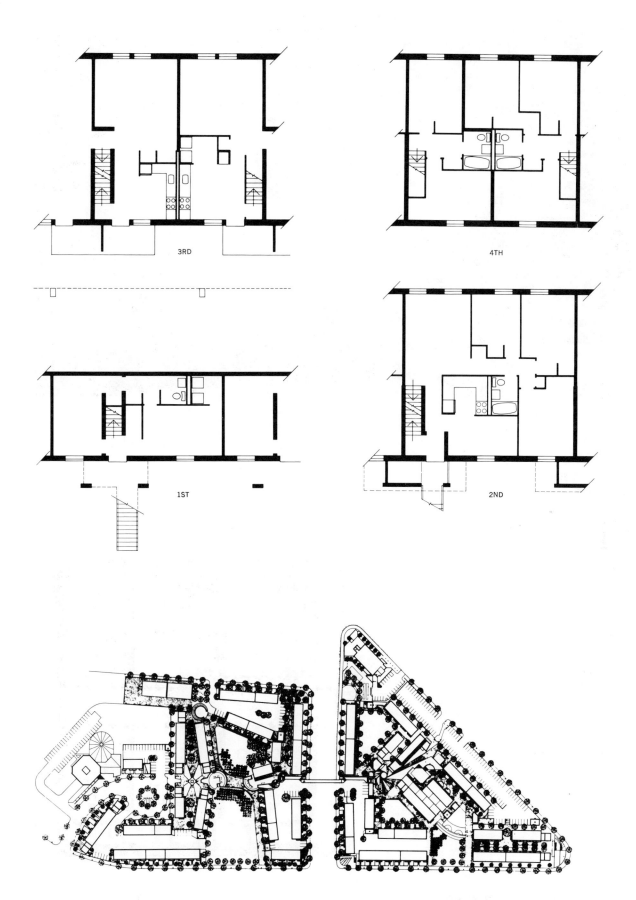

3RD

4TH

1ST

2ND

CHURCH STREET SOUTH 541

80

LOVETT SQUARE
Houston, Texas

Architect:
WM. T. CANNADY & ASSOCIATES
Houston, Texas

Number of dwelling units: 36
     24—two bedroom
     12—two bedroom plus study
Gross floor area: 90,000 sf
  (incl. 30,000 sf garage)
Construction cost: $2,254,000
              $25.00/sf
              $62,610/unit
Year of bid: 1978
Site area: 1.43 acres
            25 units/acre
User: middle-upper income
Financing: conventional

Photo credit: Rick Gardner

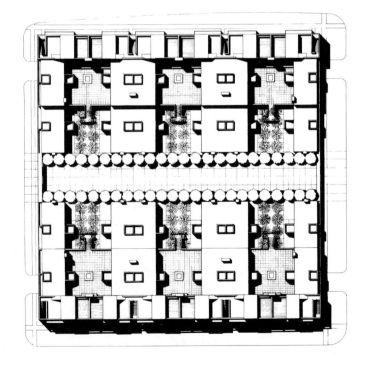

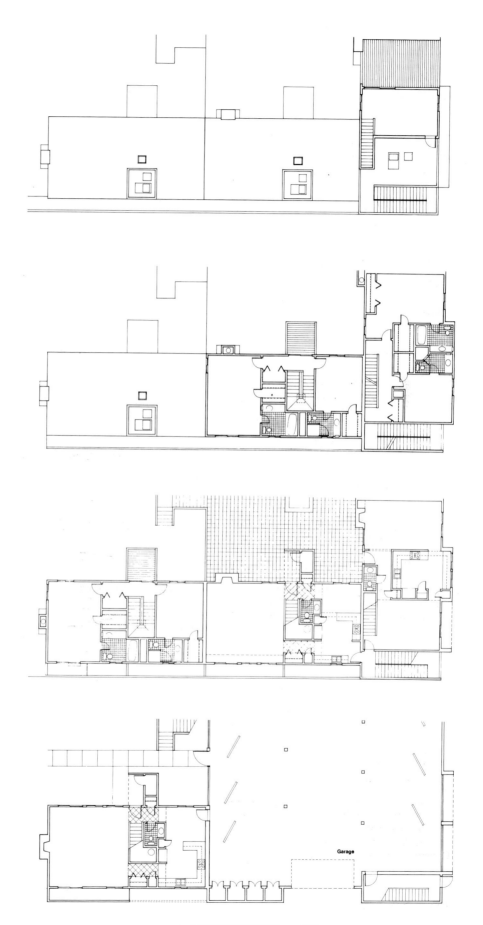

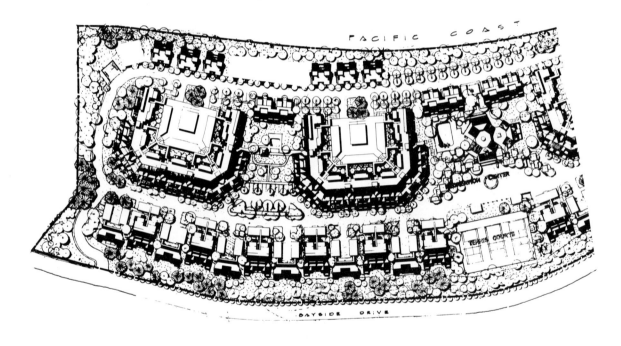

81

PROMONTORY POINT
Newport Beach, California

Architect:
FISHER–FRIEDMAN–ASSOCIATES
San Francisco, California

Number of dwelling units:	520	Year of bid:	1974
190—one bedroom		Site area:	30 acres
330—two bedroom			17.33 units/acre
Gross floor area:	793,789 sf	User:	upper income
Construction cost:	$22,000,000	Financing:	conventional
	$27.71/sf		
	$42,310/unit		

Photo credit: Joshua Friewald

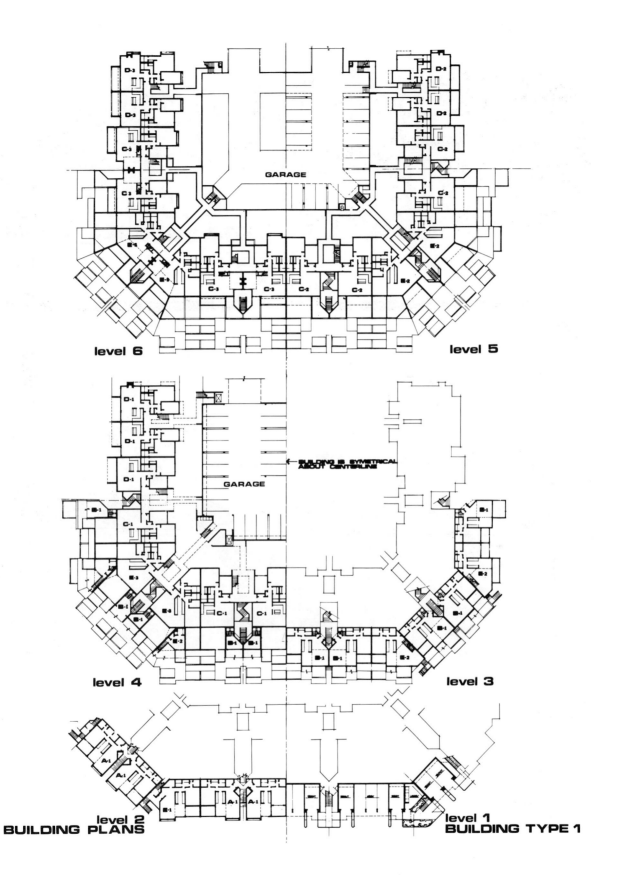

level 6

GARAGE

level 5

level 4

GARAGE

BUILDING IS SYMETRICAL
ABOUT CENTERLINE

level 3

level 2
BUILDING PLANS

level 1
BUILDING TYPE 1

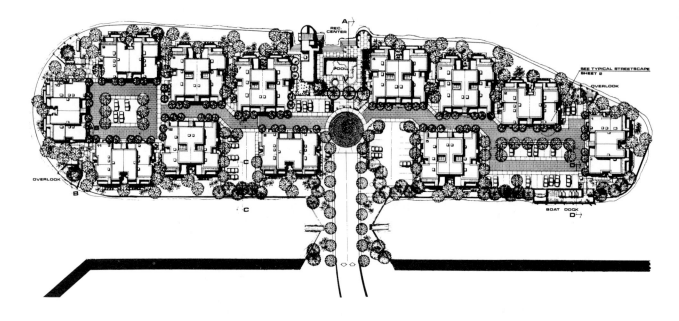

82

THE ISLANDS
Foster City, California

Architect:
FISHER–FRIEDMAN–ASSOCIATES
San Francisco, California

Number of dwelling units: 246
   202—two bedroom
    44—three bedroom
  Gross floor area: 473,210 sf
Construction cost: $18,500,000
          $39.09/sf
          $72,200/unit
  Year of bid: 1973

Site area: 15.5 acres
          15.87 units/acre
User: upper income
Financing: conventional

Photo credit: Joshua Friewald

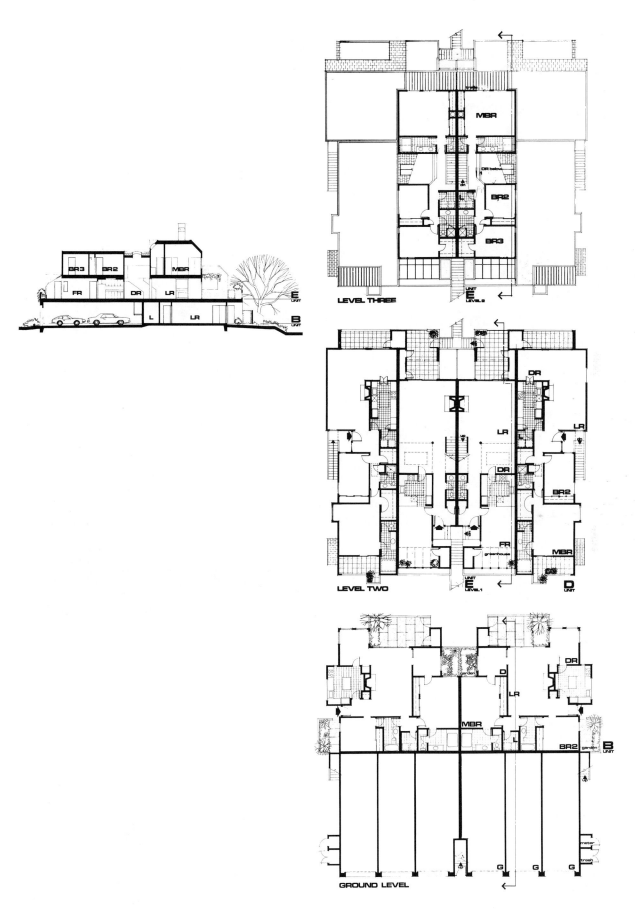

BR3 BR2 MBR
FR DR LR
L LR
E UNIT
B UNIT

MBR
DR below
BR2
BR3
LEVEL THREE
UNIT E LEVEL 2

DR
LR
LR
DR
LR
BR2
FR
greenhouse
MBR
LEVEL TWO
UNIT E LEVEL 1
D UNIT

DR
D
LR
garden
MBR
BR2 garden
B UNIT
garden
meter
trash
G G G
GROUND LEVEL

THE ISLANDS 547

83

PENN'S LANDING SQUARE
Philadelphia, Pennsylvania

Architect:
LOUIS SAUER ASSOCIATES
Philadelphia, Pennsylvania

Number of dwelling units: 103
  Apartments:
    17—three bedroom
    1—four bedroom
  Row houses:
    45—one bedroom
    32—two bedroom
    8—three bedroom
  Gross floor area: 220,480 sf
  (including garage for 123 cars)
Construction cost: $3,732,000
                     $16.92/sf
                     $36,230/unit
    Year of bid: 1971
    Site area: 2.3 acres
                 44.8 units/acre
        User: upper income
  Financing: conventional

Photo credit: David Hirsch

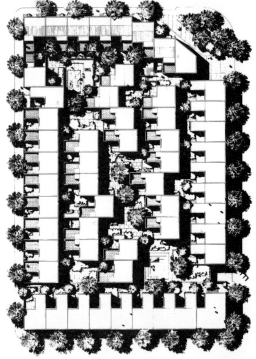

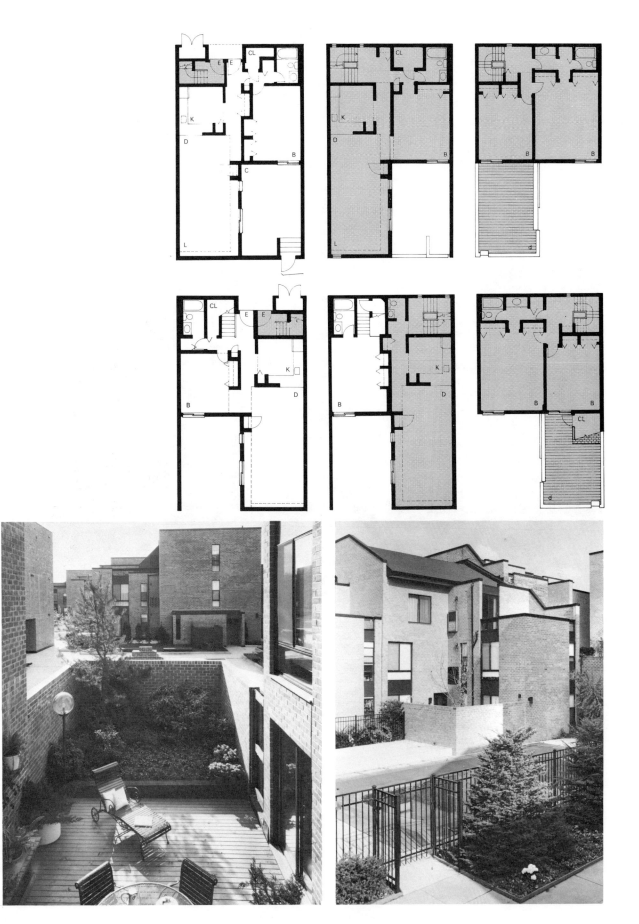

84

LOMBARD CONDOS
Philadelphia, Pennsylvania

Architect:
LOUIS SAUER ASSOCIATES
Philadelphia, Pennsylvania

Number of dwelling units: 16 (8@2)
   8—two bedroom plus den
   8—two bedroom plus den plus greenhouse
  Gross floor area: 30,000 sf
  (parking off site)
Construction cost: $800,000
               $26.66/sf
               $50,000/unit
    Year of bid: 1978
     Site area: .16 acre
             100 units/acre
        User: middle to upper income
  Financing: conventional

Photo credit: Robert Harris

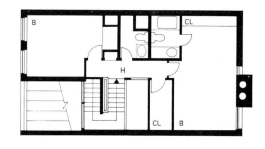

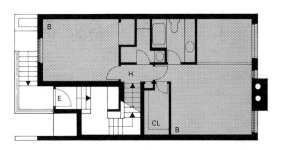

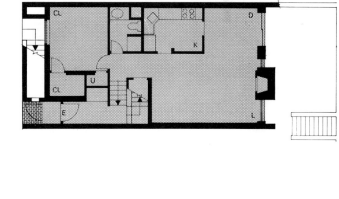

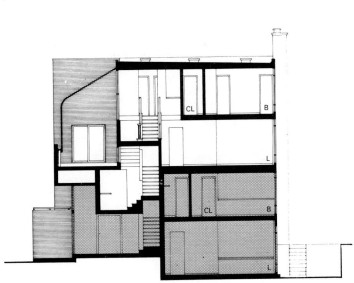

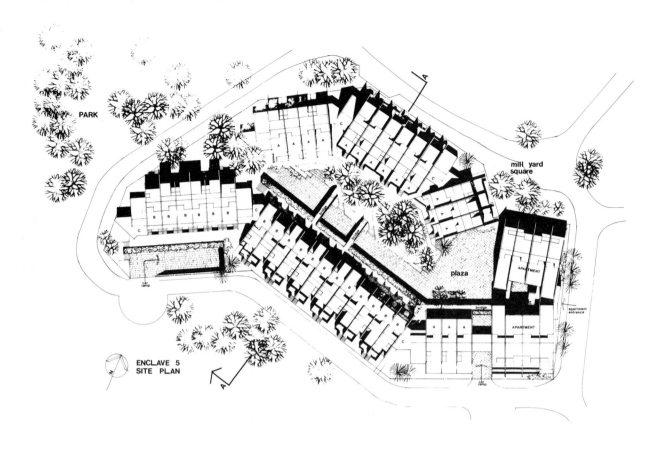

85

ENCLAVE 5
SITE PLAN

PARK

mill yard
square

plaza

APARTMENT

APARTMENT

bridge

apartment
entrance

car ramp

car ramp

FALSE CREEK COOPERATIVE
Vancouver, British Columbia

Architect:
HENRIQUEZ & PARTNERS
Vancouver, British Columbia

Number of dwelling units: 170
    12—one bedroom
    98—two bedroom
    38—three bedroom
    22—four bedroom
  Gross floor area: 170,000 sf
Construction cost: $7,000,000
              $41.18/sf
              $41,180/unit
    Year of bid: 1976
      Density: 35 to 45 units/acre
        User: low income
   Financing: Government
           (Canada Mortgage & Housing Corporation)

Photo credit: Simon Scott

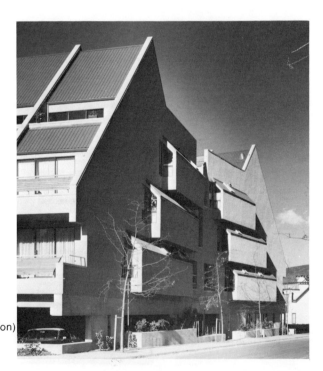

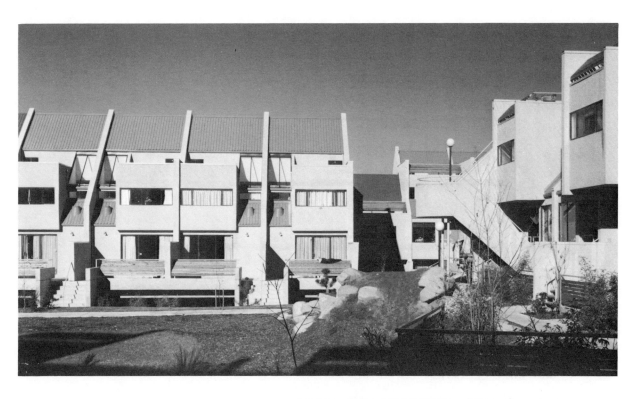

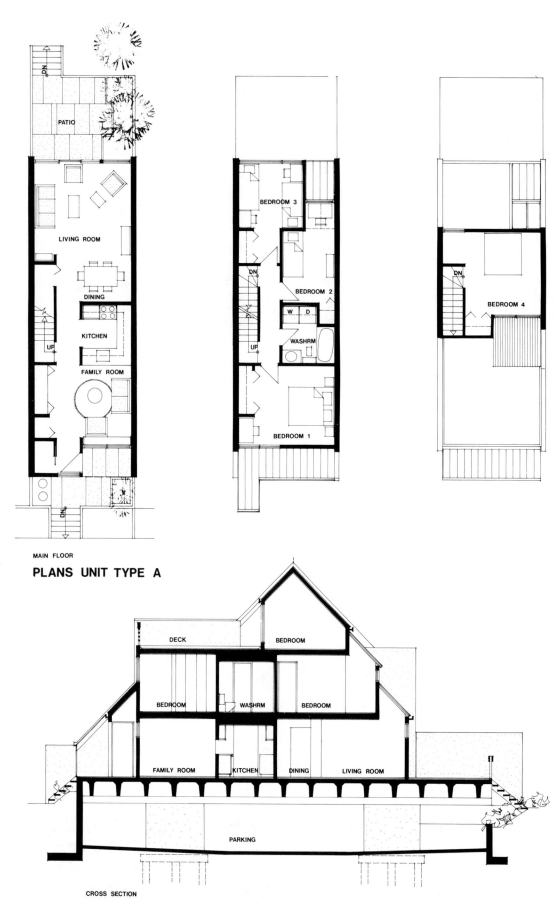

MAIN FLOOR

PLANS UNIT TYPE A

LIVING ROOM

DINING

KITCHEN

FAMILY ROOM

PATIO

DN

UP

BEDROOM 3

DN

BEDROOM 2

W   D

WASHRM

UP

BEDROOM 1

DN

BEDROOM 4

CROSS SECTION

SECTION & ELEVATION UNIT TYPE A

DECK   BEDROOM

BEDROOM   WASHRM   BEDROOM

FAMILY ROOM   KITCHEN   DINING   LIVING ROOM

PARKING

554   **LOWRISE—WALKUP/MIXED**

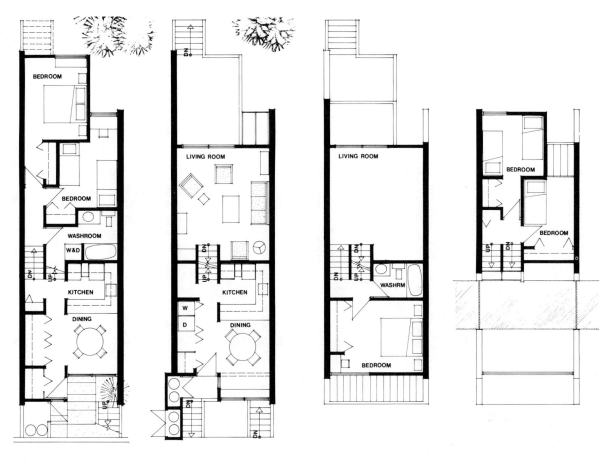

LOWER UNIT   LOWER UNIT / UPPER UNIT   UPPER UNIT   UPPER UNIT – TOP FLOOR

UNIT TYPE B

SECTION UNIT TYPE B

FALSE CREEK COOPERATIVE   555

86

COLDSPRING NEW TOWN
Baltimore, Maryland

Architect:
MOSHE SAFDIE AND ASSOCIATES INC.
Boston, Massachusetts

Number of dwelling units: 124
    74—two- and four-bedroom maisonettes
    48—three-bedroom row houses
    2—three-bedroom bridge units
Gross floor area (incl. decks):   224,000 sf
Construction cost (incl. decks): $6,750,000
                    $30.13/sf
                    $54,430/unit

Year of bid: 1976
Site area: 6 acres
            20.66 units/acre
User: middle and upper income
Financing: City of Baltimore bond issue

Photo credit: Moshe Safdie and Assoc.

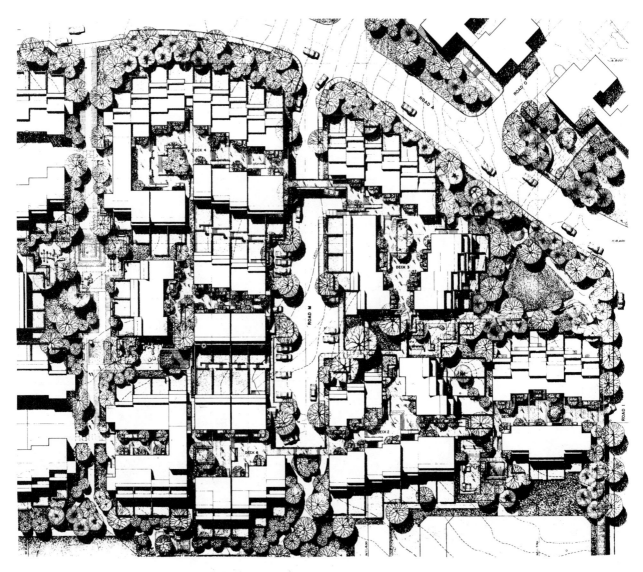

87

560   **LOWRISE—WALKUP/MIXED**

MARCUS GARVEY PARK VILLAGE
Brownsville, New York

Architect:
THE INSTITUTE FOR ARCHITECTURE AND URBAN STUDIES/DAVID TODD &
ASSOCIATES
(Architects: Arthur Baker, Kenneth Frampton; Planner: Peter Wolf; Supervising Architect: Leland
   Taliaferro) Prototype Studies office, Chief of Architecture N.Y. State Urban Development Corp.
New York, New York

Number of dwelling units: 625
      23—efficiency
      63—one bedroom
   291—two bedroom
   180—three bedroom
      40—four bedroom
      28—five bedroom
            Construction cost: $22,650,000 (including 5000 sf community space; 800 sf
                              commercial; 12,000 sf day-care; open on-grade parking)
                              $36,240/unit
            Year of bid: 1973
            Site area: 12.5 acres
                        50 units/acre
                  User: low income
            Financing: UDC

Photo credit: Norman McGrath

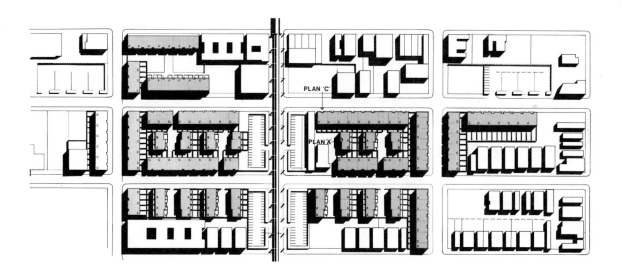

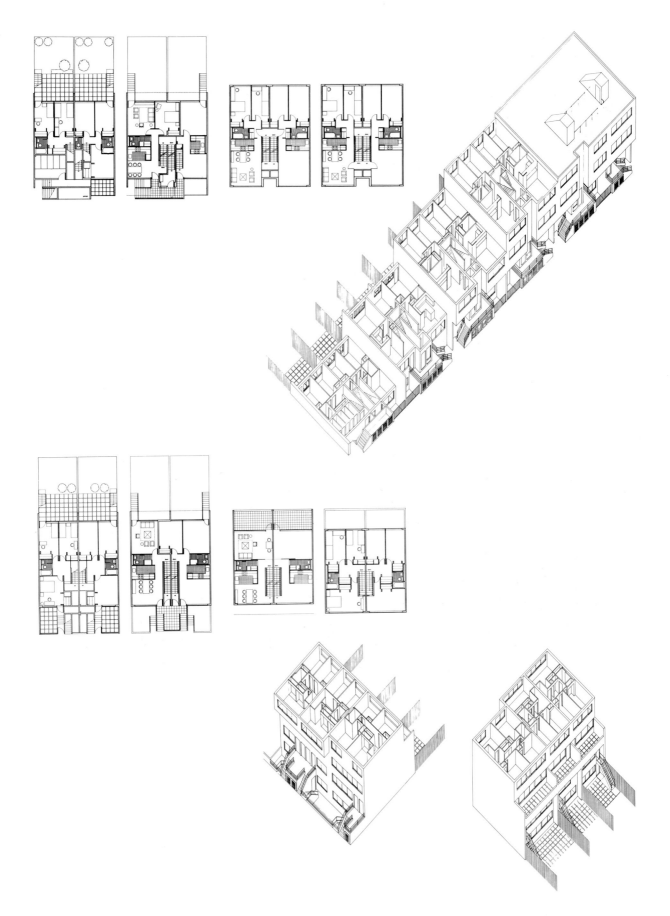

BIBLIOGRAPHY

HOUSING

Davis, Sam, ed.: *The Form of Housing* (New York: Van Nostrand Reinhold, 1977).

DeChiara, Joseph and Koppelman, Lee: *Manual of Housing/Planning and Design Criteria* (Englewood Cliffs, N.J.: Prentice-Hall, 1975).

Deilman, Harald, Kirschenman, Jörg C., and Pfeiffer, Herbert: *The Dwelling* (Stuttgart: Karl Kramer, 1973).

Engstrom, Robert and Putnam, Marc: *Planning and Design of Townhouses and Condominiums* (Washington, D.C.: Urban Land Institute, 1979).

Institute for Architecture and Urban Studies, New York State Urban Development Corporation: *Another Chance for Housing: Low-Rise Alternatives* (New York: Museum of Modern Art, 1973).

Jacobs, Jane: *Death and Life of Great American Cities* (New York: Random House, 1961).

Kirschenmann, Jorg C. and Muschalek, Christian: *Residential Districts* (New York: Watson-Guptill, 1980).

Newman, Oscar: *Defensible Space* (New York: Macmillan, 1972).

Newman, Oscar: *Community of Interest* (New York: Anchor/Doubleday, 1980).

Schmitt, Karl Wilhelm: *Multistory Housing* (New York: Praeger, 1966).

Sherwood, Roger: *Modern Housing Prototypes* (Cambridge, Mass.: Harvard University Press, 1978).

PLANNING, SITE PLANNING

Ashcraft, Norman and Scheflen, Albert E.: *People Space* (New York: Anchor Doubleday, 1976).

Ashihara, Yoshinobu: *Exterior Design in Architecture* (New York: Van Nostrand Reinhold, 1970).

Barnett, Jonathan: *Urban Design as Public Policy* (New York: Architectural Record Books, 1974).

Catanese, Anthony J. and Snyder, James C., eds.: *Introduction to Urban Planning* (New York: McGraw-Hill, 1979).

Chermayeff, Serge and Alexander, Christopher: *Community and Privacy* (New York: Anchor/Doubleday, 1965).

Cullen, Gordon: *Townscape* (New York: Reinhold, 1961).

DeChiara, Joseph and Koppelman, Lee: *Site Planning Standards* (New York: McGraw-Hill, 1978).

Halprin, Lawrence: *Cities* (Cambridge, Mass.: M.I.T. Press, 1972).

Lynch, Kevin: *Site Planning* (Cambridge, Mass.: M.I.T. Press, 1971).

Mercer, Charles: *Living in Cities* (Baltimore: Penquin, 1975).

Reilly, William K., ed.: *The Use of Land* (New York: Thomas Y. Crowell, 1973).

Rubenstein, Harvey M.: *A Guide to Site and Environmental Planning*, 2nd ed. (New York: Wiley, 1980).

Untermann, Richard and Small, Robert: *Site Planning for Cluster Housing* (New York: Van Nostrand Reinhold, 1977).

Whyte, William: *The Last Landscape* (New York: Anchor/Doubleday, 1970).

REFERENCE SOURCES

Callender, John Hancock, ed.: *Time-Saver Standards for Architectural Design Data* (New York: McGraw-Hill, latest edition).

DeChiara, Joseph and Callender, John Hancock, eds.: *Time-Saver Standards for Building Types* (New York: McGraw-Hill, latest edition).

H.U.D. Minimum Property Standards (U.S. Department of Housing and Urban Development, latest edition).

Kira, Alexander: *The Bathroom* (New York: Viking, 1976).

BIBLIOGRAPHY

Newman, Oscar and Johnston, Stephen: *Model Security Code for Residential Areas* (New York: Institute for Community Design Analysis, 1974).

Ramsey, Charles G. and Sleeper, Harold R.: *Architectural Graphic Standards* (New York: Wiley, latest edition).

HOUSING AND ENVIRONMENTAL CONTROL

Banham, Reyner: *The Architecture of the Well-Tempered Environment* (Chicago: University of Chicago Press, 1969).

Fitch, James Marston: *American Building, The Environmental Forces That Shape It* (Boston: Houghton Mifflin, 1972).

THE GAME PLAYERS

Mayer, Martin: *The Builders* (New York: W. W. Norton, 1978).

ZONING

Babcock, Richard F.: *The Zoning Game* (Madison: University of Wisconsin Press, 1969).

Urban Design Council of the City of New York: *Housing Quality, A Program for Zoning Reform* (New York, 1973).

LANDSCAPE

Laurie, Michael: *An Introduction to Landscape Architecture* (New York: American Elsevier, 1975).

Robinette, Gary O.: *Plants/People/And Environmental Quality* (Washington, D.C.: U.S. Department of Interior/National Park Service, 1972).

Simonds, John Ormsbee: *Landscape Architecture* (New York: McGraw-Hill, 1961).

Tandy, Cliff: *Handbook of Urban Landscape* (London: Architectural Press, 1973).

THEORY

Arnheim, Rudolf: *The Dynamics of Architectural Form* (Berkeley: University of California Press, 1977).

Blake, Peter: *Form Follows Fiasco* (Boston: Little, Brown, 1977).

Boudon, Philippe: *Lived-In Architecture* (Cambridge, Mass.: M.I.T. Press, 1972).

Brett, Lionel: *Architecture in a Crowded World* (New York: Schocken, 1971).

Brolin, Brent C.: *Architecture in Context* (New York: Van Nostrand Reinhold, 1980).

Brolin, Brent C.: *The Failure of Modern Architecture* (New York: Van Nostrand Reinhold, 1976).

Moore, Charles and Allen, Gerald: *Dimensions* (New York: Architectural Record Books, 1976).

Norberg-Schulz, Christian: *Intentions in Architecture* (Cambridge, Mass.: M.I.T. Press, 1965).

Rasmussen, Steen Eiler: *Experiencing Architecture* (Cambridge, Mass.: M.I.T. Press, 1959).

Rowe, Colin: *The Mathematics of the Ideal Villa and Other Assays* (Cambridge, Mass.: M.I.T. Press, 1976).

Scruton, Roger: *The Aesthetics of Architecture* (Princeton, N.J.: Princeton University Press, 1979).

Venturi, Robert: *Complexity and Contradiction in Architecture* (New York: Museum of Modern Art, 1966).

HISTORY

Benevolo, Leonardo: *History of Modern Architecture* (Cambridge, Mass.: M.I.T. Press, 1976).

Eckardt, Wolf von: *A Place to Live* (New York: Dell, 1967).

Frampton, Kenneth: *Modern Architecture, a Critical History* (New York: Oxford University Press, 1980).

Giedion, Sifgried: *Space, Time and Architecture*, 5th ed. (Cambridge, Mass.: Harvard University Press, 1967).

Jencks, Charles: *Modern Movements in Architecture* (New York: Anchor/Doubleday, 1973).

Roth, M. Leland: *A Concise History of American Architecture* (New York: Harper & Row, 1979).

Schoenauer Norbert: *6000 Years of Housing* (New York: Garland STPM, 1980).

Scully, Vincent: *American Architecture and Urbanism* (New York: Praeger, 1969).

Stern, Robert A. M.: *New Directions in American Architecture* (New York: George Braziller, 1969).

Tafuri, Manfredo and DalCo, Francesco: *Modern Architecture* (New York: Harry N. Abrams, 1979).

ELDERLY

Barry, John R. and Wingrove, C. Ray: *Let's Learn about Aging: A Book of Readings* (Cambridge, Mass., Schenkman, 1977).

Bednar, Michael J., ed.: *Barrier-Free Environments* (Stroudsburg, Pa.: Dowden, Hutchinson and Ross, 1977).

Birren, James E.: *Handbook on Aging and the Individual* (Chicago: University of Chicago Press, 1960).

Byerts, Thomas O. and Conway, Don, eds.: *Behavioral Requirements for Housing for the Elderly* (Washington, D.C.: American Institute of Architects, 1973).

Butler, Robert N.: *Why Survive? Being Old in America* (New York: Harper & Row, 1975).

Green, Isaac, *et al.*: *Housing for the Elderly, The Development and Design Process* (New York: Van Nostrand Reinhold, 1975).

Howell, Sandra C.: *Designing for Aging: Patterns of Use* (Cambridge, Mass.: M.I.T. Press, 1980).

Koncelik, Joseph A.: *Designing the Open Nursing Home* (Stroudsburg, Pa.: Dowden, Hutchinson and Ross, 1976).

Lawton, M. Powell: *Planning and Managing Housing for the Elderly* (New York: Wiley, 1975).

Lawton, M. Powell, Newcomer, Robert J. and Byerts, Thomas O., eds.: *Planning for an Aging Society: Design of Facilities and Services* (Stroudsburg, Pa.: Dowden, Hutchinson and Ross, 1976).

Pastalan, Leon A. and Carson, Daniel H., eds.: *Spatial Behavior of Older People* (Ann Arbor, Mich.: Institute of Gerontology, University of Michigan, 1970).

Regnier, Victor, ed.: *Environmental Concerns of the Aged* (Los Angeles: University of Southern California Press, 1977).

HANDICAPPED

American Society of Landscape Architects Foundation and H.U.D.: *Barrier Free Site Design* (Washington, D.C.: U.S. Government Printing Office, 1976).

ANSI A117.1: *Making Building Accessible and Usable by the Physically Handicapped* (New York: American National Standards Institute, 1971).

Goldsmith, Selwyn: *Designing for the Disabled*, 2nd. ed. (New York: McGraw-Hill, 1968).

Harkness, Sarah P. and Groom, James N.: *Building Without Barriers for the Disabled* (New York: Whitney Library of Design, Watson-Guptill, 1976).

Jones, Michael A.: *Accessibility Standards* (Springfield, Ill.: Capital Development Board, State of Illinois, 1978).

Kliment, Stephen A.: *Into the Mainstream, A Syllabus for a Barrier-Free Environment* (Washington, D.C.: The American Institute of Architects, 1975).

Mace, Ronald L. in Laslett, Betsy, ed.: *An Illustrated Handbook of the Handicapped Section of the North Carolina State Building Code* (Raleigh, N.C.: North Carolina Building Code Council and North Carolina Department of Insurance, 1974).

Olson, Sharon C. and Meredith, Diane K.: *Wheelchair Interiors* (Chicago: National Easter Seal Society for Crippled Children and Adults, 1973).

Sorensen, Robert James: *Design for Accessibility* (New York: McGraw-Hill, 1979).

STRUCTURAL

Angerer, Fred: *Surface Structures In Building* (New York: Reinhold, 1961).

American Concrete Institute: *Manual of Concrete Practice* (Detroit, Mich.: 1979).

Corkill, Philip A., Puderbaugh, and Sawyers: *Structure and Architectural Design* (Iowa City, Iowa: Sernoll, 1965).

BIBLIOGRAPHY

Cowan, Henry: *Historical Outline of Architectural Science* (Iowa City, Iowa: Sernoll, 1965).

Cross, Hardy: *Engineers and Ivory Towers* (New York: Arno, 1952).

Engel, Heineich: *Structure Systems* (New York: Praeger, 1968).

Gaylord, Edwin Henry and Gaylord, Charles Nelson, eds.: *Structural Engineering Handbook* (New York: McGraw-Hill, 1968).

Hertel, Heinrich: *Structure, Form, Movement* (New York: Reinhold, 1966).

Howard, H. Seymour: *Structures: An Architect's Approach* (New York: McGraw-Hill, 1966).

Lin, T. Y. and Stotesbury, S. D.: *Structural Concepts and Systems for Architects and Engineers* (New York, John Wiley & Sons, 1981).

Parker, Harry: *Simplified Site Engineering for Architects and Builders* (New York: Wiley, 1954).

Parker, Harry: *Simplified Mechanics and Strength of Materials*, 3rd ed. (New York: Wiley, 1977).

Parker, Harry: *Simplified Design of Structural Steel*, 4th ed. (New York: Wiley, 1974).

Parker, Harry: *Simplified Design of Structural Wood* (New York: Wiley, 1979).

Parker, Harry: *Simplified Design of Reinforced Concrete*, 4th ed. (New York: Wiley, 1976).

Parker, Harry: *Simplified Engineering for Architects and Builders*, 5th ed. (New York: Wiley, 1975).

Parker, Harry: *Simplified Design of Roof Trusses for Architects and Builders*, 2nd ed. (New York: Wiley, 1953).

Salvadori, Mario G. and Heller, Robert: *Structure in Architecture* (Englewood Cliffs, N.J.: Prentice-Hall, 1963).

Salvadori, Mario G. and Levy, M.: *Structural Design in Architecture* (Englewood Cliffs, N.J.: Prentice-Hall, 1967).

Sandstrom, G.E.: *Man The Builder* (New York: McGraw-Hill, 1970).

Schild, Erich: *Structural Failure in Residential Buildings*, Vol. II (New York: Halsted Press, 1979).

Torroja, Eduardo: *Philosophy of Structures* (Berkeley: University of California Press, 1958).

Wachsmann, Konrad: *The Turning Point of Building* (New York: Reinhold, 1961).

Zuk, William: *Concepts of Structure* (Huntington, N.Y.: Krieger, 1963).

MECHANICAL AND ELECTRICAL

American Society of Heating, Refrigerating and Air Conditioning Engineers: *Fundamentals* (New York: 1977).

American Society of Heating, Refrigerating and Air Conditioning Engineers: *Systems* (New York: 1980).

American Society of Heating, Refrigerating and Air Conditioning Engineers: *Equipment* (New York: 1975).

American Society of Heating, Refrigerating and Air Conditioning Engineers: *Applications* (New York: 1974).

Emerick, Robert H.: *Troubleshooters' Handbook for Mechanical Systems* (New York: McGraw-Hill, 1969).

Keller, William J.: Fan Engineering (Buffalo, N.Y.: Buffalo Forge Co., 1970).

Lenk, John D.: *Handbook of Simplified Electrical Wiring Design* (Englewood Cliffs, N.J.: Prentice-Hall, 1975).

McGuiness, William J., Stein, Benjamin, and Reynolds, John S.: *Mechanical and Electrical Equipment for Buildings*, 6th ed. (New York: Wiley, 1980).

National Electrical Code, (Boston: National Fire Protection Association, current issue).

Steel, Ernest W.: *Water Supply and Sewerage*, 2nd ed. (New York: McGraw-Hill, 1947).

Uniform Plumbing Code, 15th ed. (Los Angeles: International Association of Plumbing and Mechanical Officials, 1979).

Wilkes, Gordon B.: *Heat Insulation* (New York: Wiley, 1950).

SOCIAL AND BEHAVIORAL

Alexander, C. *et al.: A Pattern Language* (New York: Oxford University Press, 1976).

Baldassare, M: *Residential Crowding in Urban America* (Berkeley: University of California Press, 1979).

Bechtel, R.: *Enclosing Behavior* (Stroudsburg, Pa.: Dowden, Hutchinson & Ross, 1977).

Becker, Franklin: *Design for Living: The Resident's View of Multi-Family Housing* (Ithaca, N.Y.: Center for Urban Development Research, Cornell University, 1974).

Becker, Franklin: *Housing Messages* (Stroudsburg, Pa.: Dowden, Hutchinson & Ross, 1977).

Bennet, Corwin: *Spaces for People: Human Factors in Design* (Englewood Cliffs, N.J.: Prentice-Hall, 1977).

Canter, D: *Psychology for Architects* (New York: Halsted Press, 1974).

Cooper, Clare: *Easter Hill Village* (New York: Free Press, 1975).

Francescato, G., Weideman, S., Anderson, J.R. and Chenowith, R.: *Residents' Dissatisfaction in HUD-Assisted Housing: Design and Management Factors* (Washington, D.C.: HUD, 1979).

Hall, Edward T.: *The Hidden Dimension* (New York: Anchor/Doubleday, 1969).

Lansing, John B., Marans, Robert W., and Zehner, Robert B.: *Planned Residential Environments* (Ann Arbor, Mich.: Survey Research Institute, Institute for Socail Research, University of Michigan, 1970).

Lee, T.: *Psychology and Environment* (London: Methuen, 1976).

Michelson, W.: *Behavioral Research Methods in Environmental Design* (Strondsburg, Pa.: Damden, Hutchinson and Ross, 1972).

Newman, Oscar: *Community of Interest* (Garden City, N.Y.: Anchor/Doubleday, 1980).

Newman, Oscar: *Defensible Space* (New York: MacMillan, 1972).

Panero, J. and Zelnick, M.: *Human Dimension and Interior Space* (New York: Whitney Library of Design, 1979).

Zeisel, J.: *Inquiry by Design* (Monterey, Ca.: Brooks/Cole, 1981).

REAL ESTATE

American Institute of Real Estate Appraisers: *The Appraisal of Real Estate*, 7th ed. (Chicago: 1978).

O'Mara, W. Paul: *Residential Development Handbook* (Washington, D.C.: Urban Land Institute, 1978).

Philippo, Gene: *The Professional Guide to Real Estate Development* (Homewood, Ill.: Dow Jones–Irwin, 1976).

Seldon, Maury and Swesnik, Richard H.: *Real Estate Investment Strategy*, 2d ed. (New York: Wiley, 1979).

FINANCING

Beaton, William R.: *Real Estate Finance* (Englewood Cliffs, N.J.: Prentice-Hall, 1975).

Greer, Gaylon E.: *The Real Estate Investor and the Federal Income Tax* (New York: Wiley, 1978).

Maisel, Sherman J. and Roulac, Stephen E.: *Real Estate Investment and Finance* (New York: McGraw-Hill, 1976).

Messner, Stephen D., *et al.*: *Marketing Investment Real Estate: Finance, Taxation, Techniques* (Chicago: Realtors National Marketing Institute of the National Association of Realtors, 1975).

INDEX

INDEX

INDEX

INDEX